Further praise for The Sustainability Handbook

'This is a truly comprehensive review of sustainable development as it relates to organizations large and small. This book will help managers think about the impact of their business on the people they employ, their customers, their shareholders, the environment and society at large. It also puts the many tools and guidelines in a context allowing for thoughtful selection.'
Sir Mark Moody-Stuart, Chairman, Anglo American, Former Chairman, Royal Dutch/Shell

'By far the best book on sustainability I have read in the last ten years. The book is unique in that it goes well beyond making the business case for sustainability. It is filled with practical techniques, tips and tools to 'operationalize' these concepts into the plans, programs, and performance of any organization. Great advice for both the seasoned veteran and energetic newcomer on action steps for driving continuous improvement in an organization's economic, social, and environmental performance.'
George Nagel, Senior Director, Environment, Health & Safety Strategies and Outreach, Bristol-Myers Squibb Company

'Blackburn has produced an impressive and comprehensive work on sustainability and business practice. The book is deep and wide, and contains numerous insights into how corporate environmental and social responsibility is being internalized by many companies and can be profitable for many others. A real first in the literature.'
Dennis J. Aigner, Professor of Economics, Paul Merage School of Business, University of California

'A very complete and detailed account of how to take the difficult concept of sustainable development, move it from the confines of the international forums and academia and make it a valuable tool to help ensure a more just, equitable, and environmentally safe planet.'
Alberto Ninio, Lead Counsel, Environmental and International Law, Legal Vice Presidency, The World Bank

'Bill Blackburn has accomplished a rare feat: he has crafted the perfect reference for both the academic and the executive. Readers are made critically aware of the importance of considering the ramifications of decisions that are not made with sustainability in mind. *The Sustainability Handbook* should be required reading for MBA students and seasoned executives.'
Allen White, Senior Fellow, Tellus Institute, Co-Founder and former CEO, Global Reporting Initiative, Co-Founder and Director, Corporation 20/20

'Blackburn's tenacious and relentless focus on results and his readiness to adopt and apply new thinking allowed him to achieve much over his years as a leader in the EHS field. His book will be a valuable resource for others who really do want to make a difference. It is full of ideas that will make you think and act differently. Read it, if you care!'
Brian Kraus, CEO, ERM Certification and Verification Services

'Blackburn is a powerful voice for a common-sense approach to sustainability. He presents a strong social and business case for adopting sustainable practices, and demonstrates its significant contributions to individual and corporate well-being. It's practical, clear, comprehensive, and compelling.'
Scott Charon, LEED AP, Project Manager, New Product Development, Herman Miller Inc.

'This book is an essential guide for practitioners who are trying to wade through the myriad of terms, frameworks, claims and counter-claims about the importance of sustainability initiatives. Blackburn has hit a home run with this book. He tells us what sustainability is, why organizations should pursue it, and how they can approach it to improve their chances of long-term success. It is full of useful checklists, model language and frameworks and strategies for implementation. The book is a valuable reference guide on many levels—both to academics and practitioners who are new to sustainability as well as to the well-seasoned sustainability professional.'
Mark A. Cohen, Justin Potter Professor of American Competitive Enterprise, Owen Graduate School of Management, Vanderbilt University

'Bill Blackburn is a recognized expert and leader in the environmental arena, including on sustainability and corporate responsibility. Bill's career as head of EHS at Baxter Healthcare makes him particularly qualified to comment on how companies should and will manage toward sustainability and ensuring that their behavior on social, economic, and environmental matters is responsible. Bill's new book is a good read for any environmental legal practitioner or business manager, and certainly will add to their understanding of the relevant issues.'
Vail T. Thorne, Senior Environmental, Health & Safety Counsel, The Coca-Cola Company

'With all the short-term results, Blackburn opens the reader's eyes to the long-term risks and opportunities that lay in wait. Readers will strengthen their organization's operations and relationships by following the advice in this book.'
Ernst Ligteringen, Chief Executive, Global Reporting Initiative, Amsterdam

'Bill fully understands maintaining a sustainability operating and management system, from an experienced and practical experience. His style helps the reader understand the impact of sustainability now, and for the future, and the path to pursue it in reality. This Guide is long overdue!'
Erin Elizabeth Kreis, Manager, Corporate Relations, General Motors Public Policy Center

'This handbook provides a wealth of information and practical ideas on how to translate sustainable development into the day-to-day operations of corporation and other organizations. Building on more than 25 years of management, consulting and legal experience, Bill Blackburn has provided an invaluable resource for adding value—environmentally, economically and socially sustainable value—to any organization's work.'
John C. Dernbach, Professor of Law, Widener University Law School

'*The Sustainability Handbook* is the first complete, practical book about sustainability for all types of organizations. Corporations, NGOs and government agencies alike will find the tools invaluable in their efforts to achieve economic, social and environmental responsibility.'
George P. Nassos, Director, MS in Environmental Management Program and Center for Sustainable Enterprise, Stuart Graduate School of Business, Illinois Institute of Technology

'Blackburn is a uniquely qualified author. This book is told from the perspective of one who has both led a successful sustainability initiative within a major global corporation as well as worked closely with global multi-stakeholder NGOs like CERES.'
Mindy Lubber, President, Coalition for Environmentally Responsible Economies (CERES)

THE SUSTAINABILITY HANDBOOK

By William R. Blackburn

publishing for a sustainable future

First published by Earthscan in the UK and USA in 2007
Reprinted 2008, 2009

Copyright © 2007 Environmental Law Institute
2000 L Street NW, Washington DC 20036

ISBN 978-1-84407-495-2

Cover design by Andrew Corbett

For a full list of publications please contact:

Earthscan
Dunstan House
14A St. Cross Street
London EC1N 8XA, UK
Tel: +44 (0)20 7841 1930
Fax: +44 (0)20 7242 1474
E-mail: earthinfo@earthscan.co.uk
Web: **www.earthscan.co.uk**

22883 Quicksilver Drive, Sterling, VA 20166-2012, USA

Earthscan publishes in association with the International Institute for
Environment and Development

A catalogue record for this book is available from the British Library

Library of Congress Cataloging-in-Publication Data has been applied
for

At Earthscan we strive to minimise our environmental impacts and
carbon footprint through reducing waste, recycling and offsetting
our CO_2 emissions, including those created through publication of
this book, For more details of our environmental policy, see
www.earthscan.co.uk.

This book was printed in the UK by
TJ International, an ISO 14001 accredited
company. The paper used is FSC certified
and the inks are vegetable based.

FSC
Mixed Sources
Product group from well-managed
forests and other controlled sources
Cert no. SGS-COC-2482
www.fsc.org
© 1996 Forest Stewardship Council

Dedication

To Sara Jean, whose love and support (and tolerance for towers of research materials stacked in my home office) made this book possible.

The Sustainability Handbook:
The Complete Management Guide to Achieving Social, Economic, and Environmental Responsibility

Table of Contents

*See www.WBlackburnConsulting.com for a model syllabus
for a college-level course.*

Acknowledgments

My three-year effort of researching and writing this book has not been easy. Like those who climb Mount Everest, I found my progress stalled, redirected, or reversed from time to time by obstacles that were tough to predict at the outset. And like such climbers, I relied on a team of skilled and knowledgeable experts to help me to the end. I thank them all for their belief in this project, for their generous contributions, and for the encouragement they provided me along the way.

I owe a special debt of gratitude to Carolyn Fischer, Dick MacLean, William D'Alessandro, and Donna Schmid who tenaciously read the drafts from front to back, pointing out the rough spots needing repair. Carolyn, my superb editor at the Environmental Law Institute (ELI), gave her all to the project. Dick, along with Frank Friedman and Gib Hedstrom, all respected, seasoned veterans of the corporate environmental arena, helped keep the text grounded in the real world. Donna joined another friend of our family, Andrew Fisher, in offering views from a quite different perspective—the perspective of two gifted young writers unfettered by the biases of the past. William, a long-time reporter on environmental and sustainability issues, served as a good foil for identifying gaps in my information and arguments. Margery Moore, also from the environmental publishing business, lent her expertise on the selection and use of information technology. Bob Willard, a well-known author on sustainability in his own right, also suggested important improvements. I witnessed first hand the benefits of paying all those expensive tuition bills for my daughter Laura's education in business and design when she produced many of the more difficult graphics for the book, and guided me by the hand through a few episodes of computer hell. I would also like to thank Linda Johnson, Bill Straub, and April King at ELI, who were responsible for making the book visually coherent.

Various teammates from my days at Baxter International Inc. reviewed significant portions of the draft, providing the same type of candid, useful feedback (based no doubt in their firm belief of my fallibility) that enabled the company to become so well regarded in the fields of sustainability and environment, health, and safety. Those teammates included Bob Seguy (now of Enviance), Ron Meissen, Peter Etienne, Jenni Cawein, Mike Cycyota, Lisa Keltner, Sue Miller, Dennis Shoji (now of

Edward Life Sciences), and Caroline Gelderloos. Good friends Jaime Einstein and the late Jean-Pierre Henri, former international lawyers for Baxter, offered insight on the cultural challenges of effecting change within a modern transnational corporation.

Graduate business school professors George Nassos, Mark Cohen, and Dennis Aigner reviewed various parts of the book from their academic perches. Patricia Jerman and Dave Newport, two people who manage university sustainability initiatives, helped with the text on collegiate sustainability programs. Chuck Bennett of The Conference Board and Dee Woodhull of ORC Worldwide injected some enlightening views on a number of topics, including how to drive corporate performance, based on their studies and experiences within their global business associations. I was also aided by teammates from two organizations: Tauni Brooker, who is a fellow member of the Stakeholder Council of the Global Reporting Initiative, and Jeffrey Smith, who, like me, is active in the American Bar Association's sustainability initiatives. Other assistance came from Vail Thorne, Arlo Brady, Staffan Söderberg, Nicholas Eisenberg, Cathy Crain, and Chris Bell, as well as from the many people quoted and cited throughout the book.

Special thanks go to Scott Schang and John Thompson of ELI, who believed in this book from the beginning, and served as the patient guides, skillfully leading me through the thicket of the publication process.

Finally, I must not forget the fine leaders I have worked under over the years—particularly those mentors who imparted to me important lessons about organizational management. These mentors have included Hans deWaal and the late Ivan Bogert of the former environmental consulting firm, Clinton Bogert Associates, and Ray Murphy, John Gaither, Tom Schuman, Art Staubitz, and Marsh Abbey of Baxter. In many ways, their lessons live on in this publication.

—W.R.B.

About the Author

For over 30 years, William R. (Bill) Blackburn has been involved with the management of global programs on environment, health, and safety (EHS) as well as on programs on sustainability as that concept has emerged. He is a frequent lecturer around the world on these topics.

Until 2003, Blackburn was vice president and chief counsel of Corporate Environment, Health, and Safety at Baxter International Inc., a global manufacturer and distributor of medical products based in Deerfield, Illinois. As a sustainability leader at Baxter, Blackburn led efforts pioneering effective sustainability performance metrics; transparent sustainability reports; innovative management standards; unique environmental cost and income statements; and sound emergency response programs. Baxter's operations received over 300 external awards for EHS excellence while Blackburn guided the company's program. Prior to joining Baxter in 1978, Blackburn was employed as the general counsel at Clinton Bogert Associates, an environmental engineering firm based in New Jersey.

Today, Blackburn continues his work on EHS and sustainability issues as the president of a consulting firm, William Blackburn Consulting, Ltd. His firm advises organizations on the performance, structure, strategy, planning, and development of programs related to sustainability, EHS, and crisis management/emergency response. His clients include: large, small, and struggling companies; nonprofit organizations; local governments; trade and professional associations; and multi-stakeholder coalitions.

In 1973, Blackburn received his J.D. in law from the University of Iowa and three years prior, in 1970, he received a B.S. in aerospace engineering from Iowa State University. He received law licenses in the District of Columbia, Illinois, and New Jersey and a professional engineers' license in New Jersey.

Blackburn serves as: a member of the management team of the Stake-holder Council, Global Reporting Initiative; an expert delegate on the Working Group on the Guidance on Social Responsibility of the International Organization for Standardization (ISO 26000); a vice chair of the American Bar Association's Subcommittee on Sustainable Development within the Section on Environment, Energy, and Resources; and a member of the board of advisors for the Environmental Management Program and Center for Sustainable Enterprise, Stuart Graduate School of Business, Illinois Institute of Technology. He is a former chairman of the Chief EHS Officers Council of The Conference Board, a U.S. business association.

For more information on Blackburn and his firm, visit his website at www.WBlackburnConsulting.com, where a detailed table of contents for the book and a model syllabus for a college-level course can be found. Alternatively, contact him at WRB@WBlackburnConsulting.com.

Introduction and Executive Summary

"We shall require a substantially new manner of thinking if mankind is to survive."[1]

—Albert Einstein

This book could have been titled *How Organizations Can Use Sustainable Development to Their Advantage* or simply, *Sustainable Development for Dummies*. *Sustainable development*, or the shorthand *sustainability* used in this book, is a concept of growing popularity aimed at producing long-term global well-being through the wise use and management of economic and natural resources, and through respect for people and other living things. Sustainability is a concept describing mankind's ability to create a world for humans and non-humans that environmentally, socially, and economically provides for a current population's needs without damaging the ability of future generations to take care of themselves. At the outset, the book provides background information on the topic and its importance to business. It then proposes an approach for managing companies in an efficient, holistic way that takes into account important sustainability trends shaping our world of tomorrow. It is a handbook filled with explanations, practical strategies, checklists, forms, tips, and reference information. To a large extent, the text is as much about smart management techniques as it is about the topic of sustainability.

The book is written with large companies in mind, although Chapter 12 tells how the lessons can be applied to companies that are small or in financial difficulty. Chapters 13, 14, and 15 explain how nongovernmental organizations (NGOs), governmental organizations, and colleges and universities can approach sustainability, too. These four chapters are filled with best-practice examples which should prove particularly useful to readers interested in those organizations. Other readers, including those from large corporations, may find the ideas and strategies presented there can stimulate new thinking for them as well.

The book is geared both for people who know nothing about sustainability as well as seasoned experts who are anxious to hone their approach to the concept. The former are advised to read Appendix 1 first.

That part of the book provides an overview of three dozen major sustainability trends—things like globalization, the growth of NGOs, wealth distribution, population, resource depletion, pollution, corporate governance, green products and marketing, and socially responsible investing (SRI). Those who are knowledgeable about these trends may still find this to be a handy reference.

Chapter 1 talks about some common views on sustainability held by executives today. It candidly discusses the misconceptions that business leaders and others often have about the concept. Chapter 2 helps clear the air by providing an operational definition of sustainability, one that can be used as the basis for targeted action. The premise of the book is that companies can improve their chances of success—and survival—by integrating sustainability into their operations and decisionmaking in a consistent manner. The book offers the sustainability operating system (SOS), as one way this can be done.

"Oh, no! Not *another* management system standard!" I hear you say. "We've already had our fill of ISO, EMAS, OHSAS, and a litany of other alphabet-soup processes!" Fortunately, the SOS offered here is not another add-on system. It's a general business system that can encompass all others into a common process that serves sustainability as well as the purposes of manufacturing, design, sales, finance, human resources, and any other function or business unit. It is a broad-based system, one that can increase uniformity, coordination, and efficiency rather than detract from it. It's an improved approach, too, aimed not just at continual improvement—going from, say, *really really bad* to just *really bad*—but designed for achieving quantum leaps in performance to *good* or better. It incorporates the important tools of Talent Management and the Big Picture Review often overlooked in other systems standards. Even if not adopted wholesale, the SOS can be used to achieve the same ends by serving as a good checklist against which existing management systems can be judged and improved.

So what is an SOS? It's a process of proactive, holistic organizational management for purposes of achieving sustainability for both the organization and society. Chapters 4 and 5 explain the SOS in detail. Some of its critical elements can be captured under the following four categories, which are depicted in Figure 4.1.

1. *The Drivers.* These elements assure the organization's efforts toward sustainability are constantly propelled forward. They include the following:

- *A champion/leader.* A good champion/leader is critical to the success of a sustainability initiative within a company. But what does it take to be a successful champion/leader? Thoughts on this are offered in Chapter 4.

- *Approach for selling management on sustainability.* Chapter 4 also suggests sales arguments and strategies. It borrows points from Chapter 3 about the business value of an SOS.

- *Accountability mechanisms.* Fair, effective methods for holding management and other employees accountable for sustainability performance are essential to ongoing improvement. Chapter 9 reviews some of those methods.

2. *The Efficient Enablers.* These elements help ensure that people and groups within the organization are properly equipped to undertake coordinated action toward sustainability in an efficient and effective way. These elements include:

- *Organizational structure.* Chapter 4 explains the advantages of using a virtual sustainability organization, rather than a formal structure. It suggests roles and responsibilities of various players and notes where teams may be helpful.

- *Deployment and integration.* Chapter 8 delves into what are often the most important and most overlooked ingredients for a successful sustainability initiative. How do you roll out an SOS to the field so it sticks? What do you do if someone slams the door in your face? The chapter answers those questions and discusses the needs and challenges for deployment and integration within individual corporate departments.

3. *The Pathway.* Pathway elements chart the course toward sustainability. They include the following:

- *Vision, values, and policy.* These elements are needed to clarify what the organization is trying to accomplish through its SOS process and related programs. They define the desired end state.

Chapter 4 offers a model sustainability vision and policy that can serve as a starting point for the development of an organization's own version. It also presents guidance on whether or not the organization should adopt the Global Compact, Earth Charter, or other external code. Summaries of many of the more popular sustainability-related codes are provided in Appendix 2.

- *Operating system standards.* Chapter 5 presents a set of unique SOS standards. These standards describe a holistic, organizationwide process for improvement that considers sustainability trends. The chapter examines why management standards often fail to drive performance and offers some solutions.

- *Strategic planning for aligned priorities.* Chapter 6 explains how planning can improve organizational efficiency and effectiveness. It suggests some companywide and department-level planning processes and presents tools that can be used for them.

4. *The Evaluators.* These elements help us periodically judge the sustainability performance of an organization so it may adjust its efforts for optimal results. These elements include:

- *Indicators and goals.* Chapter 7 explains the various types of sustainability metrics and other indicators. It offers a process for selecting the indicators and goals most appropriate for the organization. The concept of the "collective directional goal" is introduced. Appendix 7 presents a broad collection of sustainability metrics commonly used by companies, local governments, and universities.

- *Measuring and reporting progress.* Measurement and reporting are essential elements of any process of continual improvement. Chapter 9 discusses how to monitor progress toward sustainability. Do you need an information technology system for this purpose? This chapter helps you determine if you do, and shows you how to select the one you need. Chapter 10 outlines challenges and approaches to sustainability reporting. The author draws on a dozen years of reporting experience to provide practical tips for communicating sustainability information. The chapter also reviews the legal implications of reporting.

- *Stakeholder engagement and feedback.* Without stakeholder
  engagement and feedback, management becomes myopic in its
  views and organizationally incestuous in its thinking. Over
  time, this can become a recipe for trouble. Chapter 11 presents
  guidelines for selecting and effectively engaging stakeholders
  under various circumstances.

The book lays out these elements roughly in the order they would be
addressed by one who is introducing sustainability to an organization for
the first time. It need not be read front to back, however. Those interested
in a specific topic—say metrics, for example—can go directly to the
chapter on the topic to learn more. To help crystallize the lessons for practical use, a follow-up checklist for action is provided at the end of each
chapter. Chapter 16 closes with some tips on how to keep the initiative
alive—how to assure the SOS itself remains sustainable.

So why should an organization do all this? What's the value of an
SOS? The answer is provided in Chapter 3 through two models that examine the role or purpose of business relative to its stakeholders. First is
the "Show-Me-the-Money Model," which presumes that the sole purpose of business is to make as much money as possible for as long as possible. The unique Baxter International Inc. environmental financial statement—a tool the author was instrumental in developing—is presented. It
and a host of other real-life examples are used to bolster the claim that a
march toward sustainability can contribute to bottom-line financial results. Next, the "Quid Pro Quo Model" is presented. This model says
business must give something to its stakeholders in order to receive from
them what it needs to be successful over the long term.

Throughout the book, the author shares insights gained over 25 years
in the management of global environmental, health, and safety (EHS)
and of sustainability programs and in observing others do so. You will
learn of the obstacles commonly faced in the march toward sustainability, and hear how leading organizations have responded to these challenges in building their own sustainability programs.

In short, the wealth of information provided by this book should enable you to thoroughly understand sustainability and use it where you
work—use it to protect and grow assets, strengthen financial performance, and shape an organization to be admired by all.

Endnote to Introduction and Executive Summary

1. This quote is attributed to the brilliant physicist, Albert Einstein, who lived from 1879 to 1955.

CHAPTER 1

Addressing the Confusion About Sustainability: The Typical Executive View

"If you cry 'Forward!' you must without fail make plain in what direction to go. Don't you see that if, without doing so, you call out the word to a monk and a revolutionary, they will go in directions precisely opposite?"[1]

—Anton Chekhov

Consider these typical responses you might hear from business executives about sustainability:

"The business of business is business, not sustainability."

"Sustainability is nice to do if you can afford it, but we are running a lean organization here and don't have the time or money for such things."

"Sustainability is about good citizenship and good public relations. We have always tried to be a good corporate citizen. There's really nothing more we need to do."

"Sustainability seems to encompass everything under the sun. It's just more tree-hugger mumbo jumbo."

"We're in a U.S. service business. Sustainability is not for us. It's for those big international manufacturers."

"What is sustainability?"

For sustainability advocates, this isn't encouraging. The picture was rosier for them in the 1990s when President William J. Clinton appointed a council to study and publicize sustainability. But in recent years, the U.S. government's focus on it has subsided as terrorism and war have dominated the agenda.

So is sustainability just a fad?

No. Quite the contrary. There is plenty of evidence the concept is here to stay. In government circles in Australia, Canada, Europe, and several other regions, sustainability has been gaining momentum. Attention to it has also been on the rise among leading businesses, academic institutions, and other sectors in the United States and abroad. More than 70% of large companies surveyed by PricewaterhouseCoopers in 2002 reported that sustainability was important or very important to them, and nearly 9 of 10 respondents believed there would be more emphasis on it in the near future.[2] World leaders like United Kingdom (U.K.) Prime Minister Tony Blair and former United Nations (U.N.) Secretary-General Kofi Annan promoted it. Over the past few years, sustainability conferences have been held throughout the world—even in places like Chile, China, Croatia, Iceland, Kenya, Morocco, Palestine, and United Arab Emirates.[3] Forty major banks around the world have committed to consider sustainability effects in making major investment decisions.[4] Wangari Maathai, a crusader for poor women and the environment in her native Kenya, acknowledged the importance of the concept in her acceptance of the Nobel Peace Prize in 2004.[5] It was included in U.N. resolutions on the recovery and rebuilding of Iraq.[6] The European Commission issued a "green paper" on it in 2001 and chartered an organization to determine how to further it.[7] In recent years there has been a blizzard of discussion and debate among business, activists, and academics about it. Books, articles, and conferences abound on the topic. In 2006, there were over 60 million entries on sustainable development on the Internet, up eightfold from 2003.

History of Sustainability

But even with all this attention to sustainability, much confusion remains about it in business circles. The concept—really a blend of concepts—first emerged in Stockholm during the 1972 U.N. Conference on the Human Environment. There, industrialized and developing nations debated which was more important: environmental protection or economic development.[8] This was a time when the environmental movement was bursting on the scene, 10 years after Rachel Carson published *Silent Spring*,[9] a powerful book describing the dangers of pesticides to wildlife and humans. The same year of the Stockholm meeting, the United States passed five major pieces of environmental legislation. Only a year later, India would witness the Chipko citizen uprising against deforestation. Within this setting, the debates at Stockholm gave birth to the notion that both environmental protection and economic development were inextricably linked. That idea was refined through extensive discussions in U.N. circles over the many years that followed.

In the late 1970s and the decade thereafter, other momentous events sparked public outcries about the need for environmental responsibility. These outcries were coupled with growing demands for open, transparent communication from industry and government about environmental risks. This was the time of the Love Canal toxic waste debacle in New York and the deadly Bhopal release in India. It was also the period of public anger over the massive Alaskan oil spill from the *Exxon Valdez* oil tanker and the disastrous radiation release at the Chernobyl nuclear power plant in the Soviet Union. In the United States, these headline events inspired a number of laws, including one requiring industry to file annual public reports on their inventories and releases of toxic materials—data that proved shocking to many communities.

But environmental issues were not the only concern. The Apartheid racial segregation policies of South Africa were coming under attack from Rev. Dr. Leon Sullivan, a Philadelphia clergyman and civil rights leader, and from other religious and student activists as well. The movement gained momentum in 1976 when South African police fired on student demonstrators at Soweto. A burgeoning number of universities, pension funds, and local governments in Europe and the United States began dropping their investments in companies that refused to recognize human rights and equal opportunity in their South African operations. The seeds of Apartheid's demise were being sown, and "socially responsible investing" was finding new meaning. Meanwhile, a new disease, acquired immune deficiency syndrome (AIDS), was beginning its devastating rampage.

These issues were the backdrop for the Brundtland Commission, a group appointed by the United Nations to propose strategies for improving human well-being without threatening the environment. In 1987, the commission published its report containing the definition of sustainable development most widely used today: "Development that meets the needs of the present without compromising the ability of future generations to meet their own needs."[10] Five years later, the concept was fleshed out in 27 principles in the Rio Declaration on Environment and Development,[11] the work product of the Rio Earth Summit—the U.N Conference on Environment and Development in Rio de Janeiro. The declaration recited the economic and environmental concerns that had been the main focus of sustainability, but added social topics like peace, poverty, and the role of women and indigenous people.[12] In 1997, Briton John Elkington introduced a definitional term drawn from financial accounting: the triple bottom line (TBL). By this he meant that to reach sustainability, one must achieve not only economic "bottom-line" performance but environmental and social performance as well.[13] When the Global Reporting Initiative (GRI) issued its draft *Sustainability Reporting Guidelines* for organizations in 1999, it, too, assumed sustainability entailed all three TBL elements. The final versions published in 2000 and 2002 continued that assumption.[14]

In recent years, other developments have refined the dimensions of sustainable development. High-profile incidents involving sweatshops in Asia have given rise to voluntary inspection and certification programs targeted at operations supplying products to transnational companies. Pressures from activists have led to other certification programs on fair trade, lumber, fishing, and agricultural products. Labor and environmental groups have appeared together in front-page photos of demonstrations against global trade policies. Financial scandals at Enron Corporation, Tyco International, Ltd., and WorldCom have highlighted the importance of good corporate governance. Organic food and hybrid cars are no longer novelties but big business. Product and packaging take-back laws have extended the responsibility of producers across Europe. Climate change is now a threat backed by serious science, and an issue of growing investor concern. Rating groups have exploded on the scene to evaluate company social and environmental performance to satisfy growing legions of socially responsible investors. The GRI, a coalition of investors, activists, business, and other organizations, has helped make sustainability reporting commonplace among major companies. Activist and public interest groups—known as NGOs—have gained considerable voice and power. With their creative use of coalitions and the Internet, their role continues to expand. All of this has been encircled within the concept of sustainability.

Resources and Respect

Indeed, trends and events ascribed to sustainability, and the scores of definitions of it, have reflected a common theme about its meaning. We shall use that theme to craft the meaning of sustainability for purposes of this book. We shall call this meaning the "2Rs," which stand for:

Resources: the wise use and management of economic and natural resources; and

Respect: respect for people and other living things.

The aim of the 2Rs from an organization's perspective is *long-term well-being, both for society as a whole as well as for itself.* A more in-depth explanation and examination of the 2Rs is given in Chapter 2.

Selecting the Term: Sustainability? Corporate Social Responsibility? Something Else?

Sustainability and *sustainable development* are two terms that cover the 2Rs as it applies to organizations. But there are other terms, too. *Corporate social responsibility (CSR), organizational social responsibility (OSR), social responsibility, corporate responsibility, corporate social investment, corporate citizenship, global corporate citizenship,* and *sustainable growth* are sometimes used to mean the same thing. While sustainability, as we have seen, originated from a concern about the balance between the environment and economics, the terms related to responsibility and citizenship have generally sprung from the tradition of corporate philanthropy. With the advent of the TBL, all those concepts have been drifting together.

Still, there are many who insist that these terms carry different meanings.[15] In one sense, *social responsibility* is but one of the three parts of the TBL that covers community and employee issues and the like. But the term is often used in a broader sense, too. Some relegate sustainable development or sustainability to the larger societal focus of the TBL and 2Rs, and consider social responsibility to cover the company perspective on the same topics.[16] For example, the draft *Guidance on Social Responsibility* of the International Organization for Standardization (ISO) defines *social responsibility* to be

> actions of an organization to take responsibility for the impacts of its activities on society and the environment, where these actions are consistent with the interests of society and sustainable development; are based on ethical behavior, compliance with applicable law, and intergovernmental instruments; and are integrated into the ongoing activities of an organization.[17]

Think also of *socially responsible investing*, which has come to mean investing in companies taking into account not only their financial performance but that on environmental, social (in the narrow sense), and governance matters as well.

CSR—a term of growing popularity, especially in Europe—is occasionally used in a way that excludes environmental responsibility, although the more popular usage includes it. Indeed, documents labeled "CSR reports" often cover the same TBL scope as those called "sustainability reports." Some other variations of CSR exclude economic responsibility, however. For instance, the European Commission Green Paper defines it as "a concept whereby companies integrate social and environmental concerns in their business operation and in their interaction with their stakeholders."[18]

The term *corporate responsibility* is usually thought to be synonymous with *social responsibility* in either its broad or narrow sense, or with *business ethics*. To some people, *corporate citizenship* suggests an emphasis on activities within local communities weighted more toward social concerns than environmental ones.[19] However, the most commonly cited difference between *sustainability* and the responsibility and citizenship terms is that the latter concepts sometimes exclude a company's financial viability—its need to economically prosper as a business.[20]

Companies like DuPont that use the term *sustainable growth* intend it to mean corporate sustainability as defined by the TBL, adding the word *growth* to make clear sustainability is not about stagnation. However to others, the word *growth* is to be avoided because it suggests the need to increase size or consumption, irrespective of other ways of adding value through sustainability. Some even think these words mean simply *perpetual growth* with no social or environmental emphasis at all.

Admittedly, the raft of terms can be quite confusing, especially since these fine distinctions are sometimes followed, sometimes not. You should feel free to use any term that best fits with the goals and culture of your organization. Businesses may also find more descriptive terms, like "a better company, a better world," "long-term well being," or "people, planet, and profits" to be useful in certain communications.

Regardless of the words used, however, *sustainability* and *sustainable development* should nevertheless be explained to employees because of the historical significance and since workers are bound to encounter these terms outside their organization. For our purposes, *sustainability* or *sustainable development* are the most appropriate terms given their breadth, origin, and consistent inclusion of a company's financial success. And, of course, financial success is an indispensable element of a company sustainability initiative because without it, the organization cannot contribute to the well-being of its community or employees—or do anything else for that matter. Moreover, the terms *sustainable development* and *sustainability* have become increasingly important in communications with government and industry leaders over the past decade.[21]

The Executive View: "That Sounds Nice, but . . ."

From what has been said, sustainability sounds like a warm and comforting concept. The reality is, though, few executives understand the hard-nosed business ramifications of it. Granted, a 2002-2003 survey of over 500 U.S. business executives found 8 in 10 agreeing that good corporate citizenship helps the financial bottom line and that it needs to be given a priority. But while most executives have their hearts in the right place, their actions speak louder than words. Less than one-third of those surveyed said they were increasing resources in that area and 14% were cutting them. Nearly one-half of the respondents declared the lack of resources to be a barrier to corporate citizenship within their companies.[22] Even among corporations noted for sustainability—members of the World Business Council for Sustainable Development (WBCSD)—nearly one-third claimed their management doesn't have much faith in the business case for sustainability and doesn't actively support the concept internally.[23] Examining their actions, it is apparent that many executives don't fully appreciate what a pursuit of sustainability can mean to business success and society; still fewer know how to approach it in a systematic way that realizes its maximum business value.

Business people often see sustainability programs as outside the circle of things essential for success. These programs may be looked upon as the hobby of the chief executive officer (CEO)—something to be tolerated but not taken seriously. They may be considered discretionary measures for image-polishing when times are flush, but something to be quickly jettisoned when financial results slip. Occasionally some enlightened company sets course toward sustainability, but commonly this is understood and pushed by only a few executive champions with the rest of leadership simply riding along. Even the enlightened few may struggle with how to address so broad a concept within their organizations, a concept that doesn't fit neatly into any one function or department.

On the other hand, sustainability may be taken very seriously at a few companies, especially those beaten down by the press over a dispute with activists. Frequent poundings from the media about a company's toxic emissions, unhealthy products, or unsound forestry practices—or front-page stories on its sweatshop labor, exploitative hiring policies, or overly zealous security measures—can bring the importance of sustainability to a business' front door. Executives across the organization can see first hand how sustainability issues can affect business risk, reputation, sales, and efficiency. Still, these managers may remain oblivious to the other business benefits a broader strategy on sustainability could provide. "Old school" companies under the same public relations heat may dismiss altogether any form of sustainability strategy and instead plead "victim!" and pull up the drawbridge to wait out the siege. To them, making money is job number one, happy customers and low costs are the keys to this, and these companies see no meaningful way sustainability can help achieve those ends. To them, the idea is, at best, garnish. Clearly, many people have a long way to go in grasping the value of this illusive concept to their organizations. They don't see that ignoring key sustainability trends and issues can impede a company's ability to compete. They don't understand that addressing these trends and issues systematically can open new business opportunities and protect the organization from the risk, reputational challenges, and inefficiencies that destroy shareholder value.

"If pursuing sustainability is all that important," say some business leaders, "why is it that many companies not noted for their drive toward sustainability can be so prosperous?" ExxonMobil Oil Corporation and Altria Group, Inc./Philip Morris Co. (Altria) are among the most successful corporations in the history of capitalism, yet neither has a long track record as public stars of sustainability. Does this mean a business can have no formal approach to sustainability—no SOS—and still build a successful organization? Yes. An SOS does not guarantee business success, but like other sound business aids, it can surely improve an organization's chances for achieving it. An SOS is a tool, an attitude, a philosophy that can lead to new insights and solutions to business challenges while helping address some of the world's most worrisome problems.

Nobody's Perfect

Sustainability within business is not a black-and-white thing; it's not that a company either has or doesn't have initiatives driving toward sustainability. Whether they know it or not, almost all companies have some activities that further the cause of sustainability. Those that have sustained their own financial success and provided long-term employment for many have at least part of the sustainability equation right. Unfortunately, companies that suffer adverse press because of some misstep concerning their environmental or social performance may find that bad news overshadowing anything positive they do. While the public lambastes ExxonMobil for its stand on climate change and for alleged human rights abuses by the Indonesian military it hired to secure a project, few acknowledge the company has a world-class safety program. Nor do they recognize ExxonMobil's pipeline project in Cameroon and Chad, which has shown how large development projects of transnational corporations can be structured to guarantee ongoing benefits to local citizens. Altria's extensive charitable giving is forgotten when the safety of its products is debated. Shakespeare was right: "The evil that men do lives beyond them; the good is oft interred with their bones."[24] Even so, the good that these companies have done and continue to do has helped them sustain operations through community and employee support, improved efficiencies, and in other ways.

Other companies like Shell Oil Corporation (Shell), BP (formerly British Petroleum), Hewlett-Packard (HP), Statoil (a Norway-based oil and gas producer), and Baxter lie on the opposite end of the spectrum. For years they enjoyed a solid public image in many circles when it came to sustainability. Certainly each has had many commendable accomplishments. Yet they are not perfect either. Within the past few years, all five companies suffered setbacks in credibility with investors—Shell for overstating oil reserves, Statoil for ethical improprieties in Iran, BP for Alaskan pipeline leaks and fatal refinery explosions, and Baxter and HP for failing to meet sales and earnings projections. Added to Shell's woes were well-publicized "alternative Shell reports" by Friends of the Earth, Inc., criticizing the company for what it claimed were shortcomings in fulfilling its sustainability commitment in the field.[25] Said Shell's new CEO Jeroen van der Veer: "Recent events have only reinforced the importance of embedding sustainable development consistently in our systems, processes and behavior." He added: "People who accuse us of getting distracted by sustainable development miss the mark. Indeed, I am heartened to see growing awareness in the financial community that companies—especially energy companies—ignore sustainable development concerns at their peril."[26] Fortunately all five companies are strong. Now under new leadership, all five seem on the mend, and should continue to see positive results from their attention to sustainability.

Firms like Dow Chemical Company and Procter & Gamble (P&G) that have pursued sustainability aggressively and openly have their own challenges. Still, their focus on sustainability is proving advantageous as well. But even the best of them have not reaped all the benefits that a fully deployed SOS can offer.

Views on Sustainability Reporting

Often executives gain their understanding of sustainability by skimming through sustainability reports of their own company or those of a competitor or other respected peer. They become interested in these reports primarily to keep up with the herd. Some also may be influenced by the attention given these reports by a growing number of journalists, NGOs, and rating companies. Unfortunately, too many business leaders think sustainability is merely about reporting—getting the right message in the right form to the right people who will pass judgment. But given their vague understanding of sustainability, their sensitivity to criticism, and their tight control on resources, business executives often find sustainability reporting perplexing if not daunting.

Those who consider such reporting are often dissuaded by the extensive, polished reports issued by companies they consider big liberal, elite corporations. Both the cost of publication and the effort needed for data collection seem way out of reach. A quick review of reporting guidelines issued by the GRI doesn't help.[27] Company representatives often skim over the part about materiality and mistakenly think most of the listed data must be reported to make a decent showing among peers and critics. Prospective reporters can be overwhelmed by the amount and complexity of the data they think they must gather. And the thought that some other companies may actually be reporting all this—as evidenced by their 100- to 200-page tomes—just exacerbates the frustration. In the end, some conclude they will never be able to compete and cease trying altogether.

Companies that feel they can master the publication cost and effort still may be reluctant to report for other reasons. They may believe that transparent reporting—openly discussing problems—is shark-infested waters, with the press and activists circling hungrily, intent on consuming them whole. Yet they are sophisticated enough to know that a dessert table of good stories or "greenwash" may be greeted with even less favor. They see transparency as a risk but fail to comprehend that the lack of transparency is an even bigger risk-spawning distrust and inhibiting constructive change.

Many of the organizations that do report have problems too. They struggle with what to report and what to leave out. They question how much to include in the report, how to balance Internet data with hard copy reports, how often to report, and to whom. Some go too far, producing weighty documents that few read. Exhausted by the effort, they vow never again to attempt reporting. Yet others seem to find a comfortable balance between the effort and value of reporting, viewing it as a vehicle to drive both reputation and performance. How can a company reach that balance? Chapter 10 on transparent sustainability reporting provides guidance.

Reason for Optimism

While few business executives understand the full business value of sustainability reporting or of sustainability itself, more and more are getting the message. Wal-Mart, for years the retailing giant that activists loved to hate, has more recently taken on a wide range of sustainability commitments and actions, including improvements in the energy efficiency of its fleet vehicles and facilities, reductions in solid waste and packaging, and the introduction of sustainability-certified coffee, fish, and other products. In total, the company plans to invest $500 million in sustainability projects. It has also announced initiatives to address the healthcare benefits of its employees and close the gender gap in pay and promotion. While this transformation in attitude may have been prompted at least in part by the McKinsey & Company study the company funded showing it had lost 8% of its shoppers because of its reputation, Wal-Mart executives have come to realize this approach presents real opportunities to improve public and employee relations, grow sales, cut waste, and otherwise make the company more competitive.

Said Jeff Immelt who now heads the $150 billion General Electric Company (GE), another company not formerly known for leadership on sustainability: "The world's changed. Businesses today aren't admired. Size is not respected. There's a bigger gulf today between the haves and the have-nots than ever before. It's up to us to use our platform to be a good citizen. Because not only is it a nice thing to do. It's a business imperative."[28]

Follow-up Checklist for Action: Management Views on Sustainability

☐ Informally assess the views of key management about sustainability.
☐ Identify the common points of confusion and misunderstanding. This will help you shape communication strategies later on.
☐ Identify the best term to use for communicating about sustainability inside and outside your organization.

Endnotes to Chapter 1

1. This quote by Anton Chekhov, the famous Russian dramatist and short story author, can be found in VLADIMAR ERMILOV, ANTON PAVLOVICH CHEKHOV, 1860-1904 (1950) and WILLIAM SAFIRE & LEONARD SAFIRE, GOOD ADVICE, MORE THAN 2,000 QUOTATIONS TO HELP YOU LIVE YOUR LIFE (Time Books 1982).

2. PRICEWATERHOUSECOOPERS, 2002 SUSTAINABILITY SURVEY REPORT (2002), *available at* http://www.pwcglobal.com/fas/pdfs/sustainability%20survey%20report.pdf.

3. For a list of events, see Forum on Science and Technology for Sustainability, Harvard University, *Events*, http://sustsci.harvard.edu/events.htm (last visited Jan. 13, 2005).

4. EQUATOR PRINCIPLES (2003), *available at* http://www.equator-principles.com/index.html. *See also* Latham & Watkins, *Private Lenders Commit to Apply "Equator Principles" as Environmental and Social Benchmarks for Project Funding*, CLIENT ALERT, Aug. 5, 2003.

5. Wangari Maathai, Nobel Peace Prize Acceptance Lecture (Oslo, Dec. 10, 2004), http://www.nobel.no/eng_lect_2004b.html.

6. Felicity Barringer, *U.N. Senses It Must Change, Fast, or Fade Away*, N.Y. TIMES, Sept. 19, 2003, at A3.

7. Commission of the European Communities, *Green Paper: Promoting a European Framework for Corporate Social Responsibility*, COM (2001) 366 (July 18, 2001), *available at* http://europa.eu.int/comm/off/green/index_en.htm. *See also* Commission of the European Communities, *Communication From the Commission Concerning Corporate Social Responsibility: A Business Contribution to Sustainable Development*, COM (2002) 347 (July 2, 2002), *available at* http://europa.eu.int/comm/employment_social/soc-dial/csr/csr2002_en.pdf [hereinafter EC Communication on CSR 2002]. EUROPEAN MULTISTAKEHOLDER FORUM ON CSR, FINAL RESULTS AND RECOMMENDATIONS (2004), *available at* http://forum.europa.Eu.int/irc/empl/csr_eu_multi_stakeholder_forum/info/data/en/CSR%20Forum%20final%20report.pdf.

8. U.N. Environment Programme (UNEP), *Stockholm 1972: Report of the United Nations Conference on the Human Environment*, http://www.unep.org/Documents.multilingual/Default.asp?DocumentID=97 (last visited July 7, 2006).

9. RACHEL CARSON, SILENT SPRING (1962).

10. WORLD COMMISSION ON ENVIRONMENT & DEVELOPMENT, OUR COMMON FUTURE (Oxford Univ. Press 1987).

11. U.N. CONFERENCE ON ENVIRONMENT & DEVELOPMENT, RIO DECLARATION ON ENVIRONMENT AND DEVELOPMENT (2006), *available at* http://www.unep.org/Documents/Default.asp?DocumentID=78&ArticleID=1163.

12. *Id.*

13. JOHN ELKINGTON, CANNIBALS WITH FORKS: TRIPLE BOTTOM LINE OF 21ST CENTURY BUSINESS (Capstone Ltd. 1997).

14. GRI, SUSTAINABILITY REPORTING GUIDELINES (2002), *available at* http://www.globalreporting.org/guidelines/2002/contents.asp (last visited May 18, 2006) [hereinafter GRI GUIDELINES].

15. *See, e.g.*, Thomas Loew et al., *Significance of the CSR Debate for Sustainability and the Requirements for Companies* (Institute for Ecological Economy Research GmbH, and German Federal Ministry for the Environment, Nature Conservation and Nuclear Safety 2004), http://www.ioew.de/english/publications/future-IOEW_CSR-Study_Summary.pdf (last visited Jan. 9, 2006).

16. Some consider corporate social responsibility to be the business contribution to a broader societal concept of sustainable development. *See, e.g.*, ISO Advisory Group on Social Responsibility 25 (Apr. 30, 2004) (working report on social responsibility).

17. ISO, GUIDELINES ON SOCIAL RESPONSIBILITY, ISO/WD 26000, WORKING DRAFT 2, §3.9 (2006).

18. *See* EC Communication on CSR 2002, *supra* note 7, at 5.

19. A survey of over 500 U.S. business executives found that over 8 in 10 believed ethical business practices, treating employees well, providing jobs and profits, and producing good products and services were very important to corporate citizenship. Less than 6 in 10 believed a good environmental record was very important to corporate citizenship. *See* THE CENTER FOR CORPORATE CITIZENSHIP AT BOSTON COLLEGE AND THE U.S. CHAMBER OF COMMERCE CENTER FOR CORPORATE CITIZENSHIP, THE STATE OF CORPORATE CITIZENSHIP IN THE U.S.: A VIEW FROM INSIDE 2003-2004 (2004), *available at* http://www.bcccc.net/ [hereinafter BOSTON COLLEGE-USCC CORPORATE CITIZENSHIP SURVEY].

20. See, e.g., the definition of CSR at EC Communication on CSR 2002, *supra* note 7, at 5. *See also* INTERNATIONAL INSTITUTE FOR SUSTAINABLE DEVELOPMENT, ISSUE BRIEFING NOTE: PERCEPTIONS AND DEFINITIONS OF SOCIAL RESPONSIBILITY 8 (2004), *available at* http://www.pacinst.org/inni/corporate_social_responsibility/standards_definitions.pdf.

21. In GlobeScan surveys, 300 sustainability experts from around the world were asked in 1996 and 2002 whether the potency of the term "sustainable development" was positively influencing key government and industry decisionmakers. In 2002, 55% of all experts—three-fourths of those from Asia, over one-half in Europe and North America—agreed the potency was increasing, up from only one-third six years earlier. Only one-sixth said the potency was decreasing, down from double that amount in 1996. *See* GlobeScan Inc., *Assessing Sustainable Development: Potency of Term*

"Sustainable Development," *in* Survey of Sustainability Experts 2002-1, at 5 (2002), *available at* http://www.globescan.com/.

22. *See* Boston College-USCC Corporate Citizenship Survey, *supra* note 19.

23. WBCSD, *Members Give Their Views on the Business Case for Sustainable Development,* WBCSD News, Oct. 17, 2003, *available at* http:// www.wbcsd.ch/templates/TemplateWBCSD2/layout.asp?type=p&MenuId= Mzcx&doOpen=1&ClickMenu=RightMenu&CurPage=21&SortOrder= pubdate%20desc,%20sector%20asc.

24. William Shakespeare, Julius Caesar act 3, sc. 2.

25. *See, e.g.,* Friends of the Earth, Inc., Lessons Not Learned—The Other Shell Report 2004 (2005), *available at* http://www.foe.co.uk/ campaigns/corporates/case_studies/shell/index.html. Shell has vigorously disputed many of these claims. *See Shell Response to the "Other Shell Report,"* http://www.shell.com/othershellreport (last visited Jan. 9, 2006).

26. John Elkington et al., *Lessons Learned: Jeroen van der Veer, in* Risk and Opportunity Best Practice in Non-Financial Reporting: The Global Reporters 2004 Survey of Corporate Sustainability Reporting 15 (2004), *available at* http://www.sustainability.com/publications/ engaging/Risk-Opportunity-Exe-Summary.pdf.

27. *See* GRI Guidelines, *supra* note 14. The third edition of the guidelines (G3) was issued in October 2006.

28. Marc Gunther, *Money and Morals at GE,* Fortune, Nov. 1, 2004, *available at* http://www.cof.org/files/Documents/Education_Collaborations/ Money_and_Morals_at_GE.doc.

CHAPTER 2

Determining Scope: An Operational
Definition of Sustainability

"If you don't know where you're going, you just might not get there."[1]
—Yogi Berra

The plan sounded good: bring employment and development to northern Mexico by enacting a law enabling companies to set up special corporations, called maquiladoras.[2] These corporations could establish collaborating "twin" facilities on each side of the U.S.-Mexican border and ship duty-free raw materials, product components, and assemblies from the U.S. operations to their Mexican counterparts. There in Mexico, hand work or other processing could be done before shipping the finished product back to the North. Employment, development, and social progress would flow to many Mexican families. Everyone would win.

Indeed, business did flourish in northern Mexico, but the reality of maquiladoras in practice left much to be desired. Towns became crowded with the wave of new residents seeking work. Water and sewerage systems, garbage disposal, and other basic services were overwhelmed. Squalid shanty towns erupted. Although many responsible U.S. companies and their suppliers flocked to take advantage of Mexico's maquiladora law, many others with weaker social values or economic resources also arrived. Serious health problems from pollution became commonplace. This was far from what planners had envisioned.

It was in this setting in the early 1990s that fierce debate arose over the proposed North America Free Trade Agreement (NAFTA).[3] Here was an agreement that would take the idea of free trade in the border region and expand it to the entire country—in fact to three countries: Canada, Mexico, and the United States. The questions for the Mexican maquiladora communities were: Would this agreement spread the same ills that arose years earlier in the wake of the maquiladora pact? Would this just make a bad situation worse?

As the controversy raged on, religious, labor, and other social groups sympathetic to the plight of the Mexicans began to wade in. They publicly grilled U.S. companies with operations already in Mexico or intentions to locate there. Some of the questions asked were: What wages will you pay? What contributions will you make to the community? Will you help address water, sewer, and education needs? What type of pollutants will you generate and how will you handle them? What has been your record on employee safety and working conditions? Will you use local suppliers and, if so, how will you treat them? In short, are you the kind of corporate citizen we want to have as a long-term neighbor?

Intuitive and Literal Definitions of Sustainability

What these groups were really asking was this: Is your company working toward sustainable development or against it? Their worries about NAFTA provide an intuitive understanding of sustainability and why it is important. Simply stated, if an issue is something a maquila activist would have raised, it is most likely part of sustainability. Concerns about sustainability were the activists' concerns. They feared fleeting, parasitic businesses that would degrade their community's economic, social, and environmental health. In essence what the activists wanted to know was, would the company follow the 2Rs?

Indeed, as the maquila activists would envision it, sustainability is not a term of stagnation but a term of progress to a better life. The *development* in *sustainable development*—often dropped for shorthand convenience—connotes this sense of hopeful progress. It suggests an evolving process that restores the balance needed for long-term organizational and societal well-being.

The 2Rs' definition of sustainability proposed here encompasses the version put forth by the U.N. Brundtland Commission (a sufficient legacy for future generations) as well as Elkington's TBL (economic, social, and environmental performance). It also appears consistent with several other noteworthy definitions that have been put forth by others:

- *International Institute for Sustainable Development (IISD).* A business variation of the Brundtland definition was published by the IISD and others in 1992 which states: "Adopting business strategies and activities that meet the needs of the enterprise and its stakeholders today while protecting, sustaining and enhancing the human and natural resources that will be needed in the future."[4]

- *WBCSD eco-efficiency + CSR.* The WBCSD, a coalition of 170 international companies committed to sustainable development, looks at sustainability as a combination of two other concepts. One is "eco-efficiency," a term they coined in 1991 linking financial and environmental performance to create more value with less adverse impact.[5] The other term is "corporate social responsibility," which the WBCSD defines as "the business commitment to contribute to sustainable economic development, working with employees, their families, the local community, and society at large to improve their quality of life."[6] The council asserts that the drive toward sustainability is best furthered by focusing on these concepts, along with the use of innovation and technology, the management of ecosystems, and the design of markets.

• *Forum for the Future (Forum)/Sustainability-Integrated Guidelines for Management (SIGMA).* Another meaning of sustainability has been suggested by Forum. This meaning was adopted for SIGMA, an initiative launched by the U.K. Department of Trade and Industry in partnership with Forum, the British Standards Institution, and AccountAbility (a U.K.-based international professional institute, formerly The Institute of Social and Ethical Accountability). According to Forum, organizations pursue sustainability by actively managing and enhancing five types of assets: (1) natural capital (the environment); (2) human capital (people); (3) social capital (social relationships and structures); (4) manufactured capital (fixed assets); and (5) financial capital (profit and loss, sales, shares, cash, etc.). Sustainability is achieved by living off the *income* (flows or outputs) from these capitals rather than by degrading the capitals themselves.[7]

• *U.K. government.* The U.K. government says the goal of sustainable development is "to enable all people throughout the world to satisfy their basic needs and enjoy a better quality [of] life, without compromising the quality of life of future generations." For the U.K. government itself, this goal is to be pursued "in an integrated way through a sustainable, innovative and productive economy that delivers high levels of employment; and a just society that promotes social inclusion, sustainable communities, and personal wellbeing." At the same time, the goal must be achieved "in ways that protect and enhance the physical and natural environment, and use resources and energy as efficiently as possible."[8]

- *World Conservation Union (WCU), UNEP, and World Wildlife Fund for Nature (WWF).* In 1991, the WCU, UNEP, and the WWF offered the following definition of sustainability: "Improving the quality of life while living within the earth's carrying capacities."[9]

- *U.N. Secretary-General.* Then-Secretary-General Annan characterized sustainability in a way that focuses on its benefits: "Far from being a burden, sustainable development is an exceptional opportunity—economically, to build markets and create jobs; socially, to bring people in from the margins; and politically, to give every man and woman a voice, and a choice, in deciding their own future."[10]

These and scores of other definitions that have emerged have suggested the following important aspects of sustainability that must be considered when designing and implementing an SOS:

- *Multiple geographic levels.* If sustainability is to be accomplished, it must be done through people and their organizations at the local, regional, and global levels.

- *Moving target.* The sustainability of societies and organizations, like good personal health, is a moving target that requires ongoing attention.

- *Easier to see failure than success.* Metrics and other indicators can help gauge progress toward sustainability, but only to a point. Unfortunately, it is difficult to tell when sustainability is achieved. A society or an organization may be sustainable for one's lifetime, but will its processes, practices, and adaptability enable it to survive for decades—even centuries—beyond? It's hard to tell. In that sense, sustainability—as one colleague claims—is "like democracy . . . a lofty goal whose realization eludes us."[11] It's much easier to tell when organizations and societies fail the sustainability challenge, when they cease to exist because of shortcomings in managing economic or natural resources or because of their lack of respect for people or other living things. According to Pulitzer Prize-winning author Prof. Jared Diamond, the Mayan, Anasazi, and Easter Island societies suffered that fate.[12] Businesses also frequently come unwound for those reasons, too. Whether you are a society or organization, a failure to achieve sustainability means either complete annihilation or, at best, being assimilated by your rivals. That result is usually easy to spot.

- *Shaping rather than stopping change.* Of course, people can prevent some but not all turnover in societies and companies. But the quest for sustainability is not about halting change. Rather, it is about anticipating, planning for, and helping shape change—creating sustainable change. It is also about making transitions with the least amount of harm and suffering for humans and other forms of life, the least amount of social upheaval. The big concern, of course, is keeping Homo sapiens off the extinction hit list. At the very least, we don't want to add ourselves to that list by our own hand through a nuclear holocaust or by more subtle means that slowly erode the foundations of life. But mere survival is not enough. Life that is "nasty, brutish, and short"—to quote Thomas Hobbes[13]—is not what we are after. We want life of mutual respect and well-being—for everyone now and in the future. From the perspective of companies and other organizations, the goal is to anticipate and facilitate change in the development of products, services, processes, and practices to support the sustainability of society. The idea for such enterprises, of course, is to not only accomplish this goal, but to also become successful survivors as well.

- *Economic sustainability more urgent but not more important.* From a company's perspective, is economic sustainability—often the ultimate undoing of a business—more important than social or environmental sustainability? It cannot be denied that economic performance often lies at the top of a company's priority list and that lack of that performance is commonly fatal for a CEO's career. But the question is like asking, which is more important to human life: air, water, or food? Air to a human, like money to a company, is the thing most urgently needed for survival. But a person's lack of water and food, like a company's inadequate social and environmental performance, can eventually prove deadly as well. As we will see in Chapter 3, the failure of a business to appreciate its social and environmental risks and opportunities can significantly retard economic performance and weaken its competitive position.

- *Interdependence of sustainability elements.* Sustainability elements—respect and resources in the case of the 2Rs or economic, social, and environmental considerations in the case of the TBL—are not independent, isolated concepts but closely related. Certainly tax policy and other economic incentives can have profound effects on how business serves or harms environmental or social interests. Business ethics, union rights, and sweatshop practices pose economic and social concerns. Drought-caused starvation can bring environmental and social problems together in a disastrous way. Perhaps no better example of the tie among the environment, poverty, and social conflict comes from Nobel peace laureate Maathai, the Kenyan activist who mobilized women to plant 30 million trees across her homeland while promoting human rights. Maathai observed:

  > When I started, I was addressing the needs of rural women—firewood, building materials, food, vegetation. In the course of time, I saw the link between environment and good governance. A corrupt, evil government will support (unsustainable) logging and deforestation. I saw that when these resources are degraded, people fight. There's fighting between pastoral communities and farming communities. I did not step out to work for peace, but for peace to work we needed this.[14]

- *Collaboration essential for success.* Given these interdependencies and other complexities of sustainability issues, no one sector—not government, not business, not NGOs—can master them on its own. The quest for sustainability must be a joint effort. Where organizations take these lessons and apply them collaboratively, the positive impact of their efforts will be multiplied.

Operational Definition of Sustainability: Questions, Policy, and Topics

Unfortunately, none of these definitions previously discussed provides sufficient direction to translate sustainability into practical action. For example, how can the reader divine more from the Brundtland meaning—*development that meets the needs of the present without compromising the ability of future generations to meet their own needs?* What are the true needs of the present generation? Under the TBL definition—economic, social, and environmental responsibility—what do we mean by each of these three components? What topics do each embrace?

These broad definitions provide no other suggestions about how to implement sustainability within a company. They don't tell us what sustainability is and is not at an operating level. To discern that, we will need to dig deeper as noted in Figure 2.1, examining the expected sustainability behaviors of the organization and the topics those behaviors typically touch. To identify the behaviors, it is useful to approach the matter as a maquila activist by asking a few fundamental questions. Those questions can be framed around the TBL definition and linked to the 2Rs as follows:

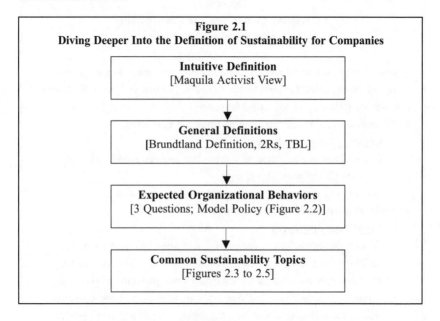

Figure 2.1
Diving Deeper Into the Definition of Sustainability for Companies

Intuitive Definition
[Maquila Activist View]

General Definitions
[Brundtland Definition, 2Rs, TBL]

Expected Organizational Behaviors
[3 Questions; Model Policy (Figure 2.2)]

Common Sustainability Topics
[Figures 2.3 to 2.5]

- *Question concerning economic success (the wise use of financial resources):* Do our business activities promote sustainable economic health for the company and the global community?

- *Question concerning social responsibility (respect for people):* Do we conduct our business in a manner that contributes to the well-being of our employees and the global community?

- *Question concerning environmental responsibility (respect for life and the wise use and management of natural resources):* Do we manage our operations in a way that is protective of the

environment to help ensure the earth can sustain future generations and the company's ability to meet future needs?

These questions imply certain, more specific obligations of a company—obligations that can be captured in a model sustainability policy
like that presented in Figure 2.2. The topics commonly covered under
these policy obligations are listed in Figures 2.3 to 2.5.

Figure 2.2
A Company Commitment to Sustainability
(A Model Sustainability Policy)

<u>Vision:</u> It is in the best interests of our company and society as a whole that our
company moves along the path to sustainability. To that end, we will strive to
achieve the following vision of performance:

1. Economic success: the wise use of financial resources

   a. <u>Company Economic Prosperity</u>

   Our business is positioned to survive and prosper economically.

   b. <u>Community Economic Prosperity</u>

   We help our community survive and prosper economically.

2. Social responsibility: respect for people

   a. <u>Respect for Employees</u>

   We treat our employees in a respectful, fair, non-exploitative way, especially with regard to compensation and benefits; promotion; training;
   open, constructive dialogue with management; involvement in decisionmaking; working conditions that are safe, healthy, and non-coercive;
   rights of association, collective bargaining, and privacy; employment-
   termination practices; and work-life balance.

   b. <u>Diversity, Fair Hiring Practices</u>

   We promote diversity and use hiring practices that are fair, responsible,
   non-discriminatory, and non-exploitative for our employees, board
   members, and suppliers.

   c. <u>Responsible Governance</u>

   We manage our risks properly, use our economic power responsibly, and
   operate our business in a way that is ethical and legal.

Figure 2.2 (continued)

d. Respect for Stakeholders

We are transparent, respectful, and fair to local populations, investors, suppliers, and other stakeholders outside our organization who may be affected by our operations. We work collaboratively with our communities to enhance the well-being of others.

e. Fair Dealing With Customers

We are honest and fair with our customers, competing fairly for their business, respecting their privacy, and providing them safe and effective products and services under the conditions we promise.

3. Environmental responsibility: respect for life and the wise management and use of natural resources

a. Resource Conservation

We conserve our use of natural resources to the extent practicable.

b. Waste Prevention and Management

We reduce to the extent practicable the quantity and degree of hazard of the wastes we generate from our operations, and handle them in a safe, legal, and responsible way to minimize their environmental effects.

c. Environmental Risk Control and Restoration

We minimize the risk of spills and other potentially harmful environmental incidents, restore the environment where damaged by us, and enhance it to better support biodiversity.

d. Reduction of Supply Chain Impacts

We work with others in our supply chain to help assure adverse environmental impacts and risks associated with our products and services are reduced and properly controlled, and environmental benefits optimized.

e. Collaboration With Communities

We collaborate with our communities to protect and improve the environment.

Figure 2.3
Examples of Economic Topics

Brand strength	Dividends	Retained earnings
Capital expenditures	Liabilities	Return on investment
Cash flow	Local purchasing	Sales
Community donations	Market share	Taxes
Credit rating	Profits	Tax subsidies
Debt and interest	R&D investment	Wages

Figure 2.4
Examples of Social Topics

Access to company
 products and services
 by the disabled
Access to company
 products and services
 by the poor
Access to healthcare
 by the poor
Anti-sexual harassment
 policies
Antitrust practices
Bioterrorism
Board diversity
Bribery and corruption
Charitable donations
Child labor
Community education
Community outreach
Consumer privacy
Corporate governance
Dependent care benefits
Digital divide in e-access
Disaster relief
Disciplinary practices
Emergency preparedness
Employee assistance
 programs
Employee benefits

Employee diversity
Employee layoff policies
Employee privacy
Employee relations
Employee shared values
Employee training and
 development
Employee turnover
Employee wellness
 programs
Employee work-life
 balance
Employment
Ethics
Fair advertising
 and labeling
Fair wages
Flexible work options
Food product nutrition,
 obesity
Forced labor
Helping the
 disadvantaged
Human rights
 (security policies, etc.)
Impacts on local cultures
Indigenous rights
Indoor air pollution

Industrial hygiene
Legal compliance
 on social topics
Non-discrimination
 policies
Occupational health
Political contributions
Predatory lending
Producer responsibility
Product labeling
Product quality
Product safety
Product usefulness
Securities regulation
Socially responsible
 sales & marketing
 practices
Supplier diversity
Supplier work practices
Support for community
 services
Transparent public
 reporting
Union relations
Worker violence
Workplace safety

Figure 2.5
Examples of Environmental Topics

Air pollution	Greenhouse gases	Product energy use
Animal rights	Invasive species	Radio-frequency exposure
Biodiversity	Litter, visual pollution	Recycling
Chemical spills	Natural habitat	Renewable energy and
Compliance with	restoration	materials
environmental laws	Natural resource	Responsible land use
and permits	usage	Soil contamination
Cultural heritage sites	Noise	Soil erosion/depletion
Customer disposal of	Odors	Spill prevention
products	Ozone-depleting	Vibration
Endangered species	substances	Waste disposal
Energy conservation	Packaging reduction	Water conservation
Environmentally	Pollution prevention	Water pollution
sensitive design	Precautionary Principle	Wetlands protection
Genetically modified	Product and packaging	Wildlife conservation
organisms	take-back	

These questions, obligations, and topics underscore two important points about sustainability as it applies to organizations. First, as shown in Figure 2.6, each of the three overarching areas of sustainability has an internal and an external aspect. Each organization must help assure the sustainability of itself as well as that of the external society. This acknowledges that as we will see in the next chapter, the long-term success and survival of organizations is dependent upon the long-term success and survival of the communities in which they operate. It demands that companies go beyond their internal silos to understand, be a part of, and help improve the external world upon which they depend.

Figure 2.6
Examples of Internal and External Aspects of Sustainability

TBL Component	2R's Component	Internal (Company) Aspect	External (Societal) Aspect
Economic	Wise use of economic resources	Achieving economic success of company	Achieving economic prosperity of society
Environmental	Wise use of natural resources	Leaving enough resources to meet current and future needs of company	Leaving enough resources to meet current and future needs of society
	Respect for living things	Treating living things with respect within company operations (e.g., respecting animal rights)	Protecting ecosystems so living things can survive in the environment
		Preventing and controlling pollution within company property (sometimes considered part of social sustainability)	Preventing and controlling pollution of the external environment
Social	Respect for people	Respecting the needs of people inside the company	Respecting the needs of people outside the company

Second, the wide range of questions posed emphasizes sustainability's broad reach into nearly every corner of company operations and society. In fact, for many organizations, this breadth may appear too overwhelming to manage. Early American pioneers on the westward wagon trains had an expression for it: seeing the elephant. For those of 150 years ago who were about to begin their trek, the "elephant" represented a new and bizarre experience that lay ahead. But for the many who struggled along the trail and eventually turned back, *seeing the elephant* came to mean seeing the experience as hardship and wanting no more of it. Like dejected 19th-century travelers, some companies of today take one glance at sustainability, immediately see the elephant, and proceed no farther. But as the pioneers taught us, the difficult paths often bring great rewards, not just for the initial travelers, but for those who come after them. Indeed, that is the promise of the path toward sustainability. For those who remain concerned about the "elephant," Chapter 6 provides a logical process for prioritizing efforts to assure they produce good business value without overtaxing resources.

But what is the business value that can be provided through a quest for sustainability? Let us turn to that issue next.

Follow-up Checklist for Action: An Operational Definition of Sustainability

☐ Review the model sustainability policy (Figure 2.2) and the lists of sustainability topics (Figures 2.3 to 2.5) and modify them to address the sustainability obligations and topics relevant to your organization.

Endnotes to Chapter 2

1. This quote and many others by the famous New York Yankee catcher can be found in, YOGI BERRA, THE YOGI BOOK: "I REALLY DIDN'T SAY EVERYTHING I SAID" (1998).

2. *Decree for the Development and Operation of the Maquiladora Export Industry* (the Maquiladora Decree), Mexico, *Diario Oficial*, December 22, 1989, amended January 1, 1994, June 1, 1998, November 13, 1998, October 30, 2000, December 31, 2000, and May 12, 2003. *See* Office of North American Free Trade Act (NAFTA), *Frequently Asked Questions and Answers (FAQs) About Maquiladoras* (NAFTA Facts Document No. 8313), http://www.mac.doc.gov/nafta/8313.htm (last visited Jan. 9, 2006).

3. Dec. 17, 1992, Can.-Mex.-U.S., 107 Stat. 2057, 32 I.L.M. 289 (1993); 19 U.S.C. §3312 (1994), *available at* http://www.dfait-maeci.gc.ca/nafta-alena/menu-en.asp (approving and implementing NAFTA).

4. IISD ET AL., BUSINESS STRATEGY FOR SUSTAINABLE DEVELOPMENT (1992), *available at* http://www.bsdglobal.com/tools/strategies.asp.

5. WBCSD, *Eco-Efficiency*, http://www.wbcsd.ch/templates/Template WBCSD1/layout.asp?type=p&MenuId=MzI4&doOpen=1&ClickMenu= LeftMenu (last visited Jan. 9, 2006). According to the WBCSD, eco-efficiency is achieved through pollution prevention, greater reuse and recycling of wastes, and making products more resource-efficient to produce and use. It may also come about through leasing products or selling their function rather than selling the products themselves, improving product durability and recyclability, and using networks and virtual organizations to share resources.

6. WBCSD, CROSS-CUTTING THEMES (2003), *available at* http://www.wbcsd.ch/DocRoot/MtdNqMsKPWluRQKihmC6/cross-cutting.pdf.

7. SIGMA, *The SIGMA Project*, http://www.projectsigma.com/ (last visited Jan. 9, 2006). *See also* Appendix 3.9 and Appendix 8.3, Figure A8.3.8. for more information about SIGMA and the five capitals.

8. FOOD & RURAL AFFAIRS, U.K. SECRETARY OF STATE FOR ENVIRONMENT, SECURING THE FUTURE: DELIVERING U.K. SUSTAINABLE DEVELOPMENT STRATEGY: THE U.K. GOVERNMENT SUSTAINABLE DEVELOPMENT STRATEGY 16 (2005), *available at* http://www.sustainable-development.gov.uk/publications/uk-strategy/uk-strategy-2005.htm.

9. WCU ET AL., CARING FOR EARTH: A STRATEGY FOR SUSTAINABLE LIVING (WCU 1991), *available at* http://www.iucn.org/bookstore/WorldconStrat.htm.

10. Kofi Annan, U.N. Secretary-General, *From Doha to Johannesburg by Way of Monterrey: How Development Can Be Achieved and Sustained in the 21st Century*, Speech to the London School of Economics and

Political Science (Feb. 25, 2003), *available at* http://www.lse.ac.uk/Press/archive/Kofi_Annan_at_LSE.htm.

11. ALAN ATKISSON, THE COMPASS OF SUSTAINABILITY (1998), *available at* http://www.atkisson.com/.

12. *See* JARED DIAMOND, COLLAPSE: HOW SOCIETIES CHOOSE TO FAIL OR SUCCEED (Viking Press 2005).

13. The complete quote can be found in Hobbes' masterpiece, THOMAS HOBBES, LEVIATHAN ch. 13 (1651).

14. Vicki Hallett, *Her Trees Bring Peace*, U.S. NEWS & WORLD REP., Jan. 10, 2005, at 56.

CHAPTER 3

The Value of Sustainability: Why Bother?

"Problems are only opportunities in work clothes."[1]
—Henry Kaiser

As they say in my neighborhood, the only sure things in life are death, taxes, and that the Chicago Cubs baseball team will once again fail to win the World Series championship. There are no such certainties in business; the adoption of a sustainability initiative does not ensure success. This is particularly true of the company that views sustainability only in terms of its public relations value—such shallow sustainability programs don't last. However, if used as the foundation of a business operating system, as described in Chapters 4 and 5, sustainability can make a business stronger and more competitive. It can strengthen risk management, compliance, productivity, and credibility. It can help a firm avoid many problems of the past, seize new opportunities for the future, and become part of the lifeblood of the company that continues to contribute in good times and bad. While the benefit of an SOS will vary from company to company, all who make a serious effort to implement one should find the effort well worth the investment.

The value of an SOS is at the heart of the business case for pursuing sustainability. Much has been written about this elusive case—the Holy Grail of social activists. The problem is that pursuing sustainability is not just about going after one issue. As we learned in Chapter 2, it's really about many issues, each with a different priority and business justification. For example, reducing waste for the purpose of cutting cost—something with visible short- and long-term financial benefits—is almost always more attractive to a business than furthering biodiversity. It is hopeless to search for overarching arguments that support aggressive advancement on all sustainability topics. Instead, one must first define an SOS, which enables a company to comb through topics, applying evaluation criteria to determine which topics deserve attention and which do not. In other words, with an SOS, one has a way of examining the business case for sustainability on a topic-by-topic basis from the unique viewpoint of each company.

Business Value Versus Ethical Value

Does this mean that sustainability issues like biodiversity will always be ignored because they have a lower business value with most companies? Not necessarily. One objective of an SOS is to modify decisionmaking on important matters so that all relevant, significant sustainability issues are considered. Designs of new facilities and products should identify and address relevant biodiversity impacts, for example. Of course, this doesn't mean every company should contribute to a "save-the-whales" fund. But an SOS can help determine if and when a company should do so. An SOS is a cyclical process that year after year works down through the priority of actions that contribute to sustainability and company success. In early years, the SOS may point to productivity, legal compliance, and high risk issues as those to be addressed. Later, after the top issues have been mastered, action can be taken on those of lower priority. These actions may well involve programs to control lower level risks or enhance or protect the company's new-found reputation for social consciousness. At this later stage of the SOS, a save-the-whales program may be considered. Such an initiative may fit nicely with the theme, culture, and reputational goals of a company in the fishing industry, but not with one manufacturing farm equipment. All companies cannot take on all sustainability issues. Most companies simply don't have the resources, and as with any organizational endeavor, focus is the key to achievement.

If companies are to address sustainability issues according to the priorities they set, what is to prevent them from conveniently ignoring some important ethical issue simply because there is no money in it for them? Nothing. Certainly there will be companies that do just that for any number of reasons. A few business leaders—the most culpable—will choose to break the law, be dishonest, or adopt other "career-limiting" strategies. Other executives may display benign neglect; like slave owners of centuries past, they may continue unsavory conduct because they lack the creativity, ambition, or courage to find a morally upright way of doing business. Thus, the SOS is not for them. It is for those who are eager for business success while adhering to high standards of ethics. It is for the vast majority of business leaders—the ones who want to "do well by doing good."

Framing the Business Case: Five Questions

So how do we make the business case for establishing an SOS? In essence, we must show that attractive nuggets of business value are waiting to be found in the hills of sustainability, attractive enough to support a prospecting expedition there.

Unfortunately, many executives who ask about the business case for sustainability are not thinking about a process for prospecting for big nuggets of business value—their view is much narrower. What they are thinking about is the business justification for preparing a sophisticated annual sustainability report. They find the "case for sustainability" wanting because they have yet to see good examples where such a report generated identifiable increases in sales, stock price, or worker motivation. But this type of analysis misses the point. The value of reporting is based on the value of an SOS. We must establish the latter first.

The business case for both an SOS and sustainability reporting can be built by working through this sequence of easy questions:

1. Should business operations and functions perform short- and long-term planning in a way that anticipates future trends and considers the needs of those who make a company successful?
2. Should this planning involve a process by which operational and functional groups identify business risks and opportunities and prioritize them for action?
3. Should business managers be accountable for setting and achieving performance goals designed to realize these identified, high-value priorities?
4. Should progress toward these goals be periodically measured and reported within the organization?
5. Should the company use this collected information to its best advantage in enhancing its credibility with interested employees, customers, suppliers, investors, governments, and communities?

The answers to these questions should be obvious. They ask about common techniques of good management. That's the point: an SOS *is* simply good management. An SOS naturally flows from positive answers to Questions 1-4. Question 4 speaks to internal reporting as a tool for constructive change. Question 5 assumes that an SOS has already been justified on its own merits. In essence, Question 5 asks whether the company feels it should spend some added time and money to take advantage of information it has already obtained for internal management reasons. If the answer to Question 5 is "yes," then the only issue remaining is how much time and money should be devoted to this effort. In some cases, a simple website page or short computer-generated report may be all a company feels it can produce for its stakeholders. Companies should not be embarrassed to start off in this way. In the eyes of many peers and NGOs, the companies that do so would be considered leaders, showing their non-reporting brethren how easy communicating with the public can be. Because few resources are required to make already collected data available to the public, the business case for reporting shouldn't be a difficult one. With experience, the value of sustainability reporting and the justification for a more sophisticated approach to it should become increasingly apparent. We will talk more about reporting in Chapter 10. For now, let's jump back to the business case for an SOS.

The Show-Me-the-Money Model: Using Sustainability to Make Money

An SOS is a systematic, efficient way of identifying and pursing high-priority sustainability issues—a method for prospecting for business value. Therefore, the imperative for adopting an SOS can be best justified by reviewing the results an SOS can produce—the nuggets likely to be found in the search. Real-life examples demonstrate how a proactive approach to various sustainability topics can strengthen a business and how neglecting these topics can hurt it. These examples can be conveniently examined through two models which depict the factors that contribute to business success.

The first model—the Show-Me-the-Money Model—is diagrammed in Figure 3.1. It is based on the views of Nobel Prize-winning economist, Milton Friedman. It was he who said: "So the question is, do corporate executives, provided they stay within the law, have responsibilities in their business activities other than to make as much money for their stockholders as possible? And my answer to that is, no they do not."[2] While many companies strongly disagree with Friedman, let us assume for the moment that he is right, that increased profits and cash flow are the primary objectives of business, and that a business' primary obligation is to provide increasing financial returns to its investors in the form of ever-higher stock prices and dividends. If this is so, then we must look at the following key factors which drive profits, stock price, and dividends:

Factor 1: Reputation and brand strength;
Factor 2: Competitive, effective, and desirable products and services; new markets;
Factor 3: Productivity;
Factor 4: Operational burden and interference;
Factor 5: Supply chain costs;
Factor 6: Cost of capital (lender and investor appeal); and
Factor 7: Legal liability.

These items are listed as sales and cost factors in Figure 3.1. Let us consider each of these factors in turn, review how they might be affected by a company's drive toward sustainability, and identify the business value that emerges from that relationship.

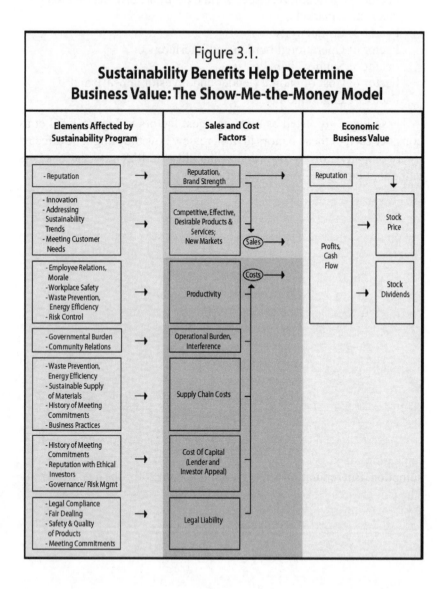

Figure 3.1.
**Sustainability Benefits Help Determine
Business Value: The Show-Me-the-Money Model**

Factor 1: Reputation and Brand Strength

Business-case argument: *Sustainability performance determines reputation, and reputation has a significant effect on sales and stock price. Studies show that one-fourth to one-third of a company's public reputation is based on social and environmental performance.*

Reputation as a Valuable Asset, Significantly Affecting Sales, Stock Price, and Market Value

Reputation has many definitions. In general, it can be considered the "net result of the interaction of all experiences, impressions, beliefs, feelings and knowledge that stakeholders have about the performance of a company."[3] A strong company reputation can be beneficial in many ways. In a 2003 survey commissioned by Hill & Knowlton, over 250 senior executives from around the world were asked to list the benefits derived from building and maintaining their company's reputation. The top five responses were:

1. ability to recruit and retain employees;
2. ability to generate additional sales;
3. ability to facilitate transactions and partnerships;
4. ability to charge premium prices; and
5. enhanced stock price performance.

Six in 10 executives said reputation was much more important in this regard than it was five years earlier.[4] Taking these five responses, let us more closely examine items 2, 4, and 5 related to sales, pricing, and share value.

Certainly most people would agree that company and product (brand) reputation can affect sales. The advertising industry was built on that assumption. But reputation affects pricing, too. In 2003, the business group The Conference Board organized a meeting among 18 CEOs and other senior executives from major international organizations to discuss future business challenges. Several attendees said they felt cost-cutting would be become so common in the future and costs and pricing so transparent to customers, that brand differentiation would become the only true pricing power remaining.[5] If they are right, reputation will become even more valuable in the future.

As Figure 3.1 suggests, reputation not only influences sales and the price of goods and services but the price of a company's stock as well. A number of studies confirm this, although they differ widely about the extent of the correlation. These studies measure the strength of a reputation or brand and compare it with market value (stock price × number of shares outstanding) and other financial measures. Reputation strength can be determined in a variety of ways. The following three are among the more popular:

- *Brand valuation by Interbrand.* Interbrand is a unit of advertising group Omnicom. Interbrand's method takes into account the projected future earnings of the brand as well as its basic strength. Brand strength is determined from an analysis of brand and market characteristics and legal factors.[6]
- Fortune *magazine's criteria for most admired companies. Fortune* relies on a survey of 10,000 directors, executives, and analysts which asks them to rank other companies on a scale of 1 to 10 in each of nine different categories, including social responsibility.[7]
- *Harris-Fombrun reputation quotient (RQ).* This technique was developed by Charles Fombrun, professor emeritus of management at the Stern School of Business of New York University and executive director of the Reputation Institute, in collaboration with Harris Interactive, the worldwide polling and consulting firm. A company's RQ is determined by surveying 600 or so consumers, investors, employees, and members of the general public to obtain their perceptions about the organization based on 20 attributes classified under the following 6 dimensions:

1. *Emotional appeal*: how much the company is liked, admired, and respected;
2. *Products and services*: perceptions of the quality, innovation, value, and reliability of the company's products and services;
3. *Financial performance*: perceptions of the company's profitability, prospects, and risk;
4. *Vision and leadership*: how much the company demonstrates a clear vision and strong leadership;
5. *Workplace environment*: perceptions of the quality of a company's employees, how good it is as an employer, and how well it is managed; and
6. *Social responsibility*: perceptions of the company as a

good citizen in its dealings with communities, employees, and the environment.[8]

What is a company's reputation worth? Research has shown that between 50 and 90% of a company's market value can be attributed to reputation and other intangibles.[9] Based on Interbrand's methodology, the Coca-Cola brand was most valuable in 2005 at $67 billion.[10] While critics can quibble about that valuation, most would concede that the value of reputation in many industries is enormous. Most telling is the remark from John Stuart, former CEO of Quaker Oats Company: "If this business were split up, I would give you the land and bricks and mortar, and I would take the brands and trademarks and I would fare better than you."[11]

If reputation is valuable, it naturally follows that change in a company's reputation will affect its market value. Indeed, studies have confirmed that. A comparison of the 1999 and 2000 RQs for 35 companies showed an average 28% slide in market value among those companies whose RQ scores dropped, and an average gain of 8% among those with rising RQ scores.[12] A review conducted at the University of Texas at Austin found that a 60% difference in reputation score translated to a 7% difference in market value.[13]

The Impact of Social and Environmental Performance on Overall Reputation

We've established that reputation and brand are valuable, but what contribution does a company's sustainability efforts make to that value? Arguably most of a company's reputation is based on its sustainability performance. Remember, by *sustainability* we mean not only environmental performance, philanthropy, and other traditional matters of social consciousness, but also mainstream company issues like financial performance, governance, and product quality. The term also includes open and honest behavior and communications, which are essential for showing respect for others and fulfilling sustainability's demand for social responsibility.

If sustainability performance determines much of reputation, is the economic component of sustainability the main determinant? What part of reputation is based on social and environmental activities—commonly referred to as *social responsibility*?

Professor Fombrun's Reputation Institute provided some insights in a 1999 study of public impressions of U.S. companies. That study disclosed that perceptions about a company's social responsibility and workplace environment—the two dimensions most closely related to a company's reputation on sustainability—had an average correlation of 35% and 23%, respectively, to a company's overall reputation. The products and services category, which also has some sustainability aspects, rated 37%.[14]

Results similar to those reported by the Reputation Institute were also found by BT, a leader in corporate social responsibility. Their studies reveal that over one-quarter of their corporate reputation with customers was driven by their socially responsible activities. BT determined that without these activities, its customer satisfaction ratings would drop by approximately 10%. They believe this would have a direct impact on sales, particularly since socially concerned customers tend to be more affluent than average and therefore more likely to spend larger sums on communication equipment and services.[15]

In Hill & Knowlton's 2003 global executive survey, 8 in 10 business leaders said they felt social responsibility initiatives contributed to their company's reputation in at least a moderate way, and 3 in 10 believed the contribution was significant.[16] In a follow-up survey a year later, 175 executives were asked to identify the single most important factor driving their company's reputation in the marketplace other than financial and operational performance. The top factor—the reputation of the CEO and the management team—drew 30% of the responses. But three factors related to sustainability garnered a total of nearly half of the votes: (1) workplace policies and practices, general treatment of employees (21%); (2) transparent and strong governance controls (17%); and (3) track record of socially responsible behavior (9%). Media coverage came in at 14%, industry and financial analysis reports at 5%, and reputation of the board at 3%.

The link between social responsibility and overall reputation is not just conjecture, but can be demonstrated from brand and reputation analyses. Figure 3.2 shows three top-10 lists of companies ranked according to brand strength and other measures of general reputation. The listed companies are marked to indicate those that also appear on one of three top-10 lists for social responsibility. Although each of the brand and reputation analyses produced different lists, over one-half of the 30 entries on the three lists were also included in the top-10 rankings for social responsibility. Microsoft, the only company listed in all three columns of the table, was ranked at the top on both the 2004 and 2005 surveys for social responsibility jointly conducted by PricewaterhouseCoopers and the *Financial Times*.[17] Obviously, advertising can have its impact on reputation, too. Event sponsorships and other promotional activities by Philip Morris and its parent Altria no doubt continue to help propel the Marlboro brand into its high ranking notwithstanding the social stigma of the tobacco industry.

Figure 3.2 The Top Ten for Reputation and Brand Strength Versus The Top Ten for Social Responsibility			
Rank	***Fortune* Global Most Admired Companies-2006**[18]	**Companies With Top HarrisInteractive-Fombrun RQ in the United States-2005**[19]	**Interbrand Top Brands-2004**[20]
1	General Electric(2)	Johnson & Johnson(2)	Coca-Cola(2)(3)
2	Toyota(2)	Coca-Cola(2)(3)	Microsoft(2)(3)
3	Procter & Gamble(3)	Google	IBM(2)(3)
4	FedEx	United Parcel Service(1)	General Electric(2)
5	Johnson & Johnson(2)	3M	Intel
6	Microsoft(2)(3)	Sony	Nokia
7	Dell	Microsoft(2)(3)	Disney(2)
8	Berkshire Hathaway	General Mills	McDonald's(2)(3)
9	Apple Computer	FedEx(1)	Toyota(2)
10	Wal-Mart	Intel	Marlboro/Altria
(1)= Company ranked among the top 10 for the social responsibility component of *Fortune*'s Global Most Admired Companies list for 2006.[21] (2)= Company ranked among the top 10 for community commitment in the 2005 PricewaterhouseCoopers-*Financial Times* survey of CEOs, NGOs, and media.[22] (3)= Company ranked among the top 10 for social responsibility in the 2004 PricewaterhouseCoopers-*Financial Times* survey of NGOs and media.[23]			

The Direct Effect of Social and Environmental Reputation on Sales and Stock Price

As we've seen, social and environmental performance affects a company's general reputation, and general reputation affects sales and stock price. But if we single out the social and environmental component of a company's reputation—often referred to as simply *social responsibility*, what direct effect does that have on sales and stock price? A few studies have tried to answer that question.

The following customer surveys examined the link with sales:

- *2003 survey of British general consumers*: Eighty-four percent of those questioned indicated that when deciding to buy a product or service from a company, it was at least fairly important that the company show a high degree of social responsibility. To 4 of 10, this was *very important*.[24]
- *2004 international survey of business buyer representatives*: Approximately 45% of respondents said a supplier's performance on social responsibility was important in their purchasing decisions, although admittedly many other factors, such as those associated with the product, communications, and the quality of management, ranked higher.[25]
- *2004 survey of 1,000 Americans*: Eighty-six percent reported they would be likely to change brands to another of about the same quality and price if the other brand was associated with a social cause. But that result must be placed in context. The respondents reported they valued the following positive corporate actions even more than social responsibility (although one could argue that social responsibility includes the last three items):

  1. providing good quality products and services (valued by 98% of respondents);
  2. offering fair-priced products and services (97%);
  3. paying adequate employee benefits (93%);
  4. upholding the law (93%); and
  5. respecting human rights in manufacturing (93%).[26]

So while product price and quality may remain of paramount importance in the minds of customers, social and environmental performance is also of serious concern. Companies with comparable, competitively priced products may find their organization's sustainability performance to be a critical differentiator. Certainly that has been true for the U.K.-based bank, Co-operative Financial Services (CFS). Thirty-six percent of the CFS' account customers said that the bank's ethical and sustainability policies were the most important reason they opened and maintained an account with them.[27]

A company's social and environmental performance also affects the demand for its shares, and such performance is drawing increasing attention from money managers. Later in this chapter we will review the results of investor surveys and learn more about the small but fast-growing area of socially responsible investing (SRI).

While the survey results of consumers and—as we will see—investors are impressive, they must be viewed in perspective. The interesting questions not asked in these studies are (1) how often has the surveyed party actually changed products or investments because of a company's social responsibility practices, and (2) how well did the respondent know about the social responsibility performance of the company and its competitors? Still, this data discloses the sympathies if not the behaviors of critical stakeholder groups—employees, customers, and investors. Those sympathies should be taken into account in business decisionmaking.

Harm to Reputation and Financial Results From Negative Environmental and Social Performance

It's clear that social responsibility and other sustainability initiatives can have a positive effect on reputation, but a perceived lack of responsibility can have an even more pronounced effect in harming it. The following studies reinforce this point:

- *2003 global survey of business executives*: Respondents believed unethical corporate behavior was ranked along with product and service problems as the biggest threats to their company's reputation.[28]
- *2004 survey of 1,000 Americans*: Ninety percent of those questioned indicated that if a company behaved illegally or unethically, they would consider switching to another company's products or services (although, again, it's not clear how many actually have).[29]

If the corporate sin riles powerful public activist groups, the slide in social and environmental reputation can accelerate and prove quite painful. Chiquita Brands International, one of the world's largest banana producers and distributors, knows this only too well. Over its 100-year history, Chiquita and its predecessor companies had become known as the "octopus" for the broad reach and power they held over their employees and the governments of the countries—primarily in Latin America—that were home to its plantations. At various times the company had been implicated in political corruption, deforestation, water pollution, discrimination, inadequate worker health and safety, the suppression of trade unions, and other improprieties. The organization had earned a reputation for being closed and defensive to criticism. This all came to a head in the 1990s, when environmentalists in Costa Rica engaged the company in a bitter dispute over its farming practices. At the same time, European activists waged a media and consumer campaign targeting the company's trade union relations and pesticide use. Work stoppages became common. To make matters worse, toward the end of the decade, Chiquita suffered a dramatic collapse in banana prices and found itself embroiled in a serious trade dispute over access to European markets. As a consequence, the company's stock price plunged over 90%, forcing new management to slash costs and restructure the company's debt under bankruptcy protection.

However, Chiquita is determined to make a comeback. It has proclaimed a set of core values, which encompass, among other things, open and honest communication, stakeholder dialogue, and respect for people. A drive toward sustainability is now a key part of its strategy. It has worked with the nonprofit Rainforest Alliance to arrange third-party certification audits of its operations against three sets of standards: (1) Social Accountability (SA) 8000, the international labor and human rights standard; (2) the Better Banana Project Standard, the sustainable land use practices written by the Rainforest Alliance; and (3) the EURPGAP food safety standard. Audit results are reported openly and in considerable detail in its sustainability reports. It is now on track to complete its certification goals, and has reduced employee days on strike by 70%. In addition, $5 million are being added to the financial bottom line each year through reduced agrichemical use. What is more, Chiquita's actions have done much to satisfy those socially and environmentally concerned buyers in northern Europe—buyers who account for over half of Chiquita's sales in that region. Although sales and profitability have improved significantly, tough competition, trade tariffs, and the uncertainties of weather and other agricultural risks still pose challenges. Though its struggles are not over, Chiquita has emerged from bankruptcy armed with a new attitude and approach that will greatly improve its chances of success.[30]

As the Chiquita example shows, a company's social and environmental performance can have a significant impact on its reputation, which, in turn, can have profound consequences for financial performance. Although the precise extent and value of these correlations may be difficult to measure, they cannot be ignored.

Boosting Social Reputation and Business Value Through
Strategically Planned Philanthropy

One type of socially responsible activity—philanthropy—is commonly used by companies to boost reputation. Perhaps it should be no surprise to see Microsoft on all three lists of reputational measure in Figure 3.2. They not only do lots of things right, but their founder has funded a $27 billion foundation that gives enormous sums to various social causes. Although not in the same league as Bill Gates, corporate giving has been one way some companies have helped build their reputations. Three of the top four corporate givers for 2004 are listed in Figure 3.2: Wal-Mart ($188 million in donations); Johnson & Johnson Company ($122 million); and Marlboro's parent company, Altria ($113 million).[31]

If properly planned, philanthropy can enhance a company's reputation and serve other business objectives as well. Contributions can improve a corporation's image with a particular segment of consumers—women, youth, retirees, young parents, and the like. (For more information on this and other types of "cause-related marketing," see Appendix 1.29.) This is no doubt one reason the cosmetics company Avon Products, Inc. funds breast cancer programs in 50 countries, sponsoring research, donating medical equipment, and subsidizing mammograms. It may also be why medical-products giant Abbott Laboratories, Inc. has spent $35 million improving 82 regional health centers and training 1,300 health care workers to test, counsel, and treat AIDS patients in Tanzania. Philanthropic projects like Abbott's initiative can also enable a company to build credibility and relationships with government officials, potential customers, and other important decisionmakers in possible new markets. Such projects can help companies learn about the culture, customs, practices, and market characteristics of the area—knowledge that can prove invaluable later when introducing new business. In addition, firms can use philanthropy locally to strengthen their own work forces by providing them and their neighbors better health care facilities and educational opportunities. Moreover, companies that fund worker time for charitable initiatives may well be providing them valuable learning experiences about teamwork and project management that can benefit the business in the end.

Obviously corporate giving must be communicated if it is to have a beneficial effect on reputation, but care must be taken that the message doesn't backfire. Too much overt promotion of the gift can lead the public to conclude a company's motives aren't genuine, thus erasing all intended goodwill. Corporate givers must recognize that the public starts with a bias anyway. A survey of Americans revealed that only about one-fourth of them believed companies who participated in charitable or philanthropic activities were truly committed to the cause. However, the same study showed that 6 of 10 Americans were very impressed with philanthropic activities where employees volunteer their time or companies donate products or services.[32] Thus, the more personal the approach, the better the reputational result.

Strategies for Maximizing Reputational Benefits From Sustainability Performance

Injecting the personal touch is one way to maximize the reputational benefit from philanthropic activities. Companies can also improve the reputational bang for their investment by carefully evaluating and timing their social and environmental efforts. For example, organizations that take the early lead on studying and acting on tough social and environmental issues—like BP's support on climate change and Levi Strauss' action on worker conditions along its supply chain—assume the risks typical of pioneers, to be sure. But they also stand out from the crowd for their ethical courage and wisdom, thereby reaping reputational rewards only first-movers can enjoy. For those that don't step out front early, there is still reputational value in a "me-too" status. It's certainly a more comfortable position than being on the wrong side of social or environmental concerns, suffering the wrath of customers, investors, and employees.

Some types of businesses seem to have special appreciation for the value of reputation and how it can be affected by sustainability performance. Certainly, reputational concerns are a major reason why particular industries play up their sustainability performance. It's no coincidence that firms issuing public sustainability reports are often in businesses involving petrochemicals, mining, lumber, automobiles, heavy equipment, and utilities. Other common reporters can be found in the computer, food, pharmaceuticals, and cosmetics industries. Why are companies in these businesses paying more attention to their sustainability reputations? Some want to reinforce their image as a caring, safe, and environmentally sensitive business. Others are intent on protecting a strong brand. There are also those who desire to burnish their image because they find themselves in an industry that is socially or environmentally unpopular. A few may have more immediate concerns, such as countering adverse press about some unpleasant incident. Many may be thinking ahead, trying to build credibility with their stakeholders now in case such an event should occur in the future. Other proactive companies may see sustainability as a way to enhance their industry's reputation with governmental agencies and dissuade them from further regulation. This concern with reputation on sustainability is not a bad thing. From a company's perspective, a stronger reputation is of real business value. And if the effort being publicized is genuine and significant, how can these companies be faulted?

Factor 2: Competitive, Effective, and Desirable Products and Services; New Markets

Business-case argument: *Companies can spur innovation by incorporating sustainability considerations in their design processes. By coupling these "green" design processes with careful market assessments, a company can better address customer needs, produce products and services that are more competitive, and tap new markets. The result is increased sales and profits.*

To quote the old saw: "If you build a better mousetrap, customers will beat a path to your door." But what do we mean by *better?* Whether it's mousetraps, marmalade, or music boxes, a *better* product is one that does a superior job of meeting the needs and expectations of customers. A company that produces better products is one that best understands not only what customers want today but what they are likely to need in the future. "Green" design processes help cultivate that understanding by introducing sustainability issues and trends into the review. By looking at issues like demographic shifts, resource depletion, and public attitudes about genetic engineering, a company can improve the likelihood that customer appeal for a new product or service will be strong now and—even more important—sustainable over the long term. These processes may also reveal entirely new markets for a company. New markets and more attractive products mean more sales. As British Prime Minister

Blair observed with regard to climate change: "It is technological advances and economic development that will provide the realistic solution. It is the firms and countries that lead the way in adapting to this challenge that will have the competitive advantage in the future."[33]

CEO Immelt of GE is well aware of the opportunities as well. Since 2001, GE has acquired businesses in water purification and solar and wind energy. It is planning to earn $20 billion a year by 2010 from the sale of more energy-efficient (and less-polluting) locomotives, jet engines, coal-fired power plants, washing machines, and other equipment. Explains Immelt: "The economics of scarcity are going to drive lots of technological innovation over the next 10, 20, 30 years. This (focus on sustainability-related businesses) is an approach to growing the company faster."[34]

Green Design Defined

Green design processes can help companies realize the visions of leaders like Blair and Immelt. These processes are grounded on two sustainability objectives:

1. *Improving the efficient use of natural and economic resources all along the life cycle of the product, from material extraction to manufacture, use, and post-use disposition.* (See Figure 3.3.) This means searching for ways to provide the customer the same function or service that the product was intended to perform but at less cost and with less material and energy required in the manufacture and use of the product. (This challenge is a part of Extended Producer Responsibility discussed in Appendix 1.27.) Designers must look for approaches that minimize the quantity and degree of hazard of waste along the life cycle and make the product more economically attractive to reuse or recycle. Light-weighting products, extending their useful life, and designing them for ease of disassembly are common strategies that serve this purpose. Just-in-time manufacturing techniques also help by providing product materials and components just as they are needed in assembly thereby eliminating excess production, inventories, wastes, and costs.

2. *Providing greater respect and accommodation for the needs of people and other living things along the product life cycle.* This means designing products that are easier for customers to use and that pose less of a health and safety risk for them and for

product manufacturers, transporters, disposers, and other handlers. It also means developing products that minimize the potential harm to the environment along the product life cycle, or
even better, enhance the ability of the environment to repair and
sustain itself. Examples include the replacements DuPont developed for its ozone-depleting chlorofluorocarbons (CFCs) and
those that Great Lakes Chemical identified for its persistent,
toxic brominated fire retardants. Products that improve the
length or quality of life are desired, especially if they are not
only commercially successful, but make a difference among
the poor and starving among us—the bottom of the socioeconomic pyramid.

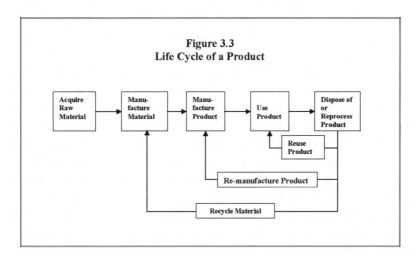

Figure 3.3
Life Cycle of a Product

The challenge with green design is to identify solutions that serve both
objectives; it is not enough that only one is served to the detriment of the
other.[35] A manufacturer who improves resource efficiency and helps the
environment by increasing carton size, enabling more product to be
packed in each, does not provide a good solution if the new cartons are so
heavy that handlers suffer back and shoulder strain in moving them. Air-
craft manufacturers can't sell more fuel-efficient planes unless they are

also safe and properly control engine noise. Medical vaccines that pre-vent a disease could arguably fit the green category unless they become so expensive that people who need them can't afford them. The answer is not to demand medical companies forego a profit and simply give vac-cines to the public; solutions to big problems cannot be based on philan-thropy alone. Instead, the challenge is to find an approach that is econom-ically sustainable—to find innovative ways to make the product at less cost while still paying production workers a decent wage. This balancing act can be tough, but nobody said green design was easy.

One company that takes green design seriously is Herman Miller, the Michigan-based manufacturer of office furniture, often considered among the most innovative companies in the nation. Under its design-for-environment (DfE) process, the company evaluates all new product proposals under a special rating system. Reviewers score each product component in three different areas: (1) "material chemistry," that is, the degree of environmental and health risk posed by the material; (2) ability to be disassembled; and (3) recyclability, which covers both recycled content and the ability to be recycled. Component ratings in each area are converted to percentage scores which are then weighted based on com-ponent mass. A total score is then determined for each area and for the product as a whole. According to Scott Charon, the company's project manager in New Product Development: "The overall goal is to continu-ally improve each product score, finding safer, more environmentally at-tractive alternatives to problematic components. The key to our success so far has been excellent management support, clear goals, dedicated ex-perts, and a good database and rating scheme." In addition to the DfE analysis, Herman Miller's design process also includes extensive studies on human factors associated with the use of their products.

The process has produced some remarkable results. For example, the Aeron, the highly popular office chair with black webbed seating and exoskeletal frame, has become the benchmark for back safety and com-fort. A newer chair, an Aeron-inspired, lower cost alternative called the Mirra, is perhaps the most environmentally friendly chair of its kind on the market. The company's marketing people see the environmental features of this popular product as a significant competitive advantage and therefore are devoting about one-third of their marketing messag-ing to them.[36]

Stimulating Innovation With Sustainability Initiatives

As Herman Miller demonstrates, producing good green designs—like producing good designs in general—requires considerable innovation. Innovation is not only stimulated by green design criteria and processes but also by the internal social programs companies adopt. In a 2004 study sponsored by the National Urban League, a New York-based civil rights group, two-thirds of the U.S. employees surveyed said diversity improved creativity and innovation—two factors that can enhance productivity and lead to better products and services.[37]

Studies by Harvard University creativity expert Prof. Teresa Amabile suggest that a company's respect for employees can facilitate innovation, too. Professor Amabile and her team collected 12,000 daily journal entries from 238 people working on creative projects in 7 companies. Participants were asked to record their thoughts about their work and work environment. The conclusion: creativity is positively associated with happiness, joy, and love and negatively associated with anger, fear, and anxiety. Tormented creative geniuses—the Van Goghs of the world—are rare exceptions, not the norm. Business managers who want to spur innovation should therefore create a pleasing work environment for their employees, make a serious effort to identify and understand their concerns, and demonstrate an open, caring attitude in responding.[38] In the long run, happy employees produce happy customers and happy customers produce happy investors.

Commercially Successful Green Products

People are inclined to buy green in many circumstances. Roper Green Gauge polls taken in 1990 and 1996 showed that about one-half of U.S. consumers are interested in, and even willing to pay more for, green products.[39] Currently you can buy "green" shoes, clothing, appliances, homes, food, cars, antifreeze, toilet paper, household cleansers, computers, and a host of other items. But not every product promoted as "green" is popular enough to command a price premium. Among those that can are organic baby food and cotton, natural soft drinks, and unbleached coffee filters.

Good demand also often exists for products which people believe will offer a personal health benefit because of the absence of chemical preservatives, pesticides, herbicides, animal drugs, or other hazardous substances. Personal safety sells better than environmental consciousness.

One company that knows that lesson well is Seventh Generation, Inc., a Vermont-based company that has become the leading U.S. brand for non-toxic, environmentally safe household products. Seventh Generation had used the tagline "Products for a Healthy Planet" to sell its green detergents, cleaners, diapers, and paper goods. Eventually they switched the message to "Safer for You and the Environment" when they discovered a large number of customers were buying their products not out of concern for the environment, but because they feared consuming pesticides and being exposed to chemicals that could set off asthma attacks or allergic or chemical-sensitivity reactions.[40]

Perhaps there's no better proof that "natural" sells than the fast-growing organic food business—already a $25 billion market, primarily from sales in Europe, Japan, and the United States.[41] Organic foods include crops that have not been: (1) developed through bioengineering; (2) grown using conventional pesticides or herbicides, fertilizers made with synthetic ingredients, or sewage sludge; or (3) otherwise treated with chemicals or radiation. The "organic" label also applies to meat, poultry, eggs, and dairy products from animals that are raised on organic feed, given access to the outdoors, and given no antibiotics or growth hormones. Between 1997 and 2003, U.S. sales of organic foods rose 17 to 20% annually versus a growth of only 2 to 4% for all foods.[42] What is more, people have been willing to pay 25 to 30% more for the organic alternative.[43] Organics are no longer confined to small avant-garde shops: one of the larger players in the market, Whole Foods, has 187 stores and 39,000 employees generating over $5 billion in sales annually. While the industry has taken a positive approach to promoting organic products, emphasizing freshness and taste rather than food safety, a 2003 survey showed that nearly two-thirds of the shoppers buying them do so because they believe these foods contain fewer chemicals.[44]

Concern about chemical exposures has also led to the creation of another successful business. For years, city officials in London struggled to find a way to eliminate the sea of pigeons that were continually fouling Trafalgar Square. Poisoning, trapping, and other usual means were not acceptable, given the high visibility of the site and its popularity with tourists. An acceptable approach was eventually provided by Van Vynck Avian Solutions. This British firm, established in 1988, uses small hawks and falcons to effectively control areas overrun with pigeons, starlings, or seagulls. After the staff of falconers and their trained birds work a site for a short time, most of the nuisance birds flee. Thereafter daily site visits of but one or two hours are required to keep the area under control. At Trafalgar, the service cut city maintenance costs, reduced health concerns, and opened the square to a wide range of events which previously couldn't be held. Van Vynck has seen its business grow steadily, serving clients like the Port of Liverpool, the British Museum, and various cities and industries.[45]

Other popular green products are those that save energy costs. They include energy-efficient water heaters, furnaces, and other heating, ventilating, and air conditioning equipment. The demand for such items is particularly strong at times when energy prices are high. As energy supplies dwindle and concerns about climate change continue to grow, these products will become even more attractive. Since it's typically easy to substitute energy-efficient products for inefficient ones, usually the only real issue for customers is whether they are willing to pay a little more in price to secure long-term savings in operating costs. Indeed, the data show that many people are: In 1997, only 1% of clothes washers, none of the refrigerators, and 6% of dishwashers on the U.S. market were certified for energy efficiency under the U.S. Environmental Protection Agency's (EPA's) Energy Star® program. By 2004, these certified products had captured market shares of 25, 33, and 86%, respectively.[46]

Energy efficiency became a critical selling point in the auto industry during the fuel crisis of the 1970s. Then, Japanese automakers with their fuel-efficient cars took large bites of market share from their American rivals, a loss the Americans never fully regained. The Japanese are favorably positioned once again as the market in new gasoline-electric hybrid vehicles takes a leap forward. Toyota, the current leader in hybrid car production with its popular Prius, continues to refine that car to make it more powerful, fuel-efficient, and comfortable. The company's marketing strategy for the Prius was explained by Toyota Motor Manufacturing Canada Inc.'s (Toyota Canada's) managing director, Stephan Beatty: "If you take two vehicles and price them comparably, operate them the same way, maintain them with the same frequency, obtain the same performance and reliability, and offer similar styling, we know the . . . consumer will choose the one that uses less fuel and creates fewer emissions."[47]

Certainly the Prius has been a hit. It was named *Motor Trend Magazine*'s 2004 Car of the Year. Over 50,000 of them were sold in the United

States in 2004, and the rate of sales doubled for 2005. The success of the Prius and the second-place American Honda Motor Company (Honda) hybrids and their ability to command a $3,000 average price premium has spurred Ford Motor Company, Nissan Motor Company, and General Motors Corporation to enter the competition. J.D. Power and Associates estimates 35 hybrid models will be available to U.S. consumers by 2008, over 50 by 2012. Projections vary widely about how much of the auto market the hybrids will eventually command: J.D. Power forecasts an annual sales plateau of 3% (roughly 500,000 U.S. cars) by 2010; the global consulting firm Booz Allen Hamilton says hybrids will take 80% of the market by 2015. Future gas prices and manufacturing-cost differentials between the hybrids and their non-hybrid counterparts will likely determine the outcome.[48]

Energy efficiency has also played a role in green real estate development, but such development has a broader appeal to sustainability as well. A good example is the 667-acre Prairie Crossing residential development in Grayslake, Illinois, 40 miles north of Chicago. The property was purchased by Chicago printer and conservationist Gaylord Donnelley in 1987 and has been developed by his nephew, former Inland Steel Company executive George Ranney Jr., and George's wife Victoria, a landscape historian. Their vision was a conservation community built around 10 sustainability principles:

1. Environmental protection and enhancement;
2. A healthy lifestyle;
3. A sense of place;
4. A sense of community;
5. Economic and racial diversity;
6. Convenient and efficient transportation;
7. Energy conservation;
8. Life-long learning and education;
9. Aesthetic design and high quality of construction; and
10. Financial stability.

The site consists of 360 farm-style homes nestled in clustered communities surrounded by 470 acres of open space—primarily wild prairie, wetlands, and ponds. It boasts a 22-acre lake with a beach and bird-nesting island, 10 miles of trails, garden plots, an organic farm and farmer's market, and a horse stable. A renovated century-old barn serves as a community center. For city commuters, two train stations are located at the edge of the development. An outpatient hospital facility is also on the perimeter. The Prairie Crossings Institute furthers the community's goal for life-long learning, focusing on sustainability, smart growth, and protecting nature. A special environmental charter school integrates environmental education into the class work for 300 students in kindergarten through seventh grade. The school is 40% more energy efficient than most similar structures, is heated by water circulated through geothermal wells, and contains a number of other green features. Homes are constructed to conserve water and use only one-half the energy of other new houses in the area. Prairie Crossing levies 0.5% of the sales price—an average of $1,500—to fund a foundation that maintains the prairie and wetlands on-site and across a 2,500-acre string of contiguous protected lands. Eight percent of home buyers have been African American versus 1% in the surrounding area. The Ranneys would like to see more, although they acknowledge house prices may be an obstacle to some.

A Prairie Crossing home sells in the $200,000 to $500,000 range, approximately one-third higher than the competition. They cost nearly 20% more to build due to the higher level of finishes, upgrades, and other features which are standard there but typically optional elsewhere. The remainder of the premium—approaching 15% of the price—is being paid by buyers because of their attraction to the lower operating costs of the homes and the development's ambiance and sustainability orientation. Once the vision of the community began to take shape, new houses sold as fast as they could be constructed. Says Victoria Ranney: "Very often families come here because of the farm, the sense of community and because they believe as strongly as we do in our guiding principles."[49]

Preferences for Green Products and Services by Governments and Companies

Green products and products made with green processes have a built-in advantage with some customers. Executive Order No. 13101, signed in 1998 by President Clinton, requires federal executive agencies to use EPA's *Guidance on Environmentally Preferable Purchasing* in their procurement of products and services.[50] The Agency stresses five guiding principles for environmental preferable purchasing (EPP):

1. Product selection must be based on product performance, price, *and* environmental attributes;
2. Products that prevent pollution will be favored;

3. The environmental evaluation must look at multiple environmental characteristics across the product's life cycle;
4. The selection must be based on a comparison of attributes and impacts among competing products; and
5. The evaluation must be based on good environmental performance information.

The EPP guidance spells out certain product attributes that agencies are asked to consider in making purchasing decisions. These attributes are listed in Figure 3.4. The Agency maintains a website of standards, guidelines, contract specifications, vendor and product lists, and other EPP information. (Bear in mind, however, this site is merely a collection of information from other sources; the Agency has not verified the appropriateness or accuracy of the product criteria or lists on the site.)[51] Companies are advised to look closely at the EPP criteria if they want to be more competitive in seeking some of the $200 billion in product sales made each year to the U.S. government.

Green purchasing initiatives are being implemented by other governmental bodies as well, especially in Denmark, Japan, and the United Kingdom. As these initiatives spread, corporate sustainability personnel are more frequently being called upon to help their organization's compete for valuable government contracts. During its fiscal year 2004-2005, the CSR group at U.K.-based BT was asked to provide support on nearly £3 billion in bids for government and corporate telecommunications business, up from £1 billion the previous year.[52] More information is provided on government green procurement programs in Chapter 14. EPP programs at universities are discussed in Chapter 15.

Major corporations like Ford and General Motors now require their suppliers to provide products only from sites that have an ISO 14001 environmental management system (EMS). Unilever expects its suppliers of farm produce to meet certain sustainability requirements. Other companies, responding to customer demand and pressure from NGOs, have also begun asking for products certified under various environmental and social criteria. Wal-Mart requests its leading suppliers to join with company executives, environmentalists, and regulators in one of its many special networks formed to identify or develop successful green products. A very recent development is surfacing which involves companies feeling pressured by Wal-Mart to become sustainable. This "phenomenon" is known as the "Wal-Mart effect." The development is suggesting that becoming sustainable is no longer an *elective or voluntary* choice for companies.

Figure 3.4 **Environmental Product Attributes to Be Considered in Procurements by U.S. Executive Agencies**[53]	
A. Natural Resource Use *(minimize these)* -Ecosystem impacts -Energy consumption -Water consumption -Non-renewable resource consumption -Renewable resource consumption B. Human Health and Ecological Stressors *(minimize these)* -Bioaccumulative pollutants -Chemical releases -Ambient air releases -Indoor environmental releases -Conventional pollutants released to water -Hazardous waste -Non-hazardous waste -Other stressors	C. Hazard Factors Associated With Materials *(minimize these)* -Human health hazards (acute toxicity, carcinogenicity, developmental/ reproductive toxicity, immunotoxicity, irritancy, neurotoxicity, sensitization, corrosivity, flammability, reactivity, other chronic toxicity) -Ecological hazards (aquatic toxicity, avian toxicity, terrestrial species toxicity) D. Positive Attributes *(maximize these)* -Recycled content -Recyclability -Product disassembly potential -Durability -Reusability -Reconditioned or re-manufactured -Take-back -Bio-based -Energy efficiency -Water efficiency -Other attributes with positive environmental effects

Procurements are not just being geared to environmental conditions, however; social action is also being demanded. For example, the stodgy world of law firms is being challenged by the call for greater diversity in their ranks—a call coming from some of their biggest corporate clients. As major companies like Sara Lee Corporation, Shell, and BellSouth Corporation have watched their base of consumers and employees grow increasingly diverse, they have begun to pressure their service providers to do the same, making their outside law firms a prime target. Sara Lee's general counsel, Roderick Palmore, and Shell's counterpart, Catherine Lamboley, have been among those in the forefront of this movement. They have led the charge not just because they see such action as an ethical imperative, but because of pragmatic business reasons as well. They know that a law firm with a good mix of people of each gender and vary-ing races will bring a variety of perspectives to its legal team and believe such a mix better reflects the spectrum of views among the workers and customers of their own companies. They are also mindful that the U.S. buying power among African Americans, Asian Americans, and Hispan-ics is growing, and is expected to surge from approximately $1.8 trillion in 2004 to nearly $2.5 trillion by 2009—a 40% increase.[54] Moreover, these business leaders believe that diversity within hired firms will ulti-mately result in more innovative solutions.[55]

For these and other reasons, in 1999, Charles Morgan, then BellSouth general counsel, began circulating among his peers a written commit-ment called, "Diversity in the Workplace: A Statement of Principle." Over 500 companies signed. In 2004, General Counsel Palmore sent his own "Call to Action" to fellow general counsels, asking them to promise to give more business to diverse firms and drop firms that aren't making adequate progress toward a mixed staff. As of 2005, over 70 general counsels had made the pledge. In the future, law firms seeking large cor-porate clients should not be surprised to see selection criteria like that of Shell—criteria focused on quality, professionalism, cost-effectiveness, *and diversity.*[56]

The Growing Demand for Sustainability-Certified Products and Services

The desire for products conforming to certain sustainability criteria has prompted a dramatic growth in environmental and social product stan-dards and certifying bodies. Think of SA 8000 and the Better Banana Project Standards used by the Rainforest Alliance in certifying Chiquita's banana farms. Here are some other popular environmentally oriented certification programs:

- The Forest Stewardship Council (FSC)—founded in 1993 by environmental groups, the timber industry, foresters, indigenous peoples, and community groups from 25 countries—worked with Home Depot and others to certify wood products coming from sustainable forestry practices.[57] A more industry-oriented counterpart—the Sustainable Forestry Initiative—was started a year later by the American Forest and Paper Association.
- The Marine Stewardship Council is an independent, global nonprofit organization that certifies fish products obtained from

fisheries that meet its environmental standard. It was founded in 1997 by Unilever, the world's largest buyer of seafood, and WWF, the international conservation organization, and spun off into a fully independent organization in 1999.

- The U.S. Green Building Council's Leadership in Energy and Environmental Design (LEED)™ program, developed with the help of Johnson Controls and others, provides standards, a rating system, and a certification program for buildings with good eco-designs and operations. Green-building certifications are also offered by a number of local and regional groups, including the "Built Green" organizations sponsored by builders associations in Seattle and Colorado.[58]

- Other certification programs have targeted specific environmental concerns. For example, the Chlorine-Free Products Association endorses items—like paper and water treatment systems—that typically require chlorine but are made or operated without it. The Chlorine-Free Paper Consortium provides similar review and approval of paper products.

- The U.S. government certifies energy-conserving products under its Energy Star® program. That program carries considerable weight, especially since the government's insistence in the 1990s that it would only buy Energy Star®-certified computers stampeded the whole personal computer industry toward energy-conserving designs.[59] According to EPA, in 2003 alone, Energy Star® projects for household products and other items conserved enough energy to power 20 million homes, cut greenhouse gas emissions equivalent to those of 18 million cars—all the while saving Americans $8 billion.[60]

While the vast majority of sustainability-related labeling and certification programs have been limited to environmental concerns, some are beginning to encompass nonenvironmental issues, too. The Rainforest Alliance has certified coffee sold by Kraft Foods, Sara Lee, P&G, and Starbucks, representing that the coffee was not only grown using good sustainability practices but was traded under fair business practices as well.[61] The Consumer's Choice Council, a nonprofit association of 65 environmental, consumer, and human rights organizations from 25 different countries, also includes within its charter the certification of organically grown fair-trade coffee. The demand for certified "sustainable" coffee has been rising significantly over the last few years, growing 20% annually in Britain, for example. As of 2005, it accounted for 4% of all coffee purchased there and 20% of the premium roast and ground coffee.[62]

Widely accepted standards for fair-trade and sustainable production have been issued by the Fairtrade Labeling Organizations International (FLOI). Fair-trade certifications have gone to pineapples from India, mangos from Peru, oranges from Egypt, honey from Chile, bananas from Ghana, and footballs from Pakistan—covering altogether 800,000 producers in 40 countries.[63] A group of nine international standard-setting and accreditation organizations formed the International Social and Environmental Accreditation and Labeling (ISEAL) Alliance, which establishes voluntary standards and verification programs around best social and environmental production practices.

The business benefit of "social certifications" is well known to DeBeers, the world's number one source of gems. In the late 1990s, human rights, academic, and religious groups, among others, claimed that the company and other diamond producers were buying "conflict diamonds"—those gems sold by guerilla forces in Angola and Sierra Leone to fund bloody rebellions. The United Nations had banned trading in those stones, but there was no effective way to determine which diamonds were from illegal sources. With the escalation of the issue in 2001, DeBeers faced a 21% drop in sales even though it claimed no involvement with the contraband gems. The company then took the offensive by leading an industrywide effort to draft a code of conduct and certification process, called the Kimberley Process, which could be used to verify that the diamonds did not come from rebel forces. It also established a "Supplier of Choice Program" to advance best ethical practices among its suppliers. With these new programs in place, DeBeers saw a 16% rebound in sales the following year.[64] But progress on the issue didn't stop there. In 2003, U.S. President George W. Bush signed into law the *Clean Diamond Trade Act*, joining 50 other nations in support of the Kimberley Process.[65]

Successful Business Models for Serving the Poor

As the DeBeers case shows, the demand for sustainability-friendly products and services is not just directed to those with environmental advantages, but may also extend to those providing social benefits. Consider also the Grameen Bank, founded in Bangladesh by economist and Nobel

Peace Prize winner Muhammad Yunus, which has been highly successful in the microcredit business it started in the 1970s. The company was
the first to institutionalize a Microfinance Institution (MFI) to provide
small-scale financial services to the poor, managing loans as little as $50,
and accepting savings deposits as small as $5. Because of the small sums
handled, interest rates on some loans are higher than typically offered by
banks—20% for loans for income-generating items, for example, but
considerably less than the usurious rates poor customers would otherwise have to pay street lenders. Housing loans are set at 8%, student loans
at 5%, and loans for "struggling members" (beggars) are interest free.
Borrowers are urged to adopt the *Sixteen Decisions*, a set of practical
goals concerning education, health, and other areas of social responsibility (sanitary latrine, education for children, safe drinking water, no
dowry, etc.). However, no legal documents are signed and no one is sued
for default. To encourage repayment, the bank uses peer pressure rather
than legal recourse. Borrowers are engaged in groups of five. The bank
extends loans to two of them first, monitors their performance for six
weeks, then issues loans to the others if performance has been satisfactory. Annual repayment rates are typically 95% or higher. The bank has
made money in all but three of the last 20 years. Grameen has issued over
$4 billion in loans since its inception. It now has 1,200 branches serving
44,000 villages in Bangladesh. The number of borrowers has grown to
over three million, 95% of whom are women.[66] This success has
spawned more MFIs by others. They are now found in 58 countries.[67]

The Grameen organization has also established separate independent
companies that focus on other needs of the rural poor, such as education,
energy, and internet and phone communications. These companies play a
part in an overall strategy that also involves lending programs at the
bank. For example, under the "telephone-ladies" program, over 40,000
people have borrowed money from the bank to buy mobile phones from
Grameen Telecom, a not-for-profit sales agent for the phones. The
phones are then rented for short periods by local villagers as needed. In
this way, phone service has been brought to over half of the villages that
previously had none. These phones now account for over 16% of the total
air time of Grameen Phone, another entity in the family which is now the
largest telephone company in Bangladesh.

The Grameen experience reinforces the message of Michigan Prof.
C.K. Prahalad, author of *The Fortune at the Bottom of the Pyramid*: "If

we stop thinking of the poor as victims or as a burden and start recognizing them as resilient and creative entrepreneurs and value-conscious consumers, a whole new world of opportunity will open up."[68] Indeed, new attitudes and ways of thinking are essential to serve the four billion people of the world who lie at the bottom of the economic pyramid, earning less than $2 a day. This challenge of "corporate social opportunity" has become a focus for some major firms. For example, companies like P&G and Unilever have jumped into the burgeoning market among the poor for single-serve sachets, selling shampoos and matches for a penny a package, detergents and soaps for 4 cents, toothpaste for 10 cents. Single-serve shampoo now makes up two-thirds of the total shampoo market in India. This business is also creating opportunities for the economically disadvantaged. For example, Unilever selects and trains entrepreneurial women from remote Indian villages to introduce and distribute its products there.[69]

As the sachet business and Grameen show, companies cannot be successful at the bottom of the pyramid relying on traditional ways of doing business. Just as "social entrepreneur" Yunus had to find a new business model to provide banking for the poor, new approaches have been developed to help those suffering from debilitating medical problems. Dr. G. Venkataswamy, former head of the Department of Ophthalmology at the Government Medical College in Madurai, India, began searching for a way to bring down the cost of surgery for the nine million in his home country with blinding cataracts. The surgery cost as much as $2,500 to $3,000 in the United States and was well out of reach for the impoverished people of India. Dr. V, as he is affectionately called, became inspired by the McDonald's hamburger chain and its techniques for efficient and consistent production. His idea was to buy good equipment, develop procedures, establish rigorous training programs, and use paramedics to free up doctors so they could focus on surgeries and patient counseling. Starting with a modest private 11-bed clinic in 1976, Dr. V's Aravind Eye Care System now has five hospitals providing nearly 200,000 lens replacements a year. Through his process, each doctor performs approximately 2,600 operations annually compared to the national average of about 400. Patient outcomes rank with those from the best eye clinics in the world. The cost per surgery: $25. The poorest 60% receive their operations for free, their costs covered by the remaining 40% who pay $50 to $300, depending upon income. To bring down the cost of the intra-ocular lenses and eye pharmaceuticals and sutures, the Aravind group set up a manufacturing facility called Aurolab. Lenses which typically cost $80-$100 are now being produced for under $5. The factory not only makes a profit, but has become one of the world's largest suppliers of lenses, with roughly 20% of the market.[70]

One person instrumental in establishing Aurolab was David Green, the founder and leader of Project Impact, a nonprofit group in Berkeley, California, that helps create businesses to improve society. He has also been the main driver behind the development of a high-quality, affordable hearing aid to help the 250 million people around the world estimated to have disabling hearing loss. By using off-the-shelf chips and components and avoiding all marketing, Green has been able to produce a digital hearing aid at Aurolab for only $50—dramatically less than the $1,600 a comparable device would sell for in the United States. Following Dr. V's model for cataract surgery, Green is selling the hearing aids in India for $118 to those who can pay in order to subsidize the very poor, who obtain them below cost or for free.[71]

But business geared to the poor is not just a concept for the Third World; sustainability-minded entrepreneurs can also find good opportunities in industrialized nations. This was underscored in a 1998 joint study of retail markets in six major U.S. inner cities conducted by the Initiative for a Competitive Inner City—a U.S. nonprofit organization founded by Harvard Business School Prof. Michael E. Porter—along with the Boston Consulting Group and PricewaterhouseCoopers. It showed that inner-city households account for $85 billion, or 7%, of all annual U.S. retail spending, but that more than one-fourth of that demand is not being met by neighborhood retailers. Because of high population density, the purchasing power of these poor regions is actually greater than in many affluent suburbs, hitting $71 million per square mile in the Boston inner city, for example, compared with $12 million per square mile for the rest of the metro area. As the report noted: "[I]nner cities represent the largest and closest emerging market in the world."[72] Indeed, many companies have found great success there. The organizations on the 2004 list of the "Inner City 100"—the 100 fastest growing U.S. inner-city private companies identified by *Inc. Magazine*—enjoyed an average growth rate of 850% between 1998 and 2002.[73]

Retailing giant Wal-Mart understands the opportunity. It sees urban low-income areas as its next frontier for sales. In 2004, for example, it convinced Chicago city officials to allow it to locate a new store in the Austin neighborhood, one of the poorest in the city. Two factors no doubt helped secure the approval, overcoming objections of labor activists who opposed the company's low wages. One factor was the prospect of several hundred new jobs for the low-income community. The second factor, according to the city's Planning and Development Department, was that Austin residents were spending approximately $150 million outside their area due to limited retail choices.[74]

Of course, risks abound for industries trying to serve those at the bottom of the economic pyramid. Companies can be criticized as predatory capitalists rather than creative saviors if they try to entice the poor to buy needless luxuries or take their hard earned cash without investing some of it back in the local community. Huge research and development and general overhead costs may prohibit the typical large corporation from competing with the likes of Aravind or Aurolab. Plans to adapt existing European or U.S. products for poor consumers may meet with dismal failure because costs are too high or product storage, transportation, and operating conditions are much harsher than expected. Product labeling and marketing can become big challenges given the illiteracy of the consumers and lack of television, radio, or other traditional channels of communication. Companies may not have the experience or inclination to create a new sales structures based on door-to-door methods or Amway-like home sales. And, of course, operations in developing countries may be stymied by governmental corruption. But even with these obstacles, many transnational companies will eventually find themselves courting the bottom-tier consumers. Where else can they go for long-term growth? Besides, these markets may well be the incubators for design and operational innovations of wider application—the so-called disruptive technologies that shake up the competition with new ever higher ratios of product value to cost.

Lessons From Green Product Failures

Unfortunately, not every business strategy aimed at social or environmental responsibility works. As noted in Figure 3.5, some products or services touted as green may not sell if they cost significantly more—remember, economics is part of the sustainability balance—or offer less quality or performance or greater inconvenience than the competing product. Customer attitudes, whether or not based in fact, also come into play. A 2003 study in the United Kingdom disclosed that consumers were willing to buy certain products with recycled-paper content, but not others. Toilet paper, facial tissue, and kitchen paper towels with recycled content were okay. Feminine hygiene products were not, primarily because of negative perceptions about performance, appearance, and safety.[75] When Iceland, the frozen food retailer, switched to selling only organic vegetables that carried a higher price than its usual non-organic varieties, sales plunged. Much of the clientele at Iceland were very cost-conscious, and this new approach eliminated the main reason they were shopping there.[76] Unilever, the Anglo-Dutch food and detergent company, had to admit failure in its effort to market fish from more sustainable sources. Despite their best efforts at promoting New Zealand hoki, they found their customers still preferred cod and haddock. Unilever and the supermarkets it serves are now revising their strategy to develop more creative ways to market hoki and to educate consumers about the role they can play in achieving sustainability of fish stocks for future generations.[77]

Figure 3.5
Lessons About Green Products

1. Customers will pay more for added safety of food and hygiene- and health-related products, for a more natural living environment, and for lower life-cycle costs.
2. Products and services for the poor must break barriers on cost/pricing either through low volume per unit or low-cost operations.
3. Many customers will avoid products with a highly publicized social or environmental stigma.
4. A small percentage of customers will pay more for a green product than a comparable non-green product for ethical reasons; some commercial customers may also pay a premium for such products if they can gain a clear reputational advantage with their own customers or other important stakeholders.
5. If none of the above provisions apply, the purchasing decision is most likely to be controlled by the primary factors of cost, function, quality, or style, rather than by any difference in social or environmental advantages. But among products or services that are comparable on the primary factors, the social and environmental advantages and the seller's cause-based marketing can be strong differentiating factors.

One company that knows what it takes to produce a successful green product is Whirlpool Corporation. However, much of its learning came from a product that wasn't a marketplace success. The company had been incorporating energy and water concerns in product development since the 1970s, so it was only natural that it would jump into a contest to build a green refrigerator when it was announced in the early 1990s. Billed the Super Efficient Refrigerator Program (SERP), the competition involved a winner-take-all $30 million prize, funded by 24 electric utility companies. It was to be awarded to the company that could develop and distribute the best refrigerator that was free of ozone-depleting CFCs and at least 25% more energy efficient than called for under the 1993 U.S. Department of Energy (DOE) standards. The good news for Whirlpool was that it won the contest in 1993; however, the bad news was that when the $100 utility rebate for buyers dried up in 1997, so did sales. What went wrong? The problem was the refrigerator size specified for the contest was only sufficient for households of modest size and means; it wasn't large enough for most families. Given all the work that went into designing and producing the award winner, it could not be priced low enough to attract those households. Although the SERP refrigerator was not a commercial success, Whirlpool came away with new, valuable knowledge about what customers want in green appliances and how to design them.

Over the years that followed, Whirlpool went on to produce marketable refrigerators that use no more energy than a 60-watt bulb. The company also found great success with its Duet® stackable clothes washers and dryers. The Duet washer consumes only one-half the water and one-third the electricity of a conventional washer. It has other advantages, too. It uses a special washing motion that is gentle enough to handle silk, cashmere, and other delicate fabrics. In addition, with its front-loading design it has a capacity large enough to handle king-size comforters and area rugs. The matching dryer was designed to provide faster drying time, equal to the washing time, and with no over-drying that can damage clothes. Said Whirlpool executive Tom Catania:

> Unlike the SERP refrigerator, with our Duet washer-dryer units we were able to come up with "no regrets" technology, mixing green design with the attractive styling and improved performance a customer would want. Customers have been willing to pay a premium for the Duet because they can see they are getting more for their money. The green aspects of the equipment help us now and in the future. If

public concerns about energy and water resources continue to grow, our market is not only protected but strengthened. But beyond that, we feel good about helping the environment. We know our customers do, too.[78]

Another green product that initially faltered in the marketplace was organic cotton clothing. In the mid-1990s, companies like Gap and Levi Strauss attempted to sell some of it but retreated when consumers refused to buy because of the higher prices and uninteresting styles. Patagonia, the California outdoor apparel maker, converted its entire cotton line to organic in 1994, but few other manufacturers followed. By 2005, however, more than 250 brands were offering organic cotton clothing, up from under 100 only three years before. What changed? For one thing, the cost of organic cotton became more competitive, especially from locations like India where labor is cheap and organic farms have been in operation for some years. For another, fashion designers like Oscar de la Renta found ways to use organic cotton and other eco-friendly fibers in stylish designs. These developments encouraged Nike to set a goal of using organic fibers for at least 5% of its cotton-based garments by 2010. The British retailer, Marks & Spencer targeted 5% for its private label line by 2012. While less than 1% of the cotton produced worldwide is organic, that will climb significantly if organic cotton apparel suppliers like Under the Canopy have their way. Said Marci Zaroff, founder of the firm: "The ultimate business model is no compromise. If you can give people fit and style and value and also appeal to their values, it's not: 'Why would I buy it?' It's: 'Why wouldn't I buy it?'"[79]

While environmental and other sustainability issues can help with the marketing of certain products, they can also complicate the marketing of others. For more information on challenges posed by green power, genetically modified crops, and polyvinyl chloride (PVC), see Appendix 1.28.

Certainly a green product or service strategy is not without risk. But not going green has its risks too, especially where young people are concerned. The youth of today—the adult consumers of tomorrow—are the first generation to grow up learning about environmental problems. Unlike many of their parents, they are eager to walk the talk: a U.S. survey by Infocus Environmental discovered that one in three parents have changed their buying habits because of what their children taught them about the environment.[80] Teenagers were among the most active boycotters of McDonald's and Starkist tuna, forcing McDonald's to

eliminate their "clamshell" Styrofoam hamburger containers and the
Heinz Corporation to sell only dolphin-free tuna.[81] Students at the University of Wisconsin and several other colleges organized demonstrations to communicate their displeasure with the hazardous materials in
Dell computers, prompting the company to begin sponsoring local computer collection and recycling programs.[82] A two-year campaign led by
high school and college students convinced office-supply giant Staples
to move toward the sale of forest-friendly paper. This was after 600 protests at company stores, tens of thousands of letters and calls to the CEO,
and nationwide news coverage.[83]

The lesson here is that green product and service strategies present opportunities as well as risks. But designs for sustainability are really designs for the future, designs that play to those particular needs of society
that will become more important as time goes on. More and more people
are beginning to see the merits of such strategies: witness the growth of
green procurement preferences in government and corporate circles, the
increasing popularity of sustainability-related certification programs,
and the rise of new business models for serving the poor. With proper
market evaluations, the business risks of going green can be controlled.
Those like Toyota that offer green products that are competitively priced
and perform as well as if not better than their non-green alternatives will
be ideally positioned to seize the market opportunities that will surely
come. Woe be to the competitor left on the sideline.

Factor 3: Productivity

<u>Business-case argument</u>: *Many aspects of sustainability if properly ad-
dressed can help improve business efficiency, which bolsters profits.*

The concept is simple: a manufacturing or other business process that is
as productive as it can be has little if any waste, no accidents, and a
well-trained, motivated work force. Pollution and the unproductive use
of energy are merely lost economic and natural resources. Accidents and
unmotivated employees produce wasteful diversions of human effort.
Explosions, fires, and spills are needless—sometimes tragic—interruptions and economic losses. All of this should be intuitively obvious.
Real-world examples abound.

Big Savings From Eco-Efficiency

As noted in Figure 3.6, companies can use a variety of eco-efficiency techniques to increase their productivity and profitability. One company that has done a particularly good job of that through green product design is Xerox Corporation, the maker of copy machines and related products. The company designs equipment so that up to 60% of the parts are the same as found in previous models. Components are made with sufficient durability so they can be repeatedly reused. Before each reclaimed part is reinstalled, however, it is specially tested to affirm it continues to perform as required. When a copy machine is returned, 70 to 90% of the components by weight is reused either in the same model or a newer version, which cuts the energy, material, and labor that go into each new machine, as well as the waste and pollution that would arise from component manufacture. Savings in resources means savings in costs, and in Xerox's case, this amounts to several hundred million dollars a year.[84]

Perhaps the best known examples of how green initiatives can enhance productivity come from Dow and 3M Corporation. Under 3M's Pollution Prevention Pays program which began in 1975, the company has implemented over 5,000 projects aimed at eliminating pollution, either through product changes, process modification, equipment redesign, or the recycling or reuse of waste materials. Altogether, these projects have prevented more than 1.1 million tons of pollutants and saved the company over $950 million.[85] Dow's Waste Reduction Always Pays (WRAP) program has saved it roughly $1 billion through approximately 400 projects implemented since the program began in 1986. These projects cut waste by 230,000 tons, wastewater by 13 million tons, and energy by 8 trillion British thermal units. The company's initiatives to reduce accidents and spills are expected to save another $130 million on an investment of $90 million.[86]

Dow and 3M are just two of many companies that are seeing good returns not only through pollution prevention, but through energy conservation as well. Firms such as DuPont, IBM, and STMicroelectronics are routinely improving their energy efficiency by 6% annually with savings often paying back the investment in two to three years. How much more can be done? According to energy conservation expert Amory Lovins, we should be able to profitably cut our oil and gas consumption rates in half and trim our energy usage rate by nearly three-fourths. History provides some encouragement: the United States now uses over 40% less energy and 50% less oil per dollar of real gross domestic product than it did in 1975.[87]

Productivity improvements have also been documented for green building design.[88] In 2003, several California state agencies commissioned a study of 33 buildings in the state that had been certified to the LEED green building criteria. LEED criteria address such things as energy and water conservation, pollution prevention, and the use of environmentally friendly materials. They also cover indoor environmental quality—which entails temperature control, natural lighting, and the reduction of indoor air pollution. The review was for the purpose of analyzing the construction and operating costs of these green buildings and comparing them with the costs for similar structures built to conventional designs. The study revealed that the construction costs for green buildings were on average 2% higher, but this was more than offset by savings in operating cost. Over the 20-year life cycle of the buildings, the savings averaged more than 20% of the total construction cost, or 10 times the cost premium. Savings in excess of 30% were found for buildings certified to the highest LEED criteria—gold and platinum. While some savings was due to reductions in water and energy use, most was attributed to productivity improvements. For example, a study at Herman Miller showed a 7% increase in the productivity of workers after they moved to a green day-lit facility.[89] Lockheed Martin Corporation saw even better results when it installed sophisticated day-lighting. It not only cut its lighting energy costs by three-fourths, but experienced a 15% drop in absenteeism and a 15% improvement in worker productivity the first year.[90]

Figure 3.6
Eco-Efficiency Measures That Often Improve Productivity of Processes
and Profitability of Products and Services

1. Reducing material intensity (less material per unit)
2. Reducing energy intensity (less energy per unit)
3. Reducing the dispersion of toxic substances into the environment (reducing the degree of hazard and quantity of toxic substances per unit; recapturing toxic substances; preventing the release of toxic substances that do not readily biodegrade to a harmless state)
4. Improving recyclability (improving ease of disassembly; avoiding multi-layer materials or other material combinations that cannot be recycled with pure material)
5. Increasing the service intensity of products and services (increasing functional value per unit of product or service hour)
6. Improving the quality and durability of products (reducing defect and repair rates; lengthening product life; increasing number of uses per product)
7. Maximizing the percentage of resources that are from renewable sources (can save costs in long run due to reliability of supply)

Source: Based on eco-efficiency concepts of the WBCSD.[91]

The financial advantages of green buildings can be further enhanced by incentives offered by some state and local governments. Special tax credits and expedited permitting may be available for such buildings in some locations. Communities like Arlington, Virginia, and Portland, Oregon, offer additional densities (floor-area ratios) for buildings meeting certain green criteria.[92] Energy-efficient mortgages, which are available through the Federal Housing Authority and other lending authorities, enable a borrower to raise the mortgage amount to cover the cost of energy improvements without qualifying for the added amount or making an additional down payment.[93]

The financial benefits from energy conservation and pollution prevention activities, while already attractive, will become even more so in the future. As the supply of fossil fuels dwindles over the years to come (see Appendix 1.14), energy and petrochemical costs will continue to climb. In turn, this will raise the financial payback for energy conservation measures and pollution prevention activities involving petroleum-based substances.

Government action on climate change may also affect the payback rates on energy- and waste-reduction projects. (See an overview on climate change in Appendix 1.15.) Regulators may well resort to a "cap-and-trade" mechanism for transferring credits that entitle a company to emit a certain amount of greenhouse gases. Companies that don't lower their emissions to reach their assigned targets (caps) must make up the difference by buying emission credits from someone else. Companies can earn a surplus of credits to sell by cutting emissions below their caps. These emission reductions can be achieved in a number of ways, including from energy conservation projects, which chop the use of fossil fuels and the associated release of carbon dioxide (CO_2), and from waste-reduction and process-efficiency projects, which lower use and emissions of various listed greenhouse gas chemicals—primarily modern Freon™ replacements. Cap-and-trade was successfully used in the United States to cut sulfur dioxide emissions contributing to acid rain. It is being implemented for carbon emissions in the European Union to help them meet their commitment under the Kyoto Protocol on climate change. Over the years to come, as more countries see the need to address climate change, cap-and-trade is likely to be a tool of choice. A voluntary program for trading carbon credits is being tested by the Chicago Climate Exchange.[94] Experts believe such a program is likely to be mandatory in the United States in the future.

Documenting Benefits Through the Baxter Environmental Financial Statement

Since the early 1990s, Baxter has tracked the cost and savings associated with its environmentally beneficial activities and published it annually in an environmental financial statement. The statement for 2004, which is presented in Figure 3.7, and those for previous years show that but for these activities, Baxter would have spent on average over $80 million more per year—approximately $800 million in total.[95] This savings has been accompanied by the following environmental improvements:

1. Ninety-nine percent reduction in air toxics since 1988 through material substitutions, alternative technologies, and improved processes;
2. Reduction of hazardous and non-hazardous waste by three-fourths per unit of production since 1989;

3. Reduction of packaging by over one-third per unit since 1990; and

4. Reduction of energy by more than one-fifth per unit since 1996, with associated reductions in greenhouse gases.[96]

The financial statement captures the economic consequences of these achievements. The data is presented in three main categories. The first is *Environmental Costs of the Basic Program*. These are the expenses for maintaining a proactive environmental program. These expenses cover the costs for environmental, energy, and packaging professionals and for acquiring, maintaining, and operating pollution controls. Since the statement is framed like an income statement, capital costs for controls are shown as depreciation. Any dramatic increases or decreases in *Total Costs of the Basic Program* not explained by acquisitions or divestitures should raise alarms. Significant cost increases should be checked to see if they are truly necessary. Big declines in costs should be evaluated to assure that the company hasn't cut corners it will regret later.

Next are *Remediation, Waste, and Other Response Costs*. These are "reactive" program costs. In a perfect world with no fines, wastes, and cleanups, these costs would be zero—which, of course, is the target. In the real world of business, though, with its acquisitions and ever-changing circumstances, this is not a reasonable expectation. Good environmental performance would normally be reflected in the continual decline of these costs over the years. A large acquisition or number of small ones would be one of the few good reasons why they might rise. Seeing these costs jump a year or two after significant cuts in basic program costs may suggest that the cuts have been too deep and did not really improve the overall economic efficiency of the company. Notable increases in costs for settlements of government claims (fines, etc.) and waste disposal may be a clue that compliance and waste prevention warrant more attention and a greater allocation of available resources.

Figure 3.7 Baxter Environmental Financial Statement 2004: Estimated Environmental Costs and Savings Worldwide ($ in millions)[97]			
ENVIRONMENTAL COSTS			
Costs of Basic Program	**2004**	**2003**	**2002**
Corporate Environmental—General and Shared Multidivisional Costs	1.2	1.2	1.3
Auditors and Attorneys Fees	0.3	0.3	0.4
Energy Professionals and Programs for Energy Reductions	1.0	0.9	1.0
Corporate Environmental—Information Technology	0.3	0.5	0.6
Division/Regional/Facility Environmental Professionals and Programs	6.3	5.4	5.2
Packaging Professionals and Programs for Packaging Reductions	1.0	1.0	1.3
Pollution Controls—Operations and Maintenance	3.2	2.8	3.0
Pollution Controls—Depreciation	0.8	0.8	0.9
Total Costs of Basic Program	≈14	≈13	≈14
Remediation, Waste, and Other Response Costs			
(Proactive environmental action will minimize these costs.)			
Attorneys Fees for Cleanup Claims, Notice of Violations	0.1	0.7	0.5
Settlements of Government Claims	0.0	0.0	0.0
Waste Disposal	6.2	6.8	6.8
Environmental Fees for Packaging	1.0	1.0	0.6
Remediation/Cleanup—On-site	0.1	0.4	0.4
Remediation/Cleanup—Off-site	0.2	0.1	0.0
Total Remediation, Waste, and Other Response Costs	≈8	≈9	≈8
TOTAL ENVIRONMENTAL COSTS	≈22	≈22	≈22
ENVIRONMENTAL SAVINGS			
Income, Savings, and Cost Avoidance From Report-Year Initiatives			
Air Toxics Cost Reductions	0.0	0.0	0.0
Hazardous Waste Disposal Cost Reductions	0.7	(0.4)	(0.0)
Hazardous Waste Material Cost Reductions	2.0	(1.6)	(0.3)
Non-hazardous Waste Disposal Cost Reductions	0.7	0.5	(0.9)
Non-hazardous Waste Material Cost Reductions	5.0	6.5	3.1
Recycling Income	3.0	2.9	1.9
Energy Conservation Cost Savings	9.2	4.2	3.4
Packaging Cost Reductions	2.9	1.7	2.4
Water Conservation Cost Savings	1.0	0.9	0.3
TOTAL REPORT-YEAR ENVIRONMENTAL SAVINGS	≈25	≈19	≈12
—As a Percentage of the Costs of Basic Program	≈180%	≈145%	≈85%
SUMMARY INCOME, SAVINGS, AND COST AVOIDANCE			
Total Report-Year Environmental $ Benefit	≈25	≈19	≈12
Cost Avoidance in Report Year From Efforts Initiated in the Six Years Prior to Report Year	≈57	≈40	≈42
TOTAL INCOME, SAVINGS, AND COST AVOIDANCE IN REPORT YEAR	≈82	≈59	≈54

Income, Saving, and Cost Avoidance shows the benefits of environmentally friendly activities. *Income* is revenue received by the company—money taken in. *Savings* is simply the reduction in actual cost between the report year and the prior year. When costs go up, savings is
negative. *Cost avoidance,* on the other hand, is the additional cost, other
than the report year's savings, that was not incurred but would have been
if the waste reduction activity had not taken place. The methodology for
calculating savings and cost avoidance is explained in Appendix 5.

When an item under *Income, Savings, and Cost Avoidance* goes negative, as Hazardous Waste Material Cost Reductions did in 2002 and
2003, this is a red flag that productivity, efficiency, and environmental
performance are declining in those areas, and that more aggressive action is needed to bring performance back on track. The slippage in 2002
and 2003 did, in fact, help prompt more aggressive action on those
wastes, which, in turn, produced good environmental and economic results in 2004.

The growth of year-over-year savings in the energy area shows that the
integrated energy/greenhouse gas reduction efforts have accelerated and
are gaining traction. To help achieve savings in energy costs, Baxter's
Facilities Engineering Services group conducts energy audits evaluating
site operations against the latest techniques and technologies for minimizing energy use. The identified cost savings opportunities have ranged
from $140,000 to $600,000 per site with good returns on investment. As
shown in the financial statement, total savings and cost avoidance from
these energy projects was over $9 million in 2004.

The final line of the financial statement shows *Total Income, Savings,
and Cost Avoidance in the Report Year.* This includes not only the results
from the report-year activities, but also cost avoidance in the report year
that resulted from efforts initiated over six years prior to the report year.
The benefits were totaled over seven years because that was the rough
approximation of the useful life of most of Baxter's waste- and packag-
ing-reduction projects and other improvements in operations and products. Looking at the economic benefits over that period is like examining
an accountant's net present value calculation, except instead of speculat-
ing about the future financial impact of a waste-reduction project at the
time it is proposed, one actually measures that impact annually over time.
Like net present value, cost avoidance acknowledges that economic benefits accrue long after a project is implemented. If a pound of waste re-

duced today saves a dollar this year, we will not have to pay that dollar next year or the year after, as well. Based on this analysis, the total economic benefit in 2004 from environmentally beneficial activities at Baxter from 1998-2004 is shown to approach an estimated $82 million. Further details on the calculation of this component of the statement are provided in Appendix 5.

The total numbers are presented here as rounded approximations to account for the degree of accuracy in reporting. Indeed, many costs and savings were omitted because there was no credible way to measure them with any confidence. Costs for environmentally driven materials research were excluded under the assumption that they would be offset by increased sales, which are not accounted for in the statement. Likewise, the capital costs for modifying processes, other than the addition of pollution controls, were ignored because it was thought these costs would be countered by savings from increased production efficiencies not covered in the statement. On the savings side of the ledger, the big omission was the avoidance of costs for problems that did not occur because of the proactive program—an estimate that would be beyond the grasp of even the best fortune tellers. In the end, though, the financial statement serves its purpose as an awareness tool showing good environmental programs can make good business sense. Moreover, it underscores that within a company, environmental and economic success often rise or fall together.

Productivity Improvements From Safety Programs and Other Internal Social Initiatives

Baxter's environmental financial statement and the cases cited earlier show that productivity can be significantly improved through environmentally beneficial activities. But productivity can be enhanced through other sustainability initiatives, too. Consider workplace safety, for instance. In some countries like Australia, Canada, France, Ireland, Japan, and the United States, employers pay for worker compensation insurance or contribute to similar funds that pay partial salaries and medical, rehabilitation, and other direct costs of employees injured on the job. The price for this coverage—now averaging over 45 cents per worker hour in the United States,[98] or nearly $1 billion per week for all employers[99]—is determined at least in part by the employer's claims history. The more injury claims, the higher the insurance bill.

However, this is not the only economic burden an employer bears from accidents. Expenses for ambulance and other emergency response services may be incurred. Severe cases may involve property damage, fines, legal fees, and other liabilities. Such cases may also have a significant impact on the company's reputation and employee morale. They can cause business disruption, too, which can lead to missed sales opportunities and other indirect losses. Frequently there are expenses for training, salaries, and occasionally overtime wages for workers who fill in for injured employees. Valuable internal administrative time must be diverted to handle injury claims and any resulting organizational trauma. Several U.S. studies have estimated that the average of these indirect costs may be as high as two to three times direct costs.[100] On the other hand, if the workplace becomes safer and there are fewer and less severe accidents, then productivity rises and many of these costs melt away. Hard Rock Café, for example, saved approximately $400,000 in 2001 by reducing its injury rates faster than its industry average.[101] Intel's rigorous construction safety program reaped even greater benefit—by cutting accident rates on its construction sites by 95% since 1994, the company chopped $30 million in costs under its Owner-Controlled Insurance Program through which it self-insures for contractor accidents.[102] GE reduced its annual cost of injuries by over $50 million by dropping its accident rates three-fourths from 1996 to 2004.[103]

A focus on safety can enhance productivity in other ways, too. Health and safety hazards that exist in a production process are typically awkward, dangerous, and sometimes unnecessary process steps. Searching for these hazards and eliminating them often results in a simpler, quicker, more streamlined and efficient process with less downtime and waste. The consequential savings from these process improvements can often dwarf the more traditional direct and indirect cost savings associated with safety. Indeed, from many different perspectives, safety pays.

Like good safety programs, company programs that strengthen ethical business practices can also prove financially worthwhile. For example, programs aimed at preventing bribes can cut the risk of significant fines, civil penalties, legal fees, and lost business that may follow in their wake. Since bribes are unreliable in their effect, they become an expensive and inefficient way to secure business. A study of over 3,000 firms in 59 countries by the World Economic Forum found companies reporting higher levels of bribery regularly spent more time negotiating approvals and taxes with officials than did more honest firms.[104] Bribes prompt bureaucrats to invent new rules and obstructions which lead to greater uncertainty and hassles. A company that condones bribery to outsiders also tacitly encourages internal skimming and pilfering. Transparency International found that as much as one-fifth of the money intended for bribes in Tanzania never reached its target but ended up in the pockets of company employees.[105] Firms with strong ethical programs avoid these nonproductive expenses and inefficiencies.

A drive toward sustainability can improve a company's productivity in other ways as well. Corporations that take their environmental and social responsibilities seriously, while at the same time assuring their own economic success, are companies that people want to work for. There is plenty of evidence supporting this:

- *2003 survey of British workers:* When Britons were asked how important it was for their own employers to be responsible to society and the environment, 92% said it was at least fairly important. Six in 10 felt it was very important.[106]
- *2004 survey of 1,000 Americans:* Eight in 10 people said a company's commitment to a social issue is important in deciding where to work.[107]
- *2003 survey of 800 North American and European graduate business students:* Intellectual challenge was identified by the students as most important in their choice of jobs, with compensation rating 80% as important. However, corporate reputation for ethics and caring about employees scored third at 77%. Moreover, over 97% of the students said they would be willing to give up an average of 14% of their financial package to work for a company with a better reputation for social responsibility and ethics.[108]
- *Student public commitment:* Scholars at over 100 universities in the United States and elsewhere are now promoting the Graduation Pledge, under which graduates commit to investigate and take into account the environmental and social consequences of any job they are offered.[109]

The conclusion from all this is clear: employees and potential employees alike are truly concerned about the social responsibility of an employer. Companies with strong sustainability programs will have an edge in competing for the best workers. By attracting and retaining top talent, companies can realize significant competitive advantages in productivity as well as innovation, which, as Figure 3.1 depicts, is critical to financial success.

Indeed, happy workers tend to be productive workers who are less likely to leave their jobs. Job satisfaction is also enhanced when companies make their workers feel wanted. Firms that make workers of all races, religions, and sexual persuasions feel at home will be more competitive in the long run. With the declining fertility rates in industrialized nations (see Appendix 1.8), companies will be looking to minority, non-native, gay, and older workers to fulfill needs for talent. Those corporations that offer a work environment conducive to people of many backgrounds and beliefs will be able to attract and keep workers with the knowledge, skills, and motivation that will make them most productive. Such an environment can also help stop the financial bleeding that companies experience when turnover is high. Consider this: for consulting giant Deloitte and Touche, every 1% reduction in employee turnover translates to a $22 million savings.[110]

One company that has seen social responsibility translate into productivity improvement is B&Q, the British do-it-yourself home improvement retailer. In the late 1980s, the company began to recognize certain trends:

1. The company work force of 35,000 was primarily young;
2. It was becoming difficult to recruit enough workers to keep up with company growth;
3. Staff turnover was highest among young workers;
4. Customers favored older workers, perceiving them to be more service-oriented and knowledgeable about do-it-yourself projects and products; and
5. Within the next few decades the number of Britons aged 55 to 65 would increase by one-quarter and those in their 20s would drop 20%; the steepest growth in available work force was going to come from those over 45.

In 1989 the company decided to experiment by opening a large store in Macclesfield, England, staffed entirely by people over 50. A year later, the University of Warwick conducted a benchmarking study of this store and four other comparable B&Q retail facilities. Here's what they found at Macclesfield: (1) profits were 18% higher; (2) staff turnover was six times lower; (3) absenteeism was 39% less; (4) shrinkage was 58% below the others; and (5) customers perceived the service was better.[111] (But the lessons from Macclesfield are not unique. A study of 360 workers in the United States found that contrary to the stereotype, older workers exhibited a stronger willingness and commitment to learn than their younger co-workers. Seniors were also more open to changes that would benefit the organization.)[112]

Not only has B&Q declared it wants to be the company of first choice for older workers and customers, but one for the disabled as well. Its disability program includes staff training, special customer service, access for the disabled to the store and goods, products with accessible design features, and special recruitment and employment policies. B&Q's "Agenda for Action" strategy incorporates commitments concerning the disabled, as well as those on age, gender, cultural diversity, and quality of life. Progress against these commitments is communicated annually. Overseeing the initiative is a diversity manger who reports directly to the CEO.[113]

Controlling Risk of Incidents With an SOS to Protect Productivity

A proactive approach to sustainability through the use of an SOS enables a company to prevent and best manage risks that can cripple its business, diverting endless hours of management time, halting critical operations, and causing big financial loss. Fires, explosions, strikes, public unrest, and scandals can devastate even the strongest of enterprises. So can boycotts, lawsuits, press attacks, environmental incidents, and fines. These harmful consequences are more likely to befall firms that ignore sustainability trends and fail to address relevant sustainability issues. Corporations must examine how their operations and products may be affected by climate change, corporate governance, and population shifts. They must be mindful of child labor, worker rights, and hazardous materials. Many must consider dwindling supplies of raw materials, fish stocks, fresh water, and agricultural lands. In doing so, companies can follow the lead of Coca-Cola. Because the soft-drink supplier is highly dependent upon a steady supply of good water, it has undertaken a comprehensive assessment of their future water needs and prepared a plan to address them.[114] By properly managing their sustainability issues, firms like Coca-Cola can reduce the risks to their productivity—and perhaps even to their own survival.

Telecommunications giant BT is one company that is taking its sustainability risks seriously. Its CSR group routinely undertakes a risk assessment with management examining sustainability issues like climate change, breach of integrity (à la Enron), outsourcing of jobs, electronic privacy, and supply chain risks (working conditions, etc.). As new issues arise, they are plotted on a graph showing the likelihood of occurrence versus the estimated financial impact of the issue over three years. The graph not only depicts the gross risk but, more importantly, the "net risk" after mitigating measures are taken. The review team discusses the higher risk issues and evaluates the cost and effectiveness of mitigation. Ultimately they decide what risk level and mitigating measures are appropriate for each issue, and then apply that across the organization. The CSR group also works with the businesses to conduct "health checks," whereby they prioritize sustainability risks and opportunities that may apply to the development of products and services. Individual functions, such as those covering EHS, ethics, and human resources, undertake similar reviews with management on internal operational risks and opportunities associated with sustainability.[115]

For major corporations, the identification and management of sustainability risks is not just a matter of good management. With the U.K. Combined Code and U.S. Sarbanes-Oxley raising standards of corporate governance, there are growing expectations—and legal duties—demanding a more active role by corporate boards in enterprise risk management (ERM),[116] and sustainability risks should be part of that.

An SOS is quite suited for incorporating an ERM, as well as eco-efficiency, safety, anti-bribery, diversity, and other sustainability initiatives. As Figure 3.1 indicates, these measures can lower cost and make a company stronger and more productive.

Factor 4: Operational Burden and Interference

Business-case argument: *A company that neglects sustainability concerns invites public distrust, which can lead to greater regulation, operational burden, and cost. By proactively addressing these concerns, a company can often ease this burden.*

Businesses that play the ostrich and ignore sustainability do so at their own peril. One or two incidents can flair up when least suspected, setting off public outrage and spurring prescriptive government action. The surge in U.S. environmental legislation in the 1980s was prompted by incidents like the Love Canal waste-site contamination in New York, the deadly gas release at Bhopal, India, and the *Exxon Valdez* oil spill in Alaska. The Sarbanes-Oxley law, which imposes strict standards of governance on corporations, was adopted by the U.S. Congress in response to financial scandals at Enron, WorldCom, and Tyco. Governments can also grow impatient with business behavior that is not scandalous but merely non-responsive on sustainability issues. The United Kingdom adopted new rules requiring that large British companies include environmental and social information in their public financial reports. Was it a coincidence these rules were approved after three-quarters of top British businesses ignored Prime Minister Blair's plea that they voluntarily begin publishing environmental reports?

Companies that are proactive in addressing sustainability help remove justification for prescriptive laws. If laws are eventually passed anyway, these firms may well reap favorable publicity for being forward-thinking. Moreover, they will have designed a functional approach which can serve as a model for regulators and make their own compliance readily achievable. In any case, such firms will have been able to address the issues at their own time and pace rather than under the whip of some arbitrary, inconvenient deadline dictated by authorities. A proactive approach reduces the burden on employees and keeps management of company matters more in the hands of the business managers rather than in the hands of government. What is more, it can provide a real competitive advantage.

Baxter's program for removing all single-walled underground petroleum and hazardous materials tanks was a classic example of this. In the late 1980s, Baxter realized it had approximately 175 of these tanks around the world and that sooner or later each would leak. Leaks would mean soil contamination and perhaps even the fouling of groundwater. As time went on, the extent of contamination would only grow worse. Experience had shown that it cost on average $20,000 to remove a tank that wasn't leaking and restore the site. However, the cost was likely to be over $100,000 if the tank was leaking and causing soil contamination—well in excess of $500,000 if groundwater contamination was involved. By removing the tanks before the tank regulations took effect, Baxter avoided extensive monitoring, recordkeeping, and reporting obligations. More important, the total removal program cost $10 million, well shy of the $20 to $80 million that would have been incurred if removal of each tank would have been postponed until it leaked.[117]

Likewise, those companies that decided early on to screen the sites to which they sent hazardous waste saw a benefit. By identifying poorly operated disposal sites and not sending waste there, waste generators avoided being named later as parties potentially responsible for site cleanup under the so-called U.S. Superfund law and other "polluter-pays" legislation. Many American companies that did not take this proactive approach before the enactment of Superfund eventually faced cleanup claims and suffered extensive administrative, legal, and financial burdens in resolving them.

Preempting environmental regulation also appears to have been a wise strategy for Toyota and Honda. The European Union and Japan have both made strong commitments to lower CO_2 emissions from vehicles as part of their commitment to the Kyoto Protocol on climate change. California also has begun to regulate such emissions as well. Anticipating these trends and the waning of fossil fuel supplies, both auto makers have been pioneers in producing hybrid-electric and other high fuel-economy vehicles. The two companies now have less of a climb than most of their competitors in meeting the emission and fuel-economy regulations that are likely to emerge. A study by the World Resources Institute (WRI) and Sustainable Asset Management (SAM) estimated that Toyota would see an increase in net earnings of around 8% by 2015 as a result of these regulations. The impact on Honda was projected at around a 3% earnings growth. The forecast for their American competitors was not so bright: their earnings were projected to *drop* 7 to 10% under the new rules.[118]

A pro-sustainability approach can also lower a company's legal burden in other ways. Many laws, including those governing hazardous waste and emergency response, are applicable to operations that store or use over a certain quantity of some potentially hazardous materials. Through innovative process modifications and other measures, the amount of these materials that are used can often be reduced or even eliminated, significantly cutting a company's regulatory burden.

Organizations that are serious about their environmental and social responsibilities can receive other regulatory benefits as well. For example, companies that voluntarily adopt an EMS and maintain good compliance records may qualify for EPA's Performance Track program. This program grants facilities additional flexibility under certain Agency rules and exempts them from routine inspections.[119] Oregon and Wisconsin have initiatives similar to EPA's Performance Track, which give qualifying companies greater leeway on regulatory requirements and enforcement. In Virginia, companies with model environmental programs are eligible for special professional assistance as well as low interest loans and discounted permit fees.[120] Other regulatory and tax relief for sustainability-oriented companies may also be available. Where it doesn't exist, companies should consider lobbying government for it because opportunities for competitive advantage may be there for the asking.

Being progressive in the drive toward sustainability can also pay dividends when it comes to seeking and maintaining the support of local governments. Companies that build a solid reputation of social and environmental responsibility with community authorities are likely to find these authorities more sympathetic than they otherwise might be when the company wants to build or expand operations or close them. Reducing these obstacles means easier implementation of business plans and, as Figure 3.1 shows, lower costs.

Factor 5: Supply Chain Costs

Business-case argument: *By working proactively on sustainability issues with their suppliers and contractors, a company can help assure that critical supplies and services will be available on an ongoing basis and that supply chain costs are properly controlled.*

Government is not the only stakeholder that can affect a company's financial success—suppliers can too. Collaborations between corporations and their suppliers can lead to more environmentally safe raw materials and product designs that pose less risk and cost in manufacture, handling, and use. Where hazardous materials are used in the manufacture of a product, expensive controls and additional cautionary procedures often must be employed. The cost of handling, storing, and disposing of such materials will generally be many times that of nonhazardous alternatives. For example, years ago many suppliers cleaned metal components with Freon™ or other CFC solvents. But as CFCs were phased out and their price began to soar, suppliers often found they could simply substitute water and detergent or benign citrus-based cleaners, saving millions of dollars. With lower production costs, these suppliers could be more competitive, keeping prices flat or even passing some of the cost savings up the supply chain to the product producer and, eventually, the customer.

Similarly, producer-supplier projects involving the reduction of component packaging can not only save the supplier the cost of packaging materials, but also help the end-product producer cut costs for the storage and disposal of the waste packaging. Vendors that develop oriented-fiber technology for corrugated boxes and new, stronger designer plastics enable their manufacturing customers to use light-weight products and packaging, taking both cost and material out of the supply chain and waste stream.

Financial and environmental benefits have also resulted from "peak shaving," whereby electrical power generators entice their industrial customers to install small, clean-burning natural gas standby power generators to be used at times of peak energy demand. Large manufacturers often improve efficiency by having multiple standby units on-site, which are brought on-line as the need arises. With the use of these generators, power companies have avoided the environmental impact and huge cost of power plant expansions needed to handle peak loads. In turn, this has enabled the power companies to offer their peak-shaving customers significantly lower rates.

Sustainability is also furthered by just-in-time (JIT) inventory arrangements. Under these arrangements, suppliers deliver materials and components to producers at the time they are needed, and producers do the same for the products they deliver to retailers. JIT not only saves money, but avoids the squandering of production and distribution resources and the generation of wastes for products the market doesn't need.

These and other financially and environmentally attractive measures have become the focus of the Green Suppliers Network (GSN), a program of EPA and the U.S. Department of Commerce. One GSN initiative commenced with Baxter International examining how its suppliers could address pollution prevention and other environmental concerns while at the same time implementing "lean manufacturing" principles. Lean manufacturing is a process that continually identifies, reduces, and eliminates non-value-added activities, materials, and other resources in manufacturing processes to improve quality and efficiency. Through the GSN program, government funding is provided to train suppliers on this "lean and clean" approach. The GSN is now working with a growing number of other industry sectors—including automotive, aerospace, office furniture, and heavy equipment—to help drive environmental cost out of their supply chains.[121]

Sustainability programs by suppliers can also help assure the continual supply of needed materials to their customers, minimizing the risk of costly interruptions. Producers that fail to probe the accident rates and safety fines of their suppliers, especially in sole-sourcing arrangements, may be exposing themselves to excessive risk of supply disruption from fires, explosions, or other safety disasters. A pattern of serious incidents will often continue in the absence of a dramatic shift in management emphasis on safety. Think of the Phillips Petroleum plastics plant near the Houston shipping channel. A 1989 explosion there killed 23 employees and prompted a $4 million fine from the Occupational Safety and Health Administration (OSHA). Another blast in 1999 killed two and a third in 2000 injured over 70. With some diligent inquiry, customers who depended on the plant for their polyethylene or polypropylene in 2000 might have been well aware of the risks.

Accidents are not the only sustainability-related threat to the continued flow of reasonably priced supplies. Resources that are particularly hazardous or dwindling should also be suspect. Companies that obtain components with lead, hexavalent chromium, mercury, or cadmium, or that are made with the use of CFCs should be aware of the growing regulatory pressures around the globe to eliminate those materials. Producers that rely on fish, water, petroleum products, exotic woods, or other shrinking commodities must periodically assess the supply trends and the potential future impact these trends may have on the company. Companies that don't incorporate sustainability concerns into their supply chain strategies may be putting their future competitiveness and financial success in serious jeopardy.

Starbucks is one company that has taken this message to heart. It decided that the coffee farms that take good care of their employees and land are the most responsive and responsible suppliers. Consequently, it scores its suppliers on 20 measures directed to responsible environmental and social practices. Those firms that score well may earn long-term contracts and up to a 5% premium on the contract price for their coffee.[122]

Indeed, environmental and economic factors are not the only ones that can affect supply chain costs; another aspect of sustainability—respect for people—can too. Suppliers won't trust business customers who are dishonest or unreliable. Such customers pose a greater level of uncertainty and risk for suppliers—risk that may be covered by them through higher prices. If the behavior of a company is so disreputable, the uncertainty and risk so great, suppliers will cease doing business with it altogether. Likewise, suppliers with similarly poor reputations will find fewer business customers who are willing to risk their own reputations and success on such unreliable sources.

As Figure 3.1 suggests, these issues of respect, as well as the wise use of natural and economic resources, affect the supply chain in a way that influences its overall financial success.

Factor 6: Cost of Capital (Lender and Investor Appeal)

Business-case argument: *A significant and growing number of investors and lenders are making investment and lending decisions based not only on traditional financial analysis, but on an evaluation of company social and environmental performance as well. In order to remain attractive to these money providers and keep the cost of capital low, companies should properly manage their sustainability risks.*

The idea that markets add cost to address risk and uncertainty also holds true for the financial community. Investors and lenders will expect greater returns on their investments and loans if a company's ability to pay becomes threatened. Strikes, customer outrage and boycotts, and catastrophic fires and explosions can cast doubt on a company's ability to perform, as can large legal liabilities, possible debarment from government contracts, and shortage of critical supplies. Through a proactive approach to sustainability, a company can help reduce these risks, putting investors and lenders more at ease and thereby reducing the cost of capital.

Traditionally, lending rates and stock prices move, sometimes dramatically, in response to new significant risks encountered by companies seeking funding in the form of debt (loans) or equity (stock). Share prices may tumble when labor disputes arise or securities scandals erupt. In recent years, a growing number of investors and lenders have tried to gain deeper insights about the likelihood of such risks by probing the ethical, environmental, and social performance of the companies they fund. They do this not only to better protect their investments, but also to respond to increasing demands from their own constituents that financial support be provided only to those organizations that are ethically sound. A new generation of individual investor is emerging—a generation that understands that money talks and can do some social good if invested wisely. These investors feel they can gain the financial returns they need—or even improve them—by placing their money in companies and projects that are helping society rather than harming it.

Growth of SRI

A 2000 survey found that over one-fourth of Americans who own corporate stocks either directly or indirectly (through mutual funds) had bought or sold shares on the basis of companies' employment practices, community involvement, or business ethics, and that another 10% considered doing so.[123] In the United States, socially responsible investing—sometimes called *SRI, social investing, ethical investing, mission-based investing*, or *natural investing*—grew 40% faster than all professionally managed U.S. investments from 1995 to 2005, surging from $640 billion to $2,290 billion. As of 2005, SRI represented $1 of every $10 of managed portfolio investments in the United States.[124] Most of this money was in *screened investments*—securities selected because of their financial as well as one or more social or environmental factors. Some was also devoted to investments supported by *advocacy* by stockholders who use dialogue and resolutions to pursue various environmental, governance, or other social issues with corporations. A small percentage of these funds went for sustainability-oriented *community projects*. (See Appendix 1.32 for more information on SRI and its trends.)

The SRI movement in Europe has been rapidly developing over the last few years, proving itself to be one of the world's most advanced financial markets for this kind of investment. The European SRI market was estimated at €360 billion ($430 billion) in 2005, with many of the financial institutions in the region offering a wide range of SRI products. The United Kingdom remains the European leader on SRI, in large measure because of the active role of the huge government pension funds.[125]

The growth of SRI is expected to continue over the next decade. A 2004 survey of over 190 mainstream investment managers worldwide found that 9 of 10 believed investor advocacy would become a mainstream practice within 10 years. Nearly three-fourths of the respondents thought the use of social and environmental performance information in investment processes and strategies would become mainstream in that time as well. Almost two-thirds said the same thing about the use of such information for screening stocks for investment.[126]

Recent History of SRI

Although some form of SRI has been practiced over hundreds of years, springing primarily from religious traditions, the concept first gained broad visibility in the 1970s and 1980s as U.S. investors used it to apply economic pressure on South Africa to end Apartheid. The success in South Africa served as a strong reminder to religious groups, labor unions, foundations, universities, and other organizations that they too could use their funds to further their own social agendas. Many used it to raise concerns about dangerous environmental releases in the wake of Bhopal, Chernobyl, and the *Exxon Valdez* incidents. Others applied SRI to address the threats of ozone depletion and climate change. Marquee corporate scandals like those of Enron, WorldCom, Arthur Andersen, and Tyco have encouraged investors to look beyond the economic bottom line to governance, ethics, and other areas of sustainability performance. Such a review, they believe, helps in evaluating the values and quality of management as part of the assessment of investment risk.

Key Organizations Driving the SRI Movement

A number of key organizations help guide the SRI movement, such as the following:

- The Investor Responsibility Research Center (IRRC), an independent 80-person research firm focusing on corporate governance and responsibility, advises institutional investors collectively managing over $5 billion.
- The Interfaith Center on Corporate Responsibility (ICCR) comprises 275 faith-based institutional investors with a total portfolio of approximately $110 billion.
- The International Interfaith Investment Group (3iG) was launched in 2005 by 27 members representing 7 world religions and an array of banks, philanthropies, and SRI organizations. It works with religious leaders around the world to encourage investments grounded in values of justice and faith. 3iG is optimistic it can persuade these leaders to allocate to SRI at least $1 trillion of their more than $7 trillion in assets.

- The Coalition for Environmentally Responsible Economies (CERES) is a U.S. coalition of environmental, investor, and advocacy groups representing $300 billion in invested capital.
- A number of U.S. pension funds and organized labor groups, such as the Service Employees International Union (SEIU), come together through the Council of Institutional Investors (CII) to coordinate efforts on corporate governance and social issues.
- The International Institutional Investors Advisory Group (IIIAG) serves a similar role among its three huge members: the California Public Employees Retirement System (CalPERS), the largest pension fund in the U.S. with 1.4 million members and over $150 billion in assets; the Teachers Insurance and Annuity Association-College Retirement Equities Fund (TIAA-CREF), a U.S. investment and insurance organization for those in education; and the U.K.-based *Hermes Pension Management Ltd*.
- Other major players in the SRI field include the New York State Common Retirement Fund, the New York State Comptroller's Office and the Connecticut Retirement and Trust Plans.
- The Social Investment Forum (SIF) operates the Shareholder Action Network (SAN), a U.S. group that arranges collaboration among many activist groups on shareholder resolutions. SIF also hosts the Social Investment Research Analyst Network (SIRAN), a network supporting more than 100 North American social research analysts from 30 investment firms, research providers, and affiliated investor groups.
- The *Enhanced Analytics Initiative* is a joint effort among four European and global fund managers representing over €800 billion ($1.0452 trillion) in managed assets. Under this initiative, the fund managers agree to allocate 5% of their broker commissions based on how well brokers integrate the analysis of intangibles and extra-financial issues, including those related to sustainability, into their investment practices.
- The United Nations has taken up the cause of SRI, as well. UNEP's Finance Initiative (UNEP FI) is a partnership between the United Nations and more than 200 firms across the global financial services sector. It uses working groups, training programs, and research to develop and promote linkages between

sustainability and financial performance. In 2004, UNEP FI launched its Responsible Investment Initiative with 12 firms, committing to help mainstream fund managers identify and respond to social and environmental issues in their investment selections. That same year, the United Nations Global Compact published a report entitled *Who Cares Wins—Connecting Financial Markets to a Changing World,* which advocated similar improvements across the investment community. The report was endorsed by 20 major investment companies.[127]

• In addition to these organizations, a host of *investment rating firms*, like Innovest, KLD and Calvert Group, conduct social screening evaluations of companies targeted for investment.

Screening Programs for Loans, Securities, Mutual Funds, and Indexes

Screening of loan applications for some sustainability issues has become routine. For example, most banks now closely evaluate lending proposals involving real estate to ascertain the presence of environmental contaminants that may require expensive remediation. Large financial institutions often have permanent staff assigned to oversee these due diligence reviews. A number of well-known banks have gone beyond that to screen their investment projects against the *Equator Principles*, a voluntary financial guideline developed by 10 major banks with the assistance of the World Bank and its private-sector investment arm, the International Finance Corporation (IFC). Under the principles, banks agree to impose certain environmental and social standards of the IFC and World Bank when funding any project of $10 million or more. Forty major banks, including Barclays, Citigroup, and Credit Suisse, have made this commitment.[128]

The screening of stocks for sustainability issues is also popular. Investors select screened securities based on their financial performance as well as one or more ethical, social, or environmental factors—such as the company's environmental practices, the nature of its products, or its record on employee-relations or human-rights. Many screened investments exclude stocks in companies involved with "sin products" such as tobacco, weapons, gambling, or alcohol. Because there is no consensus definition of "socially responsible," the screening criteria—and the lists of companies meeting them—vary widely.

Social screening of stocks rose tenfold from 1995 to 2005. These investments increased continually until 2003, then dipped about one-fifth between then and 2005 due primarily to the decline in single-issue screening by separate accounts for individual and institutional investors. Some speculate this decline was due in part to the significant drop in screening for tobacco in the wake of the large multi-state settlements with the tobacco industry, and in part because SRI investors are preferring to remain stockholders rather than shun stocks, so they can advocate for change through resolutions and dialogue.[129]

In contrast with the decline in investments in screened separate accounts, the amount in socially screened mutual funds continued its climb from 1995, moving up a healthy 18% in the two years following 2003. With over 200 ethical mutual funds reported in 2005, about the same as two years earlier, the United States still leads all countries in the SRI field.[130] However, throughout Europe there were over 375 SRI funds in 2005, with assets up 27% from a year earlier. The largest fund investment there is in the United Kingdom, followed by France, Italy, and Sweden.[131] Significant screened funds can also be found in Australia, Canada, and Japan, while other SRI funds exist in Brazil, Hong Kong, Malaysia, Singapore, South Africa, South Korea, and Taiwan. Only a very small percentage of SRI fund assets are in securities from emerging markets, in part because of inadequate disclosure of environmental and social information from companies located there.[132]

The growth of SRI has given birth to a surge in investment indexes and analysts to help ethical investors place their bets. All these SRI indexes operate like the well-known regular index, Standard and Poor's (S&P) 500, offering investors benchmarks against which they can compare other groups of stocks. Investment firms may actually acquire the stocks reflected in the index and provide them to investors as an indexed fund. Typically the indexing organization will compile information on companies from a number of sources: direct surveys and interviews with company officials; company financial and sustainability reports; and government records, to name a few. Once the data are compiled, it is reviewed and scored by staff personnel.

One of the oldest screened index funds, the Domini 400 Social Index launched in 1990, is made up of roughly 400 large company stocks that pass multiple broad-based reviews. In 1999, the Dow Jones Indexes and the Switzerland-based SAM Sustainability Group launched the Dow

Jones Sustainability World Index (DJSWI), now made up of over 300 companies from 23 countries—the socially screened subset of the 2,500 largest companies in the Dow Jones Global Index. Within two years of its establishment, financial institutions in 11 countries had created investment funds based on the DJSWI. Outside the United States, London's FTSE4Good index series is popular. So is the Business in the Environment (BiE) index of Corporate Environmental Engagement, an index run by the London-based Business in the Community. Thirty institutional investors use the sustainability performance indices of Vigeo, a rating group from France. Twenty-eight institutions rely on ratings from the Sustainable Investment Research International (SiRi) Group, which comprises SRI research organizations from 11 different countries. Morningstar Japan KK, a financial research and evaluation firm, established the MS-SRI, a stock index of 150 socially responsible companies. In South Africa, the Johannesburg Securities Exchange launched its own SRI index, too.

Benefits of SRI for Investors and Companies

Certainly much has been written about the performance of SRI funds versus conventional funds, with many claiming the former provide superior returns[133] and some alleging just the opposite.[134] A review of 52 studies of SRI performance published between 1972 and 1997 found a significant positive correlation between corporate social and financial performance, suggesting that excellence in both are mutually reinforcing and associated with good management and a strong corporate reputation.[135] On the other hand, a study of the performance of 103 German, U.K., and U.S. ethical funds from 1990 to 2001 found no statistically appreciable difference between the risk-adjusted returns of SRI funds and conventional funds. Interestingly, the authors of the study did find significantly better performance by SRI funds that had been in operation for three years or more versus those that were younger, which suggests that there may be greater advantages to SRI as this segment of investing matures.[136] Regardless of which studies you believe, at the very least an investor should be able to invest according to conscience and not be penalized.

From a company's perspective, there are real benefits to being selected by an SRI mutual fund. Not only does the firm see positive publicity and the demand for its stock rise somewhat, but history shows that investors in SRI mutual funds, unlike those owning unscreened versions, are more likely to stick with their investments through down markets.[137] (See Figure 3.8, which shows the flow of funds into regular and socially responsible mutual funds during the 2001-2003 recession. During the post-recession period 2003-2005, the rate of increase in asset flows into SRI mutual funds continued to keep pace with that of unscreened funds.)[138] There is a price for this, however: a company selected for investment must respond to ever-growing requests for SRI information and remain proactive on environmental and social issues in order to stay in favor. These are not easy tasks. By ignoring these requests, though, a company turns its back on a chorus of investors whose voices are growing louder—not a promising strategy for long-term corporate success. In the world of SRI, corporations can run but they cannot hide.

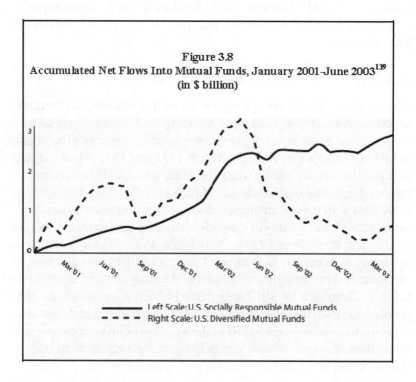

Figure 3.8
Accumulated Net Flows Into Mutual Funds, January 2001–June 2003[139]
(in $ billion)

———— Left Scale: U.S. Socially Responsible Mutual Funds
- - - - Right Scale: U.S. Diversified Mutual Funds

Investor Preference for Companies With Strong Governance

On the shareholder advocacy side of SRI, the large majority of sustainability resolutions have addressed corporate governance. (See Appendix 1.33 for more information on SRI related to corporate governance.) "Corporate governance," a term originally coined in the mid-1980s to describe the role of the audit committees of corporate boards, now refers to a broad range of rules, policies, and practices that boards use to fulfill their management duties and other responsibilities to stockholders and other stakeholders.[140] The topic has gained considerable attention in recent years with the much-publicized abuse of power by certain corporate leaders. This attention has come not just from socially responsible investors, but from mainstream stockholders who are concerned about protecting their investments from financial ruin and securing improved returns. A 2001 study for the National Bureau of Economic Research, which evaluated the performance of 1,500 companies throughout the 1990s and scored them against a governance index, found that corporations with the best governance scores financially outperformed those with the worst by 8.5%.[141] Likewise, a 2002 survey of the investment community by *Business Week* disclosed that the "best corporate boards"—those operating according to guidelines commonly adopted by governance experts—outperformed the worst, especially in down markets.[142]

Given this, it should be no surprise that investors would be willing to pay more for those companies with strong governance practices. In fact, a 2002 global investor opinion survey by McKinsey & Company reported that an "overwhelming majority of investors are prepared to pay a premium for companies exhibiting high governance standards. Purchase premiums averaged 12-14% in North America and Western Europe; 20-25% in Asia and Latin America; and over 30% in Eastern Europe and Africa."[143] Because investors are increasingly seeing poor governance as a serious business risk, mainstream corporate credit-rating firms such as Moody's Investors Service and S&P have begun offering corporate governance assessments as part of their rating services.[144] For the same reason, the infusion of foreign and institutional capital into businesses in some developing nations, which heavily relied on state and family funds in the past, is bringing more attention to governance there.[145] Clearly, companies that want to keep their cost of capital low would be well advised to keep their governance programs strong.

Factor 7: Legal Liability

Business-case argument: *Companies guided by sustainability princi-ples are less likely to incur crippling legal liabilities which can wipe out profits.*

As depicted in Figure 3.1, a company's financial returns—even its entire existence—may be threaten by legal liabilities flowing from sustain-ability-associated issues. Poor governance practices may prompt share-holder lawsuits with sizeable claims. Cendant Corporation's 1998 settle-ment netted shareholders a whopping $3.3 billion. Lawsuits over ethical improprieties can also sink a company, as they did Enron accountants, Arthur Andersen. The sale of dangerous products or unsafe food or drugs can result in product liability actions that can bring a company to its knees, too. Think about the 70 companies driven to bankruptcy because of asbestos litigation.[146] Even those that survive can find the burden tough to swallow. AAB reported charges of over $1 billion for asbes-tos-related personal injury claims for 2001-2003.[147] Tobacco companies have felt the heat, too, agreeing in 1998 to pay $246 billion over 25 years to resolve a lawsuit brought by 46 states. The theft of patents or copy-rights and the failure to fulfill contract commitments can also result in court actions that vaporize profits. Unfair business dealing can lead to an-titrust suits that break up the company and impose stiff fines. Discrimina-tion lawsuits can not only tarnish a firm's reputation but require large payouts as well. Just ask Coca-Cola ($192 million), Denny's ($54 mil-lion), and Abercrombie & Fitch ($40 million).[148] Where anti-sustain-ability behavior rises to criminal action—as it did for some executives at Enron and WorldCom—large fines may be coupled with the imprison-ment of key executives.

Criminal and civil penalties can also be stiff for environmental infrac-tions. For example, in 2005, EPA collected over $250 million in criminal and civil penalties and sent defendants to jail for a total of 186 years. In addition, the Agency had outstanding commitments from violators to pay $10 billion for environmental cleanups and other corrective ac-tions.[149] While environmental liabilities have been generally only a con-cern in the United States, this is beginning to change as polluter-pays laws are being adopted elsewhere.[150]

Where serious permit violations are proven, courts may not only seek penalties but halt operations or demand other action that can hurt a company financially. Human rights violations may be subject to litigation, too. Indeed, a number of high profile cases of this type have been brought against companies in U.S. federal court. These cases allege that the company defendants tolerated egregious breaches of human rights by government military and other forces retained to provide security services on company projects in developing countries.[151]

A company can avoid many of these painful consequences—including the diversion of funds and valuable employee time—if it is guided by values and processes supporting the respect of people and other living things and the wise use of resources. Having proactive regulatory-compliance and risk-management programs—a part of any good SOS—can make a big difference, too, not only in reducing the likelihood of problems but in lessening the harm if some impropriety does occur. The U.S. government has even formalized that principle, indicating in its *Sentencing Guidelines* that the severity of penalties for federal crimes can be reduced where companies show they have an "effective compliance and ethics program."[152] (See more on the U.S. *Sentencing Guidelines* in Appendix 3.26.) Among other things, such compliance and risk control programs should encompass comprehensive due diligence reviews of proposed business acquisitions examining performance and risks around a broad range of sustainability topics.

Linkage Between Company Sustainability Obligations and Financial Success Factors

We have now completed our review of the seven cost and sales factors from the Show-Me-the-Money Model, Figure 3.1. We have seen how sustainability-oriented action can contribute to these factors and, therefore, to a company's overall financial success. The examples of these actions have been scattered across the whole spectrum of a company's sustainability obligations—everything from resource conservation and eco-efficiency to employee diversity and philanthropy. But how does the full list of a company's sustainability obligations—those identified in the model policy, Figure 2.2—contribute to these financial factors. Can all of them contribute to financial success? Figure 3.9 suggests they can. In later chapters we will learn how an organization can use an SOS to identify and implement specific actions that not only help fulfill its sustainability obligations, but also realize the greatest business value. In the end, a company should be able to place its own value-contributing initiatives on many of the Xs of Figure 3.9.

Figure 3.9
Linkage of Company Sustainability Obligations to Financial Success Factors
(x= significant linkage between obligation and success factor)

Policy (from Figure 2.2)	Financial Success Factors (from Figure 3.1)						
	1. Stronger Reputation	2. More Competitive Products; New Markets	3. Improved Productivity	4. Reduced Operational Burden	5. Reduced Supply Chain Costs	6. Reduced Cost of Capital	7. Reduced Legal Liability
1. Economic Responsibility							
1.a. Company Economic Prosperity	x	x	x	x	x	x	x
1.b. Community Economic Prosperity	x	x		x			
2. Social Responsibility							
2.a. Respect for Employees	x	x	x	x			x
2.b. Diversity, Fair Hiring Practices	x	x	x				x
2.c. Responsible Governance	x		x	x		x	x

Figure 3.9 (cont.)
Linkage of Company Sustainability Obligations to Financial Success Factors
(x= significant linkage between obligation and success factor)

Policy (from Figure 2.2)	Financial Success Factors (from Figure 3.1)						
	1. Stronger Reputation	2. More Competitive Products; New Markets	3. Improved Productivity	4. Reduced Operational Burden	5. Reduced Supply Chain Costs	6. Reduced Cost of Capital	7. Reduced Legal Liability
2.e. Fair Dealing With Customers	x	x			x		x
3. Environmental Responsibility							
3.a. Resource Conservation	x		x				
3.b. Waste Prevention & Mgmt.	x		x				x
3.c. Envtl. Risk Control & Restoration	x		x				x
3.d. Reduction of Supply Chain Impacts	x	x			x		x
3.e. Collaboration With Communities	x			x			

Sustainability Initiatives That Don't Contribute to Financial Success

Does the Show-Me-the-Money Model say that all activities by a company that help social interests or the environment ultimately lead to financial success? Of course not. As noted in Figure 3.10, sustainability-oriented actions to aid various stakeholders don't necessarily promote the sustainability of the company itself. Steep taxes may assist communities, high wages may aid workers, and prompt payment may help vendors, but at some point these things may become more than a company can reasonably bear. Sustainability is about balance. Without balance there is no survival. A company that works only to benefit its customers, leaving no profits for its investors will soon dry up. Finding the right balance to achieve both organizational and societal sustainability is the goal, and principles of honesty, openness, and fairness should light the path.

In deciding where to draw the line between societal sustainability and self-interest, great care should be taken by business to assure that societal needs are not taken too lightly. Sometimes conventional wisdom within business about what is beneficial is simply wrong. Installing pollution controls that do not reduce the consumption of materials may bite the company's financial results, but it may also buy valuable good will from the community and greater public support for the operation. Moreover, it may be viewed as a strong statement by management about the ethical need to reduce waste—something that helps motivate employees to search for other waste reduction projects that *are* economically attractive.

Figure 3.10
Some Issues That Favor Sustainability Outside the Organization
But Adversely Affect Direct Economic Business Value

- High taxes
- High wages
- Pollution controls that do not reduce material usage
- Cleanup of past contamination
- Prompt payment of bills

Consider also the lesson Henry Ford taught us in 1913. That year, the pioneer auto maker doubled the wages of his workers to the unheard of rate of $5 per day and cut their workday from nine hours to eight. The change had the intended effect: it attracted better workers and dramatically cut the high labor turnover that was bleeding the company of efficiency. But there were other motives, too. Said Ford: "If you cut wages, you just cut the number of your customers." Under the new strategy—and contrary to the general thinking of the times—Ford's business boomed.[153]

Quid Pro Quo Model: Using Sustainability to Garner Critical Support From Stakeholders

The effect that pro-sustainability action has on the attitudes and motivation of employees and other stakeholders should not be dismissed as unimportant. Companies rely on their stakeholders to provide what companies need in order to prosper. Stakeholders look to companies for certain things, too. It is this mutually beneficial relationship that is the basis for the second model illustrating the business value of an SOS. This model is named *Quid Pro Quo* after the Latin phrase for "something for something." Using this model as depicted in Figure 3.11, we can examine the "something" that each of the key stakeholders—employees, investors/lenders, customer/suppliers, and communities/governments—need from a company and the "something" those stakeholders provide to the company in return. This "something" is the benefits that are exchanged between company and stakeholder as part of the social—and to some extent, legal—contract between them. The model shows that attention to sustainability—to respect for people and the wise use and management of resources—plays a critical role in maintaining the support of key stakeholders—support that ultimately determines a firm's fate. So let us review Figure 3.11, examining the deliverables that are expected to pass between a company and each of the four key stakeholder groups.

Figure 3.11

What Stakeholders Need From and Provide to Business: The Quid Pro Quo Model

Sustainability Aspect	Stakeholders								
	Employees		Investors/Lenders		Supply Chain (Customers, Suppliers)		Communities/ Governments		
	Need	Provide	Need	Provide	Need	Provide	Need	Provide	
Wise Use and Mgmt of Economic and Natural Resources*	- Fair Wages - Tools - Training	- Reliable, Motivated Labor	- Good Reliable Management - Good Return on Investment at Reasonable Risk	- Money For Operations	Suppliers: - Sales Revenue Customers: - Good Quality, Safe Products Properly Delivered - Reasonable Total Product Cost	Suppliers: - Good Quality, Safe Supplies Properly Delivered - Reasonable Total Supply Cost Customers: - Sales Revenue	- Taxes - Total Wages - Local Purchasing - Prudent Use Of Natural Resources	- Authorization to Operate - Support Services	
Respect for People and Other Life**	- Safe and Healthy Working Conditions - Employee Development - Ethical Treatment - Diversity - Management Transparency - Non-Intimidation - Employee Benefits - Recognition for Contributions	- Trust - Safe Workplace - Behavior - Ethics - Transparency	- Consistent Meeting of Commitments - Good Business Oversight (Governance) - Management Transparency and Ethics	- Trust - Good Business Practices (Ethics) - Long-Term Support	Both: - Trust - Consistent Meeting of Commitments - Good Business Practices; Fair Dealing - Reasonable Use of Economic Power - Transparency Customers: - Accountability for Harm From Products	Both: - Trust - Consistent Meeting of Commitments - Good Business Practices; Fair Dealing - Reasonable Use of Economic Power - Transparency Suppliers: - Accountability for Harm From Supplies	- Remediation of Environmental Harm - Pollution Prevention - Protection of Biodiversity - Community Safety, Emergency Response - Support for Community Social Programs - Responsible Use of Economic Power - Transparency	- Trust - Community Safety, Stability - Law Enforcement - Fair Treatment - Transparency	

* Comparable to the economic and environmental responsibilities under the Triple Bottom Line and to natural, manufactured and financial capital under the Forum for the Future/SIGMA approach to sustainability.

** Comparable to environmental and social responsibilities under the Triple Bottom Line and to human and social capital.

Employees

Consider first the quid pro quo between a company and its employees. A company wants good labor resources—workers who are reliable and motivated. It desires their trust and confidence, and expects them to behave in a way that is safe, ethical, and open and honest (transparent).

Employees, for their part, want their employers to furnish fair wages and the tools and training for their jobs. From the respect side of the 2Rs, workers expect, among other things, safe and healthy working conditions, skills development, ethical treatment, and support for work force diversity. They also desire transparency by management, a non-intimidating work environment, and basic employee benefits. Companies that fall significantly short in fulfilling employees' expectations will find it difficult to attract and motivate people to provide what the business needs from them. If employees are too disappointed in their employer's behavior, they will scale back their own performance through crippling strikes or other labor action.

Investors and Lenders

Another important stakeholder group includes those who provide funding. Businesses want their lenders and investors to provide essential capital through a trusting, ethical, long-term business relationship. This kind of relationship is most likely to develop when a company has capable, reliable, transparent management, and effective governance processes—all characteristics of a sustainability-oriented company. It's also essential that a company show economic sustainability, compiling a solid record of meeting its business commitments and providing a good return to investors. Organizations that fail to demonstrate these skills, behaviors, and performance will not be able to attract the reasonably priced funding needed to operate and grow the business.

Suppliers and Customers

The next stakeholders of concern are those suppliers and customers that serve on each end of the company's supply chain. In many respects, the relationship between a company and its suppliers is the reverse of that between the company and its customers. Suppliers depend on the companies they serve for sales revenue; companies depend on their customers for the same. Both companies and customers need good quality, safe products and services delivered to them at the time and place required.

Both expect not to be gouged on pricing and total overall costs, including the seller's price for the product as well as associated hidden costs for storage, handling, and disposal after use. When the product or supplies are faulty or cause harm, buyers expect their sellers to redress the problem. For the supply process to work properly and efficiently, all links in the chain of supply must be characterized by relationships of trust, with each party upholding its reputation for consistently meeting commitments. As noted in the discussion on Factor 5 of the Show-Me-the-Money Model, good ethics, fair dealing, and transparency are also needed to sustain a supply chain. In addition, parties in the chain who possess superior economic power must use that power responsibly and stay within antitrust laws and other expected norms. A company that pursues a sustainability agenda, demonstrating respect and the ability to manage and deliver resources as promised, should be able to attract the type of suppliers and customers who can help assure the company's long-term success.

Communities and Governments

Last, but certainly not least, are the external enablers of business: communities and governments. Through formal and informal means, these entities grant a company its authorization to operate. They typically furnish police, fire, water, sewerage, and other essential support services. Companies count on them to provide a trusting, safe, stable environment in which business can flourish. To prosper, companies also need the fair treatment, honesty, and openness of these public groups.

In return, the firm must meet a long list of community needs which are essential for the community's own sustainability. At a minimum, a company must provide funding to governments and their citizens in the form of reasonable taxes and wages. However, to garner solid support, a business must go beyond this, donating time, money, or other resources for social causes, and hiring local contractors and suppliers. To be trusted, a company must not threaten the health or safety of local citizens or despoil their environment, but rather protect biodiversity, use natural resources wisely, and prevent and control harmful pollution. Where environmental damage is done, the company is obligated to remedy the situation. A business must be constantly prepared to address emergencies that may hurt employees, neighbors, and the environment, and must take other measures to prevent and mitigate catastrophic risks. Companies also must not abuse their economic power in dealing with communities and governments. Issues must be resolved without intimidation though open and honest communication. A firm that shows respect to its community and fulfills its financial and other duties to government, is likely to find the favor returned in the form of long-term trusting relationships that support business success.

Self-Interest Versus a Higher Calling

To some, what has just been described concerning stakeholder-company behavior is Nirvana—the state of perfect harmony rarely found in the real world. Still, few would disagree that this is the conduct that most parties desire, and if provided, would do much to solidify the vital relationships that sustain business. While the Quid Pro Quo Model is based on self-interest—you get what you sow—there is also a higher sense of obligation to much of this conduct—a moral calling. For corporations and their stakeholders to be truly successful in the pursuit of sustainability, they must answer this calling. They must make sustainability-oriented behavior the commonly expected action, a part of the moral fiber of their organizations. Once that is achieved, much of the debate about the business case for sustainability will become moot, having gone the way of the debates on the business case for barring robber-baron practices, dangerous patent medicines, and the bondage of human slavery.

Follow-up Checklist for Action: The Value of Sustainability

☐ Review Chapter 3 to identify the arguments and examples showing the value of an SOS that are likely to be most relevant and of greatest interest to key management personnel in your organization.

☐ Identify examples from within your own organization that show the business value of sustainability-oriented action. These examples and those from this chapter will be incorporated in one or more presentations for management, as discussed in Chapter 4.

☐ Begin thinking about how your organization might realize more benefits and better control risks of the type discussed in this chapter; save those ideas for consideration during strategic planing as discussed in Chapter 5.

Endnotes to Chapter 3

1. Quote attributed to famous U.S. industrialist, Henry Kaiser, who lived from 1882-1967.

2. *Milton Friedman Responds*, CHEMTECH, Feb. 1974, at 72, *available at* http://www.bartleby.com/73/143.html (interview by Milton Friedman with John McClaughry, Contributing Editor, *Business and Society Review*).

3. RENE KIM & ERIK VAN DAM, THE ADDED VALUE OF CORPORATE SOCIAL RESPONSIBILITY: A REPORT FOR NIDO NATIONAL INITIATIVE FOR SUSTAINABLE DEVELOPMENT 18-19 (NIDO 2003) [hereinafter NIDO REPUTATION STUDY].

4. HILL & KNOWLTON AND THE ECONOMIST INTELLIGENCE UNIT, CORPORATE REPUTATION WATCH 2004 (2004), *available at* http://www.hillandknowlton.com/crw/.

5. ESTHER V. RUDIS, THE CEO CHALLENGE 2003: TOP MARKETPLACE AND MANAGEMENT ISSUES 11 (The Conference Board 2003).

6. Interbrand considers the following seven factors in evaluating brand security and growth prospects: (1) volatility of consumer preference in that market; (2) age of brand; (3) market leadership position; (4) long-term profit trend; (5) investment and support provided the brand; (6) geographic breadth of brand appeal; and (7) legal protection. *See* INTERBRAND, BRAND VALUATION AND ITS APPLICATION (2000), *available at* http://www.poolonline.com/archive/iss6fea5.html and BUILDING-BRANDS LTD., BRAND VALUATION: THE SEVEN COMPONENTS OF BRAND STRENGTH (2005), *available at* http://www.buildingbrands.com/didyouknow/11_brand_valuation.shtml.

7. The factors used in the *Fortune* survey are the following: (1) innovation; (2) employee talent; (3) use of corporate assets; (4) social responsibility; (5) quality of management; (6) financial soundness; (7) long-term investment value; (8) quality of products/services; and (9) globalness. *See* http://www.fortune.com (last visited Jan. 9, 2006).

8. The 20 attributes include 3 for Emotional Appeal (Feel Good About, Admire and Respect, and Trust), 4 for Products and Services (High Quality, Innovative, Value for Money, and Stands Behind), 4 for Financial Performance (Outperforms Competitors, Record of Profitability, Low Risk Investment, and Growth Prospects), 3 for Vision and Leadership (Market Opportunities, Excellent Leadership, and Clear Vision for the Future), 3 for Workplace Environment (Rewards Employees Fairly, Good Place to Work, and Good Employees), and 3 for Social Responsibility (Supports Good Causes, Environmental Responsibility, and Community Responsibility). For a further discussion of the RQ methodology, see Charles J. Fombrun & Christopher B. Foss, *The Reputation Quotient, Part 1: Developing a Reputation Quotient, in* THE GAUGE (2001), *available at*

http://www.reputationinstitute.com/press/01_15_14_GUAGE.pdf [here-inafter RQ STUDY]; HARRISINTERACTIVE, THE ANNUAL RQ 2004—METHODOLOGICAL OVERVIEW (2004) and HarrisInteractive, *Reputation Management: A Critical, but Often Overlooked, Component of Business Growth*, http://www.harrisinteractive.com/ expertise/reputation.asp.

9. JONATHAN LOW & PAMELA COHEN KALAFUT, INVISIBLE ADVANTAGE (Perseus Press 2002).

10. *The 100 Top Brands*, BUS. WK., Aug. 1, 2005, at 90.

11. JONATHAN LOW & PAMELA COHEN KALAFUT, INVISIBLE ADVANTAGE (Perseus Press 2002).

12. *See* RQ STUDY, *supra* note 8. SustainAbility, *Programs: The Business Case—Brand Value and Reputation*, http://www.sustainability.com/ business-case/definitions.asp.

13. *See* RQ STUDY, *supra* note 8.

14. *See* NIDO REPUTATION STUDY, *supra* note 3.

15. BT Group, untitled presentation on how BT's corporate social responsibility initiatives affect customer satisfaction, at http://www.btplc.com/ Societyandenvironment/Originalthinking/BusinessCase.pdf (last visited Jan. 9, 2006). *See also* Chris Tuppen, *Satisfying Customers Through Corporate Social Responsibility*, EBF (Autumn 2002), Lori Ioannou & Stan L. Friedman, *Corporate America's Social Conscience*, FORTUNE, May 26, 2003, at S4, and Allen White, *Sustainability and the Accountable Corporation*, ENVIRONMENT, Oct. 1999, at 32.

16. Opinion Research, Hill & Knowlton, and Korn/Ferry International, *Corporate Reputation Watch: Summary of Findings*, Sept. 2003, http://www. hillandknowlton.com/crw/index/survey [hereinafter *Hill & Knowlton Corporate Reputation Watch 2003*].

17. PRICEWATERHOUSECOOPERS & FINANCIAL TIMES, THE WORLD'S MOST RESPECTED COMPANIES SURVEY 2004—NGO-WORLD, CORPORATE SOCIAL RESPONSIBILITY (2004), *available at* http://news.ft.com [hereinafter PwC-FT SURVEY 2004]. PRICEWATERHOUSECOOPERS & FINANCIAL TIMES, THE WORLD'S MOST RESPECTED COMPANIES SURVEY 2005—WORLD-COMMUNITY COMMITMENT (2005), *available at* http:// news.ft.com [hereinafter PwC-FT SURVEY 2005].

18. Anne Fisher, *The Most Admired Companies*, FORTUNE, Mar. 6, 2006, at 72.

19. RQ STUDY, *supra* note 8.

20. *The 100 Top Brands, supra* note 10, at 90-94.

21. *Fortune: Global Most Admired Companies—Best and Worse: Social Responsibility—Most Admired*, CNNMoney.com, http://money.cnn.com/

magazines/fortune/globalmostadmired/best_worst/best4.html (last visited Mar. 28, 2006).

22. PwC-FT Survey 2005, *supra* note 17.

23. PwC-FT Survey 2004, *supra* note 17.

24. *See* JENNY DAWKINS, MORI, THE PUBLIC'S VIEW OF CORPORATE RE-
SPONSIBILITY 2003 (2004), *available at* http://www.mori.com/pubinfo/
jld/publics-views-of-corporate-responsibilty.pdf [hereinafter MORI
BRITISH SURVEY 2003].

25. MPG International, *Sustainable Motivation: Attitudinal and Behavioral
Drivers for Action* (Report on a UNEP project sponsored by ESOMAR,
the World Association of Research Professionals), http://www.mpgintl.
com/sustain/english/MPG_Intl_Sustainable_Motivation_Report.pdf.
This finding from the MPG survey was consistent with the results of a
2003 survey of the British general public by the MORI organization,
which was also cited in the MPG report. *See also* MORI BRITISH SURVEY
2003, *supra* note 24.

26. CONE INC., MULTI-YEAR STUDY FINDS 21% INCREASE IN AMERICANS
WHO SAY CORPORATE SUPPORT OF SOCIAL ISSUES IS IMPORTANT IN
BUILDING TRUST (2004), *available at* http://www.causemarketingforum.
com/page.asp?ID=330 [hereinafter CONE 2004 SURVEY].

27. CO-OPERATIVE FINANCIAL SERVICES, SUSTAINABILITY REPORT 2003, at
33 (2004), *available at* http://www.cfs.co.uk/sustainability2003/.

28. *Hill & Knowlton Corporate Reputation Watch 2003, supra* note 16.

29. CONE 2004 SURVEY, *supra* note 26.

30. Chiquita Brands International, Inc., *Corporate Responsibility-Living Our
Core Values: Corporate Responsibility Reports*, http://www.chiquita.com/
corpres/CRReports.asp. Chiquita Brands International, Inc., *Press Releases: Chiquita Achieves SA8000 and EUREGAP Certification of Its Banana Farms in Colombia, Costa Rica, and Panama*, http://www.chiquita.
com/announcements/releases/pr040217b.asp. Jem Bendell, *Analysis:
Chiquita's Path From Pariah to Paradigm*, ETHICAL CORPORATION ON-
LINE, Mar. 13, 2003, http://www.ethicalcorp.com/content.asp?Content
ID=434. Chiquita Brands International, Inc., http://www.chiquita.com/
(last visited Feb. 14, 2005).

31. *Special Report—Philanthropy 2005: Smarter Corporate Giving*, BUS.
WK. ONLINE, Nov. 28, 2005, http://www.businessweek.com/.

32. HILL & KNOWLTON, 2001 CORPORATE CITIZEN WATCH SURVEY (2001),
available from JSloan@hillandknowlton.com (last contacted Feb. 15,
2005).

33. Gavin Cordon, PA News, *Africa and Climate Change Top Blair's G8
Agenda*, SCOTSMAN (U.K.) (Dec. 29, 2004), *available at* http://climateark.
org/articles/reader.asp?linkid=37734.

34. Marc Gunther, *Money and Morals at GE*, FORTUNE, Nov. 1, 2004, *available at* http://www.ge.com/en/company/investor/ge_social_responsibility_ and_citizenship.htm. *See also* Daniel Fisher, *GE Turns Green*, FORBES, Aug. 15, 2005, at 80-85.

35. "Green design" as used in this book goes beyond the concept of "cleaner production," which is defined by UNEP as "the continuous application of an integrated preventive environmental strategy to process, product and services to increase overall efficiency and reduce risks for humans and the environment." Green design is not just a preventive strategy, but one for seizing opportunities to serve environmental, social, and economic interests for the purpose of creating greater well-being. *See* UNEP, CLEANER PRODUCTION — KEY ELEMENTS (2001), *available at* http://www.uneptie. org/pc/cp/understanding_cp/home.htm.

36. *A Seat at the Table*, GREENBUSINESS LETTER, Apr. 2002, at 1, 6, 7. Herman Miller's green design system was developed with the help of famous green design experts William McDonough and Michael Braungart. For more on their approach, see WILLIAM McDONOUGH & MICHAEL BRAUNGART, CRADLE TO CRADLE (North Point Press 2002). *See also* Peter Hall, *The Next Icon*, METROPOLIS, July 2003, at 124, *available at* www.metropolismag.com. Interview by William Blackburn with Scott Charon and Gabe Wing, Herman Miller, in Holland, Mich. (May 31, 2005).

37. Deepti Hajela, *Survey: Diversity Programs Falling Short*, DAILY HERALD (Illinois), June 26, 2004, at C1.

38. Bill Breen, *The 6 Myths of Creativity*, FAST COMPANY, Dec. 2004, at 75, *available at* http://www.fastcompany.com/magazine/89/creativity.html.

39. T.L. Speer, *Growing the Green Market*, AM. DEMOGRAPHICS, Aug. 1997. *See also* RUDD MAYER ET AL., PROMOTING RENEWABLE ENERGY IN A MARKET ENVIRONMENT: A COMMUNITY-BASED APPROACH FOR AGGRE-GATING GREEN DEMAND (Land and Water Fund of the Rockies/U.S. Department of Energy Report, 1997), *available at* http://www.eere.energy. gov/greenpower/law_intro.html [hereinafter GREEN ENERGY REPORT].

40. Barry Estabrook, *Clean 'n' Green*, ONEARTH, Winter 2004, *available at* http://www.nrdc.org/onearth/04win/sevgen1.asp. *See also* http://www. seventhgeneration.com (last visited Jan. 9, 2006).

41. Ion Exchange Enviro Farms Ltd., *Why Organic-Organic Markets*, http://www.ionenviro.com/organicmarkets.html (last visited Jan. 9, 2006). Organic Monitor, *Research News Index: Global Organic Food Sales—U.S. $26 Billion and Rising*, Nov. 6, 2001, *available at* http:// www.organicmonitor.com/.

42. Organic Trade Association, *The OTA 2004 Manufacturer Survey Overview*, http://www.ota.com/pics/documents/2004SurveyOverview.pdf (last visited Jan. 9, 2006).

43. Amy Bernard Satterfield, *Frozen Organic Produce Sales Hot: Consumers Willing to Pay Extra for Healthy Food Choices*, NAT. GROCERY BUYER, Apr./May 2003, *available at* http://www.newhope.com/naturalcategory buyer/ncb_backs/apr-may_03/frozen.cfm.

44. *The Packers*, 2003 FRESH TRENDS, *cited in* Charles M. Benbrook, *Why Food Safety Will Continue Driving Growth in Demand for Organic Food*, Jan. 24, 2003, http://www.biotech-info.net/Ecofarm_Food_Safety.pdf.

45. Van Vynck Avian Solutions, http://www.vanvynckpestcontrol.co.uk/pages/about.shtml (last visited Jan. 9, 2006).

46. Cheryl Lu-Lien Tan, *New Incentives for Being Green*, WALL ST. J., Aug. 4, 2005, at D1, D3.

47. Jeremy Cato, *Toyota Still in Drivers Seat as Hybrid Segment Swells: Environment, Drivers Both Winners as Models Move Into Mainstream*, STAR PHOENIX, Sept. 12, 2003.

48. *Id. See also* Jim Mateja, *Ford to Expand "Green" Offerings*, CHI. TRIB., Jan. 11, 2005, at C3. *Sales Numbers and Forecasts for Hybrid Vehicles*, HYBRIDCARS.COM, http://www.hybridcars.com/sales-numbers.html (last visited Jan. 9, 2006). Matthew Wootten, *Hybrid-Powered Cars: The Light Is Turning Green*, BULL & BEAR FIN. REP., 2005, http://www.thebullandbear.com/articles/2004/0704-hybrid.html (last visited Jan. 9, 2006).

49. Interview by William Blackburn with Victoria and Ben Ranney, Grayslake, Ill. (Mar. 22, 2004). *Prairie Crossing, A Conservation Community: About Prairie Crossing*, http://www.prairiecrossing.com/pc/site/about-us.html. Letter from Christopher Leinberger, Managing Director, Robert Charles Lesser & Co., to George Ranney Jr. (Aug. 24, 1999). John Handley, *Experiment on the Prairie*, CHI. TRIB. (Real Estate), Sept. 29, 2002 (reprint). Jodi Cohen, *Green Day Dawns for Pupils*, CHI. TRIB., Jan. 4, 2005, at B1. David Dunlap, *Developing a Suburb, With Principles*, N.Y. TIMES, July 11, 1999 (reprint).

50. Exec. Order No. 13101, 63 Fed. Reg. 49642-51 (Sept. 14, 1998), *available at* http://www.epa.gov/opptintr/epp/pubs/13101.pdf (last visited Jan. 9, 2006).

51. U.S. EPA, *Environmentally Preferable Purchasing: Database on Environmental Information for Products and Services*, http://www.epa.gov/oppt/epp/tools/database.htm (last visited Jan. 9, 2006). *See also* ANSI Government Affairs, *Environmentally Preferable Purchasing*, http://www.ansi.org/government_affairs/laws_policies/epp.aspx?menuid=6 (last visited Jan. 9, 2006).

52. Interview by William Blackburn with Chris Tuppen, CSR, BT, London (Mar. 7, 2005) [hereinafter BT Interview 2005].

53. U.S. EPA, *Environmentally Preferable Purchasing: Database on Environmental Information for Products and Services*, http://www.epa.gov/oppt/epp/tools/database.htm (last visited Jan. 9, 2006). *See also* ANSI

Government Affairs, *Environmentally Preferable Purchasing*, http://www. ansi.org/government_affairs/laws_policies/epp.aspx?menuid=6 (last visited Jan. 9, 2006).

54. The National Organization for Diversity in Sales and Marketing, *Home Page*, http://www.minoritymarketshare.com/?id=facts (last visited Jan. 9, 2006).

55. A 2005 survey of 5,500 U.S. workers conducted for the National Urban League found 65% of the respondents agreeing that diversity improved creativity and innovation. *See* THE NATIONAL URBAN LEAGUE, DIVERSITY PRACTICES THAT WORK: THE AMERICAN WORKER SPEAKS (2004), *available at* http://www.nul.org/.

56. Molly McDonough, *Demanding Diversity—Corporate Pressure Is Changing the Racial Mix at Some Law Firms*, ABA J., Mar. 2005, at 52-58.

57. Home Depot found that when priced the same, its certified plywood outsold the non-certified product by a wide margin in both liberal and rural communities. Even when priced more, the certified plywood was still preferred by one-third of all customers. *See* JARED DIAMOND, COLLAPSE: HOW SOCIETIES CHOOSE TO FAIL OR SUCCEED 475-76 (Viking 2005).

58. For links to a wide range of green building programs and information, see Built Green Colorado, *Other Related Sites,* http://www.builtgreen.org/sites/default.htm (last visited Jan. 9, 2006). *See also* American Institute of Architects, Denver Chapter, *The Sustainable Design Resource Guide*, http://www.aiacolorado.org/SDRG/home.htm (last visited Jan. 9, 2006).

59. ATMOSPHERIC POLLUTION PREVENTION DIVISION, U.S. EPA, ENERGY STAR OFFICE PRODUCTS PROGRAM (1998).

60. U.S. EPA, PROTECTING THE ENVIRONMENT—TOGETHER: ENERGY STAR AND OTHER VOLUNTARY PROGRAMS, 2003 ANNUAL REPORT (2004), *available at* http://www.energystar.gov/ia/news/downloads/annual_report_2003.pdf (last visited Jan. 9, 2006).

61. Associated Press, *Kraft to Sell Fair-Trade Coffee*, STATE (Columbia, S.C.), Oct. 9, 2003, at B7.

62. *Row Brews Over Kenco's Sustainable Coffee*, ENDS REP., Dec. 2004, at 38.

63. Fairtrade Labeling Organizations International, *Home Page*, http://www.fairtrade.net (last visited Jan. 9, 2006).

64. Peggy Anne Salz, *Branding Your Reputation*, FORTUNE, July 21, 2003, at S10-11.

65. Statement by President George W. Bush, The White House (Apr. 25, 2003), *available at* http://www.whitehouse.gov/news/releases/2003/04/20030425-9.html.

66. Grameen Bank, *Home Page*, http://www.grameen-info.org/bank/index. html (last visited Jan. 9, 2006).

67. WORLDWATCH INSTITUTE, VITAL SIGNS 2001, at 110 (W.W. Norton & Co. 2001), *available at* http://www.worldwatch.org/pubs/vs/ (last visited Jan. 9, 2006).

68. C.K. PRAHALAD, THE FORTUNE AT THE BOTTOM OF THE PYRAMID: ERADICATING POVERTY THROUGH PROFITS (Wharton School Publishing 2005).

69. *Id.* at 1-19, 207-35.

70. *Id.* at 265-86.

71. Brian Dumaine, *See Me! Hear Me!*, FORTUNE, Oct. 27, 2003, *available at* http://money.cnn.com/magazines/fortune/fortune_archive/2003/10/27/ 351684/index.htm (last visited Jan. 9, 2006). Project Impact, *Home Page*, http://www.project-impact.net/ (last visited Jan. 9, 2006).

72. Press Release, Initiative for a Competitive Inner City (ICIC), The Boston Consulting Group, and Price Waterhouse, $85 Billion Retail Opportunity in America's Inner Cities, Boston (June 11, 1998), *available at* http:// www.icic.org/vsm/bin/smRenderFS.php?PHPSESSID=cde2d2695f0eed 92d1bce8e5a1f614cb&cerror=NO_SESSION.

73. *About Inner City 100*, http://www.innercity100.org/About.asp (last visited Jan. 9, 2006).

74. Antonio Olivo, *Wal-Mart Wages Grass-Roots Campaign to Crack Chicago*, CHI. TRIB., May 23, 2004, at 1, 17. Dan Mihalopoulos, *Wal-Mart Gets Half a Loaf: West Side Store OKd; South Side Site Gets Shelved*, CHI. TRIB., May 27, 2004, at 1.

75. Press Release, Waste & Resources Action Program, Boosting Markets for Recycled Paper, July 18, 2003, *available at* http://www.mediacentre. info/Content_Frame.html (last visited Jan. 9, 2006).

76. Aison Maitland, *Business Also Benefits From Helping the Poor: Potential Markets Can Be Productive, But the Pathway to Success Is Seldom Easy*, FIN. TIMES, Sept. 29, 2003, at 5.

77. Roland Gribben, *Conservation Fails Taste Test: Supermarkets and Suppliers Struggle to Sell Greener Products to Reluctant Consumers*, DAILY TELEGRAPH (U.K.), Sept. 18, 2003.

78. Telephone Interview by William Blackburn with Tom Catania, Government Affairs, Whirlpool Corporation, Benton Harbor, Mich. (Aug. 2, 2004). Steve Willis, Director Global Environment, Health & Safety, Whirlpool Corporation, *Emerging Customer Expectations Regarding Product Performance and the Environment*, Presented at AHC Group Conference, Phoenix, Ariz. (Jan. 22, 2004). Whirlpool, *Introducing Resource Friendly Brands From Whirlpool Brand*, http://www.energy. whirlpool.com/ (last visited Jan. 9, 2006).

79. E-mail from Kathy Robinson, Under the Canopy, to William Blackburn (Sept. 12, 2004). *Quoted in* Amy Cortese, *Wearing Eco-Politics on Your Sleeve*, N.Y. TIMES, Mar. 20, 2005, at 7.

80. GREEN ENERGY REPORT, *supra* note 39.

81. *Id.*

82. Chuck Nowlen, *Recycling Programs Offers Dell Grants—Protesters Say Health Risk Still There*, CAPITAL TIMES, Nov. 18, 2003, at 1C.

83. Press Release, Eco-Sense & Free the Planet!, Office Supply Superstore Staples Inc. Agrees to Historic Endangered Forest and Recycling Standard (2002), *available at* http://www.benladner.com/access/press/austaples.htm (last visited Jan. 9, 2006) (Eco-Sense and Free the Planet! are environmental groups affiliated with American University, Washington, D.C.).

84. Xerox, *Xerox Equipment Remanufacture & Parts Reuse*, http://www.Xerox.com/go/xrx/template/020e.jsp?view=Programs&cat=Equipment%20Remanufacture&Xcntry=USA&Xlang=en_US (last visited Jan. 9, 2006).

85. 3M, *Pollution Prevention Pays (3P)*, http://solutions.3m.com/wps/portal/!ut/p/kcxml/04_Sj9SPykssy0xPLMnMz0vM0Q9KzYsPDdaPOI8yizeINzR21y_IcFQEAPUi-n0! (last visited Jan. 9, 2006).

86. The Dow Chemical Co., *Dow Global Public Report 2003: Environmental Stewardship*, http://www.dow.com/publicreport/2003/stewardship/case.htm (last visited Jan. 9, 2006).

87. Interview with Amory Lovins, *Voices of Innovation: Amory Lovins*, BUS. WK. ONLINE, Oct. 11, 2004, http://www.businessweek.com/magazine/content/04_41/b3903468.htm (last visited Jan. 9, 2006).

88. See Chapter 14, fig. 14.5, for a list of some common green building principles.

89. GREG KATS ET AL., THE COSTS AND FINANCIAL BENEFITS OF GREEN BUILDINGS (2003), *available at* http://www.cap-e.com/ewebeditpro/items/O59F3259.pdf.

90. PAUL HAWKEN ET AL., NATURAL CAPITALISM 88-89 (Little, Brown & Co. 1999) [hereinafter NATURAL CAPITALISM].

91. WBCSD, *Eco-Efficiency*, http://www.wbcsd.ch/templates/TemplateWBCSD1/layout.asp?type=p&MenuId=MzI4&doOpen=1&ClickMenu=LeftMenu (last visited Jan. 9, 2006).

92. *See, e.g.,* Edna Sussman, *Green Buildings: An Overview and Recent Developments*, TRENDS — ABA SECTION OF ENVIRONMENT, ENERGY, AND RESOURCE NEWSL., May/June 2005, at 8, 9.

93. Homes and Communities, U.S. Department of Housing & Urban Development, *FHA Energy-Efficient Mortgages*, Oct. 26, 2001, http://www.hud.

gov/offices/cpd/energyenviron/energy/apply/fha.cfm (last visited Feb. 4, 2006).

94. Chicago Climate Exchange, *Home Page*, http://www.chicagoclimatex. com/ (last visited Jan. 9, 2006).

95. BAXTER INTERNATIONAL INC., SUSTAINABILITY REPORT 2004 (2005), *available at* http://www.baxter.com/about_baxter/sustainability/ (last visited Jan. 9, 2006) [hereinafter BAXTER ENVIRONMENTAL PERFORMANCE 2004]. BAXTER INTERNATIONAL INC., SUSTAINABILITY REPORT 2000 (2001), BAXTER INTERNATIONAL INC., SUSTAINABILITY REPORT 2001 (2002), BAXTER INTERNATIONAL INC., SUSTAINABILITY REPORT 2002 (2003), Baxter International, Inc., *Sustainability Report 2003* (2004) (web-based only). BAXTER INTERNATIONAL INC., ENVIRONMENTAL, HEALTH, AND SAFETY REPORT, BAXTER INTERNATIONAL INC., ENVIRONMENTAL, HEALTH, AND SAFETY REPORT (1998), and BAXTER INTERNATIONAL INC., ENVIRONMENTAL, HEALTH, AND SAFETY REPORT (1999). BAXTER INTERNATIONAL INC., ENVIRONMENTAL PERFORMANCE REPORT 1994 (1995) and BAXTER INTERNATIONAL INC., ENVIRONMENTAL PERFORMANCE REPORT 1995 (1996).

96. *See* BAXTER ENVIRONMENTAL PERFORMANCE 2004, *supra* note 95.

97. *Id.* BAXTER INTERNATIONAL INC., ENVIRONMENTAL, HEALTH, AND SAFETY REPORT 1996 (1997). Details on the cost avoidance from initiatives completed in prior years and definitions of terms are provided at http://www.Baxter.com/about_baxter/sustainability/our_environment/ performance_at_a_glance/E16_Environmental_Financial_Statement.pdf (last visited Jan. 10, 2006).

98. U.S. Department of Labor, Bureau of Labor Statistics, *Table 1. Civilian Workers, by Major Occupational Group*, Dec. 9, 2005, http://www.bls. gov/news.release/ecec.t01.htm (last visited Jan. 10, 2006).

99. Liberty Mutual Group, *New Study Reveals Financial Burden of Workplace Injuries Growing Faster Than Inflation*, Oct. 23, 2003, http://www. Libertymutual.com/omapps/ContentServer?pagename=CorporateInternet/ Page/PressReleaseOrange&cid=1029415782133&prid=1058288766202 &pagestyle=Orange&dir=/ResearchCenter/RCHomePage/RCNewsEvents/ RCNewsReleases/2003/RCPR2003WorkplaceSafetyIndex2 (last visited Jan. 10, 2006) [hereinafter *Liberty Mutual Safety Study*].

100. See J. PAUL LEIGH ET AL., COSTS OF OCCUPATIONAL INJURIES AND ILL-NESSES 8-10 (Univ. of Michigan Press 2000), which finds that an employers' indirect costs of a disabled worker are 0.38 times the direct costs. In 1998, Occupational Health Research, an occupational health consultancy, reported on a study showing that preventive, medical, wage replacement, and administrative costs for employee healthcare were 8-12% of payroll, with "half again as much in lost productivity." They also cited another study indicating that average indirect disability costs were over 100% of

average direct benefit payments; more specifically, actual direct benefit payment averaged 4% of payroll, with disability management averaging 1.2%, and the hidden costs, including lost productivity, 3%. *See* Occupational Health Research, *Operational Strategies: Integrated Disability Management*, OCCUPATIONAL HEALTH TRACKER, Spring 1998, *available at* http://www.systoc.com/tracker/1998Editions/spring1998.pdf. See also Monroe Berkowitz, *Full Cost of Disability—Results, Trends and Assessment*, INSIGHT, Feb. 17, 1997, at 1-4, *available at* http://www.unum.com/dislab/insight32/main.html, which says that indirect costs of a worker disability were about two times that of direct costs. Indirect costs excluded consequential property and product loss but included safety and wellness program costs. Miriam Basch Scott, *On Disability Management: Insurers, Support Services Focus on Enabling Return to Work From Disability*, EMPLOYEE BENEFIT PLAN REV., Mar. 2000, at 16-22, reports that indirect costs were 3.2 times the direct costs of workers compensation.

101. *Liberty Mutual Safety Study, supra* note 99.

102. E-mail from Bradley Burris, Health & Productivity Business Systems Manager, Intel Corporation, to William Blackburn (Feb. 23, 2005).

103. GE, GE 2005 CITIZENSHIP REPORT—OUR ACTIONS (2005), *available at* http://www.ge.com/files/usa/company/investor/downloads/ge_citizenship_overview_10202004.pdf.

104. BSR, *Issue Brief: Corruption and Bribery*, Oct. 2003, http://www.bsr.org/CSRResources/IssueBriefsList.cfm.

105. *Id.*

106. MORI BRITISH SURVEY 2003, *supra* note 24.

107. CONE 2004 SURVEY, *supra* note 26.

108. David Montgomery & Catherine Ramus, *Corporate Social Responsibility Reputation Effects on MBA Job Choice* (GSB Research Paper No. 1805, 2003) (available by e-mailing: research_papers@gsb.stanford.edu). *See also* Alice LaPlante, *MBA Graduates Want to Work for Caring and Ethical Employers* (Stanford Graduate School of Business: Research, 2004), *available at* http://www.gsb.stanford.edu/news/research/hr_mbajobchoice.shtml (last visited January 10, 2006).

109. To learn more about the *Graduation Pledge,* see Chapter 10.

110. Melissa Master, *Limits to Diversity, in* ACROSS THE BOARD 34-39 (The Conference Board 2003).

111. B&Q, *Is Age a Barrier to Employment?* http://www.diy.com/diy/jsp/aboutbandq/2004/social_responsibility/pdfs/age_policy.pdf (last visited July 15, 2006).

112. 2005 study by Tracey Rizzuto, assistant professor of psychology at Louisiana State University, *cited in* Carol Kleiman, *Older Workers More Willing to Tackle Tech Changes*, CHI. TRIB., May 24, 2005, at 2.

113. B & Q, *Respect for the Diversity of People*, http://www.diy.com/diy/jsp/
bq/templates/content_lookup.jsp?content=/aboutbandq/2004/social_
responsibility/respect_diversity.jsp&menu=aboutbandq (last visited Jan.
10, 2006).

114. *See* Vail T. Thorne, *Water Scarcity and Its Impact on Water Rights: A Real
Concern for Multinational Companies?* (Presented at the American Bar
Association, Section of Environment, Energy, and Resources, 32nd An-
nual Conference on Environmental Law, Keystone, Colo., Mar. 14, 2003).

115. *See* BT Interview, *supra* note 52.

116. See Appendixes 2.6.3 (the U.K. Combined Code) and 2.6.6 (Sarbanes-
Oxley Act), for discussion of some enterprise risk management programs.

117. BAXTER INTERNATIONAL INC., STATE OF THE ENVIRONMENTAL PROGRAM
REPORT 1995, at 20-21 (1996).

118. DUNCAN AUSTIN ET AL., CHANGING DRIVERS: THE IMPACT OF CLIMATE
CHANGE ON COMPETITIVENESS AND VALUE CREATION IN THE AUTO-
MOTIVE INDUSTRY (WRI & SAM 2004), *available at* http://pdf.wri.org/
changing_drivers_full_report.pdf.

119. U.S. EPA, *National Environmental Performance Track*, http://www.epa.
gov/performancetrack/ (last visited Jan. 10, 2006).

120. *See* Steve Parascandola & J.P. Sevilla, *State Incentive Programs Promote
Environmental Stewardship*, TRENDS — ABA SECTION OF ENVIRONMEN-
TAL, ENERGY, AND RESOURCES NEWSL., Sept./Oct. 2005, at 13.

121. U.S. EPA, *Pollution Prevention: Green Suppliers Network*, http://www.
epa.gov/p2/programs/gsn.htm (last visited Mar. 18, 2005). GreenBiz.com,
Baxter Spearheads Green Supplier Network for Health Care, July 7, 2004,
http://www.greenbiz.com/news/news_third.cfm?NewsID=26937 (last
visited Jan. 10, 2006).

122. STARBUCKS COFFEE CO., STRIKING THE BALANCE: CORPORATE SOCIAL
RESPONSIBILITY REPORT — FISCAL 2004 ANNUAL REPORT (2005), *avail-
able at* http://www.starbucks.com/aboutus/csrannualreport.asp (last vis-
ited Jan. 10, 2006). *See also* Elliot Schrage, *Supply and the Brand*, HARV.
BUS. REV. (JUNE 2004), *Harvard Business Review OnPoint*, Reprint No.
F0406B, http://www.hbr.org (last visited Jan. 10, 2006).

123. SOCIAL INVESTMENT FORUM (SIF), 2001 REPORT ON SOCIALLY RE-
SPONSIBLE INVESTING TRENDS IN THE UNITED STATES (Social Investment Forum Foundation (SIFF) & SIF 2001), *available at* http://www.
socialinvest.org/Areas/research/trends/SRI_Trends_Report_2001.pdf
(last visited Jan. 10, 2006).

124. SIF, 2005 REPORT ON SOCIALLY RESPONSIBLE INVESTING TRENDS
IN THE UNITED STATES (SIFF & SIF 2006), *available at* http://www.
socialinvest.org/areas/research/trends/sri_trends_report_2005.pdf (last
visited Jan. 10, 2006) [hereinafter, 2005 U.S. SRI STUDY].

125. *Id.* EUROPEAN SUSTAINABLE AND RESPONSIBLE INVESTMENT FORUM (EUROSIF), SOCIALLY RESPONSIBLE INVESTMENT AMONG EUROPEAN INVESTORS—2003 REPORT (2003), *available at* http://www.eurosif.org/pub2/lib/2003/10/srirept/eurosif-srireprt-2003-all.pdf (last visited Mar. 16, 2005). *See also* SIRI GROUP & AVANZI SRI RESEARCH, GREEN, SOCIAL, AND ETHICAL FUNDS IN EUROPE 2003 (2003), *available at* http://www.sricompass.org/trends/Factsandfigures/ (last visited Mar. 15, 2005) [hereinafter GREEN, SOCIAL, AND ETHICAL FUNDS].

126. Jane Ambachtsheer, Mercer Investment Consulting, Inc., *SRI: What Do Investment Managers Think?*, Mar. 21, 2005), http://www.merceric.com/summary.jhtml?originUrl=/home.jhtml&idContent=1174905. Only about one-third of the U.S. respondents agreed that the use of environmental and social information in investment practice and for screening stocks would become mainstream within 10 years. In contrast, the support for those statements outside the United states was particularly strong. This difference in sentiment may foretell a stronger SRI market outside the United States than inside it over the years to come. *See also* CSR EUROPE ET AL., INVESTING IN RESPONSIBLE BUSINESS: THE 2003 SURVEY OF EUROPEAN FUND MANAGERS, FINANCIAL ANALYSTS AND INVESTOR RELATIONS OFFICERS (2003), *available at* http://www.csreurope.org/pressroom/sri%20survey_page4783.aspx. Seven of 10 European fund managers and analysts questioned in this 2003 survey said they expect the SRI market to grow.

127. UNEP, *Finance Initiative*, http://www.unepfi.org/index.html (last visited Jan. 10, 2006). UNITED NATIONS & SWISS FEDERAL DEPARTMENT OF FOREIGN AFFAIRS, WHO CARES WINS—CONNECTING FINANCIAL MARKETS TO A CHANGING WORLD (2004), *available at* http://www.innovest group.com/pdfs/WhoCaresWins.pdf.

128. *See* Equator Principles, *The Equator Principles*, http://www.equator-principles.com (last visited July 23, 2006).

129. *See* 2005 U.S. SRI STUDY, *supra* note 124.

130. *Id.*

131. *Id.*

132. *Id.* Vanessa Houlder, *Prospects in Asia Are Improving: In China, Pressure From Investors Will Reinforce New Regulations*, FIN. TIMES, Oct. 16, 2003, at 2.

133. Stephanie Kendall & Todd Larsen, *Number of Large Socially Responsible Funds Earning Top Performance Marks Rises Again at Mid-2003 Mark*, SOC. INV. F. NEWS, July 29, 2003, *available at* http://www.socialinvest.org/Areas/News/2003-Q2performance.htm. Alexander Barkawi, *Sustainability Leadership—Insights From the Dow Jones Sustainability Indexes*, SUSTAINABLE DEV. INT'L, Summer 2003, at 39-40.

134. Steven F. Hayward, *The Triple Bottom Line: Companies Measure Environmental and Social Performance*, FORBES, Mar. 17, 2003, at 42.

135. Marc Orlitzky et al., *Corporate Social and Financial Performance: A Meta-Analysis*, 24 ORGANIZATION STUDIES (2003) 403-41, *available at* http://business.auckland.ac.nz/newstaffnet/profile/publications_upload/000000556_orlitzkyschmidtrynes2003os.pdf.

136. ROBERT BAUER ET AL., INTERNATIONAL EVIDENCE ON ETHICAL MUTUAL FUND PERFORMANCE AND INVESTMENT STYLE (2001), *available at* http://www.socialinvest.org/Areas/research/Moskowitz/2002_full.pdf. *See also Companies Named as Leaders in Sustainability Strive to Reward Investors*, BUS. & ENV'T, Oct. 2002, at 8.

137. *See* 2005 U.S. SRI STUDY, *supra* note 124. STEPHANIE KENDALL & TODD LARSEN, MARKET SLUMP PROVIDING UNEXPECTED BOOST TO SOCIALLY RESPONSIBLE MUTUAL FUNDS (SIF News & SIF 2002), *available at* http://www.socialinvest.org/Areas/News/020730.htm (last visited Jan. 10, 2006).

138. *See* 2005 U.S. SRI STUDY, *supra* note 124.

139. SIF, 2003 REPORT ON SOCIALLY RESPONSIBLE INVESTING TRENDS IN THE UNITED STATES 44 (SIFF & SIF 2006), *available at* http://www. socialinvest.org/areas/research/trends/sri_trends_report_2003.pdf (last visited Jan. 10, 2006) (as modified based on Communication with Don Cassidy, Senior Research Analyst, Lipper Inc., Denver, Colo. (Aug. 16, 2004).

140. BSR, ISSUE BRIEF: OVERVIEW OF BUSINESS AND CORPORATE GOVERNANCE (2003), *available at* http://www.bsr.org/CSRResources/Issue BriefsList.cfm?area=all (last visited Jan. 10, 2006).

141. *Id.*

142. *Id.*

143. *Id.*

144. Moody's Investors Service, *Rating Methodology: U.S. and Canadian Corporate Governance Assessment*, Aug. 2003, http://www.moodys. Com/moodys/cust/research/MDCdocs/20/2002000000425793.pdf?search=5&searchQuery=Governance%20Assessment&click=1 (last visited Jan. 10, 2006). S&P's, *Standard & Poor's Corporate Governance Scores—Criteria, Methodology, and Definitions*, May 20, 2002 and *Credit FAQ: Standard & Poor's Enhances Analysis of Corporate Governance*, Mar. 25, 2004, both at http://www2.standardandpoors.com/servlet/Satellite? Pagename=sp%2FPage%2FSiteSearchResultsPg&l=EN&r=1&b=10& search=site&vqt=Corporate+Governance&submit.x=9&submit.y=10 (last visited January 10, 2006).

145. *See, e.g.*, Luis Aguilar, *Corporate Governance: Does Mexico Finally Get It?*, METROPOLITAN CORPORATE COUNSEL, Jan. 2006, at 4.

146. Glenn Hess, *Key Court Cases Focus on Industry Liability Issues*, CHEM. MARKET REP., Jan. 26, 2004, at 1, 9.

147. AAB Ltd., *SEC 20-F, Amendment No. 1, Filed February 2004*, http:// www.abb.com/global/abbzh/abbzh251.nsf!OpenDatabase&db=/GLOBAL/ ABBZH/ABBZH259.NSF&v=329E&e=us&c=C04B07BB670DD6FDC 1256C4F0032D114 (last visited Jan. 10, 2006).

148. *See* Tedd Kochman, *The Legal and Practical Value of Promoting Diversity in Your Workforce*, METROPOLITAN CORPORATE COUNSEL, Mar. 2005, at 47.

149. U.S. EPA, *Compliance and Enforcement Annual Results: FY 2005 Numbers at a Glance*, http://epa.gov/compliance/data/results/annual/index. html (last visited Jan. 27, 2006).

150. *See, e.g.*, European Parliament and the Council of the European Union, *Directive 2004/35/CE on Environmental Liability With Regard to the Prevention and Remedying of Environmental Damage* (Apr. 21, 2004), http:// europa.eu.int/eur-lex/pri/en/oj/dat/2004/l_143/l_14320040430en00560075. pdf (last visited Jan. 10, 2006). *See also* Tawny Bridgeford, *The Latest on Corporate Environmental Accountability in a Third World Court*, INT'L ENVTL. L. COMM. NEWSL., Dec. 2004, at 13-17 [hereinafter Bridgeford on Corporate Accountability].

151. *See* Bridgeford on Corporate Accountability, *supra* note 150. *See also, e.g.*, William Baue, *Unocal Alien Tort Claims Act Case Settlement Boosts Corporate Accountability*, SOCIALFUNDS.COM, Dec. 16, 2004, http://www. socialfunds.com/news/article.cgi/article1591.html (last visited January 10, 2006).

152. U.S. SENTENCING GUIDELINES MANUAL—SENTENCING OF ORGANIZATIONS §§8A1.2, 88B2.1, and 8C2.5 (2004), *available at* http://www.ussc. gov/2004guid/tabconchapt8.htm (last visited Feb. 15, 2006).

153. Ford Motor Co., *An American Legend*, http://media.ford.com/newsroom/ release_display.cfm?release=81. *See also* DAN ROBERTS, A MOMENT IN TIME: HENRY FORD AND THE $5 WORKDAY: PART II (1997), *available at* http://ehistory.osu.edu/world/amit/display.cfm?amit_id=1413.

CHAPTER 4

Building an SOS: The Key Elements and Basic Structure

"You can't cross the sea merely by standing and staring at the water."[1]
—Laurence J. Peter

An oil tanker as long as five football fields is difficult to maneuver, and even at modest speeds, it may take three miles or more to bring the behemoth to a stop. Considerable care and planning are required to make the necessary turns and adjustments to deliver the ship safely to port. But this won't happen unless the crew is well trained and focused and the captain skilled and experienced. So it is when one tries to change the course of a company and bring it to some new destination—a destination like sustainability.

It's often easy to excite corporate people about a trip toward that noble goal. After all, who would disagree with changing a company to improve its management of economic and natural resources and heighten its respect for people and other living things? The thought of reaching that end sounds most pleasant, but then come the details of the trip, such as: How do we start? What are the steps? How do we convince the captain, his crew, and the entire roster of passengers that they should make this trip with us? What will sway them if they are already on course to another more familiar place?

One approach to setting a company on course to sustainability is the SOS. This approach—like piloting a tanker—requires focused, skilled, well-trained leaders and teams; careful planning and execution; and, of course, plenty of patience. Other assets are required as well. Here are some critical elements of an SOS, which are graphically depicted in Figure 4.1:

1. *The Drivers.* These are the elements that help assure the organization is continually motivated to drive forward toward sustainability. They include the following:

   • *A champion/leader.* A champion within the company must bring the idea of sustainability forward and start things moving. After the effort is underway, a leader keeps it rolling.

- *Approach for selling management on sustainability.* One person can't steer a ship or make a permanent change to a company without first having a vision of what is needed and then convincing others to help. It's this *convincing* that is the biggest initial challenge for the champion and other early supporters. It's also important for supporters to continue to sell the merits of sustainability at lower levels of the organization on an ongoing basis.
- *Accountability mechanisms.* These mechanisms are the teeth of the program. They show that the company is serious about this effort—so serious it will dole out or withhold rewards based on how well the effort progresses.

2. *The Efficient Enablers.* These elements enable the organization to undertake its sustainability efforts in a logical, coordinated, efficient way. They include:

- *Organizational structure.* A few teams of supporters are needed to move the company along its course. They must communicate the sustainability message throughout the organization, collect and compile feedback, and assure appropriate actions are being taken. Their roles must be clarified and efforts coordinated so they can optimize the effectiveness and efficiency of their work.
- *Deployment and integration.* A sustainability initiative won't be successful unless it becomes part of the culture of the organization. People in all corners of the organization must understand, accept, and support the concept. This ownership doesn't happen unless a conscious effort is made to deploy the idea into the ranks of the company and meld it into the company's existing tools, processes, procedures, programs, and values.

3. *The Pathway.* These elements, which map the path toward sustainability, are the following:

- *Vision, values, and policy.* These statements define what sustainability means within the organization. They describe the ultimate objectives of the SOS.
- *Operating system standards.* Operating system standards document the cyclical management process that serves as the

engine for change. They help the organization establish a sustainability culture and stay on course over the long term as it moves closer to achieving the vision and policy.

• *Strategic planning for aligned priorities.* One part of the operating system is strategic planning, which is essential for prioritizing among the many possible actions toward sustainability. This tool helps the organization focus its resources on those things that provide the greatest value. Alignment and coordination on these priorities across the organization are necessary to produce the most pronounced change with the least resources.

4. *The Evaluators.* Evaluator elements are needed to gauge the organization's progress toward sustainability. They enable the operation to make appropriate adjustments when performance comes up short. These elements include:

• *Indicators and goals.* Specific goals create a clear picture of our destination. Various indicators, such as earnings per share of stock, percentage of women on the board, and tons of toxic waste generated, give us a way to tell whether we are on track and making the expected progress.

• *Measuring and reporting progress.* What gets measured gets managed; what gets managed gets done. Effective measurement, analysis, and reporting provide a clear picture of progress to those inside and outside the organization. Inside, it enables the organization and those involved to receive due recognition for performance, whether good or bad, which in turn provides further motivation for achievement. Outside, it helps establish the company's credibility for being economically, socially, and environmentally responsible as well as sincere, open, and honest.

• *Stakeholder engagement and feedback.* This element of an SOS gives a company a true view of how others see it. It is important that a corporation calibrate its views of itself with those of outsiders who care. This dose of reality can aid the process of constructive change and, at the same time, help build credibility with key stakeholders.

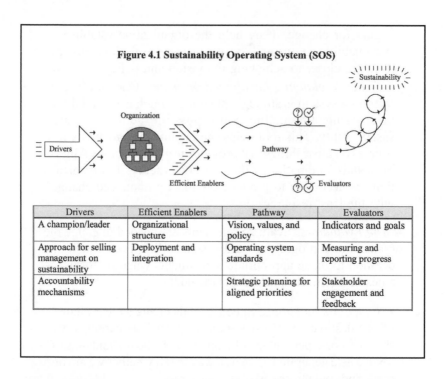

Figure 4.1 Sustainability Operating System (SOS)

Drivers	Efficient Enablers	Pathway	Evaluators
A champion/leader	Organizational structure	Vision, values, and policy	Indicators and goals
Approach for selling management on sustainability	Deployment and integration	Operating system standards	Measuring and reporting progress
Accountability mechanisms		Strategic planning for aligned priorities	Stakeholder engagement and feedback

Armed with this broad understanding of these SOS elements and their purposes, let us now examine four elements in more detail: (1) the champion/leader; (2) vision, values, and policy; (3) sales approach; and (4) organizational structure. These elements are the measures first needed to lift a sustainability initiative off the ground.

The Champion/Leader

A key internal driver is the *champion/leader*. The champion is the person who brings forward the idea of a sustainability business agenda and rallies the organization to commence action. Champions, who can come from almost anywhere in the company, are the inspired true believers, the people with the insight that sustainability is vital to the company's and society's long-term success. Their main task is to gain converts among the movers and shakers of the corporation and to create a network of other influential champions who form a "core team" to move the idea forward. Where should the champion look for core team members? The best place may be among leaders from a few business units as well as from key functions such as EHS; human resources; purchasing/supply chain;

business planning; finance; governance; government affairs/public policy; community relations; communications; philanthropy; law; and business practices/ethics. The champion and core team can help sell the merits of a sustainability goal and SOS to senior management and recommend to them the organizational structure most effective in implementing and maintaining the system.

People likely to succeed as the champion are those respected change-agents within the company who are good collaborators and communicators; are knowledgeable about the company, its business and culture; and understand and have a passion for sustainability. Seasoned, effective, admired executives with these characteristics can be most successful in leading the charge. Other good candidates are company leaders who have done well in EHS departments, or in groups responsible for community relations, business practices/ethics, corporate governance, or public affairs. Since external stakeholders play a prominent role in an SOS, it is helpful for the champion to have experience working with them in a transparent, non-defensive way.

Why don't more companies have sustainability champions? It's because champions are volunteers, and in the overworked, competitive corporate world, fewer and fewer people are raising their hands for extra work. It's also because being a champion takes courage. And finally, it's because a champion must have a working knowledge of sustainability and its benefits to a company—knowledge many employees don't have. Management can do much to help address the first issue by encouraging the prioritization of work assignments; the second, by rewarding those who show the kind of initiative and leadership a champion displays. While a natural tension exists between limiting work on the one hand, and volunteering for more of it on the other, that's exactly what champions do. And they do so guided by a sense of what adds the greatest value to the organization. They make time for the important things by carefully managing the expectations that others have of them about work deadlines and output. What about the third issue, the lack of knowledge on sustainability? This book can help in that regard, as can sustainability conferences and collegiate courses—both of which are on the rise.

Can a CEO be a champion? Yes, but not the *only* one. Two problems arise if the CEO tries to take on this task alone. First, the CEO doesn't have the time for all the focused discussions that must occur; there are simply too many competing issues. Second, the march toward sustainability would seem like it has the support of only the CEO, with others following suit merely to please the leader, not because they themselves have accepted the idea on their own terms. For these reasons, it's best to have the CEO in a supportive but visible role, providing encouragement and recognition, giving speeches and media interviews and otherwise helping the cause. This allows the "movement" to develop from within the organization while showing that the CEO is fostering an environment in which it can flourish. What happens if a champion doesn't emerge? Nothing happens—unless, of course, an inspired CEO or senior executive assigns a temporary leader to study sustainability and help gain concurrence for action.

Once the organization decides to implement an SOS, a team leader must be identified to coordinate and facilitate the companywide efforts. The leader may or may not be the champion. Whoever is selected must be motivated, knowledgeable about sustainability, trusted by the group, and process- and goal-oriented. Leaders should possess good communication, collaboration, and organizational skills and have the extra time to lead this initiative. They must also be courageous, thick-skinned, and tenacious. To be effective, they must be placed high enough in the organization—say, as vice president or one position lower. Regardless of the companywide group they report to, the leader must somehow be closely aligned with the company's strategic planning and development function. Some important duties of leaders are to assure the right people are on the supporting teams, that the roles of team members are clear, and that the teams are making adequate progress. Leaders must also balance sustainability efforts to available budgets and personnel, and when necessary, seek help from superiors to obtain additional resources and overcome other tough obstacles. Their job is not an easy one.

Vision, Values, and Policy; External Codes

What everyone will first want to know from the champion/leader is, *what* is it she is asking the company to achieve and *why* is it important that the organization achieve it? The champion will need to answer to these questions to gain converts for the cause. The leader must also be able to respond on those points to move the organization to the desired destination of sustainability. We will discuss how to answer the "why" question—how to sell management on sustainability—later in this chapter.

To explain what sustainability means to the organization, we can look back to Chapters 1 and 2. Recall that sustainability can be defined at various levels, from the conceptual to the operational as noted in Figure 2.1. A Brundtland Commission, TBL, or 2Rs definition can provide a general vision of the destination. Ultimately, however, a more specific explanation must be provided so people can understand what these concepts mean in practice. A model sustainability policy like that shown in Figure 2.2 can fill that need. Various external sustainability codes such as those described in Appendix 2 may also help.

A champion may find the use of the model sustainability policy or external codes helpful for soliciting supporters, but a leader will need more. The leader's main assignment is to work with company leaders and groups to design and implement an operating system—an SOS—that will carry the organization toward sustainability. This will involve the development of certain vision, policy, and planning documents, as shown in Figure 4.2. The starting point for company action is its mission statement and one or more documents which set forth the company's aspirations. The mission statement, commonly found at most sizeable corporations, is a short statement describing the organization's main role, typically covering its purpose and the nature of its products, services, and customers.

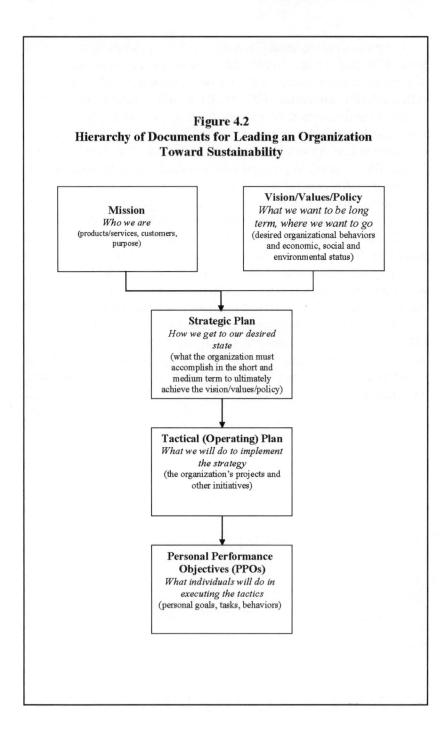

**Figure 4.2
Hierarchy of Documents for Leading an Organization
Toward Sustainability**

Mission
Who we are
(products/services, customers,
purpose)

Vision/Values/Policy
*What we want to be long
term, where we want to go*
(desired organizational behaviors
and economic, social and
environmental status)

Strategic Plan
*How we get to our desired
state*
(what the organization must
accomplish in the short and
medium term to ultimately
achieve the vision/values/policy)

Tactical (Operating) Plan
*What we will do to implement
the strategy*
(the organization's projects and
other initiatives)

**Personal Performance
Objectives (PPOs)**
*What individuals will do in
executing the tactics*
(personal goals, tasks, behaviors)

The aspirational statement may go under various names: vision, values statement, or policy, to name a few. Many companies already have such documents. Recall the 10 sustainability principles used by Prairie Crossing. Johnson & Johnson's aspirational statement, which has guided it for more that 60 years, is its one-page *Credo*. The *Credo* presents the company's commitments to its customers, employees, communities, and investors written in plain, concise language. Novo Nordisk, the Danish healthcare products company, has a five-point vision. The foundation for it is the company's articles of association, which were amended to specify that the company will "strive to conduct its activities in a financially, environmentally, and socially responsible way." Van City, the Canadian bank, looks to its two-page *Statement of Values and Commitments*, which emphasizes integrity, innovation, and responsibility. The statement also details commitments aimed at "strengthening (the company's) long-term business while contributing to the well-being of (its) members, staff, communities, and the environment." Another Canadian firm, Mountain Equipment Co-op, has a sustainability policy organized in three parts: *What We Believe*, *What We're Going to Do*, and *How We're Going to Do It*. Shell promotes its nine *Business Principles*; Toyota, its seven *Guiding Principles*. S.C. Johnson & Sons has captured its values in a half-page document entitled, *This We Believe—Our Guiding Corporate Philosophy*. B&Q, the U.K. do-it-yourself chain store, has 12 *Core Values*, reinforcing its vision "to improve the quality of life for all the people (its) business touches."

If your company has a document like this, then it should be compared with the model sustainability policy (Figure 2.2) to determine what if any changes may be needed to fully capture a commitment to sustainability. Linking sustainability into a company's existing core documents is a convenient way of helping employees build on the familiar past and thereby ease the transition to sustainability. On the other hand, if the existing statements have generally been ignored in the company or are too general to form the basis for action, then a separate sustainability policy should be considered. Dow has taken this approach, creating not just one guiding document on sustainability but two. Its *Sustainable Development Guiding Principles* consist of eight commitments supporting its vision "to achieve financial, environmental, and social excellence in all parts of the world where (the company does) business." In addition, it has a similar 12-point *Sustainable Development Operating Plan*, which is a mix of policy statements and strategic plan provisions. For example, it includes, among other things, a commitment to develop and produce "value-added, essential-to-life products that positively contribute to a sustainable society." Functionally, the operating plan serves the desired result, however, creating the foundation for a number of implementation plans developed by Dow's various businesses, functions, and sites.[2]

The Dow documents, the statements of other companies, and Figure 2.2 are all good sources for a company seeking to draft its own policy or guiding principles covering sustainability. Ideally, every company should have its own document of this type—one it has birthed and fully embraces and that is tailored to its own operations and values. Such a document will make more sense to the organization than some external voluntary code and may therefore be more readily followed. However, that is not to say external codes should be ignored. Indeed, there are many ways they can prove valuable in defining a company's vision of sustainability.

Types of Codes

"Voluntary codes," as we will use the term, entail any of a variety of codes, standards, and guidelines developed by NGOs, business groups, and other organizations. Voluntary codes related to sustainability are of four types. First are *codes of organizational behavior*. They are behavioral or ethics-like standards that the issuers believe organizations should follow. These codes are commonly framed as a series of obligations written in a style similar to that of the model sustainability policy, and they may be broad or specific in scope. The U.N. Global Compact is an example of a broad code of this type. Some of the more popular sustainability-related codes of organizational behavior are listed in Figure 4.3 and summarized in Appendix 2, highlighting provisions that may be more challenging to fulfill.

Figure 4.3
Sustainability-Related Codes of Organizational Behavior
Summarized in Appendix 2
(Appendix number for each code is noted below.)

2.1 General Sustainability Codes
2.1.1 U.N. Global Compact
2.1.2 The Earth Charter
2.1.3 Global Sullivan Principles of Corporate Social Responsibility
2.1.4 OECD Guidelines for Multinational Enterprises
2.1.5 Social Venture Network's Standards for Corporate Responsibility
2.1.6 Caux Round Table's Principles for Business
2.1.7 Principles for Global Corporate Responsibility: Benchmarks for Measuring Business Performance
2.1.8 U.S. Department of Commerce Manual of Business Ethics for Emerging Markets
2.1.9 Nippon Keidanren's Charter of Corporate Behavior

2.2 Environmental Codes
2.2.1 The CERES Principles
2.2.2 ICC Charter for Sustainable Development
2.2.3 Position Statement of Pew Center's Business Environmental Leadership Council
2.2.4 Responsible Care® Global Charter

2.3 Human Rights, Labor, and Other Social Codes
2.3.1 U.N. Universal Declaration of Human Rights
2.3.2 Amnesty International's Human Rights Principles for Companies
2.3.3 U.N. Norms on the Responsibilities of Transnational Corporations and Other Business Enterprises With Regard to Human Rights (draft)
2.3.4 U.S.-U.K. Voluntary Principles on Security and Human Rights
2.3.5 ILO Tripartite Declaration of Principles Concerning Multinational Enterprises and Social Policy
2.3.6 European Union Charter of Fundamental Rights
2.3.7 Social Accountability 8000
2.3.8 Fair Labor Association's Workplace Code of Conduct

2.3 Human Rights, Labor, and Other Social Codes—continued
2.3.9 Worker Rights Consortium's Model Code of Conduct
2.3.10 WRAP Apparel Certification Principles
2.3.11 Ethical Trading Initiative's Base Code

2.4 Marketing and Advertising Codes
2.4.1 ICC International Codes of Marketing and Advertising Practice
2.4.2 Better Business Bureau and Other U.S. Marketing and Advertising Codes
2.4.3 British Code of Advertising, Sales Promotion, and Direct Marketing
2.4.4 Canadian Direct Marketing Association Code of Ethics and Standards of Practice

2.5 Anti-Corruption Codes
2.5.1 OECD Convention for Combating Bribery of Foreign Officials in International Business Transactions
2.5.2 U.N. Convention Against Corruption
2.5.3 ICC Rules of Conduct to Combat Extortion and Bribery
2.5.4 Transparency International's Business Principles for Countering Bribery
2.5.5 AS 8001-2003 Fraud and Corruption Control Standard

2.6 Governance Codes
2.6.1 OECD Principles of Corporate Governance
2.6.2 Council of Institutional Investors' Corporate Governance Policies
2.6.3 The U.K. Combined Code
2.6.4 King II Code of Corporate Practices and Conduct
2.6.5 AS 8000-2003 Australian Good Governance Principles
2.6.6 Sarbanes-Oxley Act
2.6.7 Other Governance Codes

2.7 Industry-Specific Codes

Another type of code, the *product certification standard*, sets forth the conditions under which a product must be produced in order to receive a particular certification. These standards, which were reviewed in Chapter 3, cover various aspects of production, such as labor and fair trade practices and sustainable forestry and agriculture.

Process standards present a methodology by which companies can achieve some end, such as improving performance. ISO 9001 and ISO 14001 are two popular examples. These and other sustainability-related management systems standards are discussed in Chapter 5 and listed and summarized in Appendix 3. Process standards may have a specific focus, covering such things as report verification or the management of quality, EHS, or labor rights. Other process standards may have a broad scope, encompassing social responsibility, sustainability or—as in the case of the Baldridge Award criteria—even the entire management of the business.

Finally, *reporting guidelines and standards*, like those of the GRI, provide guidance to organizations on what they should voluntarily disclose to the public concerning their sustainability policies, practices, and performance. Reporting standards and standards for report verification are further discussed in Chapter 10.

The Benefits of Using Codes

Companies may realize internal and external benefits by using voluntary codes in their quest for sustainability. Here are some of those benefits:

1. *Ease of adoption.* Like internal sustainability policies, voluntary codes can paint the vision for moving a company toward sustainability. Such codes—especially those already adopted by well-respected peer organizations—may present a smoother path to management approval than a company-specific policy that may take months to draft and approve. "Look," you say to the CEO, "this code represents the consensus of three dozen important outside groups. Moreover, 35 well-respected corporations have already signed on. They don't have a problem with it. In addition, it is a code that is highly regarded by many of our socially sensitive stakeholders." That argument can often be persuasive. But even if it is, you will still need to discuss the code with key constituencies within the company, explaining what it means to the business and securing their support for implemen-

tation. If some knotty provision of a code holds up its internal approval, you can always pluck a few noncontroversial provisions from it to insert in the company's own policy, then use the same argument to support those proposed amendments.

2. *Benchmarking for improvement.* Whether or not a company formally endorses a code, it may reap internal value by simply benchmarking against the code to find opportunities for improving its own policy, objectives, and practices.

3. *Enhanced internal visibility of an initiative.* Within a company, a commitment that has been publicly proclaimed takes on much greater importance than one that has not. A public commitment to meet some recognized code places the company in the spotlight. It puts at risk the company's reputation for meeting its goals and raises the consequences of failure, which in turn provides extra motivation for performance. However in most cases, the heat of outside scrutiny is not what it could be. The United Nations and other code-setting groups often lack the resources or desire to evaluate company conformance. Indeed, many of these groups measure success more by the quantity of code endorsers than the quality.[3]

4. *Strengthens reputation with external stakeholders.* The external value of a code comes from the public endorsement itself. By publicly adopting a code, the company signals to its external stakeholders the values it embraces. If these values align with those of its stakeholders, the company's reputation can be enhanced in their eyes.

5. *Opens communication with external stakeholders.* A company may also find that by signing on to a code like the CERES Principles, it gains access to a regular forum for discussing matters with the issuing authority as well as other endorsers and supporters of the code. Such a forum can facilitate useful benchmarking and stakeholder dialogue.

6. *Magnifies voice for change.* Endorsements are also a way the company can lend its voice to a choir calling for specific changes in business practices, values, or culture. For example, 38 major corporations who believe business should be proactively combating climate change found a common voice in the principles of the Business Environmental Leadership Council of the Pew

Center for Global Climate Change.[4] Through this endorsement, these companies have helped promote action on climate change and, at the same time, have bolstered their reputations as environmental leaders and responsible corporate citizens.

Determining Which Codes to Adopt

If voluntary codes can add business value, how does a company determine which ones to endorse? Each company must answer that by assessing the potential value of particular codes to its organization. Initially a company may be drawn to a code because it has been supported by a number of industry peers, because it has gained considerable publicity, or—as in the case of the Pew Center principles—because it involves some topic of particular interest. Once a code comes into the sights of the company, it can be assessed by posing certain questions:

1. *Is the topic relevant and material to the company?* A chemical company may want to pursue the ISO 14001 environmental management standard or the Responsible Care® Global Charter. A human rights code like SA 8000 may be of interest to a business with production in developing nations. Appliance makers might consider the U.S. Energy Star® certification standards. Furniture makers, lumber supply companies, and paper producers may look to the standards of the FSC or Sustainable Forestry Initiative. Firms with global operations should think about the U.N. Global Compact.

2. *Is this an important area where improvement or companywide consistency is needed?* A company that is persuaded to pursue a sustainability agenda might bring internal and external attention to that objective by adopting a broad code on sustainability. If a company has performed poorly in an area such as governance and needs greater focus on that topic across the organization, it could be helped by adopting an external governance code. This move could prove especially beneficial if the deficiency has become a public issue and the company desperately wants to show it is committed to achieve best demonstrated practices.

3. *What burden is imposed on endorsing companies? Does the company have the resources to meet the code requirements?* Some companies adopt codes simply for the publicity value and with little real intention of assessing their own conformance to

the standard and closing the identified gaps. That's a dangerous strategy. It can seriously backfire, threatening the company's credibility, especially if some serious noncompliance comes to public attention through an unexpected incident or at the hands of a disgruntled worker. A company should endorse a code only if it is committed to fulfilling the code obligations—it must look before it leaps. Some codes may require reporting or third-party audits, while others might demand extensive changes in the practices of the business and its suppliers. But is the company prepared to do this? That's the key question.

4. *Is the code sufficiently flexible and not overly prescriptive?* A company may find from careful review that certain provisions of a code are too prescriptive or otherwise impracticable. However, before dropping the standard from further consideration, the company should review its objections with the issuing body, and perhaps a few organizations that have endorsed the code, to clarify the meaning and ramifications of the objectionable provisions. Say a company is concerned about the U.N. Global Compact's provisions on the precautionary approach and the right to collective bargaining. If the company discusses these provisions with the U.N. representatives, it may find they are comfortable with the company's position on the issues even though it may not be what some labor unions or environmentalists would prefer. Of course, there is a limit as to how far a company should go in this regard. Certainly it should not endorse a code if the only way it can do so is by ignoring a key provision or giving it an interpretation that is distorted beyond reason. To do otherwise is hypocrisy. Moreover, it leaves the company's credibility and reputation vulnerable to attack. If an external code isn't flexible enough to be workable, the company may want to develop one of its own.

5. *How much credibility does the code and its issuing body have with company management and key stakeholders?* The ISO standards, the Global Compact, and the GRI Sustainability Reporting Guidelines all carry a cachet that most other voluntary codes lack. An endorsement of these codes by a company sends a message that many stakeholders understand. Company management may well be impressed with the support these codes already enjoy with other major companies. The credibility of a

code among company personnel will also be enhanced if the CEO personally knows a leader of the issuing authority—such as the U.N. Secretary-General if the code is the Global Compact, or the chairman of GRI's board of directors in the case of the GRI Sustainability Reporting Guidelines.

6. *Will future amendments to the code be likely, and will the company be expected to conform to them?* Nobody likes to be the victim of the old "bait and switch," where one product is advertised and something else delivered at the time of sale. Companies need to explore the likelihood that a code will be significantly amended and how often such amendments are likely to occur. If significant amendments are probable, then you should understand the amendment process, including the involvement allowed for your company and other businesses. While companies have every right to drop a code they have previously endorsed, this can be awkward and invite questions the company may prefer to avoid.

7. *Is the company already supporting an internal or external code on the same topic?* If the company has already adopted one code, the addition of a second similar one can sometimes pose conflicts or confusion. A company with ISO 14001 that later adopts the Occupation Health and Safety Assessment Series (OHSAS) 18001 may bewilder EHS people in the field who struggle to discern the difference between an ISO aspects analysis and an OHSAS risk assessment. This confusion can be minimized if the company drafts a single integrated standard that melds together the provisions of these two management systems along with any similar company requirements. Such a one-stop shop is preferred. When multiple, un-integrated initiatives of the same type are adopted, the organization tends to lose focus on them. "Code overload," confusion, and cynicism can result. Generally it's better to focus on a few important codes and execute them well rather than adopt many and deliver only mediocre conformance.

8. *Are there legal implications?* Support for a code can be of strategic importance from a legal perspective. For example, by adopting management systems standards that satisfy the U.S. *Sentencing Guidelines*, a company can help "bullet-proof" its top executives from severe penalties for any breaches of federal

law by others in the organization.[5] It can help shape future legislation or perhaps forestall it altogether. There may be other legal
issues associated with code endorsement as well. Occasionally
someone raises the fear that a particular code may create a "standard of care" in law, which, if breached, could serve as the basis
for a lawsuit in negligence. While it is possible that voluntary
codes could be admitted into evidence in courtroom proceedings
in a negligence action, generally that is limited to safety-related
situations where the code was designed to protect the life or
property of others. Besides, simply refusing to endorse these
codes may not help block liability flowing from them. Generally,
if a code is the type that is admissible, it can be admitted as evidence irrespective of whether the accused company adopts it.
And if the code reflects best practices of industry, then those
practices may be admissible even without reference to the code
itself.[6] All things considered, a company is best served by
adopting popular safety-related codes—or at least the best
practices described in them—and working to conform to their
provisions rather than shunning them and remaining exposed
to liability anyway.

Armed with these questions for evaluating voluntary codes, a company can explore some of them for possible adoption.

Selling Management on Sustainability

Defining what sustainability means to a company through a mission or
values statement, policies, or external codes is an indispensable step in
moving the organization to it. But the organization isn't going anywhere
near sustainability unless someone explains why it should. Personnel
time and other resources are too valuable to waste on an initiative that has
no merit. Someone must answer the question, "why?" Initially that falls
to the champion as she tries to recruit allies to the core team. Later it becomes the focus of the leader as she attempts to gain support from management for adopting a sustainability vision/values/policy and implementing an SOS. Finally, it becomes the charge of the leader, core team,
management, and others as they reach for broad employee support and
work to change the culture of the company.

Contents of the Sales Pitch

What should go into this sales pitch? Here are items to consider in a presentation to top management. Many of these points are also worth evaluating for presentations soliciting support from other internal groups.

1. *Reconfirm the CEO's vision.* Restate the CEO's vision for the company. Indicate that the concept of sustainability can help achieve that vision and make the company a stronger, more admired business.

2. *Offer a vision for moving the corporation toward sustainability.* Sustainability is not an easy concept to grasp quickly. As noted in Chapter 1, while a company may choose to use corporate social responsibility or other terms to describe sustainability to employees, the concept of sustainability should not be ignored. For purposes of the presentation, sustainability can first be defined broadly using the Brundtland Commission, TBL, and 2Rs. A more operational definition can then be presented in the form of the model sustainability policy of Figure 2.2, a model code drawn from Appendix 2.1 or some other version of a vision/values/policy that is drafted internally.

3. *Link the drive toward sustainability with business objectives.* Show how the sustainability commitments of Figure 2.2 (or some alternative document) tie to the top three or four business priorities of the CEO. For example, the model commitments on *Company Economic Prosperity* and on *Waste Reduction and Management* could be tied to a business priority of reducing costs. Showing a matrix similar to Figure 3.9 juxtapose the sustainability policy may be a convenient way of presenting this information.

4. *Introduce the idea of pursuing sustainability through an SOS.* Discuss the elements of an SOS, identifying what parts of the system already exist within the company and what gaps need to be filled. Talk about how much time and money such an effort may take. For companies where resources are tight, the plan should initially be modest, relying on existing people and funds as much as possible. Resource needs can be reassessed later as progress is made and the value of the effort becomes more apparent.

5. *Present the business case for pursuing an SOS.* Present the Show-Me-the-Money Model (Figure 3.1) and draw from some

practical examples of business value—especially those taken from the company itself, its competitors, or other businesses. Examples can be most enlightening if they show how sustainability helped secure a business advantage or how the lack of attention to sustainability led to failure. Review the topics listed in Figures 2.3 to 2.5 and the company examples discussed in Chapter 3 to help recall the most noteworthy incidents. If time permits, show the Quid Pro Quo Model (Figure 3.11) too, or at least speak to the concept.

6. *Create a sense of urgency for action.* If there is some public scandal or internal incident concerning ethics, governance, security, labor relations, environmental performance, or other sustainability topic that has management's attention, the presentation might mention that situation and the lessons it holds for the company. Media attention to some internal or external incident can underscore the importance of sustainability in everyday life and make the sale easier. These incidents can help create the "sense of urgency" for action, which is critical in convincing employees to leave their old comfort zones. John P. Kotter, Professor of Leadership at Harvard Business School, says that at least half of failed change efforts bungle this step.[7] Be careful, though, in discussing internal failures; avoid any implication of fault or blame that can lead to defensiveness and divert attention from the business case. Other suggestions on how to create a sense of urgency are shown in Figure 4.4.

7. *Discuss some key sustainability trends that most affect the organization and identify the challenges and opportunities those trends pose.* This can also add impetus for action. For example, a beverage manufacturer should consider the potential impact from the depletion of fresh water supplies. Large global companies may want to review how projected changes in demographics may affect recruiting and marketing strategies. Think not only about trends in population shifts and resource depletion, but in governance, extended producer responsibility, pollution, globalization, socially responsible investing, and the other issues listed in Appendix 1. Legal experts may be able to provide regulatory and enforcement trends concerning relevant topics. If the company has already engaged in some sustainability reporting, these reports may be a good starting point for this discussion

since they show how sustainability already applies to the company. Once the relevant issues and trends are identified, the following points should be made:

• These important trends and issues will increasingly affect the way the company does business.
• If the company ignores these trends and issues, it will hurt the company's ability to compete. Possible scenarios may be described which illustrate this point.
• If the company adequately addresses these trends, it will be better able to anticipate the future and the new business opportunities the future presents, and to more effectively protect itself from the risk, reputational challenges, and inefficiencies that can destroy shareholder value. This point may also be underscored with scenarios.
• The best way to address these trends and issues is systematically through an SOS and open and honest dialogue with stakeholders. If the company does this, it can become a stronger, more competitive organization.

8. *Acknowledge that an SOS is advantageous but not essential for success.* To boost credibility, concede that there are successful companies that do not openly embrace the economic-social-environmental balance that sustainability suggests, just as there were many good companies that did not openly embrace many of the business concepts that the company now takes as gospel. Use as an example Six Sigma, Lean Manufacturing, Total Quality Management, Talent Management, or other concepts valued by the company. Avoid those considered flavors of the month or outright failures. Note that some early skeptics like GE are now changing their view about sustainability.

9. *Show lists of GRI and WBCSD companies.* Observe that many respectable companies are moving along the path to sustainability to one extent or another. Show the lists of reputable companies that are members of the WBCSD as well as those that publish sustainability reports using the GRI guidelines.

10. *Use the language of business.* For example, talk about conducting an enterprise risk and opportunity assessment, protecting assets and investments, responding to the growing interest of investors, strengthening brands, and building credibility with

key constituents. Discuss the need to anticipate future trends in business planning, defuse potential issues with the public and NGOs, bullet-proof management on compliance risk, and develop products that better address future needs of customers. Finally, you might speak of seizing opportunities for business growth and achieving good returns on investment. Business people may want to see the projected financial implications of these benefits. That should be furnished if available, provided the projections are conservative. Exaggerated claims can seriously hurt a speaker's credibility and undermine the whole sales pitch.

11. *Request specific action be taken by the audience.* In speaking with the CEO or other top executive group, you might ask for comments on the draft sustainability policy and for authorization to solicit further feedback on it from other groups, with a specific date targeted for final approval. You could also request that a sustainability leader and sponsor be appointed, that a core team be formally acknowledged and supported, and that the core team be authorized to draft SOS standards for review and approval.

| **Figure 4.4** |
| **Information That Can Create a Sense of Urgency for Action on Sustainability** |

1. Examples of big problems that have arisen at companies—especially competitors—because of a lack of attention to sustainability	5. Performance results on sustainability-related metrics showing serious problems or the opportunity to realize significant value if best practices are adopted across the company
2. Examples of big successes companies—especially competitors—have realized because they addressed sustainability concerns proactively	6. Examples of how a proactive approach on sustainability can help the company deal with its current financial, reputational, or other crisis
3. Audit or consultant's reports identifying legal and other sustainability risks within the company	7. Benchmarking information showing that the company is significantly behind industry peers regarding sustainability infrastructure and performance
4. Survey results, quotes, or views of employee groups, customers, investors, or other important stakeholders indicating the company's responsibility for sustainability is important to them	8. Business risks or missed opportunities that will threaten the company due to sustainability trends (see Appendix 1) unless action is taken

A short presentation should be prepared for management to lay out the most persuasive information drawn from the above suggestions, with extra time allowed for discussion. How do you tell what information is most persuasive? Review the draft with the core team as well as a trusted member of upper management.

Whether preparing the presentation for management or for other groups, you should customize it for the audience, playing to what is familiar and relevant to them, particularly with respect to values, goals, tools (Lean Manufacturing, Six Sigma, Total Quality Management, etc.), and issues. In addition, you will need to tailor it to the time allowed. It's usually a good idea to solicit feedback on the draft from others known for their ability to influence the audience you are trying to persuade. If the agenda permits, think about drawing in a "testimonial" speaker—some credible facility manager or other business person from inside or outside the company. Their purpose would be to talk about their own first-hand experience in reaping the benefits of sustainability or in struggling with a difficult situation where a sustainability-oriented approach would have helped.

Sequencing of the Sales Effort: The "Snowball" Strategy

The sales presentation should be tailored and used in a variety of forums to gain broad support across the organization for sustainability in general and the SOS in particular. Unless the grounds are properly prepared in this way, the SOS will find no fertile soil in which to take root and bear fruit over the long term. The grounds can be most effectively prepared if the task is undertaken in a strategic way, building from the support of one group to improve the chances of gaining it from others. Occasionally, a champion of some issue will go directly to the CEO and find the CEO inspired to pursue the matter. If that occurs on the issue of an SOS, then the champion will still need to circle back to gain the support of others in upper management and to recruit core team members. Many in both groups may be somewhat resentful that they weren't involved in the initial decisionmaking. This can be unfortunate, since both groups will be critical to the successful deployment of the SOS throughout the organization. Another disadvantage of having the champion go to the CEO straight away is that the presentation will not have been thoroughly vetted by the core team—the people who can provide useful insights on how to strengthen and trim the presentation to give it maximum impact. In addition, without the core team behind her, the champion's appeal to the CEO is weakened, thus reducing the chances of a favorable outcome. A rejection by the CEO creates an awkward predicament for the champion about how next to proceed.

All things considered, the safest course may be to follow the sequence noted in Figure 4.5. Using this strategy, potential core team members who are thought easiest to persuade are approached first so a groundswell of support can build quickly. At this early stage, the champion would avoid those who may subvert the initiative because of concerns about "turf" or because they feel it interferes with their own personal agenda. They can be brought in later after a critical mass of company leaders is already on board. As the sales effort proceeds, the growth in the number of enthusiastic core team members may have a snowball effect, convincing many doubters to join the cause.

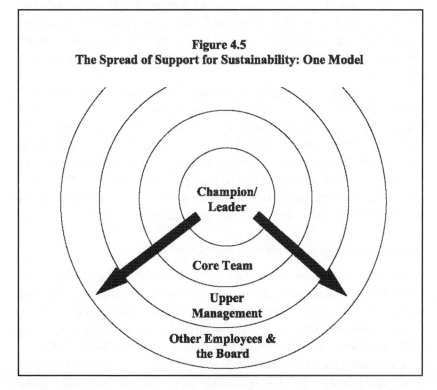

Figure 4.5
The Spread of Support for Sustainability: One Model

Champion/
Leader

Core Team

Upper
Management

Other Employees &
the Board

After the core team has been rallied, the next step is to approach the CEO and the executive staff. Before a meeting with them, the champion or members of the core team might want to speak with some of the CEO's trusted staff members one on one to preview the presentation—or at least the gist of it—and solicit feedback. These pre-meetings can significantly improve the odds of success. If stiff resistance is encountered from some in senior management during the preview, strategies can be devised to deal with their concerns. It is better to flush out these sensitivities early—and even postpone the meeting and regroup if necessary—than to walk into a buzz saw of high-level opposition unprepared.

After the CEO and her team have agreed to support an SOS, then the planning and prioritization exercises we will discuss in Chapter 6 can be facilitated by core team members. These exercises are intended for the staffs of the core team members themselves as well as with other functional groups not represented on the team. The positive outcomes of these exercises can be shared with other less experienced, less supportive groups to show them the benefits of the process. Publicizing early successes can build critical momentum for the effort. Once the core team, senior management, and functional teams are trained on the SOS and its value, these groups can be recruited to help deploy the programs to the field.

This strategy of starting at the middle of the organization creates a solid force of managers with companywide responsibilities—the core team—who can continue to stoke the sustainability fires at the most critical level of the company. It is this level—lower level vice presidents, along with directors and general managers—that Professor Kotter has found to be the biggest obstacle to change.[8] The position in the middle also offers the important advantage of closer proximity and easier access to those above and below who can make change happen.

Other Techniques for Gaining Management Buy-In

Besides the staff meetings of the CEO and key functional leaders, other forums may also prove useful in gaining buy-in from management. One tactic is to bring management to meetings with stockholders and key customers who are interested in sustainability. Respected outside speakers, especially those with corporate experience, can be influential, too.

Even better than having top managers listen is having them talk. Arranging for them to speak at well-attended external and internal engagements can help in several ways. First, and perhaps foremost, these engagements can provide executives an opportunity to deepen their own understanding of sustainability and their commitment to it. This naturally happens as they work with inside experts to prepare their remarks and find audiences who are receptive to the message. Their speeches can also serve as the basis for articles and other subsequent communications within the company targeted for all employees. Finally, this approach furthers the overall objective of making top management the chief salespeople for sustainability.

But speeches aren't the only techniques for convincing management and other employees to support a sustainability initiative. With the help of the sustainability leader or core team members, top managers can provide phone and e-mail messages about company incidents and accomplishments tied to sustainability. These messages can help keep the issue visible and provide both listeners and message-givers a better appreciation of its practical scope. Company brochures, newsletters, reports, media interviews, employee meetings, celebrations, and other recognition events can achieve the same aim. Management involvement in them will reinforce how important sustainability is to the organization. Business leaders can also underscore this importance by adding an update on sustainability performance as a regular agenda item for their staff meetings. Other techniques for rolling out the SOS and gaining employee buy-in are discussed in Chapter 8. Corporate communications experts usually can advise on how to use these and other communications tools to best advantage.

To some, this scattershot of communication may seem like overkill. But according to Professor Kotter: "Most leaders undercommunicate their change vision by a factor of 10." This communication, he adds, is not just speeches and memos but, more important, behaviors. As he observes: "People watch their bosses—particularly their immediate bosses—very closely."[9]

If All Else Fails

What happens if despite your best efforts in following all these suggestions, key members of management aren't buying what you are selling? If this happens because the company has fallen on tough financial times, then Chapter 12 may hold some answers. If it's for other reasons, then help may be found in the lessons from Chapter 8 for dealing with those who resist the rollout of the SOS. The first and most critical step in overcoming this resistance is acquiring a good understanding of why management opposes your proposal. They may articulate reasons, which you will need to probe. However, there may also be other reasons they don't reveal, which you may only discover from discussions with others.

Gaining Support From the Board

Once top management is sold on an SOS, the next stop is the board of directors. It's not unusual for the board or its public policy committee or other subgroup to periodically receive status updates or issue briefings from various functional leaders of the company. These leaders may, for example, be those from EHS; philanthropy; human resources; business practices/ethics; governance (corporate secretary, law); risk management; and corporate communications. Instead of providing these presentations individually at separate times, they can be linked together in a single several-hour session devoted to sustainability. A broad presentation on the company's sustainability policy, SOS, or other sustainability strategies can kick off the session. This can be followed by individual discussions by each functional leader which address the achievements, challenges, and plans within the function. This is also a good opportunity to capture the key risks across the organization—something boards are increasingly being asked to examine as part of an enterprise risk management program for good governance. This multifunctional approach gives the board a better grasp of sustainability as it applies to the company. Moreover, the mere fact that sustainability is being discussed at board level raises the visibility of the issue across the corporation and creates high-level expectations of further progress. Providing the board with these updates at least annually helps assure that visibility and progress continue.

Organizational Structure: Multidisciplinary Teams

If an SOS will provide great value to a corporation, does that warrant hiring a large centralized staff of people to execute and oversee it? Generally it does not. However, many companies—P&G, Suncor Energy, Inc., British Columbia Hydro (BC Hydro), Alcan Corporation, Ontario Power Generation Inc., Nike, Inc., Intel Corporation, Starbucks, Dow, DuPont, Toshiba Corporation, Stora Enso, HP, and ABN AMRO Holdings, to name a few—have appointed directors or vice presidents of sustainability, CSR, or global citizenship. Many others have dedicated sustainability managers. Some of these executives have only small supporting staffs who work with the company's functional departments and businesses through various sustainability teams. Whether a company needs a full-time sustainability leader or someone who has only a portion of her time devoted to that function depends upon the size and complexity of the company and the extent and visibility of its public risks. In any event, a company that wants to adopt an SOS and undertake internal and external communication around sustainability would be hard pressed to succeed without a named leader.

One of the progressive companies on sustainability tried centralizing the function but later had second thoughts. Shell initially established a separate sustainable development and planning function at the corporate level. It also had sustainability managers positioned at the division and local levels and assigned to major projects. Later, though, the company melded the corporate group with EHS, and reassigned some auxiliary sustainability roles to human resources and communications. At the business (division) level, sustainability functions were merged with either EHS or strategy groups. Although the new organization no longer has a dedicated corporate group, many of the reassigned sustainability people maintain their full-time sustainability roles. Their primary function continues to be integrating environmental and social considerations into decisionmaking and representing Shell externally on sustainability matters.[10]

BT and DuPont formed separate sustainability functions at the corporate level focusing primarily on sustainability issues concerning products, services, and business planning, as well as external stakeholder matters. These corporate groups coordinate various multifunctional and cross-business teams to achieve company objectives. Other companies, like IBM, have no dedicated sustainability function but work through similar teams to report on sustainability and coordinate progress.

Indeed, multidisciplinary teams offer some important advantages. First, sustainability by its nature is a multidisciplinary issue. Think of the 10 dozen sustainability topics identified in Chapter 2. With an agenda almost as broad as the business itself, sustainability can be too large to manage under a single function. Second, a multidisciplinary structure means that each participating member has a seat at the table where the concept of sustainability and its implementation are routinely discussed. Over time, this produces a solid base of influential managers across the company, many of whom possess a relatively deep understanding of sustainability in a corporate setting. Third, the multidisciplinary structure helps ensure that sustainability plans are thoroughly evaluated from many perspectives and therefore more likely to succeed. Fourth, with sustainability achievements typically broadcast both inside and outside the company, some healthy competition for good results is likely to arise among team members. This competition keeps members motivated and efforts moving forward. Finally, the multidisciplinary approach helps assure that a critical mass of support and action on sustainability remains even though one or two functions may be undergoing reorganization or other disruptive changes.

To create a multidisciplinary approach, a sizeable company may want to establish a core team, deployment team, and report distributors network, or comparable groups, as described below.

Core Team

As previously mentioned, one of the first jobs of the champion is to recruit the core team to help generate and maintain support for the sustainability initiative. This leadership team is at the heart of the company's sustainability initiative. In addition to advocating internally, the core team can promote the company's sustainability efforts outside the company, establish the SOS, and craft the strategy and tactics for its implementation. It can also oversee and collect feedback on the operation of the SOS, and make adjustments as necessary. In addition, the team may compile the companywide strategic plan for sustainability after gathering needed input from others. Members should be experienced leaders within their functions or business units who know the company well, are good team players, and have the authority to speak for their organizations. Membership may change somewhat with the appointment of a leader and the shift of team focus from advocacy to planning. When this shift occurs, the leader may want to add members with strategic planning experience or extensive knowledge of management systems.

Deployment Team

After the core team establishes the infrastructure for pursuing sustainability, various groups must evaluate the business opportunities and risks posed by sustainability, set their own sustainability objectives and measures, and report progress against them. This is the job of the deployment team members. This team includes the core team plus representatives of other groups that will participate in these tasks. Depending on what is to be reported, these other groups may include quality, research and development, sales and marketing/distribution, security, manufacturing, engineering, and other functions and business units.

Report Distributors Network

Although the core and deployment teams are broad, they still may not cover all internal groups that distribute the company's sustainability reports—or data from them—to key stakeholders. To assure the reports meet the needs of these groups, the leader can establish a team or network to provide input on report content. This report distributors network may include not only the company communications department, but government affairs (which may provide the information to legislators), investor relations (investors), sales and marketing (customers), human resources (new recruits), and business development (buyers and sellers of parts of the business, joint venture partners, and government officials), among others. To provide the needed input, these represented groups should, in turn, gather feedback from their own stakeholders. This feedback may also prove valuable to the core and deployment teams in setting strategic and tactical priorities. Sample memberships for the core and deployment teams and report distributors network are provided in Figure 4.6.

Figure 4.6 Sample Membership for Sustainability Teams			
Function/Group Providing Representative	Core Team	Deployment Team	Report Distributors Network
Business Development (Mergers and Acquisitions)			x
Business Planning	x	x	
Charitable Giving; Foundation	x	x	
Communications; Public Relations	x	x	x
Community Relations	x	x	
Corporate Governance; Corporate Secretary	x	x	
Environment, Health & Safety	x	x	
Ethics/Business Practices	x	x	
Facilities Engineering/ Energy Management		x	
Finance	x	x	
Government Affairs/ Public Policy	x		x
Human Resources; Employee Relations	x	x	x
Internal Audit		x	
Investor Relations			x
Law/Compliance	x	x	
Manufacturing		x	
Quality		x	
Research & Development		x	
Risk Management		x	
Sales and Marketing/ Distribution		x	x
Security		x	
Supply Chain/Supplier Management/Purchasing	x	x	
A few key business units	x	x	

Other Team Structures

Of course, each company must organize its teams and select team members that best serve the organization's own needs. In the end, the only thing that matters is that the right people are assigned to work together to accomplish the roles identified in Figure 4.7. Dow, for example, addresses many of these responsibilities through a team of 12 global implementation leaders drawn from various groups around the company. Each leader is responsible for tracking and spearheading efforts on a different part of its 12-point Sustainable Development Operating Plan.[11]

Figure 4.7
Structural Elements That Can Support an SOS

Structural Element	Role
Sustainability leader	Encourage and coordinate the development, implementation, and ongoing performance of the SOS across the organization; chair the core and deployment teams; represent the organization on sustainability issues
Executive sponsor	Coach the leader and core team to maximize their effectiveness; serve as their advocate among upper management
Core team	Help design and promote the SOS and assure its ongoing effectiveness; recommend the key companywide strategic objectives and goals for sustainability; provide support on planning
Deployment team	Deploy the SOS to the field; collect and compile sustainability performance data; coordinate the communication between the field and the core team
Report distributors network	Distribute the organization's sustainability performance information to key stakeholder groups; communicate stakeholder information needs and other feedback to the core team and leader
Board oversight committee	Oversee the performance and effectiveness of the SOS from the board level; determine effectiveness of governance programs and other sustainability risk-control programs

BT has a CSR steering group that champions major initiatives, assesses risk, and agrees on key performance indicators and strategic targets concerning social and environmental matters. The group is made up of CSR champions nominated by the business units and seven support functions (human resources, corporate governance, health and safety, group property, communications, internal audit, and procurement). Two subcommittees of the steering group—the environmental policy implementation committee and the corporate responsibility (CR) team—are responsible for raising issues and implementing programs.[12]

Toshiba has five companywide teams under the umbrella of its CSR governance committee. These teams focus on: (1) corporate citizenship; (2) risk compliance; (3) corporate environmental management; (4) human rights and employee satisfaction; and (5) customer satisfaction promotion.[13]

Vodafone Group (Vodafone) assigns senior executives from its operating companies and group functions to drive its sustainability initiatives. Key players are top executives in the Group Supply Chain, Group Marketing, and Group Human Resources departments. Social and environmental specialists on the corporate CSR team help plan and coordinate these initiatives. The leaders of the individual operating units are responsible for implementation. Goal-setting and progress are monitored through formal quarterly performance reviews, where the senior management of the group and operating companies meet to evaluate performance of local operating companies. A group corporate affairs director, to whom the group CR director reports, is a member of the Executive Committee that provides oversight and support for the effort.[14]

Nike's vice president for CR manages a group that includes CR planning, CR finance, compliance, and community affairs. Product sustainability people from the operating groups and a representative from the Nike Foundation also participate on the team. The work of this team is, in turn, guided by the CR Business Leadership Team, consisting of various operations vice presidents, the general counsel, and the vice president of CR. A CR committee of the board of directors reviews progress four times a year. At the operational level, CR representatives work closely with other functions, such as those responsible for law, labor, and EHS compliance, environmental initiatives, corporate communications, government affairs, human resources, reporting, stakeholder engagement, and strategy development.[15]

At HP, the Corporate Affairs and Global Citizenship Group manages sustainability issues and addresses risk using cross-business, cross-geography councils that focus on the following topics: environmental strategies and sustainability; supply chain; standards of business conduct; and privacy.[16]

Organizing the Board for Sustainability

Many corporations have a board committee responsible for public policy or public interest matters. McDonald's calls theirs the CR Committee. Whatever its name, this committee commonly oversees the company's social and environmental activities. According to surveys conducted for the Dow Jones Sustainability Index, roughly one in five companies in the index has a board-level committee of this type.[17] Firms also typically have a finance committee which addresses internal financial matters and an audit committee which focuses on compliance with legal and auditing standards. The audit committee is also often charged with examining the company's governance programs. These three committees can cover the full range of sustainability issues. One of them should be assigned responsibility for evaluating the adequacy of the company's infrastructure and systems for managing sustainability matters. While at first glance the public policy committee may seem like the logical choice, the audit committee may end up playing a major role, too, given the growing focus by regulators on governance and enterprise risk management. Nevertheless, the board should decide which committee follows sustainability.

More progress is being made in this regard in some regions than in others. In a Hill & Knowlton global survey of senior executives conducted in 2004, over one-fourth of the European business leaders and over one-fifth of those from Asia reported that their boards were playing an important role in managing CSR initiatives. By contrast, only 4% of the American respondents said their boards were doing so.[18]

Some progressive companies have designed the make-up of their boards to better manage sustainability-related issues. A number have named labor and environmental directors. Suncor, the company that extracts petroleum from oil sands in western Canada, has gone so far as to elect a representative of indigenous peoples. If certain stakeholder groups are likely to have a significant impact on the business, they too should be considered when the company slates board candidates. Including these groups is an effective way of assuring that the interests of these stakeholders are considered in high-level decisionmaking.

Structure at Small Companies

If a financially challenged company needs to form two or three new teams like these, how can it do so without adding resources? Is this really something a small or struggling business can afford? Perhaps the better question would be, is the formation of these teams something the company can afford to ignore? After all, these teams should simply be helping members undertake what all good business leaders do anyway, which is: prioritize opportunities and threats; set priorities for action; measure results; and communicate transparently with key stakeholders. These efforts may be as extensive or as broad as the organization desires. For small companies where people wear many hats, the teams may be much smaller and the efforts less ambitious.

Code of Conduct for Good Teamwork

The success of teams will depend upon the skill and motivation of their members, and, most importantly, their teamwork. Team members with hidden agendas, jealousies, or poor interpersonal skills or who are not willing to do their part, can destroy team dynamics, efficiency, and effectiveness. To help assure this doesn't happen, one of the first things a team may want to do is develop a code of conduct that outlines what each member expects of fellow members. See the example in Figure 4.8. Team meetings may start with a review of the code and conclude with a brief discussion of how well these values have been upheld. The few minutes it takes to do this may pay big dividends in team productivity and satisfaction.

Figure 4.8
Model Code of Conduct for a Sustainability Team

We will:

1. Make all decisions focusing on what's best for the organization overall instead of what's best for individuals or their groups; put the goal of the team ahead of individual goals.

2. Work together in a manner that is honest, open-minded, helpful, and trusting of fellow team members.

3. Show respect to each other in all of our interactions; be sensitive to cultural differences.

4. Recognize both individual and team achievements, including adherence to this code of conduct.

5. Make all reasonable efforts to participate in meetings, conference calls, and other team activities.

6. Meet our individual commitments to the team, or if that's not possible for reasons beyond our control, communicate that to the team as soon as possible.

7. Give and receive feedback respectfully, balancing positive encouragement with constructive coaching.

8. Be focused and efficient in meeting our objectives; at the end of major meetings, review how well we adhered to this code of conduct in order to improve overall team performance.

9. Be constructive; offer different options or solutions when challenging the suggestions or views of others.

10. Keep up to date on sustainability and its major issues, and work to move our organization toward it.

The Sponsor

Another part of the support organization for sustainability is the *sponsor.* If the leader needs help, this is the person she can turn to. The sponsor can be the CEO or some other member of senior management who can provide advice on the best way to maneuver through the corporate maze to get things done. If there is some roadblock to progress, the sponsor can use her influence and authority to help eliminate it. If there are some doors that need opening, she can provide the key. Without a trusted and skilled sponsor, a sustainability initiative can become mired down in corporate politics and rust away on the side of the road.

The sponsor is important. But so are the champion/leader and the teams and other groups noted in Figure 4.7. Working together, they can be the force that changes the company, making sustainability one of its basic values and the foundation for long-term success.

**Follow-up Checklist for Action: Key Elements and Basic Structure
of an SOS**

☐ Speak with those department or function leaders within the organization who may be knowledgeable about sustainability and supportive of the concept to see if they would like to help promote a sustainability initiative within the organization.

☐ Have the sustainability champion(s) and a small core team of supporters define in a vision, statement of values, or policy document what sustainability means within the organization. To do this, they draw from the model sustainability policy (Figure 2.2) and relevant external codes as well as any that are currently used by the company itself and other respected peer organizations.

☐ Incorporate the proposed vision/values/policy in a "sales" presentation advocating the adoption of an SOS. Prepare the presentation following the guidance of this chapter.

☐ Use the presentation to gain participation from other people who may be needed on the core team. Also refine and use the presentation for seeking formal support for an SOS from the CEO and others in upper management.

☐ Persuade management to appoint a sustainability leader and upper-management sponsor to help promote and guide the development of an SOS for the organization. Obtain management backing for the core team, various support teams, and any needed resources.

☐ Create appropriate teams supplementing the core team to help with the deployment of the SOS (deployment team) and with the engagement of various external stakeholders about the company's sustainability reporting and performance (report distributors network).

☐ Work with the core team and management to finalize the vision/values/policy on sustainability for the company. Review it with the board of directors.

☐ Work with the core team to assess the merits of endorsing external sustainability-related codes using the evaluation criteria provided in this chapter. Seek management's endorsement of any codes recommended.

☐ Work with the CEO and the board to determine how oversight for sustainability matters should be handled within the board.

☐ Ask the CEO, other management, the core team, and others to spread the word throughout the organization about the sustainability vision/values/policy, the SOS, and the value of these sustainability initiatives to the company. Prepare materials they can use for this purpose.

☐ Recognize early successes and use them to help build further support.

Endnotes to Chapter 4

1. This quote is by Vancouver native Laurence Peter, who was an educator and perhaps best known for his formulation of the Peter Principle which states: "In a hierarchy, every employee tends to rise to his level of incompetence." LAURENCE J. PETER, THE PETER PRINCIPLE (1969).

2. DOW, THE DOW CHEMICAL COMPANY 2003 GLOBAL REPORTING INITIATIVE REPORT (2004), *available at* http://www.dow.com/commitments/pbreports/index.htm [hereinafter DOW 2003 GRI REPORT]. *See also* DOW, THE DOW CHEMICAL COMPANY 2004 GLOBAL REPORTING INITIATIVE REPORT (2005), *available at* http://www.dow.com/commitments/pbreports/index.htm.

3. *See* Pete Engardio, *Commentary: Global Compact, Little Impact*, BUS. WK. ONLINE, July 12, 2004, http://www.businessweek.com/@@6BTk0 oQQnKIFZxcA/magazine/content/04_28/b3891132_mz021.htm (last visited Jan. 10, 2006). Pete Engardio, *Online Extra: Kofi Annan's Business Plan (Extended)*, BUS. WK. ONLINE, July 12, 2004, http://www. Businessweek.com/@@6BTk0oQQnKIFZxcA/magazine/content/04_ 28/b3891135_mz021.htm (last visited Jan. 10, 2006). Pete Engardio, *Online Extra: Raising the Bar for Corporate Behavior*, BUS. WK. ONLINE, July 12, 2004, http://www.businessweek.com/@@6BTk0oQQnKIFZxcA/ magazine/content/04_28/b3891136_mz021.htm (last visited Jan. 10, 2006). Pete Engardio, *Two Views of the Global Compact*, BUS. WK. ONLINE, July 20, 2004, http://www.businessweek.com/bwdaily/dnflash/ jul2004/nf20040720_9215_db039.htm (last visited Jan. 10, 2006).

4. Pew Center for Global Climate Change, *Business Environmental Leadership Council*, http://www.pewclimate.org/companies_leading_the_way_ belc/index.cfm (last visited Jan. 10, 2006).

5. See more on the U.S. *Sentencing Guidelines* in Appendix 3.26. They are also further discussed under *Factor 7: Legal Liability, supra* Chapter 3.

6. *See* J.D. LEE & BARRY LINDAHL, 1 MODERN TORT LAW—LIABILITY AND LITIGATION 3-104 to 3-113 (Thomson West 2002).

7. John P. Kotter, *Winning at Change*, LEADER TO LEADER, Fall 1998, http://www.pfdf.org/leaderbooks/l2l/fall98/kotter.html (last visited Jan. 10, 2006).

8. *Id.*

9. *Id.*

10. E-mail from Mark Weintraub, Sustainable Development Strategy, Policy, and Reporting, Shell International B.V., The Hague, The Netherlands, to William Blackburn (Dec. 10, 2004). E-mail from Mark Wade, Sustainable Development Group of Human Resources, Shell International Ltd., London, England, to William Blackburn (Nov. 11, 2002).

11. *See* DOW 2003 GRI REPORT, *supra* note 2.

12. BT, *Business Principles, in* BT SOCIAL AND ENVIRONMENTAL REPORT (2005), *available at* http://www.btplc.com/Societyandenvironment/ Socialandenvironmentreport/PDFdownloads/PDFdownloads.htm.

13. TOSHIBA, CORPORATE SOCIAL RESPONSIBILITY REPORT 2005, at 17 (2005), *available at* http://www.toshiba.co.jp/csr/en/report/index.htm.

14. VODAFONE, CORPORATE SOCIAL RESPONSIBILITY REPORT 2004/2005—WE SAID, WE HAVE, WE WILL 6 (2005), *available at* http://www.vodafone. Com/section_article/0,3035,CATEGORY_ID%253D304%2526LANGUAGE_ ID%253D0%2526CONTENT_ID%253D265246,00.html?.

15. NIKE, CORPORATE RESPONSIBILITY REPORT—FY04, at 7-8 (2004), *available at* http://www.nike.com/nikebiz/nikebiz.jhtml?page=29&item= fy04.

16. HP, 2005 ABRIDGED GLOBAL CITIZENSHIP REPORT—HP's GLOBAL CITIZENSHIP PRIORITIES 5 (2005), *available at* http://www.hp.com/ hpinfo/globalcitizenship/gcreport/downloads.html.

17. Philip Mirvis & Bradley Googins, *The Best of the Good*, HARV. BUS. REV., Dec. 2004, and *Harvard Business Review OnPoint*, Reprint no. F0412F, *available at* http://www.hbr.org.

18. HILL & KNOWLTON, GLOBAL EXECUTIVE SURVEY (2004).

Chapter 5

SOS Standards: The Roadmap for Change

"It is not necessary to change. Survival is not mandatory."[1]
—W. Edwards Deming

You have defined a vision of sustainability for your organization. You have convinced company management that the journey toward sustainability is worthwhile. A leader has been appointed and support teams have been organized and motivated to sail the corporate ship on its way. Now what? The next step is to chart the pathway to this elusive destination, to define a process that will extract the greatest business value from the effort year after year. This sustainability management process or "operating system" should be mapped out, recorded in some way—such as in a set of system standards—and communicated to all who will be involved in implementing and measuring sustainability performance. SOS standards let participants understand the overall process and their role in it. Together with a sustainability policy, the standards serve as a constitution of sorts, setting the values, relationships, and approach that can successfully guide the organization over the long term regardless of circumstance, regardless of people. Like a constitution, the SOS standards should be institutionalized in a written document. Recording the process also makes it easier for the leader to solicit feedback on it and amend it over time to improve its efficiency and effectiveness.

The core team may want to share the SOS standards with external stakeholders who are targeted to provide feedback. This shows the stakeholders how the company will constructively use their input. Telling stakeholders about these standards also underscores that sustainability is not merely a public relations concern as it may be in other organizations, but something more serious: a basis for running the business.

Natural Evolution of SOS From Reporting

Companies pursuing a sustainability agenda often try to omit this step, devising an approach to sustainability reporting before they devise an approach to sustainability itself. Some do this because they believe reporting is the essence of a corporate sustainability program; others may go straight to sustainability reporting because they are already doing a public environmental or social report and it's easy to convince the company to expand that report for greater coverage and value. Some may believe public reporting will help management and other employees better understand the nature of sustainability, thus laying the groundwork for more aggressive efforts later on.

Even if a company starts with sustainability reporting, sooner or later it will be led back to an SOS. Reporting companies that fill their publications only with good stories or "greenwash" will gain little value from the effort: their reputations will be tarnished and, in time, stakeholders will likely scrutinize their performance and press them for greater transparency on problems and progress. An SOS will help such companies respond. Other companies that start by transparently reporting their strengths and opportunities for improvement will eventually develop a routine for gap identification and closure. Over the years, that will evolve to an SOS-type process as well.

In the end, both transparent and nontransparent reporters will find it much more efficient and productive to spell out their SOS standards and continue to refine them as experience is gained with the process. These standards should help ensure that efforts are coordinated, aligned, and timely and that resources are focused on stated priorities and not squandered on lower value whims. Properly implemented, the SOS standards will prove a powerful engine for driving change toward sustainability.

Advantages of Management System Standards

How do we know that management system standards can drive this change? Baxter's experience over the last few decades provides some insight.

In the late 1980s, while Baxter was exploring ways to revitalize its environmental programs, its environmental leaders began to wonder why some facilities were consistently able to comply with the law, effectively manage risks, and aggressively reduce and prevent waste, while other sites had a dismal record on this. They noticed from their audits that the successful facilities often used some tools, followed certain practices, or displayed particular characteristics that their less successful counterparts did not. Among these elements of success were the following:

1. A process for identifying regulatory and company requirements;
2. Rational goal-setting;
3. Well-considered implementation plans;

4. Effective training programs;
5. Integrated change-management processes;
6. Adequate resources;
7. Sound methods for tracking progress versus deadlines;
8. Thorough self-assessment processes; and
9. Management reviews and visible support (including holding subordinates accountable for performance).

Armed with this benchmarking information, Baxter's corporate environmental team drafted a set of facility "state-of-the-art" environmental management standards incorporating these elements of success. Top management proclaimed the goal that North American sites achieve full conformance to those standards within three years and that sites elsewhere—those that historically had no environmental programs—do so within six years. Similar interlocking management system standards were also developed for the division and corporate levels, which were to be met within three years.

As a result of this approach, environmental performance at Baxter accelerated. By the end of 1993, 99% of the domestic operations had achieved the standards, producing the following results from 1989 levels:

• 93% reduction in toxic air emissions;
• 53% reduction in nonhazardous waste disposal per unit of production;
• 39% reduction in hazardous waste disposal per unit of production;
• 85% reduction in quarterly exceedances of wastewater limits;
• 95% removal of underground hazardous substance tanks;
• 11% reduction in packaging per unit of product;
• 66% of targeted space covered with energy-conserving lighting; and
• More than $75 million in savings from the above actions.[2]

Over the years that followed, the company rolled out the standards to its facilities outside North America. Later, after the environmental function merged with health and safety, new internal EHS management standards were developed that reflected some additional processes—such as an aspects analysis—which were drawn from the then-new ISO 14001 EMS standards. Finally, the focus shifted to an approach melding ISO and OHSAS 18001, a similar management standard for health and safety. Throughout this evolution of EHS management systems at

Baxter, the company remained steadfast in its belief that if properly crafted and applied, such systems would produce good results.

Richard Guimond, former vice president of Environment, Health, and Safety at Motorola Inc., agrees, but notes that the benefits of management system standards can be more subtle, too.

> If a company really wants to improve its performance, management system standards can help. That was our experience at Motorola. We found that if you identify a standard that people can embrace, it not only encourages them to focus on the things that are important, but offers other benefits as well. It brings a consistent, disciplined approach that can be integrated across the organization—something that might be difficult to achieve otherwise. Why is that important? Because when you have this alignment—when everyone is moving in the same direction—you end up with greater productivity and more impressive results.[3]

Some other advantages of management system standards are listed in Figure 5.1.

Figure 5.1
Some Advantages of Management System Standards

1. Focuses organization on priorities for action
2. Provides an institutional memory for the process of improvement
3. Infuses organizational discipline for improvement
4. Helps prevent backsliding of performance
5. Facilitates constructive cultural change
6. Aligns efforts across the organization for greater impact
7. Improves consistency and efficiency
8. Serves as a framework for spreading best practices

Today, management system standards abound. Many are based on the old "plan-do-check-act" process loop that became popular in quality circles several decades ago and more recently in EHS. In essence, these standards require that some prioritization process be followed in developing a policy and plan for action (plan); that action be taken to implement the plan and operate under it (do); that progress be measured, reported, and analyzed to identify gaps (check); that corrective and preventive actions be taken and adjustments made to the sustainability policy and programs (act); and that the whole process be periodically repeated. Some of the more noteworthy management system standards are listed in Figure 5.2 and summarized in Appendix 3.

Figure 5.2
Sustainability-Related Management System Standards
Summarized in Appendix 3
(Appendix number for each code is noted below.)

3.1 ISO 9001 Quality Management System Standard	3.15 IFC Social and Environmental Management System
3.2 ISO 14001 Environmental Management System Standard	3.16 Austrian Model CSR Management System Guide ON-V 23
3.3 ISO 26000 Social Responsibility Guidance Standard (proposed)	3.17 Mexican Standard IMNC SAST 004 Social Responsibility System Guideline (draft)
3.4 OHSAS 18001	3.18 AFNOR Guide SD 21000
3.5 ILO Guidelines on OSH Management Systems	3.19 Q-RES Management Model
3.6 ANSI Z10 OHS Management System	3.20 German Values Management System Standard
3.7 EMAS	3.21 U.K. Investors in People Standard
3.8 Responsible Care® Management Standards	3.22 SA 8000
3.9 SIGMA Management Framework	3.23 The Natural Step Framework
3.10 BS 8900 Sustainability Management Guidelines (proposed)	3.24 Reitaku Ethics Compliance Standard 2000
3.11 Baldridge Award Criteria	3.25 ISO 27001 and 28000 Security Management System Standards
3.12 Australian Business Excellence Framework	3.26 Compliance Program Elements of the U.S. *Sentencing Guidelines*
3.13 AS 8000 through 8004 Australian Governance Series Standards (including CSR Standard)	3.27 U.S. EPA Compliance-Focused Environmental Management System
3.14 U.S. Department of Energy Performance-Based Management Handbook	

Developing an SOS Standard

If a company is serious about gaining business value from efforts aimed at sustainability, one way to help assure this happens year after year is through an SOS that draws from some of the best features of established management systems standards as well as from those things that experience has shown drive performance.

Each company should develop its own SOS standards that take advantage of the structure, tools, and systems that have already proven successful. If the organization believes ISO 9001 or 14001 has served them well, those standards can be adjusted and extended to other aspects of sustainability. A similar approach was taken by the Sonoma (California) Coast Division of wine maker Ernest & Julio Gallo. A company that follows this strategy can compare their own systems standards with the model SOS standards of Figure 5.3 to identify what, if anything, is missing from their own standards and evaluate the merits of amending them. Note that unlike most established management systems standards, the model is geared for the entire organization, not just individual facilities. Because an SOS is the road map for moving toward sustainability over the long term, the version of the SOS standards adopted by the company should be communicated to all who will be involved.

Figure 5.3
Model Sustainability Operating System (SOS) Standards

1. Scope and Purpose

1.1 *Scope.* This standard applies at the organizationwide level, although all or a part of some processes may also be undertaken by individual facilities, divisions, or other business units.

1.2 *Purpose.* This standard describes a process enabling the Organization to continually progress toward Sustainable Development while deriving attractive business value, benefitting society and, in particular, improving the chances that both the Organization and society will meet their long-term needs.

2. Definitions

2.1 *Key Group.* Functions and business units within an Organization which are identified by the Organization as key to preparing and implementing plans under this SOS. Functions may include groups such as EHS; human resources; purchasing; distribution/supply chain; governance; government affairs/public policy; law; community relations; communications; philanthropy; ethics/business practices; investor relations; finance; business planning; quality; research and development; sales and marketing; security; manufacturing; and engineering.
Comment: *See Figure 4.6 for some suggested teams and their memberships.*

2.2 *Organization.* A company or other entity to which these SOS standards apply.

2.3 *Sustainability, Sustainable Development.* A concept promoting the wise management and use of natural and economic resources and respect for people and other living things. Companies pursue Sustainability to improve the global long-term well-being of their own Organization and society.

2.4 *Sustainability Operating System (SOS).* The management process described by the SOS standards.

3. Policy; Description of Management Process

3.1 *Policy.* The Organization shall develop and communicate a policy setting forth the vision of Sustainability principles of performance which it aspires to achieve
Comment: *For model policies, see Figure 2.2 above, and the appendix to the 2002 SD Planner published by the Global Environmental Management Initiative.*[4] *Also see the discussion on vision, values, policies, and codes in Chapter 4.*

3.2 *Management Process Description.* The management process to be used by the organization in achieving its Sustainability policy shall be recorded and communicated to all who are involved in executing it.
Comment: *This Figure 5.3 is an example of such a process.*

Figure 5.3 (cont.)
Model Sustainability Operating System (SOS) Standards

4. Planning

Comment: See Chapter 6 for further discussion on planning.

4.1 *Identifying and Evaluating Requirements.* The Organization shall have a process for identifying the legal requirements that apply to its operations as well as the relevant requirements of any codes, policies, or procedures, whether written by itself or others, to which it voluntarily subscribes. The Organization shall also have a process for effectively communicating the identified requirements to employees and others responsible for meeting, monitoring, and enforcing them.

4.2 *Prioritizing Issues/Topics.* Each Key Group will identify the issues or topics under the Sustainability policy that are within the responsibility of the group and that the members of the group believe are most important to the Organization. This prioritization shall consider the following at a minimum:

(1) the importance of each issue to the Organization's business success, considering both risks and opportunities;

(2) the attention given to the issue by management;

(3) the importance of the issue in the Organization's culture;

(4) the public visibility of the issue; the external pressure on the Organization to address it;

(5) the extent to which addressing the issue would be responsive to a Sustainability trend;

(6) the extent and lasting effect of the impact that the company could make in addressing the issue; and

(7) the ease with which the issue can be addressed.

Once Key Groups have completed their prioritization, a team of function and business-unit leaders shall examine the results and identify those Sustainability issues of highest priority across the Organization.

Comment: See Appendix 4 for model forms that can be used for this prioritization process. Chapter 6 contains an explanation of how to use these forms. Figures 2.3-2.5 list examples of Sustainability issues and topics.

4.3 *Talent Management Review.* Each Key Group shall annually assess the specific strengths, needs, and capabilities of their staffs to determine whether they are able to fulfill their duties in achieving the near and long-term Sustainability objectives of the function and that part of the Sustainability policy related to the function. In addition, each Key Group shall more generally assess the strengths, needs, and capabilities of the Organization's other employees to do their part in achieving these objectives and policy requirements. The group shall then prepare and implement an action plan as needed to close any identified gaps.

4.4 *Pre-Planning Review.* Annually each leader responsible for Sustainability planning within a Key Group shall review and discuss the following information with the group's planning team:

Figure 5.3 (cont.)
Model Sustainability Operating System (SOS) Standards

(1) previous year's audit trends, regulatory enforcement data, litigation, and other information showing the extent of conformance by the Organization with the identified requirements that are administered by the group;

(2) the previous year's results of the Organization against its key business objectives and goals;

(3) any new business objectives and goals of the Organization;

(4) prospects ahead for the Organization and its industry;

(5) progress versus the group's last plans, objectives, and goals;

(6) latest list of high-priority Sustainability issues identified by the group, which specially highlights those posing the greatest risk of harm to the Organization;

(7) list of lower priority or longer term Sustainability objectives of the group that were previously identified but postponed for action;

(8) any significant changes over the last year in the Organization, its strategies, and policies;

(9) any significant changes over the last year in relevant Sustainability trends;

(10) any significant changes in the legal or other requirements that apply to the group;

(11) organizational strengths and needs identified from the last Talent Management Review;

(12) the results of any management or other employee surveys or feedback that may be relevant to the group;

(13) the results of any external stakeholder feedback that may be relevant to the group, including customer surveys and the ratings from socially responsible investment firms;

(14) information on the Sustainability performance of the group's counterparts in other comparable organizations; and

(15) reasonably possible alternative scenarios about the impact of Sustainability trends on the Organization over the decades to come.

Comment: *It may be most manageable for each Key Group to break its Pre-Planning Review into several sessions, such as a "Review of Business Performance and Goals" in January, a "Sustainability Performance Review" by the group during the first quarter of the year, and a "Big Picture Review" covering Sustainability trends and issues, changes in requirements, benchmarking information, and scenario planning.*

Figure 5.3 (cont.)
Model Sustainability Operating System (SOS) Standards

4.5 *Objectives*. After completing its Pre-Planning Review, each Key Group will identify measurable Sustainability performance objectives for achieving note-worthy improvement in areas where the review—especially internally and exter-nally benchmarked levels of performance—suggests that such improvement is needed. The time frame for the objectives may be annual or multi-year. For each multi-year objective, an annual target will be identified for progressing toward that objective. Before each Key Group finalizes its Sustainability objectives, it will review them for consistency with the business strategic plan for the Organi-zation, and discuss their feasibility with management representatives and others responsible for achieving the objectives.

Comment: *See Chapter 7 for a discussion on goal-setting. Examples of met-rics and goals are provided in Appendix 7 and in Sustainability reports avail-able from companies listed as reporters on the websites of the GRI (http://www.globalreporting.org/guidelines/reports/search.asp) and CERES (http://www.ceres.org/reports/corporate_reports.htm).*

4.6 *Strategic Plan*. An organizationwide Sustainability planning team shall re-view the list of high-priority Sustainability risks, issues, and objectives prepared by each Key Group and select the highest priority strategic objectives for organi-zationwide focus. The selected objectives, along with a list of the highest priority risks, shall be shared with top management and considered in the strategic plan for the overall business. After the business strategic plan is finalized, each Key Group will establish a Sustainability strategic plan that is consistent with it.

Comment: *See Chapter 6 for a discussion of strategic planning. The list of high-est priority risks can be used in preparing an enterprise risk management report for top management and the board of directors.*

4.7 *Tactical Plan*. Each Key Group will develop a tactical plan identifying the projects and other planned actions it will complete to meet its Sustainability stra-tegic plan. Each tactical plan shall identify the scope of each intended action, the plan for development and deployment, the parties responsible for imple-mentation, and the schedule. Progress against the plan shall be tracked and re-ported quarterly.

5. Implementation and Operation
5.1 *Structure and Responsibility*.
Comment: *See Chapter 4 for further discussion on organizational structure.*
5.1.1 *Sustainability Leader*. A Sustainability leader shall be appointed by the Organization to oversee the establishment and implementation of the SOS, to co-ordinate and facilitate the collaborative efforts required under it, and to assure that the process is working effectively. The leader shall be positioned high enough within the Organization to be able to effectively execute his or her duties.

Figure 5.3 (cont.)
Model Sustainability Operating System (SOS) Standards

5.1.2 *Executive Sponsor.* An executive sponsor shall be appointed by the Organization to serve as the senior-executive advisor to the Sustainability leader and teams, and to represent and promote the Sustainability initiative in senior executive discussions. The sponsor shall be someone reporting directly to the CEO.

5.1.3 *Group Leaders.* A Sustainability leader/representative shall be designated for each Key Group. Each leader will be a senior executive within their group who is authorized to speak for the group and commit its resources to implement this SOS.

5.1.4 *Teams.* The Organization shall appoint teams of function and business-unit leaders as appropriate for the development, implementation, and deployment of strategies, plans, and tactics developed under the SOS.

Comment: *The Organization may want to consider different multidisciplinary teams for Sustainability planning, deployment, and reporting, respectively, as discussed in Chapter 4.*

5.1.5 *Roles and Responsibilities.* The Organization shall define and effectively communicate the roles and responsibilities of the Sustainability leader, group leaders, and teams to assure their efforts are coordinated efficiently to achieve the purpose of this SOS.

5.2 *Deployment and Integration.* The Organization shall establish effective training, communication, tools, guidance, and other measures needed to properly deploy to employees, contractors, and other appropriate parties the relevant responsibilities for fulfilling the Sustainability policy, for achieving the Sustainability objectives, and for complying with law and other requirements to which the Organization subscribes. To the extent practicable, these deployed responsibilities shall be integrated into established programs, processes, procedures, and practices used by the parties.

Comment: *See Chapter 8 for a discussion on deployment and integration.*

5.3 *Resources.* Top management shall provide the human, technical, and other resources needed to establish and operate this SOS and to achieve the Sustainability objectives.

5.4 *Change Management.* A change-management process shall be established by the Organization to assure that Sustainability considerations are taken into account in decisionmaking concerning proposed changes in facilities, services, processes, and products and in the acquisition or deletion of such items.

Comment: *See Chapter 8 for a discussion on integrating Sustainability concerns into change-management procedures.*

5.5 *Emergency/Crisis Response.* Appropriate plans and processes shall be adopted by the Organization to help assure it is prepared to quickly and effectively address possible facility emergencies and organization crises in a way as consistent as reasonably possible with the Sustainability policy. Drills shall be conducted at least annually to test the plans, processes, and procedures. Feedback from drills and actual emergencies and crises shall be evaluated, and appropriate changes made to response plans as warranted.

Figure 5.3 (cont.)
Model Sustainability Operating System (SOS) Standards

Comment: See Chapter 8 for further discussion on integrating Sustainability concerns into emergency/crisis response.

5.6 *Documentation/Recordkeeping.* The Organization shall document the policies, requirements, plans, goals, progress and performance reports, analysis results, and audits required by this SOS. It shall also document other key information required by this SOS where such documentation is mandated by law; where procedures are complex and designed to prevent potentially significant harm to people, property, the environment, the community, or the Organization; where needed to show trends or progress; and where the information must be precisely communicated to various people over time. Documents that contain private or other confidential information shall be so marked and stored in a secure location. The Organization shall establish document-retention periods conforming to legal requirements and shall cull and destroy or archive documents once they have been maintained for the requisite period.

Comment: See discussions later in this chapter on how to avoid the common problem of overdocumentation.

5.7 *Procedures and Other Operational Controls.* Operating and maintenance criteria and procedures shall be specified for operations and activities where needed to help prevent significant deviations from the Sustainability policy, especially those deviations that may involve great harm to people, property, the environment, the community, or the Organization.

5.8 *Fostering Ongoing Management Support.* The Sustainability leader and function leaders shall undertake such periodic communications and other measures as needed to foster ongoing support for this SOS by the Organization's CEO and other senior management.

Comment: See Chapter 4 for a discussion of how to communicate to management about the value of an SOS.

5.9 *Demonstrated Management Commitment.* Management at all levels of the Organization shall routinely and visibly demonstrate to their subordinates a commitment to the Sustainability policy, this SOS, and to the Sustainability objectives identified by the Organization.

6. Monitoring and Corrective and Preventive Action

6.1 *Assessment of Conformity.* The Organization shall establish processes for assessing its conformance with:

    (1) legal requirements;

    (2) the Sustainability policy;

    (3) this SOS, and the internal and external standards, codes, and other requirements to which the Organization voluntarily subscribes;

    (4) good risk identification and management practices; and

    (5) best Sustainability practices.

Figure 5.3 (cont.)
Model Sustainability Operating System (SOS) Standards

Processes for evaluating conformance with requirements shall be designed so as to assure no conflict of interest by the evaluators.

Comment: See Chapter 9 for a discussion of auditing and other assessment processes.

6.2 *Monitoring and Measurement.* The Organization shall identify those characteristics and other measures of its Sustainability performance and supporting activities that it will periodically monitor and report either internally or externally. These measures will address at least the following:

(1) progress under Sustainability goals and other objectives;

(2) progress under the strategic and tactical plans;

(3) any survey results related to Sustainability performance;

(4) results of audits by internal and external experts;

(5) record of regulatory compliance, including agency inspections, notices of violation, enforcement actions and fines; and

(6) litigation and significant public controversies arising out of Sustainability issues.

Where monitoring equipment is required for measurement, such equipment shall be properly maintained and calibrated at appropriate intervals, and maintenance and calibration records shall be maintained.

Comment: See Chapter 7 for a discussion of metrics and goals, and Chapter 9 for a review of monitoring processes.

6.3 *Incident Investigation.* The Organization shall define and implement procedures and responsibilities for investigating accidents, spills, legal and ethical violations, and significant nonconformances with the Sustainability policy and other voluntary requirements to which the Organization subscribes.

6.4 *Preventive and Corrective Action.* The Organization shall define and implement procedures and responsibilities for developing, recording, and tracking preventive and corrective actions to address the incidents described in Section 6.3.

Comment: See Chapter 9 for a discussion on developing and tracking corrective and preventive actions.

7. Analysis and Reporting

Comment: See Chapter 10 for a discussion on internal and external reporting on Sustainability performance.

7.1 *Internal Reporting.* The Sustainability leader and team will at least annually report to the Organization's management, including the CEO and board of directors, on the following:

(1) the Organization's Sustainability risks;

(2) the Organization's Sustainability performance, including the reasons for success or failure;

(3) business benefits derived from the progress toward Sustainability;

Figure 5.3 (cont.)
Model Sustainability Operating System (SOS) Standards

(4) any obstacles to further progress;

(5) suitability, adequacy, and effectiveness of this SOS; and

(6) planned measures to overcome obstacles and enhance progress.

Each Key Group will provide a similar report to its management and staff concerning the group's area of responsibility for Sustainability. Reports shall also be periodically provided to the Organization's business units, regions, facilities, and departments on their own Sustainability performance.

7.2 *External Reporting*. At least annually, the Organization shall publicly report its Sustainability risks and performance in a way that is open, honest, reliable, relevant, material, complete, timely, and responsive to the most important concerns of key stakeholders.

8. Recognition and Accountability. Individual and group performance against Sustainability objectives and goals will be considered by the Organization as a significant part of performance affecting decisions about compensation, promotion, and other rewards as well as discipline. Awards or other special recognition shall be granted to those who demonstrate superior Sustainability performance.
Comment: See the discussion in Chapter 9 on accountability mechanisms.

9. Management and Stakeholder Feedback. At least annually, the Organization shall undertake discussions, meetings, surveys, or other communications with management and a representative group of employees, as well as with customers, suppliers, investors, communities, governments, and other stakeholders, as appropriate, to solicit candid feedback on its Sustainability risks, performance, and reporting. This feedback will be documented for later use in planning.
Comment: See Chapter 11 on stakeholder involvement.

10. Continuation of Process Cycle. At least annually, after management and stakeholders have reviewed the Organization's Sustainability performance and provided feedback, the Sustainability leader and team will reexamine the Sustainability policy and this SOS to determine whether adjustments are warranted. After any changes are made, the steps of the SOS shall be repeated.
Comment: See Figure 5.7 for a flow chart of a model SOS process.

Possible Concerns by Management About an SOS

When the sustainability leader and core team attempt to sell management on the wisdom of adopting an SOS, it would not be unusual for some top executives—or managers in the ranks, for that matter—to have reservations about adopting this new set of management system standards. These reservations are likely to come in the form of the following questions:

> 1. Our organization already follows ISO 9001, ISO 14001, OHSAS 18001, and a number of other management system standards. Why do we need another one adding to the bureaucracy?
> 2. From my experience, management systems are more about paper than progress. How are we going to implement an SOS without generating more volumes of needless documents?
> 3. From what I see and hear, management systems often don't help deliver performance. How are we going to assure that an SOS does?

Let us explore how to respond to each of these concerns.

Avoiding Management System Overload

Appendix 3 lists a variety of management system standards that a company may adopt. An SOS—whether adopted as a new standard or built by modifying an existing one—can tie standards like these together into a single overarching approach. This adds consistency, alignment, and efficiency across the organization while not disturbing the ISO or other certifications that the company believes are important. This consistency may well open up new opportunities for groups to work together, sharing resources and tools to improve performance. What is more, a companywide SOS helps spread best management practices across functions and business units. In this way, for example, new and improved methods of tracking corrective actions for production quality can benefit more than just the quality group. An organizationwide SOS also creates a framework that can be harnessed to develop an enterprise risk management program of the type promoted in governance circles.

Minimizing the Documentation Burden

A common problem with implementing management system standards is the overreliance on documentation and the underemphasis on in-field behavior and performance. A management system is not a 50-pound binder of procedures but rather what happens on the shop floor and with nearby neighbors. Documentation should be limited to that information mentioned in Section 5.6 of the model SOS standard (Figure 5.3).

In deciding whether documentation is warranted, common sense should rule. Somehow day after day, people successfully start their cars, drive to the grocery store, buy food, return home, and prepare meals. The only documentation needed to achieve that entire process may be some recipes or microwaving instructions. Stored away somewhere are operating manuals for the car and the stove. Looking at common situations like this can help make practical sense of when documentation is truly needed. More often than not, good training information is more useful than an elaborate procedure, and one-page cartoon-like instructions posted on a machine are more helpful than detailed textual instructions filed in a notebook.

Getting Management Systems to Deliver Superior Performance

Overdocumentation is not the only common problem inhibiting the effectiveness of management system standards. As noted in Figure 5.4, there are many others. One lies in adopting standards for the wrong reason. Managers who are intent on using the standards to improve their operations will often find success. Those who use them merely to meet a customer demand or just for the status will often cut corners, seek lenient reviewers, or otherwise "game the system"—doing the least amount possible to get the prized certification. These managers usually come up short on results. With management system standards as with many things in life, you get out of it according to what you put into it.

Figure 5.4
Seven Common Reasons Why Management Systems Fail to Deliver Superior Performance

Management Issues
1. Organization has wrong reason for obtaining the management system.
2. System focuses on continuous improvement rather than absolute performance versus benchmarks ("sustainable quantum leaps").
3. Management is lulled into believing its certified management system can operate with little help and excessively cuts number or skill-level of those administering it.

Evaluator (Auditor) Issues
4. Evaluators overemphasize documentation, underemphasize field interviews aimed at the effectiveness of deployment down at the point of decisionmaking and action.
5. Evaluators judge the system on what it is likely to provide, not what it has consistently provided.
6. Evaluators lack good professional judgment of system outputs (compliance, risk management, productivity).
7. Evaluators fail to spot and address overarching root causes for inadequate performance.

Management system standards also fail from weak auditing technique in assessing the effectiveness of the process and identifying needed corrections. As Figure 5.5 shows, a properly designed management process or system is like a good production machine. The main purpose of both is to provide good output consistently and efficiently. While some deficiencies of a machine may be spotted during a physical inspection during shutdown, most surface when the machine is in operation and fails to make products according to specification at the anticipated rate. The real test of a machine's effectiveness is determined by looking at its output. Likewise, to determine the effectiveness of an overall management system, one must closely examine the consistency and nature of the output: compliance, risk control, and productivity (employee morale, waste and accident reduction, etc.). Too often auditors don't do this. Sometimes this is because they aren't sufficiently experienced to pass judgment about the suitability of the output. They may not know enough about the topic to assess compliance, risk, and productivity or to identify the overall root causes when performance is lacking. Other times, it's because the auditors are ignoring the "wet ink syndrome" and accepting management systems even though the procedures were drafted only a short time ago and there has been no track record of consistently good performance.

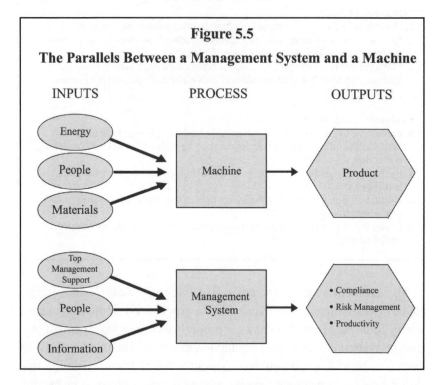

Figure 5.5

The Parallels Between a Management System and a Machine

Or the problem may be that the auditors devote too much effort to studying procedures and other documents when they should be examining the results produced by the system. Granted, some review of documents is necessary, especially those showing past performance and regulatory compliance, but auditors should spend most of their on-site time interviewing and observing the behavior of line workers and their supervisors, learning how the management system works in practice at the point of decisionmaking and action. Effective systems auditing is not simply dashing through a yes-no checklist.

Given the nature of most management system standards, auditors may feel they are limited to judging the output of a system by whether performance is inching forward in "continual improvement" rather than delivering good overall performance as judged against benchmarked operations. This is a mistake. Poor performance is still poor performance, even though it's improving. Going from really, really bad to just really bad is nothing to cheer about. It's a sign that the process remains broken and needs repair. What is needed in such cases is not just continual improvement but a "sustainable quantum leap" in performance.

Occasionally an organization will be lucky enough to go for a period of years without a problem even though its management system appears incomplete. Does this mean the system (the machine) is good enough and further improvement is not needed? Maybe. Informal systems established through long-standing practices, good communications, and strong organizational culture may be sufficient to provide consistently good performance. But in that case, the informal system is still a system—and a complete and effective one—even though it is not recorded anywhere. The real question is whether the system is likely to continue to provide consistently good performance if there are personnel changes, power outages, or any of a wide range of possible circumstances that the operation has so far been fortunate enough to avoid. If the answer to this question is "no," then the good performance of the past is not enough and systems improvements must be made.

Sometimes a machine's product output is lousy even though the machine itself is in perfect operating condition. In those cases, one must check the adequacy of the inputs to the machine: the energy source; materials; and the people operating and maintaining it. For a management system, the inputs are top management support, people, and information. Where a management system isn't delivering good performance and problems with inputs are suspected, these inputs must also be probed by interview and examination to search for root causes. Such a review often reveals broad-based deficiencies in management support, personnel competency, tools, training, roles and responsibilities, accountability, or resources. Effectively evaluating system inputs and spotting and addressing overarching root causes are critical to achieving superior long-term performance.

Figure 5.6 reveals how important the evaluation of inputs and root causes can be. It shows the results of three views—one by a corporation (Intel) and two by business groups (The Conference Board and ORC Worldwide). Each party identified the factors that they believed most contribute to improving safety performance in companies. While each party generally supported the usefulness of all factors listed in Figure 5.6, each emphasized particular factors that were of special importance.

The important factors selected by all three were management support, training, resources, and clear roles and responsibilities. Most of the other factors were deemed important by two of the parties. Indeed, the listed actions do help drive performance. Intel used these factors to cut the occupational injury rate among its operations by 90% and at its construction sites by 95%. Baxter benchmarked safety performance among its peers to develop a set of best safety practices that included similar items. It used those practices to cut the rate of serious accidents in half in three years.

Program Element	Organizations Viewing Element as Critical to Safety Performance		
	Conference Board[5]	ORC[6]	Intel[7]
1. Leadership			
1.1 Visible support of the CEO	x	x	x
1.2 Management action (conducting safety inspections, shutting down unsafe sites, imposing discipline for knowing breaches of safety rules, etc.)	x	x	x
1.3 Management coaching and feedback on safe behavior	x	x	
1.4 Providing adequate safety resources	x	x	
1.5 Fostering a trusting relationship among employees so they promptly disclose accidents, safety issues, and recommendations	x		
2. Solid programs			
2.1 Good training	x		x
2.2 Prompt, thorough investigation of accidents and implementation of corrective and preventive action; rigorous analysis of data and use of findings to improve performance	x	x	x
2.3 Integration of best practices into management systems, specifications, processes, etc.	x		x
2.4 Use of occupational health professional to assist with the management of injury cases	x		
2.5 Job hazard analysis	x	x	x
2.6 Clear roles and responsibilities	x	x	
2.7 Short- and long-term goals and objectives		x	x
2.8 Leading and lagging indicators		x	x
3. Individual commitment			
3.1 Attitude that no injury is acceptable or unavoidable, and that safety is everyone's personal responsibility			x
3.2 Employee involvement in safety program	x	x	x
3.3 Employee-management safety committee	x		
4. Continual improvement			
4.1 Sharing problems and solutions across organization	x		x
4.2 Assuring programs are adjusted until they deliver continual improvement in performance		x	x

Figure 5.6
What Drives Safety Performance: Three Views

But these factors are not unique to safety; they are equally critical to achieving good ethical and regulatory compliance, diversity improvement, and financial and other sustainability results. That's the reason these factors and others from Figure 5.6 are addressed proactively in the model SOS standard (Figure 5.3). See, for example, Sections 4.3 (talent competency), 4.5 (use of data to plan improvement), 5.1.5 (roles and responsibilities), 5.2 (training, tools, and integration), 5.3 (resources), 5.9 (visible management commitment), 6.1 (assessment of compliance and risk), 6.4 (preventive and corrective action), and 8 (accountability). The formula for success is clear: be serious about improvement; implement the model SOS standard or something like it; and establish a program to effectively assess system performance. If a company does that, it should be well on track to delivering desired results.

But being on track now and staying on track over the long term are two different things. Sometimes managers start off well and their operations even pass a third-party audit with flying colors but they still end up with disappointing results. This can happen when managers become lulled into a false sense of security, mistakenly concluding the system has been confirmed to be in good running order and can now operate with little assistance. The skilled people who were administering the system are reassigned and either not replaced or replaced by lower skilled, less-expensive personnel. While it is true that more skilled resources are needed to build a system than maintain it, management can easily go overboard in the cut-back to the point the system erodes and eventually fails. When cut-backs occur, system outputs must be monitored with special care to assure performance continues to meet the company's expectations.

The Role of Stakeholders in Evaluating Management Systems

Of course, the results desired by a company may not be the results that everyone else would like it to produce. The adequacy of an organization's management system performance must be judged by a wider audience than just its own managers and auditors. Too often companies begin to believe their own public relations press and discount criticisms bubbling up from outsiders or sometimes even from their own employees. A company must keep a good ear to these voices and take them seriously, no matter how unjustified they may seem. It is a mistake to think of stakeholder relations as merely a matter of who is scientifically right or wrong.

As Monsanto Company found with its troublesome venture into genetically modified crops (discussed in Appendix 1.28), the emotion of stakeholders can be a more powerful force than the business logic of the company.[8] See Chapter 11 for further discussion on stakeholder involvement.

SOS Process Schedule

One of the practical challenges of implementing operating system standards is how to link the elements together in a cogent schedule that allows for the logical and efficient flow of information and decisionmaking. Figure 5.7 shows how that may be done. The schedule ties operating system elements with other typical business processes, such as budgeting and personal performance reviews. Notice that the Pre-Planning Review (Section 4.4 of Figure 5.3) is divided into five parts in the schedule: (1) Talent Management Review; (2) Review of Business Performance and New Business Goals; (3) Big Picture Review; (4) Sustainability Performance Review; and (5) Stakeholder Feedback on Sustainability Performance and Report. After these steps are completed, strategic objectives and goals can be identified and incorporated into business-unit, function, and companywide strategic plans. All of these steps are discussed in more detail in the next chapter.

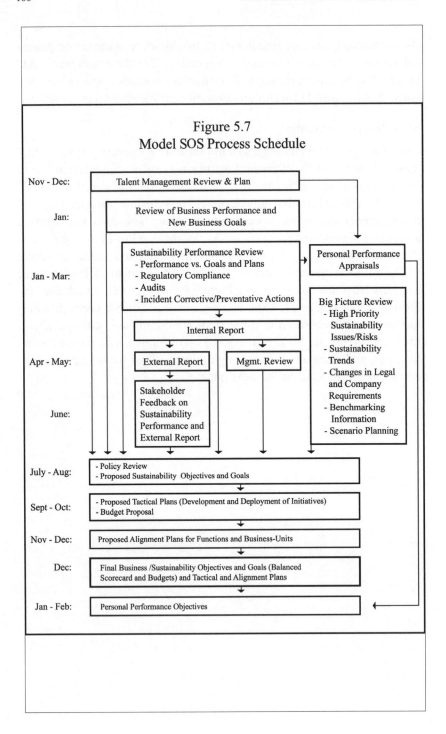

Figure 5.7
Model SOS Process Schedule

After the first cycle through the system, subsequent cycles may only require the updating of original plans rather than completely redrafting them. While most system steps are intended to be updated or re-done annually, the Big Picture Review and perhaps the Stakeholder Feedback might be undertaken every two or three years.

Once the SOS is laid out in a rational schedule, implemented throughout the organization, and debugged to the point it is performing smoothly, a company should notice a significant difference. It should see an improvement in business efficiency, alignment, and productivity; an improvement in finding business opportunities and addressing risks; and an improvement in the respect it commands from employees and others who can bring it success.

Follow-up Checklist for Action: SOS Standards

☐ Determine what management system standards are already in use in your organization.

☐ If your organization uses management system standards, locate managers who have used them and determine what they perceive as the strengths and weaknesses of those standards.

☐ Study the model SOS standards (Figure 5.3) and the management systems summaries of Appendix 3 to determine what standards might be a good base for the development of SOS standards that would apply across your organization. Discuss this with the core team and any internal people who have a working familiarity with management systems.

☐ Using sales strategies from Chapter 4 and the information from this chapter, prepare a presentation proposing an approach for developing appropriate SOS standards.

☐ Determine if there are specific groups receptive to trying the SOS standards as a pilot, and, if so, incorporate such a pilot in the proposal.

☐ Seek the necessary management approval to develop and implement SOS standards as proposed.

☐ Establish a team to prepare the SOS standards, and prepare them for implementation.

☐ As the standards are being developed, work with any internal or external auditing groups to assure their approach to management systems assessments will be effective. In particular, help assure the approach addresses the common shortcomings noted in Figure 5.4.

☐ Implement the SOS as planned and approved.

☐ Every year or two, evaluate the SOS and improve it as appropriate.

Endnotes to Chapter 5

1. Quote attributed to U.S. business advisor, physicist, statistician, and author W. Edwards Deming, who lived from 1900-1993, and was renowned for his systematic approach to problem solving.

2. BAXTER INTERNATIONAL INC., ENVIRONMENTAL PERFORMANCE REPORT: 1993 (1994).

3. E-mail from Richard Guimond, Vice President, Environment, Health & Safety, Motorola Inc., to William Blackburn (Mar. 28, 2005).

4. STEPHEN POLTORZYCKI ET AL., EXPLORING PATHWAYS TO A SUSTAINABLE ENTERPRISE: SD PLANNER™ USER GUIDE app.: Definition of Sub-Elements (GEMI 2002), *available at* http://www.gemi.org/sd/.

5. MEREDITH WHITING & CHARLES BENNETT, DRIVING TO "0": BEST PRACTICES IN CORPORATE SAFETY AND HEALTH (The Conference Board 2003). This study was based on a survey of EHS leaders at companies who are members of The Conference Board's Chief EHS Officer Councils.

6. ORC Worldwide, *Part II: Management System Elements, in* ORC MEMBER COMPANY SAFETY AND HEALTH BENCHMARKING MODEL (2005). These elements were identified based on the views of experienced health and safety professions at ORC (a global business association and consulting organization), as well as those of over a dozen of its member companies. ORC plans to conduct surveys and analysis related to these systems elements over the years to come.

7. E-mail from Bradley Burris, Health and Productivity Business Systems Manager, Intel Corporation, to William R. Blackburn (Feb. 23, 2005).

8. ERIK SIMANIS & STUART HART, MONSANTO COMPANY (A) AND (B): QUEST FOR SUSTAINABILITY (World Resources Institute 2000).

Chapter 6

Strategic Planning for Focused Sustainability Improvement

"Strategy without tactics is the slowest route to victory.
Tactics without strategy is the noise before defeat."[1]
—Sun Tzu

Purpose and Benefits of Strategic Planning by Functional Groups

Why do companies prepare strategic plans? The simple answer is that a failure to plan is planning to fail. Without a strategic plan, business managers allocate resources to whatever priorities they think appropriate. For a large company, this means a thousand different managers directing their teams in a thousand different directions. Strategic planning enables a business to do what management consultant Stephen Covey recommends: "Put first things first." As Covey observes in his national bestseller, *The 7 Habits of Highly Effective People*: "I am personally persuaded that the essence of the best thinking in the area of time management can be captured in a single phrase: Organize and execute around priorities."[2] Strategic planning enables an organization to do just that. It brings an organizational cohesion and focus of resources to high-priority objectives, improving the chances of accomplishing them with the least time, effort, and money. As noted in Figure 6.1, such planning has other merits as well.

Business people often concede that strategic planning at the top levels of a company makes good sense. Yet many think it a waste of time for functions like human resources, purchasing, EHS, or business practices. For some reason, they believe this tool for improving organizational effectiveness and efficiency would be of little benefit within smaller, more focused parts of the company. They are mistaken. In a 2001-2003 study, Proudfoot Consulting, a U.K.-based firm specializing in operational improvement, analyzed 1,440 projects in Australia, France, Germany, South Africa, Spain, the United Kingdom, and the United States and spent 10,000 hours observing how people worked. They found that an average of 87 working days per person were lost each year through inefficiency, with the main cause—present in over 40% of the cases—being poor management planning or inadequate monitoring of how plans were executed.[3] Good planning pays, even within departments, functions, or other subunits of an organization.

Figure 6.1
The Purposes and Benefits of Good Strategic Planning

1. Raises awareness about threats and opportunities; helps the organization confront the brutal reality
2. Aligns the organization around a common direction and set of priorities; improves teamwork and job satisfaction
3. Eliminates low-value work
4. Improves organizational efficiency and productivity
5. Provides a basis for allocating resources
6. Defines a baseline and direction for measuring progress
7. Helps instill confidence in the leadership ability of top managers
8. Enables subordinates to understand the importance of their role in achieving the organization's major objectives
9. Brings new ideas and creativity to the surface for the benefit of the organization
10. Establishes accountability for performance

Many corporate functional groups avoid strategic planning because they don't know how to do it and they see it as some high-level, arcane science. Or they may fail to appreciate its benefits and see no reason to do it. Most are simply overwhelmed with work. As the saying goes, it's hard to think about draining the swamp when you are up to your (ears) in alligators. Department leaders may find it too awkward to ask their internal customers to lower expectations about department performance for a period so resources can be diverted to drain the swamp. Occasionally leaders see merit in planning but try to avoid the time commitment by delegating most of the plan preparation to a team of subordinates. That can be a problem. While some supportive tasks can be done by others, and teams can be used to generate ideas, the job of envisioning and debating final strategies and goals cannot be handed over. Decisionmaking on how resources will be applied to priorities is the primary role of management, and thus it requires their personal involvement. The answer for leaders is to just do it: do the planning as efficiently as possible. Ask your customers to be understanding of the time you are taking to improve your operations. It may help to solicit input from them for use in the planning. At least it will show you are trying to improve for their benefit, too.

General Process for Sustainability Planning

Indeed, if a company is committed to exploring the risks and opportunities associated with sustainability, then strategic planning is a critical tool for bringing focus to that effort. That is why it is included as Section 4 of the Model Sustainability Operating System Standards (Figure 5.3) and is featured prominently in the Model Sustainability Process Schedule (Figure 5.7). This planning may be done in different ways. The best ways involve a process that is both bottom-up—with various functional specialties providing recommended objectives and goals in their areas—as well as top-down—with the CEO and executive team laying out the broad direction for the business and incorporating the specialists' recommendations as appropriate.

Using our model approach, for example, which is diagrammed in Figure 6.3, the sustainability leader and core team would kick off the planning with some guidance to each member of the deployment team (DT). DT members would then identify with their own respective groups (DT member groups) the issues or topics under the company's sustainability policy that are within the responsibility of their function and that members of their function believe are most important to the organization. (See the lists of topics in Figures 2.3 to 2.5. See also Appendix 6 for a sampling of issues that might arise for the functional groups listed in Figure 6.2.) Each DT member group would also develop a list of prioritized risks and a set of recommended sustainability objectives and goals within their scope of responsibility. Once each group completes its prioritization, the core team—or committee drawn from it—would examine the results and collectively identify those sustainability objectives and goals of highest priority across the company and recommend them to the executive planning team for inclusion in the companywide strategic plan. After the companywide strategic plan is finalized, the core team would help guide the DT member groups in preparing their own strategic and tactical plans to implement the agreed-upon strategies. DT member groups would also work with functions and business units that may not have been involved in the process earlier to assure sustainability issues of special importance to those functions and units are properly addressed in their plans.

Figure 6.2
Functional Groups for Which Sustainability Issues Are Listed in Appendix 6
(Appendix number for each function is noted below.)

6.1 Business Development (Mergers and Acquisitions)

6.2 Business Planning

6.3 Charitable Giving; Foundation

6.4 Communications; Public Relations; Community Relations

6.5 Corporate Governance; Corporate Secretary

6.6 EHS

6.7 Ethics; Business Practices

6.8 Facilities Engineering; Energy Management

6.9 Finance

6.10 Government Affairs; Public Policy

6.11 Human Resources; Employee Relations

6.12 Information Technology (IT)

6.13 Internal Audit

6.14 Investor Relations

6.15 Law

6.16 Manufacturing

6.17 Quality

6.18 Research and Development; Product Design

6.19 Risk Management

6.20 Sales and Marketing; Distribution

6.21 Security

6.22 Supply Chain (Supplier Management; Purchasing)

A variation of this approach is used by HP. A number of planning teams from their Corporate Affairs group, other corporate functions, and business units create strategic business plans based on the company's framework of priority areas for global citizenship. Then representatives from the business organization and key functions integrate key aspects of each plan into their respective plans.[4]

Ideally the planning teams for each DT member group and similar organizations should be made up of those with good business and professional judgment who reflect the appropriate diversity of geographies, areas of specialization, and job levels so as to be representative of the make-up of the companywide group. A human resources (HR) planning team, for example, could consist of the company HR vice president from Europe, a benefits specialist from the United States, and personal development expert from Asia, and a compensation manager from Latin America. The team should be augmented with others as needed to provide the necessary planning-facilitation skills and knowledge about the business, sustainability, and the SOS. A small planning team of four to six people is ideal, with a wider range of experts and support teams furnishing suggestions in specific areas. This second tier of support can include the key people who will execute the tactics that flow from the strategic plan. The support teams should also contain those who are familiar with the needs and challenges faced by employees down in the ranks and on the assembly room floor. The key is to garner broad involvement in the plan so it is well considered and enjoys widespread ownership and support in implementation.

Discussions by the planning teams will likely bounce between strategies and tactics in an iterative way. This can help the teams identify strategies and explore their ramifications, but it can also lead to confusion about the difference between strategies and tactics. The objectives for the strategic plan are those that define *what* needs to happen (e.g., increase by 5% the employees who are women), rather than the tactics of *how* it is to happen (e.g., target qualified women in recruiting). Focusing on the *what* at the strategy stage can spawn more creative thinking about the *how* later during tactical planning.

Planners often have the tendency to "reverse plan," that is, look at the budget, determine what projects they can do that fits within those resource constraints, then concoct a strategy to justify the tactics. That certainly makes the process easier, but doesn't align the organization's direction with the current circumstances and those likely ahead. Nor does it optimize the positive impact that can be achieved with the resources available. Moreover, it usurps the role of upper management. Top executives rely on subordinate groups and functional experts to recommend the best course of action for the organization, considering the relevant risks and opportunities. If the organization is best served, for example, by having an expensive software program that produces better record-keeping and efficiency in managing personnel documents, then upper management expects the HR department to propose it, even if it means exceeding the generally expected budget level. Upper management can then decide whether the need for the software justifies budget relief in light of the company's strategic direction and competing demands for resources. That is their job. If budget relief is not possible, then the HR department can always reevaluate its other priorities and the timing, scope, and alternatives for the software to see if such a project is feasible for the budget year. If it isn't, the project must be shelved until later. But even if that happens, at least upper management has begun to understand the HR department's new emerging needs and may be more inclined to approve a solution in the future.

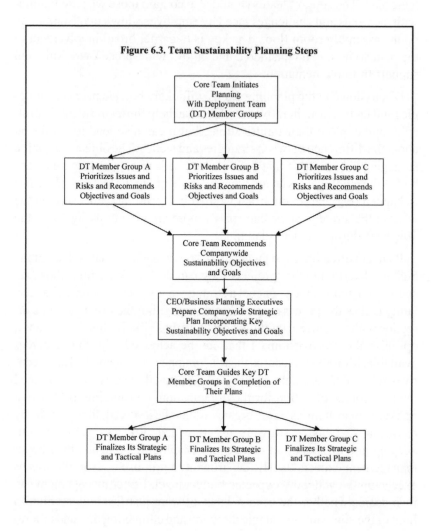

Figure 6.3. Team Sustainability Planning Steps

Strategic planning commonly considers initiatives to be accomplished over the next three to five years, with the expected progress against that strategy—and the goals, tactics, and budgets supporting it—more precisely defined for the planning year. Once a plan is prepared, it is usually reviewed and updated annually, unless some major acquisition, divestiture, or major financial upheaval causes it to be done sooner. Some companies use contingency planning to consider the possibility of such upheavals as well as better-than-expected financial prospects. They prepare, but keep in reserve, worst-case and best-case plans, submitting for approval the version that assumes the most likely circumstances. This can help reduce the panicked scrambling that can result if conditions radically change. A look at worst, best, and likely scenarios some 10 to 20 years out is also sometimes undertaken through "scenario planning," which we will examine shortly. Other companies have shifted their strategic planning to be more of a rolling or continuous process, where various key issues are examined in some depth over the course of the year, and the strategic plan and budgets are adjusted at various times of the year as decisions are made on those issues.[5]

Prioritization Process

Organizations that begin to understand sustainability and commence planning around it will not be wanting for suggestions for action. But of course a company can't do everything at once. As William Shakespeare observed: "Small to great matters must give way."[6] Indeed, prioritization is essential throughout the process for narrowing the scope of sustainability from what is desired to what can be done.

Any prioritization exercise requires four things to be successful: (1) a clear understanding of the purpose of the ranking; (2) knowledgeable evaluators; (3) good ranking criteria; and (4) an appropriate prioritization technique. The purpose of the prioritization varies, depending upon the stage of planning. It may be required to evaluate the threats and opportunities of sustainability trends, to rank sustainability risks, or to select strategic objectives and goals or tactical projects.

Infusing the planners with the right knowledge requires some pre-planning work, as shown in Sections 4.3 through 4.4 of the Model SOS Standards (Figure 5.3). That work is geared to providing planners with a wide variety of relevant information, including that on sustainability trends, the company, and its employees, other stakeholders, and industry.

Pre-Planning Information and Processes

Rather than overwhelming planners with a mass of pre-planning data all at once, it is more effective to break the information into logical segments and communicate and discuss it in a few sessions held over the course of the year. One way to organize and schedule these review sessions is depicted in the Model Sustainability Process Schedule (Figure 5.7). Some of the short reviews can be incorporated in staff meetings. Others, like the Talent Management Review, may warrant a separate meeting. The purpose and content of these reviews are as follows:

Talent Management Review

This review is best held among the leaders within a function or business unit to evaluate the performance of personnel, and to identify their training and development needs and their suitability for their positions. This is also a good time to reexamine employee career paths and succession plans. In addition, the leaders can determine whether the organization possesses the knowledge, skills, experience, and attitudes needed to complete the strategic plan and meet other current and future needs. An experienced human resources expert can help assure these issues are properly explored. The website for the U.K. Investors in People Management System has information and tools that may be helpful. (See Appendix 3.21.)

The Talent Management Review is often most conveniently conducted late in the year when performance reviews and development plans for individuals are assessed, and before new personal objectives are prepared for the coming year. If the review shows that human resources are not adequate to meet the objectives, then either the HR capabilities must be modified—such as through training or reassigning personnel—or the objectives must be changed, at least over the short term until the necessary human resources can be developed or acquired.

At the conclusion of the review, a confidential plan of action should be prepared listing the follow-up to be taken with regard to reviewed personnel. This might include special work assignments, training, personal coaching, or other development measures for certain individuals, as well as new training strategies, personal feedback processes, or other actions to be implemented across the function. The groupwide actions, if strategic in nature, should be incorporated in the group's strategic plan.

If done properly, a Talent Management Review can be a powerful tool for improving organizational efficiency and performance. Unfortunately, it can also deteriorate into a dysfunctional round of accusations and defensive rebuttals, judgments based on politics rather than merit, or an exchange of pleasantries that avoid the real issues. However, there are several things that can be done to head off these problems. One is to agree in advance upon criteria that will guide discussion on individual performance. These criteria may touch different aspects of results, responsiveness, and respect. Some are suggested in Figure 6.4. Performance discussions can then be confined to these criteria. Weaknesses should be covered with individual development plans and strengths reinforced with complements and, if appropriate, rewards. Development measures involving special coaching, training, or work experience should be considered. Workers who are not meeting expectations or not adequately responding through development plans should be targeted for reassignment, or if necessary, removal. Every effort should be made to find new, more challenging roles for rising stars.

Figure 6.4
Possible Employee Success Criteria for Use in Talent Management Review

Respect	Results	Responsiveness
Integrity, ethics	Leadership	Value creation
Communications	Innovation	Customer satisfaction
Listening, empathy	Courage, tenacity	Managing expectations
Teamwork	Ability to make tough decisions	Personal initiative
Conflict resolution		Ability to prioritize
Constructive attitude	Business acumen	Continuous improvement
Objectivity	Planning	
Developing the talent of others	Execution on commitments	
	Ability to manage projects and programs	

Another step to help keep the review session on track is to develop a code of conduct for the session, which limits hearsay and defensiveness and assures that feedback is provided constructively, respectfully, and confidentially. A third step is to identify a trusted facilitator who can assure the code is followed, tough issues are discussed, and agreed actions are confidentially recorded. Finally, the leader can set the tone at the outset by opening herself to a critique of her own strengths and improvement opportunities from the review group, even probing sensitive areas for input. Other members of the review team can request similar feedback from the team. While this live, around-the-table feedback can be awkward at first, in the end, it can produce greater trust among the group, enhance their feedback skills, and provide valuable coaching to each member. However, it's not for managers who are overly defensive or political, or emotionally immature.

All employees involved in preparing and executing a group's strategic plan should be covered by a Talent Management Review, whether undertaken by the group's leadership team or at some lower level. The first review may require some time, but subsequent annual reviews can go faster since much of the discussion will be mere updates.

After individual performance is assessed and development plans formulated, the talent review team should look at any trends that may have emerged, such as special training that appears to be needed at a companywide, division, or regional level. Also, the inventory of talent can be compared with the organization's changing needs to assure the right people will be on board with the right knowledge and skills in the future. Action plans arising from these discussions should also be recorded for follow-up.

Review of Business Performance and Goals

When the annual financial results of the business are released, typically in January, this can be melded into the planning. So can the new sales and earnings targets which are also issued around the beginning of the year. This is also an appropriate time to review the financial prospects for the industry as a whole and what factors may be stimulating or restraining the growth of this business segment. The outcome of this review may well affect the priority of some proposed objectives.

Sustainability Performance Review

This review can encompass not only how well the organization performed against its sustainability goals and plans, but information on performance trends, strengths, and top needs. This information may be gleaned from audits, litigation, agency inspections, and various incidents, as well as from the corrective and preventive actions for them. A list of the lower priority long-term sustainability objectives that were postponed during planning in earlier years should be brought to the table again to see if any items warrant inclusion in the new plans in light of the latest performance trends.

Big Picture Review

Someone in the organization—the sustainability leader and core team in our model—should communicate information about relevant sustainability trends to the planning teams. Information of this type is summarized in Appendix 1. Many of these trends are also covered in the *Vital Signs* books that are periodically issued by the Worldwatch Institute.[7] The Dutch drug, chemicals, and materials company DSM has developed its own Sustainability Issue Tracker for use in its strategic planning.[8]

The primary purpose of a Big Picture Review is to assess these trends and their potential impact on the company. But this review also presents a good opportunity to evaluate other information as well. This could include, for example, noteworthy changes in legal or company requirements occurring since the last review. It could also encompass an evaluation of short and projected long-term trends for the company and its business sector. Another useful addition is comparative information about sustainability performance gleaned from internal and external benchmarking. All this information provides a good basis for several planning techniques, such as scenario planning, back-casting, and strengths, weaknesses, opportunities, and threats (SWOT) analysis, which can be tacked onto the end of the Big Picture Review if time permits or conducted later.

Scenario planning is a tool used extensively by Shell.[9] It is a multidisciplinary exercise for researching and brainstorming alternative, reasonably possible scenarios that may substantially affect the company over the decades to come. Given the long timeframes involved, the scenarios must not be too precise. Once the scenarios are identified, planners examine the risks and opportunities that each scenario poses for the company and suggest strategies that should be adopted now as a consequence. As the future plays out, strategies are adjusted accordingly. Scenarios are often prepared for best-case, worst-case, and most-probable-case assumptions.

Back-casting builds from long- or short-term scenario planning. It follows from the advice of Covey: "Begin with the end in mind."[10] Once the organization defines what it wants to achieve or look like at some point in the future, then it can work backwards to identify the incremental steps it must take to reach that desired state. If the vision is challenging enough, this can help shake the company out of its business-as-usual or continuous-improvement mentality to embrace more radical change.

SWOT analysis is a process used by planners which enables them to identify objectives and actions to protect the organization from serious threats and enable it to seize attractive opportunities. An example of how that might be done for sustainability trends is shown in Figure 6.5. Form C in Appendix 4 can help with the identification of opportunities and threats (risks) arising from those trends. In addition to using this information for strategic planning, the list of risks developed from this process can be prioritized and used in an enterprise risk management assessment.

Figure 6.5
Sample SWOT Analysis for Sustainability Issues

Issue	Strength	Weakness	Opportunity	Threat	Possible Objectives
Depletion of Fresh Water Resources	1. Some water conservation projects underway 2. Internal engineering expertise	No long-term water rights secured in some growth regions; some communities serving our factories have poor water supply infrastructure	1. Water conservation projects can save money, help secure supply 2. More on-site water treatment and reuse are possible 3. May be able to secure long-term water rights in some locations	1. Water shortage could jeopardize operations 2. Some competitors have long-term water rights	Investigate water risks on site-by-site basis and develop actions to address them; consider more aggressive water treatment, reuse, and conservation programs using internal engineers; explore possibility of securing long-term water supplies in high-risk areas while respecting community needs
Supplier Labor Practices in Developing Nations	Some suppliers are certified	1. Labor practices of some suppliers are unknown 2. Labor surveillance programs not well developed	1. New customers possible if supplier practices are certified 2. Good supplier labor practices can create more stable work force, more reliable supply	1. Poor labor practices can create scandal, hurt company's business 2. Supplier labor unrest can interrupt supply	Develop and implement surveillance program for labor rights evaluation at high-risk sites; benchmark among other companies to identify best practices
Changing U.S. Population Profile	Some departments have good record on diversity	1. Poor representation of minorities in upper management 2. No marketing studies on future opportunities with minority customers	1. Can attract best minority workers 2. Can build new markets with certain minorities	Company may be out of step with needs and preferences of certain minorities, which will be growing segment of work force and customers	Strengthen diversity programs, especially among upper management and the board; explore implications and opportunities of a more culturally sensitive approach to marketing

Management Feedback Review

Upper management's feedback on the organization's sustainability performance is another critical piece of information needed for planning. That feedback is most conveniently obtained at the time top management reviews the organization's internal sustainability performance report—typically undertaken around the time of the annual stockholders' meeting in the second quarter of the year. Feedback should not only be obtained from upper management but from the board itself. All too often sustainability leaders are blocked from directly engaging with these top layers of management. That's unfortunate because it can lead to the misalignment of the SOS with the direction and strategies of the company, which in turn can significantly diminish the business value the SOS can produce. For that reason, one of the chief roles of the executive sponsor must be to assure this access is available.

Stakeholder Feedback Review

Another pre-planning activity is soliciting feedback from key stakeholders. At a minimum, input should be requested of employees and customers. The views of investors, government representatives, neighbors, suppliers, or activists may also help, depending upon the nature of issues facing the company. Written surveys can be used if some documentation of progress is desired, but it's simpler and sometimes more effective to solicit comments live as part of a conference, meeting, or phone call already scheduled for other business purposes. Before the feedback is obtained, the targeted stakeholders should be given the latest report on the company's sustainability performance. Comments can then be sought on the company's past performance and new goals, as well as on the form and content of the report itself. Plans for stakeholder interviews or surveys should be shared with the report distributors network to identify and coordinate the inquiries. (See Chapter 11 for more information on stakeholder feedback.)

Criteria for Prioritizing Sustainability Issues

Once planners have acquired the necessary knowledge base for prioritizing sustainability issues, they must then decide on the criteria to use for the ranking. In selecting priorities for action from among the sustainability topics listed in Figures 2.3 to 2.5, those that are obviously irrelevant should be dropped and others added as they come to mind in light of the company's sustainability policy. One way to rank the issues—and the objectives and goals that follow—is to give priority to those which:

1. Are important to business success (they add value regarding productivity; employee relations; reputation; control of legal, financial, or other risks; sales growth; innovation; new markets; or license to operate);
2. Are of greatest concern to management;
3. Are consistent with the company culture (as reflected in the company's vision, policies, goals, stated values, and general communications from management);
4. Are of public concern (such as governance issues after Enron and WorldCom, emergency preparedness after 9/11, energy conservation after a big regional blackout or surge in energy prices);
5. Make strategic sense in light of the sustainability trends (such as a coal supplier looking at climate change, a plastics manufacturer examining the depletion of petroleum stocks, a employee recruiter considering population trends, a public relations consultant studying the growing influence of activist groups);
6. Provide the greatest, longest lasting beneficial impact; and
7. Are easiest to implement.

Issues that have been in the public eye recently may offer top opportunities for action. Of utmost concern will be those things which can significantly affect the ability of the company to do business. They might include serious legal or public relations problems or operational or product issues posing serious threats to life. Actual crisis will garner the most attention, but realistic potential risks can find good support too. All lend a sense of urgency for action, which is helpful in effecting change.

Slightly lower on the list but also worth considering are matters that will help secure business growth or prevent the loss of business. Here's where customer dialogue can be useful. Is product quality hurting sales? Is a fair-trade certification needed for a vegetable supplier to sell to a major customer? Does demand for growth suggest that business should be expanded to developing nations? If so, these issues should make the to-do list.

Further down but also attractive are those issues that can improve efficiency and reduce cost. Product and packaging material reduction and waste and accident prevention are good examples. Finally, there are those many items, like cause-related marketing (see Appendix 1.29), which can strengthen the company's reputation with key constituencies. For these, the evaluation should focus on what can be done that will provide the greatest, longest term impact for the resources expended.

Techniques for Reaching Consensus on Priorities

With ranking criteria in place, planners well informed, and the reason for prioritizing clearly understood, the only remaining step for prioritization is to identify an appropriate technique for agreeing on the priorities. Without such a technique, the planning team may face a stalemate on the direction forward or walk away disgruntled over a selection process that was undemocratic. Here are a few of the many techniques that can be used to bring a team into agreement on priorities, whether on issues, objectives, goals, or tactics:

Ratings on Appendix 4 Forms. Forms A, B, and C presented in Appendix 4 are designed for ranking sustainability topics for action. Form A is for prioritizing the 100 or so sustainability topics found in Figures 2.3 to 2.5 to develop a manageable list for action. This form incorporates input from Forms B and C. Form B assesses the importance of each topic to business success. Form C is for identifying and rating the opportunities and risks posed to the business by various sustainability trends. Form C is the place to answer questions like: Will the trend concerning growth in global business competition pose a serious risk for the company? Are large powerful transnational competitors likely to invade local markets? Is there an opportunity for the company to expand into new foreign markets itself? Forms A and B can be modified slightly to rank goals, objectives, and tactical projects as well.

The three forms may be used as-is, modified as desired, or simply used as a guide for discussion, with the conclusions documented in some other way. The documentation is useful because the conclusions not only serve the prioritization process but provide a basis for strategic and tactical planning.

Value-Resources Mapping Process. This technique relies on the broad judgment of the evaluators/planners to rate the value of an objective, target, issue, or risk versus the resource burden (time and money) required to address it. Figure 6.6 graphically shows how this technique works. The items being ranked are each scored from 1 to 4 for two characteristics. The first is *value*, with a 4 rating given to items that are essential or of great value, a 0 to those of little or no value. Value scores can be based on a wide range of criteria. Forms A and B of Appendix 4 provide factors that can be used formally or informally for this purpose. The other scoring is for *resources*, that is, the time and money needed to address the objective, target, issue, or risk. A rating of 4 is given to those items requiring few resources and 0 to those demanding many. Here again, the ratings may be formal—relying on cost and time estimates—or informal. Once an item is scored for value and resources, the two scores are multiplied to give a value-resources score for each item. The value-resources scores from each planner are then compiled and averaged. Items are ranked by these average scores, with a score of 16 being the most preferred and 0, the least. A cut-off score can be set for dropping low-priority items.

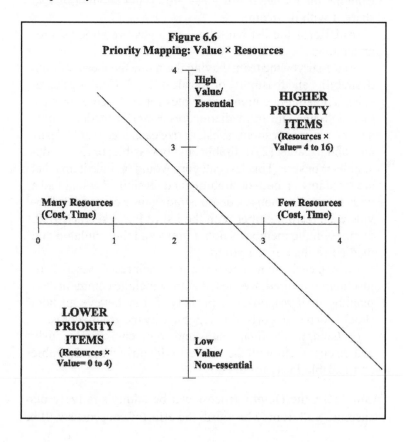

Figure 6.6
Priority Mapping: Value × Resources

3. *Voted dots process.* One simple way to prioritize among alternatives is through "sticker voting." This involves giving each planner a certain number of colored round stickers and letting the planner place any number of their stickers on any of the proposed items they feel are of greatest merit in light of the prioritization criteria. The proposals are then ranked according to the number of dot votes they receive.

4. *Delphi process.* If planners fear that creativity may be stymied by dominant individuals, endless debate, or group pressure for conformity, a Delphi technique or some modification of it can be considered. The technique involves the following steps:

(a) Confidentially survey the planning team for ideas. Compile the master list of ideas preserving anonymity, and share it with the team.

(b) Discuss the list with the team to assure all ideas are understood.

(c) Re-survey the team, having them rate the ideas for both desirability and feasibility on a scale of 1 to 5. Compile the results, tabulating the number of votes for each score for each idea, and calculate the median scores. From the median scores and the range of responses, categorize each idea as: (1) desirable and feasible; (2) desirable but not feasible; or (3) not desirable or unsure. This last category would include items that are rated low on both desirability and feasibility or that had a wide range of responses, demonstrating little consensus. Provide each team member with the list of items so classified, along with the member's own ratings and the tabulated and median ratings of the group.

(d) Ask each member to reevaluate their responses and adjust them if desired. Request that they include comments explaining their responses, especially if they believe an item should not be categorized as suggested by the group scores.

(e) Compile the final results and comments anonymously and discuss them with the full team. Identify those desirable and feasible ideas for action.[11]

Admittedly, the Delphi process can be administratively burdensome. Still, it may be worth the effort if consensus will be

difficult to achieve or there is a particularly strong need to stimulate innovation.

Using a selected prioritization technique, the planning teams can develop
sustainability objectives and goals for their own use and recommend
them for inclusion in the company's strategic plan.

Strategic Planning Formats: The Balanced Scorecard and Alignment Tools

To the extent possible, each group proposing strategic sustainability objectives and goals should present their information in the same format
and under the same overarching strategic categories used for the
companywide strategic plan. This will help show how the sustainability
initiatives align with the business objectives. For example, if the business
uses a stakeholder-oriented balanced scorecard format—such as that
shown in Figure 6.7—to present its objectives, then each specific business unit and each function like EHS should use a similar format, such as
that shown in Figure 6.8. A dozen or so specific objectives should be set
for the company and each business unit and function, respectively. Care
must be taken that the organization does not take on too many objectives
and end up being spread too thin and become unfocused. Each companywide and group objective should also be accompanied by a specific
measurable goal or some other explanation as to how the fulfillment of
the objective will be determined. In the next chapter, we will review how
to set these goals. Ultimately, each business unit and functional department must finalize their own plans and assure they are aligned with the
companywide plan.

Figure 6.7
Companywide Balanced Scorecard

Employee Objectives *Build the best global team in our industry*	Financial (Investor/Lender) Objectives *Deliver significant shareholder return*	Supply Chain (Customer/Supplier) Objectives *Create sustainable win-win customer relationships*	Citizenship (Community/ Government) Objectives *Improve lives in local global communities*
Share talent and learning across the company to improve business results Goal:_____	Achieve profitable, sustainable, and capital-efficient growth targets in sales, earnings per share, cash flow and margins Goal:	Consistently evaluate and meet agreed customer and product-quality requirements Goal:_____	Establish the company as a community leader Goal:_____
Ensure frequent, open two-way feedback and communication Goal:_____	Invest targeted funds in R& D and capital projects to drive long-term sustainable growth while achieving short-term commitments Goal:_____	Continually identify unmet needs of current and future customers Goal:_____	Facilitate the participation of employees in their communities Goal:_____
Attract, develop and retain the best talent to achieve current and future results Goal:_____	Deliver superior shareholder returns that exceed the average for our industry Goal:_____	Develop and launch innovative products and services to meet customer, product-quality and financial needs Goal:	Reduce waste and achieve targeted improved efficiencies in energy, packaging and water use Goal:_____
Create an environment that motivates, develops and rewards individuals for living the company's shared values and achieving results Goal:	Improve cost efficiency by achieving targets for days sales outstanding, inventory turns, and costs of supplies and travel Goal:	Improve the quality and frequency of customer feedback and the responsiveness of the company to it Goal:	Increase global access to our products so as to improve the quality of lives Goal:_____
Ensure safety in the workplace Goal:_____	Grow sales faster than general & administrative overhead Goal:_____	Improve the pipeline of products to serve developing markets Goal:_____	Increase the number of foundation grants to new organizations, especially those in new locations Goal:

Figure 6.8			
Environment, Health, and Safety Balanced Scorecard			
Employee Objectives *Build a more effective EHS program to better protect, develop and respect employees*	**Financial (Investor/Lender) Objectives** *Improve EHS operational excellence through a risk-based, value-focused approach*	**Supply Chain (Customer/Supplier) Objectives** *Anticipate and align EHS initiatives with the needs of external customers and suppliers to create better customer outcomes*	**Citizenship (Community/ Government) Objectives** *Reduce the environmental impact of our operations and better engage our key external stakeholders*
More effectively share best EHS practices across the organization Goal:_____	Implement integrated EHS management systems consistent with ISO 14001 and OHSAS 18001 Goal:_____	Strengthen processes for gathering and responding to input from customers on the EHS aspects of our products and services Goal:_____	Achieve targeted improvements in the eco-efficiency of operations regarding energy, water, hazardous and nonhazardous waste, and packaging Goal:
Strengthen the assessment and effectiveness of EHS training programs Goal:_____	Strengthen EHS risk management tools and programs Goal:_____	Improve processes and tools for considering EHS in product design and development Goal:	Enhance communications to and from external stakeholders Goal:
Strengthen Six Sigma skills among EHS personnel Goal:_____	Improve speed and effectiveness of EHS processes for integrating new facilities/businesses Goal:_____	Strengthen compliance with European packaging and electronic take-back laws Goal:	Provide community outreach support on EHS education Goal:_____
Promote a healthy work-life balance Goal:_____	Improve the EHS strategic planning process Goal:_____	Expand programs for assessing and improving supplier sensitivity to EHS issues Goal:_____	Improve systems for identifying and assessing community concerns about the EHS aspects of our operations Goal:
Sustainably improve safety performance and culture to drive toward world class results Goal:_____	Help identify and achieve opportunities for business savings and improved efficiency (see env. objectives) Goal:_____	Work with selected suppliers to implement Lean Manufacturing principles while reducing environmental impacts Goal:	Raise factory manager awareness about good stakeholder engagement practices Goal:_____

Aligning Plans With Sustainability Concepts

While it is important for functions and business units to show a close link between their own strategic plans and that of the entire company, it is also worthwhile to show employees how both plans align with sustainability concepts. Figure 6.9 presents one way that can be done. In developing a linkage document like this, the objectives of the plan are compared with the provisions of the sustainability policy. When we juxtapose the objectives of our model scorecards with the provisions of the model sustainability policy (Figure 2.2), we find, for example, certain financial and citizenship objectives of the scorecards will help fulfill the economic leg of our sustainability policy. The financial objectives are clearly aimed at assuring the company's economic prosperity (Section 1.A of Figure 2.2). Charitable donations under the company's citizenship objectives (see Figure 6.7) also align with economic sustainability since they contribute to community economic prosperity (Section 1.B of Figure 2.2). A full comparison produces a matrix like Figure 6.9. This enables all to see that by implementing its strategic plan (scorecard), the company is working toward sustainability.

Figure 6.9 Alignment of Sustainability Issues With Balanced Scorecard Objectives				
Sustainability Issues	**Balanced Scorecard Objectives**			
	Employee	Financial (Investor/Lender)	Supply Chain (Customer/Supplier)	Citizenship (Community/Government)
Economic (Wise use of economic resources)		x		x
Social (Respect for people)	x		x	x
Environmental (Respect for living things; wise use of natural resources)			x	x

Another way to show the strategic plan links with sustainability is to identify certain obvious sustainability issues as overarching themes for the company to address in its planning over the long term. P&G selected as its themes water and health and hygiene—water, because 85% of its products require the use of water, and the company has considerable expertise in this area, and health and hygiene because many of the company's products improve health and well-being, and are used to clean skin, clothing, and homes. These were themes that could involve all the company's businesses and regions and could stimulate new ideas about products, services, and initiatives. Moreover, by looking for products suitable for the poor slum-dwellers of the developing world, and designing ways to reach those consumers, the company might well gain valuable insights about how to improve its core businesses.[12]

Like P&G, HP established long-term strategic themes—theirs framed around environment, privacy, e-inclusion, and education. They selected these themes based on their importance to the business, the information technology sector, and society.[13]

Aligning Implementation in Large Organizations

Once the strategic objectives and goals are defined, then the next phase of planning concerns how to achieve them. For a large company, several different groups—corporate, division, or regional organizations, for example—may be involved in implementing the objectives. In such cases, an alignment document such as Figure 6.10 may be helpful. By agreeing to such a document, all groups will have the map for proceeding in a coordinated, efficient, supportive way to achieve their common objective. This alignment is necessary to produce the most pronounced change in the shortest time and to expedite the companywide cultural transformation toward sustainability. Without it, different parts of the company may begin to work at cross purposes, stymieing progress and efficiency and stoking fires of destructive infighting and competition.

Figure 6.10
Aligned Companywide Implementation Plan:
Environment, Health, and Safety Balanced Scorecard--
Employee Objectives

Companywide Objectives	Corporate EHS Group Implementation	Business Unit A Implementation	Business Region 1 Implementation
More effectively share best EHS practices across the organization	Share facility non-conformance log information across the EHS organization; share information on practices of award-winning facilities	Collect best practices during facility reviews and post on Web	Cover best practices in all future regional EHS meetings
Strengthen the assessment and effectiveness of EHS training programs	Lead team of division EHS leaders and company training experts to develop tools for assessing effectiveness of training; review trends on audit items regarding training needs and include in planning	Use effectiveness tools in field training	Use effectiveness tools in field training
Strengthen programs for developing EHS personnel	Lead EHS talent management review and planning; update Corporate EHS job descriptions	Participate in talent management review and planning; update divisional EHS job descriptions	Participate in EHS talent management review and planning; update regional EHS job descriptions
Promote a healthy work-life balance	Periodically solicit feedback and suggestions from EHS team; assure managers are prioritizing work	Periodically solicit feedback and suggestions from EHS team; assure managers are prioritizing work	Periodically solicit feedback and suggestions from EHS team; assure managers are prioritizing work
Sustainably improve safety performance and culture to drive toward world class results	Lead team in preparing new tools for health and safety risk assessment; review 6 top opportunity sites against best safety practices; review safety performance quarterly with CEO staff	Conduct workplace safety and health risk assessments and behavior-based training in 25% of sites; participate in 4 top-opportunity site reviews	Provide 3 regional training sessions on behavior-based safety and health and safety risk assessment; participate in 2 top opportunity site reviews

The Tactical Plan

The specific details of the coordinated path forward can be captured in tactical or operating plans prepared by each DT member group.[14] Figure 6.11 shows how a tactical plan for the EHS function might be crafted for one objective—safety improvement. P&G uses a similar approach called STAR, which calls for planners to specify the steps, timing, assistance, and responsibility needed to accomplish an objective. A plan like this is useful in showing the activities various teams and individuals will undertake to fulfill the objective. Since the tactical plan defines the extent of effort anticipated, it should be carefully reviewed before being finalized. If the effort demanded by the draft plan appears to exceed available resources, which is often the case, the added resources must be obtained or the plan scaled back accordingly. The rule should be, *if in doubt, cut it out.* There will never be a shortage of priorities to add if resources free up later.

Figure 6.11
Companywide EHS Tactical Plan

Strategic Objective	Team Tactic/Project/Activity	Responsible Team/Individual	Schedule
Sustainably improve safety performance and culture to drive toward world class results Goal: Less than 0.10 lost-time cases and 0.35 recordable cases per 100 full-time employees	1. Improved health and safety risk assessment tools	Risk Assessment Team (Tom Blanco, leader)	Tool development: -Define needs-- Feb 1 -Draft tool-- May 1 -Final tool-- July 1 Tool deployment: -Training mat'ls--Aug.1 -Pilot test--Sept 15 -Communicate final--Nov 1
		Region 1 EHS (Tanya Brown) Business Unit A EHS (Sue Green)	Field implementation: -Regional training--Dec 1 - Site assistance-- 25% sites per quarter starting beginning of next year
	2. Review 6 top-opportunity sites against best safety practices	Corporate EHS (Sam Blue)	Develop plan: -Identify sites-- Jan 15 -Develop review process--Mar.1 Deploy process: -Train regional and divisional reviewers--April 15
		Site Review Teams (team leaders to be identified by Sam Blue)	Field implementation: -Conduct site reviews--one per month July 1-Dec 1

Listing the names of responsible people in the tactical plan helps assure ownership and accountability for the work. Ownership can be best instilled if these people actually prepare the tactical plan for their project, or at least review and concur on it before it's finalized. Since the same parties may not be responsible for all phases of project development and rollout, the assignments and schedules should be arranged in the plan under three categories: (1) project development; (2) the preparation of training materials and other deployment tools; and (3) field implementation. This helps guarantee that each phase—and the resources required for it—are considered in planning and budgeting.

The Role of Aspects Analyses and Risk Assessments in Planning

For those organizations with ISO 14001, OHSAS 18001, or other EHS management systems, the question naturally occurs, where does aspects analysis or risk assessment fit in the planning process? Under ISO 14001, an organization must identify its environmental aspects that it can control or influence, and then determine which aspects may have a significant impact on the environment. An *aspect* is an element of a product, service, or activity that can have a beneficial or adverse impact on the environment. Aspects cause impacts. So, for example, the manufacture of water-saving devices is an aspect that causes the beneficial impact of water conservation. The burning of fossil fuels is an aspect that causes the adverse impacts of climate change and the depletion of natural resources. Under ISO, aspects determined to be significant are to be considered when the organization sets its objectives.[15]

Likewise, OHSAS 18001 calls for organizations to identify its hazards, assess its risks, and determine what measures are necessary to control those risks. A *hazard* is generally considered to be the potential to cause harm, such as the potential for a hazardous substance to cause harm under certain circumstances. A *risk* is the actual likelihood of a certain degree of harm (adverse impact) under specific circumstances. The information on hazards, risks, and controls is also to be considered when the organization sets its objectives.[16]

Aspects analysis and risk assessments fit nicely into the planning process. In the identification of key sustainability issues (see Form B of Appendix 4 and Figures 2.3 to 2.5), a company must take into account the internal economic, social, and environmental impacts—both negative (risks) and positive—posed by those issues. The organization must also consider external impacts, especially as they relate to key sustainability trends (see Form C of Appendix 4 and Appendix 1). Of course, this requires some general understanding of the nature of the organization's products, services, and activities, which is why the use of a multifunctional core team is useful. Those issues which need attention and pose a significant impact from an organizationwide perspective must go into the company's strategic plan. As the plan is deployed across the organization, individual functions, facilities, divisions, and other business units can look more closely at those issues and address them as they relate to the relevant aspects of their own products, services, and activities. These units must also look at other issues that may not have made the cut for companywide attention, but are significant for the unit nevertheless. It is this kind of evaluation which can lie behind the identification of specific control measures and other projects and initiatives that become a part of the unit's tactical plan.

Tracking Progress

After each DT member group finalizes its tactical plan, progress under each plan must be tracked. Responsible parties should provide periodic updates to some central source, whether that's a person who compiles the information or a website. In any case, someone should be assigned to review the input to assure it's clear and complete. The frequency of review depends on the urgency of the issue. Under normal circumstances, the review might be quarterly, which is often enough to spot and address obstacles, yet not so often as to pose an unnecessary burden. Quarterly status reports should be widely available to participants. Some teams have found they can obtain a quick understanding of overall status by color-coding the tactical items in a summary matrix, using green to designate those items on schedule, yellow for those slightly behind schedule or facing some difficulty, and red for those clearly late. The report should be evaluated carefully by a small executive team within the group so prompt adjustments can be made to the plan items, resources, or personnel assignments, if necessary.

Those organizations that want to record and track their sustainability tactical plans by computer should consider using the GEMI SD Planner™[17], a software tool and guidebook published by the Global Environmental Management Initiative (GEMI). GEMI is a U.S. organization made up of approximately 40 major corporations chartered with providing information and tools to help companies achieve excellence in EHS and corporate citizenship. Figure 6.12 shows how the GEMI SD Planner program is structured. A number of sustainability elements are identified under the TBL categories—social, economic, and environmental. Each element is defined. These definitions are published together in one document comparable to the model sustainability policy of Figure 2.2, and appended to the user guide. Targeted levels of performance under each element are selected from 17 "stages of practice" presented under 5 categories. These categories are arranged in order of program maturity, with the first category (Prepare) reflecting initial phases of program development, such as compliance with law. The last category (Champion) contains leadership phases, such as public policy involvement. Progress is tracked through self assessment by selecting the current stage of practice and comparing it to the targeted stage. The program allows the user to modify the element and sub-element definitions and enter customized tactical plans (action items) for each stage of practice of each sub-element. Whether or not a user likes the categories presented in the GEMI SD Planner, she may well find its computerized format a good one for tracking progress under a sustainability tactical plan.

Figure 6.12
Sustainability Elements and Stages of Practice From
Global Environmental Management Initiative (GEMI) SD Planner™[18]

Sustainability Elements	Stage of Practice																
	1-Prepare				2-Commit				3-Implement			4-Integrate			5-Champion		
	Compliance with law	Assessment of current practice	Information gathering	Response to stakeholder concerns	Formal commitment	Proactive policies	Focused programs	Stakeholder dialogue	Management systems	Comprehensive programs	Stakeholder reporting	Integration into business processes	Supply chain management	Stakeholder communications	Proactive programs	External partnerships	Public policy involvement
SOCIAL																	
1.Employee well-being																	
1.1 Employee rights																	
1.2 Responsible Workplace Practices																	
1.3 Employee Health & Safety																	
1.4 Work Life Balance																	
1.5 Respect for Diversity																	
1.6 Employee Compensation																	
2. Quality of Life																	
2.1 Social Equity																	
2.2 Basic Human Needs																	
2.3 Human Capital																	
3. Business Ethics																	
3.1 Basic Human Rights																	
3.2 Positive Impact																	
3.3 Local Cultures & Indigenous People																	
3.4 Fair and Free Competition																	

Figure 6.12
Sustainability Elements and Stages of Practice From
Global Environmental Management Initiative (GEMI) SD Planner™

Sustainability Elements	Stage of Practice																
	1-Prepare				2-Commit				3-Implement			4-Integrate			5-Champion		
	Compliance with law	Assessment of current practice	Information gathering	Response to stakeholder concerns	Formal commitment	Proactive policies	Focused programs	Stakeholder dialogue	Management systems	Comprehensive programs	Stakeholder reporting	Integration into business processes	Supply chain management	Stakeholder communications	Proactive programs	External partnerships	Public policy involvement
ECONOMIC																	
4. Shareholder Value Creation																	
4.1 Competitive Return & Protection of Assets																	
4.2 Reputation & Brand																	
5. Economic Development																	
5.1 Stimulating Local Development																	
5.2 Supporting Disadvantaged Communities																	
ENVIRON- MENTAL																	
6. Env. Impact Minimization																	
6.1 Emissions & Waste																	
6.2 Operational Incidents																	
6.3 Products & Services																	
7. Natural Resources Protection																	
7.1 Biological Resources																	
7.2 Energy																	
7.3 Water																	
7.4 Raw Materials																	

Personal Performance Objectives

Although quite specific, tactical plans by themselves provide no accountability for performance. To secure that all-important accountability, personal performance objectives (PPOs) are needed. (See the example in Figure 6.13.) PPOs align individual responsibility with the tactical and strategic plans. They spell out what each employee is expected to do to contribute to the plan. This helps the employee focus on those things that can most help the organization meet its goals. Employees who do well against their PPOs should receive extra salary, greater opportunities for advancement, or other rewards. This more firmly links the employee's personal interests with those of the company. Moreover, if the employee works for a company, with an SOS, her PPOs will provide more than just ethical and altruistic motivation to move the organization toward sustainability. Indeed, with all employees tied to PPOs, with all PPOs tied to tactical and strategic plans, and with all plans tied to sustainability through an SOS, the forces propelling the organization toward sustainability can be potent. Like metal filings on a paper over a strong magnet, this linkage enables everyone to become aligned to a common point.

Figure 6.13
Sample Personal Performance Objectives for an EHS Manager

1. Provide subordinates with frequent coaching and candid quarterly performance reviews; work with them to develop constructive personal development plans.
2. Visit 4 facilities among the 20 with the highest lost-time accident rates and review their practices against best safety practices. Coach these sites to help them achieve at least a 10% reduction in such rates.
3. Identify at least $500,000 in financially attractive opportunities for cost savings through pollution prevention or other beneficial environmental practices. Work with the facilities to realize these opportunities.
4. Work with the purchasing department to evaluate the top-four local suppliers of high-risk supplies against the new sustainability criteria. Share any best practices identified.
5. Fulfill assigned obligations under the job description and the department's tactical plan.
6. Keep spending within approved budget limits.
7. Perform work in accordance with the company's shared values and employee success criteria.

Planning in Small Organizations

Ideally, strategic and tactical planning for sustainability should be melded into the general business planning process. This is especially true for small companies. For those organizations, it is wise to have the business planning representative work with someone versed in relevant sustainability issues to design a process that builds on the planning process already in place. The small firm may find it sufficient simply to incorporate consideration of Forms A-C (Appendix 4) in whatever planning process exists. In companies where planning is weak, the tools and considerations presented in this chapter may well prompt improvements in overall business planning, helping save much of the person-years of valuable employee time lost to misalignment, inefficiency, and ineffectiveness.

Follow-up Checklist for Action: Strategic Planning

☐ Sustainability leader discusses with the core team the purpose, process, and tools for strategic and tactical planning; the core team agrees on the process, tools, and schedule, tying them to the approach and timing used for the companywide strategic plan.

☐ Core team members discuss the planning process, tools, and schedule with the DT and their member groups.

☐ DT member groups identify the people responsible for performing the pre-planning work discussed in this chapter.

☐ DT member groups proceed through the planning process as agreed, developing proposed objectives, goals, and tactical plans, as well as identifying major risks to the business.

☐ Core team (or a committee of it) collects the proposed sustainability objectives, goals, and risks from the DT member groups and recommends some sustainability objectives and goals to the CEO/executive team for incorporation in the companywide strategic plan.

☐ After the companywide plan is finalized, the core team works with the DT member groups and other business units and functions, as appropriate, to guide them in finalizing the strategic and tactical plans for their groups and preparing intergroup aligning documents.

☐ Core team compiles and reviews the high sustainability risks furnished by the DT member groups and provides a list to the company's Governance and/or Risk Management groups for incorporation in an enterprise risk management assessment for upper management and the board.

☐ Employees develop PPOs aligned with their group's strategic and tactical plans.

☐ DT member groups track and report progress against their strategic and tactical plans; employees and their supervisors track progress on PPOs.

Endnotes to Chapter 6

1. Quote attributed to a Chinese military strategist who lived circa 500 B.C.

2. STEPHEN R. COVEY, THE 7 HABITS OF HIGHLY EFFECTIVE PEOPLE 149 (Simon & Shuster Inc. 1990) [hereinafter COVEY 7 HABITS].

3. PROUDFOOT CONSULTING, MISSING MILLIONS—HOW COMPANIES MIS-MANAGE THEIR MOST VALUABLE RESOURCE (2003), *discussed in Wasted Labour Costs Millions*, COMPANY & SHAREHOLDER, Nov. 2003, at 65.

4. HP, 2005 ABRIDGED GLOBAL CITIZENSHIP REPORT—HP'S GLOBAL CITIZENSHIP PRIORITIES 5 (2005), *available at* http://www.hp.com/hpinfo/globalcitizenship/gcreport/downloads.html [hereinafter HP CITIZENSHIP REPORT 2005].

5. *See, e.g.*, Michael Mankins & Richard Steele, *Stop Making Plans; Start Making Decisions*, HARV. BUS. REV., Jan. 2006, at 76-84.

6. William Shakespeare, *Anthony and Cleopatra*, act ii, sc 2.

7. *See, e.g.,* THE WORLDWATCH INSTITUTE, VITAL SIGNS 2005 (W.W. Norton & Co. 2005), *available at* http://www.worldwatch.org/pubs/vs/.

8. Royal DSM N.V., *Sustainability in Business, in* TRIPLE P REPORT 2004: PEOPLE, PLANET, PROFIT (2005), *available at* http://www.dsm.com/en_US/html/sustainability/triplep04.htm.

9. SHELL INT'L LTD., SHELL GLOBAL SCENARIOS TO 2025 (2005), *available at* http://www.shell.com/home/Framework?siteId=royal-en&FC3=/royal-en/html/iwgen/our_strategy/scenarios/dir_scenarios_28022005.html&FC2=/royal-en/html/iwgen/leftnavs/zzz_lhn5_4_0.html.

10. *See* COVEY 7 HABITS, *supra* note 2, at 95.

11. To learn how Dalhousie University in Canada used the Delphi technique to develop its environmental action plan, see Tarah Wright, *Giving "Teeth" to an Environmental Policy—A Delphi Study at Dalhousie University*, presented at the Environmental Management for Sustainable Universities Conference, Monterrey, N.L., Mexico, June 9-11, 2004. *See also* N.C. DALKEY, DELPHI (The Rand Corporation 1967).

12. P&G, SUSTAINABILITY REPORT 2005—LINKING OPPORTUNITY WITH RESPONSIBILITY 61 (2005), *available at* http://www.pg.com/company/our_commitment/sustainability.jhtml.

13. *See* HP CITIZENSHIP REPORT 2005, *supra* note 4, at 4, 5.

14. See Figure 4.6 for examples of such groups.

15. ISO, ISO 14001: 2004 (2004), *available at* http://www.iso.ch/iso/en/CatalogueDetailPage.CatalogueDetail?CSNUMBER=31807&ICS1=13&ICS2=20&ICS3=10 (last visited Feb. 1, 2006). *See also* Appendix 3.2. International Organization for Standardization, *ISO 14004: 2004* (2004) §§3.7, 3.8, and 4.3.1, http://www.iso.ch/iso/en/CatalogueDetailPage.

CatalogueDetail?CSNUMBER=31808&ICS1=13&ICS2=20&ICS3=10 (last visited Feb. 1, 2006).

16. OHSAS 18001 §4.3.1. See Appendix 3.4 of this book for the citation and a summary of the standard. Center for Occupational & Environmental Health, *Hazard and Risk*, http://www.coeh. man.ac.uk/teaching_learning/resources/hazard.php.

17. STEPHEN POLTORZYCKI ET AL., EXPLORING PATHWAYS TO A SUSTAINABLE ENTERPRISE: SD PLANNER™ USER GUIDE app.: Definition of Sub-Elements (GEMI 2002), *available at* http://www.gemi.org/sd/.

18. *Id.*

Chapter 7

Selecting Goals and Indicators

"If you don't keep score, you're only practicing."[1]
—Vince Lombardi

Importance of a Clear and Elevating Goal

In the late 1980s, two experts on teamwork, Dr. Carl Larson and Dr. Frank LaFasto, undertook a study of 75 diverse high-performing teams—world-class cardiac surgery teams, championship college football teams, Antarctic expeditional teams, military units, accomplished business teams, and others.[2] The purpose of the study was to see if there are certain characteristics, practices, or features that consistently contributed to team success. Although Larson and LaFasto identified eight different elements that helped many teams to some extent, there was one element that each team possessed, one clearly more important than the others: a clear and elevating goal. Each team had a specific performance objective framed so that all members knew unequivocally whether or not it had been achieved. And each of these objectives was *elevating*—either in terms of being personally challenging or in the sense of being important and creating a sense of urgency. But it's not enough to say: "We will put a man on the moon by the end of the decade." Leaders must show they are taking reasonable steps to enable their teams to meet that goal. Without that support, the goal is hollow—a farce—even demoralizing.

Indeed, clear, inspiring goals visibly supported by management are essential tools for any company desiring to move its entire team of employees to a new way of thinking and acting. Such goals provide a yardstick for measuring progress and enable a company to make mid-course corrections in resources or tactics if progress drags. When a significant portion of bonuses, salary increases, or other rewards are attached to performance against specific goals, a powerful accountability mechanism is created, tugging at both the hearts and the minds of affected employees and instilling the focus and motivation essential for moving an organization toward its objective.

Setting inspiring, effective goals is definitely a challenge for business. A 2004 Harris Interactive poll of 23,000 U.S. industrial employees found that only one in five was enthusiastic about their department's and organization's goals.[3] For four out of five of the respondents, the goals were simply not working. Indeed, as noted in Figure 7.1, there are many reasons why goals fail. However, by giving more attention to goal-setting, companies can improve goal effectiveness, gain the advantages listed in Figure 7.2 and, at the same time, strengthen a tool critical to their march toward sustainability.

Figure 7.1
Why Goals and Other Indicators Fail to Deliver Performance

1. The measures aren't credible with intended data users because:
   a. the measures are based on unreliable, sparse, or old data
   b. the measures are being collected, compiled, and/or reported by people who are not trained or held accountable for doing so
   c. the meaning of the measures isn't clear
   d. the measures are not thought to be valuable or a priority by those who must perform to produce the desired results, or are not linked to important objectives of those people
   e. the people whose performance is needed for results are not aware of the measured results
   f. there are confounding factors other than those intended to be stimulated or controlled that affect the results; the cause-effect relationship is unclear; the actions needed to improve performance under the measure are not clear
2. The use of the measures isn't readily visible; management isn't interested in the results
3. There are too many measures or they are reported too frequently, which overwhelms data compilers and users
4. Results are reported too infrequently to keep the organization on course
5. There are too few measures and their context relative to other factors isn't well understood, e.g., having sales figures without profit figures
6. Not enough time is allowed for corrective actions to take effect; goals are too short term
7. There is no accountability or recognition for performance under the measure
8. Goal targets are unrealistic
9. The goals drive the wrong performance
10. The results aren't reported clearly or with sufficient detail and explanation
11. The results aren't used to make business decisions

Figure 7.2
Benefits and Purposes of Measurable Goals

1. Focuses organization on a common mission, enhances teamwork
2. Helps define accountability for action
3. Documents accomplishments; marks point of success
4. Serves as basis for granting rewards
5. Motivates people to perform
6. Provides early warning device for alerting organization if performance is slipping
7. Helps organizations manage and improve processes
8. Reveals the strengths and opportunities for improvement in tactics, programs, processes, people, and organizations
9. Makes personal performance evaluations more objective
10. Guides organization in allocating resources
11. Demonstrates responsiveness to stakeholders

Goal-setting should be part of the strategic and tactical planning process. Goals that are inspiring and simple, measurable, achievable, relevant, and time-based (SMART) should be included with each strategic objective so everyone can know whether or not the objective was achieved. The Balanced Scorecard (Figure 6.7) shows how that can be done. A plan with such goals framed around sustainability issues brings a company's sustainability policy to life; without such goals, the company statement becomes a mere "trophy policy," which—like the moose head hung on the wall to impress visitors—is simply dead.

Ideally, an individual worker should be asked to achieve no more than five goals, but given the number of hats most employees wear these days, it is not unusual to see them manage eight or more. If an employee is made responsible for more than five goals, the supervisor should help rank or weigh them to assure the most important ones receive proper emphasis.

Objectives, Goals, Targets, Indicators, and Metrics: What Do They All Mean?

Figure 7.3 is a rough depiction of the relationship among goals, metrics, and indicators as used in common parlance. The term indicator means different things to different people. To some, it is synonymous with metric, parameter, or statistic. Most often, however, it carries a broader con-

notation, suggesting a communication about some performance, characteristic, or condition that enables people to make decisions or value judgments about something—such as an activity, effort, result, situation, person, or thing. Borrowing from ISO 14031's definition of *environmental
indicator,* we can say that a *sustainability indicator* is: "A specific expression that provides information about an organization's
sustainability performance, efforts to influence that performance, or
sustainability conditions . . . ."[4]

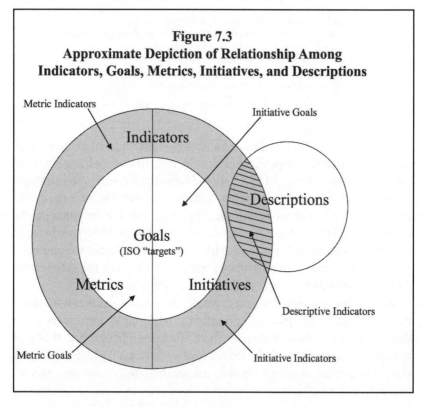

Figure 7.3
**Approximate Depiction of Relationship Among
Indicators, Goals, Metrics, Initiatives, and Descriptions**

For our purposes, there are three types of indicators:

1. *Metric indicator* (or just *metric*)—a quantitative standard of
measure or rating. Metrics are often expressed numerically, but
can be communicated through other measures, such as the A, B,
C, D, and F grades familiar to students, or high, medium, and low
ratings. Examples of metrics are provided in Appendix 7.

2. *Initiative indicator*—statement of status about a discrete project or task. This type of indicator would include, for example, an indication of whether a new human rights training program for security personnel has been developed.

3. *Descriptive indicator*—a qualitative description of conditions. A statement describing the elements of a company's existing SOS would be a descriptive indicator that helps readers judge a company's commitment to sustainability.[5]

A metric or initiative indicator critical to the success of an organization is called a key performance indicator (KPI). KPIs would include, for example, the measurable goals used for determining whether a company met its Balanced Scorecard (Figure 6.7) objectives. KPIs are not merely restricted to company-level performance; they can also be developed for subunits of an organization or for specific projects or activities.

Goals are indicators expressed as commitments to achieve some final level of performance or status. Since goals are directed to some end, one must be able to determine if that end has been achieved. The most common goals are metrics and initiatives expressed as commitments. "Score at least an 85% favorability rating on customer surveys by April 1" is a metric goal. An example of an initiative goal is "prepare a supplier diversity manual by January 31." A commitment to reach some described condition, such as "achieve good teamwork among core team members," is also an initiative goal, assuming there is some way to determine if it has been met. If this objective is adopted without any intention to survey members or otherwise gather feedback from them on progress, then this is just an aspirational or values statement and not a formal goal.

While a company and each of its functional departments should have only a few strategic goals, they will have many more goals in their tactical plans. In fact, most tactical objectives are nothing more than specific projects or other initiatives expressed as initiative goals. Consider the example of a tactical plan goal that reads: "Conduct employee-diversity training at a company leadership conference in northern Europe by September 15." Tactical plans may contain metric goals, too, such as: "Train one-fourth of the company's Chinese workforce on the organization's new ethics policy each quarter."

Baxter's goal to achieve a state-of-the-art environmental program in Canada, Puerto Rico, and the United States by the end of 1993, and in the rest of the world by the end of 1996, was a clear and elevating initiative goal supported by several metric goals. Those goals included having facilities and divisions in those regions conform to 100% of the applicable company management systems standards by the target dates, as well as achieving specific companywide reductions in hazardous waste, toxic air emissions, and packaging by 1996. Each unit was annually scored versus the management standards to track and encourage progress. Management compensation was linked with the achievement of the goals. This strategy produced the superior results recounted in Chapter 5.

The terms *indicators, goals*, and *metrics* as defined above reflect the way these terms are commonly used. The concept of *indicator* employed here is consistent with the way it is used by the GRI and formally defined in ISO 14001 and 14004. However, ISO also sometimes uses the term *indicator* in place of *metric*. What some might call annual or interim *goals*, ISO calls *targets*. It occasionally substitutes the word *goal* for its formal term *objective*, which refers to a longer term policy-like commitment of intent which may or may not be quantified. In ISO's view, the relationship among indicators, targets, and objectives is as shown in Figure 7.4.

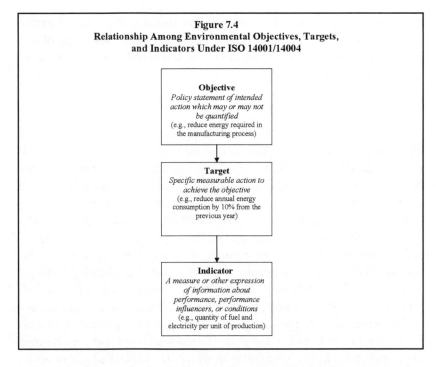

Figure 7.4
Relationship Among Environmental Objectives, Targets,
and Indicators Under ISO 14001/14004

Objective
Policy statement of intended
action which may or may not
be quantified
(e.g., reduce energy required in
the manufacturing process)

Target
Specific measurable action to
achieve the objective
(e.g., reduce annual energy
consumption by 10% from the
previous year)

Indicator
A measure or other expression
of information about
performance, performance
influencers, or conditions
(e.g., quantity of fuel and
electricity per unit of production)

One can debate whether indicators flow from measurable goals or vice versa, and whether goals need to be measurable at all. In practice, a number of indicators are usually proposed during planning, some are selected for use in crafting measurable goals, and then the target values of the goals are negotiated and approved.

While the terminology around various sustainability measures can be confusing, the key is to understand the concepts, then use a consistent terminology across the company. If a consistent terminology is already in place, follow it, while bearing in mind how the various terms are used elsewhere.

Other Types of Goals

Multi-Year Goals

Since most sustainability objectives cannot be fully accomplished within a single year, multi-year goals are recommended. A set of 5- or 10-year goals tells employees that this is a long-term strategic effort which will require some sustained focus and cultural change. Long-term goals also have the advantage of avoiding much of the research and sales effort that must be made to sell an entirely new goal each year. Still, some of this work is needed to establish annual targets and each business unit's allocation under them.

Collective Directional Goals

Long-term goals have some disadvantages, however. If the business changes dramatically, the opportunities for improvement may be significantly reduced, making the goal futile and unmotivating. Or the goal may be so easy to achieve that some operations reach their long-term goals early then sit on their hands not pursuing additional improvements. The long-term *collective directional goal* resolves these concerns. It is *collective* in that it depends on each part of the organization to contribute its share of the improvement according to its unique opportunities. It is *directional* because it is not absolute: If it is accomplished early, the target will be extended. On the other hand, if the goal later seems out of reach, it will be modified downward, provided circumstances have significantly and unexpectedly changed and all business units have given their best efforts but still can't achieve the goal. Communicating these expectations at the outset can help assure that employees stay motivated and progress is optimized. Annual targets against the goals are set to keep proper attention on the effort and allow for recognition and accountability for short-term performance.

Zero Goals

DuPont and some other companies have taken a different approach to long-term goals with the introduction of clear and elevating *zero goals*. Targets are set at zero for accidents, waste disposal, and regulatory noncompliance, thereby removing any implication that some level of them is to be tolerated. These goals can be inspiring as statements of philosophy or attitude, to be sure. Indeed, the idea that the job is not done until all accidents, wastes, and violations are eliminated is a general position management should espouse regardless of the goals. And on a facility basis, zero goals can often be achieved: certainly many sites have gone a number of years without any significant injuries or notices of violation. However, nobody really expects a large corporation to be able to reach that performance on a companywide basis. In that respect, these goals lose some credibility and effectiveness. From a companywide perspective, it is best to complement zero goals with realistic annual stretch goals to which clear accountabilities are attached.

Implied Goals

As previously noted, a company can have goals not based on metrics. It can also have metrics not tied to goals—at least explicit ones. For instance, let's say the companywide performance within your function is well below par. Your leadership team suggests this may be due to the high turnover in field managers, so you begin to measure this turnover. After the data is collected, the results seem excessive, so you make additional measurements to determine the main reasons for the turnover. You discover that too many professionals are leaving to take higher paying jobs at other companies. In response, you reassess and upgrade the manager position and establish new job qualifications, career paths, a job-posting process, and an annual job-satisfaction survey. Thereafter, you continue these measurements. If your preventive actions are effective, you should see a significant reduction in turnover and a higher percentage of it attributed to internal promotions.

This example shows how metrics can be used as management performance indicators for root-cause analysis. Although no explicit numerical goal was set in this case, an informal measure, such as the turnover rate among all company employees, could be used as a benchmark or *implied goal* to determine whether action is warranted. Once the problem is studied, corrective and preventive actions are taken, and performance reaches acceptable levels, this indicator can be dropped. Other metrics may also have implied goals or benchmark levels which mark unacceptable levels of performance and trigger action. If a metric has no explicit or implied goal or doesn't otherwise aid in decisionmaking, it should be eliminated. Metrics take time to develop, measure, and analyze, and competitive companies can't waste resources gathering data that has no purpose.

Setting Metric Goals

The trick of setting a good metric goal is finding a target that is achievable, not hopelessly beyond grasp, and yet challenging enough to stimulate real effort and innovative thinking—one that optimizes the rate of improvement without sacrificing attention to other key goals.

There are several ways to identify reasonable targets. One is to study the historical performance of the company and simply assume the same rate of improvement for the future. Or the target can be based on the past results of one or more of the better performing facilities—an approach that can encourage the widespread adoption of the best practices of these superior performers.

External benchmarks, which can be pulled from the reports of other companies or the government, may be helpful, too. A good place to identify goals of other businesses is in the public sustainability reports listed on, and available through, the GRI website.[6] For example, if you look at the reports of a number of companies and find they have been able to achieve roughly a 25% improvement in workplace safety each year, then a 25% improvement may be a good starting point for discussions about an annual safety goal at your company. However, if your company is just now introducing programs to strengthen its safety culture, perhaps a lower goal may be warranted, which could be increased annually as momentum builds. Likewise, government information on population and workforce diversity can present a starting point for determining a diversity-improvement goal.

Where performance against a goal will be dictated primarily by the installation of pollution controls or other major technical projects, the target can be determined by estimating the impact of those projects. On the other hand, where a wide variety of tactics will be needed to achieve a goal, the goal can be set by compiling the estimates from individual business units or facilities about their own opportunities for improvement. A variation of this approach is to base the target on expert evaluation of the opportunities at a few representative sites. Where site or project information is tallied, the results can be rounded upward to provide a company-wide target with a little stretch. Sometimes several of these techniques can be employed together, providing a cross-calibration to affirm the reasonableness of the target.

Other Types of Indicators

Indicators may be classified in several different ways in addition to the metric-initiative-description categories mentioned earlier. Other classifications of indicators are discussed below. Bear in mind as you review the following text, a goal is simply a type of indicator for which an expected level of performance is set. Consequently much of the guidance offered here on indicators is also relevant to goals.

Condition Versus Performance Indicators

The ISO 14031 environmental performance evaluation guidelines distinguish between *environmental condition indicators* and *environmental performance indicators*.[7] The former include a measure of a quality or property of a component in the environment, such as the concentration of contaminants in groundwater in milligrams per liter. The latter may be classified as either *operational performance indicators*—such as the gallons of fuel burned or the weight of hazardous waste generated per unit of product—or as *management performance indicators,* which focus on costs, personnel, training, maintenance, audits, or other management mechanisms or capabilities.

These indicator categories can be extended beyond the environment to sustainability as well: *sustainability management* and *operational performance indicators* would thus be those used for measuring internal conditions and performance; *sustainability condition indicators*, for tracking environmental, social, or economic conditions that are outside the organization but affected by it.

The vast majority of metrics publicized by companies are performance indicators rather than condition indicators. Condition indicators are commonly published by governments and social institutions. Companies do use environmental condition indicators but mostly for internal purposes, such as to determine the adequacy of cleanup efforts for soil, groundwater, or surface water contamination. They are also used in air pollution modeling needed to secure air permits for certain large emission sources. While this kind of data may be publicly communicated in local hearings and other limited discussions, because of its limited relevance, it is rarely reported in global sustainability reports.

One company that has used sustainability condition indicators is Suncor. Their 2005 sustainability report presents an interesting table showing the percentage impact they had on total provincial and nation-wide levels (conditions) for employment, charitable donations, and oil and gas production. Other condition indicators used by Suncor include the company's share of the total water use within the watershed; its portion of national forested lands disturbed by its development; and its percentage of its industry's emissions of greenhouse gases and other air pollutants within the province and nation.[8]

Leading Versus Lagging Indicators

Performance indicators may be *lagging or leading indicators*. Lagging indicators record the outcome of a company's processes, such as earnings per share (operational indicator), the pounds of waste generated (operational indicator), the percentage of its employees who are minorities (operational indicator), and the cost of pollution prevention (P2) projects (management indicator).

Leading indicators measure the attitudes, behaviors, efforts, or conditions that may eventually affect the outcome of concern. They provide early warning about where a company must shore up efforts to improve or sustain performance. Leading indicators include, for example, the following:

- The number of sites in full compliance with a company's management system standards (a management indicator which may later affect risks and regulatory compliance);
- The percentage of operations completing diversity training (a management indicator which may later affect diversity hiring practices); and
- Customer inventory levels (an operational indicator which may later affect sales).

By tracking and reporting the rate of change of lagging indicators, they can be used like leading indicators to gain a sense of future direction in performance. For example, a company can keep a list of its 10 sites that have improved the most over the last quarter and another of those 10 sites whose performance has slipped the most. Looking at these lists and the rates of change noted on them, one can project future performance and decide where best to apply resources. A factory operating at good levels but with performance that is slipping dramatically may well need more attention than one with poor performance that is improving rapidly.

Absolute Versus Ratio Metrics

Metrics can be designed to capture *absolute* values or may be used together in ratios showing *percentage, average, concentration,* or *per-unit* values. Absolute metrics record total weight, volume, area, distance, money, time, number, or other single parameter. They are most useful in communicating the total impact of the organization on the global sustainability of society. Percentage metrics communicate the percentage of absolute values, such as the percentage of board members who are women. Concentrations are expressed as milligrams per liter, people per square mile, or other quantity per spatial unit.

Per-unit metrics are normalized values expressed as either *intensities* or *efficiencies*. Efficiencies reveal the value gained for the sustainability burden incurred. They are determined by dividing units of production or service value (e.g., tons of steel produced) by the units of sustainability performance (e.g., pounds of waste generated). Intensities are the inverse of efficiencies, displaying sustainability burden per unit of value, such as pounds of waste generated per ton of steel produced. Efficiencies go up and intensities go down when performance improves. Examples of units of production activity and service value are shown in Appendix 7.1.1. Some common units of sustainability performance for companies as well as suggested ratio metrics are listed in Appendices 7.1.2 through 7.1.5.

Indexes

One problem with sustainability metrics is that so many of them may apply to a particular operation. The challenge when sustainability performance is measured under a number of metric goals is to find a way to combine these measures into a single metric that provides a quick picture of overall status—a metric that can be used to compare the general sustainability performance of a facility or other business unit with that of its peers. Indeed, without a measure of overall performance, it is difficult to determine in a consistent, objective way, the extent of bonuses or pay increases to be awarded managers who are being judged under a number of sustainability goals. An index can address these concerns.

Indexes may be designed in different ways. A simple version sets the baseline performance level for each measure at 0 and each target level at 100, then tracks progress along that continuum, adding the scores for all measures to compute a total index score for the operation. The problem with this approach is that all items being measured are given equal weight regardless of importance.

To overcome that problem, the Eastman Kodak Company developed an index with weighted scoring for environmental performance. A variation of their approach is shown in Figure 7.5. By identifying the level of performance for each measured result and multiplying that by its assigned weight, a weighted score for the measure is determined. The sum of the weighted scores for all items gives the overall weighted score that can be used to rank performance for benchmarking, compensation, or other reasons. Watercare Services Limited, a water supply and wastewater treatment company in New Zealand, uses an interesting variation on that approach. For each of its key objectives, it identifies 1 to 5 indicators, then sets 10 milestones or projects for each indicator. A score of 1 to 10 is given each indicator depending upon how many of the 10 milestones and projects have been completed. Each indicator is also weighted. Using the indicator scores and weights, an average weighted score is calculated for each objective.[9]

Figure 7.5 Method of Calculating a Sustainability Performance Index Score													
Progress Measures	Performance Level										Calculations		
	1	2	3	4	5	6	7	8	9	10	Actual Value	Level x Wt.= Score	
Recordable Injury Rate	≥1.20	1.10	1.00	.90	.80	.70	.60	.50	.40	.30	.55	7	30	210
Wastewater Exceedances	≥9	8	7	6	5	4	3	2	1	0	0	10	25	250
% Staff Trained on Diversity	≤55	60	65	70	75	80	85	90	95	100	83	6	20	120
Budget Performance (% Favorable)	≤-4	-2	0	2	4	6	8	10	12	≥14	-1	2	25	50
Source: Eastman Kodak[10]	Base-line			Goal			Stretch Goal	Total=		100	630 of 1,000

As with most indexes, the downside of the Eastman Kodak-Watercare approach is securing organizational buy-in for the assigned performance levels and weights, both of which demand subjective evaluation. In addition, the approach requires an additional administrative effort for designing, explaining, and completing the index forms. Also, it doesn't consider special circumstances beyond the control of the manager that help or hurt performance. That is not necessarily a bad thing, though, because it places sustainability performance on equal footing with financial performance. A big advantage is that once the table is set up, the accountability for results is fixed and most debate about the characterization and consequence of year-end performance is eliminated.

Indexes for Risk Rankings

An index based on weighted scoring can be the metric of choice for identifying the level of risk posed by a site or business unit, which, in turn, determines the level of resources, program complexity, audit priority, and general attention to be given an operation. Scoring can be based on historical or prospective information about its regulatory compliance, public relations, emergency incidents, and audit performance. Such scoring can also consider personnel competence, site hazards, size, and the surrounding environment, among other things.

Indexes for Audit Scores

Index scores are also sometimes used to measure audit performance. Audit index scores can be established by assigning weights to various characteristics of audit items, such as type, severity, extent of recurrence, degree of hazard, and time unresolved. Special weighting may be warranted for items posing risk of serious harm or concerning major program gaps, such as a lack of visible management support or weak self-assessment or corrective-action processes. A simpler non-index scoring method—one used by Baxter—involves just reporting the number of major, minor, and repeat audit items, categorized as regulatory, company requirement, or best practice. Classification of items by subject matter can also prove useful, especially in setting training priorities and planning program improvements.

Selecting Indicators

With all these types of indicators, how does one select those that are best for a particular company? A number of factors must be considered:

1. *Relevance to key organizational objectives and decisionmaking.* Indicators should directly or indirectly further the organization's key objectives. For a business, these objectives are often related to such issues as productivity, product appeal, growth, compliance, risk control, and reputation. They may be found in the organization's Balanced Scorecard (see Figures 6.7 and 6.8)

or other strategic planning documents, or in its statement of values or set of policies. When trying to identify sustainability indicators that support a company's objectives, it may be helpful to compare the objectives with the sample sustainability metrics provided in Appendix 7 and with the sustainability issues related to business success that are contained in Figures 3.1, 3.9, and 3.11. So, for example, if cost control and improved productivity are high priorities for the company, then metrics tied to savings from energy conservation, pollution prevention, and safety could be attractive. Sustainability and stakeholder trends within the organization can be another place to look for relevant indicators. If regulatory compliance has been wanting in critical areas, the selected measures should focus on that. If customer and stockholder relations are of concern, metrics related to surveys of these stakeholder groups may be useful. Whatever the metric, it must be viewed as important to the business—particularly to the people involved in measuring and delivering performance.

It's not enough, though, that the metric be associated with some business interest; a metric is only truly relevant to that interest if it measures something the organization can control or use in decisionmaking to help achieve or protect a desired outcome. For example, a trucking company may find it more useful measuring fuel efficiency in ton-miles per liter of fuel than in miles per liter, since fuel efficiency of a truck naturally goes down as its load increases. Moreover, measuring ton-miles per liter encourages practices—such as packing trucks more fully—that will maximize the economic and environmental value gained for the fuel purchased. Likewise, tracking the weight of disposed waste may prompt increased recycling, which is admirable but not nearly as sustainable or economically attractive as sound P2. A metric geared to waste generation levels would be a more effective way to encourage P2 and therefore more relevant to a business' financial and environmental interests. The point is, a company has little need for a metric that doesn't help much in achieving the desired business objective.

2. *Scope and location of operations.* Metrics for individual facility performance may not work for companywide performance, especially if intensity or efficiency metrics are used. Pounds of hazardous waste per liter of product may be appropriated for a

soft drink factory but not for the company as a whole if it is diversified and also has sites making snack foods and kitchen utensils. Employee diversity measures that work quite well in Europe and the United States may be problematic for locations in Africa, Asia, and the Caribbean, where there is a different mix of racial, religious, and employment issues.

3. *Purpose of measurement.* If a company wants to track reductions in air emissions of dioxin because of public concerns about community health effects, an absolute measure of emissions, rather than just intensity or efficiency metrics, would best address this concern. Concentration indicators would be preferred, however, if the concern was employee exposures to dioxin on a production line. An organization attempting to maintain and hone its already superior performance may desire leading indicators that detect early evidence of program erosion, such as those framed around training, resources, and the extent of conformance with operating system standards. If the objective is to track customer or employee opinions or attitudes, a metric built around survey scores may be most helpful.

A company that wants to build a strong ethics program would be wise to avoid a goal for reducing the number of calls to the ethics hotline. While this might be a sign that ethical behavior is improving, it would tend to dissuade management from encouraging hotline use. That would be unfortunate. An increased number of hotline complaints may actually be a good thing, signaling that employees are feeling more comfortable about coming forward—a critical element of a strong program. A more effective goal could be framed around ethics training, personal adherence to the ethics code, or some confirmation that all known issues of significance have been disclosed.

Indicators used to drive performance would be different than those for exploring possible root causes of performance failure. For instance, let's say a few site audits point to a decline in regulatory compliance that seems related to a cut-back in training, prompting the management to worry that this decline may be widespread. A company in this position could begin measuring training-related data, such as budgets, expenses, or training hours per employee, and compare this with the results from audits and agency inspections to see if a correlation exists between training resources and performance. If a correlation is found and the problem is discovered to be widespread, the collected data could be used to establish benchmark levels of training appropriate for various types and sizes of operations. Facilities falling below these benchmarks would be suspect and could be moved up the priority list for the next compliance audits.

4. *Vulnerability to illusory results.* The fourth consideration is whether the metric might produce illusory results or encourage manipulation and gamesmanship rather than motivating the desired behavior. Baxter was concerned about misleading metrics in 1989 when it set a goal aimed at reducing emissions of toxic air pollutants, including ethylene oxide (EtO) gas used to sterilize its medical products. To cut EtO emissions, the company adopted a multi-pronged approach, modifying the sterilization process, using more diluted EtO blends in place of pure EtO, and introducing alternative sterilization techniques. At the same time, though, the company was negotiating agreements with outside EtO sterilization contractors to meet some of its needs and was afraid this outsourcing would distort its true performance. To assure reported results were complete, the company measured not only its own EtO emissions, but the off-site contractor emissions associated with processing its products.

Other common metrics can also produce distortions if care is not taken. Currency rate fluctuations may affect profits of a transnational corporation (TNC). Consequently, their impact should be tracked and, where significant, reported to provide a more accurate picture of business financial performance. Similarly, a multi-product company wanting to improve overall waste efficiencies or intensities should be mindful of changes in product mix that may alter the results. One way to avoid the product-mix issue and drive waste-reduction and resource-conservation projects is to measure or estimate the baseline quantity once, then simply track the impact of the improvement projects as they are completed. This approach can be particularly useful if the total quantity—tons of packaging, for example—is large and difficult to track.

Measuring serious injuries where employees lose days away from work may be worthwhile, but if this causes a supervisor to simply reassign injured workers to other menial tasks without addressing underlying safety issues, then the purpose of the metric may be undermined. In that case, the metric can be broadened to also encompass injuries where the victims were reassigned. Alternatively, the company could look at all injuries whether or not they involve lost time.

So how do you know if the metric is producing illusory results? Follow up on significant changes in performance—both good and bad—to understand why the change occurred. This probing will not only reveal sham results but also confirm legitimate improvements. Moreover, it will uncover problems and best practices that can be shared across the organization to accelerate performance.

5. *Clarity.* The measurement must be easily understood by the intended audiences, both inside and outside the organization. These audiences must know what results reflect good performance and what are below par. A metric in common use among major companies and institutions should be preferred over one that is new and specially designed. For example, it is better to use tons of CO_2 equivalents to measure greenhouse gases than to concoct some other measure that is unfamiliar to others and lacks comparability. Clarity can be a problem with indexes, too. But while indexes may be useful for benchmarking and determining merit increases in compensation, they may be confusing to the public. A number of simple individual metrics are generally easier for them to understand.

6. *Suitability for benchmarking.* Suitability for benchmarking is another reason to opt for popular metrics over some new or obscure ones. Benchmarking can help highlight best practices and inject a dose of reality about how good a company's performance really is. Total charitable contributions may appear impressive at first blush, but not seem so great when expressed as a percentage of pre-tax profits and compared with the contributions of other companies on that basis. However, care must be taken that the measures provide for an apples-to-apples comparison. Comparing fines paid per billion dollars of revenue may be fair, but looking at the percentage reduction in waste may not, especially if one company undertook an aggressive waste-reduc-

tion initiative and picked much of its low-hanging fruit well before the latest waste baselines were set. Days sales outstanding (DSO)—the average period for paying invoices—may look bad for a company in contrast with that of a neighboring firm, suggesting the former is unduly harming suppliers for its own gain. However, the picture might not look so shameful if the review examines the ratio of days payables outstanding (DPO)—the average period for receiving payment from buyers—to DSO, and it reveals the company is paying its suppliers as fast as it is receiving payment itself.

7. *Obstacles to intended use.* Does the metric call for personal data that is private, technical numbers that are proprietary, or other information legally protected from disclosure? Will the information incite union workers? Might this data reveal the need to change something the organization cannot or would not change? Does it unfavorably complicate some current litigation or business negotiation? Where special sensitivities like these are suspected, appropriate counsel should be sought before the metric is adopted.

8. *Administrative burden.* A large administrative burden posed by an indicator can render it infeasible. This burden entails designing and implementing an approach to collect the data, train data providers and compilers, and evaluate the accuracy of reported data. It also involves following up on suspicious data, encouraging late reporters to submit their findings, and compiling and arranging the data for use. What is a tolerable burden? That depends on the value of the measure. Some strategies may help reduce the load, however. For example, if a company is already collecting injury and illness data from a majority of its sites to comply with the rules of OSHA, then the least burdensome way to collect safety data worldwide may be to extend current U.S. metrics and systems to non-U.S. operations—something commonly done for precisely this reason. Also, where the administrative burden initially seems too high, alternative approaches can be examined with a view to the degree of accuracy needed. Can small sites be dropped? Can minor sources of data within a site be ignored? Typically 85 to 90% of desired data is sufficient for most decisionmaking purposes. Moreover, missing data can

sometimes be reasonably estimated using surrogate measures or benchmarking information. For instance, if no significant process changes have been made, the inflation-discounted percentage growth in the value of production of a factory may be a good approximation for its percentage growth in waste generation.

But even with all these simplifications, the burden of collecting the data may still be too great to justify the metric. More often than not, though, the burden is underestimated. For this reason, it's wise to collect data under a new metric first on a pilot basis restricted to just a few operations before taking data collection companywide.

9. *Reliability of information source.* Planners who are developing metrics and goals must always think ahead, asking themselves how the data will be collected, who will provide it, and when it can be provided. If the source of information will be uncertain or unreliable, or the data can't be obtained when needed, the measure should be dropped, or at least postponed until the feasibility of data collection can be tested in a small pilot study.

Prioritizing Indicators

Once proposed performance indicators are evaluated in light of these nine factors, they can be prioritized for use. If many indicators have been proposed, it is essential this be done. As performance measurement expert Mark Graham Brown noted: "Having too much data is the most common and most serious problem an organization can have with its measurement system."[11] An overload of measures can dilute their potency and overwhelm those in charge of achieving, measuring, and reporting performance. Some priority measures—particularly those deemed least relevant to driving the most critical changes in performance—can be postponed for later adoption or dropped altogether. The KPIs that remain can be tracked in a brief report or "dashboard," as discussed in Chapter 10. Their visibility may also be strengthened by setting target values for them as formal goals.

Developing Complementary Goals and Other Indicators

By strategically linking complementary goals and other indicators, each can be strengthened. The following paragraphs illustrate how this can be done.

Linking Environmental and Social Goals to Financial Benefit

Goals can have extra motivational impact if they are aligned or linked with each other so a single effort can provide double benefit. The prime example is tying EHS goals to financial goals. This strategy tugs on both the hearts and minds of employees and broadens the appeal of the EHS goals to financial managers and others who otherwise would have little interest. Figure 7.6 shows, for example, how financial targets may be associated with environmental and safety goals.

Figure 7.6
Baxter's 2005 Environment and Safety Goals and Associated Savings Targets

Parameter	Reduction Target (%)	Base Year	Target 2005 Savings and Cost Avoidance ($ million)
Air toxic emissions per unit of production	80	1996	1
Hazardous and regulated waste generation per unit of production	35	1996	4
Non-hazardous waste per unit of production	35	1996	15
Energy use (and associated GHG) per unit of production	30	1996	30
Packaging materials per unit	20	1995	25
Employee work-related lost-day cases per 200,000 work hours	60	1996 }	
Rate for all employee work-related injuries and illnesses per 200,000 work hours	50	1999 }	25
TOTAL			100

Using Complementary Goals to Eliminate Undesirable Results

A fast-food restaurant that just measures and rewards its staff based on how fast they satisfy customer orders may soon find itself lacking in cleanliness and food quality. Having metrics and goals that address all the critical success factors—like speed, quality, cost, and compliance—is a way to assure that overall performance doesn't suffer at the expense of a single goal. Tying specific goals to each Balanced Scorecard objective also helps assure proper balance is maintained.

Using Indicators at Different Levels of the Organization

Except in the most highly decentralized companies, facility-level goals on establishing a management system can be strengthened if they are complemented with goals for establishing supportive interlocking systems at the business-unit and corporate levels. Likewise, a company that truly wants to improve employee development should set goals around it at all levels, although the timing of the rollout may dictate a staggered start.

Complementary goals may be worthwhile not only for different levels of the organization but also for different levels of employees. Generally, goals for management should include performance results, such as improving the score on an employee survey. Management might also have tactical targets around activities and behaviors that show their visible support for the objective. Targets of this type could include, for example, adopting new policies, sponsoring training, giving speeches, and coaching subordinates. Goals for lower level workers should be primarily oriented to their activities and behaviors that contribute to performance. For a company goal on employee development, employee-level measures might touch on completing training and working with supervisors to prepare personal development plans.

Using Different Types of Indicators to Address the Same Issue

A mix of metric, initiative, and descriptive indicators can be a good way to attack an objective comprehensively. In most cases, strategic metric goals will be supported by tactical initiative indicators on projects. For example, a metric goal to *allocate 25% of supplier spending to minority- and women-owned vendors* could be supported by an initiative indicator to measure the status of projects identified to help achieve that goal, such as a project of revising supplier evaluation criteria. A descriptive indicator calling for a short summary of the extent of implementation of the supplier program could round out the picture of progress toward the goal.

Lagging indicators on waste reduction and product quality can be augmented with leading indicators on the implementation of quality and EMS. If these measures are maintained for some time, they can provide a basis for assessing the effectiveness of the systems in producing results.

Using Different Indicators for Cause and Effect

We've already seen how metrics may be used to evaluate the cause-effect relationship between regulatory compliance and training. Combinations of cause and effect indicators can drive performance in other areas as well. Metrics on energy usage and cost can complement greenhouse gas metrics nicely, since the burning of fossil fuels contributes such gases. The cost metric can reveal the economic consequence, too, providing even more reasons to reduce fuel consumption.

The international Organization for Economic Cooperation and Development (OECD), the European Environmental Agency, and other environmental authorities favor a chain of environmental cause-effect metrics—termed DPSIR, which is the acronym for drivers, pressures, state, impact, and responses.[12] Figure 7.7 shows an example of this approach, noting how different metric topics might be used if fish stocks were being examined. Metric chains like this can be appropriate for companies as well.

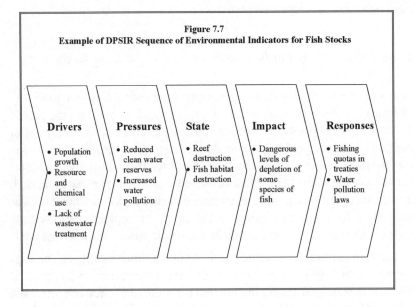

Figure 7.7
Example of DPSIR Sequence of Environmental Indicators for Fish Stocks

Drivers	Pressures	State	Impact	Responses
• Population growth • Resource and chemical use • Lack of wastewater treatment	• Reduced clean water reserves • Increased water pollution	• Reef destruction • Fish habitat destruction	• Dangerous levels of depletion of some species of fish	• Fishing quotas in treaties • Water pollution laws

Using Indicators by Stage of Process

The World Bank, DOE, and others use another sequence of indicators—this one examining various stages of a process.[13] Indicators are presented on inputs, the process itself, outputs, outcomes, and impacts. An example framed around regulatory compliance training is shown in Figure 7.8.

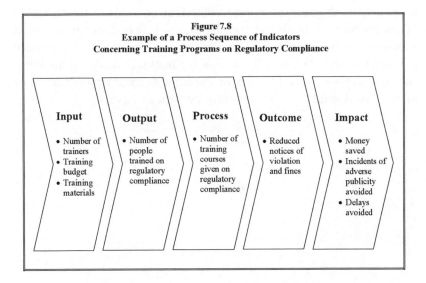

Figure 7.8
Example of a Process Sequence of Indicators
Concerning Training Programs on Regulatory Compliance

Input	Output	Process	Outcome	Impact
• Number of trainers • Training budget • Training materials	• Number of people trained on regulatory compliance	• Number of training courses given on regulatory compliance	• Reduced notices of violation and fines	• Money saved • Incidents of adverse publicity avoided • Delays avoided

Using Indicators Across the Supply Chain

Complementary indicators can also be spread across the supply chain. For example, product quality measures might begin with data on raw materials from the supplier, move to various metrics for tracking quality during the manufacturing and distribution processes, then look at product defects discovered by customers.

Using Indicators by Stage of Program Development

Indicators can be laid out in a multi-year plan as the program of concern proceeds through various levels of maturity. Environmental managers responsible for controlling air pollution emissions might track regulatory compliance first. Once that is mastered, risk control could be monitored.

Later, measurements might be directed to P2 and other ways to improve productivity. Finally a company could explore business opportunities, measuring the external marketability of its unique solutions to controlling air emissions. A good set of sustainability indicators of this type have been issued by Ethos, a Brazilian-based NGO with over 950 company members.[14]

Figure 7.9 offers a tool for tracking progress toward the development of a management system across various units of an organization. As noted in the instructions, a scoring method can be used to reflect the level of development of the system at each business unit or department as well as across the entire company. The scoring can also reveal which stage of the management system still requires considerable work within a unit and companywide. The form can be modified to incorporate different or more refined stages of program development as desired.

Figure 7.9
Form for Tracking Status of Development of Management System

Company/ Corporate Functional Department/ Division/ Region/ Facility/ Other Business Unit	1. Planning and Defining Requirements — Effective approach for defining what is to be achieved			2. Implementing Requirements — Effective approach for implementing what is to be achieved			3. Monitoring Progress — Effective approach for monitoring progress toward what is to be achieved			4. Addressing Monitoring Results — Effective approach for addressing results of monitoring (corrective and preventive action planning)		
	Substantially in place	Partially in place	Very little in place	Substantially in place	Partially in place	Very little in place	Substantially in place	Partially in place	Very little in place	Substantially in place	Partially in place	Very little in place

Notes:
1.
2.
3.

Instructions

Review this form with personnel who are knowledgeable about the status of the management system in the organizational unit listed, and check the box under each of the four categories that best describes the status of the management system in place there. In assessing this status, consider both the breadth of the system (what portion of the unit is covered) as well as the depth of the system (the average extent of development). For example a business unit with a system fully in place in only a very few of its facilities would rate the same as a system spread across all its facilities but which is only developed to a very small extent. If desired, a scoring system can be used with this form, for example, allocating a score of 2 for *Fully* or *Substantially in place*, 1 for *Partially in place*, and 0 for *None* or *Very little in place*. A score of 8 would mean everything is in place as required. By multiplying 8 times the number of departments or business units to be covered, a targeted total score for the company can be identified. By comparing the sum of the scores of all the units with the total target score for the company, a percentage implementation of the system across the company can be determined.

Role of Stakeholders in Selecting Goals and Indicators

As previously mentioned, each goal should support some strategic purpose that the organization determines is important enough to warrant its investment of resources. If that purpose is to help satisfy customers, employees, or other groups of stakeholders, those stakeholders should be consulted to determine if the achievement of the goal might increase their satisfaction. If several different goals and supportive indicators are being considered, stakeholders who are potentially affected can help identify those measurements that are likely to have the greatest impact.

A few words of caution, though: You should not ask for stakeholder feedback if you have already made up your mind about the goal and are not open to change. This can destroy credibility. Also, you will need to anticipate resistance from special groups that may be hurt if performance is poor. For example, unions may oppose safety goals if employee members are likely to see pay increases cut if accidents rise. Attaching financial consequences to managers rather than shop-floor employees might be the answer. This has the added benefit of not inhibiting the reporting of injuries by such employees. Also, unions might reject goals to reduce absenteeism or lost time due to injuries if they think this may cause injured workers to be rushed back to work when not fully recovered. To assuage their fear, case review procedures can be drafted, and healthcare workers trusted by both the union and the employer can be assigned to do these reviews. Likewise, suppliers might fight quality or diversity goals tied to contract payments if they believe the goals will be difficult to meet. In those cases, rewarding the supplier with a special bonus if the goal is achieved might be more palatable. While dialogue with external stakeholders can pose problems, in the end it often produces a more stimulating goal and effective result.

Feedback should also be solicited from those key individuals and groups within the company who are expected to perform or oversee the work toward the goal. If a facility, region, division, or other business unit is expected to contribute a particular level of performance, that share should be identified, agreed upon, and listed with other performance measures for which the unit is accountable. If this buy-in and clarity isn't established up front, progress toward the goal can be seriously retarded.

Getting this buy-in can be fraught with problems, however. The biggest one is sandbagging—the practice of intentionally underestimating the capability of the organization. Sandbagging is done for the purpose of assuring only minimal effort is needed to avoid adverse consequences and reap the rewards. Internal and external benchmarking can sometimes help break down this charade. Goals with sliding scale performance metrics, such as those presented in the index depicted in Figure 7.5, may help somewhat. The best remedy, however, is a strong leader familiar with the organization's operations and capabilities who can push back on the sandbaggers and coax them into stretch goals by appealing to their competitive nature and integrity.

Final Administrative Details

Before a metric goal or other key indicator is accepted, the questions presented in Figure 7.10 should be answered. Identifying in advance who is responsible for these issues will avoid headaches later on.

Also to be resolved in advance are the circumstances under which goal baselines should be adjusted. This becomes an issue when product lines, facilities, or business units are acquired from, or divested to, outside organizations, or when operations are started up or closed. Assume a company with 1.00 injuries per 200,000 work hours sets a goal to reduce this rate by 70% to a target of 0.30 between 2005 and 2010. Then in 2008, the company buys a new business with an injury rate of 2.00. Should the new merged business restate its own target? Weighing the impact on the measurement and the burden of data restatement, a company might elect to recalculate its safety target only if the acquisition or divestiture involved 5% or more of the company workforce. On the other hand, a company that has a goal to cut hazardous waste generation by 30% and later sells a facility could agree to drop that facility's waste from the baseline altogether if that can be done with little administrative effort. However, if the company closes the facility and distributes the production to its other sites, the companywide baseline could justifiably remain unaltered. The baseline could also remain unchanged if a small new operating plant is built, a new product line added, or production naturally grows, provided the size of the addition is small relative to the size of the overall business. These are but a few examples of the issues that may arise with baselines.

Figure 7.10
Goal and Indicator Implementation Issues

1. Where will the data be obtained?
2. Who will provide the data?
3. How and when will the data be supplied?
4. Who will supply instructions to the data providers and answer their questions?
5. Who will review and compile the collected data?
6. Who will track the timeliness and accuracy of data supplied?
7. How will data providers be held accountable for meeting reporting requirements?
8. How will the data be converted and presented in the performance report?
9. Who will convert the data and prepare the information for the report?
10. Who will maintain any needed documentation on the raw data and its conversion, and how long and where will it be kept? (If the data will be reported publicly, documentation should be kept for at least several years.)
11. Who will periodically assess the effectiveness of the goal/indicator and the data collection process in meeting the intended purpose, and recommend any needed improvements?
12. How can goals/indicators and data-collection processes be modified if needed?

Once a goal or other key indicator is set, organizational and stakeholder support is garnered, and the administrative details are planned, the goal or indicator can be rolled out for implementation. But just as care must be taken in developing a goal, it is also essential for its rollout. Indeed, that care can be the difference between an organization's success and failure in achieving its own objectives and pushing toward sustainability. Let us next examine how that rollout should be done through deployment, integration, and alignment.

Follow-up Checklist for Action: Selecting Goals and Indicators

☐ Resolve what terminology to use to cover objectives, goals, metrics, indicators, and related items.

☐ Include discussion of indicators and goals in planning meetings discussed in Chapter 6.

☐ Planning teams consider indicators and goals appropriate for key objectives, taking into account guidance of this chapter and lists of metrics in Appendices 7.1.1 to 7.1.5.

☐ Planning teams and management assure the clear assignment of responsibilities noted in Figure 7.10 for deploying, measuring, and reporting on identified goals and other key indicators. (See Chapter 8 for more information on deployment and Chapter 10 for more information on reporting.)

☐ Reevaluate effectiveness of goals and other indicators in follow-up planning sessions.

Endnotes to Chapter 7

1. Quote attributed to the legendary National Football League coach, Vince Lombardi, who lived from 1913 to 1970.

2. CARL E. LARSON & FRANK M.J. LAFASTO, TEAMWORK: WHAT MUST GO RIGHT/WHAT CAN GO WRONG 27-38 (SAGE Publications, Inc. 1989).

3. Harris Interactive, http://www.harrisinteractive.com/. *See also* Get Ready for the 8th Habit, FORTUNE, Nov. 29, 2004, at 160, 162.

4. *See* ISO, ISO 14031: ENVIRONMENTAL MANAGEMENT: ENVIRONMENTAL PERFORMANCE EVALUATION — GUIDELINES (1999) (ISO 14031:1999(E)), *available at* http://www.iso.ch/iso/en/CatalogueDetail Page.CatalogueDetail?CSNUMBER=23149 [hereinafter ISO 14031]. This definition is an amalgam of those for "environmental performance indicator," "management performance indicator," "operational performance indicator," and "environmental condition indicator."

5. For examples of sustainability-related descriptive indicators, see INSTITUTO ETHOS DE EMPRESAS E RESPONSABILIDADE SOCIAL, ETHOS BUSINESS SOCIAL RESPONSIBILITY INDICATORS 2004 (2004), *available at* http://www.ethos.org.br/DesktopDefault.aspx?TabID=3597&Alias= ethos&Lang=pt-BR [hereinafter ETHOS INDICATORS 2004].

6. GRI, *Organizations Using the Guidelines*, http://www.globalreporting. org/guidelines/reporters_all.asp. Another good website for locating company reports is CorporateRegister.com, http://www.corporateregister. com/data/companies.pl?com=121 (last visited July 18, 2006).

7. *See* ISO 14031, *supra* note 4.

8. SUNCOR, 2005 REPORT ON SUSTAINABILITY: OUR JOURNEY TOWARD SUSTAINABLE DEVELOPMENT — STEPPING FORWARD THROUGH INNOVATION AND TECHNOLOGY (2005), *available at* http://www.suncor.com/ data/1/rec_docs/616_Suncor%20SD%20Report_2005%20.pdf.

9. WATERCARE, ANNUAL REPORT 2004—CONSTANT PROGRESS, CONTINUOUS SUCCESS (2005) and WATERCARE, ANNUAL REPORT 2005—WATERSHED: AN INTEGRATED APPROACH (2006), *both available at* http://www. watercare.co.nz/default,publications.sm.

10. GEMI, MEASURING ENVIRONMENTAL PERFORMANCE: A PRIMER AND SURVEY OF METRICS IN USE app. C (1998), *available at* http://www.gemi. org/MET_101.pdf.

11. MARK GRAHAM BROWN, KEEPING SCORE: USING THE RIGHT METRICS TO DRIVE WORLD-CLASS PERFORMANCE (Amacom 1996).

12. *See, e.g.*, European Environmental Agency, *Indicators*, http://themes. eea.eu.int/indicators/all_indicators_box?sort_by=dpsir. *See also* A. WARHURST, SUSTAINABILITY INDICATORS AND SUSTAINABILITY PERFORMANCE MANAGEMENT 36 (IIED & WBCSD 2002).

13. WILL ARTLEY & SUZANNE STROH, DOE, THE PERFORMANCE-BASED
    MANAGEMENT HANDBOOK, VOLUME TWO, ESTABLISHING AN INTE-
    GRATED PERFORMANCE MEASUREMENT SYSTEM 36 (2001), *available at*
    http://www.orau.gov/pbm/pbmhandbook/pbmhandbook.html.

14. *See* ETHOS INDICATORS 2004, *supra* note 5.

Chapter 8
_____

Bringing Sustainability to the Front Line: Deployment, Integration, and Alignment

> *"Many people regard execution as detail work that's beneath the dignity of a business leader. That's wrong. To the contrary, it's a leader's most important job."*[1]
> —Larry Bossidy

Why Things Don't Get Done

Teenagers know that it's one thing to say you will clean up your bedroom; it's another thing to actually do it. As the famous 18th-century Scottish poet Robert Burns noted: "The best laid plans of mice and men often go awry."[2] Unfortunately, when that happens, when plans are not properly executed, unpleasant consequences often follow, not the least of which is disappointing those around you—parents if you are the teenager; superiors, subordinates, and stakeholders if you are a company employee.

Execution is what gives life to ideas like an SOS. Getting things done takes people, organizations, ideas, and plans—but that's not all. When it comes to a system like an SOS, execution won't be complete until the system becomes part of the culture of the organization—a way of doing business, part of its life-blood rather than a separate appendage that is the exclusive domain of a particular department or function. People in all corners of the company must accept the system as their own and know their role in implementing it. This gives the system a critical mass of support which keeps it alive for the long term, through good times and bad, and regardless of changes in leadership or other personnel.

Unfortunately, this broad ownership often fails to materialize with many company initiatives. One reason it may fail is because no one effectively *deployed* the initiative into the ranks of employees and *integrated* it into the company's existing tools, processes, procedures, programs, and values. It also may fail because efforts have not been *aligned* across the organization and people haven't been convinced to pull together. Without this alignment, the power of the leader's message and her ability to effect cultural change are significantly diminished. As with executing other company visions, in order to successfully execute our vision for sustainability, to properly implement an SOS, we need deployment, integration, and alignment—the actions for planting sustainability deep and wide throughout the organization.

Business teams often devote considerable effort to plan the development of some new program, policy, or tool but give little thought to the rollout. They celebrate the completion of the work product, then make a posting on the company's website or in a manual and consider the job done. When companywide adherence to the policy or use of the tool is poor, they shake their heads in wonder. They blame noncompliant employees for shirking their duties without considering that most of the fault may lie closer to home. No one bothers to tally the wasteful losses from poor deployment, integration, and alignment—how much delay is caused in achieving conformance, how much work is wasted in audits, explanations, and other follow-up. Often this is chalked up to "the way business is done." And with the next rollout, the waste and delay are perpetuated. Careful planning of deployment, integration, and alignment can save much of that waste and grief. Let us see what those measures entail.

Deployment: Rollout Tools and Field Implementation

Deployment is about spreading some practice, procedure, program, or tool across an organization. Typically deployment comes in two stages:

> 1. *Developing and testing rollout tools:* planning and preparing those communication and training aids and tactics needed to roll out the initiative (see Figure 8.1 for examples of common deployment tools); and
> 2. *Field implementation:* using the tools in the field to convey understanding, responsibility, and accountability to others.

Each stage warrants careful consideration.

Figure 8.1
Common Deployment Tools

Audit checklists
Award celebrations
Award criteria
Brochures
Customer testimonial
Diagrams, drawings
Display booths at company fairs
Employee announcements board
Employee meeting discussions
E-reports
E-training programs (live, on-demand, simulations, interactive, etc.)
Executive speeches
Exhibits, models, samples
Films, photos
Frequently asked questions
Learning maps
Manuals
Memos
Model personal performance objectives
Newsletters, magazines
Phone mail messages
Posters, flags
Press releases
Promotional items (calendars, pens, etc.)
Self-assessment checklists
Skits, role-playing performances
Symbolic activities (tree planting, public donation, etc.)
Tapes, CDs, other recordings
Training-evaluation forms, tests
Training presentations
Train-the-trainer presentations, guides
Websites

Developing and Testing Rollout Tools

Let's say we want to roll out a new sustainability policy like Figure 2.2. The first thing we must do is decide what we want to accomplish with the rollout. Perhaps we want to familiarize people in the organization with the content and meaning of the policy, and explain to them what an SOS is. We may also want to discuss why it should be adopted, and prepare employees for later stages of the SOS rollout. Once we've decided *what* we want to deploy, the next thing for us to determine is *how* to deploy it and *who* will do it. Figure 8.1 provides some methods we can consider. In our case, we might develop appropriate training materials, as well as tools for testing the effectiveness of the training. We may also need to prepare and conduct train-the-trainer sessions, perhaps pilot the training at a few sites, and adjust the training based on the feedback received. To spread the message more broadly, we may want to ask our communications department to draft articles on the policy and SOS for the company's newsletter and website, and prepare some remarks on it for a CEO speech. If the policy is one to be covered in audits, then someone may want to prepare self-assessment checklists or other tools for follow-up evaluation. Finally, we might identify and communicate the names and phone numbers of experts who will be on call to answer questions.

Those in charge of the policy rollout must identify which people to target. Is it just the communications function, or are we also concerned about research and development, human resources, business development, EHS, quality, finance, and other groups? Must *every* employee be involved somehow? Planners must determine how far the deployment will extend vertically—that is, across corporate, regional, divisional, and facility levels. They must also define how far the rollout will reach horizontally across departments and functions at each level. A good way to mark off these boundaries for deployment is by asking, who at what levels must implement, support, and use the tool or initiative being deployed in order for the organization to achieve its objective. In the case of a sustainability policy and SOS, as in many other instances, a multi-tiered approach will most likely be warranted, with all employees acquiring some understanding of the matter, and specific groups receiving more in-depth training.

After the planners identify the groups to be covered by the deployment, they must sort out how the deployment tools and training will be delivered to them. For large organizations, this typically is done through a series of trainings or other communications that course through the company from one department or level to another. Figure 8.2 shows one example of the paths that deployment of a sustainability initiative might take in a large corporation. Once deployment reaches a particular business unit or facility, someone there will need to spread the initiative to fellow members of those organizations. Those selected for this task should be able to rely on guidance provided by the planners of the companywide deployment.

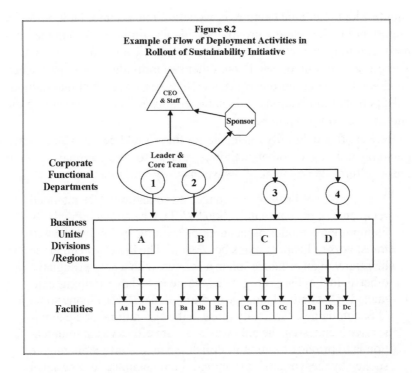

Figure 8.2
Example of Flow of Deployment Activities in
Rollout of Sustainability Initiative

If a wide range of groups or regions are to be targeted for the deployment, appropriate flexibility must usually be designed into the deployment tools to account for the location, size, risk, complexity, and type of operation. For example, flexible fill-in-the-blank provisions and optional clauses can be incorporated into memos, standard procedures, announcements, or other written documents. Training materials and films can be prepared in various languages. Simplified versions of tools can be developed for small operations. This kind of flexibility can significantly improve the chances the deployment will be well received across the organization.

Cultural factors—the collective values, beliefs, attitudes, and behaviors of the target group—may also play a role in the design of deployment strategies and tools.[3] The factors identified below are particularly important for deployments across countries but may also be a concern when deploying across different employee categories. The approach taken with Americans may not work for Latin Americans, just as the one for shop-floor workers may not be effective with the academic crowd in research and development. One caution, however: While cultural factors can be important in addressing a group, individuals within that group may exhibit cultural characteristics that vary significantly from the norm. Therefore, a rollout to the CEO or other key individual, especially when conducted on a one-on-one basis, should take into account that individual's personal motivations and characteristics rather than assuming the cultural stereotype applies.

Here are five culturally related issues that should be considered when planning training or other activities related to international or other cross-cultural deployment of a sustainability initiative:

> 1. *Language.* What is the language and education of the intended recipients of the communication? Will we be able to effectively communicate model procedures or training in English or will translators or local speakers be needed? The lower you go in the hierarchy of an organization in a country with a native language other than English, the greater the need to have training conducted in the native language of the audience. Even among some U.S. companies, especially those in the agricultural or cleaning-service businesses, the only way to assure effective communication is to provide training in Polish, Spanish, or other language spoken by the workers. If training is being planned for low-level illiterate workers, then role playing and skits can be a useful part of oral training.

A few other language questions:

> • *Are we using slang or jargon that is not understood locally?* Unless we are in Japan, the United States, or some Spanish-speaking Caribbean country, listeners probably won't comprehend what is meant by "hitting it out of the park" or "made it to first base." If soccer, not baseball, is the sport of choice, then soccer analogies should be used.

> • *Is technical data presented in feet and pounds when the audience understands only meters and kilograms?*

> • *Are we properly attuned to differences in the meaning of words?* For example, if a U.S. business person says a proposal *bombed* or was *tabled*, a U.K. citizen would think she meant just the opposite of what was intended. Do all parties attribute the same meaning and weight to the words "yes" and "no"? In some

places, people use those words the same way an American would use the words "I see" or "uh huh," just to acknowledge they are listening. In India, the Middle East, and northern Africa, it is uncommon to receive "no" in answer to a serious request. In Brazil, "no" is rarely the final word; there is always room for further negotiation.

2. *Authoritarian (trainer-orientation) versus participative (participant-orientation) approach.* Training sessions planned around extensive group discussion, team breakouts, feedback, and debate may work well in Australia, Canada, South Africa, the United States, or western Europe—societies that are generally egalitarian and internally competitive. Participatory sessions may not work so well in the Arabic Middle East, Asia, eastern Europe, Latin America, or northern Africa, where hierarchy is more respected, open confrontation less tolerated, and more emphasis is placed on relationships than tasks. Deployment techniques involving face-to-face interaction are more valuable among the relationship-oriented cultures than among the more egalitarian, participative, task-oriented cultures. However, a good presenter who uses the local language and has carefully planned the session can often do wonders in persuading an audience to participate.

3. *Perceptions about legal and voluntary standards, detailed procedures.* The United States is noted for its regulatory-legal emphasis with strong enforcement for noncompliance. In contrast, Europeans and Latin Americans generally see regulations and standards more as guidelines. China, Japan, and northern Europe value ISO and other voluntary standards and detailed procedures more than the United States does. Many in the United States are suspicious of such standards, believing they are too rigid and bureaucratic, and fearing that somehow the public may hold users accountable for strict compliance. When standards or procedures are rolled out internationally, deployment planners must try to anticipate objections of this type. Where resistance is likely to occur—especially those places where strong opposition to similar initiatives has been voiced in the past—planners should develop ways to address it in the deployment materials and approach, such as by allocating more time to discussing the purpose, value, and implications of the initiative.

4. *Cultural/political predisposition for the issue.* For a variety of reasons, the people of some regions and cultures may be predisposed to favor a particular issue or to oppose it. This may be due to social, economic, or political conditions; some historical event; or a recent disaster or scandal. In poor nations, economic development and social equality will typically be of greater interest than environmental matters. Northern Europeans may be more concerned about product environmental issues than those from Asia, Latin America, or the United States. A plea for strong corporate governance may find more sympathetic ears in the United Kingdom and the United States than elsewhere. Of course, the predominant attitude of any particular group may run counter to the popular view within their region. Nevertheless, those planning deployment should be alert to these regional and cultural attitudes and be prepared to address them candidly in the approach and tools for rollout.

5. *Time-related issues.* Deadlines may be considered mere guidelines in Latin America and northern Africa unless accompanied by live discussion and frequent follow-up.

Other issues concerning time—or, to be more specific, timing—also come into deployment planning, such as the following:

• *If a series of tools are to be deployed, are they properly sequenced taking into account priorities and whether certain items must be mastered before others are introduced?* For example, if a new ethics program is to be rolled out, some broad training on the purposes and organization of the program should occur before the rollout of online learning programs on specific topics like sexual harassment, privacy, or nondiscrimination.

• *Are competing deadlines or assignments being placed on employees?* For example, will the target audience be consumed learning about the new e-program for personal performance objectives or undergoing a big quality audit at the same time you are planning a sizeable rollout to them?

• *Should the rollout of an initiative be made to all affected parts of the organization at roughly the same time, or should it be deployed to some parts of the organization before others?* A simultaneous deployment is usually preferred for its speed and efficiency. As a practical matter, however, a phased approach may be needed if the deployment team lacks the resources to do it all at once. Then too, a phased rollout may be better if speed is not critical and either the deployment is complicated or some parts of the business may resist it. Under such circumstances, the initiative can be first deployed to those influential parts of the organization where the rollout is likely to be easiest and the chances of acceptance the greatest. This can build a momentum of peer support for the initiative among business units, reducing the obstacles to later deployment. The odds of success can also be enhanced by applying the lessons from early deployments to improve those that follow.

• Finally, *will the deployment of some tool be scheduled for completion just before people are expected to use it so they can quickly apply the lessons learned?* If there will be a big delay between training and use, can that be corrected? If not, what arrangements will be made for helping those who need refresher training?

To effectively plan a deployment, these questions must be answered.

Field Implementation

Once the essential rollout tools and planning are ready, field implementation can begin. Ideally, the deployment planning team will select well in advance those who will perform the training and coaching in the field. Cultural considerations may play a role, here too, leading to a preference for local people as trainers or co-trainers. Sometimes, however, cultural considerations may be trumped by company policies, such as those promoting equal opportunities for women and minorities. When that happens, special care should be given to planning the rollout timing and content. A pre-visit call between high-level executives from the training and target groups may help lay a foundation for success. The target group executive can also contribute in other ways, such as by sending a memo or voicemail message to her group to introduce and support the trainer, or by expressing that support in a short introductory speech at the outset of training.

Visible Management Support

Indeed, visible management participation in deployment sends a strong message that the initiative and training should be taken seriously. It can foster greater cooperation and more active engagement of employees in the effort. But to be effective, this participation must be more than "do as I say"; it must be "do as I do." Management must model the behavior they want from others, and show they are willing to do whatever they can to support the initiative. They must demonstrate that what is being rolled out truly matters. That's because what matters to a supervisor—the person who dispenses salary and career rewards—most often matters to subordinates.

Follow-Up

Field implementation doesn't end after the first round of training. Follow-up discussions, reviews, audits, or tests should be conducted to evaluate the effectiveness of the training. Someone must determine if the message stuck, if people are performing as hoped. If not, the deployment approach must be reevaluated and a new, more effective one implemented. In addition, an arrangement must be made for refresher training, if needed, and for communicating the information to employees who join the organization later.

Integration

If deployment is the method for casting ideas broadly across an organization, integration is the method for planting them deeply. Strictly speaking, integration is a part of field implementation. It usually starts with generic introductory training. Then the deployment representative and one or more target group representatives collaborate in identifying the existing policies, standards, procedures, programs, practices, structures, and tools of the group that should be modified to incorporate the new item. Integration—mixing the new into the old as shown in Figure 8.3—is preferable to adding an entirely new tool or program, especially when it comes to employees who may already be facing more new programs than they can absorb.

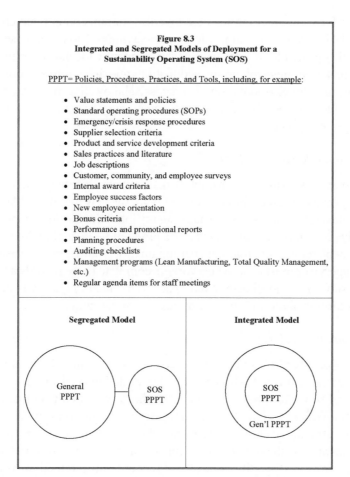

Figure 8.3
Integrated and Segregated Models of Deployment for a
Sustainability Operating System (SOS)

PPPT= Policies, Procedures, Practices, and Tools, including, for example:

- Value statements and policies
- Standard operating procedures (SOPs)
- Emergency/crisis response procedures
- Supplier selection criteria
- Product and service development criteria
- Sales practices and literature
- Job descriptions
- Customer, community, and employee surveys
- Internal award criteria
- Employee success factors
- New employee orientation
- Bonus criteria
- Performance and promotional reports
- Planning procedures
- Auditing checklists
- Management programs (Lean Manufacturing, Total Quality Management, etc.)
- Regular agenda items for staff meetings

Segregated Model   **Integrated Model**

General PPPT — SOS PPPT

SOS PPPT
Gen'l PPPT

The concept can best be understood with a few examples. Let's say an organization wants to roll out new policies respecting the privacy of certain employee records. It might integrate those policies into other existing human resource or occupational health procedures concerning recordkeeping. A company that is emphasizing a special cost-trimming program like "Lean Manufacturing" in its factories and desires to stress pollution prevention can integrate the latter into the former. Criteria for personal performance reviews could be modified to integrate a new company policy on employee development. A safety procedure could fit nicely into the standard operating procedure (SOP) for a machine. Conformance to recently enacted policies on ethics may serve as one of the criteria for some internal business award. Programs on climate change might be linked with existing energy cost-savings efforts. Likewise, sustainability principles may be included in companywide multidisciplinary programs on strategic planning, acquisitions and divestitures, recruiting, and new employee orientation. As discussed below, they may also be incorporated into compliance assurance, emergency response, and change management processes.

Reinforcing Responsibilities

Deployment with integration only works, however, if management of the target group reinforces the accountability for the new initiative. Management must resist protests of: "That's not my job!" For instance, if product quality procedures are integrated into a production procedure, line workers may be required to maintain certain quality records. In that case, the line supervisor must ensure her workers complete those records and not try to shift that recordkeeping duty back to the facility quality manager. Integration is about building in duties, not separating them.

Integration Overload

Supervisors should listen to employee concerns, though, if "integration overload" is suspected. This can often be spotted through employee surveys and from informal feedback from those who aren't routine complainers. With global market pressures driving frequent corporate downsizing, a strategy of choice is frequently downsizing of functional groups accompanied by the integration of functional responsibilities within operating groups. If quality control workers are cut, production workers may be expected to assume their duties. But when new duties are repeatedly added and none removed, employees may soon find themselves stretched so thin that even the most essential duties suffer and morale sags. If employees are at the breaking point, their supervisors can help by prioritizing their work, or, even better, by providing the guidance and tools their employees need to do this ranking themselves. Supervisors can also help by occasionally culling out old policies and practices that have lost their value. Systematizing the approach through model procedures and forms can often reduce the burden, too. Internal and external benchmarking can sometimes help find labor-saving solutions. To the extent possible, managers and deployment planners must make the integration seamless so that it becomes more about the way work is done and less a matter of adding new onerous tasks on top of old ones. Proper planning and execution in this regard can pay big dividends in efficiency. Says Dennis Shoji, senior director of Facilities/EHS at healthcare manufacturer Edwards Lifesciences: "Never underestimate the ability of an organization to take on more work. With effective deployment and integration, it is amazing what can be accomplished."[4]

Alignment

Alignment sets the guardrails of deployment. Its purpose—as represented in Figure 8.4—is to assure that all parts of the organization are moving in the same general direction, thereby enhancing efficiency and maximizing the momentum for change. If done properly, good alignment resolves internal political struggles for program direction, which, in turn, reduces inefficient, destructive intracompany competitiveness, prevents the duplication of resources, and improves teamwork. As mentioned in Chapter 5, one of the benefits of an SOS is that it stimulates alignment around common priorities, and helps harmonize different management systems that may be in place around a company.

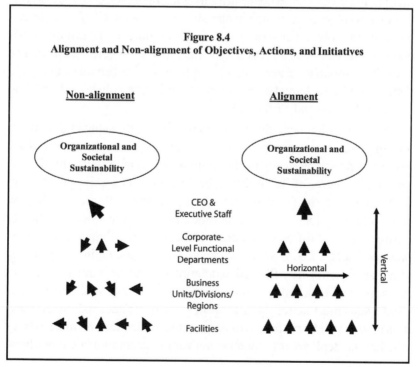

Figure 8.4
Alignment and Non-alignment of Objectives, Actions, and Initiatives

Like deployment, alignment occurs both vertically and horizontally. If we are deploying some sustainability policy, procedure, practice, or tool throughout a company, we must assure that it is aligned with the overall objectives of the corporation, and that our deployment efforts are substantially consistent across the corporate, regional, division, and facility levels (vertical alignment). Looking at Figure 8.2, we also must ensure that the rollout to division A is generally consistent with that to division B (horizontal alignment), or—even more important—that what is rolled out to facility Aa by division A is generally consistent with what is rolled out to facility Bc by division B (horizontal and vertical alignment). In Chapter 6, we saw an example of horizontal and vertical alignment in Figure 6.10. A tool like Figure 6.10 can clarify how well multiple groups are aligned to a common objective, and highlight gaps in cases where that alignment is suspect or uncertain.

Besides assuring good vertical and horizontal alignment across business levels and groups, the deployment planner must also promote good alignment *within each group*. Each group's sustainability performance metrics and goals should be in harmony with, or—even better—a part of, its business objectives, which in turn should be linked with PPOs and bonus and other reward criteria. Without this alignment, the group can become confused about direction and frustrated if expected performance doesn't materialize. Even worse, employees may become angry and demotivated if they mistakenly work toward wrong objectives and find no reward at the end of the effort.

To achieve alignment, the deployment can take the same timing, form, and approach across groups. More often that not, though, variations are made to best fit the needs of the individual business units and departments. The degree of flexibility in the deployment as well as in the item being deployed should be defined during planning. If a new policy on charitable donations is to be rolled out, planners must decide whether business units in different regions will be allowed to modify it to meet their own needs. Likewise, if a companywide goal on minority hiring is established, someone will need to determine if business units must meet the same goal or whether some variation will be allowed. Other alignment issues must be resolved as well, such as whether individual business groups will be permitted to revamp the model training materials, or whether the deployment schedule can vary to accommodate other local priorities. By clearing up these issues early, future confusion and delay can be minimized.

Special Concerns in Particular Functions

Who is responsible for deploying, integrating, and aligning sustainability initiatives across a company? Who must initiate and oversee the process? Typically, that responsibility falls to those who lead various functional groups. Appendix 6 lists some sustainability-related activities that individual functional groups may need to deploy, integrate, or align.

Sustainability in the Rollout of Cross-Functional Activities

Deployment, integration, and alignment of sustainability initiatives also come into play in a number of cross-functional activities traditionally undertaken by a company, including compliance, emergency response, and change management, as discussed below.

Compliance

Companywide regulatory compliance—an inherent part of economic, social, and environmental responsibility—can often benefit from common compliance program tools, such as noncompliance tracking logs and periodic status reviews with management. It is not unusual to see an operation struggling with compliance in one area also have problems in others, often for the same underlying reasons. A good way to proactively uncover these cross-functional compliance problems is through a companywide compliance council consisting of representatives of all functions with auditing or legal-compliance responsibilities. Besides sharing information about problem sites, business units, and compliance trends, the council can also serve as a good forum for coordinating audit schedules and for internal and external benchmarking on best auditing and compliance assurance practices.

Issues Management; Emergency Response; Risk Management

Issues management is another cross-functional area that often involves sustainability. Issues, such as serious explosions and fires, product safety problems, environmental and community disasters, government investigations, and executive criminal activity can sometimes slip into threatening situations. This may call for local emergency response or companywide crisis management involving several different functions. To address those situations, many companies have established procedures and roles for employees and teams to follow in identifying, communicating, and managing these issues. To assure a prompt and effective response, these roles and procedures must be coordinated and aligned across many functions. Those who are assigned to respond must know these roles and procedures well. Annual reviews, training, drills, and other measures can keep that knowledge fresh and assure these programs remain strong, aligned, and up to date.

Closely related to issues management is risk management. Risk management involves looking at various issues to decide which ones are significant risks, and then developing preventive and mitigating measures to reduce the significant risks to acceptable levels. Corporate boards in the United Kingdom and the United States are being asked to oversee companywide "enterprise risk management programs" as part of their governance responsibilities.[5] These ERM programs also require effective deployment, integration, and alignment around sustainability issues that pose short- and long-term threats.

Change Management

Change management is an additional cross-functional activity that is important in the rollout of a sustainability initiative. Proposed significant changes in processes, operations, facilities, organizations, products, and services should be evaluated from a sustainability perspective. This review can help assure that both the impact of sustainability issues on the change, as well as the impact of the change on sustainability, have been considered. Will certain employee or community groups be angered? Are serious financial or environmental risks involved? Are important ethical or safety concerns being ignored? Will resources and energy be used efficiently? These are the kinds of questions that may need to be asked. Besides producing better decisions, a sustainability review has side benefits: it is one of the best ways to raise awareness about sustainability and its impact on the business. Employees can repeatedly see how sustainability affects everyday operations. Using change management processes in this manner can go a long way toward infusing the sustainability ethic into the life-blood of the organization.

Overcoming Resistance: What If They Slam the Door in Your Face?

All of this guidance on deployment, integration, and alignment can help improve the speed and effectiveness of the rollout of a sustainability initiative. Still, there are always those groups or individuals who are not willing to buy what you are selling. They simply aren't inclined to embrace the concept of the SOS and sustainability goals and integrate sustainability considerations into their work. In short, given their other interests and competing priorities, they don't care enough to take action.

Before you push too hard against resisting groups, the first question to ask is: Does the adoption of the initiative by the resisting group actually add significant value to that group or to the company as a whole? If it doesn't, then the deployment to that group should be halted. On the other hand, if that question has already been seriously considered and answered by management in the affirmative, then the next question is: What can be done to convince the resisting parties to support the deployment? Earlier in Chapter 4, we discussed a number of tactics for selling the value of an SOS to upper management, including the following: gain allies; explain the importance of the initiative to the business; create a strong sense of dissatisfaction with the status quo; use their lingo; understand their business and issues; and use short-term wins to increase momentum and peer pressure. Many of the same tactics work well in overcoming resistance to deployment at lower levels, too.

However, two steps are often more effective than all the others in coaxing the doubters and resisters on board. One is to search for common ground—find ways you can use the SOS to help a group further its own interests and achieve its own goals. The second is to identify and work with the key influencers of the group. These are the people with great credibility among the group—people whose judgment the group respects. They aren't always the leaders, but do tend to be among the more popular team members. Close attention to meeting dynamics can often tell you who they are. By focusing on the influential team members, you often gain critical insight about what makes the group tick and how best to sell them on an idea. Once an influential team member demonstrates support for the initiative, many doubters will likely reevaluate their positions on the matter and in time fall in line.

Occasionally one finds a group where nothing seems to work. Their obstinate opposition may be based on any number of reasons. Often these resisters fall into one of five camps:

- *The Antagonists.* These are usually angry people who may oppose you because of some offense they believe you or your group committed against them in the past or simply because they dislike anyone from "headquarters." Fortunately, there aren't usually many antagonists in an organization; unfortunately, the rare ones you find can make your life a living hell.

- *The Overworked.* These people may personally support the idea of an SOS and of a march to sustainability in general, but they have been battered with reorganizations and staff reductions and have been asked to pick up too many responsibilities from other groups. They simply don't see how they could take on one more assignment.

- *The Procrastinators.* Like the overworked, these people tend to support an SOS. They will get to their work in *due time*, but for them, *due time* never seems to come—some other more interesting priority always seems to slip in ahead of sustainability.

- *The Nonbelievers.* These are the people who are usually supportive on other issues but haven't been persuaded that the initiative you are now trying to deploy has merit for the company or, in particular, for their part of the organization.

- *The Rocks.* Rocks sit in meetings and may act attentive. They may even seem supportive at times, but usually they don't say much. You may think you have them in your camp, but find later they don't budge, and you don't know why. It may be an issue with control or authority, and if so, working with them is like trying to move a 10-ton boulder.

How does one deal with these or other resisters? You will need to size up the situation and respond based on particular circumstances. Figure 8.5 provides some options borrowed from the military that may be worth considering. Often the response is dictated by the urgency of the matter being deployed. If it is deemed highly urgent, then you may need to "call in the big guns" right away, recognizing that you will gain the resister's conformance to your demands but not likely secure the buy-in you would like from them. Moreover, the group may resent you for going over their heads. If the matter isn't so urgent, you might adopt one of the other listed strategies which take time but eventually may bring the group to your side voluntarily with lasting ownership. The key to good deployment under tough circumstances is not only sound planning, but also patience, courage, tenacity, and keeping your eye on the objective. It's trying an approach, evaluating its effectiveness, learning from mistakes, and when needed, planning an improved approach and trying again.

Figure 8.5
What You Do If They Slam the Door in Your Face: Some Military Solutions

1. **Retreat and attack the opponent at another place where success is more likely**. Speak with another part of the opponent's organization to see if they can be persuaded.

2. **Retreat, regroup, and re-attack.** Debrief with your team to see what went wrong, correct it, and try again.

3. **Retreat, rearm, and re-attack**. Beef up the information in your presentation and try again.

4. **Retreat, seek reinforcements, and re-attack**. Recruit other allies to join you to help persuade the opponent.

5. **Call in the big guns**. Get someone high in the organization to speak with the opponent on your behalf.

6. **Create a siege**. Wait for the opponent to come to you for something you have that he wants, then negotiate to get what you want.

7. **Build a Trojan horse and wait for it to be pulled inside the fortress**. Create an award, opportunity to be covered in the company newsletter, or some other attractive benefit that can be achieved only if the opponent begins to behave in the way that you desire.

8. **Retreat and recruit another army to attack**. Have some other group try to persuade the opponent.

9. **Cultivate peace and wait for the next good opportunity to re-attack**. Back off and resume normal relations with the opponent but wait for a good time to try again.

10. **Slowly infiltrate**. Slowly gain individual converts within the opponent's organization—or move them from your organization to his—until there is a critical mass of support there.

11. **Retreat, ignore the opponent, and move on to another**. Back away and move on to some other group with the hope that the opponent will come around once he sees that many others are accepting the idea.

Deployment to Outside Organizations

Deployment, integration, and alignment of sustainability initiatives are not limited to people within the company; many on the outside may also be involved. Consultants and other experts may be called upon to supplement internal resources in the effort. Suppliers may be brought into the assignment, too. More and more organizations are seeing the merit of developing various sustainability-related programs for their suppliers, including programs on diversity, ethics, the environment, safety, working conditions, and waste reduction. This is done primarily to help the supplier control costs and to reduce the risk of incidents that can interrupt supply and cause harmful spillover publicity for the company. Deployment of programs to suppliers can be through supplier conferences or by many other means. Novo Nordisk developed a small booklet on sustainable supply chain management, a special website of tools, and a supplier audit program, among other things, to aid in its rollout of supplier initiatives.[6]

Other outside groups, such as trade and professional associations, can also be involved in sustainability matters on behalf of a company or group of companies. Business for Social Responsibility (BSR), the WBCSD, CSR Europe, and GEMI are four business organizations in the forefront of the cause. Other mainstream trade associations, like the American Chemistry Council, are promoting sustainability as a business theme. Through organizations like these, companies with sustainability agendas work with other like-minded companies to research and share best strategies for dealing with some of the difficult sustainability challenges of our day.

A good example where an outside organization helped companies further their sustainability interests is the Sustainable Mobility Project sponsored by the WBCSD. Under this project, eight automobile makers, three energy companies, and a tire manufacturer worked with the council to identify the challenges and solutions for achieving sustainability in the transportation of people and goods. Their report, *Mobility 2030*, maps the difficult course to sustainability for their industries, and suggests how progress toward it might be measured.[7] As this project shows, respected companies and professionals all moving in the same direction can bring momentum to the cause. Such an effort can help everyone better anticipate the business opportunities and challenges ahead and raise visibility for them within their respective organizations. Moreover, such collaborations can produce constructive peer pressure, providing players in the industry with some concern that if they do not act, they could be left behind the pack on the road to sustainability and future business success.

Public interest or activist groups—NGOs—can also play an important role in a company's deployment of sustainability programs. Company departments responsible for community relations, public relations, and marketing may find ways NGOs can help. For example, this help may be certifying products or operations—as the Rainforest Alliance did for Chiquita—participating in stewardship councils, or aiding with green labeling or cause-related marketing as discussed in Appendix 1.29. Indeed, companies may discover a host of strategies involving NGOs that can further their business and, at the same time, advance the cause of sustainability. Those opportunities are explored further in Chapter 11.

A company that gives careful thought and attention to executing its sustainability objectives—that does a good job of deploying, integrating, and aligning—will improve its chances of a successful rollout. But success will remain out of reach unless there is good follow-up to check on the effectiveness of the deployment and whether expectations are being met. Leaders must assure efforts stay on track and that people keep motivated to achieve the goal. In the next chapter we will learn how to do just that.

**Follow-up Checklist for Action:
Deployment, Integration, and Alignment**

☐ Define what is to be deployed—a sustainability policy or an SOS procedure, practice, or tool, for example.

☐ Define the objective and scope of deployment in a formal or informal plan, identifying what is to be deployed to whom for what purpose by when.

☐ Assure the deployment plan will result in proper alignment of the policy, procedure, practice, or tool vertically and horizontally across the organization.

☐ Assure that the sustainability objectives and goals of the business units are aligned with those of the company.

☐ Assure that the sustainability objectives and goals of the business units are aligned with, or integrated in, their own business goals and objectives.

☐ Encourage the integration of sustainability-related considerations in PPOs and bonus or other reward criteria.

☐ Assure the deployment plan includes integrating the deployed policy, procedure, practice, or tool into existing policies, procedures, practices, and tools as noted in Figure 8.3.

☐ Prepare training and awareness materials and tools, considering the list of tools in Figure 8.1.

☐ Arrange for any necessary translations of materials and otherwise assure the deployment materials and approach are culturally appropriate.

☐ Identify internal experts who can respond to questions about the thing being deployed.

☐ Prepare train-the-trainer materials and tools.

☐ Identify and train the trainers.

☐ Develop methods and tools for evaluating training effectiveness.

☐ Pilot the training and other rollout activities at a few sites, evaluate the feedback, and make adjustments as needed.

☐ Execute the deployment as planned.

☐ Be prepared to respond as noted in Figure 8.5 if the deployment meets with significant resistance.

Endnotes to Chapter 8

1. Larry Bossidy is the former chairman and CEO of Honeywell International and Allied Signal and vice chairman and division leader at GE. LARRY BOSSIDY & RAM CHARAN (WITH CHARLES BURCK), EXECUTION: THE DISCIPLINE OF GETTING THINGS DONE 1 (Crown Business 2002).

2. The saying is adapted from a line in the poem, *To a Mouse*, by Robert Burns.

3. *See* TRAINING MANAGEMENT CORPORATION, DOING BUSINESS INTERNATIONALLY: MANAGING CULTURE FOR COMPETITIVE ADVANTAGE (1999).

4. E-mail from Dennis Shoji, Senior Director of Facilities/EHS, Edwards Lifesciences, to William Blackburn (Apr. 27, 2005).

5. See Appendices 2.6.3, 2.6.6, 6.5, and 6.18 and the section of Chapter 3 on risk management for more information on enterprise risk management programs.

6. Novo Nordisk, *Our Approach to Sustainable Supply Chain Management*, http://suppliertoolbox.novonordisk.com/approach/approach.asp.

7. WBCSD, *Sustainable Mobility*, http://www.wbcsd.ch/templates/Template WBCSD4/layout.asp?type=p&MenuId=ODE&doOpen=1&ClickMenu= LeftMenu.

Chapter 9

Data Systems, Auditing, and Other Monitoring and Accountability Mechanisms

"As soon as the boss decides he wants his workers to do something, he has two problems: (getting them to) do it and monitoring what they do."[1]
—Robert Krulwich

So far your efforts have been a success. You've sold management on the benefits of an SOS, created the structure to support it, and developed indicators, goals, and the plans that define the way forward. You've rolled all this out to the regions, divisions, and facilities with good deployment, integration, and alignment. Now that this hard work is done and the SOS has been well planted in the field, isn't it time to sit back, drink lemonade, and watch the plantings grow to a fruitful harvest? Is there really anything left to do until you reap the benefits of the SOS at year-end?

Anyone familiar with agriculture knows that planting and harvesting are the two seasons of intense activity, but there's also work to be done in the interim. Weeds must be removed; pests must be controlled. In some places, irrigation is needed. Steps must be taken to assure the objective of a rich bounty is fulfilled.

This is also true about an SOS. Progress in growing an SOS within an organization must be monitored so adjustments can be made if the growth doesn't meet expectations. Along the way, things must be done to encourage progress toward the objective. For an SOS, that encouragement and motivation comes in the form of accountability—the clear assignment of responsibility and the duty to report and explain results with meaningful rewards granted or withheld based on performance.[2]

While monitoring and accountability within a company can take many different forms, each has its own challenges.

Types of Monitoring; Common Problems

Monitoring includes measuring performance versus goals as well as other means of periodic oversight and evaluation of conditions or performance. It may be undertaken in a variety of ways, such as through inspections, audits, interviews, observations, or measurements. Monitoring can be *qualitative*—based on good informed judgment—or *quantitative*—based on measurement. Two qualitative evaluations that can be important are the periodic assessments of teamwork and communication. The greatest plans in the world go nowhere if these two things are missing. But qualitative monitoring has its drawbacks: Since it is based on judgment, it can sometimes lead to disagreement and debate, creating resentment rather than more enthusiastic support.

Quantitative monitoring—tracking things like air pollution concentrations, discrimination claims, and earnings per share—can pose problems, too. Numerical measurements are not always simple, and data integrity can be particularly troubling. Instructions to the field may be weak creating confusion about what is to be reported. A tally of the minorities recently hired or hazardous waste generated will make little sense if no one has defined what a *minority* and *hazardous waste* are. Monitoring can also be hampered by reporters who are new to the process or untrained, and by virus-infected reporting software. If the data is being collected on a global basis, kilograms may be mistakenly reported as pounds and other units of measure may become mixed. Other major difficulties can arise simply because those who designed the data request form didn't understand how the data is collected in the field.

The biggest problems with measurement come from infrequent reporting and lack of feedback. Facilities that take a "tax-return" approach to reporting—throwing invoices, scraps of correspondence, and other data into a shoe box for sorting out at the end of the year—have a difficult time recalling all the lessons learned the year before. They may not be familiar enough with the data to know what values are reasonable and which ones may reflect an error of a slipped decimal point. Even worse, problems with bad, incomplete, or delayed data can languish unresolved for years if no one is tracking the problems or providing feedback to the field on them. An investment of time to address these issues proactively can pay big dividends in the long run. In addition, entering data quarterly or monthly can help by keeping users familiar with the data and systems.

Data Collection and Management Systems: How Do You Know What to Buy?

Some companies have computerized data systems with "guard rails" that flag suspicious data and compile reports on late filers. This can significantly improve data quality and timeliness. Some of these systems are expensive, however. Other organizations may rely on simple Lotus Notes® or Excel® spreadsheets or other elementary approaches, according to their needs. Each can be an effective means of monitoring if used in the right situation with proper encouragement, guidance, feedback, and support. Ultimately, however, users must be persuaded that the application aids their work and is superior to other solutions at hand. In the end, user acceptance is the key to success.

Companies sometimes make the mistake of assuming that technology can cure all ills. They find their monitoring systems to be inefficient and frustrating and see technology as the answer. They believe an Information Technology (IT) expert can apply computer magic to improve the quality and speed of the effort or that some new software will provide the miracle cure. However, they eventually discover the old saying is true: "Garbage in, garbage out." Data quality and timeliness will remain problems unless users have good training and coaching and a clear accountability for performance. Organizations that skimp on these things shouldn't be surprised if their information systems fall short of expectations. For that reason, it's wise to include the costs for adequate training and assistance in the budget for system startup.

Model Process for Selecting and Implementing IT for Monitoring and Managing Sustainability Performance

With these caveats and the right application, IT can significantly improve an organization's efficiency and effectiveness, enabling it to better focus its resources for superior performance. But the selection of the technology solution should not be treated lightly. If chosen and implemented without enough forethought, IT systems for sustainability management can become big black holes, sucking inordinate money and effort from the organization and providing more headaches than value. This is a particular risk where IT products are purchased off the shelf before sustainability plans, goals, and management systems are well defined. To avoid these pitfalls, a company should follow a methodical process in evaluating, selecting, and implementing its IT systems. The following steps outline how this might be done:

1. *Prioritize data needs and identify providers.* Review the strategic and tactical plan and goals to identify current information and communication needs, and those likely over the next five

years. Prioritize those needs, giving great weight to what's easiest to fulfill. Identify who will provide the data, who will evaluate and compile it, and who will use it. If possible, involve people from these groups in the discussions.

2. *Map information processes.* Define the processes needed to collect, manage, and use the identified information. See Figure 9.1 for some typical information management processes or functions. In many cases, a combination of these processes will be used in an integrated way to manage a particular program. For example, an audit program might use document templates for audit reports and notification letters, the document-control function for exchanging and finalizing individual reports, and the storage function for holding old reports and certain supporting documentation. Personnel databases could be tapped to assemble distribution lists for reports. Online reference libraries may hold the latest regulations and audit checklists. A calendar-reminder system and an automatic e-mail reminder function could track and notify audit participants of key deadlines for finalizing reports, returning action plans, and other steps. A process for tracking corrective and preventive actions could be used to follow the planned actions for resolving the audit items. Delays in closing out items could be flagged through an automatic notification system. An Internet-based survey could collect feedback on the audit at its conclusion. Large audit programs might automate all of these processes, while smaller ones may automate only a few and handle the rest manually.

Figure 9.1
Checklist of Functions for Monitoring and Managing Sustainability
Performance That Can Be Automated With IT

1. Document Management Functions

☐ Shared Templates. Shared templates for model reports, letters, memos, procedures, policies, manuals, audit text, and other documents, with flexibility regarding modification of templates and ability to use the organization's existing internal templates.

☐ Document Control.
-Control of document creation, security, and integration, such as providing review and editing by multiple parties;
-Limiting access to drafts and ability to make changes;
-Tracking drafts;
-Linking documents to plans, activities, tasks, responsibilities, training, management system standards, and other documents and databases.

☐ Record Storage and Management. Storage and archiving data, reports, and other records for regulatory, due diligence, liability control, business continuity, and other reasons, with index and automatic reminders for record-retention and record-destruction reviews.

2. Management of Reference Materials

☐ Reference Libraries. Reference libraries with an index and links to other useful resources, including access to latest regulations and company requirements, and automated notifications of new requirements.

☐ Material Safety Data Sheet Management.
-Creating, importing, and maintaining material safety data sheets or chemical information sheets on raw materials and company's products;
-Automatically sending the information sheets to internal personnel who use a covered material and to customers who purchase a covered product.

3. Progress Monitoring Functions

☐ Project Management.
-Project management, including identification of milestones, tasks, and responsible parties;
-Tracking progress and closeout;
-Linking strategic plan to tactical (operating) plan to individual projects.

☐ Change Management Reviews. Tracking progress of sustainability reviews of new or changed products, services, processes, and facilities.

☐ Regulatory Follow-Up. Tracking government inspections and claims, regulatory and permit exceedances, and the follow-up on them.

Figure 9.1—Continued
Checklist of Functions for Monitoring and Managing Sustainability
Performance That Can Be Automated With IT

4. Information Analysis Functions

☐ Data Analysis.
  -Querying databases;
  -Reporting on trends and comparative analysis of data to spot gaps and
  opportunities.

☐ Root-Cause Analysis.

☐ Risk Analysis; Prioritization.
  -Risk and aspects/impacts analysis;
  -Processes for prioritizing projects and issues.

5. Survey Management Functions

☐ Investor Survey Response. Internet-based systems for importing and compiling company data needed to respond to investor and rating-company questionnaires. Such systems have the functionality similar to that provided by
  OneReport™ (SRI World Group) and StakeholderEngage (NeoRep).

☐ Stakeholder Surveys. Internet-based surveys for collecting the views of employees and other stakeholders, with automated compilation and analysis
  of results.

6. Other Information Management Functions

☐ Multilingual Conversion of Documents.

☐ Management of Personnel Information. Tracking personnel, titles, functions, distribution lists, and passwords.

☐ General Communications. Improving speed and extent of communication
  among staff at multiple locations.

☐ Information Security Controls. Imposing security controls on access to confidential information.

☐ Material and Product Classification. Classifying raw materials and products
  for regulatory, environmental, and health reasons.

☐ Tracking Items. Using bar code readers or other devices to input labeling
  data to track materials, wastes, and other items.

☐ Compiling Remote Monitoring and Inspection Data. Using mobile devices,
  such as personal digital assistants (PDAs), pocket personal computers (PCs)
  and tablets, and other wireless devices for entering monitoring, inspection,
  and other data from a variety of remote locations.

3. *Define detailed requirements.* Flesh out the other details of the information requirements, such as key deadlines and milestones and language and security needs. Keep in mind the skill levels, equipment, and other limitations of the data providers.

4. *Identify gaps.* Identify the gaps between identified process and information needs and current practice. Determine what you need that you don't have.

5. *Target processes for IT solutions.* Identify those processes where the time and effort for them are so great, or where errors or lapses are so frequent, and the value of the information so important as to warrant consideration of an IT solution. Involve IT experts in this and subsequent discussions. If possible, involve them even earlier—from the very beginning of step 1, above—to provide them a more complete understanding of the substantive needs that must be addressed by the IT solution.

6. *Define linkage requirements.* Identify requirements for linking with other existing and proposed information systems.

7. *Assess technological solutions.* Assess possible technological solutions in light of: (1) identified requirements, including relevant considerations from Figure 9.2; and (2) the likely useful life of the solution, given the trends in IT. Evaluate what can be provided with possible modifications to existing systems. Review other commercially available solutions as well.

Figure 9.2
**Checklist of Considerations in Selecting IT Solutions for Monitoring and
Managing Sustainability Performance**

1. Ability to Meet Basic Requirements
☐ Meeting High-Priority Requirements.
   -Ability of the system to meet the high-priority data requirements of
   various users;
   -Ability to jettison identified lower priority projects if budgets become tight.
☐ Meeting System Objectives. Ability of the system to meet the clear state-
   ment of overall objectives.
☐ Fulfilling Needed Functions. Capability of the system to fulfill the desired
   functions. (See Figure 9.1 for examples.)
☐ Appropriate for Geographic Focus. Ability to operate on a global, national,
   regional, or local basis, as required.
☐ Compatibility With Organizational Structure. System architecture reflects
   the extent of decentralization of the organization and processes, and the extent of the facility and business-unit autonomy. These factors can affect the
   extent of review and approval to be given compiled data, for example. They
   may also influence the choice between a stand-alone PC solution and a network solution.
☐ Database Size. Database size limitations of system.
☐ System Life. Likely life of the system given the trends in technology relevant
   to the application.

2. System Compatibility Issues
☐ Compatibility With Other Systems.
   -Needed compatibilities with other systems, such as government systems,
   Excel® spreadsheets, Access® databases, and resource planning systems like
   Peoplesoft®, Oracle®, and SAP databases;
   -Need for integration with the company's operating system or with systems
   of other organizations within the company.
☐ Needed Mobility.
   -Portability of information;
   -Ability to link with mobile devices (PDA, pocket PC, wireless, etc.) for
   data entry.

3. User Concerns
☐ Value to Data Users and Providers. Value to data users as well as to data providers. A broad user base helps maintain cost-effectiveness of the system and
   the political support for it. Making collected data available in forms useful to
   providers can expand the user base and help create support for the system.

Figure 9.2—Continued
Checklist of Considerations in Selecting IT Solutions for Monitoring and Managing Sustainability Performance

☐ Ease of Use.
   -Ease of use and intuitiveness of the system;
   -Minimization of steps to accomplish data tasks;
   -Acronyms and jargon avoided or clarified.
☐ Limitations of User Technology. Bandwidth, equipment, or other limitations among system users.
☐ Trial Use. Availability of system for trial use with sample database.

4. Flexibility Considerations
☐ Flexibility to Address Changing Data Needs. Flexibility to customize reports and system to future, currently unknown data needs.
☐ Ease of Changing Administrative Data. Ease in accommodating day-to-day changes in personnel, their roles, the organization, passwords, and other administrative details.
☐ Flexibility for Growth. Flexibility of system architecture to accommodate growth and other changes.

5. Special Features
☐ Security Features.
   -Security features, restrictions for single or multi-level access;
   -Encryption capabilities.
☐ Data Display Capability. Capability for producing clear graphical reports, dashboards, and other displays of data.

6. Vendor Service Considerations
☐ Training.
   -Training needs addressed;
   -Training provided by vendor for current and new users.
☐ Proactive Field Support. Arrangements for proactive (versus reactive) field support/customer service.
☐ Vendor Accessibility. Accessibility of the vendor to address difficult problems.
☐ Technical Capability of Vendor. Technical capability of vendor to fix problems of the types that may arise; capabilities of vendor's assigned project leader.
☐ Vendor Contacts and Communications.
   -Identifying good point people for assuring effective communications between the internal team and vendors, especially if service is outsourced off shore;
   -Planning and budgeting for communications arrangements.

Figure 9.2—Continued
Checklist of Considerations in Selecting IT Solutions for Monitoring and Managing Sustainability Performance

☐ Updates.
-Periodic system updates are provided;
-Seamlessness with which system updates are made.

7. Resource Considerations
☐ Stability of Vendor. Stability, age, and financial strength of the company that is providing the software and support. Ask:
-Who are the owners?
-How likely are they to remain in business?
-How are sales growing relative to expenses?
-What is the percentage of gross sales that the vendor reinvests into the product?
-What is the financial strength of the vendor as reflected in its latest credit-rating report?
☐ Licensing Limitations.
☐ Software and Service Costs.
-Costs of software development or licenses:
  • Are group or multi-year discounts offered?
  • Are support, debugging, maintenance, training, startup, other on-site technical assistance, and ongoing communications and coordination included?
-Costs of importing or converting data from the old system to the new.
-Note regarding U.S. costs as of 2004: *total final cost for an elaborate custom-built system can be three to five times the initial capital outlay. Licensing costs typically run $250 to $1,250 per user, depending upon the number of users, the capability of the system and the provider.*[3]
☐ Needed Internal Resources. Internal skills and resources needed to support the system.

---

8. *Detail merits and costs of alternatives.* Detail the benefits, shortcomings, five-year costs, and estimated return on investment of top-ranked alternative approaches. Answer the following questions with the help of an IT expert:

• Will a simple approach be sufficient, such as using Lotus Notes®, an Excel® spreadsheet, or an Access® database? Or will the proposed solution be infeasible because of requirements for database size, systems compatibility, or security?

- Can the needs for automated report submittal, data aggregation, and verification be accommodated?
- Can the system provide the desired error screening and process control?
- Will the company's enterprise resource planning system, like those provided by SAP, Peoplesoft®, or Oracle®, be flexible enough to meet most needs? Or will the company prefer more specialized off-the-shelf systems?

9. *Prioritize options.* Prioritize the optional solutions, identifying contingencies for different assumed scenarios of business financial health (budget availability) at certain points in the future. Have a strong bias for simplicity, which can aid user acceptance and the return on investment. Consider a phased implementation, starting with a small scale and moving to other parts of the project as results and funding allow.

10. *Establish a 3x5 Plan.* Draft a "3x5 Plan," identifying the (1) IT system developments, (2) needed personnel, and (3) budgets required for the current year and each of the coming four years. Include the costs for new technology at the end of the useful life of the system. Review and adjust it as needed every three to six months. This tool helps you make better business decisions about the system by allowing you to understand the impact of today's IT initiatives on future resource needs and budgets. Depreciation charges can mount up fast. Share this information at least annually with those who will be expected to fund the system.

11. *Secure management approval.* Review proposals and the 3x5 Plan with an executive sponsor, and secure other necessary approvals.

12. *Test and assess solution.* Review mock-ups and run pilots with actual users who represent the range of duties and skills of the people who will use the system. Take other appropriate measures to test the system, as well. Carefully collect user feedback. Evaluate the results and adjust the project as needed.

13. *Identify process and data owners.* Identify the people or positions that will have ownership for various information processes and data. These are usually the company's functional experts who review and use the data. Clearly articulate their roles. If possible, make them responsible for both the content and user

training for their part of the system. Assure they see this as a primary responsibility.

14. *Train users*. Train all users on the system, using simulations of realistic facts and circumstances likely to be encountered by the users. Schedule training close to the time the users will begin entering or retrieving data from the system. If the organization is large and global, consider rolling out the system over a six- to nine-month period, emphasizing that this training is an important part of personal development. Review training logs to see who has yet to receive training and follow up to close those gaps.

15. *Assure effectiveness of training*. Assure the training of users has been effective and that they are properly using the system; hold them accountable. Check on the quality of data when visiting sites and as part of scheduled audits. Provide additional training if needed. Assure that sustainability leaders at all levels are promoting use of the system by all targeted users.

16. *Check alignment with organizational needs*. Periodically check to assure the system remains aligned with organizational needs at all levels. Frequently communicate with users. Track user feedback, system problems, vendor responsiveness, opportunities for system improvement, and changes in the organization and its business priorities.

17. *Promote the system*. Continually assess and communicate the value and successes of the system.

18. *Improve training and procedures*. Continually improve training and procedures to enhance the efficiency and effectiveness of the system and the processes it serves.

19. *Evaluate new technologies*. Every few years, review the latest technologies and the cost benefit of shifting to other systems.

20. *Adopt new solutions*. Shift to a new, better solution when persuaded by an objective cost-benefit analysis. This change must be properly timed, however. On the one hand, you want to avoid confusing and frustrating users by bombarding them with frequent extensive changes in the system. On the other, you shouldn't fall in love with a system for years if it isn't serving the

best interests of the organization. Your IT expert can help you decide the proper pace of change.

Overcoming Data Overload

Even with good planning processes, some companies hit the wall of information overload. They find that with "system creep" over the years, they are now asking for too much data from too many people and trying to automate more than needed. This sometimes results in big, lumbering obsolete IT systems that become stretched to the limits and hard to master. Under these circumstances, users may find the system lowering their efficiency and raising their frustration, rather than the reverse. The way out of this difficulty is through teamwork and ruthless prioritization. Metrics can be ranked by evaluating their relationship to the hierarchy of goals and objectives from strategic and tactical plans. A finer cut can be made by further assessing the measures against the criteria for business value found in Form B (Appendix 4). This ranking should be done with involvement of data submitters, data compilers, data users, and IT experts. Working together, these parties can identify the easiest and most valuable approach that meets their collective needs and those of the company, whether that is an Internet-based system, a simple commercially available software, or a solution that doesn't involve computers at all. Indeed, the non-computerized option is often taken too lightly. It should be seriously weighed for monitoring in small companies and for situations that don't involve the repetitive submittal, compilation, presentation, or storage of large amounts of data.

Another way to help control information overload is to manage the timing of changes in the information to be reported. Frequent changes in information requirements, like frequent changes in information technologies, can confuse and frustrate users. While people are often eager to fix problems and roll out new metrics, the response should be paced to accommodate the resources available and to allow proper absorption and use in the field. Since the introduction of new metrics is tied to strategic and tactical planning, the appropriate rate of change should be resolved at the planning stage with some reasonable cushion of time built in. Later, if planners identify changes in data reporting that are too important to postpone, the plans can be revisited.

Auditing

Monitoring as described above contemplates that facilities or other performers in the field will report their own performance data to an oversight group. But monitoring may also be accomplished by auditors or
other third-party evaluators who collect, assess, and report the performance information themselves. Since auditing is such an important
monitoring tool for any sustainability program, we will examine it in
some depth.

When to Do an Independent Audit

Auditing is warranted when a company seeks a new, fresh assessment of
gaps in compliance, risk control, or efficiency. It is also used when a
third-party opinion is desired to add credibility to a performance report or
certify conformance to an ISO or other recognized standard. Then too,
the opinion of a respected auditing professional can add considerable
weight to an internal plea for improvement that management has been reluctant to hear. Moreover, a program of independent audits can serve as a
mitigating factor under the U.S. *Sentencing Guidelines* (see Appendix
3.26) in setting penalties for a violation of federal regulation.

To obtain the best results for the investment, third-party audits should
be part of a portfolio of other reviews, such as self-audits by the site itself
and daily, weekly, and monthly checklist inspections by various departments. The third-party assessment can help improve the other review
processes, which in turn leads to a greater sense of ownership, empowerment, and motivation by employees of the audited operation.

Management-by-Audit; Achieving the Right Balance

Generally, audits should not be undertaken unless management is committed to address whatever findings may result. From a legal and moral
perspective, there is nothing worse than knowing about a violation of law
or serious threat to people or property and doing nothing about it. This
can change an innocent oversight to a serious criminal matter. Auditing
can also be inappropriate if it becomes so excessive it no longer serves as
a method for sampling performance, but a substitute for good management. Management-by-audit can bring on audit fatigue, reversing the
gains of deployment and empowerment, and suppressing the motivation
of managers. It can prompt the targeted entity to abandon any critical
self-analysis and initiative for improvement, instead drifting into a hiber-

nation of non-activity as soon as the hot glare of the audit has cooled. The attitude becomes: "Let's postpone that action until the auditors get here. If we start something now, the auditors might soon tell us it's wrong and we'd just have to start over."

On the other hand, failure to commission an audit in the face of suspected impropriety can allow a bad problem to worsen, increasing the odds of more severe legal and public relations damage later. Such a failure can also be ethically reprehensible—and career limiting. On balance, auditing by qualified experts done at frequencies based on risk can be a good thing for a company, providing an honest understanding of problems and prompting constructive change. This kind of auditing should be an important part of any sustainability program.

Types of Audits

Audits may be of several different types:

- *Compliance audits* assess conformance to regulations and government permits and licenses.
- *Internal standards audits* review how well the organization meets requirements it has developed for itself.
- *External standards audits* assess the extent of conformance with an outside standard to which the organization subscribes.
- A *management systems audit* is a type of internal or external standards audit. It evaluates an organization's adherence to a process described in an internal management standard or to an external one, such as ISO 9001, ISO 14001, SA 8000, OHSAS 18001, or the SOS standard from Chapter 5. ISO 19011 provides general guidance on how a management systems audit might be conducted.[4]
- *Risk/best practices assessments* are audits that examine potential liabilities and risks of harm to people and property, and seek out commendable approaches that can be shared with others.
- *Productivity assessments* are conducted to spot opportunities to improve efficiency, typically through energy conservation, waste reduction, material substitution, or process change. Six Sigma and other quality tools are often used to ferret out these opportunities.

A particular type of audit may be done separately or combined with one or more other types. Management systems audits are most effectively performed together with compliance, risk/best practice, and internal or external standards audits. This way the systems can be judged by their output, revealing more clearly the patterns of underlying root causes. (See further discussion on this in Chapter 5.) If time is a limiting factor, then it is better to examine particular topics or parts of the operation to evaluate legal and policy compliance, risk, and productivity in an integrated way, rather than to just evaluate one of those aspects of performance across the entire site or organization. An integrated audit does a superior job of getting to the root cause of the problems and identifying a permanent solution for them. For example, if training on regulations, company policies, and risk-control measures is shown to be weak, it is not enough to simply conduct that training. That is like cutting weeds without pulling their roots: the problem will simply sprout up again later. The underlying reason for the training weakness—be it a shortage of resources, lack of management support, or poor trainer skills—must also be uncovered and addressed. That is the only way to create a properly tuned system that will deliver consistently good performance over the long term.

Audits may also be *internal* or *external*. Internal audits are conducted by the organization's own people; external audits, by consultants or other independent entities outside the organization. Internal audits may be *self-assessments*—reviews of an operation conducted by its own personnel. Or they may be *independent internal assessments* undertaken by a special internal auditing group or another part of the organization that is independent of the operation being reviewed.

Each of these types of audits and auditors offers advantages and disadvantages. Periodic self-assessments can help assure an operation remains well aware of its compliance status and takes ownership for its performance gaps instead of being defensive about them. Self-assessments are relatively inexpensive because the auditors are already on staff. And since self-assessment auditors come from the operation's own organization, they have the advantage of being intimately familiar with its activities, personnel, practices, and culture. But they have disadvantages, too. On difficult issues, auditors drawn from the audited operation may be more susceptible than independent auditors to subtle or overt influence from the operation's management. Furthermore, because self-assessment auditors generally do not conduct audits on a regular basis, they typically do not possess the same technical skills or breadth of experience as a full-time independent internal or external auditor. Independent auditors, on the other hand, can help cross-fertilize ideas among facilities, departments, and—in the case of external auditors—companies. While internal independent assessments may be less expensive than external ones, the former may not carry the same credibility or impact as the latter. Because of their expertise and independence, specially qualified external auditors are commonly required for formal certifications under ISO, Eco-Management and Audit Scheme (EMAS), and certain product and fair trade standards. Given the pros and cons of the various types of audits and auditors, many large companies use a complement of these types for best overall effect.

Audits also vary as to the amount of forewarning given the audited operation. Notices of several months or more can provide extra motivation for a previously unaudited facility to get its house in order. After the operation has responded to the audit, fulfilled all requirements, and developed all required programs, a short-notice spot check can be conducted. Despite the element of surprise, facilities often favor these short-notice reviews, especially if they offer the opportunity for well-performing sites to avoid a full-blown audit and all the preparation it entails. The advantage of such reviews is that they catch the procrastinating site that is allowing programs to erode until just before the audit is announced. Sites that do poorly on a short-notice audit should expect a full audit to follow soon.

Selecting Auditors

In selecting auditors, the organization should pick people who have good auditing, writing, and interpersonal skills and who are knowledgeable about the subject being reviewed. It is not enough for an auditor to claim she is skilled in "systems"; she must also demonstrate expertise in the discipline of concern: environmental issues for ISO 14001; health and safety issues for OHSAS 18001; employment-related issues for SA 8000; and finance for a financial audit. Without expertise in the discipline, the auditor will be unable to adequately judge the severity of risk present or evaluate how well the system works in consistently producing the expected output. Auditors should also have the appropriate language skills and possess knowledge of the industry and company to which the site belongs.

Often a team is needed to capture all required expertise or to expedite the review. Where a team is used, a lead auditor should be named and the leader's scope of authority defined. One or more site representatives should be named to accompany the audit team. These representatives should be people who are open to criticism and dedicated to improvement.

Sometimes it's difficult to locate site representatives with this attitude. That's because management often views audits as a test for their operations; their main objective is to make a good showing with few items resulting. Site representatives may hesitate to disclose issues, thinking they will be viewed as traitors to their own organizations if they do. To help head off that problem, the audit leader should tell site management and audit participants before the audit commences that the audit report will include observations about the teamwork displayed among the participants, and the candidness shown by the site. If good teamwork and openness result, this should be clearly noted in the report. However, if significant problems arise in this regard, they should be dealt with firmly but prudently—perhaps most effectively behind closed doors. If an egregious cover-up is detected on a matter of importance, it should be swiftly and forcefully addressed as a major ethical impropriety, and, where an intentional breach of law is involved, as a potential criminal concern.

Getting the Most From Your Auditors

Auditors have the responsibility to find problems. In some assessments, they are also charged with helping the audited entity find solutions. Using an auditor as a consultant has its pluses and minuses. It is good to hear opinions from an expert auditor about the course of action that will resolve a deficiency. This can provide valuable training and produce a solution that not only taps the knowledge of a recognized expert, but expedites the resolution of the audit. But an auditor's role as a consultant can go too far. That happens if the organization finds itself relinquishing to the auditor most of the creative thinking about solutions. This overdelegation can reduce the capacity and inclination of the organization to solve its own problems in the future. It is a step toward the destructive management-by-audit.

The dual role of auditor and consultant can raise conflicts of interest, too. The auditor-consultant may be tempted to provide inordinate focus on uncovering items on which she can consult. Or the consulting side of the business can grow to the point where it begins to compromise the independence of the auditor. This latter problem—allegedly a factor leading to the Enron-Arthur Andersen financial scandal—was addressed by Congress when it enacted the Sarbanes-Oxley Act of 2002.[5] That law now severely limits the non-auditing services allowed by independent auditors who verify company financial statements. Similar restrictions on consulting work have been imposed on ISO auditors since 1996.[6]

Given the pros and cons of auditor-consultants, what should a company do? The simple answer is to use reasonable prudence in tapping your auditor's expertise to gain an in-depth understanding of the issues and their possible solutions. At the same time, you must respect the legal and registration requirements that apply. Moreover, you must not let your organization abandon its primary responsibility for determining solutions to the issues raised.

Other things can be done to assure that auditors are most productive and helpful. Well before the on-site audit begins, the auditor should obtain the basic information about the features and characteristics of the operation to be audited. Part of this exercise involves obtaining and studying in advance key documents, such as plans, permits, past audit reports, government inspection reports, self-audits, and completed checklists. Auditors should also review at this stage nonconformance logs or other open-item lists and closeout reports. From the study of this data, gaps and questions can be identified. After this review is completed, an audit checklist can be prepared. Armed with this checklist, the audit team can prioritize the areas for on-site review and assign each area to one or more team members. This audit plan can serve as an on-site working guide for the audit team, subject to change based on field observations. While some additional documents may be reviewed on location, most of the site work should involve discussions with line workers, supervisors, and managers to discover how decisions are made, things are done, and problems addressed.

Cautions About Cursory and Survey Audits

Occasionally a company will want a quick snapshot of issues for planning purposes. This may involve a cursory walk through a facility and interviews with management and a few key employees. Or it may entail a survey appraisal and group discussion about the extent to which certain practices have been adopted. While these reviews can be useful, care must be taken that they do not lull the organization into thinking all significant issues have been identified and addressed. Since opinions don't always reflect fact, if that kind of assurance is desired, a more complete site appraisal must be undertaken.

The Audit Report

Whatever type of audit is performed, the report of findings should be written clearly and succinctly so readers can quickly grasp each deficiency. It should classify items by subject matter (bioethics, hazardous waste, diversity, etc.) and type (regulatory, company requirement, best management practice, etc.). It should also characterize them as *regular* or *major* (or other term reflecting unacceptably high risk), and note whether they are a repeat of an item observed during a previous audit. By capturing this information on all audits, the organization will have a database from which to spot companywide trends—something of great value during planning. Observed best practices should be noted for balance. To assure accuracy of the facts, the draft report should be reviewed by key audit participants and site representatives before it is finalized.

An audit cover memorandum or one-page executive summary, which discusses major items and captures overall trends and root causes, can be especially useful to management. The summary can address, for example, the capability of the operation to identify, prioritize, and resolve issues on its own. It can also touch on how well the organization has identified its priorities and deployed, integrated, and aligned its efforts around them.

Final audit reports should be shared with the auditors, the other key audit participants, and those in management who participated in the audit or have responsibility over the operations or functions that were reviewed. Internal legal counsel should also receive a copy, especially if significant regulatory or liability matters are involved. In addition, certain noteworthy audit issues and their solutions should be communicated in some general way to other parts of the organization that may have the same problems. Having others check their own operations for these issues can produce better compliance and risk control across the company. What is more, if the issues are legal ones, this can lessen the likelihood of liability and of willful, repeat, or knowing violation of law—something that could develop if the same deficiency later arises elsewhere.

Some in the U.S. legal profession argue that distribution of audit report information should be tightly restricted and that each report be marked "Confidential Attorney-Client Privileged Material." This legal claim of privilege from disclosure is appropriate in those rare cases involving highly sensitive audits commissioned by a lawyer for the purpose of rendering legal advice.[7] In those unusual situations, distribution of the report should be limited only to legal counsel, to those who need to verify the reported facts, and to those who must act on the advice. Sharing it with others may waive the privilege of confidentiality.[8]

In most cases, however, severe constraints on the distribution of audit reports do more harm than good, especially if they interfere with the resolution of the issues and fail to engage company officials who can prevent recurrence. Moreover, the confidentiality of the vast majority of reports simply cannot be legally protected anyway. This is because most reports are not undertaken at the request of a lawyer for the purpose of offering legal advice. To be prudent, though, companies may want to mark each audit report as privileged and send a copy to an attorney and only those audit participants and management who have a good reason to know. These actions will provide some basis for a claim of privilege—albeit a weak one—in the rare instance the government or some other party seeks the report. While this justification is unlikely to succeed in court, it is usually enough to create a bargaining position from which to negotiate a more palatable partial, limited disclosure of the report.

The final audit report should be issued with the corrective and preventive action (CAPA) plan identifying who will do what by when to resolve each item and prevent its recurrence. The audit manager should periodically review progress against the plan until all items are addressed to the satisfaction of the lead auditor.

Tracking Audit Items

The process and tools for tracking open items can take many forms. A written or e-based status report can be prepared by the audited site and sent to the manager responsible for overseeing audits who then manually tracks the closure of items. This is the usual approach at small companies. In contrast, at some large companies, audit items, action plans, and status reports are posted in a protected companywide database designed to sort and compile information on the audit trends of individual facilities, divisions, regions, and the company as a whole. These systems are powerful tools that can help organizations decide where best to allocate resources. Unfortunately, this capability comes at a significant cost.

Companies that track several dozen or more audits a year have added challenges. For them, it's not practical for high-level management, legal counsel, or others who are responsible for many sites to receive the status reports on all audits. What they need is a report that provides an update on the open items that warrant their attention. These items would include the major ones that pose serious risk of harm, liability, adverse publicity, or agency action. Less urgent issues that languish for an extensive period may also be covered, such as regulatory items that remain unresolved for more than 60 days or nonregulatory matters open for more than 6 months.

Indeed, communication with management is a key element of a successful audit program. If poor results from an agency inspection or other circumstances cast doubts about a facility's performance, those concerns should be discussed openly with the facility's management before the audit occurs. Insights from this discussion can prove quite useful in dissecting the root causes of problems discovered at the facility. Live discussions with facility management and their superiors are also recommended after the audit is concluded. Good performance can be commended and weaknesses more fully explained. These discussions are a good time to inform management about the issues, answer their questions, and to dispel any destructive rumors, paranoia, or suspicions that can fester and grow if left unaddressed. Without this communication, some operations managers can remain blinded by the unwavering belief their organization can do no wrong.

Other Accountability Mechanisms

An audit is one powerful accountability mechanism that can bring the responsibility of organizational performance to the doorstep of management. It is one of many carrots and sticks that can keep the organization focused and motivated to achieve sustainability objectives. But there are other accountability mechanisms as well. The purpose of each is to show everyone the company is serious about these objectives—so serious it will dole out or withhold rewards based on how well the objectives are being addressed. These mechanisms should be applied to groups and individuals alike to recognize performance, creativity, and personal initiative.

On the surface the most important mechanism is tying adjustments in base pay, bonuses, and opportunities for advancement to performance against objectives. Certainly this is a strong motivator for many employees. Other rewards for exceptional performance may include special awards, recognition luncheons, and articles in the company newsletter. More meaningful rewards can be those that are subtler, such as granting top performers the opportunity to showcase their efforts in key forums—especially those forums attended by top management. These opportunities are especially prized by facility managers who are continually struggling to distinguish themselves from their peers in order to claw their way to the top. But among the most powerful motivators is a simple one: caring. Most employees will go to great lengths to help an organization and to satisfy a manager who they believe truly cares about their well being. Emotional benefits can be more powerful than financial ones. In short, rewards need not be expensive; more often than not, it's the thought that counts.

That is not to say it is always easy to develop effective accountability mechanisms. As Figure 9.3 indicates, many things can undermine the effectiveness of such mechanisms. Care must be taken to avoid these pitfalls.

Figure 9.3
Factors That Can Undermine Accountability and Inhibit Good Performance

1. *Lack of management follow-through on rewards or penalties:* Unless the consequences are promptly reinforced, they lose their motivational impact.

2. *Favoritism:* If performance is judged with an unfair bias, employees will become de-motivated and hold management in contempt.

3. *Hidden agendas:* If the object of accountability is not on improvement of the organization but on some personal benefit for management, employees will not see it as a legitimate goal.

4. *Lack of resources:* Accountability won't have any effect if employees are unable to perform because of a lack of time, training, knowledge, or other necessary resources.

5. *Lack of clear objectives:* If direction of desired performance isn't clear, accountability mechanisms will just frustrate employees.

6. *Unrealistic objectives:* If accountability is tied to objectives that realistically cannot be achieved, this will de-motivate employees.

7. *Easy performance target:* If the maximum reward is easy to achieve, the motivation to perform beyond that level will be diminished.

8. *Too many objectives:* If employees are spread too thin, they won't be able to achieve the objectives for which they are accountable.

9. *Insignificant accountability consequences:* Unless the consequences for employees are perceived by them to be significant, the accountability mechanism won't have much motivational effect.

10. *Lack of control by the accountable party:* If employees cannot deliver, control, or influence the performance for which they are held accountable, motivating them to achieve that performance will do little good.

Care must also be taken in selecting the type of mechanism. What works well for one group of people or culture may have no affect on another. Recall the discussion in Chapter 3 about the Grameen bank for the poor. Normally, a bank might threaten a lawsuit to collect on a defaulted loan. However, bringing such a suit against Grameen's impoverished borrowers would have had little consequence, given the small sums involved and the lack of borrower assets. By dealing with groups of five borrowers at a time and conditioning the loans to some on the payment by others, the bank creates a powerful peer pressure that produces a much better response than the threat of litigation.

Peer acclaim through group and individual awards can also be a potent stimulant to perform. Such programs not only inspire excellence but present a wealth of benchmarking opportunities as well. Since peers will want to know how they can achieve similar attention, a best practice achievement should be publicized broadly and in some detail.

But accountability is not just about rewarding good performance; it is also about making poor performance most undesirable. One mechanism—peer and public criticism—can provide the bite of accountability when performance is well below expected levels. An executive who understands that well is Lee Scott, CEO of Wal-Mart, a company that in recent years has faced a series of highly publicized problems concerning illegal workers, discrimination litigation, and other matters. Said Scott: "We can't just fall back on the idea that we should have some leeway because we don't mean to do any harm. We're going to be judged on how we react to racism, or sexism, or these other issues when we find them going on, and I tell everyone we have to react more dramatically and in a less forgiving, harsher way to behaviors that don't measure up."[9]

Group accountability and motivation through peer and public scrutiny can be facilitated proactively through a company's own external and internal reports on its sustainability performance. Such reports can focus on the performance of a single functional department—such as business practices, human resources, corporate governance, or quality—or of a facility, region, division, or other business unit. Particularly effective are periodic reports showing how a unit's performance compares with internal and external peers. Lists of the top-10 and bottom-10 performers can help motivate laggards to be sure, but sometimes those reports don't tell the full story. A more complete understanding can be had if the comparison also includes lists of those that have improved the most and slipped the most. This information not only helps motivate action but provides early warning of program turnaround or erosion. The business units covered in such reports are naturally sensitive about them, especially since these reports usually don't allow for extensive explanation. For that reason, even the most transparent companies don't communicate such rankings outside their organizations. However, some do publish tables listing their facilities and their respective performance against certain EHS metrics. Even though they lack rankings, these tables are powerful stimulants for action. Where is the plant manager who wants to see inferior performance numbers published for his facility alongside superior ones from his peers?

Besides their motivating role as an accountability tool, sustainability performance reports serve other important functions as well. In the next chapter, we will examine those functions and see how sustainability reporting can best fulfill them.

Follow-up Checklist for Action: Monitoring and Accountability

☐ Identify the qualitative and quantitative monitoring that may be appropriate for tracking performance toward sustainability objectives and goals.

☐ Identify the processes needed to collect, manage, and use data to achieve the objectives and goals, and determine what functions from Figure 9.1 are involved in those processes.

☐ Identify the data processes where the time and effort for them are so great, or where errors or lapses so frequent, and the value of information so important as to warrant consideration of an IT solution.

☐ Using the guidance of this chapter, and considering the available funding and support and the estimated return on investment, determine if an IT solution is warranted, and if so, what solution to pursue.

☐ If an IT solution is selected, implement it and follow up as suggested in the model process described in this chapter.

☐ Prioritize data needs and manage the timing of systems changes to deal with any data overload problems.

☐ Determine if auditing is needed to supplement monitoring and accountability mechanisms. If so, implement the auditing following the guidance of this chapter.

☐ Adopt performance reports, reward programs, and other accountability mechanisms needed to stimulate performance. Reevaluate them annually and, if necessary, adjust them.

Endnotes to Chapter 9

1. The quote is from the article, *Motivating Help*, N.Y. TIMES, July 4, 1982.

2. DOE defines accountability as:

   The obligation a person, group, or organization assumes for the execution of authority and/or the fulfillment of responsibility. This obligation includes:

   • Answering—providing an explanation or justification—for the execution of that authority and/or fulfillment of that responsibility,
   • Reporting on the results of that execution and/or fulfillment, and
   • Assuming liability for those results.

   See WILL ARTLEY ET AL., THE PERFORMANCE-BASED MANAGEMENT HANDBOOK, VOLUME ONE, ESTABLISHING AND MAINTAINING A PERFORMANCE-BASED MANAGEMENT PROGRAM 21 (2001), *available at* http://www.orau.gov/pbm/pbmhandbook/pbmhandbook.html.

3. Global Environment & Technology Foundation, *Environmental Management System Software: EMS Software Assessment* (EPA & American Association of Port Authorities 2004). Robert Seguy, Baxter International Inc., *Making a Business Benefit Case of Having Adequate EHS Strategy and Tools in Place*, Marcus Evans Conference on EHS Management Implementation, Amsterdam (Mar. 10, 2004). Interview with Nicholas Eisenberger, CEO, Ecos Technologies, Inc., by William R. Blackburn (July 21, 2004).

4. ISO, BS EN ISO 19011: 2002, GUIDELINES FOR QUALITY AND/OR ENVIRONMENTAL MANAGEMENT SYSTEMS AUDITING (2002), *available at* http://www.iso14000-iso14001-environmental-management.com/iso-19011.htm.

5. Sarbanes-Oxley Act of 2002, Pub. L. No. 107-204, 116 Stat. 745 (2002) (codified as amended at scattered sections of 15 U.S.C.). *See also* Appendix 2.6.6. for a summary of key provisions of this Act.

6. ISO, ISO/IEC GUIDE 62 (1996) (for quality management systems) and ISO, ISO/IEC GUIDE 66 (1999) (for EMS), *both available at* http://www.iso.org/iso/en/ISOOnline.frontpage. These guides will be replaced by ISO/IEC 17021. INTERNATIONAL ACCREDITATION FORUM, INC. (IAF), IAF GUIDANCE ON THE APPLICATION OF ISO/IEC GUIDE 62: 1996 (2003) and IAF, IAF GUIDANCE ON THE APPLICATION OF ISO/IEC GUIDE 66 (2003), *both available at* http://www.iaf.nu/.

7. *See, e.g.*, Upjohn Co. v. United States, 449 U.S. 383 (1981).

8. See discussion in *In re Horowitz*, 482 F.2d 72, 82 n.10 (2d Cir. 1973).

9. Brent Schlender, *Wal-Mart's $288 Billion Meeting*, FORTUNE, Apr. 18, 2005, at 91-106.

Chapter 10

Transparent Sustainability Reporting

"Sunlight is said to be the best of disinfectants."[1]
—Justice Louis D. Brandeis

Reasons for Transparent Reporting

Primary school students understand performance reports. Even at that young age, they see clearly the relationship between these reports and accountability. Mothers and fathers beam with pride when good scores appear on their child's report card from school. Extra money, treats, or other rewards may result. On the other hand, a report showing poor performance can prompt great displeasure in the household, causing parents to cut their child's valued play time and liberties to make room for extra study. To teachers, these reports are a critical tool for improving scholastic results. They know that shining a light on performance can produce the heat of accountability which heightens the likelihood of constructive change.

Driving Constructive Change

The idea that *"light brings heat brings change"* applies to a company's sustainability performance as well. The light of internal and external reporting on performance helps drive internal change in several ways. First, it forces a company to identify its sustainability issues and assess the gaps. By communicating the gaps internally, company sustainability leaders can show managers and employees what needs to be done and rally broad support for action. In this regard, the sustainability report serves as part of the "check" in the plan-do-check-act process that is popular with quality and environmental management professionals. As an essential element of the SOS, reporting helps a company realize the benefits of an SOS discussed in Chapter 3.

Change is also affected by sustainability reports through benchmarking and positive encouragement. The report and the process of gathering data for it can surface those groups that are delivering superior performance. Moreover, reporting can help pinpoint what was done to achieve these good results, presenting the path for success to others inside and outside the organization who are eager for similar results and acclaim.

Finally, sustainability reports spur change because they invite scrutiny and reaction to performance by stakeholders from whom a company needs support. Like students who don't want to disappoint their parents, companies are often willing to extend extra effort to keep employees, customers, and investors satisfied and to avoid the wrath of the all-too-critical public. Business-unit managers know that both the CEO and important stakeholders may read the report, and they don't want to let them down. Rather, most managers are eager to show they can run all aspects of their business just as good as, if not better than, their peers. Their egos and competitive nature are powerful forces which can be stimulated by a candid sustainability report.

But it's not just the executive ranks that can be influenced by these reports. Workers at all levels take pride when they see the name of their company, division, or facility linked with successful, socially responsible performance. Moreover, they tend to work even harder when they realize their efforts are being applauded in this way. This enthusiasm for action can be best channeled for enhanced performance if the report is balanced, providing acclaim when warranted but also openly discussing specific opportunities for improvement. The trick is to develop a report—or a complementary collection of internal and external reports—which best stimulates all these forces for constructive change.

Building Stakeholder Trust Through Transparency

Besides driving internal change, another reason to report on sustainability performance is to build trust and credibility with key stakeholders. As we saw in Figure 3.11, a trusting relationship is essential for building good support among those stakeholders—the employees, customers, suppliers, investors, and communities—that determine a company's success. Unfortunately, much is wanting in this regard: only one-third or less of the respondents in several public surveys said they thought companies were trustworthy.[2] To gain trust, a company must demonstrate transparency, that is, openness, honesty, and enlightened self-criticism. A sustainability report is a good place to start.

Writers who seek to be transparent must be mindful of not only what goes in their reports, but what is left out. A publication of only positive stories will do more harm than good. The public knows that business life is filled with ups and downs, and that a glossy report of great achievements reveals only part of the picture. Moreover, such a report invites uncomfortable questions: Is the company undertaking a cover-up of actions that have or will harm key stakeholders or are otherwise embarrassing? Does the company's culture discourage employees from speaking out about weaknesses and failures? Is communication so poor that company officials simply don't have a clue about the problems that exist? Transparency is more than just telling the truth; it is truthfully telling the whole story before others tell it. It is about talking with stakeholders to understand their concerns and then responding to them candidly with complete and accurate information.

The most embarrassing or unpleasant issues are often the most important issues to discuss. Certainly that's the message from a 2003 survey of 56 NGOs, where nearly 4 out of 5 respondents said that sustainability reports were "very" or "fairly" useful, but less than one-half considered them believable. The most effective way to improve the credibility of reports, according to the survey, is to acknowledge noncompliance, poor performance, and significant problems.[3] This information may include some executive impropriety, a product quality problem, an unpopular lobbying position, or some union activity. If the situation smells bad or is widely covered by the media, then it is probably ripe for disclosure unless, of course, the information is proprietary. Indeed, a legal review is essential before releasing any sensitive information. Unfortunately, all too often companies are overly cautious about disclosure only to find their reputations and stakeholder relationships suffer when the information is later revealed.

To avoid suspicion, a company should produce a report that identifies not only significant achievements, but the weaknesses in its performance and the steps it will take to address them. Data must be presented fairly, not with distorted graphs or metrics. The information must be reliable and communicated in a timely manner. Whatever is stated in a sustainability report must be consistent with what is said in the company's financial reports and elsewhere. Report writers must exercise particular care in this regard. To assure conformance with securities regulations, writers should use virtually the same language in the sustainability report as used in the financial report to discuss potential environmental liabilities and other sensitive financial issues. A few reporters go so far as to include in their sustainability reports the same standard disclaimer they use in their financial reports about future projections of performance—so-called *forward-looking statements*.[4] To be prudent, significant inconsistencies between the current sustainability report and earlier versions should be explained.

By openly sharing information on issues of actual and potential concern, a reporting company can convey its good-faith intentions as well as its perspective, educating stakeholders about the practical obstacles to achieving desired outcomes. The ABN AMRO bank in the Netherlands did this quite effectively in its 2003 report through a series of sidebars labeled "The Dilemma," discussing client-related issues concerning such things as animal rights, military defense equipment, and environmental degradation in a developing country. Likewise, a company that supports diversity, climate change, or another sustainability objective but which is having trouble meeting its goals should explain its difficulties. Stakeholders know that companies aren't perfect and that progress often does not proceed at an even pace. When they read sustainability reports that are transparent, they are typically consoled by how conscientious the organization is in identifying and addressing issues on its own. This strengthens the reporting company's credibility, and tends to quiet external criticism—an outcome than can be a great relief to managers who have been beleaguered with unfavorable press. Occasionally these managers will misread the situation, though, lulling themselves into believing the problem has gone away when it really hasn't. While transparency may boost credibility, it also requires follow-up since it raises the expectation that the company will address the problems noted and do better in the future. If the company doesn't make a good-faith effort to remedy the problems in a timely manner, then the gains in credibility may be lost and the company's reputation diminished even more than if it hadn't been transparent in the first place.

Then too, there is always the slim possibility that candid reporting could prompt an unfavorable response. When that happens, weak-kneed companies may retreat from transparency; strong ones do not. Instead they see these barbs as part of a healthy stakeholder-dialogue process that accelerates constructive change, which, in turn, reaffirms the company's appreciation for transparency. Experienced companies acknowledge that the heat generated by transparency, even though unpleasant, rarely approaches the intensity of criticism that would result if the problem was initially disclosed by others. It is an attitude like this that keeps companies such as Shell committed to transparent reporting in the wake of past criticisms of its sustainability performance. Nike, too, has seen the wisdom of continuing to publish reports every two years—with increasing emphasis on transparency—even though it cut back communication for a time amidst controversy over statements it made about its labor practices in developing regions. These two leaders, perhaps more than others, have come to know the true value of open communication.

Building Reputation Through Consistent Communications

Transparent sustainability reporting cannot only enhance a company's reputation by building trust and credibility with stakeholders, but it can also strengthen it by fostering consistent communication from across the company about the organization, its sustainability results, and the company's positions and policies on controversial issues. This keeps company spokespeople "on message" when they are speaking publicly about the company and reduces the risk of communicating inaccurately or inconsistently. As a reference publication, these reports prove quite useful in responding to public inquiries, saving hours of time that otherwise would be required to compile needed data on an ad hoc basis.

The Reasons Companies Give for Reporting

The reasons for public transparent sustainability reporting—to spur internal change, and enhance the company's credibility and reputation with stakeholders—were voiced in a slightly different way in a 2002 survey of over 200 business leaders from 50 countries. Their top four reasons for reporting were, in this order:

1. Improve stakeholder relations;
2. Improve management of sustainability issues;
3. Protect license to operate; and
4. Enhance reputation.[5]

Figure 10.1 lists these and other reasons often cited for openly communicating on sustainability issues.

Figure 10.1
Why Companies Transparently Report
About Their Sustainability Performance

1. Drives constructive change in the management of sustainability issues
2. Educates employees on the issues
3. Aligns the organization on areas of needed improvement
4. Hastens the resolution of problems before they magnify
5. Builds stakeholder trust
6. Enhances company reputation for honesty
7. Strengthens relationships with stakeholders

While the financial benefits of sustainability reporting are difficult to show—few can say they added x new customers because of their publication—these studies show that the companies involved in such reporting realize important intangible benefits, benefits that contribute to business success. Observed Phil Knight, founder and chairman of Nike: "Just producing the (Nike 2004 Corporate Responsibility) Report proved to us that the value of reporting goes far beyond transparency. It becomes a tool for improving both our management of business and in giving us clues about what to do next."[6]

Why Companies Don't Report Transparently; How to Reverse That

If transparent sustainability reporting is such a good thing, why aren't more companies doing it? Chapter 1 provided some executive perspectives on that, and in this chapter, Figure 10.2 captures most of the reasons. Generally it's because of fear of adverse consequences or because the company doesn't believe candid reporting on a particular issue is important enough to warrant action.

So how does one convince peers within an organization to move more toward transparent reporting? One way is to begin being transparent with internal reports not subject to the scrutiny of outside stakeholders. Once the internal reports show improvement is being made, then externally communicating a mix of accomplishments and opportunities for improvement may be easier to sell. Examples of transparent text from the sustainability reports of companies such as Shell, Nike, Chiquita, ABN AMRO, Ben & Jerry's, Motorola, and Ford may offer some solace to those who are still concerned about repercussions. Those who are concerned may be further encouraged if made aware of the broad multi-stakeholder support for various transparency programs. A good example is the Extractive Industries Transparency Initiative (EITI), a program endorsed by governments, investment groups, NGOs, and companies. EITI advocates that oil and mining companies publicize what they pay the governments of developing countries and that those governments disclose what they receive.[7] Other tactics can work, too. One is to have important customers, investors, or other stakeholders commend the company for its transparency. Another is to share written or live testimonials from executives inside or outside the company who have seen the advantage of open communication. As a groundswell of support for transparency builds among key managers, more progress can be made.

If company executives are resisting transparent reporting because they think the cost and effort would be too great, the section on strategies for controlling reporting costs and effort that appears later in this chapter may offer a solution.

Figure 10.2
Why Companies Don't Transparently Report
Certain Significant Sustainability Performance Issues

1. Embarrassed about performance
2. Key competitors aren't reporting on the issue; no competitive advantage
3. Afraid of releasing proprietary information that could hurt business
4. Concerned about reporting information that could create a security risk
5. Concerned about possible litigation on the issue
6. Afraid it will stir up certain stakeholders and create public relations problems
7. Afraid the media will criticize the company for its failings
8. Don't fully understand the issue
9. Not aware of the issue
10. Believe their trade association is adequately addressing the issue
11. Believe the issue isn't significant/material enough to be a priority
12. Not concerned about improving performance on the issue
13. Believe the cost and effort of reporting would be excessive

Internal Reporting

To be most effective in driving constructive change, external sustainability reports, typically issued every year or two, should complement and
build from more frequent internal reports. Monthly or quarterly internal
progress reports enable a company to quickly shift resources or take
other actions to ensure commitments are met. Transparent internal reporting—especially reports comparing performance among business
units, facilities, or departments—boosts accountability and motivation
and helps identify leaders early for benchmarking purposes. In addition,
internal reports can track efforts to reduce employee turnover, strengthen
training, improve the timeliness and quality of reporting, or implement
other corrective actions for addressing the root cause of poor performance. Issues like this, while important, often do not command enough
stakeholder interest to be included in external reports.

Internal reports can take many forms. Some follow a balanced scorecard format. Others may be bar or line graphs, pie charts, tables, or dial
gauges. Bull's eye charts are effective for showing related metrics, like
sales and costs, where you are trying to maximize one and minimize the
other. Color-coded stoplight indicators are also commonly used to show
progress (e.g., green = on schedule, yellow = slightly behind, and red =
seriously behind). A combination of these methods can be incorporated
into a one-page "dashboard" to provide management a quick look at
progress versus a number of key commitments. BC Hydro uses dashboards quite effectively, publishing a summary dashboard along with
supporting dashboards that provide details on individual metrics.[8] GE
and Johnson & Johnson also favor them.

With the proper coordination of internal and external reporting and appropriate attention to the needs of the audiences, a company can bring organizational focus to achieving its sustainability goals. Good reporting
will support strategic objectives and goals, and the underlying actions
needed to achieve them. Reporting that doesn't do this is a waste of time.

Mandatory Public Reporting

Some companies publicly report on sustainability because they are enlightened about the benefits; others do so because legally they have to.
Indeed, as discussed below, a growing number of laws are requiring companies to reveal environmental and social information.

Pollutant-Disclosure Laws

Laws requiring companies to report pollutant information to the government have been around for many years. Early laws of this type weren't designed for the wide disclosure of information to the public. However, that changed in 1986 in the United States with the enactment of the Emergency Planning and Community Right-To-Know Act (EPCRA), which mandated annual public reporting of toxic pollutant releases to the environment.[9] Toxic release inventory (TRI) reporting under EPCRA—credited with helping cut reported emissions in half between 1988 and 2000—gave rise to similar programs elsewhere. Many U.S. states now have their own "right-to-know" legislation. Canada, the Czech Republic, Hungary, Norway, Poland, and Yugoslavia have national registers of environmental emissions as well. Denmark, Japan, and the Netherlands also require annual reporting of environmental data by companies. The environmental information being collected under TRI and other environmental laws is not just being made available by the government; other organizations are disseminating it, too. NGOs like Environmental Defense, and SRI analysts like the ICCR and Innovest, compile this information and include it in the company environmental performance evaluations they provide to the public or investment clients.[10]

On a broader scale, the OECD has been chartered to promote the development of TRI-like pollutant release and transfer registers (PRTRs) among the OECD Member countries. The case for PRTRs was given a significant boost with the adoption of the so-called Aarhus Convention on Access to Information, Public Participation in Decision-Making, and Access to Justice in Environmental Matters, which was signed by 43 European and western Asian countries as well as the European Community, becoming effective in 2001. The convention, commits its signatories to assure ready access by the public to information about environmental conditions that may affect them.[11] A legally binding protocol on PRTR was adopted by the Parties in 2003 and is likely to take effect in 2007. As an interim step, the European Commission is moving forward on its European Pollution Emission Register, a less ambitious alternative to a full-blown PRTR.

Social and Environmental Information in Financial Reports

Publicly traded companies have long been required by law to periodically disclose certain financial results. Traditionally, such laws have required the reporting of environmental and social issues only if they pose a potentially material financial impact on the company. For example, in the United States, companies have commonly revealed fines over $100,000 (as required by a special rule of the Securities and Exchange Commission (SEC)) as well as multimillion dollar liabilities for the cleanup of contaminated disposal sites and other properties.[12] But historically, enforcement of these rules has been lax, providing little incentive for strict compliance.[13] However, recent developments have been prompting companies, especially those in the United States, to give these rules more attention. New insurance policies for directors and officers' liability are now excluding coverage for inadequate environmental disclosures.[14] The importance of that exclusion has been magnified by the Sarbanes-Oxley Act of 2002, which requires chief executives and financial officers to certify that the financial reports fairly present the company's financial picture, subjecting those who falsely certify to criminal penalties. Detection of violations on the reporting of environmental fines, liabilities, and costs has been enhanced over the last few years through greater sharing of information between the SEC and EPA. On top of all that, NGOs, socially responsible investors, and other governance advocates have been turning up the heat, demanding that companies more thoroughly report their sustainability risks and that regulators more closely scrutinize such disclosures, publicize shortfalls, and aggressively enforce their own rules.[15]

But public financial reporting laws are not just limited to financial performance anymore. Responding to the growing popularity of SRI, a number of countries have modified their financial reporting requirements to add environmental and social information. The New Economic Regulations (Nouvelles Regulations Economiques or NRE) adopted by France in 2001, impose this integrated annual reporting on corporations listed on the French stock exchange. Among the required disclosures is an explanation on how the company engages environmental activist groups, consumer groups, educational institutions, and impacted populations on sustainability issues of concern.[16]

A 2005 U.K. law, adopted pursuant to the 2003 European Union Accounts Modernization Directive, requires the largest companies in the country to include within their annual financial reports a Business Review, providing a comprehensive analysis of the development and performance of the company and its position at year-end. The law stipulates that an analysis related to environmental and employee matters be inserted where needed to help understand the review information.[17] In 2006, the U.K. legislature approved amendments to the law, which call for companies to report on supply chain, social and community issues, and to include information about the effectiveness of the organization's policies on the covered sustainability topics. Large companies must also provide, where appropriate, an analysis of KPIs related to their employee, supplier, and environmental matters and social and community issues.[18] The country's Accounting Standards Board issued guidance in 2006 on how to prepare text in financial reports on such non-financial topics. U.K. DEFRA, for its part, published reporting guidelines on environmental KPIs that could be considered in preparing a Business Review.[19]

In South Africa, the King Commission recommended in its Code on Corporate Governance that all companies listed on the Johannesburg Securities Exchange use the GRI reporting principles for disclosing economic, social, and environmental performance.[20] As of 2003, 85% of South Africa's largest 100 corporations were reporting at least annually on their sustainability policies and practices, although most of these disclosures were general in nature.[21] The Canadian Securities Administrators, a group of provincial securities authorities, issued model national securities reporting requirements calling for companies to identify any social and environmental policies they have adopted which are fundamental to operations, and to describe the steps companies have taken to implement them.[22] Financial reports in Sweden must include a brief statement on the company's environmental aspects, as well as information on gender diversity, employee sick leave, and governance issues. Australia and Norway also require companies to include environmental statements in their financial reports.[23]

In 2002, the European Parliament's Employment Committee—following up on the European Commission's Green Paper, *Promoting a European Framework for Corporate Social Responsibility*—recommended that companies operating within the European Union be required to issue independently verified environmental and social reports along side their financial reports. However, Parliament's Industry Committee opposed mandated reporting, favoring instead voluntary efforts to comply with existing nonbinding codes, such as the one adopted by the OECD.[24]

Voluntary Sustainability Reporting Initiatives

Certainly voluntary initiatives can be influential in encouraging companies to report on sustainability. For example, companies that are members of the American Chemistry Council must implement a Responsible Care® Management System, which requires them to periodically report to their stakeholders on the performance of the system and to provide information on health, safety, security, and environmental risks. This information is made available to the public through the Responsible Care® Tracking and Performance website.[25]

EMAS—a voluntary environmental management standard discussed in Appendix 3.7—also requires participating companies to publish a public, externally verified "environmental statement" describing the organization's environmental policy, programs, and management systems as well as its significant environmental impacts and their effects, and environmental goals and performance results.[26]

In addition to Responsible Care® and EMAS, there are over 30 other frameworks for voluntary environmental and sustainability reporting.[27] Guidance has been issued in Australia, Austria, Canada, Germany, Hong Kong, Japan, the Netherlands, and the United Kingdom.[28] Of all these initiatives, the most notable is the GRI, a worldwide collaborative effort among activists, investors, companies, and various professional associations.[29]

GRI Guidelines

GRI was started in 1997 by CERES—itself a U.S.-based multi-stakeholder group—and UNEP, bringing together those who were interested in establishing and promoting a generally accepted framework for voluntary reporting on sustainability. As of 2003, approximately one-half of the world's 100 largest companies were publishing environmental, social, or sustainability reports, and 2 out of 5 of them were referring to GRI for guidance—approximately the same ratio of GRI users among large companies reporting on sustainability in 2004-2005.[30] By 2006, GRI's Sustainability Reporting Guidelines were being employed to some extent by over 850 companies, with approximately 20% of them being self-declared "in-accordance" reporters that applied the guidelines fully as intended.[31] While use of the guidelines has grown steadily, the total percentage of companies engaged in GRI reporting—or sustainability reporting in general, for that matter—remains very small. But there are powerful forces trying to change that. For example, in 2004, 18 North American research analysts representing more than $230 billion in assets pressed all publicly traded companies to prepare GRI reports because, as they said, "current financial disclosure requirements do not reveal all of the risks, liabilities, or advantages associated with a corporation's activities."[32] Public sustainability reporting under GRI guidelines has also been a popular subject for activist-shareholder resolutions. (See Appendix 1.32 for more on that subject.)

While good sustainability reports can be prepared without adhering to GRI, companies will find few other ways to determine the consensus expectations of a wide range of stakeholders from around the world—something particularly challenging for the typical transnational corporation. Although the use of GRI is no substitute for actual dialogue between a company and its own stakeholders, it does offer a perspective even broader than dialogue can produce, helping report writers anticipate issues their own customers, investors, and employees may raise in the future.

GRI's guidelines are prepared through an extensive, global multi-stakeholder process. They call for sustainability reports to be prepared in accordance with certain principles on report content (materiality, stakeholder inclusiveness, sustainability context,[33] completeness) and on the quality of reported information (balance, comparability, accuracy, timeliness, reliability, clarity). The guidelines ask for information on the reporting entity's strategy, organizational profile, governance, and stakeholder engagement, as well as its commitments and management approach on sustainability matters. In addition, the guidelines list specific performance indicators spread across the TBL categories: economic, environmental, and social (labor, human rights, society, product responsibility). Reporters are to use those indicators that may reasonably be considered important (material) to their own decisionmaking and to their stakeholders. A standard content index is to be provided by reporters to facilitate comparison among reports. Guidance on assurance is offered for those who want their reports verified by third parties. The third edition of the GRI Sustainability Reporting Guidelines (G3) emerged in October 2006.

In addition to its basic reporting guidelines, GRI publishes sector supplements for specific industries and reporting entities, and has technical protocols which provide explanatory information on each of the

performance indicators. GRI also provides a website where reporters
may register their reports under various categories according to the extent of adherence to the guidelines.[34]

Sustainability Reporting Statistics and Trends

The general trend for company reporting on sustainability issues is upward. In 1995, approximately 200 environmental, social, or sustainability reports were issued. That number soared to approximately 1,600
by 2003.[35] Among all reports published between 1990 and 2003, nearly
60% came from Europe, 20% from the Americas, and another 20% from
Asia and Australia. Only 2% came from Africa and the Middle East.[36]
Since 1992, U.K. companies published the most reports, followed in order by those from the United States, Japan, Germany, Australia, and Canada.[37] Chemical companies produced more reports than those of other industries. The next five rankings went to firms in the electricity, oil and
gas, mining, transport, and banking businesses. This is probably due to
the high visibility of the social and environmental impacts of their operations and—in the case of banking—the financial, reputational, and legal
risks associated with funding projects with such controversial impacts.
The majority of reports now include both environmental and social content, with pure environmental reports declining from three-fourths of all
reports in 1995 to around 15% in 2004.[38] As of 2005, 52% of the world's
top 250 corporations issued an environmental, social, or sustainability
report, a jump from 35% in 1999. If financial reports with social or environmental content are included, the 2005 percentage climbs to 64%.[39]
Over 80% of the U.K. companies in the Financial Times Stock Exchange
(FTSE) 100 stock index were producing reports as of 2005, with most of
the others publishing short statements on some aspect of sustainability in
their financial reports or on their websites.[40] This unusually high percentage was no doubt influenced by the flurry of legislation and government
and standards-body guidance issued in the United Kingdom on the inclusion of environmental and social information in financial reports.

    While the overall uptake of sustainability-related reporting over the
last decade has been dramatic among large, highly visible companies, especially in North America and western Europe, the rate of growth in reporting has declined over the last few years. For the pace of acceptance to
increase so that reporting is adopted by a significant portion of businesses over the next decade, three things must occur. First, new, more

streamlined, less resource-intensive approaches, such as those discussed below, will be needed. Second, governments, customers, and investors must more aggressively encourage companies to report. Finally, the 35 or so organizations granting awards and recognition for sustainability reporting will need to redefine reporting excellence by shifting their criteria to emphasize materiality, transparency, and succinctness and de-emphasize the exhaustive coverage of issues.

Deciding Whether to Report Publicly; Low-Cost Strategies

Given the benefits of reporting, many companies might find it worthwhile to produce some sort of public document on their sustainability policies and performance, even if that consists of only one page of highlights. With the right knowledge, creativity, skill, and prioritization, most companies should be able to meet the typical challenges to reporting listed in Figure 10.3. Still, there are some situations where public reporting may not be warranted. For example, reporting would be hard to justify for a small company of only a few employees that is not concerned with public relations. Reporting would also be unwise for companies that feel only stories about success should be published. In such cases, the benefits of the report might easily be outweighed by the harm from critics who would likely view the document as mere greenwash.

Figure 10.3
Top Challenges in Sustainability Reporting
According to Petroleum Industry Companies[41]

1. Determining:

    a. How to measure or estimate performance for indicators
    b. How to define indicators
    c. What indicators to report
    d. What activities to include in performance measurements
    e. How much information to share with the public

2. The cost, effort, and speed of collecting data

The Polaroid Reporting Strategy

What about a company in financial straits and or other crisis that strains its resources? Should they report? The Polaroid experience provides some good insights. Polaroid is a Massachusetts-based company that annually produces and sells approximately $1 billion of instant-imaging film and related products. It manufactures in five countries and distributes globally. In 2001, the company filed for bankruptcy, with its business reeling from a heavy debt load and severe competition from digital cameras and one-hour photo shops. A year later, after downsizing by half, Polaroid emerged from bankruptcy as a privately owned organization. As it weathered this dramatic change, it considered whether or not to continue its long history of sustainability reporting, having issued its first annual environmental report in 1989 and its first GRI sustainability report in 1998. According to Stephen Greene, Polaroid's former product stewardship and environmental manager, the company debated the pros and cons of going forward.[42] Weighing in favor of reporting, he said, was that stakeholders had come to expect an annual report and that the company had made a commitment to report as a signatory to CERES. Moreover, despite the troubling times, the company had good information to share that could bolster its reputation and boost the spirits of employees. Then too, the transparent communication of needed improvements could help rebuild the trust that had been so damaged by its financial problems and downsizing. Weighing against reporting, according to Greene, were the severe workforce reductions and organizational changes that left little time or money for anything beyond basic business functions. Also, with so many people leaving, key information had disappeared. What information was available from previous years was now of little value given the radical alternation of the business.

In the end, the value of sustainability reporting was just too great for the company to abandon it altogether. The solution for Polaroid was to skip reporting the 2001 data and to prepare a 23-page scaled-down report on 2002 performance and a 28-page report for 2003.[43] Instead of communicating on the whole range of GRI indicators, the company focused on the information shown in Figure 10.4. A report on 2004 performance similar to the 2003 version was issued in early 2006, some months after the company was acquired by others.[44] Why did the company continue reporting after the business changed hands? Perhaps one reason was to help support the company's strong brand, which the new owners intend to expand to a wide range of consumer electronics.[45]

Figure 10.4
Sustainability Information Reported by Polaroid for 2002, 2003, and 2004

General: CEO statement
                       Vision, strategy, and practices
                       Company profile
                       EHS management systems and structure
                       Key EHS policies

Economic: Revenues (private company)*

Social: Safety statistics
                       Charitable donations
                       Sale of business, restructuring

Environmental: Energy usage
                       Water usage
                       TRI toxic releases (by plant)
                       Hazardous and non-hazardous waste generation
                       Greenhouse gas emissions
                       Emissions of key air pollutants
                       Regulatory compliance (environmental excursions)
                       Supplier evaluation criteria
                       Ozone-depleting chemicals usage
                       Key priorities and accomplishments for report year
                       Key priorities for upcoming year**

---

* reported for 2002 only
** reported for 2003 and 2004 only

As Polaroid demonstrated, the depth and frequency of reporting can be altered to align with changes in resources and priorities. A company that is financially flush and geared to fast growth will have a different perspective than one that is struggling and trying to slash costs. A small business will need to take an approach different than a large one. Companies with strong brand names may value the reputational benefits of reporting more than others. Each will strike its own cost-benefit balance when it comes to sustainability reporting. Fortunately, options exist for a wide range of circumstances.

A Key Determinant of Cost and Effort: Report Size

The cost and effort in reporting is generally directly proportional to the size of the report. A survey of member companies of GEMI found a reasonable effort devoted to EHS and sustainability reporting in 2001: the average report length was 23 pages, with only 2 of the 29 respondents issuing reports in excess of 40 pages.[46] However, because GEMI was inquiring about EHS reports, it was not clear how much social information beyond EHS was included in those reports.

But a survey of global sustainability reporters revealed a starkly different picture the following year. The U.K. firm SustainAbility in its review of the top-50 sustainability reports discovered that reports averaged 86 pages in length that year—a startling rise of no less than 45% for the same type of reports they examined two years earlier.[47] They speculated this "carpet bombing" may have been due to companies trying to meet the broad reporting criteria of GRI or various ratings groups. However, they found that a higher page count didn't necessarily mean a better report. Indeed, some of the top publications were 40 pages or so.

In 2004, SustainAbility found the average report size had dropped slightly, but still weighed in at a hefty 72 pages. They attributed the reduction to two practices: One was the fact that some writers were cramming more text on each page—a practice that only makes the data less inviting. The other was that more information was being placed on the companies' websites—which can be good or bad, depending upon how the layout is designed (more on that later).[48] Overall, though, many report writers don't seem to be appreciating what Winston Churchill supposedly once said: "The length of this document defends it well against the risk of being read." Communication that is transmitted but not read or heard is no communication at all.

Costs of Reports

Since the size, design, and coverage of reports varies greatly, so do the costs. According to GEMI's 2001 survey, report costs reached more than $200,000 for a few members. Others, however, were able to report for only a few thousand dollars. The average cost among all respondents was $116,000—approximately $87,000 for preparation and development and $29,000 for printing and distribution.

Another 2001 study—this one of 44 U.K. companies, mostly FTSE 350 firms—showed total average costs of the same magnitude—around

$135,000, but with a broad range of $10,000 to $780,000. About $35,000 of that average (range of $1,000 to $600,000) was attributed to information technology systems and planning.[49] Four companies that issued only website-based reports paid on average only $16,000. Total average costs varied significantly from sector to sector, with the low being $14,000 for the banking, finance, and investment group and the high, $235,000, for metals and mining. This higher cost was no doubt due to the latter group having more issues and risks to cover and greater public scrutiny of their sustainability performance.

At the highest end were the 2001 reports prepared by Rio Tinto and Shell, which, according to a GRI survey, hit nearly $1 million and $3 million, respectively.[50] A large share of Shell's cost was associated with worldwide data verification by two major financial accounting firms.

But few companies have sustainability budgets like those of Shell or Rio Tinto and many can ill afford the six- or seven-figure costs typically incurred for the verification of some financial reports, so less rigorous approaches are commonly used. The 2001 U.K. reporting-cost survey found the price for third-party verification ranging from approximately $1,500 to $150,000, with the average being approximately $12,000.[51] While a $1,500 verification may be able to cover little more than the data compilation and presentation processes at the headquarters of a very small company, the $12,000 figure is a more reasonable estimate for such a headquarters review at a moderately sized multinational corporation. For good assurability, however, the evaluation of headquarters processes should be supported by the sampling of data-collection practices at the facility level, which would cost more.

What conclusions can be drawn from this mixed data? There are six:

1. *Variations in use of internal resources.* The wide range of costs is likely due not only to variations in report scope, length, and medium, but also to the difference in the use of internal resources for which costs may not have been tallied. Most significant of these internal resources are those for data verification, website design, and the design and development of information management systems. A more useful comparison would capture and better categorize both external as well as internal costs.

2. *Separating planning and monitoring costs.* As noted in Chapter 3, the business case for reporting should be built on the busi-

ness case for an SOS. The cost for strategic planning and for creating and operating an information management system should not be laid at the feet of the report, but justified as part of the internal management and accountability process. When the costs for these activities are mixed with reporting costs, it misplaces the real value of data collection and distorts the costs of reporting.

3. *Placing costs in perspective.* Shell's costs of $3 million must be placed in perspective. Three million dollars represents only about 0.0015% of their 2003 sales of $202 billion and 0.025% of their profits of $12.5 billion. Had they chosen a less expensive approach to verification (see further discussion on that, below), their costs would have been even less.

4. *Expected global company costs.* A reasonably profitable global company with billion-dollar-plus sales should expect to spend $100,000 to $250,000 or so for a typical website and hard-copy report of the type produced by its peers. Of course, much simpler, less costly alternatives are also available.

5. *More visibility, more cost.* Companies in industries with high public visibility of their sustainability performance should anticipate having more extensive, more expensive reports than those in industries attracting little visibility. Since the former have more at stake, the cost of this "insurance" is justified.

6. *Cost is no barrier.* With so many companies reporting for a cost of $20,000 or less, the cost factor for producing at least some sort of sustainability report does not seem to be a barrier. Even companies with superior sustainability programs and performance should be able to provide a valuable report at a very modest price.

Strategies for Controlling Reporting Costs and Effort

So how can a company approach sustainability reporting if its management is concerned about the extent and cost of the effort? Here are seven suggestions:

1. *Start small; piggyback on existing publications.* Rely on internal resources for writing, publication, design, and other services where possible. At the lowest end, consider a simple addition to the company external website and/or print a brochure or single page of bullet points. For example, Starbucks annually publishes an attractive two-sided, five-fold brochure to communicate its sustainability performance to customers in its coffee shops. Another option is to incorporate the report in an existing publication, such as an annual financial report or company newsletter or magazine. Perhaps one edition of the employee newsletter per year can be devoted to a sustainability theme. If some mailed communication is deemed a must, consider mailing a post card notification of the availability of the report on the company's website. Or distribute a compact disk (CD) of the report rather than a hard copy. With some creativity, each of these media can be used to provide an appealing report.

2. *Use available data.* Another strategy to keep costs and efforts manageable—especially for companies that are just beginning to report—is to do what Polaroid did for their 2002 and 2004 publications: rely heavily on data that is already available. Safety data and emissions of toxic and other key air pollutants are collected and reported in the United States as required by law. Waste can be determined from reports filed with the government and from waste hauler billings. Energy usage is commonly available from power company invoices. Compliance information is typically of high visibility within a company and a matter of public record. Company foundations maintain detailed accounts on charitable giving. Affirmative action records may be tapped to report on diversity. Other reports abound with information on financial performance.

3. *Reduce frequency.* Changing reporting frequency is a step several companies have taken when money is scarce. Some like Polaroid have skipped one year and resumed annual reporting when the company's circumstances improved. Others have shifted to reporting every two years as a regular practice.

4. *Narrow scope.* The effort can also be controlled by limiting the geographic or organizational scope of the report. This is

commonly done by new transnational reporters. They may report on performance of a single division or just in their home
country or local region for a year or two on a pilot basis before
expanding the coverage to all global operations. Reporting on
joint ventures and supplier issues can likewise be phased in.

5. *Prioritize content.* One of the best ways to keep the costs and
time for reporting under control is to prioritize the information to
be included. Actually, every company that reports on
sustainability should do this as part of its normal report-planning
process. Suggestions on how to do that are provided in the discussion below on report content. When resources are tight, reporters can always cut lower priority information. Of course,
they should not be too quick to drop the collection of data if the
decision about not reporting it is likely to be reversed within the
next year or so.

6. *Cut the fancy stuff.* While artistic graphics, bright colors, and
scenic photos can make a report engaging, they aren't necessary.
DuPont produces a photo-less GRI report in a simple type-writ-
ten, question-and-answer format. Dow does the same, although
it publishes a more traditional report as well. Many of the
small-company reports mentioned in Chapter 12 are also simple
black and white Microsoft Word® documents. Low-glitz reports
can still help a company manage its sustainability issues and provide a convenient source of data for those inside and outside the
company who want to investigate or communicate the company's performance. Once management sees the data may be
valuable for employees and customers, the money for a more
engaging publication may follow. In the meantime, the company can continue to compile a reliable history of its sustainability performance.

7. *Change verification strategy.* The vast majority of companies
cannot justify the time and effort required to secure a full third-
party verification of their sustainability data using approaches as
rigorous as those applied to financial data. Fortunately, there are
many options. One, of course, is to do what many companies do:
have no external verification at all, but simply ask those who are
involved in collecting and compiling the data to document and

double check their work. The problem with unverified reports, though, is that they may be viewed skeptically by some readers. A slightly better approach is to have internal people—preferably those not involved in handling the data—assess the quality of data collection, compilation, and presentation practices with oversight from a team of independent volunteers selected from among NGOs or other external stakeholders. A cost-effective way to further improve assurance is to hire professional third-party auditors to review data compilation and presentation processes at headquarters and rely on others already in the field to assess the data being collected and reported there. Some companies like Baxter International ask their auditors who are conducting ISO 14001 or 9001 assessments to tack on the review of sustainability information while they are in the field. Others like Novo Nordisk use their financial auditors the same way. Another way for keeping costs low is to have the headquarters review undertaken by field auditors already familiar with the company and its programs. But purists like Rio Tinto don't do this; to avoid the hint of bias, they prefer the more expensive route of retaining a separate consultant for this purpose. A cost-conscious strategy used by a number of organizations is to verify only part of the reported information. Or some data can be verified one year and other data the next. Even for those who seek verification of all report information, starting small and phasing in additional portions of the data over time may be the most prudent approach.

Taken together, the prioritization and the other steps mentioned above should provide all but the smallest companies with enough flexibility to report despite the usual constraints on resources.

Process for Preparing a Public Report

For any significant sustainability reporting effort, the initial action is usually securing management approval for it and its costs. Chapter 4 offers some tips on how to gain this needed support. Once that approval is secured, the reporting process begins.

All too often the reporting process is framed around communications departments gathering data from the EHS function; drafting some nice promotional articles; and then submitting the text to lawyers who aggressively edit it themselves. Between the lawyers and communications professionals, little content on company shortcomings makes the cut. Unfortunately, the resulting report then leans too much toward puffery to be taken seriously, which actually hurts the company's credibility more than it helps. A more reasonable approach for most sizeable companies—one aimed at producing a report that is candid, useful, and effective—would include the steps shown in Figure 10.5 and described below. Ideally, the final report that emerges should be clear, engaging, candid, accurate, insightful, and concise. It should hit the issues of greatest interest to stakeholders, tell the full story, and, of course, have a cost that is within the budgetary limit.

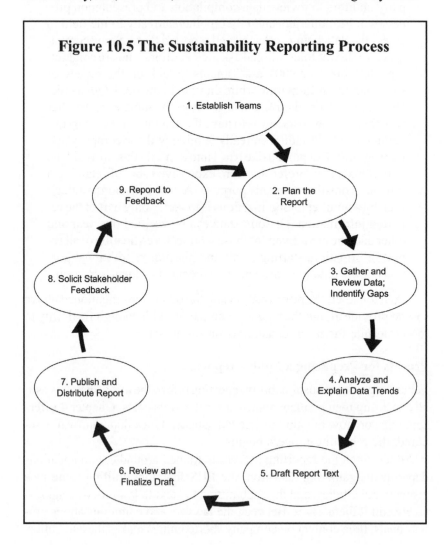

Figure 10.5 The Sustainability Reporting Process

Step 1: Establish Teams

As discussed in Chapter 4, a company would be wise to identify a sustainability leader and create a deployment team responsible for rolling out the SOS and collecting report data. In addition, a report distributors network may be formed from those internal groups that will distribute the report to key stakeholders. These representatives can provide feedback on report content based on the needs of their stakeholders. A small report preparation team is commonly established as well. For most large companies, this team consists of editors, graphic/layout designers, writers and key reviewers, most often including the sustainability leader and others from corporate communications, EHS, and outside firms. Members of the report preparation team will gather feedback on content from the report distributors network, and interact with deployment team members to collect and discuss report data. Before the work commences, team members should clearly understand and accept their duties and deadlines.

This team arrangement assumes a full sustainability report will be prepared. However, first-time reporters may want to limit the scope of their report to one or two areas, such as governance or EHS, or just the environment or health and safety, to gain practical experience with reporting before launching a comprehensive report covering economic, social, and environmental matters. If the report is of narrowed scope, the teams can be scaled back appropriately.

Step 2: Plan the Report; Monitor Performance

The report preparation team may work with the deployment team and others as appropriate to plan the details for the report as listed in Figure 10.6 and discussed later in this chapter. An action plan listing tasks, responsible parties, deadlines, and budgets should emerge from this planning. The leader of the report preparation team or some other assigned manager should track performance against the action plan to assure appropriate progress is being made.

Step 3: Gather and Review Data; Identify Gaps

Once the report has been planned, the information needs defined, and the sources of that information identified, the next step is to gather and review the data. This includes collecting any needed photos and artwork, too. As discussed in Chapter 9, there are many ways to acquire and review information for a report. Experts from the groups providing data should check it to assure it is complete and reasonably accurate. A good technique for detecting errors in facility data is to compare reported numbers to those reported by the same facility for other years, as well as to those reported by other comparable facilities. Where data doesn't exist, it can often be reasonably estimated using these same comparisons.

Shortly after the data collection and review is completed and field people have had a chance to decompress from that hectic process, a follow-up discussion should be held to dissect the process and recommend improvements. This is also a good time to review the changes needed in data collection for the next report.

Step 4: Analyze and Explain Data Trends

At the same time reviewers are evaluating raw data, they should also be trying to understand it. Some questions they might attempt to answer are: Why is the number so big or so small? Which sites and operations were the largest contributors to the companywide performance? What caused the most significant changes in data? Are any common themes apparent? If performance on important objectives has deviated dramatically from what was expected, the reasons for the deviation should be explained in the report. Those responsible for delivering performance must understand the causes, too. Where performance has been disappointing, they should take corrective and preventive actions to address it. If the performance gap will likely be of major concern to stakeholders, it may be worthwhile to discuss that response plan in the report. On the other hand, if performance has been unexpectedly good, the reasons for that should be captured so the learning can be shared across the organization.

Step 5: Draft Report Text

The next step is for the report preparation team to prepare the initial draft of text, exhibits, and photos for publication. In some cases, deployment team members may prepare draft graphs, tables, and text for editing by the preparation team. Planners should resist the temptation to shrink the size of print and graphics to squeeze more words on the page. This can produce a report that is too dense and not engaging. Of course, if text is too long, more pages can always be added, provided the budget allows. The better approach, however, is to edit down the text or cut some of the low-priority content altogether.

Step 6: Review and Finalize Draft

Content providers should have a chance to review edited text and the report layout to assure it is accurate and conveys the right messages. Legal review should be completed at this time, too, to assure proprietary information isn't being disclosed and that the text doesn't breach securities, privacy, or copyright laws or present other legal problems. Key managers of the operations covered by the report should also preview the copy so they aren't surprised later. The roles of reviewers and editors must be clear, however, especially if deployment team members have provided the initial draft of the text. People often have a strong pride of authorship. The final decisionmakers on editorial changes should be identified early in the process to avoid later conflict.

Step 7: Publish and Distribute Report

Once the report is published, it should be distributed according to the agreed distribution plan. To save costs and effort, those in the company who will be sending out the reports should determine whether the reports must be mailed individually or whether there are cheaper or more expedient ways of delivering them. For example, reports may be added to other mailings that will be going out around the same time, or boxes of reports may be sent to specific people at each facility who will distribute the reports there. Sales and government affairs people may want to personally deliver copies to customers and legislators when they meet with them. Some copies may be distributed directly at large meetings.

If the report will only be published on the company's website, it may be desirable to compile a distribution list of e-mail addresses so a notification about the report can be sent out along with the Internet link to it. If the report is noteworthy, the company's communications people may want to prepare a press release on it and forward it to key media contacts who are interested in the social, environmental, and sustainability matters of business. For the internal distribution, a letter on the report from the CEO to key managers can raise attention to the publication. This message might request that managers cascade the information down to line employees. Supplementary communication tools can be prepared to inform employees about sustainability and the company's performance on it so they can use this information with their own stakeholders.

Step 8: Solicit Stakeholder Feedback

After stakeholders have had a chance to review the report, someone should solicit feedback from them about the company, its sustainability performance, and the report itself. The request may also include inquiry about which companies the stakeholders think have produced excellent reports and why they liked these documents. This feedback is commonly collected through self-addressed reply cards included in hard-copy reports and through an e-survey for reports posted on the company's website. Members of the company's report distributors network can be recruited to solicit comments directly from customers and other stakeholders to whom they sent the report. Special meetings or conference calls can be used to collect input from NGO coalitions like CERES or other stakeholder organizations. Focus group discussions with employees may also be useful. These varied forms of feedback are a key part of the SOS. Chapter 11 discusses many other ways companies may engage stakeholders to obtain it.

The report team can gain other insights by reviewing the latest public surveys and other studies of stakeholder views on corporate sustainability reporting. Two good examples are the *2003 Global Stakeholder Report* issued by the consulting firms ECC Kohtes Klewes and Fishburn Hedges and the follow-up report issued in 2005 by Pleon Kohtes Klewes.[52] These reports not only provide useful information on stakeholder opinions, but also present survey questions companies may want to consider for the next survey of their own stakeholders.

Another way for companies to obtain valuable feedback on their sustainability report is to have it evaluated under one or more of the many recognition and award programs for sustainability reporting. The U.K. consulting firm SustainAbility works with UNEP and the S&P to evaluate and rank the top reports globally. Their ratings and analysis published every two years provides a good overview of reporting strengths, weaknesses, and trends.[53] The Roberts Environmental Center at Claremont McKenna College in California ranks sustainability reports under its *Pacific Sustainability Index*, a scored rating based on 140 questions addressing intent, reporting, and performance in the social and environmental areas. Its website contains the scoring sheet for the index, the ratings on individual reports with links to those reports, and the center's review of reporting by industry sector.[54] The Association of Chartered Certified Accountants (ACCA) issued a similar report with

CorporateRegister.com in 2004, identifying best-practice reporters and containing a wide range of global and regional reporting statistics.[55] ACCA offers reporting awards in various countries in Asia, Australia, Europe, and North America, including a joint award program with CERES in the United States. It also teams up with over a dozen other European groups to administer the European Sustainability Reporting Awards program. The CorporateRegister.com website lists over 35 reporting award programs that may be considered.[56]

Step 9: Respond to Feedback as Appropriate

The final step in the reporting cycle is to compile, discuss, and evaluate the feedback that has been obtained. A plan can then be developed in response, which can be melded into the broader SOS planning process for the following year. The action plan for reporting must not only consider the feedback on the report itself, but also the commentary on the company's sustainability performance and issues. This input may affect the content of the next report as well as the communication strategy for it. To assure its stakeholder feedback was properly addressed in its sustainability report, the U.K.-based Co-operative Financial Services included a table describing each key stakeholder group, what matters to them most about the company, and where information of interest to them is published in the report.[57]

Planning the Report

As with most initiatives, careful planning can improve the chances that a sustainability report will fulfill the company's expectations and those of its stakeholders. The planning considerations in Figure 10.6 warrant special attention. Let us review each in turn.

Figure 10.6 **Report Planning Considerations**	
1. Audiences	7. Schedule
2. Scope	8. Title and theme
3. Medium: Website or hard copy?	9. Structure, organization
4. Size	10. Content
5. Quantity of reports; distribution plan	11. Reporting tone and philosophy
6. Budget	12. Verification

Audiences

The target audiences must be defined so the report content can be tailored to their interests. Occasionally a sustainability report will be prepared for just one or two stakeholder groups, such as employees and customers. More often than not, though, reports are intended for a variety of stakeholders. Companies responding to the 2001 GEMI survey said employees were the primary audience for their reports, followed by shareholders, customers, and management. Important secondary audiences were the general public, NGOs, neighbors, government agencies, suppliers, and academics. A 2005 survey of nearly 500 report users around the globe produced a slightly different finding. Those respondents believed the top audience to be shareholders/investors followed by employees. Customers were third and the media, fourth.[58]

Report planners may be surprised to learn exactly how their reports are used by their audience. A large 2003 global study of external stakeholders who read reports found that most use them for benchmarking. This involves primarily consultants and company employees involved in report preparation who want to compare sustainability performance and reporting practices among organizations. The second most common reason for reading sustainability reports was academic, including research, teaching, and thesis writing, while the third was for obtaining general information about the company. The remaining purposes were, in order: consultancy work, investment fund selection, journalistic activity, and lastly, stakeholder dialogue.[59] While planners may initially be disappointed to see report use by investors, journalists, and other key stakeholders trailing on the list, they should be consoled by the fact that academics and consultants are often important influencers of these other groups.

Decisions about target audience will also help determine what language to use for the report. Most global reports are printed in English—the language of business. But a report in English isn't as effective as one in the native language of an important customer in, for example, China. The internal report distributors network can be a good sounding board for evaluating the cost-effectiveness of issuing reports in various languages. Shell and Dow have found publishing such reports to be useful. In Shell's case, the local operating units have so valued the report that they request and pay for these translated versions themselves.

Scope

Report planners must define which operations, geographies and time frames will be covered by the document. For instance, they must determine whether all of the company's operating units and regions will be addressed or just some of them. They must decide if only companywide data will be conveyed or if business-segment performance information will also be provided as Suncor has done. In addition, they must resolve whether facility-specific information will be communicated, either as part of the companywide report as Polaroid and StoraEnso (the Scandinavian forestry-products company) do, or in separate regional and facility reports of the type produced by DuPont, Dow, and Shell.

Other scope, or as GRI terms it, "boundary" issues concern joint ventures and the supply chain. Will joint ventures be captured in the report, and if so, will all of them be covered or just those where the company has a controlling interest? If some aspects of supplier or contractor performance will be covered, how far down the supply chain will the report extend? Will the suppliers' own vendors be included, too? What about a contractor's subcontractors? As a rule of thumb, the greater the degree of control by the company over the operation and the greater the potential sustainability impacts of that operation, the greater the justification for including that operation in the report. First-time reporters often narrow the scope and expand it over time as needs dictate and resources allow.

But scope is not just about organization and operations; it is about time frames as well. Most sustainability performance reports address the company's performance over the last two or (preferably) three years. Where goals are involved, base-year information is also commonly furnished. However, if different time frames are used for different performance measures, that should be made clear in the report.

Many reports go beyond past performance to discuss future plans, too. Vodafone presented information in its 2005 report arranged under the headings: "we said" (last year), "we have" (this year), and "we will" (next year). Co-operative Financial Services organized its 2003 and 2004 reports to show the goals and performance for the report year as well as the targets for the following year and the names of employees responsible for each target.

Medium: Website or Hard Copy?

Another question facing planners is what medium or media to use to communicate the information. The popular options include full hard-copy reports, hard-copy summaries, and website reports. Less commonly used alternatives are CDs, films, and audiotapes.

As noted in Figure 10.7, electronic Internet-based reporting has its advantages and disadvantages vis-à-vis hard-copy reports. One of the best reasons for using the company's website is the elimination of the cost and time of printing and shipping hard copies. This reduces the impact on the environment, too—at least from the publisher's perspective. (Of course, the publisher has no control over how many copies readers download and print.)

Figure 10.7
Advantages and Disadvantages of Hard-Copy and Website-Based
Sustainability Reports

Medium	Advantages	Disadvantages
Hard copy	-Doesn't require equipment to read -Portable -Familiar medium for all readers -Ease in evaluating and marking up report by rating organizations, award judges, and other reviewers -Can be distributed during meetings and left with business cards for promotional purposes -Typically more engaging to the reader; more likely to be examined	-Printing and shipping cost -Storage space -Environmental impact of printing and shipping -Extra copies require time and expense to produce -Difficulty in correcting and updating data
Website-based	-No printing or distribution cost (unless postcard announcements are sent) -Ease of correcting, updating data, making design changes -Linking to company's other website documents and to websites of other organizations -Quick links from index to text (especially for GRI indicator index) -Ease in preparing translated versions -Immediate, unlimited access by all readers globally -Ready access to past reports	-Requires computer and Internet access -Can be awkward for reading long documents -Navigation can be frustrating -Crosslinks may give impression of disjointed report -May be difficult to locate on website

Another key advantage is that website reports are readily accessible worldwide—provided the reader has access to the Internet, is inclined to use it, and can readily find the report from the company's home page. Unfortunately, all too often, this is not the case. While computers are common among the middle and upper classes of industrialized nations, only about 10% of the global population has access to them (see Appendix 1.3 concerning the "digital divide"). If local community groups are an important audience for the report, hard copies should be considered.

A website-posting strategy also won't do if the document is hidden in an obscure location many mouse-clicks deep on the company's home page. Easy access to the report from the home page is desirable if the document is to serve its purpose. A few companies achieve this by providing a prominent link on the home page to the company's sustainability site where current and past reports are kept, along with other information on governance, ethics, EHS, and other sustainability topics. This is superior to the usual practice of providing access through sites termed "About Us" or "Company Information." Access can be further facilitated by including the website address for the report in related press releases, customer bills, sales literature, and other communications. The address can also be incorporated in the automatic signature information on e-mails from core team members and other key company personnel, and linked on the websites of GRI (if their guidelines were used) and other stakeholder and industry groups.

Once the content is prepared and the layout designed, website reports require considerably less time and effort to publish than hard-copy reports. For that reason, website data can be fresher, issued more frequently, and corrected with little inconvenience. On the other hand, readers expect data posted on the company's website to be reliable and relatively current, although historical reports can prove of interest, too. In any case, it's imperative that all posted reports, data sheets, and other documents be clearly dated. Stale, undated information or hastily posted data that is inaccurate can hurt credibility with readers, defeating the very purpose for posting it.

Another major benefit of website-based reports is that the report itself—or the site on which it is posted—can be provided in hyper text markup language (html) and hyperlinked to additional information posted elsewhere, making report size less an issue. For example, a report might tie in company policies, position papers, past reports, articles, and other background documents, thereby avoiding the need to republish this data from year to year and reducing report clutter, size, and cost. International Paper's website has tiered links that lead to detailed performance information on its individual pulp and paper mills and a subsidiary. For more creative and diverse presentations, short films and audio broadcasts can even be inserted. Website reports can also be linked to external codes and other information on sites of outside organizations. One caution, though: as the amount and complexity of overall content grow, the report and linked information must be carefully designed so it doesn't become incoherent, burdensome to navigate, or overwhelming. Making the full report and key sections of it available in portable document format (pdf) for downloading can help because full pdf reports are highly desired by the serious reader who is likely to print them. Indeed, they should be designed with that use in mind. This means reducing or removing photos and less important exhibits that may slow downloading and printing, which can be a real problem for those without high-speed computer service. It also means designing the report—especially the graphs—with the contrast and patterns needed for a legible black-and-white print-out. If the report is intended to be read online, long articles and multiple-column designs should be avoided.

Website reports offer other advantages as well. With the Internet, it is easier to issue the same report in many languages. Some website reports even offer readers the opportunity to custom-select content to form a report specific to their own needs. Those scanning a report can use the site search engine to quickly locate special words or topics of interest. Readers who want available hard-copy documents can easily order them online. The Internet also reduces the burden of providing and compiling feedback compared with that posed by reply postcards and other methods. Interactive websites like *Tell Shell* enable readers to engage in dialogue with the company, which helps clarify their concerns and assure proper response. While such interactive sites can be useful, they must be designed and monitored to ensure they do not become chat rooms for interpersonal communication unrelated to sustainability.

From all these considerations, website reports seem to offer more advantages than hard-copy reports. Certainly, that's what many companies think. While the majority of sustainability-related reports were issued only in hard copy in 1999, by 2003 only about 5% were. By then nearly 60% were provided only on the Internet. Still, many companies using the Internet acknowledge there are situations where a hard-copy report better meets communication needs, which is why over 35% of reporters published reports in both formats.[60] While a few companies have issued reports—or the background data for them—on CD, that practice is unlikely to take hold. This is because users still must go to a computer to read the disk information. Since most computer owners have access to the Internet, they can just as easily pull the data from a website.

Given all these options, what should a company do? If money is tight, a printable website report may be the best solution. When the company needs hard copies, it can always print them from the computer. Where resources allow, however, a company should consider a dual strategy: producing an engaging, short, formally printed summary report to fill the need for hard copies, while publishing a more complete pdf report with other linked information on the company website. This is a cost-effective way of providing something for everybody.

Some companies, like Novo Nordisk, Novozymes, Dofasco, and Novartis, have gone a step further with their reporting strategy, using it to promote the integration of sustainability into the mainstream of the business. They have done this by including sustainability performance as part of their annual financial report. As investors, securities agencies, and stock exchanges become more interested in governance and the management of sustainability risks and issues, the pressure to follow this practice will mount. This approach does pose drawbacks, however: the space allotted for social and environmental material is often limited because much of the report is already filled with financial information mandated by securities laws and accounting standards. But if one follows the recommended strategy and publishes only summary information in hardcopy format, this is a convenient way to accomplish that goal. The company's website can still furnish the details. All things considered, the integrated report is a step in the right direction—one that emphasizes that sustainability issues are business issues.

Size

As previously mentioned, reports must not be so long that they discourage people from reading them. A well-designed hard-copy report—including pdf versions printed from the company's website—can still be engaging if they have less than 50 pages. Even at 50 pages, the full report will rarely be read cover to cover, except by a few consultants, rating groups, or competitors. Most readers will spend less than 30 minutes to skim the document, reading only those parts of interest.[61] Stakeholders particularly like a concise report smaller than 50 pages which refers readers to websites and other places where more details can be obtained on specific topics.[62] Shell's 2004 report of 34 pages and Vodafone's 2004/2005 report of 35 pages show that a report can be slim but meaty. Short report summaries can also be filled with useful information. Good examples are the 2005 BT report, which was 21 pages, HP's 24-page 2005 report, and Baxter's 26-page report for 2004. P&G's 2005 single-sheet, double-foldout summary of eight pages is perhaps the best example of a brief, engaging, readable handout.

Setting the size of the hard-copy and website reports early in the planning process helps planners stay within budget. It also forces prioritization of content, which results in a more attractive publication with greater impact.

Quantity of Reports; Distribution Plan

Planners must agree on the number of any hard-copy reports, CDs, announcement cards on report availability, or other items to be distributed. This can be developed from discussions with the deployment team and the report distributors network. Estimates should consider the items to be given to employees as well as distributed to stakeholders at key conferences, seminars, trade shows, and other gatherings. The report preparation team must also identify the internal or external parties who will be responsible for distributing the reports to stakeholders, issuing press releases, and performing other duties associated with the release of the report. Moreover, it must assure the distribution is coordinated so key stakeholders are neither overlooked nor sent copies from more than one source.

Budget

Before reporting can begin, budget moneys must be available to complete the task. The budgets must consider any costs for designing hard-copy and website reports, and printing and distributing the former. To properly estimate these costs, some assumptions must be made about report media and size, the complexity of design, and the need for the services of outside photographers and graphics designers. Printing and distribution costs will depend on the number of hard copies involved. If reports will be verified by third parties or new data collection systems installed, someone must assure those costs will be covered, too.

Schedule

The final part of planning is setting the schedule. This should be undertaken with the end in mind. If the report is to be produced as a companion piece to the annual financial report, the schedule should be set to deliver the sustainability report when the financial report issues. If the report will be released at the annual stockholders meeting or some key trade show, the dates of those events should control. Or the company may want to have the report available by the deadline for some award application. Whether it be these dates or others, the final deadline is often set according to a company communications strategy.

Planners must also consider the other end of the schedule: data collection. If some information is collected from government reports or supplier invoices, the timing of their receipt must be incorporated into the schedule. If critical data is not being routinely collected, the time to establish a new collection process must be factored in.

Toyota resolves its scheduling problems by using different periods of reporting for different types of information. The company's report issued in 2005 covered data from April 2004 to March 2005 and major developments as of June 2005. It publishes the Japanese version of the report during the summer and the English version in autumn.[63]

Shell adopted a different strategy to deal with their scheduling challenges. Their objective is to issue their sustainability report at the same time they produce their annual financial report during the first half of April. The problem is that EHS data cannot be verified until the middle of March, leaving only about three weeks thereafter to finalize, publish, and distribute the report. To resolve this, Shell begins its report preparation process around July of the previous year. By September, the feature articles are drafted, the general text for each section is completed, and the report layout and graph formats are finalized. Appropriate space is left for discussing year-end metrics and inserting the latest performance results in graphs and tables. As soon as the previous year's results are finalized in mid-March, that data is quickly added to the report and the document is shipped to the printer for final publication.[64]

Other companies try to speed up their reporting by scrutinizing performance at the end of the third quarter. They do that to develop an estimate of year-end results and ferret out and resolve problems with data quality. This expedites the completion of the report when the year-end data finally arrives during the first quarter of the following year.

Title and Theme

Planners will need to determine the title and theme of the report. If the sustainability report is simply part of an annual financial report, then a common theme will be needed for the overall publication. Novartis' *Annual Report 2004—Caring and Curing* is an example. For stand-alone sustainability reports, companies will sometimes link the title, theme, and design to that of the annual financial report and other companion documents. The cover of Novo Nordisk's publication, *Sustainability Report 2003—What Does BEING THERE Mean to You?*, bore a different color but the same design and theme as its financial report and its report on special issues and product developments. Bringing the theme and schedules of the financial and sustainability reports into sync can also be a good interim step toward publishing a fully integrated financial-sustainability report—which is exactly what Novo Nordisk did in 2004. Businesses may also tie the theme to key values the company espouses.

Here are a variety of report titles and themes that have been used in the past:

2004 Sustainability Report—Living Our Values (Johnson Controls)

Sustainability Report 2005—Linking Opportunity with Responsibility (P&G)

Sustainability Report 2004—Making the Right Choices (BP)

Corporate Social Responsibility Report 2005: Committed to People, Committed to the Future (Toshiba)

Corporate Responsibility Report 2004/2005—We Said, We Have, We Will (Vodafone)

2003/2004 Corporate Citizenship Report: Our Principles, Progress, and Performance—Connecting With Society (Ford)

Global Citizenship Report 2004—Continuity and Commitment (Intel)

BT Social and Environmental Report, 2005—Let's Make a Better World (BT)

DuPont Economic, Environmental, and Social Performance Data in the Global Reporting Initiative Format—July 2005 Update (DuPont)

The Shell Report 2004—Meeting the Energy Challenge: Our Progress in Contributing to Sustainable Development (Shell)

2004 Corporate Report—Focused on Tomorrow (Dow)

Public Report 2004—Earning Your Goodwill (S.C. Johnson)

Structure, Organization

The report preparation team must decide how the report will be organized. This starts with consideration of the theme and becomes an iterative process with the selection of content. In many reports, separate chapters are presented on the TBL categories of economic, social, and environmental responsibility with subtopics under each. Figures 2.3, 2.4, and 2.5 and the layout of GRI's TBL performance indicators provide some idea of how the subtopics might be grouped. The TBL structure may work well for reporting on GRI indicators but not so well when talking about innovation or presenting some profiles on facilities or programs. Certain topics don't fit neatly into one of the TBL categories but span two or all three of them. For instance, product safety is a social concern, but when it involves exposure to chemical substances, it may also have environmental ramifications. Supplier programs may be aimed at improving minority procurements—a social issue—as well as reducing environmental impacts. Energy conservation activities help address climate change but also have a positive effect on economic performance. Feature stories on facilities or departments may cut across all three areas.

Companies commonly adopt one of two strategies to address the difficulties with the TBL approach: either group the topic according to the aspect that is most noteworthy or most emphasized by the company, or go beyond the TBL by adding or changing chapter headings to address the broader nature of the topic. A few businesses ignore the TBL categories altogether and structure their reports by key business units, as DuPont did for 2002. Others, like Van City and Johnson Controls, build their reports around their sustainability values or goals. Ford designed a report showing how it was fulfilling its business principles. A few organizations pattern their reports after some external sustainability code they endorse. For example, one version of Dow's report consisted of plain-text responses to the GRI criteria listed in numerical order. DuPont's report for 2004 uses this same format. GE took a novel approach for its 2004 report, posting a 63-page document designed as a presentation readily usable as a PowerPoint® slide show. The report was arranged under sections on portfolio, strategy, investor overview, citizenship, social, EHS, economic, and summary. However, the company reverted to a more traditional reporting format for 2005.

Most reports, whether arranged according to the TBL or otherwise, include the following elements:

• Table of contents or index
• Letter from the CEO or president
• Company values and sustainability commitments (some-
times termed "vision and strategy")
• Performance scorecard or other summary
• Scope of the report
• Profile of the company, its products, and services
• Governance structure and management system or approach
• Stakeholder engagement activities
• Sustainability performance and focus for the future
• Glossary of acronyms and terms

A number of companies add these elements, too:

• Verification statement
• Index or table cross-referencing report content to GRI guidelines, the Global Compact, or other standards or codes endorsed
by the company.

Content

The intended content of the report—text, graphs, tables, artwork, photos—must be identified and placed in the report structure. Since content
may suggest structure and vice versa, several drafts of the outline for a
new report are often needed to finalize both. The following considerations may help when trying to decide what content to include:

Process for Prioritizing Content

While Figures 2.3, 2.4, and 2.5 offer ideas for topics that may be covered,
a report that covered all of them would be too long and unfocused. Information that could possibly be incorporated in the report must therefore be
prioritized. Much of that prioritization should occur early on, through the
sustainability strategic planning process discussed in Chapter 6, which
links sustainability initiatives with the needs of the business. The key
sustainability risks and opportunities identified from that planning, the
goals and objectives resulting from it, and the performance against those
goals and objectives are all high-priority topics for any sustainability report. Moreover, reporting on them helps establish the company's accountability to its stakeholders and promotes constructive internal
change. Stakeholder feedback—another important factor in prioritizing
content—should also have been a part of that planning.[65] Any report in-

formation that stakeholders say helps build the credibility of the company would be particularly valuable. High-priority content may also be identified through a media or Internet search to spot the issues most frequently associated with the company.

At Shell, this prioritization occurs in several phases. First their report team identifies how much space each functional group (Human Resources, EHS, Business Practices, and others) will be allowed in the report. This allocation is determined by the public commitments that require a progress update and the issues and locations of highest priority to internal and external stakeholders. The public commitments are based on company goals and key performance indicators. The process of ranking issues and locations starts with each function reviewing the following to prioritize information for its part of the report: (1) Shell's own high-priority issues and locations drawn from its business-risk and issues-management processes; and (2) stakeholder feedback from *Tell Shell*, reader surveys, media review, stakeholder sessions, and others sources. After the content is initially ranked, senior management reevaluates it based on the latest business developments prior to inclusion in the report.[66]

Nike uses the following criteria to decide what information is important enough to report:

> • Major impacts and issues based on internal life-cycle and impact analyses
> • Policies and commitments drawn from the GRI Sustainability Reporting Guidelines and Nike's Code of Conduct
> • Peer benchmarks taken from the sustainability reports of business peers
> • Information used in internal processes to manage corporate responsibility issues
> • Priority issues identified from stakeholder input gathered by the company's report-review committee and through the company's stakeholder forum.[67]

Whether a company decides to use the Shell or Nike approach or adopt some other method for prioritizing report content, the selected process should be spelled out during planning.

Information Relevance and Materiality

There are other prioritizing factors, too. Topics must not only be *relevant* to the business and sustainability—that is, affect them in some way—but also be *material*—that is, significant enough to matter. Information is material if it is so important it may affect decisions by management or affect the support for or judgment about the company by employees, investors, or other key stakeholders. Data relating to the company's performance against its public commitments or to any serious noncompliance with law or company policy are usually relevant and material, as are issues posing a significant impact on finances and those commonly discussed in the sustainability reports of business peers. The top concerns about the company expressed by employees, investors, community activists, or other key constituencies are also typically relevant and material issues.

Consider a few other examples illustrating these concepts. Forced labor is relevant to sustainability but may not be relevant to the vast majority of businesses with operations only in industrialized nations. However, it may be both relevant and material for certain companies contracting with operations in developing nations. The social impacts of businesses on local cultures—also relevant to sustainability—may be relevant and material for extractives companies (oil, mining, forestry, etc.) with large operations in aboriginal lands. Likewise, a chain of mega stores in an industrialized nation may find the economic effects of their new operations on local businesses quite controversial and, therefore, both relevant and material to the business and sustainability. But for many other firms, the issue of social and economic impacts on local cultures may be relevant (present) but immaterial (not significant enough to warrant attention).

Reported data must not only be relevant to sustainability and the company, but relevant to the message the company is trying to convey. This is a particular concern when data comparisons are provided. Stakeholders like to see a company's performance for the report year compared with that of the two previous years. Where numerical goals are involved, they also want to know the performance values for baseline years. However, this comparison isn't relevant to the message that the company reduced the environmental effects of the operations if, in fact, the company merely shifted those effects elsewhere by divesting a sizeable portion of the business or outsourcing major operations. In such cases, the baseline levels should be restated to make the data relevant or, if doing so is quite onerous, the cause of the data improvement should be prominently explained.

Reporting companies must use judgment, however, in adjusting data to account for organizational change. For example, if a downsizing occurs, several sites are closed, and their operations dispersed among those remaining, there is no need to restate companywide data because the operations have remained within the company and the change is therefore not relevant to overall performance. Likewise, if the business change has only an insignificant (immaterial) impact on the company's sustainability performance, no restatement or explanation would be warranted.

Information Availability and Reliability

Besides relevance and materiality, the *availability* and *reliability* of data are other important considerations for prioritizing content. Information that is difficult to obtain can be too costly and burdensome to provide, and may delay the publication. Data may be beyond reach if it invades privacy or discloses confidential business secrets. Some material may as a practical matter be unavailable because it's simply too embarrassing for an organization still uncomfortable with full transparency.

Information that isn't reliable should be shunned because it can threaten company credibility. Credibility can also be hurt if data is represented to be more precise than it really is. This can happen if an estimated value is depicted to too many figures or if precisely measured values are added to approximate estimates and a precise number is shown as the sum. However, credibility is not the only thing at stake from misrepresentation or over-statement. Glowing depictions of performance that have not been fully substantiated may expose reporters in some jurisdictions to legal liabilities. Consider the case of *Kasky v. Nike*.[68]

Kasky Case; Documenting Data Sources

In the *Kasky* case, California anti-globalization activist Marc Kasky sued Nike, the athletic-shoe and apparel manufacturer, claiming six statements it made about its Asian labor practices in press releases, letters to the editor, and elsewhere constituted false and misleading advertising under California law. One claim by Nike, for instance, was that the company's subcontractors in Southeast Asia paid its line workers on average double the minimum wage—an allegation the company made based on a survey of approximately 60% of the factories it was using in six Asian countries. The statements had been part of the company's attempt to defend itself against bad press arising out of several third-party audits and other reports critical of working conditions at Nike factories in the region. These reports had contrasted sharply with the favorable review of 12 sites prepared by the company's consulting firm. Reversing the opinions of two lower courts, the California Supreme Court held that Nike's statements should be judged as "commercial speech." Under this ruling, Kasky could succeed if he showed Nike's remarks to be misleading regardless of intent. Nike had asked that the statements be declared "noncommercial speech," a more forgiving standard under which the company could be held liable only upon proof that the statements were a deliberate or reckless falsehood. The U.S. Supreme Court refused to hear the case, leaving it to the lower state court to decide if, indeed, the statements were misleading. In 2003, before the lower court could act, a settlement agreement was reached under which Nike agreed to contribute $1.5 million to the Fair Labor Association, an industry-sponsored nonprofit organization that promotes conformance to international labor standards and improved working conditions worldwide.

Although this litigation discouraged Nike from issuing further public statements about its sustainability performance for a while, fortunately it did not have a long-term effect on the company or other businesses. The company resumed public sustainability reporting in 2005 with a top quality report.

Reporting companies should remain aware, however, that customers, investors, and other stakeholders are increasingly relying on sustainability performance, that it is increasingly becoming a competitive issue, and that it could receive external scrutiny—legal or otherwise. For that reason, it is important that companies document the source of their sustainability performance data and assure it is reasonably accurate. Issues likely to be controversial should warrant special attention. The report planning phase is a good time to resolve how this will be done and who will do it. With the proper supporting documentation in place, a sustainability report can actually help prevent the type of claims asserted by Kasky by providing a single companywide source of reliable information for use by company spokespeople across the organization.

GRI and Other Reporting Standards

Broad generic reporting standards produced by multi-stakeholder groups can also suggest issues that may be worth reporting or at least should be considered in the prioritization process. As previously noted, the GRI

Sustainability Reporting Guidelines are the most prominent of these standards.[69] Companies can cover the GRI-requested information in a single report or—as Shell began doing in 2004—spread the GRI content across its sustainability report, financial reports, and website.

The Sunshine Standards, developed by the Stakeholder Alliance, an NGO coalition, are also worthy of consideration. These pre-GRI standards were synthesized from a number of other reporting guidelines and codes of conduct. Although they do not enjoy the popularity or reputation of GRI, these standards may be useful in framing an overall communication strategy around sustainability because they identify information needed for customers, employees, and communities, respectively.[70]

Graphs, Tables, and Photos

Report planning should also identify what graphs, tables, and photos are needed. These items should be placed near the text that relates to them and be relevant to the point made in their caption. Because good, appropriate photos can be difficult to obtain, this too should be addressed during planning. Suppliers offer stock photos that can be used for a fee, but, of course, they won't be unique to the company. Sometimes, photos can be reused from other companywide publications or from those prepared by a division or facility. An internal photo contest can be run to collect interesting shots, although this is no guarantee the pictures will be of publishable quality. A professional photographer may be needed for special, high-quality pictures.

Planners should look for opportunities to use graphs and tables more effectively than text to communicate certain messages. They should see if information from tables can be better expressed in graphs. Possibilities may also exist to consolidate or combine graphs and tables to save space, provided the result isn't too complicated and confusing. Care must be taken to assure all depictions are not misleading—something that is likely to occur if only absolute or per-unit performance data, and not both, are provided. The real test is whether the data is presented fairly and the meaning from the figure is clear. A caption on a graph or chart that recites the message it depicts, such as "Charitable Contributions Up 12%," can help readers more quickly and forcefully grasp the message you are trying to convey.

Benchmarking Information

Report planners need to decide what, if any, benchmarking information should be included in the report. A company's sustainability performance can be most honestly and transparently represented in relation to that of other companies, especially those in the same industry. This adds credibility to the report. Unfortunately, most reports omit this comparison, either because it won't be flattering to the reporting company, because they don't want to start a public comparison war among peers, or, most often, because a fair apples-to-apples perspective is not readily available.

Safety performance is one area where several companies do show their results along side industrywide data or that of other companies. Safety statistics are ripe for such benchmarking for several reasons. First, most global companies use metrics from OSHA for internal purposes. Second, these metrics are presented in rates, such as the number of accidents or number of days away from work due to accidents, all normalized per 200,000 work hours—equivalent to that of 100 full-time employees. (Some European agencies use one million work hours.) Third, the OSHA metrics have definitions and guidelines to explain how to consistently classify accidents into various categories. Finally, industry averages on various metrics are available from OHSA itself or from benchmarking studies routinely undertaken by industry groups like ORC Worldwide.

Other areas can also be considered for benchmarking. Although not commonly seen, the percentage of pre-tax profits donated to charity is another fair, normalized measure. It could be easily calculated for an industry segment from company financial and charitable foundation reports. The amount of fines paid per billion dollars of revenue is another possible benchmarking metric.

Comparisons can also be made in the diversity area, for example, showing the percentage of board directors, management, and regular employees who are women, various minorities, or disabled. Another popular diversity metric that can be compared is the percentage of procurement dollars spent with minority- or women-owned suppliers. Benchmarking on diversity can be applied to operations in the United States and western Europe where it has meaning. There, governments publish statistics on diversity among industry employees and the general population. Among certain Latin American countries and in other multi-cultural, multi-racial societies, these comparisons may not be appropriate, either because diversity is already an accepted way of life there or because industry data is not available. For the typical transnational corporation, a measure of racial diversity on a global basis is meaningless. For such companies it may still be appropriate to report on gender diversity and perhaps on the percentage of management who are expatriates. This expatriate metric can be used to show that the company develops local talent and minimizes the use of managers imported from its home country.

Unlike safety and diversity, many measures involving environmental performance can't be benchmarked in a meaningful way. Consider, for instance, the ratio of waste quantity to sales. This metric provides an ambiguous message about how well a company is pursuing pollution prevention. The ratio can change because of alternations in costs, profit margins, or the mix of products produced, among other things. For that reason, it may be of limited value for long-term year-to-year comparison within a company, let alone among companies. Theoretically it would be good to compare the performance of, say, aluminum companies, presenting the kilograms of waste per ton of aluminum produced by each company. But it is rare for two companies—even in the aluminum business—to make only the same product of the same material shaped in the same way. Rather, the typical large company makes hundreds or even thousands of different products, including a number of variations of their most popular ones. Usually the best one can do in the environmental area is to provide some internal benchmarking, showing side-by-side division or facility comparisons on the tons of various pollutants generated. Novartis and a few other companies have taken this approach.

While report planners should seriously consider including benchmarking information to boost credibility, careful thought must be given to the availability and reliability of this information and to assuring confounding factors won't significantly distort the comparison.

Looking Ahead

The report preparation team should also work with the deployment team and the report distributors network to identify any changes in content for the following year's report that may alter the data required from the field. Field operators may need a year or more to establish and debug new data-collection requirements to acquire data of sufficient quality for a public report.

Reporting Tone and Philosophy

People who are helping prepare the report and those who must approve it should not only understand why the report is being prepared, but the tone and philosophy it will reflect. For best effect, the report should be written for the lay person, in plain, readable language devoid of jargon and long sentences. It should be a serious but engaging document that candidly addresses the significant public controversies that involve the company, its products or services. Stakeholders usually appreciate a transparent review of these issues presented in a way that provides an inside look at the trade offs considered in decisionmaking. They won't like an approach that is preachy, condescending, or overly promotional. A humble, earnest, self-critical tone will not only be better received, it will buy credibility and a greater stakeholder tolerance for those future missteps that inevitably occur within a company. By discussing the report tone and philosophy with the deployment team and top management in the early stages of report planning, report preparers can manage expectations and head off potential disagreements over report content and characterizations of performance.

Verification

One question answered long ago with regard to financial reporting but unresolved among voluntary sustainability reporters is whether the reported information should be independently verified by someone outside the company. The issue is still hotly debated, with some saying it adds little value and others insisting it is essential for adding credibility, catching weaknesses in information, and avoiding problems of the type Nike faced.

Verification Trends

The companies that have sought verification have used a wide variety of approaches and verifying organizations. Approximately 60% of the verifiers for large companies are major accountancy firms; roughly 15 to 20%, technical consulting firms; and about 10%, certification companies for ISO and other standards.[71] Unfortunately, the inconsistency in approach, along with the unlimited range of verifier's statements, has undermined the credibility of verification. The reputational damage suffered by a few large accounting firms in the wake of Enron hasn't helped either. What is more, some verification statements have been so unclear, so lacking in explanation of observed weaknesses, and so peppered with highly technical exceptions, that they have added nothing but confusion.

Despite all these problems, a growing number of readers apparently want reports verified, even though few are eager to wade into the details on the scope and nature of that assurance. Certainly, the trend is toward more external verification. A 2005 survey by the accounting firm KPMG revealed that of the large companies around the world reporting on sustainability, environmental, or social performance, approximately 3 in 10 had their reports externally verified.[72] In 1999, less than 20% did so.[73] Another study found that 40% of all the hard-copy versions of sustainability-related reports published in 2003 were verified by third parties, compared with only 17% 10 years earlier.[74]

This increase in verification has been accompanied by a shift in views about how much it affects the credibility of the report and reporter. Consider the GEMI-sponsored study of five U.S. focus groups conducted in 1995. These groups—consisting of environmentalists, investors, regulators, media, and company EHS people—rated third-party attestation as number 28 on the list of report features that enhanced credibility. A balanced tone and numerous performance indicators were deemed most important.[75]

However, in 2005 a different opinion emerged from a global survey of various stakeholders interested in reporting. Over half of those respondents said the credibility of a report could be enhanced if it was verified by third parties. This was their top-rated tactic, ranked only slightly ahead of two others: being honest about mistakes and bad practices, and using an external reporting standard such as the GRI guidelines.[76]

While attitudes toward verification seem to be changing, the change appears to be occurring more in some regions than others: according to KPMG's 2005 survey, 53% of the 71 largest U.K. reporters had their reports verified, whereas only 7% of the 73 largest reporting companies from Canada and the United States had done so. France, Italy, and Spain experienced the fastest uptake in external verification among reporters between 2002 and 2005. By the end of that period, over one-half of the largest 96 reporters in those three countries were seeking third-party assurance, up from just over 30% three years earlier.[77]

The difference in views about the importance of external verification found from the 1995 U.S. survey and the global one conducted in 2003 can be explained in part by differences in regional attitudes. But these results also reflect a growing appreciation for the value of verification over the years. This trend is likely to continue with the emergence of verification standards, the increased experience with the process, and escalating pressures from various stakeholder groups.

Types of Verification

Report verification as now practiced is of two general types: those judging reported performance and those assessing the adequacy of report content.

Performance verification provides a third-party critique of the results presented in the report or otherwise observed within the company. It may be an auditing consultant's assessment about the strengths and weaknesses of the sustainability programs, such as provided in Ben & Jerry's report. Or it may be an outside group's opinion about how well the company met the group's expectations. The external assurance written by Dow's Corporate Environmental Advisory Council is a good example of that. Occasionally this type of verification will confirm the extent to which the company met a particular standard or fulfilled some other commitment. Think of the Rainforest Alliance's verification of Chiquita's conformance to the Better Banana Project Standards. The verification in Novo Nordisk's report addressed its conformance with the GRI Sustainability Reporting Guidelines and the Global Compact.

Report-content verification is more closely related to traditional verification processes used by accounting auditors for financial reports. This is the type of assurance required for environmental reports issued under EMAS. It goes to the honesty of the report, not the sustainability performance or "greenness" of the company. For sustainability reports, this kind of verification may include a review of report content, as well as the processes for collecting and presenting it, to assure they meet some or all of the following criteria:

1. *Accuracy,* including appropriate internal processes for spotting errors;
2. *Completeness* in addressing all *material* issues within the defined report scope, including the company's responsiveness in meeting the key concerns of stakeholders as well as its performance against its public commitments—such as the GRI guidelines or the Global Compact;

3. *Reliability* of information-gathering and compilation processes in consistently producing complete, accurate results, including an assessment of data systems and training related to
these processes; and

4. *Balance* and *fairness* in presenting the information, including the fair representation of data in text, charts, and graphs; the
transparent reporting of both strengths and weaknesses; the candid explanation of shortfalls in performance; the inclusion of absolute as well as normalized data; the disclosure of significant
changes in data calculation methods; and the use of consistent
conventions for reporting on new and deleted operations.

In practice, the verifications found in sustainability reports display a
wide variation in wording and coverage. Some report-content verifications are provided on a qualified or selective basis. For example, the
Shell and Suncor reports use little symbols to identify the data that has
been verified by audit. A few companies, such as Rio Tinto, Suncor, and
Co-operative Financial Services, have gone so far as to include both report-content and performance verifications in their reports. Novo
Nordisk's integrated financial-sustainability report for 2004 provided
separate verifications for its financial and non-financial reporting, both
of which were provided by its financial accounting auditors.

Verification Standards

The report-content reviews undertaken for Co-operative Financial Services, BT, and BP used the criteria of the AA 1000 Assurance Standard
developed by The Institute of Social and Ethical Accountability (AccountAbility), a U.K.-based international professional institute.[78] Probably 10 to 20% of sustainability report verifications for large companies
refer to this standard.[79] The standard serves as the basis for assuring that
the data in a company's sustainability report is material, fair and balanced, complete, and responsive to the concerns of stakeholders. AA
1000 also permits the verifying auditor to comment on performance, suggesting improvements in processes, systems, and competencies.

GRI's Sustainability Reporting Guidelines also offer criteria for
verifiers.[80] The guidelines recommend that assurance providers evaluate
the report against the GRI reporting framework, including its reporting
principles discussed earlier. The guidelines also urge verifiers to assess
whether the report provides a reasonable and balanced presentation of

performance, taking into consideration the veracity of data and the selection of content.

ISAE 3000 is another standard that may be of use to sustainability report verifiers. This standard, entitled *Assurance Engagements Other Than Audits or Reviews of Historical Financial Information*, was issued by the International Auditing and Assurance Standards Board. It provides general guidance on undertaking assurance (verification) reviews and issuing assurance reports and statements.[81] It is one of the more noteworthy international standards referred to in roughly 15 to 20% of sustainability report verifications for large companies.[82] In verifying Novo Nordisk's report, their auditors relied on ISAE 3000 as well as AA1000 and the company's own accounting policies for non-financial data.

A few reporters rely on special sustainability report verification standards issued by some national accountants' organizations and standards-setting bodies. Standards of this type are found in Australia, Germany, Japan, the Netherlands, and Sweden.[83] Where large accounting firms provide the assurance statement, they often refer to the familiar national financial reporting standards. Since such standards are designed for evaluating the financial aspects of company performance and not environmental and social aspects, their use for sustainability reports can be awkward and require considerable adjustment.

Reporting as a Balancing Act

Those who study internal and external sustainability reporting will find the secret to success to be the same as for sustainability itself—in a word: balance. Strict adherence to guidelines and standards must be weighed against the creativity and innovation that comes from greater flexibility. The needs of one stakeholder group must be considered in the context of the needs of the others. Reports must contain technical meat, but still be easy to read. Data must not be too stale, yet not rushed so quickly to print that it is riddled with errors. Public reports should be complete, but not so watered down and unstructured as to be unfocused, nor so long and dense as to be tedious. Transparency must be promoted but not by sacrificing trade secrets or personal privacy. Employees and business units should be motivated through transparency but not humiliated. Benefit must be balanced against cost and effort. Doing all of this is not easy. The companies that do this well, are the true leaders in the field.

Future Directions in Public Reporting

Where is public sustainability reporting likely to go in the future?

The adverse trends in sustainability discussed in Appendix 1 will not abate over night. They will continue to excite activist groups and other NGOs, along with investors and, ultimately, the general population and governments. Large companies who are challenged to respond will look for help from suppliers and contractors of all sizes scattered down the supply chain. In this setting, we will see the continued growth in demand for balanced, reliable, complete information on company sustainability performance.

Although social and environmental metrics will mature, they will continue to shift with the needs of the times, particularly as new ethical scandals and scientific dilemmas erupt. Following the inroads of GRI and AA 1000, additional consensus standards should emerge. More industry groups will feel compelled to develop their own versions, too. As companies try the new standards, this use will lead to further consensus on reporting expectations. Many businesses that have shunned sustainability reporting will discover the voices of their stakeholders growing too loud to ignore. The ability of small and first-time reporters to respond will become simpler as more cost-effective reporting strategies surface. Investors and NGOs, acknowledging the frustration of survey-weary companies, will join with others to identify common data needs and communication methods to lighten the load. These two groups may well spur more governments to enter the fray thereby accelerating the convergence of sustainability reporting with corporate financial reporting. This integrated reporting should gain further support as sustainability risk assessments on topics like climate change and third-world sweatshops become more a part of new enterprise risk management programs being developed for governance reasons. The involvement of governments, along with greater scrutiny of reports by critics, will increase demand for external third-party verification.

The look of reporting should change, too. The hard-copy mega reports of 100 to 200 pages should fade from the scene. They are likely to be replaced by short published summaries of extensive data offered on the Internet. Website reporting is likely to go deeper, with some metrics updated quarterly, and with more business-unit and facility information presented. Websites may well display greater integration or Internet links between sustainability data and strategies and those of the overall business. Supply chain activities, product development, and stakeholder dialogue, which will be playing a bigger role in company sustainability efforts, should receive more coverage in reports as well. Over time, sustainability reporting should become more of an accepted way of business life.

Smart companies will anticipate these trends, establish well-considered reporting processes and strategies, and capture the reputational and performance benefits a step ahead of their competitors.

Follow-up Checklist for Action: Transparent Sustainability Reporting

☐ If your company does not publicly report on sustainability, assess the advantages and disadvantages of doing so based on the information from this chapter.

☐ Assess the degree of transparency being shown by various parts of the company about sustainability performance and issues, and identify any obstacles to additional transparency that should be overcome. Work to expand transparency over time within the bounds of legal and competitive concerns.

☐ Evaluate internal reporting practices and modify them as needed to assure the appropriate transparency and to effectively drive sustainability performance.

☐ Assure the core team is familiar with the latest sustainability reporting trends and mandatory and voluntary reporting initiatives.

☐ Develop an approach to public sustainability reporting that is appropriate for the company, using low-cost strategies if needed.

☐ Using the guidance from this chapter, develop a sustainability reporting process and plan the report, assuring the effort results in a properly balanced publication.

☐ Repeat the reporting process periodically, continually improving it over the years; monitor reporting practices and trends and respond proactively to maximize benefits for the company.

Endnotes to Chapter 10

1. LOUIS D. BRANDEIS, OTHER PEOPLE'S MONEY AND HOW THE BANKERS USE IT (1914).

2. *See* Appendix 1.26.

3. BURSON-MARSTELLAR, 2003 BUILDING CEO CAPITAL (2003), *cited in NGOs Seek "Believable" CSR Reports*, BUS. & ENV'T, Jan. 2004, at 6.

4. *See, e.g.,* WISCONSIN ENERGY CORP., 2004 PERFORMANCE REPORT: FOCUS ON CUSTOMER SATISFACTION AND FINANCIAL DISCIPLINE, EXECUTION OF OUR BUSINESS PLAN, AND INVESTMENT IN OUR FUTURE 8 (2005), *available at* http://www.wec-performancereport.com/ [hereinafter Wisconsin Energy 2004 Report]. *See also* GE, CITIZENSHIP REPORT 1 (2004), *available at* http://www.ge.com/files/usa/company/investor/downloads/ge_citizenship_overview_10202004.pdf. However, GE dropped the disclaimer in its 2005 report. *See* GE CITIZENSHIP REPORT (2005), *available at* http://www.ge.com/en/citizenship/downloads/index.htm.

5. GLOBESCAN INC. (TORONTO), A GLOBESCAN SURVEY OF BUSINESS LEADERS ON SUSTAINABLE DEVELOPMENT—HIGHLIGHT REPORT (2002), *available at* http://www.bitc.org.uk/resources/research/research_publications/globescan.html. For similar findings, see also JOSEPHINE MERRICK & CONNIE CROOKSHANKS (ENVIRON U.K.), REPORT ON A SURVEY OF ENVIRONMENTAL REPORTING COSTS AND BENEFITS (2001) (DEFRA No. 64-C4650), *available at* http://www.defra.gov.uk/environment/business/envrp/environ/environ.pdf [hereinafter 2001 U.K. Reporting Costs Survey].

6. *See* NIKE, CORPORATE RESPONSIBILITY REPORT (2004) [hereinafter 2004 Nike CSR Report].

7. *Extractive Industries Transparency Initiative*, http://www.eitransparency.org/index.htm (last visited Jan. 7, 2006).

8. BC HYDRO, DASHBOARD REPORT (2004), *available at* http://www.bchydro.com/reg_files/rev_reqs_bch/bcuc_2_203_01_86_att86.pdf (last visited Jan. 7, 2006).

9. 42 U.S.C. §§11001-11050, ELR STAT. EPCRA §§301-330. See Appendix 1.34 for further discussion on this law.

10. *See, e.g.,* Environment Defense, *Scorecard: The Pollution Information Site*, http://www.scorecard.org (last visited Jan. 7, 2006).

11. UNEC, *Aarhus Convention*, http://www.unece.org/env/pp/ (last visited Jan. 7, 2006).

12. *See, e.g.,* Peter Gilbertson, *Reconciling Environmental Disclosure With Environmental Exposure: A Case for Environmental Oversight*, SPECIAL COMM. ON ENVTL. DISCLOSURE NEWSL. , Nov. 2004, at 7-15, *avail-*

able at http://www.abanet.org/environ/committees/environdisclosures/ newsletter/nov04/envdiscl1104.pdf. *See also* Jeffery Gracer & Lawrence Schnapf, *Special Committee on Environmental Disclosure: 2004 Annual Report, in* THE YEAR IN REVIEW: ENVIRONMENT, ENERGY, AND RESOURCES LAW 150-60 (American Bar Ass'n, Section of Environment, Energy, and Resources 2005) [hereinafter ABA Environmental Disclosure 2004].

13. *See* David Case, *Corporate Environmental Reporting as Informational Regulation: A Law and Economics Perspective,* UNIV. COLO. L. REV., Spring 2005, at 410, 411.

14. Tom McMahon, *Forget Past; Disclosure Inevitable Wave of Future,* ENVTL. F., Sept./Oct. 2004, at 23.

15. *See* ABA Environmental Disclosure 2004, *supra* note 12. For a summary of studies showing significant noncompliance with the environmental reporting requirements under the SEC rules, see SUSANNAH GOODMAN & TIM LITTLE, THE GAP IN GAAP: AN EVALUATION OF ENVIRONMENTAL ACCOUNTING LOOPHOLES (The Rose Foundation for Communities and the Environment 2003), *available at* http://www.rosefdn.org/images/ GAPinGAAP.pdf. *See also* SANFORD LEWIS & TIM LITTLE, FOOLING INVESTORS AND FOOLING THEMSELVES: HOW AGGRESSIVE CORPORATE ACCOUNTING AND ASSET MANAGEMENT TACTICS CAN LEAD TO ENVIRONMENTAL ACCOUNTING FRAUD (THE ROSE FOUNDATION FOR COMMUNITIES AND THE ENVIRONMENT 2004), *available at* http://www.rosefdn. org/fooling.pdf.

16. Law No. 2001-420 of May 15, 2001. *See* Mary Lou Egan et al., *France's Nouvelles Regulations Economiques: Using Government Mandates for Corporate Reporting to Promote Environmentally Sustainable Economic Development,* Paper Presented at the 25th Annual Research Conference of the Association for Public Policy and Management, Washington, D.C. (Nov. 2003), *available at* http://www.bendickegan.com/pdf/EganMauleon WolffBendick.pdf. *See also* SARJ NAHAL, BSR ANALYSIS AND TREND REPORTING: MANDATORY CSR REPORTING: FRANCE'S BOLD PLAN (BSR 2002), *available at* http://www.bsr.org/BSRResources/Magazine/ CSRTrends.cfm?DocumentID=844.

17. European Union Council and Parliament Directive 2003/51/EC, July 17, 2003, O.J. (L178)16, http://europa.eu.int/eur-lex/lex/LexUriServ/LexUri Serv.do?uri=CELEX:32003L0051:EN:NOT (last visited Mar. 27, 2006). The Companies Act 1985 (Operating and Financial Review and Directors' Report etc.) Regulations 2005, U.K. Statutory Instrument S.I. 2005/No. 1011, March 21, 2005, *as amended by* U.K. Statutory Instrument S.I. 2005/No.3442, December 14, 2005, http://www.opsi.gov.uk/stat.htm (last visited Mar. 22, 2006).

18. U.K. Department of Trade and Industry, Companies Act 2006, cl. 417, Nov. 8, 2006, *available at* http://www.opsi.gov.uk/index.htm. *See* U.K.

Department of Trade and Industry, "Companies Bill," *Better Business Framework,* http://www.dti.gov.uk/bbf/co-law-reform-bill/index.html (last visited Sept. 13, 2006).

19. 9 U.K. DEFRA, Environmental Key Performance Indicators: Reporting Guidelines for U.K. Business (2006), *available at* http://www.defra.gov.uk/environment/business/envrp/envkpi-guidelines.pdf.

20. King Committee on Corporate Governance, Executive Summary of the King Report of 2002, §5.1 (2002). *See also* William Baue & Graham Sinclair, *Johannesburg Securities Exchange Requires Compliance With King II and Global Reporting Initiative,* Social Funds.com, http:www.socialfunds.com/news/print.cgi?sfArticleId=1174 (last visited Jan. 3, 2006). See Appendix 2.6.4 for a discussion of the Code of Corporate Practices and Conduct.

21. *Companies Comply With King II,* Sunday Times online, Nov. 16, 2003, http://www.sundaytimes.co.za/Articles/TarkArticle.aspx?ID=910317 (last visited Jan. 7, 2006).

22. Canadian Securities Administrators, Continuous Disclosure Obligations, Form 51-102F2, Annual Information Form §5.1(4) (2003), *available at* http://www.osc.gov.on.ca/Regulation/Rulemaking/Current/Part5/rule_20031219_51-102_con-dis.pdf.

23. David Case, *Corporate Environmental Reporting as Informational Regulation: A Law and Economics Perspective,* U. Colo. L. Rev., Spring 2005. *See also* Association of Chartered Certified Accountants & CorporateRegister.com, Towards Transparency: Progress on Global Sustainability Reporting 2004 (2004), *available at* http://www.accaglobal.com/pdfs/environment/towards_trans_2004.pdf [hereinafter ACCA-CR Reporting Survey 2004].

24. William Fry, *Sustainability Reporting Is Becoming an Increasingly Topical Issue in the EU and Globally,* Mar. 23, 2003, http://www.williamfry.ie/article.asp?categoryID=29&articleID=167 (last visited Jan. 7, 2006).

25. American Chemistry Council, Responsible Care®, *Tracking Performance; Sharing Results,* http://www.responsiblecare-us.com/ (last visited Jan. 7, 2006). *See also* Appendices 2.2.4 and 3.8.

26. *See* Appendix 3.7. *See also* Case Article on Environmental Reporting, *supra* note 23, at 402-07.

27. *See* Folkert van der Molen, *Guidelines and Tools for Environmental Reporting,* http://www.enviroreporting.com/mjv_link2.htm (last visited Jan. 3, 2006). *See also* Case Article on Environmental Reporting, *supra* note 23, at 386-87. *See also* Association of Chartered Certified Accountants & CorporateRegister.com, Environmental, Social, and Sustainability Reporting on the World Wide Web: A Guide

TO BEST PRACTICES 39 (2001), *available at* http://www.accaglobal.com/
pdfs/environment/ACCA-RJ3-002.pdf. Other popular guidelines on
sustainability reporting include: SNOWY MOUNTAIN ENGINEERING CORP.
ET AL., A FRAMEWORK FOR PUBLIC ENVIRONMENTAL REPORTING—AN
AUSTRALIAN APPROACH (Environment Australia 2000), *available at* http://
www.natural-resources.org/minerals/generalforum/csr/docs/guidelines/
Australian%20PER%20Frame-work.pdf. BERT HEEMSKERK ET AL., SUS-
TAINABLE DEVELOPMENT REPORTING—STRIKING THE BALANCE
(WBCSD 2002), *available at* http://www.wbcsd.org/DocRoot/GGFpsq8d
GngT5K56sAur/20030106_sdreport.pdf and STRATOS INC. & GOVERN-
MENT OF CANADA, SUSTAINABILITY REPORTING TOOLKIT (2003), *avail-
able at* http://www.sustainabilityreporting.ca.

28. ACCA-CR Reporting Survey 2004, *supra* note 23, at 12. DIRECTORATE-
GENERAL FOR EMPLOYMENT AND SOCIAL AFFAIRS, EUROPEAN COMMIS-
SION, Compendium of National Public Policies on CSR in the European
Union (2004), *available at* http://europa.eu.int/comm/employment_social/
soc-dial/csr/index.htm.

29. GRI, 2002 SUSTAINABILITY REPORTING GUIDELINES (2002), *available
at* http://www.globalreporting.org/guidelines/2002.asp [hereinafter GRI
Guidelines].

30. CSR NETWORK, CSR NETWORK ANNOUNCES 2003 BENCHMARK SUR-
VEY REPORT (CSR Wire 2003), *available at* http://www.csrwire.com/
article.cgi/1875.html. KPMG GLOBAL SUSTAINABILITY SERVICES & UNIVER-
SITY OF AMSTERDAM, SURVEY OF CORPORATE RESPONSIBILITY RE-
PORTING 2005, at 5 (2005), *available at* http://www.kpmg.com/Rut2000_
prod/Documents/9/Survey2005.pdf [hereinafter KPMG-U of Amsterdam
Reporting Survey 2005].

31. GRI, *Organizations Using the Guidelines*, http://www.globalreporting.
org/guidelines/reporters/all.asp (last visited Mar. 26, 2006).

32. Social Investment Forum, *Analysts at 17 Leading Socially Responsible In-
vestment Firms Urge Stronger Corporate Reporting*, SOC. INVESTMENT F.
NEWS, Oct. 6, 2004, http://www.socialinvest.org/areas/news/100604-
CorporateReporting.htm (last visited Jan. 3, 2006).

33. Here, "sustainability context" means placing "performance in the larger
context of ecological, social, and other limits or constraints, where such
context adds significant meaning to the reported information." *See* GRI
Guidelines, *supra* note 29. A good example is Suncor's disclosure of the
percentage of Canadian boreal forest disturbed by its oil sands development. See other environmental and social examples from Suncor discussed, *supra* Chapter 7.

34. GRI Guidelines, *supra* note 29.

35. *Global Report Output by Year and Format*, CORPORATEREGISTER.COM,
Mar. 2005, http://www.corporateregister.com/charts/byformat.htm (last
visited Jan. 10, 2006).

36. ACCA-CR Reporting Survey 2004, *supra* note 23, at 9.

37. *Report Output by Country Since 1992*, CORPORATEREGISTER.COM, Mar. 2005, http://www.corporateregister.com/charts/bycountry.htm (last visited Jan. 10, 2006).

38. *Global Report Output by "Type" Since 1992*, CORPORATEREGISTER.COM, Mar. 2005, http://www.corporateregister.com/charts/bytype.htm (last visited Jan. 10, 2006).

39. KPMG-U of Amsterdam Reporting Survey 2005, *supra* note 30, at 4. KPMG Ltd. Liability Partnership, *KPMG Survey: More Top U.S. Companies Reporting on Corporate Responsibility*, CSR WIRE, June 10, 2002, http://www.csrwire.com/article.cgi/1153.html (last visited Jan. 7, 2006).

40. *Non-Financial Reporting Status of the FTSE 100*, CORPORATEREGISTER. COM, Mar. 2005, http://www.corporateregister.com/charts/FTSE.htm (last visited Jan. 10, 2006). Eighty-two percent of the FTSE 100 issued a stand-alone or Internet-based CSR/environmental/social/community report or devoted at least six pages to these topics in their annual financial reports within the previous two years.

41. BATTELL, COMPENDIUM OF SUSTAINABILITY REPORTING PRACTICES AND TRENDS FOR THE OIL AND GAS INDUSTRY (2003), *available at* http://www.oilandgasreporting.com/compendium.html.

42. Stephen Greene, Polaroid Corp., *Securing Internal Executive Support for EHS Reporting Initiatives*, Paper Presented at the Marcus Evans Conference on Reporting for EHS, Denver, Colo. (Feb. 9, 2004).

43. POLAROID CORP., 2002 SUSTAINABILITY REPORT (2004), *available at* http://www.polaroid.com/company_info/environment.jsp. POLAROID CORP., POLAROID REPORT ON THE ENVIRONMENT 2003 (2005), *available at* http://www.polaroid.com/media/com/pdfs/environment/2003environment_report_full_a0bf.pdf.

44. POLAROID CORP., POLAROID REPORT ON THE ENVIRONMENT 2004 (2006), *available at* http://www.polaroid.com/media/com/pdfs/environment/2004 environment_report_full_e4bf.pdf.

45. *See* Barney Gimbel, *Polaroid's Next Shot*, TIME, May 16, 2005, at 29.

46. RICHARD J. GUIMOND & GEORGE NAGLE, GEMI BENCHMARKING SURVEY ON EHS ANNUAL REPORTS (GEMI 2001), *available at* http://www. Gemi.org/docs/bench/EHSAnnualReports.ppt.

47. SUSTAINABILITY LTD. & UNEP—TECHNOLOGY, INDUSTRY, AND ECONOMICS DIVISION, TRUST US: THE GLOBAL REPORTERS 2002 SURVEY OF CORPORATE SUSTAINABILITY REPORTING (2002), *available at* http://www.sustainability.com/publications/engaging/trust-us.asp [hereinafter SustainAbility Report Ranking 2002].

48. SUSTAINABILITY LTD. ET AL., RISK & OPPORTUNITY—BEST PRACTICE IN NON-FINANCIAL REPORTING: THE GLOBAL REPORTERS 2004 SURVEY OF CORPORATE SUSTAINABILITY REPORTS (2004), *available at* http://www. sustainability.com/insight/research-article.asp?id=128 [hereinafter SustainAbility Report Ranking 2004].

49. *See* 2001 U.K. Reporting Costs Survey, *supra* note 5.

50. GRI, THE COST OF PREPARING A SUSTAINABILITY REPORT (2002), *available at* http://www.globalreporting.org/feedback/forum/studycosts. asp.

51. *See* 2001 UK Reporting Costs Survey, *supra* note 5.

52. ECC KOHTES KLEWES & FISHBURN HEDGES, GLOBAL STAKEHOLDER REPORT 2003: SHARED VALUES? (2003), *available at* http://www.asria. org/ref/library/csrreports/1070937536 [hereinafter ECC FH Stakeholder Survey 2003]. PLEON KOHTES KLEWES GMBH & PLEON B.V., Accounting for Good: The Global Stakeholder Report 2005 (2005), *available at* http://www.pleon.com/fileadmin/downloads/Pleon_GSR05_en.pdf [hereinafter Pleon Kohtes Klewes Stakeholder Survey 2005].

53. *See* SustainAbility Report Ranking 2002, *supra* note 47 and Sustain-Ability Report Ranking 2004, *supra* note 48.

54. Roberts Environmental Center, Claremont, McKenna College, *Corporate Environmental and Sustainability Reporting*, http://www.roberts.mckenna. edu/ (last visited Jan. 10, 2006).

55. ACCA-CR Reporting Survey 2004, *supra* note 23.

56. CorporateRegister.com, *Complete List of Awards*, http://www.corporate register.com/data/asearch.pl?a=1 (last visited Jan. 10, 2006).

57. CO-OPERATIVE FINANCIAL SERVICES, SUSTAINABILITY REPORT 2004—A YEAR IN FOCUS (2005), *available at* http://www.cfs.co.uk/images/pdf/ cfssustainabilityreport2004.pdf.

58. *See* Pleon Kohtes Klewes Stakeholder Survey 2005, *supra* note 52, at 22.

59. ECC FH Stakeholder Survey 2003, *supra* note 52.

60. CorporateRegister.com, *Global Report Output by Year,* http://www. corporateregister.com/charts/byformat.htm (last visited Jan. 10, 2006).

61. Pleon Kohtes Klewes Stakeholder Survey 2005, *supra* note 52, at 59.

62. *See id.* at 58, 60.

63. TOYOTA, ENVIRONMENTAL AND SOCIAL REPORT 2005 (2005), *available at* http://www.toyota.co.jp/en/environmental_rep/05/index.html.

64. Interview with Mark Wade, Shell, in London (June 27, 2002) [hereinafter Shell Interview].

65. See Section 4.2 of the model SOS standards (Figure 5.3) regarding prioritization of issues and topics. See also Section 9 of the standards regarding management and stakeholder feedback.

66. *See* Shell Interview, *supra* note 64. Shell, *Issues and Locations Selection Process,* approach_to_reporting/zzz_lhn.html&FC3=/royal-en/html/iwgen/environment_and)_society/reporting_and_assurance/our_approach_to_reporting/issues_selection_25052005.html (last visited Jan. 10, 2006). *See also* SHELL, THE SHELL REPORT 2004: MEETING THE ENERGY CHALLENGE — OUR PROGRESS IN CONTRIBUTING TO SUSTAINABLE DEVELOPMENT 30 (2005), *available at* http://www.shell.com/static/investor-en/downloads/publications/2005/shellreport/shellreport_2005.pdf.

67. 2004 Nike CSR Report, *supra* note 6, at 9.

68. 27 Cal. 4th 939 (Cal. 2002), 119 Cal. Rptr. 2d 296, 45 P.3d 243 (Cal. 2002), *cert. granted,* 123 S. Ct. 817, *and cert. dismissed,* 123 S. Ct. 2254 (2003).

69. *See* GRI Guidelines, *supra* note 29.

70. The Stakeholder Alliance, *The Sunshine Standards,* http://www.stakeholder alliance.org/sunstds.html (last visited Jan. 7, 2006).

71. *See* KPMG-U of Amsterdam Reporting Survey 2005, *supra* note 30, at 33. KPMG, KPMG INTERNATIONAL SURVEY OF CORPORATE SUSTAINABILITY REPORTING 2002 (2002), *available at* http://www.wimm.nl/publicaties/KPMG2002.pdf [hereinafter KPMG Reporting Survey 2002].

72. *See* KPMG-U of Amsterdam Reporting Survey 2005, *supra* note 30, at 30.

73. *See* KPMG Reporting Survey 2002, *supra* note 71.

74. *See* ACCA-CR Reporting Survey 2004, *supra* note 23, at 8.

75. IIRC, ENVIRONMENTAL REPORTING AND THIRD-PARTY STATEMENTS (GEMI 1996), *available at* http://www.cedha.org.ar/docs/gemi-reporting.pdf.

76. *See* Pleon Kohtes Klewes Stakeholder Survey 2005, *supra* note 52, at 23.

77. *See* KPMG-U of Amsterdam Reporting Survey 2005, *supra* note 30, at 31.

78. AccountAbility (Institute for Social and Ethical Accountability), AA *1000 Series Assurance Standard,* http://www.accountability.org.uk/aa1000/default.asp?pageid=52 (last visited Jan. 7, 2006).

79. *See* KPMG-U of Amsterdam Reporting Survey 2005, *supra* note 30, at 33.

80. *See* GRI Guidelines, *supra* note 29.

81. INTERNATIONAL AUDITING & ASSURANCE STANDARDS BOARD, INTERNATIONAL FEDERATION OF ACCOUNTANTS, INTERNATIONAL STANDARDS ON ASSURANCE ENGAGEMENT (ISAE) 3000: ASSURANCE ENGAGEMENTS OTHER THAN AUDITS OR REVIEWS OF HISTORICAL FINANCIAL INFORMATION (2005), *available at* http://www.ifac.org/.

82. *See* KPMG-U of Amsterdam Reporting Survey 2005, *supra* note 30, at 33.
83. *See id.* at 46.

Chapter 11

Stakeholder Engagement; The Role of NGOs

"Oh, wad some Pow'r the giftie gi'e us
To see oursels as ithers see us!"[1]
—Robert Burns

Why Organizations Should Engage With Stakeholders

Good metrics, goals, monitoring systems, and reports can improve a company's sustainability performance and make it a stronger, more competitive organization. However, to achieve superior performance, a business must do more. As James Collins points out in his best seller, *Good to Great*, a common characteristic of great companies is that they understand and confront "the brutal facts."[2] Companies that see the world only through the eyes of their management and industry associates often overlook these facts, comforted by an incestuous dialogue based more on hope than reality. Certainly no organization wants to hear unpleasant things said about it or its strategies. But great companies have the courage to listen—not only to hear what stakeholders say, but to ask for their views and to pay careful attention to the response. Such companies then reflect their stakeholders' views in strategic objectives and communications. These companies don't do this because they are masochists, but instead because it raises early warning of issues that if left unchecked, could result in reputational damage, production delays, and inefficiencies, and in stock slides from boycotts, strikes, lawsuits, and other problems. They do it because this engagement provides valuable insights that can lead to better, more workable decisions. And finally, they do it because, as we observed in Chapter 3, it creates a quid pro quo, securing the trust and support of the very people who will make their organization a success.

For these and other reasons, a growing number of companies have begun to see engagement with stakeholders—meaningful discussion, feedback, and problem-solving with them—as an essential part of their business processes. These stakeholders have included activists, communities, governments, investors, suppliers, joint venture partners, employees, and others who may affect the company or perceive they may be affected by it. Why the increasing interest in stakeholders? One reason is obvious: as most business managers would concede, stakeholders influence business decisions. See, for example, the results of a 2004 survey of 515 U.S. business executives shown in Figure 11.1. Firms that don't listen to their customers, investors, and employees usually don't last long. But there are additional factors pushing companies toward more formal processes of engagement. Certain businesses—especially those in land development, mining, waste disposal, power generation, or other heavy industry—now realize that no major development project can proceed without such engagement. Public comment and hearings are often required for necessary permits or other governmental approvals. With the implementation of the Aarhus Convention, over 40 European and West Asian countries will have additional laws guaranteeing the rights of the public to environmental information and involvement in environmental decisionmaking.[3] New financial reporting rules, like those in France, may require companies to explain what they are doing to engage stakeholders.[4] Engagement may also be mandated by funding institutions. For instance, under the World Bank's *Equator Principles*, which have been endorsed by over 35 major banks, projects costing over $10 million are financed only if it can be shown that the borrower, the government, or a third-party expert "has consulted, in a structured and culturally appropriate way, with project affected groups."[5] Moreover, the voice of the NGOs themselves has grown louder in urging companies to engage. The GRI and AA 1000 standards both call for businesses to engage their stakeholders to help identify issues for sustainability planning and reporting.

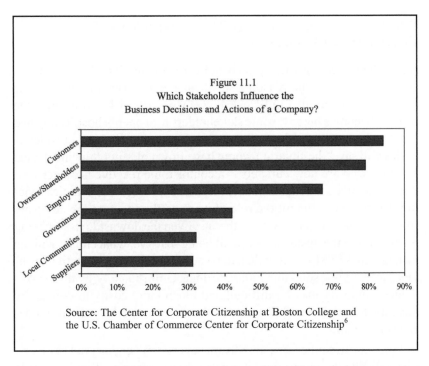

Figure 11.1
Which Stakeholders Influence the
Business Decisions and Actions of a Company?

Source: The Center for Corporate Citizenship at Boston College and
the U.S. Chamber of Commerce Center for Corporate Citizenship[6]

Companies like Dow, Suncor, BT, and Intel have found it pays to listen
to stakeholders proactively—not just when law demands it or controversy is feared, but during the regular course of business. They see this
engagement as a kind of annual checkup for assessing the health of their
organizations. Moreover, such processes demonstrate respect for the
needs of others—an ethical value at the core of sustainability. Art Gibson, while he was vice president of Environment, Health, and Safety at
Home Depot, expressed it this way:

> A company can't realize the full potential of sustainability unless the
> organization and its stakeholders are aligned on the important aspects
> of that concept in a way that brings mutual benefit. Certainly that's
> been true with regard to our sustainability-certified wood products. A
> good way to achieve that alignment is through an engagement process.
> And from our experience, a proactive well-planned process is much
> easier than a reactive one.[7]

Why Companies Don't Engage Their Stakeholders: The Engagement-Risk Dilemma

If stakeholder engagement is so beneficial, why don't all business managers endorse it? One reason is the "engagement risk-dilemma": The proactive manager that initiates engagement early risks criticism if the process becomes bumpy, some stakeholders turn openly hostile, and bad press ensues. "If only the manager hadn't encouraged these outsiders," critics will say, "the situation would have flown by smoothly undetected by those who are now enraged." In contrast, the reactive manager who doesn't act until the situation becomes quite troublesome can plead victim. He can then attempt the role of hero, battling to save the company from this "unexpected" external threat. Given the downside risk of being proactive and the upside potential of being reactive, what choice will the manager make? More often than not, she will hesitate to act until it is obvious to everyone something must be done. Unfortunately, by then stakeholder animosity may be difficult and much more costly to defuse; by then, the trust and credibility lost by the delay may take years if not decades to repair.

There are also other reasons why managers don't engage stakeholders. Many dislike the uncertainty it creates about outcomes. Some see little need to complicate their decisionmaking by giving others the power to influence it. They may feel decisions must be made and implemented as soon as possible, and there is simply no time to slow down the process to involve others. A few are blinded by their egos and adopt the patronizing view that they, rather than their critics, know what's best. Others may be unfamiliar with the engagement process and the benefits it can bring. Then too, with tight budgets, a manager may feel few resources can be spared for engagement, or—to say it another way—the interests of stakeholders are not a real priority. Another reason some managers don't engage with stakeholders is they have suffered through an unsuccessful engagement in the past and lack confidence that future engagements can be productive. (Interestingly though, as Figure 11.2 reveals, many of the obstacles to successful engagements arise from within the organization itself rather than from its stakeholders.)

Finally, business leaders may avoid initiating their own engagement because they think the local government is handling it for them. However, relying on government officials to conduct or guide stakeholder engagement can be a big mistake—particularly if the engagement is in a developing nation. Newmont Mining Corporation certainly found that to be true on a proposed mining project near Cajamarca, Peru. There, according to a Newmont spokesperson, extensive stakeholder engagement was conducted by the company along with the IFC of the World Bank, and the necessary permit was received from the Peruvian authorities. Unfortunately, at the urging of governmental co-owners of the project, the engagement did not address certain local Indian people and others who were concerned about the potential for the project to deplete and contaminate the local water supply. A two-week blockade by 8,000 protesters convinced the company to scrap the project.[8] Shell faced a similar problem when it proposed to drill oil near the small village of Obioku in Nigeria. Engagement resulted in agreements with leaders from the village and another nearby community, but work had to be halted when a third town claimed that it, rather than its two neighbors, was the rightful owner of the site.[9]

Figure 11.2
Why Stakeholder Engagement Often Fails:
Common Problems With Public Participation on Environmental Issues
in the United Kingdom[10]

1. **People in the organization are too worried about the outcome of the engagement.** Attempts by company managers to control the outcome can frustrate and discourage participants. Keeping key company managers regularly apprised of progress and strategies can put them more at ease and help avoid this problem.

2. **Poor understanding of the participation techniques available and their relative strengths and weaknesses.** Generally the more critical and controversial the objective of the engagement, the more involved stakeholders will need to be in decisionmaking to earn their buy-in. This greater involvement will require more time, expense, and relinquishment of control by the company.

3. **Lack of evaluation of the process and output.** An evaluation should be undertaken after completion of each major step of the engagement and adjustments made as needed.

4. **Poorly trained facilitators.** Training needs can vary widely. The training required for conducting a survey is not the same as that needed for a complex set of public hearings.

5. **Low awareness of the benefits and cost-effectiveness of participation.** Raising internal awareness about stakeholder engagement should be one of the first steps of any engagement program. Unless management appreciates the value of engagement, their support will be half-hearted at best and the process may not receive the attention or resources it needs.

6. **Lack of resources.** Resource needs should be identified early after the objectives of the engagement are set and the process has been thoroughly planned. These needs should be reassessed at key milestones along the process.

Encouraging Engagement; The Stakeholder Engagement Principles

Three measures can be taken to encourage companies to pursue proactive stakeholder engagement: (1) raise awareness among company management about the engagement process and its benefits; (2) assure that managers involved in engagement have the appropriate skills; and (3) make it clear that a proactive approach to engagement is encouraged and reward those managers who follow that course. To achieve the first measure, awareness presentations can be delivered to management across the company emphasizing points drawn from this chapter. The second can be accomplished by training all company people likely to be involved in the engagement on the rules of engagement, what to expect, how to behave, and how to make the engagement most effective. If the engagement is complex and much is at stake, well-experienced engagement professionals from inside or outside the company should be assigned to manage the process. Or companies can follow the lead of Novo Nordisk by appointing a vice president of Stakeholder Relations to provide the necessary expertise. Regardless of how the engagement is organized, its success will depend in large measure on whether there is sustained involvement of a committed, well-trained leader.

One way to help achieve the third measure—encouraging managers to engage—is to adopt Stakeholder Engagement Principles, which present the company's official view on the topic. An example is presented as Figure 11.3. The principles lay out the company's expectations concerning stakeholder engagement and create a yardstick by which all engagements can be evaluated. The heart of the principles should be complete, fair, open, and honest dialogue. Sham engagements, where the course of action has already been pre-determined, are clearly contrary to that and should be avoided at all cost. They can poison a stakeholder-company relationship and destroy the company's credibility.

Figure 11.3
Model Principles of Stakeholder Engagement

The company promotes proactive engagement with its stakeholders as fundamental to improving business performance and fulfilling its commitment as a good corporate citizen. When engaging stakeholders on an issue or proposed action or for general feedback, the company will adhere to the following principles to help ensure the engagement is effective.

1. **Training.** The people planning and administering engagement processes will be properly trained and possess the right knowledge and skills for their duties.
2. **Plan.** A Stakeholder Engagement Plan will be adopted for each significant stakeholder engagement. The plan will identify the objectives of the engagement, the stakeholders to be engaged, the methods of engagement, the work products expected from the process, the resources to be devoted to it, and the schedule. If the engagement involves collaboration between the company and a stakeholder organization, the plan shall also consider the terms of dissolution of the collaboration and shall be agreed to by both parties.
3. **Inclusiveness, timeliness.** The company will encourage the participation of relevant stakeholders, that is, those who have an interest in the action or decision under consideration, as well as those who would be affected by it or who may perceive they would be affected by it. Where possible, a variety of engagement methods will be offered so the full range of stakeholders may effectively participate in some way. A special effort will be made to involve effective representatives of important relevant stakeholder groups, especially those that may have a tendency to remain silent or uninvolved. Engagement planners will reflect a bias for inclusiveness in designing the methods of engagement and in defining the roles, responsibilities, and processes for managing the engagement. Of course, that preference may be tempered somewhat by the need for efficiency to assure engagement objectives can be met in a timely manner.
4. **Transparency, clarity.** The company will communicate with its stakeholders in an open and honest way. Potential conflicts of interest will be managed openly. The scope of stakeholder decisionmaking authority will be discussed early in the engagement process. If a decision has already been made and is non-negotiable, the company will say so. The company will provide stakeholders the information they need to effectively participate in engagement activities. Such information shall be presented in the manner and form that the stakeholders can most readily understand and at a time that allows for adequate review and consideration. Some means will be provided for stakeholders to obtain any needed clarification of the information provided.
5. **Listening.** The company will listen carefully to comments of stakeholders, and will hold itself open to being influenced by them. In the words of Covey, author of the best-selling *7 Habits of Highly Effective People*, the company will "seek first to understand, then to be understood."[11] It will attempt to comprehend and respond to the emotion as well as the content of the message. If key stakeholders remain quiet, the company will try to discern whether that reflects their approval or means they are intimidated or simply uninterested.
6. **Neutrality, code of conduct.** In situations likely to be highly polarized, the company will strongly consider the use of neutral, independent facilitators or conveners to manage the engagement. At the outset of hearings or other forums where controversy may erupt, the facilitator will discuss—and if possible, gain consensus on—rules of engagement or a code of conduct governing the participation of all attendees. The purpose of this code is to ensure that all participants are treated with respect and that the forum proceeds in a fair, orderly, efficient manner.

Figure 11.3—Continued
Model Principles of Stakeholder Engagement

7. **Respect, resources.** The company will work with its stakeholders to foster a
   climate of sincerity and mutual trust and respect. As part of this commitment,
   the company agrees to devote the time, resources, and priority to stakeholder
   engagement as needed to fulfill these principles and help make the engagement effective.
8. **Reporting.** The company will provide a timely report to its stakeholders on the
   results of their engagement, and will periodically communicate with them on the
   status of the actions to be taken in response.
9. **Ongoing commitment.** The company will provide ongoing opportunities for
   stakeholders to communicate concerns about the company, its operations,
   and plans.

The principles must allow for a wide variety of engagement techniques. Engagement planners must select the combination of approaches
that best fits the situation. While planning is important, companies must
remain flexible and adjust the process as it unfolds.

When planning a stakeholder engagement, a good place to start is the seven-
step framework of Figure 11.4. Each step deserves careful consideration.

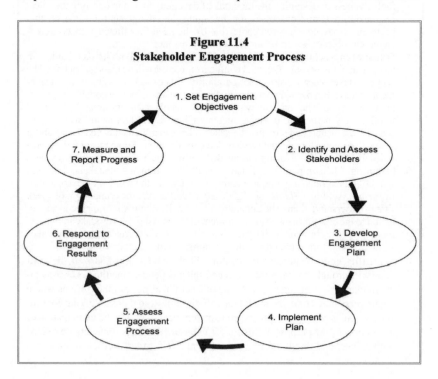

Figure 11.4
Stakeholder Engagement Process

Step 1: Set Engagement Objectives

The primary objective may be specific or broad. The objective may be to gather input on a particular project of altruistic nature undertaken to enhance company image—such as projects involving clean water or AIDS prevention for impoverished people. Or the engagement may be prompted by a controversial project or issue in the media that involves the company. In these controversial cases, the objective may be to calm stakeholder concern and repair reputational damage. If a land development or some other project is involved, the objective may be to find a way to implement the project with general public support, or at least without intense public opposition. Yet even in project- or issue-related situations, the company must also consider what it wants in a long-term relationship with its stakeholders. It is not enough to quell public outrage over the construction of a new power plant; if the company is intending to operate that plant for decades, it still must contend with the same people. In such situations, the company-stakeholder relationship should be considered a long-term marriage, not a brief blind date. While the initial objective may start as narrow and specific, focused on things such as information-gathering, learning, innovation, and decisionmaking, it may well evolve to the broader one of relationship-building. To achieve that broad goal, the engagement objective may turn out to be a composite of the benefits desired by the company and those sought by key stakeholders.

Some progressive companies have initiated stakeholder engagement without a specific project or issue in mind. They have set the broad objective of gathering constructive feedback from stakeholders on the company's sustainability performance and communications, and of addressing the concerns presented. This is the type of engagement envisioned under an SOS as a preparatory step for strategic planning.[12] The purest example of this approach has been adopted by Van City, the largest credit union in Canada. Van City conducts a "social audit" every few years, which includes focus groups, written and oral surveys, and other means to collect feedback from its employees, customers, and community leaders. The feedback is then factored into its business planning. Ford, Johnson & Johnson, Intel, BT, Suncor, and Co-operative Financial Services also periodically collect multi-stakeholder feedback on a proactive basis and use it to influence the direction of their organizations. Since 1991, Dow has worked with its Corporate Environmental Advisory Committee, a group of representatives from leading NGOs that regularly provides the company with candid counsel on a wide range of sustainability issues. BT has a similar group—its Stakeholder Leadership Panel. Johnson Controls engages NGOs through the ICCR and other groups to assess sustainability performance and communications, and to find ways to improve both. Baxter works with CERES in a similar way, using its sustainability report as the focus for discussions. Shell conducts "listening sessions" in different regions of the world with unions, human rights groups, environmental activists, think tank representatives, church groups, and other parties interested in the company's sustainability performance. The feedback is compiled and assessed for action.

Other businesses have gone beyond the objective of consultation and engage collaboratively with their stakeholders in designing solutions to problems of concern. Recall the Rainforest Alliance's role in the certification audits of Chiquita's operations. In Australia, Alcoa invited community members to help develop and oversee environmental improvement plans for its mining and smelting facilities. Johnson & Johnson's facility in Pennsylvania joined with industrial neighbors to fund annual environmental audits of their facilities by a consultant selected by the township. Audit results are openly shared and discussed at a community-industry roundtable. Suncor provides technical advice and funding to various aboriginal groups in western Canada, the region where the company extracts petroleum from oil sands. The company has established Industry Relations Corporations to help "First Nation" groups consult more effectively with industry in resolving resource-development issues. Suncor also works with these people through a Regional Issues Working Group to address housing, daycare, and other social issues, and through the Cumulative Environmental Management Association to deal with the environmental effects of industrial development.[13]

Whether broadly or narrowly defined, the engagement objectives will set the tone for the steps that follow. For that reason, engagement planners must consider these objectives carefully.

Step 2: Identify and Assess Stakeholders

Stakeholders can be identified for issue- or project-related engagements by answering several questions:

1. Who might be affected by the matter?
2. Who has been involved in similar matters in the same region in the past?

3. Who has said they would like to be involved?
4. Who has expertise that could be useful?
5. Who would be upset if excluded from the engagement?

With these questions in mind, engagement planners should be able to define the type of stakeholders they need. For example, a new land development project will be of concern to neighbors, labor groups, and government planning officials, among others. A controversy concerning product safety will typically affect customers, distributors, regulators, and perhaps some consumer safety groups. Inquiries can be made to identify the specific people who can best represent those constituencies. The organizations and people selected from this analysis, and the authorities who have worked with them in the past, may be able to suggest others who should also be involved. If the engagement objectives are more general—such as establishing a permanent advisory board for general feedback—professional colleagues might recommend candidates. An Internet or literature search and a review of speaker lists for relevant conferences may also disclose independent experts that fit the need.

During the review process, certain information should be gathered on key stakeholder organizations and their individual representatives. Figure 11.5 lists some information that may help planners shape the engagement team, techniques, and strategies to enhance the likelihood of success.

Figure 11.5 **Types of Information for Evaluating Stakeholder Organizations** **for Long or Potentially Contentious Engagement**	
1. Size and resources	12. Connections with company employees
2. Scope of operations	13. Expected position on issues, projects,
3. Knowledge and expertise	or other matters which are the subject
4. History	of the engagement
5. Organizational objectives	14. Potential risks their participation may
6. Values	pose to the company
7. Credibility	15. Information on the stakeholder's
8. Influence	individual representative likely to be
9. Outcomes of past dealings with	involved in the engagement, including
business	her education, experience, skills,
10. Willingness to engage	assertiveness, integrity, and past
11. Past relationship with company	experience in engaging with businesses

To aid in identifying and understanding the range of stakeholder organizations potentially involved in a complex project- or issue-oriented engagement, the engagement planner can try various types of mapping. For a development project, this can entail identifying on a geographical map those communities that may be adversely affected. Or stakeholders can be mapped on graphs or diagrams to show their influence, degree of opposition, and constituencies. For example, they could be plotted on a graph where the y axis represents the size or influence of a stakeholder and the x axis depicts the degree of likely support by the stakeholder for the company's proposed project or action. A single graph of this type can be prepared showing all key stakeholders, or separate graphs can be created for each major stakeholder constituency or category. Another option is to prepare a diagram showing each key stakeholder in a circle that is sized according to its relative size or influence. The circles can be plotted on a background of shaded areas coded to various constituencies. Lines of various thicknesses can be drawn connecting the circles to depict strong or weak relationships between the stakeholders.

Once a list of potential stakeholders and the information about them has been prepared, the listed people and organizations should be assessed to determine who should be urged to participate in the engagement and how best to engage them. This screening can be used to identify candidates for an advisory group or to generate invitation and distribution lists for various engagement activities. The evaluation criteria should reflect the complement of constituencies, skills, and expertise needed to fulfill the objective. The main purpose of the evaluation is not to find stakeholder representatives who are most likely to toe the company line, but rather to locate those who best represent the interests and views of various key constituencies. Sure, groups that generally support company actions may be easiest to work with, but they don't necessarily say what the company needs to hear, or stimulate the kind of constructive change that can make a company stronger. Moreover, they may not be credible enough among their peers to deliver the critical mass of support needed for the proposed action. In the long run, it's generally better to select stakeholders that are more representative—even if they are outspoken—over friendly ones with lesser peer support. Of course, if there are several stakeholder organizations or individual representatives who are equally influential with an important constituency, then the candidate that is most trustworthy, easiest to work with, and has the best listening and negotiating skills should be preferred. Even where there are more amiable choices, ignoring powerful, more controversial stakeholders should be done with caution, however. Stakeholders who are most prone to tarnishing the image of businesses will not be dissuaded from such harmful conduct merely by excluding them from discussions. Such exclusion may breed resentment and spur visible opposition rather than prevent it.

How much difficulty should a company tolerate from a tough, irascible stakeholder representative before severing the engagement? Generally, the greater the stakes, the more the company should tolerate. If the company is establishing a stakeholder advisory panel when there are no serious issues or contested projects on the table, it can afford to be more selective, picking panel members who work well with business while also being constructive, candid critics. But if a hot issue or development project is at the center of the engagement, then great caution should be taken before breaking off an association with extremists or other troublesome stakeholders. According to Peter Sandman, a well-known expert in crisis communication: "Perhaps the most common mistake companies make in their efforts to be accountable (to stakeholders) is trying to exclude the extremists." If these difficult parties are cut from the engagement process, says Sandman, this can produce two negative consequences: the moderates remaining in the engagement can be easily painted as sell-outs by their peers and lose credibility, or the moderates can start acting tough to prove they didn't sell out. The better approach for companies is to search for an acceptable way to engage the extremists and if they walk away, to continue to leave the door open for them.[14] In such situations, the company's actions about openness and inclusiveness do indeed speak louder than words to all the stakeholders who are still participating. More important, such tolerance and openness can help the remaining stakeholders preserve their credibility with their peers.

Another consideration in selecting stakeholders involves building constituencies. If, for example, a manufacturer is planning to build a new factory to make a new diabetes medication, it may want to include local diabetics or representatives of a diabetics association in the engagement process and perhaps help them organize. A company may even find it useful to help critics organize, too. Why would a company be willing to give a louder voice to its detractors? By doing this, a firm could increase participation in the engagement process, build credibility, and establish a vehicle for disseminating information and collecting valuable feedback. What is more, this can provide a forum in which critics discuss and consolidate their views, dampening the bite of extremists and expediting problem-solving.

Step 3: Develop Engagement Plan

Once the objectives have been set and key stakeholders assessed and identified, the next step is to find the techniques that can best help the company achieve its stated objectives. Examples of engagement techniques are provided in Figure 11.6. In selecting them, planners should consider the stakeholders' languages, education, and resources, as well as their locations, accessibilities, propensities, and needs. These factors can affect the selection and design of techniques in many ways. For example, engagement methods based on computers make little sense if most stakeholders don't have access to one. Written background information and surveys won't work if targeted groups are barely literate. With these groups, live theater skits and role-playing can be effective in introducing issues and stimulating discussion. If stakeholders mistrust the company, then an independent facilitator, ombudsperson, or confidential hotline may help. Stakeholders concerned about a recent disaster may find company communications by formal written reports, press releases, and meetings to be too slow, so Internet postings and chat pages may be better at that stage. Surveys might work well for groups that know and trust the company and understand the issues, but not for strangers who may be angered by the company's proposed action. For the latter, face-to-face meetings are preferred. Large open meetings won't be effective for uncovering the views of the "silent majority" who feel too intimidated to speak before a crowd. One-on-one or small focus-group discussions are better.

Figure 11.6
Some Stakeholder Engagement Techniques

Informing stakeholders with no dialogue
1. Direct notification of projects, issues, and engagement opportunities by press release, press conference, technical briefing, newspaper advertisement, or announcement distributed by mail, door-to-door, e-mail, Internet, phone, radio, or TV
2. Newspaper articles and editorials
3. Summary leaflets and bulletins
4. Newsletters (electronic or mailed, published by company or jointly with others, using existing publications or those specially established for the purpose)
5. Public sustainability and financial reports
6. Displays, models, and exhibitions in public areas and at public events
7. Videos, audio recordings
8. Radio or TV interviews with company spokespeople

Informing stakeholders with some dialogue
9. Open houses, open days, "town hall" meetings
10. Site visits and tours

Feedback by stakeholders with no or very limited exchange with company
11. Surveys (electronic or live)
12. Sustainability report feedback cards
13. Complaint hotlines

Feedback by stakeholders with some exchange with company
14. Posted written proposals and solicited requests for comments (via regular mail or Internet-based)
15. E-mail and chat-room exchanges

Short-term feedback with extensive exchange
16. Focus group meetings
17. Deliberative workshops (10-40 participants; single or multi-day)
18. Public ("town hall") meetings
19. Hearings or meetings sponsored by others (governments, trade associations, et al.)
20. Online conferences with question and answer capability
21. Conference calls
22. Video conferences

Long-term feedback with extensive exchange
23. Advisory or liaison groups (general or specific; ad hoc or permanent)
24. Community liaison officers
25. One-on-one relationships and forums for exchange

Collaborative identification of issues and design of solutions
26. Working groups or other joint stakeholder-company initiatives charged with finding mutually acceptable solutions, developing action plans, or reaching other agreements
27. Joint efforts with stakeholders to strengthen their ability to participate effectively in that role ("capacity-building")
28. Ongoing oversight or formal auditing role by stakeholders concerning company's project or site

Engagement planners must be sensitive in setting the location and time for engagement, too. Few aboriginals from the rainforest will likely join a focus-group discussion planned for the city. The costs of travel may be a barrier for some stakeholders unless compensation is provided. Working parents with children may see childcare as an obstacle to participating in evening meetings. Sessions scheduled around a popular local holiday may be poorly attended.

Engagement techniques should be selected and designed to extract information that will aid decisionmaking and problem-solving. Discussions should not just focus on stakeholder concerns about the company or its proposed action, but explore how those concerns can be addressed while allowing the company to meet its business objectives. In addition, by asking about the relative importance of various issues in a survey or focus-group meeting, a company can use the responses to help set priorities among proposed actions, and allocate resources where stakeholders need them most. Of course, to be an effective tool for decisionmaking and problem-solving, the engagement must stimulate open and honest discussion of facts, issues, and concerns. Companies should set the example by taking all reasonable measures to demonstrate that behavior themselves. Even so, firms must take care to protect proprietary information and not destroy confidences or jeopardize anyone's right of privacy.

Then too, engagement planning should address how the selected techniques can be sequenced to make them most efficient and effective. Open houses or site visits may be good informal ice-breakers where the company can deal with individuals and small groups, laying the foundation for more extensive engagement later. Some door-to-door canvassing or phone surveys may help the company focus the issues for a subsequent group meeting. Distributing information well in advance of the meeting enables stakeholders to better prepare, too. If the engagement involves a matter that is highly technical or that otherwise requires special knowledge not possessed by key stakeholders, then training or expert guidance may be needed before meaningful discussions are undertaken. These pre-meeting steps can make later engagement sessions more productive, which in turn can provide encouragement to all for further engagement.

The proper sequencing of activities can also facilitate constructive engagement with troublesome, confrontational stakeholders. For instance, ever-widening circles of trust and consensus can be built through a series of one-on-one or small-group meetings. Sessions would first be held with collaborative stakeholders. Once general consensus is established with them, meetings would be convened with their more confrontational counterparts. Eventually one or more larger meetings would be called, bringing together a wide range of collaborative and confrontational stakeholders in search of a broad consensus for action. The key to success at these large meetings is to strike the right balance between, on one hand, involving enough stakeholders to secure a critical mass of support on the direction forward, and on the other, assuring the meeting does not become so big and bureaucratic it bogs down in endless debate.

Other approaches can also be used to deal with difficult stakeholders. One is to hire a neutral third-party broker or facilitator to conduct the engagement—someone trusted by both the company and the stakeholder. Or engagement planners might find it helpful to negotiate privately with such stakeholders. This can reduce the inclination for public posturing by the parties that can erode candor and trust. Another strategy is to reach consensus with the stakeholders on a code of conduct early in the engagement process. The code would spell out how all parties will work together to achieve a productive outcome. It would emphasize respectful and constructive interaction. It could also lay out the rules about how and when the parties communicate with the media and who must approve press releases. Other ideas for code provisions can be drawn from Figure 11.3 as well as the Model Code of Conduct for a Stakeholder Team (Figure 4.8), discussed earlier. A neutral third person can monitor the parties' adherence to the code and lead a discussion on code conformance and session effectiveness at the end of each engagement meeting.

Scenario planning can sometimes be useful in designing engagement strategies and techniques on controversial matters. Armed with the stakeholder assessment information, a company can envision the various positions each stakeholder group is likely to assert, what actions each is likely to take, and how those positions and actions may be received among fellow stakeholders. Techniques and strategies can then be planned with these dynamics in mind. If a series of engagement activities is envisioned, the scenario planning can consider various possible outcomes of each stage and identify the company's response and engagement strategy that might best follow each outcome.

After the techniques are identified, an engagement plan should be prepared, especially if the engagement is likely to be contentious or drawn out. The plan can include the engagement objectives, list of stakeholders, and selected engagement techniques as well as optional ones. It can also mention engagement locations and schedules, the work products anticipated from each step of the process, and the resources needed for implementation. Altogether, the plan should enable the company to visualize how the various techniques will interlink to best achieve the objectives. The plan can also serve as the basis for estimating the resources needed for the undertaking. The document should permit an experienced professional to determine whether the scope and nature of the overall engagement are appropriate for the breadth and impact of the objective and its potential to generate controversy. Trying to engage on a tough project or issue with unreasonable constraints on time and money can be a recipe for dismal failure. And since not all engagements are successful, the downside risks of the engagement should be identified in the plan, too, in order to keep expectations realistic.

Once the plan is prepared and funded, it should be periodically reviewed and updated as necessary as the engagement proceeds. Given all that can happen during engagement, the plan should be considered a flexible guideline, not a document cast in stone.

Step 4: Implement Plan

A plan for general feedback from an advisory board may be implemented with few hitches. Engagement around hot issues or projects can be a different story. In many respects, rolling out an engagement plan in those cases is more like playing jazz than a symphony: there is a basic framework to guide you, but much of the process is improvised. New issues and stakeholders arise, while big concerns may become small ones, and small ones, big ones. Unexpected delays occur; interest and emotions ebb and flow. Political grand-standing and other side-shows pose distractions. Engagement planners must expect the unexpected and be willing to adjust quickly and move forward.

As the engagement is implemented, those who guide the process should do so with their stakeholder principles in mind. It is important that they properly manage expectations so that neither stakeholders nor company representatives become overly optimistic and therefore likely to be discouraged by the outcome. Participants should understand that a single engagement event may not end the controversy and that complete consensus among a wide range of stakeholders is rarely achieved. They should be told early on if a decision has already been made and whether it is non-negotiable. However, companies should carefully weigh any decision to pull important issues off the negotiating table because this may cause key stakeholders to drop out of the process. But even though it may be unpopular with stakeholders, it is better that the critical boundaries of decisionmaking be clarified and communicated early rather than risk serious misunderstanding and disappointment later. Openness and honesty are essential for building good, lasting relationships. Good, lasting relationships make for good, lasting solutions.

Step 5: Assess Engagement Process

As shown in Figure 11.4, assessing the engagement process follows in the wake of plan implementation. Actually, a mini-assessment should be undertaken after each phase of the plan is executed, and sometimes even in the midst of a phase. If a meeting has gone out of control, the situation must be assessed on the spot and a new course of action taken. If no one is responding to a survey, the initiator must determine why and take corrective steps. Once the plan has been fully implemented, a more complete assessment can be made. That review can consider how well the approach fulfilled the objectives, how well the engagement adhered to the principles, and what went well, what not so well. This can also be a good time to for the group to reevaluate how well it conformed to any agreed-upon code of conduct. These assessments can serve up valuable lessons, not only for improving future engagement sessions under the plan, but for designing effective engagements on future initiatives as well.

Step 6: Respond to Engagement Results

Stakeholders participate in engagement and provide their feedback because they believe the company will respond. And respond it must, using sensitivity and its own responsible judgment even when consensus is lacking. But when the dust settles, the list of items for action may also include some assigned to the stakeholders themselves. At appropriate times during the engagement process and at the end, both the company and stakeholders should identify what they will do to address the feedback they have received. These commitments should cover who will take what specific action by when and how progress will be measured.

If concerns exist about whether a particular stakeholder has enough resources or skills to perform its obligations, this should be discussed as early as possible. Capacity-building may take time. In many circumstances, it is in the company's best interests to provide funds or other resources needed for the stakeholder to complete its tasks. If the objective of the engagement is to develop a program and then pass it to a stakeholder group for on-going management, capacity-building can be critical for success. Giving a stakeholder group an important role it is not prepared to perform is a quick route to deep disappointment, resentment, and failure.

Most commitments made in follow-up to stakeholder engagement will focus on the issue, project, or other focal point of the engagement. A few may be aimed at the company-stakeholder relationship itself. All significant commitments, whatever their nature, should be recorded and communicated to all involved. Easy, non-controversial action items should be addressed first. This starts the snowball of trust rolling, helping it grow for tougher challenges ahead.

Step 7: Measure and Report Progress

As we discussed in Chapter 9, commitments are of little value unless there is accountability for meeting them, reinforced by some means of measuring and reporting progress. Periodic progress reports or review sessions are common ways of doing that for stakeholder engagement. As with the engagement techniques, the methods of measuring and reporting must be appropriate for the stakeholders involved. If it appears that key commitments cannot be fulfilled, the reasons should be fully explained and the need for further engagement explored. Once the commitments have been met, the company should publicly acknowledge the stakeholders for their contributions. A special announcement or celebration can underscore the importance of the achievement and recognize those who helped accomplish it.

Step 8: Repeat the Process

Like the SOS, the stakeholder engagement process envisioned here is a plan-do-check-act approach to improvement. Unless the company intends to sever completely its ties with the stakeholders at the end of the engagement, some provision should be made for maintaining a good on-going relationship. The engagement process of Figure 11.4 can be the framework for addressing that objective as well. Planners should bear in mind that longer term engagements may pose some special needs. For instance, to perpetuate certain complex engagements, a shared governance structure involving both company and stakeholder representatives may be needed. A reliable source of long-term funding may also be required.

Common Approaches for Engaging Various Types of Stakeholders

Because the process described above is general, it can be used under a wide range of circumstances with different types of stakeholders. Some engagement tools are designed for broad application; others are used with specific types of stakeholders in mind. Tools for broad application include the feedback cards placed in sustainability reports and the online surveys posted with Internet-based reports. Shell goes one step further with its *Tell Shell* program that allows anyone to provide candid feedback to the company via e-mail, the Internet, or regular mail.

Engagement tools commonly applied to specific stakeholder groups are discussed below.

Employees

The survey is the tool of choice for gathering feedback from employees. Ford, Dow, BT, Suncor, Van City, Novartis, and Co-operative Financial Services all use it for their workforces. BC Hydro, the Canadian power company, surveys its employees annually, asking them the same eight questions that are posed to other employees across the country in calculating the nationwide WorkCanada Employee Commitment Index (ECI). By using the ECI questions, the company can track the change in attitudes of its workers over time as well as benchmark its ECI scores with those obtained from the nationwide sampling. Some firms like Van City follow up their surveys with employee focus-group discussions to better understand the issues raised by the survey and determine how to respond. Management-employee "town meetings" are used by Ford, Baxter, and other companies as an important communication tool. They typically involve a short update by company leaders on the latest business developments, followed by a question-and-answer session. Some sessions are also broadcast live to remote locations. Volkswagen has a team of employee representatives from around the globe which frequently engages with management on matters of concern. BT has a similar organization for its European operations. Shell and other companies, especially those with unionized workforces, have "works councils" or other site-level management-labor committees. Shell and others have ombudspersons, independent counselors, and help-lines for employees who have sensitive issues to discuss with the company.

GE, Baxter, and other companies engage their employees with "upward-feedback" surveys through which employees critique their supervisors and the company. The supervisor's peers and manager are also surveyed. The results of this *360°-survey process* go to the supervisor and her manager. The surveys may be followed by live facilitated discussions between the supervisor and staff to clarify their feedback and help identify an appropriate response. Ultimately, supervisors are expected to develop and execute an action plan addressing the feedback.

If employee concerns are significant and not adequately addressed by surveys, town meetings, or other communications techniques just discussed, then a more extreme form of engagement may result: collective bargaining. Since collective bargaining is a highly regulated activity in many countries, the process should be undertaken with the help of those who are well versed in the rules. Unfortunately these rules can have the unintended effect of erecting walls between management and the bargaining employees. From a sustainability perspective, the challenge for each party is to maintain respect for the other—something enhanced through the use of good listening skills and a sincere search for mutually acceptable solutions.

Customers

Surveys are also commonly used to solicit input from customers. Both Johnson Controls and BT have extensive programs for collecting customer opinions monthly. Intel does it quarterly. Van City uses telephone surveys for regular bank patrons and mails surveys to its business clients. BT conducts 3,000 face-to-face interviews with residential customers monthly. In addition, the company retains an independent agency to canvas over 10,000 business and residential customers each month on how well their service requests were handled. BT, Van City, and Co-operative Financial Services supplement their surveys with customer focus-group or advisory committee discussions to explore specific issues. Among other techniques, Baxter uses a special Customer Advisory Council to engage on sustainability issues.

Suppliers

Co-operative Financial Services engages its suppliers through telephone surveys, while BT uses an annual supplier satisfaction survey and Statoil surveys its suppliers every other year. However, most companies that engage their suppliers do so through special meetings, conferences, or collaborative groups. Ford, for example, has established a Supplier Advisory Council for this purpose.

Communities

The approach to community stakeholders is diverse. For some companies like BT and BC Hydro that serve entire communities, the public and the customer are synonymous, and common engagement tools are used. But these and other companies may also face special concerns from neighbors living next to their operating sites. Intel and Shell have formed facilitated community advisory panels to handle those concerns. Intel and Alcoa also use other techniques, such as open houses, tours, and local meetings. A few companies, like International Paper, publish local sustainability reports as well. To gauge general public opinion, BC Hydro, Suncor, Dow, Intel, and Van City still rely on surveys.

Governments

Engagement with governments typically centers on lobbying legislators for laws favorable to the business. It also involves communicating with regulators on special projects, permits, or issues. Facility tours for key government officials are also common. Suncor takes a more proactive approach by surveying their officials every two years. Though not typical, some companies have found it useful to schedule special meetings with regulators for focused discussions not related to current projects or issues. The purpose of these meetings is to explore how to strengthen the communication and relationship between the company and the agency, and to share information on the impending developments and long-term strategies of their respective organizations.

Investors

Many companies have extensive programs for engaging mainstream investors. Some aspects of engagement—quarterly financial reports and annual public stockholder meetings, for example—may be required by law. Other usual methods include special live and web-cast conferences, regional investor meetings, and one-on-one discussions.

While these techniques are typically limited to financial matters, some companies are beginning to incorporate broader sustainability issues with their key financial information. The combined financial-sustainability reports mentioned in the previous chapter are good examples. More combined reports will be produced under France's New Economic Regulation and through related initiatives in South Africa and the United Kingdom. Vodafone, the British mobile phone company, assembled a formal road show, visiting 30 major investors and SRI funds to address their concerns proactively.[15]

For socially responsible investors, most engagement with companies is made by special company-rating groups, using questionnaires, live and phone interviews, and an occasional site visit. These activities are not undertaken with engagement in mind but for the purpose of evaluating and rating a company's sustainability performance for its investor customers. As a practical matter, however, weaknesses cited by these groups typically don't go unnoticed by company management.

As noted in Chapter 3 and Appendix 1.32, SRI is growing in popularity. For companies, this has meant an increasing barrage of inquiries from rating companies. Fortunately, GRI and a few private firms are working with companies and the SRI community with the aim of easing this survey fatigue. GRI is developing e-systems that can store and sort company sustainability information for access by rating firms and others. SRI World Group provides a system that consolidates the information requests from a number of rating groups, provides tools by which companies can report that data, and distributes customized reports on each reporting company to each participating rating firm.[16] Until such a solution is accepted across the SRI community, companies have two choices: ignore the surveys—and the fastest growing segment of investment—or respond to them. If the choice is the latter, as it is for many companies, then it pays to prepare a sustainability report so most information needed for the surveys is readily available. A report meeting the GRI guidelines will typically cover the vast majority of issues raised in such questionnaires.[17]

Activists, Public Interest Groups

In recent years, various activist and public interest groups—commonly referred to as NGOs or civil society organizations (CSOs)—have played an increasing role with companies on matters of corporate governance and other important social and environmental issues. Given the growing influence this stakeholder group has in the world of sustainability, engagement planners intending to work with them should first understand who they are dealing with. To gain that perspective, let us examine the history and characteristics of this group as well as the trends affecting them.

NGOs, CSOs: Who Are They?

NGOs and CSOs refer to a wide range of independent voluntary organizations—*excluding* governments, political parties, companies, criminal organizations, and guerilla groups—that provide services or advocacy on any of a broad range of matters. Many focus on issues related to sustainability, such as economic development, environmental protection, social justice, and quality of life. "Nongovernmental organization" or "NGO" is a term introduced in 1945 when the United Nations used it in its charter to differentiate between intergovernmental "specialized agencies" and international private (nongovernmental) organizations.[18] By the early 1970s, "NGO" passed into popular usage.

In the 1990s, the U.N. Commission on Sustainable Development sharpened the definition of NGO further by adopting for its own purposes the nine "major groups" of NGOs listed in Agenda 21, the action plan emerging from the Rio Earth Summit of 1992 (U.N. Conference on Environment and Development). The United Nations granted these groups various rights of involvement and consultation in furtherance of its policy favoring broad public participation in decisionmaking. The nine major groups include those addressing: (1) women's rights; (2) children and youth issues; (3) indigenous people and their communities; (4) worker's rights and trade unions; (5) business and industry issues; (6) science and technology; (7) farming; (8) local authorities' sustainability initiatives; and (9) other topics (environmental, etc.). While trade unions, professional and business groups, and religious organizations have, in practice, been brought under the U.N. NGO umbrella, leaders of these groups and some observers do not consider them NGOs.[19]

CSO is generally considered to be synonymous with NGO, although some people believe the term CSO includes—and NGO excludes—loose networks of individuals and groups. "Civil society organization" derives from the term "civil society," which is used in many countries outside the United States to describe the "third sector" of society, the other two being government and business.

History of NGOs

While the NGO terminology may be relatively recent, the concept is not.[20] In 1787, Thomas Clarkson and 11 other men met in a Quaker bookshop to form a society to dissuade British companies and ship owners from participating in the slave trade. Five years later, nearly 400,000 Britons were boycotting slave-grown sugar. Thanks to these and other efforts, in 1807, Parliament agreed to ban the slave trade. Clarkson's antislavery movement eventually gave rise to the World Anti-Slavery Convention in 1840, a landmark gathering that brought together citizen activists on an international basis.[21] But slavery wasn't the only topic of concern by early NGOs. The World Alliance of Young Men's Christian Associations (YMCAs) was founded in 1855, and eight years later the International Committee for the Red Cross was established.

At the end of the 19th century, Edmund Dene Morel launched another international human rights movement when he rallied clergymen, businessmen, journalists, and others to oppose Belgian King Leopold's use of forced labor in the rubber fields of the Congo. Morel revealed that the king was reaping enormous personal profits for himself from this venture. Within a decade, the control of the Congo was transferred from the king back to the Belgian government and eventually most of the egregious abuses were stopped.[22]

In the early 1900s, women's suffrage and the prohibition movement were other initiatives that gained momentum through the efforts of social activists. Within the last 50 years, NGOs played important roles in promoting U.S. civil rights, supporting the Vietnam War peace movement, and defeating apartheid in South Africa. They were also major forces behind the creation of an international criminal court and adoption of a treaty banning land mines.

As shown in Figure 11.7, NGO activity has stepped up considerably from the days of Clarkson and Morel. According to the Union of International Associations, there were approximately 25,000 active international NGOs in 2001, up from about 10,000 in 1980 and 400 a century ago. Another 18,000 entities were reported as inactive NGOs in 2001, although presumably capable of being reactivated as the need arises.[23] As of 2005, there were more than 2,600 NGOs formally accredited for consultation status with the U.N. Economic and Social Council—over double the count for 1996.[24]

The number of national and local activist groups is exploding, too. Twenty years ago, only 1 organization in Indonesia was working to protect the environment; now over 2,000 are doing so. In the Philippines, nonprofit organizations grew from 18,000 to 58,000 between 1989 and 1996.[25] Experts at the Worldwatch Institute estimate that there are now approximately two million grass-roots citizens' groups in the United States, with at least two-thirds of them having started within the last 30 years.[26]

Not only are NGOs growing in number, they are becoming more sophisticated, skilled, and specialized. Of the people working for the largest, most influential environmental NGOs, 50% have masters or law degrees and 10 to 20% have doctorates.[27] Typically NGOs are well in tune with shifting political, social, economic, and environmental trends, and use that knowledge effectively in crafting strategies. Their media relations and communications skills often rival the best in the private sector. Their ability to move quickly and form global networks is the envy of business.

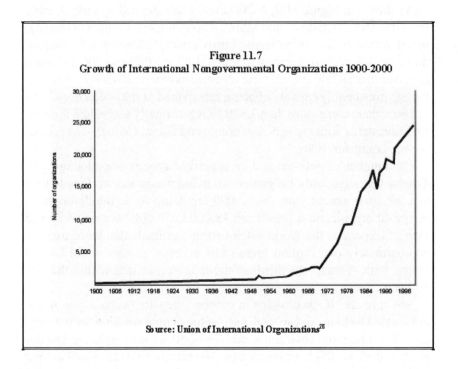

Figure 11.7
Growth of International Nongovernmental Organizations 1900-2000

Source: Union of International Organizations[28]

Types of NGOs

Today, NGOs are present in a wide variety of sizes, forms, scopes, and locations, and employ a broad range of tactics. Consider, for example, the distinctions among them described below.[29] Bear in mind, these distinctions are rarely found in pure form among the more successful NGOs. More often, these differences exist in degrees, changing over time and geographies to meet new conditions and opportunities.

Democratic Versus Self-Appointed

Some NGOs like Friends of the Earth (FoE) are democratic, granting members the right to vote for their boards. Others such as Greenpeace historically granted no voting rights to members but instead appointed their boards. Only more recently has that activist group committed to transition to elected boards. As with Greenpeace, other large NGOs are also in the midst of changing to a more democratic structure or for various reasons do not have a uniform approach across their organization.

Government-Supported Versus Nongovernment-Supported

Government funding is routinely sought by NGOs like CARE or Oxfam International, which offer humanitarian relief, and by those that help with education, healthcare, conservation, and research and development. Although less than 2% of NGO income for 1970 was from public grants, by 1988 it had soared to 35%.[30] Other groups, such as Amnesty International, will not accept direct government aid for normal operations, but instead rely on funding from members, foundations, and the sale of merchandise, credit cards, travel tours, and other services. While NGOs usually claim their views are independent of funding sources, it is not uncommon to see NGOs adjust their priorities to meet the conditions of large funders.

North Versus South

Many NGOs are based in the southern hemisphere, to be sure. They include organizations like Ethos, Acción Empresarial, the Instituto Argentino de Responsabilidad Social, and the Centro Colombiano de Responsabilidad Empresarial, among others. Large global NGOs are generally not headquartered there; rather, they tend to be based in industrialized countries in the northern hemisphere—usually in Canada, Europe, and the United States. However, these northern NGOs often operate in partnership with branches or independent groups located in the South. For instance, Oxfam has an Oxford-based secretariat but over 3,000 partner organizations below the equator.

Northern NGOs pushing issues like anti-child labor and forest preservation often find themselves at odds with their southern sisters who are desperate for family income and firewood. The social investing criteria developed by the black unions in South Africa in the 1990s rated job creation and industrial relations as the top two issues of importance. Social spending was last.[31] Even if NGOs from both regions agree on a common objective, differences in culture often require differences in approach to effect the desired change.

Tensions around objectives and approach exist not just between North and South NGOs, but also among the northern and southern members of large international NGOs. This tension is exacerbated by the fact that the northerners typically have more members and resources among their ranks and are closer to the centers of power.

Direct Action Versus Indirect Action Versus Cooperative Action

Cooperative-action NGOs tend to use dialogue, alliances, and partnerships with business as their normal way of operating. They may also provide investment funds for worthy business proposals with a social bent. NGOs of this type include the WWF, which joined with others to establish the Forest Stewardship Council (FSC) and Marine Stewardship Council. These councils work with companies to endorse products that demonstrate good sustainability practice. The Nature Conservancy and other conservation groups also assume cooperative-action strategies with businesses and private property owners to preserve environmentally attractive lands. Cooperation has certainly been a theme at Environmental Defense, American Forests, Conservation International, Natural Resources Defense Council, Inc., Rainforest Alliance, the Wildlife Habitat Council, WRI, and CERES.[32]

Indirect-action groups focus on lobbying governments and raising media and public awareness about their issues but without direct confrontation. A prime example is DATA (Debt, AIDS, Trade, Africa), founded in 2002 by U2 lead singer, Bono, along with Bobby Shriver and activists from the Jubilee 2000 Drop-the-(African Nation) Debt Campaign. DATA raises public awareness about the plight of poor African nations and lobbies the governments of wealthy countries to help their African counterparts through debt relief, increased trade, and assistance in combating the AIDS epidemic.[33]

Confrontation is, however, the modus operandi of direct-action NGOs like Greenpeace, FoE, Earth First, and the Rainforest Action Network (RAN). They create a sense of urgency around an issue by confronting companies directly through demonstrations, boycotts, lawsuits, shareholder resolutions, or other means. They are most effective against large, highly visible corporations that prize their brands and reputations. Public sympathy is one of their main weapons, and sometimes they go to extremes to get it. Think of Julia "Butterfly" Hill, the Earth First volunteer who in 1996 climbed a redwood tree in California and stayed there two years. Various NGOs kept her well supplied and assured regular press coverage by arranging the visits of a number of celebrities. Julia came down only after Pacific Lumber, tired of the adverse publicity, agreed to preserve the tree and surrounding forest.

RAN used confrontation successfully to convince Citicorp to fund projects involving renewable energy and sustainable forestry and to withhold financing for projects that degrade critical habitats. The campaign involved cable television commercials in which well-known celebrities cut up their Citi cards. The group also published a full-page newspaper advertisement claiming the CEO was an environmental villain. In addition, it staged protests at some of Citicorp's branch facilities and at Cornell University when the CEO lectured there. RAN members even chained themselves to the doors of some banks. Others rappelled down the building across the street from bank headquarters, unveiling a 60-foot banner proclaiming: "Forest destruction & global warming? We're banking on it!"[34]

Another direct-action group, People for the Ethical Treatment of Animals (PETA), has used personal intimidation as their main tactic to pressure corporate executives to change their practices on animal testing and handling. This tactic has taken many forms, including demonstrating in front of executives' homes, placing leaflets in their neighbors' mail boxes, and showing animal abuse films from projection trucks parked in the street. PETA also speaks directly with family members and neighbors of company officials, as well as with managers of the country clubs and restaurants they frequent.[35] The organization resorts to these extreme tactics because, quite frankly, they work.

Even more extreme confrontation is used by guerilla activist groups like the Animal Liberation Front and the Earth Liberation Front, which according to federal indictments handed down in 2006, have used arson and sabotage in attacks on government facilities, research centers, and private businesses. The U.S. Federal Bureau of Investigation considers groups like these to be domestic terrorist organizations. Violent groups are typically not classified as NGOs, however.[36]

By happenstance or conscious strategy, different types of NGOs often find greater success working together than by independent action. Direct-action NGOs may spur business to engage with corporative-action groups in the search for practical solutions. For example, the FSC, which certifies sustainability practices in the lumber industry, was created when the WWF began working with industry representatives at the same time other NGOs were pressuring them through direct-action tactics.[37]

NGOs that predominantly assume direct-, indirect-, or cooperative-action strategies may find themselves drifting to one of the other strategies on occasion, walking a fine line in the struggle for public credibility. Be too accommodating to business, and you may be ridiculed by fellow

NGOs as a corporate puppet. Be too confrontational and you may be viewed a scaremonger, a group that lacks accountability in the single-minded pursuit of its own objectives at the expense of the broader public good. Considerable debate about this balance goes on among NGOs, and among various factions within them. Occasionally this leads to an NGO praising a company in one instance and lambasting it in another. This is exactly what happened to Shell. For many years, FoE praised them for their commitment to sustainable development and support on climate change. Later, however, FoE issued a scathing report entitled: *Failing the Challenge—The Other Shell Report 2002*—mockingly patterned after Shell's own sustainability report—which skewered the company for the company's alleged failure to meet its sustainability commitments at the facility level.[38] Notwithstanding this example, growing numbers of NGOs are finding themselves drifting more toward the cooperative end of the spectrum in search of alliances that can achieve visible results on complex issues.

Campaign Versus Operational

Operational NGOs work to acquire funds, labor, and other resources to implement programs and projects. Campaigning NGOs, on the other hand, quickly mobilize large numbers of organizations and people for demonstrations or other activities aimed at garnering publicity and support for their cause—a strategy commonly referred to as "swarming." Campaigning NGOs helped organize 700 groups and tens of thousands of people into a mass demonstration against globalization that disrupted the Seattle Ministerial Conference of the World Trade Organization (WTO) in 1999. In the mid-1990s, the Maria Elena Cuadra Women's Movement in Nicaragua campaigned to secure 30,000 signatures in support of their code of labor and human rights protections. Their work eventually led to the adoption of these protections as law in 1998.

While the operational and campaign categories describe an NGO's general mode of operation, rarely are they exclusive: campaigning NGOs, such as those devoted to human rights and women's issues, often operate programs to help the victims of discrimination and injustice. Large operational NGOs will also regularly support campaigns.

Solo Versus Coalition

Like companies, NGOs are finding they simply don't have enough time, money, expertise, or power to achieve everything on their global wish lists. The answer for many is to get by with a little help from their friends: to pursue common causes with other like-minded NGOs. Between 1973 and 1993, the number of NGO coalitions grew from 25 to 40% of the total number of international NGOs. A classic example is GRI, which was established through collaboration among NGOs as well as businesses, investors, academics, and professional associations. Another coalition NGO is the WCU, which brings together 735 NGOs, 35 affiliates, 78 states, and 112 government agencies, as well as 10,000 scientists and other experts from 181 countries.

GRI and the WCU can be considered operational-type coalitions. However, there are campaign-type coalitions, too. One involving 350 arms-control and humanitarian groups from 23 countries was the driving force behind an international treaty banning the manufacture, distribution, and use of land mines. A coalition leader, Jodie Williams, head of the U.S.-based International Committee to Ban Land Mines, was presented the Nobel Peace Prize for her work. Another campaign-type coalition, Jubilee 2000, secured 20 million signatures in 150 countries to press for the cancellation of unpayable international debt by impoverished African nations. This was one of the broadest NGO coalitions ever, involving people as diverse as Puff Daddy and the Pope, Jesse Helms and Bono, and the Sisters of the Sacred Heart and the Spice Girls. It extracted governmental commitments for the relief of $110 billion of the debt.[39]

Some of the more effective NGO coalitions solicit businesses that support their cause to provide testimonials or directly proselytize other businesses. In the 1990s, Sunoco and General Motors, early subscribers to the CERES Principles, often joined CERES staff members in the recruitment of other company endorsers. Home Depot supported ForestEthics and Greenpeace Chile in convincing Chile-based lumber companies CMPC-Mininco and Arauco—both suppliers to Home Depot—to halt the logging of endangered species of trees.[40]

Broad Scope Versus Narrow Scope

Some NGOs focus on a particular industry (e.g., apparel, mining, forestry, health-care), while others zero in on individual companies (e.g., Nike, ExxonMobil), a specific issue (e.g., climate change, corruption), or constituency (e.g., women, workers, children). Still others confine their efforts to specific tactics, such as litigation, certification, monitoring, or developing partnerships. An NGO may assume, for example, the narrow charter of winning a particular lawsuit, a broader challenge of changing government policy, or the broadest objective of re-shaping social norms. Occasionally an NGO may work on all three perspectives, either sequentially or simultaneously.

Centralized Versus Decentralized

A number of NGOs—particularly the long-established ones like the Red Cross and the Salvation Army—are molded around a strong centralized governing body with formal bureaucracies at the local, national, and international levels. In many ways they resemble governmental or, in some cases, even military-like, organizations. The modern trend, though, is toward decentralized and networked structures that are more adaptable and responsive to local conditions, needs, and opportunities.

In essence, international NGOs are following much the same evolutionary path in structure as the modern transnational corporation. In 1929, fewer than 2% of the largest 100 non-financial companies in the United States had moved from a centralized to a decentralized multi-divisional structure; 50 years later, 84% had adopted it.[41] One NGO that has assumed a highly decentralized form is FoE, a federation with 61 groups and 5,000 local organizations. Important decisions at FoE are decided by vote, with country-level chapters casting one vote each. Taking this trend a step further, NGOs like Action Aid and Amnesty International are in almost constant reorganization in attempting to maximize their effectiveness in an ever-shifting socioeconomic-political landscape. Amnesty's formal organization consists of over 1 million members and donors, 7,500 local groups, 56 country sections, and an international secretariat with a staff of over 300. Still, it found this decentralized structure insufficient for quickly responding to prisoner abuse cases and other issues popping up around the world. To fill that need, it created Urgent Action, a network of 80,000 volunteers in some 85 countries.

The NGO as a Business

The trend toward greater decentralization is only one way NGOs are mimicking business. There are other parallels as well. This should be no surprise since both groups are encountering some of the same pressures and operating in many of the same environments. As they grow, both are challenged to develop boards and other governance structures that properly reflect the broadening diversity of their organizations. Both are facing ever-increasing competition from global rivals. In the case of NGOs, this competition is for money, staff, and publicity. To make ends meet, NGOs are competing in business markets in the sale of goods and services. More often than not, these forays into private enterprise turn out to be financially unfruitful.[42] But there are exceptions. Consider the extreme case of the American Association of Retired Persons (AARP). To fund its activities in 1996, it took in $3.8 billion for the sale of supplemental health insurance and had $13.7 billion in member investments in the association's nine mutual funds. "Social entrepreneurs" like Prof. Michael E. Porter, of Harvard Business School, are establishing NGOs that not only think like businesses, but help shape their strategies. Professor Porter's Initiative for a Competitive Inner City works to identify and promote sustainable business models that can be successful in low-income communities.

In another recent strategy that mimics business, NGOs like Habitat for Humanity, United Way of America, and the Public Broadcasting System have all hired the Interbrand consultancy to estimate the value of their "brands." They have done this primarily to show potential corporate partners how much influence their organizations have in the marketplace and the value of that influence on co-branding alliances. Habitat was able to take its 2002 brand valuation of $1.8 billion and parlay it into $39 million in donations—a rise of nearly 50% over funds collected the previous year. It also used the valuation to arrange multimillion-dollar co-sponsorships with Whirlpool and Lowe's.[43]

NGOs are not just acting like businesses; they are being treated like them as well. Financial supporters of nonprofit organizations are holding NGOs more accountable for showing measurable results, behaving more like venture capitalist than charitable donors. These and other stakeholders are demanding more transparency from NGOs about their activities and performance, a growing pressure corporations are also experiencing. These pressures have helped spawn a number of changes in the nonprofit sector. For one, it has given rise to a number of organizations and tools for measuring the value of philanthropy.[44] It has also prompted a few NGOs, including GRI, CERES, WWF, and Oxfam, to issue public reports on their sustainability performance.[45] In an attempt to show sustainable improvement, some nonprofits are shifting their emphasis away from charity—the traditional role of providing food, education, and healthcare to the masses, for example. Instead, they are exerting more ef-

forts to build infrastructure—helping communities develop their own institutions and processes, and individuals secure their own rights. Ten
Thousand Villages is one NGO trying to do that. It provides marketing
and product development assistance to those who produce craft products
in developing nations.

Political, Economic, and Social Trends Affecting NGOs

While changes in business have influenced NGOs, so have changes in
government. The cold war has ended and more nations are moving to
more capitalistic economies and democracy-leaning governance, as
much in hope of finding solutions as in appeasing the western institutions
providing financial aid. This has opened communication and increased
tolerance for debate and a broader engagement with society—the very
things NGOs are designed to deliver. With the European Union, the
United Nations, and strong free trade agreements on the scene, the development of international and interregional forms of government are
playing a more prominent role in the affairs of state, but at a level more
detached from the average citizen than ever before. This detachment
and the public sense of helplessness that often flows from it—recall the
Seattle protests—are the agar for spawning NGOs. As government institutions have become more multinational, the foundations of international law have firmed, giving NGOs added weapons for battle in this
arena. For example, think of the Aarhus Convention on Access to Information, Public Participation in Decision-Making, and Access to Justice
in Environmental Matters discussed in Chapter 10. In contrast with the
overall trend toward multinationalism, the United States—the last great
superpower—has in many respects grown more unilateral and isolated.
The absence of the United States at the international table on issues like
climate change has given more of the world stage to NGOs. That U.S.
behavior, coupled with the spread of economic globalism through
TNCs and institutions like the World Bank and WTO, have created a
growing need for global governance. NGOs have been most willing to
step in to fill this need. They have not been shy about taking on issues
like land mines and the international court of justice that have been
avoided by the United States and other governments for lack of political
will. Where standards and inspections have been called for to bring accountability to TNCs and their suppliers in developing countries,

NGOs have been quite willing to develop programs to address those needs, as well.

Modern economic and social trends have also helped shaped the climate for NGOs. While developing nations still pose a serious problem, millions of citizens in major world economies are enjoying increased individual prosperity, allowing attention to shift to the NGO agendas of environmental and social issues. Values continue to change in most industrialized countries, encouraged in part by privatization of government enterprises and other economic reforms. Modern societies are placing greater emphasis on individual responsibility and opportunity rather than reliance on the paternalism of government. The role of NGOs fits perfectly within those new values. Changes in population, resources, wealth-poverty gaps, and the spread of AIDS are also having their impact, making the need for social change more visible and dramatic. All of these factors are bringing a growing number of people to feel empowered and obligated to right the wrongs they see about them. Even religious institutions have picked up the torch, supporting the involvement of their flocks in a broad array of sustainability issues. According to the U.K.-based Alliance of Religions and Conservation, approximately 200,000 religious communities are now going beyond their traditional role of helping the poor to a broader one of also promoting environmental issues like climate change, sustainable resource use, deforestation, and biodiversity loss.[46] Certainly, this trend toward broad social self-empowerment has worked for the good, with, of course, one major exception: the rise of terrorist organizations.

Why Engage With NGOs

So why should corporations pay NGOs any mind? Why shouldn't companies simply ignore NGOs as they would any other noisy pest? The simple answer is this: NGOs have the ability to significantly help or hurt business. As President Theodore Roosevelt used to say, they have the "bully pulpit" before the public and consumers. They have more credibility than corporations, can help sway public opinion, and are constantly trying to do so. If companies—already distrusted by the public—are perceived as contributors to social ills, then much of the new enthusiasm for personal action will be directed to changing corporate behavior. In the search for the guilty, NGOs have considerable control of the spotlight.

Their endorsement of government action confers a perceived stamp of public support and legitimacy.

Indeed, governments, investors, and other stakeholders often hear a chorus of NGOs as the voice of the public. That is not to say governments are enamored of these activists. Quite the contrary, many authorities resent NGOs, seeing them as pretenders to the throne, usurpers of the power to act for the public, needlessly stirring up citizens and making their jobs harder. Still, most officials understand that NGOs are now key players in the ongoing process of democratic debate, players that are here to stay, and their views must be factored into decisionmaking.

Because of the impact NGOs have on public opinion and governments, they can have a profound effect on the regulatory burdens faced by an industry, and the resulting impacts on a company's cost, efficiency, and time to market. They can use their bully pulpits to influence a company's licenses to operate—both the formal operating permits issued by governments as well as the community's tacit acceptance of a company's presence. In a thousand different ways, NGOs can help or hinder a corporation's ability to create, market, and sell products and services.

What is more, the influence of NGOs is on the rise. Many have seen their force amplified by their power over information. This power has come from NGOs' access to scientific data on environmental, health, and social effects; from their ability to simplify and sometimes politicize the message for the public; and from their use of the Internet to broadcast information around the world in a flash. This ability to manage information, coupled with the inclination of many NGOs to serve as corporate and government watchdogs, can create unpleasant predicaments for companies that face off against them. Can a company survive by opposing a vigorous NGO attack? Sure, but typically not without suffering a damaged reputation and devoting significant resources for defense. The real problem is, while small NGOs come and go, the major ones are often tenacious and willing to wage campaigns over decades. What is more, a high-visibility fight with a corporation may only fuel more support for an NGO's efforts from a public that doesn't trust corporations in the first place.

Tips for Engaging NGOs

Given the potential effects NGOs can have on business and their propensity to focus on highly visible corporations, large companies would be wise to initiate some broad, proactive NGO engagement. Smaller organizations should consider NGO engagement, too, if projects or issues are likely to arise that may be controversial with the public or it is apparent that NGOs are targeting the business. The engagement should be undertaken with attention to the model principles, the stakeholder engagement process previously discussed, and the following suggestions:

- *Rub elbows.* To assess NGOs, you first should get to know them and have them know you. One way to do this is to participate with a group of them—especially with their leadership—in some regular forum outside the planned engagement. Subscribing to CERES and regularly attending their board meetings and conferences or becoming an Organizational Stakeholder of GRI are two ways to rub elbows with a wide range of NGOs. A number of AIDS programs and environmental initiatives also offer this opportunity. Participating in such a group enables you to personally meet the people in those NGOs who can provide insights on their own organizations and those of their peers. These insights and the relationships you may have formed with certain NGO members can make engagement planning easier and more effective.
- *Conduct an NGO impact assessment.* A large company may find it useful to go beyond the stakeholder assessment process outlined earlier and conduct an NGO impact assessment. This involves identifying the important NGOs that may be monitoring the company, the issues that concern them, and how supportive they are of the company, its policies, and performance. Background information of the type listed in Figure 11.5 can provide a more complete understanding of those organizations. The impact assessment can give you a list of NGOs to monitor. Such monitoring can help a company identify issues that are becoming ripe for engagement as well as pinpoint those NGOs to engage on those issues. It is better to be forewarned than suffer a surprise attack from some NGO campaign. Since the world of NGOs is rapidly changing, the NGO impact assessment should be repeated every few years.
- *Evaluate NGO fit.* In selecting an NGO for engagement, you should not only consider the stakeholder selection criteria previously discussed but also how well the NGO's profile fits the scope of the objective. Issues of global scope demand global

NGOs. An NGO with southern operations and perspectives should be preferred if the issue lies in that part of the world. Co-operative-action organizations would be favored unless they have low credibility with their more confrontational peers. A project-oriented NGO should be the choice if it's a joint project you intend; however, if you want collaboration on a particular issue, such as AIDS, then pick an NGO with that focus.

• *Decide between individual NGO versus panel.* Sometimes engagement with a single NGO is quite sufficient for meeting the objective. At other times, especially when broader perspectives and support are desired, it may make more sense to recruit a panel of NGOs or—as BT has done with their Stakeholder Advisory Panel—a collection of NGOs and other experts and leaders.

• *Consider the relationship with industry peer.* Aligning with some NGOs may put you at odds with other companies who oppose them, including some of your own key suppliers or customers. Be aware of this before you decide to engage, and proactively communicate with the other companies about your plans if you want to lessen the impact.

• *Play to the gallery.* Some companies find themselves arguing with NGOs in the public eye. More often than not, this doesn't help the company's image or cause. If an NGO attacks, before responding, think how your response will play to the public, your customers, and other important constituents who are watching from the gallery. These are the people you want to influence.

• *Assess NGO resources.* Most of NGOs operate on tight budgets and with people who are stretched thin. This makes it especially important for companies to assess the capability of NGOs to fulfill the commitments they make that arise from the engagement. As a general rule, don't expect an NGO to be able to manage a complex project within financial and time limits unless they have a proven record of doing so.

• *Manage company expectations.* As with any stakeholder engagement, company management must be prepared for the possibility that it may be impossible to reach agreement with some NGOs on certain topics. They also must realize that a successful engagement with an NGO on one matter doesn't mean the NGO will withhold criticism of the company on another. To deal effectively with NGOs, you need patience, understanding, and a cool head.

NGOs are a growing force. They have become legitimate players with government and industry in setting the course for society. Since they cannot be ignored, it is best for companies to understand them and acknowledge their role. This can be best accomplished through constructive engagement. Indeed, if done properly with the right forethought and appreciation of risks, engagement with NGOs—and with other important stakeholder groups, for that matter—can bring numerous benefits to a company, making it a stronger, more sustainable organization.

Follow-up Checklist for Action: Stakeholder Engagement; The Role of NGOs

☐ Review the merits of proactive stakeholder engagement with the core team and others, and brainstorm possible beneficial engagements for your organization.

☐ Prepare an awareness presentation on stakeholder engagement and its benefits, and share and discuss it with appropriate managers in the organization.

☐ Ensure that managers involved in engagement have the appropriate knowledge and skills; provide training as appropriate; retain outside experts if needed to fill gaps.

☐ Make it clear that a proactive approach to engagement is encouraged and reward those managers who follow that course; encourage upper management to adopt Model Principles of Stakeholder Engagement setting forth their expectations in this regard.

☐ Consider the techniques used by other companies for engaging various types of stakeholders and determine whether similar approaches might be worthwhile in your organization.

☐ When undertaking stakeholder engagement, follow the Principles of Stakeholder Engagement adopted by the organization as well as the Stakeholder Engagement Process shown in Figure 11.4 and described in this chapter.

☐ Ensure that the core team and the key managers of operations that may be affected by NGO action are provided background information on NGOs similar to that presented in this chapter.

☐ Conduct an NGO impact assessment if appropriate, and monitor key NGOs. If issues become ripe for engagement with certain NGOs, engage them in accordance with the recommended stakeholder engagement process as well as the special tips for NGO engagements.

Endnotes to Chapter 11

1. This quote is from the poem by Robert Burns, "To a Louse on a Lady's Bonnet," stanzas 43-44.

2. JAMES C. COLLINS, GOOD TO GREAT: WHY SOME COMPANIES MAKE THE LEAP . . . AND OTHERS DON'T (HarperCollins Publishers Inc. 2001).

3. UNEC, Convention on Access to Information, Public Participation in Decision-Making, and Access to Justice in Environmental Matters, June 25, 1998 (Aarhus Convention).

4. *See* SARJ NAHAL, BSR ANALYSIS AND TREND REPORTING: MANDATORY CSR REPORTING: FRANCE'S BOLD PLAN (BSR 2002), *available at* http://www.bsr.org/BSRResources/magazine/CSRTrends.cfm?DocumentID=844.

5. WORLD BANK, EQUATOR PRINCIPLES, STATEMENT OF PRINCIPLES §5 (2003), *available at* http://www.equator-principles.com/index/html. *See also* Latham & Watkins, *Private Lenders Commit to Apply "Equator Principles" as Environmental and Social Benchmarks for Project Funding*, CLIENT ALERT, Aug. 5, 2006.

6. CENTER FOR CORPORATE CITIZENSHIP AT BOSTON COLLEGE & U.S. CHAMBER OF COMMERCE CENTER FOR CORPORATE CITIZENSHIP, THE STATE OF CORPORATE CITIZENSHIP IN THE U.S.: A VIEW FROM INSIDE 2003-2004 (2004), *available at* http://www.bcccc.net/_uploads/documents/live/state_cc_report.pdf.

7. E-mail from Art Gibson, Home Depot, to William Blackburn (June 3, 2005).

8. The Finer Points of Stakeholder Engagement, CROSSLANDS BULL. ON BUS., L. & ENV'T, Nov. 23, 2004, *available at* http://www.crosslandsbulletin.com/.

9. Lydia Polgreen, *Blood Flows With Oil in Poor Nigerian Villages*, N.Y. TIMES, Jan. 1, 2006, at A1, 6.

10. Main points in bold drawn from *A New Age of Participatory Decision Making?*, THE ENDS REP., May 2005, at 29-32, *available at* http://www.ends.co.uk.

11. STEPHEN R. COVEY, THE 7 HABITS OF HIGHLY EFFECTIVE PEOPLE (Simon & Shuster Inc., 1990 ed.).

12. *See* Fig. 5.3, §§4.4 & 9.

13. SUNCOR ENERGY, WHAT'S AT STAKE? OUR JOURNEY TOWARD SUSTAINABLE DEVELOPMENT: 2003 REPORT ON SUSTAINABILITY (2004). *See also* SUNCOR ENERGY, 2005 REPORT ON SUSTAINABILITY: OUR JOURNEY TOWARD SUSTAINABLE DEVELOPMENT—STEPPING FORWARD THROUGH INNOVATION AND TECHNOLOGY (2005), *available at* http://www.suncor.com/data/1/rec_docs/616_Suncor%20SD%20Report_2005%20.pdf.

14. Peter Sandman, *Accountability* (2002), http://www.psandman.com/col/account.htm.

15. Alison Maitland, *Vodafone Picks Up Calls on Big Issues*, FIN. TIMES, Oct. 20, 2003, *available at* http://news.ft.com/home/us.

16. *See, e.g.*, GRI, *Digital Solutions*, http://www.globalreporting.org/software/. *See also* SRI World Group, Inc., *One Report, the Sustainability Reporting Network*, http://www.one-report.com/.

17. *See* BERT HEEMSKERK ET AL. SUSTAINABLE DEVELOPMENT REPORTING—STRIKING THE BALANCE (WBCSD 2002), *available at* http://www.wbcsd.org/DocRoot/GGFpsq8dGngT5K56sAur/20030106_sdreport.pdf.

18. Peter Willetts, *What Is a Non-Governmental Organization?* (2002), *available at* http://www.staff.city.ac.uk/p.willetts/CS-NTWKS/NGO-ART. HTM.

19. For a discussion of various definitions of NGO developed by parties other than the United Nations, see Brijesh Nalinakumari & Richard MacLean, *NGOs: A Primer on the Evolution of the Organizations That Are Setting the Next Generation of "Regulations,"* ENVTL. QUALITY MANGEMENT, Summer 2005, at 1-21.

20. For a good overview of the history and types of NGOs, see *id.*

21. Melanie Beth Oliviero & Adele Simmons, *Chapter 4: Who's Minding the Store? Global Civil Society and Corporate Responsibility*, in GLOBAL CIVIL SOCIETY 2002 (Centre for the Study of Global Governance 2002), *available at* http://www.lse.ac.uk/Depts/global/yearbook02chapters.htm [hereinafter GLOBAL CIVIL SOCIETY].

22. *Id.*

23. Helmut Anheier & Nuno Themudo, *Organisational Forms of Global Civil Society: Implications of Going Global*, in GLOBAL CIVIL SOCIETY, *supra* note 21. JAMES A. PAUL, NGOS AND GLOBAL POLICYMAKING (2000), *available at* http://www.globalpolicy.org/ngos/analysis/anal00.htm [hereinafter NGOS AND GLOBAL POLICYMAKING].

24. United Nations, *NGOs in Consultative Status With ECOSOC*, July 25, 2005, *available at* http://www.un.org/esa/coordination/ngo/pdf/INF_List. pdf. PETER WILLETTS, THE GROWTH IN THE NUMBER OF NGOS IN CONSULTATIVE STATUS WITH THE ECONOMIC AND SOCIAL COUNCIL OF THE UNITED NATIONS (2002), *available at* http://www.staff.city.ac.uk/p.willetts/NGOS/NGO-GRPH.HTM.

25. David Borenstein, *A Force in the World, Citizens Flex Social Muscle*, N.Y. TIMES, July 10, 1999, *available at* http://www.globalpolicy.org/ngos/issues/bornstei.htm.

26. Brad Knickerbocker, *Nongovernmental Organizations Are Fighting and Winning Social, Political Battles* (see *Christian Science Monitor*

website/Nando Media) (Global Policy Forum, Feb. 6, 2000), http://www.
globalpolicy.org/ngos/00role.htm (last visited Jan. 6, 2006) [hereinafter
NGOs Winning Battles].

27. Michael Yaziji, *Turning Gadflies Into Allies*, HARV. BUS. REV., Feb.
2004, *Harvard Business Review OnPoint*, Reprint No. R0402J, *available
at* http://www.hbr.org.

28. 5 Union of Int'l Ass'ns, *Statistics, Vizualizations, and Patterns, in* YEAR-
BOOK OF INTERNATIONAL ORGANIZATIONS (2002), *available at* http://
www.uia.org/, *cited in* ORGANIZATIONAL FORMS OF CSOs 194 (2002).

29. *See* ORGANIZATIONAL FORMS OF CSOs, *supra* note 28. *See* NGOs
Winning Battles, *supra* note 26.

30. *See* NGOs AND GLOBAL POLICYMAKING, *supra* note 23.

31. John Entine, *Capitalism's Trojan Horse: How the "Social Investment"
Movement Undermines Stakeholder Relations and Emboldens the
Anti-Free Market Activities of NGOs* (American Enterprise Institute for
Public Policy, 2003).

32. *See, e.g., The Power of 10: NGOs Worth Befriending*, THE GREEN BUS.
LETTER, June 2001, *available at* http://www.greenbizletter.com/gbl0601-
2.pdf.

33. *See* DATA's website at http://www.data.org/ (last visited Jan. 7, 2006).

34. Marc Gunther, *The Mosquito in the Tent: A Pesky Environmental Group
Called the Rainforest Action Network Is Getting Under the Skin of Corporate America*, FORTUNE, May 31, 2004, at 158.

35. *See* Alexander Markels, *Protesters Carry the Fight to Executives' Homes*,
N.Y. TIMES, Dec. 7, 2003, §3, at 4.

36. Michael Janofsky, *11 Indicted in Cases of Environmental Sabotage*, N.Y.
TIMES, Jan. 21, 2006, at A1, A9. *See also* Donald McNeil Jr., *At Last, a
Company Takes PETA Seriously*, N.Y. TIMES, July 25, 2005, at WK 3.

37. *See* Jonathan Cohen, *State of the Union: NGO-Business Partnership
Stakeholders, in* UNFOLDING STAKEHOLDER THINKING 112-16 (Green-
leaf Publishing 2003).

38. FoE, FAILING THE CHALLENGE—THE OTHER SHELL REPORT 2002
(2003), *available at* http://www.foe.co.uk/campaigns/corporates/case_
studies/shell/index.html.

39. Ann Pettifor, *Case Study: Campaigning for Macro-Policy Change: Jubilee 2000, in* JUSTICE, MERCY, AND HUMILITY (Tim Chester ed., Paternos-
ter 2002), *available at* http://micahchallenge.org/advocacy_resources/
documents/86.doc.

40. Hector Tobar, *Chilean Firms Accept Logging Restrictions*, CHI. TRIB.,
Nov. 13, 2003, §1, 3.

41. ORGANIZATIONAL FORMS OF CSOs, *supra* note 28.

42. *See* William Foster & Jeffrey Bradach, *Should Nonprofits Seek Profits?*, HARV. BUS. REV., Feb. 2005, at 92-100.

43. John Quelch et al., *Mining Gold in Not-for-Profit Brands*, HARV. REV. BUS., Apr. 2004, *Harvard Business Review OnPoint*, Reprint No. F0404D, *available at* http://www.hbr.org.

44. *See, e.g.*, GLOBAL LEADERS OF TOMORROW BENCHMARKING PHILAN-THROPY TASK FORCE, WORLD ECONOMIC FORUM, PHILANTHROPY MEA-SURES UP (2003), *available at* http://www.vppartners.org/learning/resources/ GLT_Report.pdf.

45. See a discussion of some NGO reports in Appendix 8.

46. WORLDWATCH INSTITUTE, VITAL SIGNS 2001 (W.W. Norton & Co., Inc. 2001), *available at* http://www.worldwatch.org/pubs/vs/.

Chapter 12

Approach to Sustainability for Small and Struggling Companies

"One kernel is felt in a hogshead; one drop of water helps to swell the ocean; a spark of fire helps to give light to the world. None are too small, too feeble, too poor to be of service. Think of this and act."[1]
—Hannah More

If you are from a large successful corporation, you may have gleaned ideas from the last 11 chapters that can help your company along the way to sustainability. But what if your firm is a small one, or one that is struggling financially? Will these ideas help you? The short answer is "yes." But your organization must modify the previously discussed strategies, tools, and approaches to make them suitable to its own circumstances and characteristics. Let us explore what adaptations may make sense for small and financially disadvantaged companies.

Approach for Small Companies

Why Small Companies Should Pursue Sustainability

Small companies have a critical role in moving our society toward sustainability. These companies, along with those of medium size, account for over 90% of businesses worldwide and are responsible for 50 to 60% of employment.[2] They tend to have more labor-intensive production than their large counterparts, which eases the transition of agricultural-based economies to more industrial ones and helps create a more equitable distribution of wealth. They serve as an incubator for entrepreneurship and innovation. Moreover, they strengthen the economic resilience of their communities. Because they can provide essential support services and products for TNCs, they make their countries more attractive to foreign investors.

The link between TNCs and their small-company suppliers is just one reason a limited but growing number of these suppliers are pursing a sustainability agenda. Large companies can no longer afford adverse publicity about child labor, poor working conditions, or environmental tragedies at contracted facilities. More and more of these companies are insisting that their suppliers demonstrate social and environmental responsibility. They insist on this not just as a matter of social conscious, but as a way to control risk to their own reputations and help ensure long-term, uninterrupted supply.

But many small companies are not linked to TNCs. Often they depend heavily on local customers, suppliers, governments, and employees for their success. Why should sustainability be of interest to locally oriented firms? The fact is, successful small companies typically focus their sustainability efforts locally. These efforts not only help cultivate and maintain essential local support, but strengthen the stability, prosperity, and health of the community to which such businesses are umbilically tied. Indeed, to the enlightened small business, sustainability offers many of the same benefits as discussed in Chapter 3, and perhaps more. Consider, for example, the words of Shane Beard, owner of Fastsigns of Naperville, Illinois, a seven-employee company that produces signs and graphics on short notice:

> When I started my Fastsigns® franchise in 1996, I didn't have a lot of money for advertising. Since most of our business comes from other organizations, I thought I should join the local Chamber of Commerce to get to know some of them. That helped. Then one day a Cub Scout leader came in looking for a sign for the troop's popcorn stand. After I gave them a big discount, the word got around. Pretty soon, people from other community organizations were showing up at my door. But these people have other jobs. So it wasn't long before they and their friends began to order signs for their businesses, too.
>
> Eventually I came to realize that community involvement was not only personally satisfying and helping improve our town, but was actually critical for my business. Now when someone needs help with a parade, pancake breakfast, or charity drive, we are there. We also sit on various community boards and committees. This has put a face on our company.
>
> Consequently, our advertising costs have gone down while our business has gone up. Currently 60% of our revenues come from referrals. And our referral customers tend to be our better customers—they buy more and keep coming back. They come back not because our prices are lowest—they aren't—but because we consistently deliver good quality signs on time—and because of our community service. That's what our customers value. And that's been our formula for success.[3]

Organizing for Sustainability

While a sustainability initiative can present special benefits to small enterprises, it also poses special challenges. Given their limited resources, small companies cannot devote much time or money to sustainability programs that offer little tangible payback. This places a premium on tapping existing resources, streamlining activities, and focusing on top strategic priorities.

The critical step to moving forward is to persuade the company leader to visibly support the sustainability initiative even though her time is in short supply. At small companies, ownership, management, and important decisionmaking are typically concentrated in a single person—the manager. So without the manager's involvement, a sustainability program cannot succeed. That involvement can be by the manager herself leading and coordinating the sustainability program, or by her working with someone else assigned to coordinate it.

In a large company, the sustainability leader would be supported by the core team and deployment team. But in a small company, usually one team will have to suffice. It may consist of only two or three people, representing groups such as finance, operations, sales and marketing, and human resources. A simple approach is to name the company's business planning team as the overall sustainability team, designating one individual to facilitate sustainability activities and reporting.

Creating a Policy, Inventory, and Plan

A small company can start on the path to sustainability with a discussion on the meaning and value of sustainability. A company sustainability policy can then be drawn from Figure 2.2, melding in the company's own values. Next, it may be useful to inventory the sustainability initiatives that the company is already supporting that help fulfill the policy. Many small companies have them. In a 2001 survey of 7,000 small and medium enterprises (SMEs) in Europe—those with fewer than 250 employees—half of the respondents reported being engaged in some socially responsible activity.[4] Most of these activities involved sponsorships or donations for sporting, cultural, health and welfare, or educational programs. As was the case with Beard's Fastsigns® business, most were undertaken for ethical or community-relations reasons.

Using the new policy and current socially responsible activities as the foundation, small companies can set new priorities for measurement, goals, and actions. They can emerge from planning discussions where stakeholder feedback, sustainability trends, and business needs are reviewed. New initiatives coming from this process should be closely tied to business strategy. Small companies will not have much time to devote to those that are not. A simplified version of the model SOS process diagramed in Figure 5.7 can serve as the framework for the plan-do-check-act planning and improvement process. Parts of the process, such as aligning plans for functions and business units, are unnecessary for small organizations; instead, alignment is required only between the company's overall business/sustainability plan and the personal performance objectives of key personnel.

Stakeholder Engagement

Unless there are serious issues with other groups, the small company should consider its employees and customers as the key stakeholders from whom to seek feedback. This feedback can be obtained live during meetings or discussions that have been scheduled for other purposes. More extended dialogue with small focus groups of eight or fewer people may also be helpful. In later years, after top employee and customer concerns have been addressed, feedback can be obtained from suppliers, community representatives, and other constituencies.

To stimulate dialogue, the company can ask its stakeholders about the three most important things the company does for the stakeholder, and that the stakeholder does for the company. It can then inquire as to how well each is delivering those things to the other. The stakeholders can also be requested to do a short SWOT analysis on the company. The SWOT should take into account any current or likely future sustainability issues that may arise. Finally, stakeholders can be questioned about the kind of sustainability information they would like the company to report.

Sustainability Reporting

Sustainability reporting by small companies should rely on simple methods. The tips on controlling reporting cost and effort discussed in Chapter 10 can help, and the GRI reporting handbook for small- and medium-sized enterprises may also provide some ideas.[5] Off-the-shelf computer spreadsheets found on most personal computers may be sufficient for collecting and compiling data. Results can be posted on the Internet and perhaps worked into a brochure or other short printout for people desiring hard copies. The following sustainability reports by small companies are also useful references:

Seaview Hotel, Isle of Wight, United Kingdom.[6] Seaview is a 16-room, 40-employee British hotel that has sought to become a model of social responsibility. This strategy has worked well in shaping the hotel's image as a site of operational, social, and environmental excellence, an image reinforced by the hotel's location in a picturesque sailing village. The environmental dimensions of its four-page report touch on the hotel's use of locally grown organic produce and its extensive recycling and reuse programs, which even include the donation of used curtains and linens. According to the report, heat, light, water, and energy are monitored. Low-voltage bulbs and high-efficiency laundry equipment are used. The social dimensions of the document address the hotel's apprenticeship program for underprivileged youth and other initiatives to help children. The economic section describes its participatory structure of management—especially with respect to financial decisions—and discusses its support for local suppliers. Various employee training and development programs are also cited. In addition, the report quotes positive feedback from restaurant critics.

Westfield Health Scheme.[7] The U.K.-based Westfield is a 100-employee nonprofit provider of health savings plans. Its 14-page sustainability report discusses its values and social and environmental programs. The document covers considerable information on employees, including development programs; health and safety programs; absence and accident rates; survey results; days of training; labor turnover; and employee numbers by age group, length of service, and gender. The text on customers addresses their growth, surveys results, complaints, and retention, and describes the company's programs to accommodate visually impaired customers. Charitable donations and employee-volunteer programs are part of the community-oriented content. Environmental topics include water, energy, paper use, waste quantities, and driver miles and training. Finally, the report looks ahead with a brief mention of next steps.

Beacon Press, United Kingdom.[8] This single-factory U.K. printing company founded in 1976 is noted for its progressive environmental programs, which produce approximately $70,000 in annual savings. Its two-page report discusses the company's 16 environmental indicators, its alcohol- and water-free printing system, and its solvent recycling program. The document also covers the company's carbon-neutral program, which involves tree planting to offset CO_2 emissions. In addition, it mentions the use of paper from forests certified by the FSC.

First Environment.[9] First Environment's 28-page sustainability report contains considerable detail about its U.S. environmental engineering services, vision, strategies, history, staff, and policies. This content makes the publication somewhat longer than you would expect for a 50-employee firm, but it gives the document extra value for business promotion purposes. The report describes in detail the firm's ISO-based integrated management system. It examines its performance on energy consumption and greenhouse gases associated with its offices and travel. The document also covers the company's use of office supplies and its management of wastes and water. Social performance is addressed through sections on wages and benefits, employee health and safety, training and career development, and workplace diversity.

Urgent Couriers.[10] Urgent Couriers is a privately owned, one-hour courier service serving the greater Auckland, New Zealand, area. It has approximately 100 contracted and hired workers. Its 30-page sustainability report for 2001 is quite extensive for a small company, especially given that the report was independently verified. The report begins with a review of the company's profile and sustainability vision, policy, and objectives. Internal social aspects of the document include survey results from hired and contracted workers and data on their turnover rates and training. Various charitable donations, sponsored community initiatives, and other outreach activities are listed as external aspects. Details about fuel usage and consequential carbon emissions are presented as the main internal environmental content. The external environmental aspects include tree plantings and other community environmental projects. Growth rates for revenues and profits are among the economic data presented. One strength of this report—something commonly missing in small-company reports—is that it candidly communicates the sustainability challenges for the coming year and identifies goals for addressing each one. Instead of preparing another extensive report, the company has continued to use this one as the foundation for pursuing its sustainability goals. For instance, to help limit greenhouse gas emissions, it converted courier vehicles to use liquefied petroleum gas. Other sustainability initiatives are discussed in the company's periodic newsletter. The firm continues to solicit stakeholder feedback through an Internet-based survey.

Tall Poppies.[11] Tall Poppies is a nine-employee training and consulting firm based in New Zealand. Its nine-page report for 2001-2002 addresses the firm's environmental, financial, and diversity performance. The environmental information is related to paper and energy usage and waste recycling. The document also presents the company's profile and sustainability values, and discusses its employee policies, supplier relationships, and professional/charitable associations. The report contains special sections entitled "Tension," which openly describe its sustainability challenges, and "Target," which list its sustainability goals.

Because of the expense, small companies generally cannot justify third-party audits of operations or verification of their reports unless required by law or an important customer or warranted because of some special risk. Endorsements of sustainability codes may be biting off more than a small organization can chew, especially if compliance is to be documented. Still, a review of the code summaries in Appendix 2 may provide some good ideas for the company when it is developing its own sustainability policy.

Other Guidance

A small- or medium-sized enterprise that wants to pursue a sustainability program may find the following two guidance documents helpful:

Enterprise3: Your Business and the Triple Bottom Line, Economic, Environmental, and Social Performance, by the New Zealand Ministry of Environment and the Sustainable Business Network.[12]

The SME Key: Unlocking Responsible Business, part of the European Business Campaign on Corporate Responsibility, an initiative of CSR Europe, the Copenhagen Centre, the International Business Leaders Forum, and various national corporate social responsibility organizations across Europe.[13]

Approach for Financially Struggling Companies

Companies large or small faced with economic troubles will find their CEOs determined—even desperate—to bring their operations back to prosperity. How will they do that? The typical reaction is to slash costs, close factories, lay off workers, and replace some of the management team. To improve profitability, business leaders may also delay payments to suppliers, get tough on collections, and reduce inventories. Some favorite acquisitions and research and development projects may be cancelled. More aggressive sales campaigns may be introduced. As CEOs grab for these common corrective strategies learned in business school, where is sustainability? If the CEO is like most in this situation, one part of sustainability—the economic sustainability of the organization—will become her obsession. But what about the other parts?

Under these circumstances, business leaders may have the knee-jerk reaction of cutting their sustainability programs, viewing them as a luxury they can no longer afford. Unfortunately, such an action may simply compound their problems. To be sure, some lower priority sustainability projects or programs may need to be dropped or postponed. But others may warrant extra attention. The question is, how can pursuing sustainability help put the company back on track? If cost cutting is needed, then waste reduction, safety improvements, and other actions to improve productivity should be accelerated. If sales and innovation are hurting, an injection of stakeholder feedback with information on sustainability trends may provide new insights for better, more attractive products and services. If the company is downsizing and facing a crisis in employee morale, sustainability initiatives to address employee transitions and job satisfaction may help.

Big companies in desperate financial condition may also want to consider adopting small-company strategies where needed. Jobs may have to be combined, and responsibilities deployed deeper into the organization. Of course, deployment should not be left until times of financial crisis. For all the reasons noted in Chapter 8, company sustainability leaders should deploy and integrate the SOS across their organizations. Then, when the economic crunch comes—as it usually will sometime in a company's history—critical knowledge, skills, and resources will already be diffused across the organization, minimizing the impact of any organizational change. While deployment can actually help the management and operation of the SOS, the common belt-tightening strategies of combining jobs and consolidating support functions at the corporate, regional, and business-unit levels may make this more difficult. These difficulties can arise if the organizational change spreads people too thin or diminishes ownership for the SOS among the units and regions that lose their own sustainability representatives. However, good deployment at the facility, work-unit, and employee levels can help keep the company on course and, to a considerable extent, offset this harm.

Large, financially pinched companies may find it necessary to adopt small-company strategies on sustainability reporting, too. Firms that have been issuing long, polished sustainability reports may want to reduce the frequency of publication and trim back and refocus their report much as Polaroid did (recall the discussion in Chapter 10).

However, one cautioned should be noted: when scrambling to respond to financial upheavals, care must be taken to not disassemble critical programs, goals, or measures that very likely will be reinstituted a few years hence. To do otherwise only whipsaws the organization and hurts morale and efficiency. While organizations in financial straits must take the actions needed to survive and prosper, they must do so prudently, in a way that doesn't convey they have abandoned important values. Indeed, it is during the tough times that a company's true values are revealed.

The biggest challenge for sustainability advocates during discouraging times is to maintain a positive outlook. Remember, even the great George Washington had to execute a strategic retreat to win his war. Times will change and, if one is watchful, new opportunities to advance the sustainability agenda will reappear.

Follow-up Checklist for Action: Approach to Sustainability for Small and Struggling Companies

If your company is a small one:

☐ Share with the company's owner/manager the potential benefits of pursuing sustainability through a simplified SOS. See Chapter 4 for ideas on how to do this.

☐ After securing support from the company owner/manager, form a small sustainability team, designating one team member to coordinate sustainability activities and reporting.

☐ With the help of the sustainability team, develop a sustainability policy drawing from Figure 2.2 and the company's own values.

☐ Take inventory of the company's current social and environmental initiatives, and—following the guidance of this chapter—plan and implement a simplified SOS.

☐ Take advantage of meetings, phone calls, and other communications to solicit input from various stakeholders—particularly employees and customers—on the company's sustainability performance and communications.

☐ Prepare and communicate a sustainability report for the company after studying the sustainability reports of small companies and the guidance in this chapter and Chapter 10. Continue to report every year or two.

If your company is a large one that is in financial difficulty:

☐ Evaluate the company's current sustainability initiatives and re-prioritize them, giving greater emphasis to those that are most appropriate for addressing company needs. This may include projects that produce cost savings, enhance efficiency, or improve employee morale. Adopt small-company strategies as needed concerning the design of the SOS, the supportive organization, and sustainability reporting.

☐ Keep a positive outlook; as financial conditions improve, be watchful for the earliest opportunities to make even further progress on sustainability.

Endnotes to Chapter 12

1. This quote is attributed to the English writer and philanthropist who lived from 1745 to 1833.

2. PETER RAYNARD & MAYA FORSTATER, CORPORATE SOCIAL RESPONSIBILITY: IMPLICATIONS FOR SMALL AND MEDIUM ENTERPRISES IN DEVELOPING COUNTRIES (Vienna, U.N. Industrial Development Organization 2002), *available at* http://www.unido.org/userfiles/BethkeK/csr.pdf.

3. Interview with Shane Beard, Fastsigns, by William R. Blackburn (Aug. 15, 2005).

4. KPMG SPECIAL SERVICES & EIM BUSINESS & POLICY RESEARCH IN THE NETHERLANDS (IN COOPERATION WITH EUROPEAN NETWORK FOR SME RESEARCH (ENSR) AND INTOMART), EUROPEAN SMEs AND SOCIAL AND ENVIRONMENTAL RESPONSIBILITY (Enterprise Director-General, European Commission, Observatory of European SMEs 2002/Nov. 4, 2002), *available at* http://europa.eu.int/comm/enterprise/enterprise_policy/analysis/doc/smes_observatory_2002_report4_en.pdf.

5. GRI, HIGH 5! COMMUNICATING YOUR BUSINESS SUCCESS THROUGH SUSTAINABILITY REPORTING (2004), *available at* http://www.global reporting.org/workgroup/sme/intro.asp.

6. SME Key (European Business Campaign on Corporate Responsibility, an initiative of CSR Europe, the Copenhagen Centre, the International Business Leaders Forum, and various national CSR organizations across Europe), http://www.smekey.org/reports/default.asp (last visited Sept. 18, 2006).

7. *Id.*

8. *Id.*

9. First Environment, *2003 CERES Report, at* http://www.firstenvironment. com/html/first_environment_literature.html (last visited Jan. 7, 2006).

10. Urgent Couriers, *Sustainable Development Report for Urgent Couriers Limited, Period 1st April 2000 to March 31st 2001*, http://www.urgent. co.nz/General/UrgentCouriersSDR.pdf (last visited Jan. 7, 2006).

11. TALL POPPIES, SEE INSIDE TALL POPPIES — OUR VISION FOR A SUSTAINABLE FUTURE (2003), *available at* http://www.tallpoppies.co.nz/tblreport. html.

12. SUSTAINABLE BUSINESS NETWORK & MINISTRY FOR THE ENVIRONMENT, ENTERPRISE3: YOUR BUSINESS AND THE TRIPLE BOTTOM LINE, ECONOMIC, ENVIRONMENTAL, AND SOCIAL PERFORMANCE (2003), *available at* http://www.mfe.govt.nz/publications/sus-dev/enterprise3-triple-bottom-line-guide-jun03.pdf.

13. Guidance and information about engaging businesses in social responsi-
    bility can be found on the Internet at http://www.smekey.org/english_
    lan/default.aspx (last visited Sept. 19, 2006).

Chapter 13

Approach to Sustainability for NGOs

"Example is not the main thing in influencing others. It is the only thing."[1]
—Albert Schweitzer

NGOs, often big advocates of corporate sustainability programs, frequently struggle to develop their own. Or at least most of them seem to have trouble implementing the facility or operations side of their programs—one common to any office-oriented business. They have the same difficulties that small companies face: limited resources and a general belief that their office operations have minimal social and environmental impact. Corporations, not NGOs, are the biggest challenge to sustainability—or so the thinking goes. But from a company perspective, this appears to be a case of NGOs not walking their talk, not setting an example that can motivate, not joining the struggle to find practical approaches to sustainability that even the small players can pursue. From this perspective, the failure of NGOs to address the sustainability of their own operations is a lost opportunity to contribute to the overall sustainability movement in a meaningful way.

Most social and environmental NGOs view the service side of their business—the advocacy, dialogue, policymaking, lobbying, reporting, and other functions they provide—as having the largest effect on sustainability. At least they hope so. Certainly that is their reason for being—their mission and vision. Typically their role is designed to build in others—in companies, governments, and other institutions—the capacity and motivation to further some aspect of sustainability. But even from the services side, NGOs may miss opportunities to drive their efforts as effectively and sustainably as can be achieved with the aid of certain SOS elements.

So how can an NGO move more aggressively toward sustainability in their operations and services? The sustainability reports of three NGOs—the Boston-based CERES, GRI from the Netherlands, and the Canadian-based IISD—provide some insights.

Sustainability Aspects of NGO Operations

CERES' sustainability reports for 2001 and 2002-2003, GRI's report for 2003-2004, and IISD's sustainable development reports for 2003-2004 and 2004-2005 provide a good account of the types of sustainability issues faced by an NGO trying to pursue sustainability in its operations. As Figure 13.1 shows, NGOs deal with the same types of sustainability issues in their operations as would a small commercial business. Indeed, many of the lessons spelled out in Chapter 12 for small companies may be useful for NGOs as well. And like small business, NGOs find that most of their operational issues have relatively small impact or are under the primary control of the building owner or others. Nevertheless, NGOs like CERES, GRI, and IISD feel compelled to address these issues in their reports not only because they believe in sustainability, but also because they want to set a good example for business and others. So it is not surprising to see these three NGOs err on the side of inclusion in deciding which operational issues to cover.

	NGO		
Figure 13.1 **Operational Sustainability Issues Addressed in the Sustainability Reports of Three NGOs** X= Performance/program covered in report XX= Issue identified in report for future measurement or program development NA= Information not available from building manager			
Issue	**CERES**[2]	**GRI**[3]	**IISD**[4]
1. Structure			
1.1 General organization, governance	X	X	X
1.2 Envtl./safety teams	X	XX	X
1.3 Key org. changes	X	X	
2. Energy usage			
2.1 Electricity usage	X	NA	X
2.2 National gas usage			X
2.3 Business trip & commuting mileage	X	X	X
3. CO_2 impacts			
3.1 CO_2 impact of energy usage/travel	X	X	X
3.2 CO_2 offsets for impacts	X	XX	X
4. Waste			
4.1 Garbage disposed	NA	X	
4.2 Waste paper recycled	X	X	X
4.3 Printer cartridges recycled		X	X
4.4 Bottles/cans recycled	X, XX		
4.5 Old computer donations	X		X
5. Employee safety			
5.1 Fire safety/drills	X	XX	
5.2 Safety information at meetings; travel safety		XX	
6. Material usage			
6.1 Paper	XX	X	X
6.2 Recycled paper	XX	X	
6.3 Water	NA	NA	X

	NGO		
Figure 13.1—Continued **Operational Sustainability Issues Addressed in the Sustainability Reports of** **Three NGOs** X= Performance/program covered in report XX= Issue identified in report for future measurement or program development NA= Information not available from building manager			
Issue	**CERES**[2]	**GRI**[3]	**IISD**[4]
7. Sustainability criteria in purchasing			
7.1 Furniture (envtl. & ergonomic design)	X	X	
7.2 Computers (energy)	X	X	
7.3 Hotels	X		
7.4 Catering/food	XX		
7.5 Printing (unionized & envtl. paper)	X	X	
7.6 Banking	X		
7.7 Telephone service	X		
7.8 Carpeting	X		
7.9 Coffee	X	X	
7.10 Recycled paper	X	X	
8. Employment practices			
8.1 Headcount	X	X	X
8.2 Employee turnover			X
8.3 Diversity (age, gender, nationality)	X, XX	X	X
8.4 Benefits	X	X	
8.5 Employee development	X		X
8.6 Internships	X	X	
8.7 Training	XX	X	X
8.8 Fair compensation	X		
8.9 Ombudsman		XX	
8.10 Nondiscrim./human rights policy		XX	X
8.11 Office air quality	XX		

Figure 13.1—Continued **Operational Sustainability Issues Addressed in the Sustainability Reports of** **Three NGOs** X= Performance/program covered in report XX= Issue identified in report for future measurement or program development NA= Information not available from building manager			

Issue	NGO		
	CERES[2]	GRI[3]	IISD[4]
8.12 Workload	X		
8.13 Community volunteer efforts	XX		
8.14 Privacy policy		X	
9. Finance			
9.1 Budget, expenses	X	X	X
9.2 Funding by source	X	X	X
10. Office space	X		
11. Report externally reviewed		X	

Sustainability Aspects of NGO Services

The services of an NGO are the means by which it fulfills its main objective, purpose, or mission and moves toward its vision for the future. As we saw in Chapter 11, an NGO may have any of a variety of environmental or social missions, typically tied to some aspect of sustainability. The range of services offered by NGOs also varies. Two NGOs with the same mission—for example, the preservation of endangered species—may offer different services to help achieve it. One may focus on research; another on preserving key habitats; still another may serve as a watchdog of forestry-company practices. All provide services to their key stakeholders—generally, their members, supporters, and the public.

Consider, for example, the three NGOs we just reviewed. In addition to their sustainability reports covering operational issues, CERES and IISD also produce reports that examine their services.[5] GRI's sustainability report covers both operations and services.[6] These reports provide a peek at how different NGOs design their services to fulfill their stated mission.

CERES' Services

CERES' 2003 and 2004 annual reports describe the organization's emphasis on "sustainable governance," which is defined as "making decisions based on all (sustainability) trends, facing all the risks, and working to preserve and grow (ecological and human) assets."[7] Most of the report text addresses CERES' sustainable governance activities in spurring corporate action on climate change. These activities entail investor meetings and conferences, and climate-risk research and reports. They also include special corporate reporting initiatives, shareholder resolutions, and dialogue with companies and industry groups. CERES' reports discuss the results of its services, that is, the corporate commitments made in response to its actions. In addition to its climate-change activities, CERES also supports GRI's initiative on public sustainability reporting and has developed a complementary approach to facility-level reporting. It continues to work with the Association of Chartered Certified Accountants in administering an annual awards program recognizing companies that produce outstanding sustainability and environmental reports. Eighty-two percent of CERES' funding was devoted to all these program services.[8]

GRI's Services

The main purpose of GRI is to encourage companies to report their sustainability performance using guidance GRI develops through a global multi-stakeholder process. In its own report, GRI describes the various activities it provides to further this purpose. One of those activities is the extensive global stakeholder engagement the organization uses to identify the reporting needs of those organizations that report, as well as those that use the reported information. GRI relies on the feedback from that engagement to improve its general reporting guidelines and to develop more specialized supplements for particular industry sectors and sustainability topics. The organization also works with the investor community and CSOs to increase the demand for reported information. GRI is exploring how it might provide new auxiliary fee-based training and other services directly to clients or indirectly through third parties—services that could increase the use of GRI's guidelines while helping make the organization more financially secure over the long term.

IISD's Service

IISD's 2003-2004 and 2004-2005 publications describe the vast array of its services related primarily to shaping governmental policy and practices on sustainable development. These services touch on trade and investment, reporting, climate change, and energy. They also cover knowledge communication, measurement and indicators, natural resource management, and economic policy. IISD addresses these topics through research, issue briefings, and advice. It also organizes and facilitates workshops and other meetings. In addition, its members participate with others in task forces aimed at developing sustainability-related policies, standards, and other tools. Some of its commendable accomplishments were: playing a key role in the development of the Millennium Ecosystem Assessment; drafting a model agreement for foreign investment for sustainable development; and developing a greenhouse gas emissions trading system for Canada. IISD intends to focus on four important areas through 2010: (1) the integration of sustainable development into institutional decisionmaking; (2) responsible ecosystem management; (3) transforming institutions through transparency, participation, and accountability; and (4) engaging new generations in sustainable development.[9]

Recommended Approach

So how should an NGO go about infusing sustainability into its own operations and services? What steps should it follow? One approach for operations is simply to mimic what a small company might do. This could start with a discussion on the meaning and value of sustainability as it applies to offices, followed by the development of an appropriately tailored sustainability policy drawing from the model policy presented in Figure 2.2.

From a services perspective, an NGO might start by considering how its mission and vision link with sustainability. It could consider endorsing the *Caux Round Table Principles for NGOs* or amending its own sustainability principles to incorporate provisions related to its services.[10] For example, these provisions might address transparency, integrity, governance, accountability, independence, and a caring philosophy. A few key metrics and goals could also be developed for both operations and services. A plan-do-check-act process of continual improvement with transparent public reporting can drive both aspects of the organization forward. To strengthen operations, feedback should be sought from employees and key suppliers. To improve services, a broader net should be cast, engaging employees, members, endorsers, funders, collaborative partners, governments, and those whose operations the NGO is trying to influence. Once collected, this feedback should be used in strategic and tactical planning. By following these steps and establishing other elements of a rudimentary SOS process, NGOs should see improved efficiency and effectiveness in both its operations and services, and enjoy a greater positive impact on the outside world.

Follow-up Checklist for Action: Approach to Sustainability for NGOs

☐ Share with the NGO leadership the potential benefits of pursuing sustainability through a simplified SOS. See Chapter 4 for ideas on how to accomplish this communication.

☐ After securing support from leadership, form a small sustainability team, designating one team member to coordinate sustainability activities and reporting.

☐ Identify the key sustainability aspects of the NGO's operations, considering Figure 13.1 and the guidance of Chapter 12, as appropriate.

☐ Adopt a sustainability policy related to those key operational aspects, drawing from the model policy in Figure 2.2 as appropriate.

☐ Consider adopting the *Caux Round Table Principles for NGOs* or a similar set of principles related to the NGO's services. Incorporate these principles in the NGO's sustainability policy for operations, if appropriate.

☐ Following the guidance of this chapter and Chapter 12, plan and implement a simplified SOS.

☐ Take advantage of meetings, phone calls, and other communications to solicit input from various stakeholders on the organization's sustainability performance and communications. Focus particularly on employees, members, supporters, and those the NGO is trying to influence. Consider this feedback in strategic and tactical planning.

☐ Prepare and communicate a sustainability report for the organization after considering the stakeholder feedback, the sustainability reports of other NGOs and small companies, the NGO's performance against its own sustainability policy, and the guidance provided in this chapter and Chapter 10. Continue to report every year or two.

Endnotes to Chapter 13

1. This quote is attributed to Albert Schweitzer, the eminent philosopher, humanitarian, theologian, musician, and medical missionary, who lived from 1875 to 1965.

2. CERES, CERES 2001 SUSTAINABILITY REPORT (2002) and CERES SUSTAINABILITY REPORT 2002-2003 (2005), *both available at* http://www.ceres.org/pub/.

3. GRI, "IT'S NOT ENOUGH TO JUST BE . . . ," GLOBAL REPORTING INITIATIVE'S FIRST SUSTAINABILITY REPORT, 1 July 2003-30 June 2004 (2005), *available at* http://www.globalreporting.org/GRISustainabilityReport/index.asp [hereinafter GRI SUSTAINABILITY REPORT 2003-2004].

4. IISD, SUSTAINABLE DEVELOPMENT REPORT 2003-2004: ASSESSING OUR ECONOMIC, SOCIAL, AND ENVIRONMENTAL PERFORMANCE (2004) and IISD, OPERATING SUSTAINABLY: FIFTEEN YEARS OF PROGRESS—SUSTAINABLE DEVELOPMENT REPORT 2004-2005 (2005), *both available at* http://www.iisd.org/about/sdreporting/.

5. CERES, 2003 ANNUAL REPORT (2004) and CERES, 2004 AND BEYOND (2005), *both available at* http://www.ceres.org/pub/ [hereinafter CERES, ANNUAL REPORTS 2003, 2004]. IISD, SUSTAINING EXCELLENCE: 2003/2004 ANNUAL REPORT (2005) and IISD, SUSTAINING EXCELLENCE FOR 15 YEARS: 2004/2005 ANNUAL REPORT (2005), *both available at* http://www.iisd.org/about/annual_report/ [hereinafter IISD ANNUAL REPORTS 2003-2004, 2004-2005].

6. *See* GRI SUSTAINABILITY REPORT 2003-2004, *supra* note 3.

7. *See* CERES ANNUAL REPORTS 2003, 2004, *supra* note 5, at 3.

8. *See id.*

9. *See* IISD ANNUAL REPORTS 2003-2004, 2004-2005, *supra* note 5.

10. CAUX ROUND TABLE, CAUX ROUND TABLE PRINCIPLES FOR NGOS (2003), *available at* http://www.cauxroundtable.org/PrinciplesforNGOs.html. See Appendix 2.1.6 for background on the Caux Round Table.

Chapter 14

Approach to Sustainability for Governmental Organizations

"You cannot escape the responsibility of tomorrow by evading it today."[1]
—Abraham Lincoln

The Impact of Government on Sustainability

Government operations have a huge impact on sustainability. The U.S. federal government possesses one-third of the nation's land and is the world's largest consumer of energy. Canada's national government is the country's biggest employer with 224,000 people on its payroll. It owns and operates 59,000 buildings and 25,000 cars and trucks. The U.K. government purchases over $15 billion of goods and services annually. Among all OECD countries, government expenditures average approximately 9% of their gross domestic products.[2]

But a government's influence on the economic, social, and environmental conditions of society goes well beyond that produced by its buildings, fleets, employment, and purchases. Like other organizations, governments also furnish products and services that can have an effect. Services and products related to sewerage, water, gas, electricity, streets, and solid waste may be provided directly through public agencies or through firms authorized by them. Influence also springs from services such as planning and development, grant funding, and the adoption and enforcement of a myriad of laws. And, of course, we can't forget tax collection. All of these services and products can make our climb toward sustainability much more difficult or much easier, depending upon the policies and practices our governments adopt. Certainly, corrupt and wasteful officials don't help the cause.

But what's in it for the government itself? Why is it in the best interests of public officials to pursue a sustainability agenda? The simple answer is, that is what their superiors—the public themselves—want in a community. They want to live in areas that are economically prosperous, socially sensitive, and environmentally responsible. They want to live where the quality of life is good—where the streets are safe, the schools are excellent, and the air is clean. And they want a place where the work is plentiful and people respect each other. That is the aim of sustainability. Moreover, the politicians who provide their constituents with a good quality of life—or at least are working hard to improve it—are likely to remain in office. Sustainability breeds sustainability.

The approach to sustainability for a public agency can mirror that of a company in many ways. This is especially true for public utilities. Utility companies, which sell their commodities and services to paying customers, are generally indistinguishable from regular corporations when it comes to sustainability issues and approaches.

On the other hand, other governmental bodies may have services and operations that bear little resemblance to those of companies. Planning and zoning commissions, the courts, and many other broad-based governmental bodies regulate and police the community and develop public policy. That's their service. Their operational issues are limited to those of a typical office. Public entities of this type may find they have more in common with NGOs than companies when it comes to sustainability strategies.

Local Agenda 21 Model Communities Program

Some authorities and collaborative groups concerned about sustainability have developed approaches tailored specifically to governments. One organization that has done this is the International Council of Local Environmental Initiatives (ICLEI). Founded in 1990 at U.N. headquarters, this association consists of more than 400 cities, towns, counties, and local government associations from around the globe. In the wake of the 1992 Earth Summit, ICLEI joined with the United Nations Development Program, the Netherlands Ministry of Foreign Affairs, and the International Development Research Centre to undertake Local Agenda 21 Model Communities Programme (LA 21 MCP).[3] This program was designed to aid local governments in implementing Agenda 21, the global action plan for sustainable development that emerged from the Earth Summit.[4] The output of MCP was a general planning framework for sustainable development for local governments, which has been tested and evaluated with various ICLEI members.[5] This framework was structured around the following seven guiding principles[6]:

1. *Partnerships.* Alliances among all stakeholders/partners are established for collective responsibility, decisionmaking, and planning.
Comment: Alliances are commonly formed through community stakeholder groups, with subcommittees and working groups addressing particular issues. Stakeholder groups may involve some of the following: women; youth; the poor; community organizations; businesses; and neighborhood associations. To be effective, these groups will need a clear understanding of their roles and the objectives of the process, as well as adequate funding and decisionmaking authority.

2. *Participation and transparency.* All major sectors of society are directly involved in sustainable development planning, and all information that relates to the LA 21 planning process is easily available.
Comment: The process must be open and accessible to all sectors of the community. Education programs for community groups and special training for government officials and staffs should be provided early in the process to help ensure effective engagement of these parties, which in turn can help secure their ownership of the resulting plan. Creativity and flexibility may be needed to engage those who are underrepresented. Open communication can often be effectively achieved through focus groups. Planning officials must be amenable to the recommendations of the stakeholder groups so that these groups will support the planning process and ultimate outcome.

3. *Systemic approach.* Solutions address underlying causes and whole systems.
Comment: The ultimate objective is to integrate sustainability concerns into the planning and decisionmaking processes of local governments, and to assure these processes have the input and involvement of a broad range of perspectives from diverse stakeholders. To do this, it may be helpful to link the LA 21 planning process with existing processes required by law. Cross-department working groups can also help.

4. *Concern for the future.* Sustainable development plans and actions address short- and long-term trends and needs.

Comment: By collecting community data and analyzing trends, planners can gain a glimpse of what may lie ahead. The planning group should study this information and then create a vision of what it would like its community to be in the long term. Plans can then be crafted to steer the community to that end.

5. *Accountability.* All stakeholders/partners are accountable for their actions.
Comment: Public engagement in defining priorities, developing plans, and monitoring progress can help ensure accountability. So can linking the LA 21 sustainability plan with the local government's formal strategic plan.

6. *Equity and justice.* Economic development must be equitable, environmentally sound, and socially just.
Comment: Special efforts should be made to engage the poor, women, youth, and other traditionally underrepresented groups in the identification and assessment of issues.

7. *Ecological limits.* All communities must learn to live within the earth's carrying capacity.
Comment: Some form of public education is needed on this point. The development of environmental indicators can help communicate progress, but should be accompanied by programs to teach the public about them. Management systems like ISO 14001 can help ensure continual improvement.

More than 2,000 communities are involved in the MCP, including places such as: Leeds, England; Hamilton, New Zealand; Hamilton, Ontario; Cape Town, South Africa; Mwanza, Tanzania; and Jinja, Uganda. To encourage additional communities to participate, the ICLEI created the *Local Agenda 21 Campaign.*[7] Governments that want to join the campaign must commit to completing five planning milestones:

1. *Multi-stakeholder group.* Establish a multi-stakeholder group to oversee and participate in the planning process.

2. *Audit.* With the participation of the stakeholder group, conduct an audit of sustainability conditions and trends in the community.

3. *Vision.* Create a sustainable community vision for the future based on the audit and assessment of priorities.

4. *Action plan.* Establish and implement an action plan which identifies clear goals, priorities, measurable targets, roles and responsibilities, funding sources, and work activities.

5. *Progress reports.* Monitor and annually evaluate and report progress under the action plan.

These milestone activities should look familiar. Indeed, many are essential parts of an SOS. For that reason, communities pursuing an MCP-like process should find that SOS tools can help them along the way.

Best SOS Practices Among Government Institutions

To obtain deeper insight to the application of sustainability to governmental entities, let us review how various public bodies have used the following SOS elements in their own sustainability programs: (1) the sustainability vision or policy; (2) team structure; (3) stakeholder engagement; (4) planning; (5) performance indicators; and (6) reporting. Then let us also see how they have integrated sustainability considerations into the elements of (7) community development and building design as well as (8) procurements.

Element 1: Sustainability Vision or Policy

The centerpiece of a public agency's sustainability plan should be its sustainability policy or guiding principles. Public authorities can look to Figure 2.2 for ideas about principles of sustainability that speak to *what* needs to be accomplished from an economic, environmental, and social perspective. They can also examine similar documents now being used by various governments. Figure 14.1 shows how the city of Hobart, Tasmania, in Australia, captured its vision of sustainability. The U.K. government's definition of *sustainable communities* (Figure 14.2) is another example of what sustainability may mean locally.

Figure 14.1
Sustainability Vision (Strategic Outcomes) of
Hobart, Tasmania, Australia, 2003-2004[8]

Hobart will be a city that—

1. Is a safe and convenient place for people, encouraging creativity and lifestyle opportunities.
2. Protects and conserves its environment and natural beauty.
3. Conserves and enhances its significant built and cultural heritage.
4. Encourages the sustainable growth and prosperity of the community.
5. As the state capital, commits itself to the development of the economic, tourism, cultural, and social life of Tasmania.
6. Prudently manages its affairs and the delivery of affordable quality services.

In addition to expressing *what* needs to be done along the path to sustainability, governmental bodies may also need implementing principles or guidelines which indicate *how* the organization will approach the matter. The first five points of the MCP planning framework discussed above are provisions of this type. Other examples can be found among the guiding principles adopted by Santa Monica, California, which are shown in Figure 14.3.

To guide its national agencies toward sustainability, the United Kingdom adopted both a vision or "goal" of what is to be achieved as well as a set of guiding principles. See Figure 14.4. The principles are a blend of the *what* and the *how*. One of the U.K. agencies—the Ministry of Defence—framed its approach around six areas:

1. *Environmentally sustainable development* (environmental appraisals and assessments) and *EMS*;
2. *Environmental protection* (biodiversity, climate change/energy, heritage, land remediation, waste, and water);
3. *Role as an employer* (diversity; health, safety and well-being; employee development; and work-life balance);
4. *Role in the community* (community involvement; volunteering); and
5. *Role in the economy* (equipment and construction procurement).[9]

Figure 14.2
U.K. Definition and Components of Sustainable Communities[10]

General definition: Sustainable communities embody the principles of sustainable development. They—

- Balance and integrate the social, economic, and environmental components of their community.
- Meet the needs of existing and future generations.
- Respect the needs of other communities in the wider region or internationally to make their communities sustainable.

Definitional components: Sustainable communities should be—

- Active, Inclusive, and Safe—fair, tolerant, and cohesive with a strong local culture and shared community activities.
- Well Run—with effective and inclusive participation, representation, and leadership.
- Environmentally Sensitive—providing places for people to live that are considerate of the environment.
- Well Designed and Built—featuring a quality built and natural environment.
- Well Connected—with good transport services and communication linking people to jobs, schools, health, and other services.
- Thriving—with a flourishing and diverse local economy.
- Well Served—with public, private, community, and voluntary services that are appropriate to people's needs and accessible to all.
- Fair for Everyone—including those in other communities, now and in the future.

Another U.K. public entity, the Royal Mail Group, designed its sustainability vision around a five-stage maturity matrix which describes the evolutionary levels of achievement to be reached in six categories: (1) integrated approach; (2) legislation and compliance; (3) measurement; (4) accountability; (5) research and innovation; and (6) sustainability. The group also has a 12-point policy—covering topics such as policy planning and objectives, risk assessment, change processes, procurement, and training—that details how operating units should work to achieve the vision.[11]

Instead of drafting their own sustainability policy, more than 2,000 local and regional governments from Europe and northern Africa have simply endorsed the *Charter of European Cities and Towns Towards Sustainability*. The *Aalborg Charter*, as it is commonly known, was drafted in Aalborg, Denmark, in 1994 at the First European Conference on Sustainable Cities and Towns. Public entities that sign the charter commit to pursue the sustainability aims of LA 21 through engagement and planning processes using a wide array of political and technical tools. The charter emphasizes that sustainable economies, social justice, and environmental sustainability are inextricably linked, that sustainability thinking must be integrated into all areas of local decisionmaking, and that cities and towns must work toward achieving sustainability in a balanced way. Special provisions cover social equity (healthcare, employment, and housing), land use and transportation planning, climate change, the investment in the natural environment, and prevention of toxic pollution. A section of the charter lists steps similar to those found in an SOS that endorsers should take in developing and implementing their LA 21 action plans. Signatories also commit to encourage and support other communities in the drive toward sustainability.[12]

Some public entities like the U.K. Royal Mail Group have adopted the U.N. Global Compact (see Appendix 2.1.1) to help guide their path toward sustainability.

Regardless of their source, a clear set of sustainability and implementing principles enables all sectors of a local or regional governmental body to align its plans and activities to a common result. With this alignment, the organization can most effectively and efficiently bring other SOS tools to bear in pursuing its vision.

Element 2: Team Structure

As we observed in Chapter 4, an organizational structure must be defined for pursuing sustainability. For governmental entities, many different structures will do. Some effective ones used by cities and national agencies are reviewed below.

City Structures

Many communities involved in the LA 21 MCP have relied on multi-department working groups to gather and assess stakeholder feedback and assist with sustainability planning. Often these groups are led by the community's planning and development department. The teams sometimes include external stakeholder representatives as well. Where they do not, stakeholder input has typically been collected through various stakeholder advisory groups. Leeds, England, took a slightly different approach, forming its own sustainable development unit, with six teams assigned to address each of the following duties: (1) conserving the historic parts of the city; (2) promoting good design; (3) promoting and managing the city's environmental programs and training; (4) landscape conservation and design; (5) planning and control of minerals extraction and waste management; and (6) overall management and support of the city's sustainable development unit and development of its sustainability policies and plans.[13] Jinja, Uganda's, sustainability planning team was divided into smaller groups to work with various sectors, such as business, NGOs, youth groups, and city departments. Johannesburg formed a stakeholder group with representatives from local and provincial government, business, labor, and the general community. The group functioned through an operating committee and five task teams. These teams focused on integrated planning and management, inner-city environment, social and economic regeneration, communication and information, and environmental management research, respectively.

Figure 14.3
Santa Monica, California's Guiding Principles on Sustainability[14]

1. The concept of sustainability guides city policy.
2. Protection, preservation, and restoration of the natural environment is a high priority for the city.
3. Environmental quality, economic health, and social security are mutually dependent.
4. All decisions have implications to the long-term sustainability of Santa Monica.
5. Community awareness, responsibility, participation, and education are key elements of a sustainable community.
6. Santa Monica recognizes its linkage with the regional, national, and global community.
7. Those sustainability issues most important to the community will be addressed first, and the most cost-effective programs and policies will be selected.
8. The city is committed to procurement decisions which minimize negative environmental and social impacts.
9. Cross-sector partnerships are necessary to achieve sustainable goals.

Structures Within National Agencies

The Royal Mail Group, the U.K. institution responsible for mail service, manages sustainability issues through corporate social responsibility groups and designated managers positioned at various levels of the organization. A CSR Governance Committee that reports to the management board oversees and sets policy on a groupwide basis. A Director of CSR manages health, safety, environmental, and social activities for the group; a Director of Diversity and Inclusion oversees diversity and disability matters. Each of these directors has a dedicated team of experts that helps develop policy. Designated executives who head CSR and Diversity and Inclusion within the group's organizational units are responsible for deploying sustainability policies and strategies. Organization-wide teams focus on charity, diversity, and disability issues. Another team guides compliance with U.K. financial and sustainability reporting laws. Dignity-and-Respect-at-Work Groups, made up of employee, management, and union representatives, address discrimination, harassment, and similar issues that affect the workplace environment.[15]

Figure 14.4
U.K. Vision and Guiding Principles on Sustainable Development
for Government Agencies[16]

Vision/goal: To enable all people throughout the world to satisfy their basic needs and enjoy a better quality life, without compromising the quality of life of future generations.

Guiding Principles: The following shared U.K. principles will be used by the government to achieve its sustainable development goal:

• Living Within Environmental Limits. Respecting the limits of the planet's environment, resources, and biodiversity—to improve our environment and ensure that the natural resources needed for life are unimpaired and remain so for future generations.

• Ensuring a Strong, Healthy, and Just Society. Meeting the diverse needs of all people in existing and future communities, promoting personal well-being, social cohesion and inclusion, and creating equal opportunity for all.

• Achieving a Sustainable Economy. Building a strong, stable, and sustainable economy which provides prosperity and opportunities for all, and in which environmental and social costs fall on those who impose them (polluter pays), and efficient resource use is incentivised.

• Promoting Good Governance. Actively promoting effective, participative systems of governance in all levels of society—engaging people's creativity, energy, and diversity.

• Using Sound Science Responsibly. Ensuring policy is developed and implemented on the basis of strong scientific evidence, while taking into account scientific uncertainty (through the precautionary principle) as well as public attitudes and values.

At the national level, a few progressive governments have designated leaders and departments responsible for furthering sustainability among government agencies, both in operations as well as policy-setting. The United Kingdom has a sustainable development unit within the Department for Environment, Food, and Rural Affairs (DEFRA) that serves this purpose. Sweden has a special Ministry of Sustainable Development. A number of countries, including the Belgium and United Kingdom, have established special councils or commissions of outside advisors who advise the government on sustainability strategies and programs.

Element 3: Stakeholder Engagement

Stakeholder engagement, a critical element of the MCP, may follow a strict process laid out under law. Public notice and hearings may be required for important governmental decisions, such as the adoption of new laws or the approval of budgets, plans, zoning variances, and certain construction and operating permits. Corporations may well be stakeholders in these engagements. However, enlightened public entities often go well beyond the statutory minimum in their engagements. A broader, more proactive approach to engagement is particularly important when the matter under consideration is a comprehensive sustainable development plan or other initiative that may have a significant impact on the economic, social, or environmental health of the community. Many find it helpful to use a variety of engagement techniques mentioned in Chapter 11. The Royal Mail Group uses surveys to help assess the views of its employees and the public. It also holds business-stakeholder workshops to encourage dialogue with a number of NGOs, and develops detailed stakeholder management plans. New Zealand's Watercare Services, the regional authority responsible for supplying water to the Auckland region, formed a special advisory group for the native Maori people so they could have a voice on major projects, including water reservoirs on ancestral lands. It also established an environmental advisory group and a variety of community liaison groups to provide input on projects and plans. The Greater Vancouver, British Columbia, Regional District (GVRD) in Canada conducted workshops to discuss governance issues with the indigenous "First Nations" groups as part of its sustainability planning. It also asked 11 issue groups to prepare reports on a wide range of topics, including agriculture and habitat, air quality and the management of greenhouse gases, energy, green buildings, and water. Other reports were prepared on economic strategy, governance and finance, growth management, housing, parks, and social issues.

Element 4: Planning

Many of lessons of Chapter 6 on infusing sustainability into strategic planning also apply to government planning. As noted earlier, public bodies, like business and NGOs, have operations as well as products and services that must be considered. Once the sustainability issues are identified and discussed through stakeholder engagement, they must be evaluated, and filtered through a prioritization process. Specific strategies, goals, performance indicators, programs, and actions must be fleshed out and aligned. The sustainability reports for 2003-2004 issued by the city of Hobart, Tasmania, and the U.K. Ministry of Defence contain good examples of how that alignment may be done.[17] The American Planning Association, a leading professional organization on community planning, has published a *Policy Guide on Planning for Sustainability* which offers useful suggestions, too.[18]

Element 5: Performance Indicators

Performance indicators, another SOS tool commonly used by corporations, can benefit governmental entities, too. Many of the GRI indicators and those identified in Appendix 7.1 are just as suitable for public bodies as they are for corporations. For governments, however, some additional factors beyond those noted in Chapter 7 may affect the selection of their yardsticks. For example, does the measure have some relevance to policy decisions? Is it likely to be of sufficient interest to the local media that they will publish and broadly publicize the results? Would the general public understand the measure? Does it link to some important community values? Does the indicator tie to local political, economic, and institutional priorities?

Appendix 7.2 provides examples of indicators used by some of the more progressive city and regional governments to monitor their advance toward sustainability. Of course, these governments are unusual. Most would find it too burdensome to track as many measures as shown there. Even Seattle has found it difficult to continue the comprehensive reporting it started in 1998. It is better that a public body select a few important measures they feel they can monitor and report every year or two rather than to take on too many and later give up the initiative in frustration.

Sustainability indicators that can be used on the national level have been developed by the European Commission, World Bank, United Nations, and the U.K. government.[19]

Element 6: Reporting

Over the last several years, governmental agencies have begun to report on their environmental and social performance and programs. Some agencies—especially those in Australia and New Zealand—have done this as an extension of the financial reports they must prepare by law. Others have published reports on the work voluntarily undertaken in sustainable development planning under LA 21. In a number of countries, reports have been prepared to show compliance with environmental or sustainability planning mandates.[20] For example, Transport Canada and other departments of the Canadian federal government were required to prepare sustainable development strategies and action plans by 1997 and update them every three years.

In the United Kingdom, local authorities are legally mandated to prepare community strategies showing how they intend to promote their area's economic, social, and environmental well-being and contribute to sustainable development of the country. All public agencies in Hong Kong and in the state of Victoria, Australia, must publish an environmental performance report annually. Some public agencies prepare sustainability reports not because they are required to, but for the same reasons that many companies voluntarily report: to drive improvement as part of a plan-do-check-act process and to enhance their reputation as a role model.

The growth in reporting among governmental bodies is one reason the GRI developed a *Sector Supplement for Public Agencies* to augment its basic sustainability reporting guidelines.[21] The supplement is intended for any tier of public agency, including ministries, federal agencies, regional governing bodies, state agencies, city councils, and departments for any geographical region. This would also include public utility companies, although several have produced nice reports using the regular GRI reporting guidelines without the supplement. That is not surprising given the close similarity in sustainability issues faced by public utilities and mainstream corporations.

Let us review a few examples of sustainability reporting in the public sector.

Watercare Services

Consider, for example, the 2002 report prepared by New Zealand's Watercare Services a local-authority trading enterprise owned by the city of Auckland and other surrounding communities for the purpose of supplying them water and treating wastewater. This 113-page document, though lengthy, rivals the best company GRI reports. It contains extensive information on the traditional areas of environmental risks and performance. It addresses corporate governance; legal compliance; and employee safety, health, training, and development. The report also discusses union relations; cultural sensitivity; and harassment prevention. It touches on customer and supplier relations, too. External relationships, including stakeholder engagement and community programs, are included, as well. The economic section presents complete financial accounts for the organization. In addition, the report contains information on important projects and a status update on the agency's long list of sustainability goals. The performance information was verified by an outside auditing firm, with special commentary by the Maori and environmental advisory groups.[22]

In 2003, the company began integrating its sustainability information into its annual report. Besides covering financial, asset management, and risk management information, the authority's 2004 and 2005 reports also address environmental care, employee issues (including health and safety), stakeholder relationships, and customer service. These reports use an innovative *sustainability performance ruler* to present weighted index scores for reporting progress against 18 sustainability objectives.[23]

Wisconsin Energy Corporation

Wisconsin Energy Corporation's (WEC's) thorough 132-page sustainability report for 2004 is another example of how far utilities can go. While WEC is a publicly traded company, its utility operations are not unlike that of governmental bodies providing those services in other parts of the world. Like Watercare Services, the company used GRI as a reference in preparing its report, which covers most of the commonly reported economic, environmental, and social information. In addition, the document addresses some more unusual topics, such as political lobbying and contributions, community programs on electrical safety, annual self-evaluation by the board, and supplier diversity. The report discusses a broad array of environmental issues, too, among them mercury emissions, biodiversity preservation, restoring and redeveloping urban properties, renewable energy, and the beneficial use of coal ash and paper-mill sludge.[24] WEC also makes its Corporate Governance Guidelines[25] and Code of Business Conduct[26] publicly available on the Internet.

The Royal Mail Group

Royal Mail issued full sustainability reports for 2004 and 2005, as well as a summary report for 2004 and large-print, Braille, and audio versions for 2005. Its long, externally verified GRI reports discuss at some length the policies and structures that have been established to manage sustainability issues within the organization. Like WEC, Royal Mail's operations—receiving, handling, storing, and transporting mail—are intrinsically tied to its operations. So it shouldn't be surprising that Royal Mail's publication, like that of WEC, touches on many of the same issues one would find in a sustainability report from business. Performance is reported in the traditional areas of environment, occupational health, safety, and diversity performance, as well as security. Volunteer programs, charitable giving, recruiting from disadvantaged groups, and special initiatives around education are featured under the social heading. The documents also provide a candid account of its regulatory noncompliance—something commonly missing from governmental sustainability reports. Specific service issues covered by the reports include the group's progress in reducing branch office closures and in assuring adequate postal service in both rural areas and poor urban communities.[27]

Australian Department of Family and Community Services; Hong Kong Architectural Services Department

Reports published by the Australian Department of Family and Community Services (ADFCS)[28] and the Hong Kong Architectural Services Department (HKASD)[29] also relied on GRI. ADFCS is charged with providing a host of services for disadvantaged families, including income and community support, disability and child care assistance, housing policy and family counseling. HKASD is responsible for designing, procuring, and maintaining public buildings for the Hong Kong government, and for advising the government on related issues. Both departments were legally bound to publish a performance report but elected to go beyond minimum requirements to address sustainability issues. However, unlike the utility reports, the ADFCS and HKASD publications more closely resemble those of NGOs than of industry.

As the ADFCS sustainability report for 2002-2003 notes: "We do not produce any significant emissions, own or manage biodiversity-rich land or water, produce significant ozone-depleting substances or manufacture products."[30] Even so, that report and the one issued by the agency the following year focus mostly on its operations and very little on its services. This is because ADFCS also issues a comprehensive annual report that covers its services and financial accounts. So why does the department also issue an annual sustainability report? One reason is to show that it "walks the talk" on human rights and respect for the individual—two themes of its core services. Accordingly, its sustainability reports cover the agency's flexible working arrangements and the workload-management programs for its staff. The documents also address the innovative recruitment and retention strategy for indigenous peoples that includes a cultural leave benefit. Organizational structure is discussed as well: a disability access coordinator assures that the concerns of the disabled are considered in the department's operations and policies, and a "diversity council" promotes diversity at senior levels.

Another reason ADFCS issues sustainability reports is that the agency is part of the prime minister's Community Business Partnership, an organization assigned to encourage TBL reporting among the country's industry. By presenting a traditional GRI-type report, it sets an example that companies could find relevant and inspiring. From that perspective, it helps that these publications cover issues common to business, such as greenhouse gases, energy usage, waste generation, and recycling, as well as water consumption, employee safety, and suppliers. In this regard, it is also noteworthy that the reports were verified by the Australian National Audit Office against both GRI's assurance principles as well as "internationally recognized financial and environmental auditing standards."

HKASD adopted a strategy for sustainability reporting that was opposite that of the Australians. The externally verified Hong Kong document emphasizes the sustainability impact of the department's services more than its operations. However, because these services include the management of the department's own buildings as well as those of its fellow agencies, the line between its services and operations is somewhat blurred. The agency's services comprise facilities development (planning, design, construction, and demolition), facilities upkeep (maintenance and renovation), monitoring, and advice. Its operations are merely the daily office activities of the organization.

HKASD's reports for 2004 and 2005 tell of the department's progress against specific objectives and targets established around EHS performance, green design, staff learning and turnover, and project delivery. A wide range of environmental metrics are presented—everything from energy and resource conservation to greenhouse gas emissions, water usage, and waste generation. Data on community volunteer programs and construction and staff safety are also reported. An unusual statistic—the number of environmental convictions of contractors—is cited along with traditional health and safety data. A significant portion of each report is devoted to case studies of environmentally and socially sensitive building design—an area emphasized through the department's assessment, rating, and award programs.

As the ADFCS and HKASD documents show, there may be good reasons to focus a sustainability report on an agency's operations or services. However, most agencies will find greatest value for themselves and their stakeholders by providing balanced coverage of both.

Element 7: Development and Building Design

A main sustainability goal of the HKASD and many other public bodies is to use and promote green building design. While green building principles often mean different things to different people, generally, they encompass the objectives listed in Figure 14.5. In short, they are designs that are economically feasible and efficient, and environmentally and socially sensitive. From a sustainability perspective, green building design, which generally incorporates green real estate development as well, is an enormously important area for governments given the large number of buildings they own and operate, and the example they set for the private sector. A government's ability to affect green design looms even greater if it sets building codes and approves real estate developments and construction.

Figure 14.5
Common Green Building Principles

1. Minimizing the use of materials and resources in construction and maintenance.
2. Incorporating used and recycled materials; reusing existing building structures.
3. Using equipment and materials that are safe and that won't pose an undue hazard when burned.
4. Using wood from certified sustainable forests.
5. Using materials indigenous to the region.
6. Incorporating safety and security concerns into design.
7. Improving energy efficiency.
8. Using clean and renewable energy sources.
9. Reducing the use of water.
10. Minimizing the quantity and degree of hazard of emissions, discharges, and wastes from construction, maintenance, and demolition.
11. Assuring good indoor air quality.
12. Preserving and promoting biodiversity in landscape design, especially with regard to plants and wildlife indigenous to the region.
13. Minimizing erosion and stormwater runoff during construction and in landscape design.
14. Creating designs that optimize occupant comfort in terms of light, heat, humidity, odors, noise, and stress.
15. Allowing for ready access by physically challenged people.
16. Preserving or restoring historical and culturally prized aspects.
17. Creating a result that is aesthetically pleasing.

Indeed, by focusing on buildings, governments can have a significant beneficial impact on a number of sustainability issues. Buildings use one-quarter of the world's wood harvest and consume 40% of all material and energy flows. Over one-half of the U.S. energy consumption and over one-third of its greenhouse gas emissions are tied directly or indirectly to the construction and operation of buildings.[31] Wetlands destruction and the depletion of water supplies and biodiversity are other adverse consequences of building construction and property development that can be halted or at least mitigated with enlightened governmental policy. For a community that wants to get serious about sustainability, green building must be close to the top of its to-do list.

Several communities, one being Portland, Oregon, way in promoting green building. Portland formally adopteu ̣ Building Policy that reads in part as follows:

> The City of Portland shall incorporate green building principles and practices into the design, construction, and operations of all City facilities, City-funded projects, and infrastructure projects to the fullest extent possible. Furthermore, the City will provide leadership and guidance to encourage the application of green building practices in private sector development. This policy is expected to yield long-term cost savings to the City's taxpayers due to substantial improvements in life-cycle performance and reduced life-cycle costs.
>
> In addition, the City shall evaluate all land purchases for future development on the basis of reducing environmental impacts that include but are not limited to transit and bicycle accessibility, urban and brownfields redevelopment, solar access, on-site stormwater mitigation capacity, and vegetation and habitat restoration.[32]

To implement this policy, Portland established the Office of Sustainable Development, Green Building Division. In addition, the city created its own Portland LEED™ Green Building Rating System based in large part on the U.S. Green Building Council's LEED™ Rating System.[33] As the city moved forward with its program, it saw that the practice of separately budgeting for construction and operations was making it difficult to invest in green building practices. Building equipment and materials selected because of their low price often end up costing more over the long term in energy and other operating costs. For that reason, Portland now applies 20- to 30-year life-cycle costing that integrates construction and operation and maintenance budgets into all building-related capital improvements.

Chicago is another city that is helping lead the charge on green building.[34] It, too, has a progressive policy and formal standard on the topic—The Chicago Standard. The city has initiated some innovative projects to stimulate the green movement among private builders. It cleaned up an old 17-acre construction-waste disposal site and rehabilitated the building that was on the site using advanced green building techniques. The structure—now the Chicago Center for Green Technology or Green Tech—was the first renovated building in the United States to receive a "platinum" rating under the LEED™ standards. It houses the city's community landscaping and job training program (Greencorps

Chicago), a manufacturer of solar panels, and an urban landscape de-sign-and-build firm.

Chicago has other green building programs, too. Special Green Roof Standards apply to new public buildings, planned developments, and privately funded structures subsidized by the city. Even city hall has a rooftop garden. The Chicago Green Bungalow Initiative showcased four different green designs that could be used in the renovation of the bungalow style of house, 80,000 of which were built in the area during the first half of the last century. The city's Green Mega Fueling Station used for fueling city vehicles is a model for environmentally friendly gas stations. Electricity for the station is provided by solar panels; alternative fuels are supplied; and a two-acre natural area helps manage stormwater runoff. The city's Mayor Richard Daley periodically presents GreenWorks Awards to recognize outstanding examples of green building in the city's private sector. One of the 2004 awards went to a project that represents the broad aspects of sustainability: Sanctuary Place, a green building erected by the Interfaith Housing Development Corporation to provide permanent housing for homeless women with substance-abuse issues.

Element 8: Procurements

With their huge purchasing power, governments can have a profound effect on the sustainability practices of their contractors, consultants, and suppliers. Public authorities in Europe spend over $1 *trillion* a year on goods, works, and services.[35] With clout like this, governments can also make a big difference in the market feasibility of green products. For instance, in 1992, only 10 manufacturers of personal computers had their products certified for energy efficiency under EPA's Energy Star® program. Six years later, virtually all manufacturers—600 in all—had Energy Star® personal computers.[36] This dramatic increase was due primarily to President Clinton's executive order requiring all federal agencies to buy only Energy Star®-certified computers. With the U.S. government purchasing one million computers a year—3% of the U.S. market—this commitment drove a whole industry toward sustainability. What is more, it saved an estimated 2.3 billion kilowatt hours of electricity—and untold costs—in 1994 and 1995 alone.[37]

The idea that governments should use sustainability criteria to select and buy goods and services is gaining ground in various corners of the globe. The practice goes by many names: *green procurement, affirmative procurement, sustainable procurement,* and *eco-procurement,* as well as *green purchasing, environmental purchasing,* and *environmentally friendly purchasing.* Today, however, most government purchasing decisions are dominated by one part of sustainability's TBL: economics. Contract awards are granted to the lowest responsible bidder. Some public authorities, like those in Portland, use *life-cycle costing,* which looks at long-term storage, transportation, operation, maintenance, and disposal costs in addition to the sales price. This helps weed out products that operate wastefully or require expensive disposal. With the emergence of sustainable procurement over the last few decades, the other two legs of the TBL have also begun to influence government purchasing. For the most part, this has meant using environmental criteria in procurements, although social issues are now being considered in a few cases as well.

Sustainable procurement has been on the upswing, especially in places like Canada, Japan, northern Europe, and to a lesser extent, in the United States. But with a few exceptions, the progress has been slow. Certainly, obstacles remain. Some entities lack the criteria, data, and knowledge for evaluating products and services for sustainability aspects. Others can't muster the time or money to do so. Most suffer from an absence of high-level political commitment and a clear strategy. Political support is often missing due to the mistaken belief that sustainability-friendly products always cost more and often don't meet performance expectations. Occasionally a shortage of tools or resources prevents deployment of national programs to local levels. And while a few governments seem to be making good progress, it is rare for them to have any measurement systems to confirm that.

Notwithstanding these difficulties, a number of organizations are moving forward on sustainable procurement. Let us examine a few of the more progressive efforts.

ICLEI Procura+ Campaign[38]

The ICLEI is promoting its *Procura+ Sustainable Procurement Campaign.* Under the campaign, ICLEI encourages its local government members to adopt a type of plan-do-check-act process to manage their purchasing programs for sustainability. This process consists of five steps:

    1. Inventory the amount and costs of procurements and any sustainability criteria already used;

2. Set specific targets for improvement based on what the organization can reasonably achieve (e.g., 70% of purchased timber from certified sustainable forests by 2010);
3. Develop an action plan that takes into account staff resources and the duration of existing contracts;
4. Deploy and implement the plan in the various administrative units, allowing time for training, communication, and consultation; and
5. Monitor and report results to local political authorities and globally through ICLEI.

Public authorities that join Procura obtain a special campaign manual for implementing the program. Program information includes criteria for evaluating products in six groups: (1) electricity from renewable sources; (2) energy-efficient computers; (3) organic foods; (4) energy-efficient buildings; (5) health-oriented cleaning services; and (6) and quality-oriented public transport services with low emissions. Subscribers can also call on ICLEI's sustainable procurement staff for product information and other support. In addition, members gain access to *BIG-Net*, the Buy It Green Network for sustainable procurement professionals in Europe. With good participation, ICLEI expects Procura+ will result in over $600 million in savings on energy, water, and waste bills. For those green products that may be more expensive than their non-green competitors, ICLEI criteria caps additional costs at 5%.

Japanese Programs[39]

Procura presents a good model for building a green purchasing program. However, the best implemented models are to be found in Japan—the undisputed national leader in green procurement. The movement there got off to a good start in 1996 with the creation of the Green Purchasing Network (GPN), a multi-stakeholder group including the Ministry of Environment and over 360 local governments, and 2,200 companies, as well as 270 nonprofit consumer groups, environmental NGOs, and cooperative associations. The primary purpose of the GPN is to promote green procurement among central and local governments, companies, and consumers. It does that in a number of ways. Its task groups have developed purchasing guidelines on office paper and supplies, computers, office furniture, and copiers and fax machines. Guidelines also cover toilet tissue, automobiles, refrigerators, washing machines, and lighting fixtures and bulbs. Others address TVs, air conditioners, uniforms, printing services, and hotels. GPN maintains a comparative database on the Internet, containing over 11,000 products in the guideline categories. In addition, the network holds seminars, publishes a newsletter, and even runs media ads to keep awareness high. It shares best practices and presents awards for excellent programs. It regularly conducts surveys to track progress on green procurement and measure its own effectiveness.

A cornerstone of Japan's GPN is its *Basic Principles for Green Purchasing,* which guide decisionmaking on procurements. Those principles are shown in Figure 14.6.

The role of GPN—and of green procurement in Japan—gained a big boost in 2000 when a national law was adopted requiring governmental bodies at all levels to undertake green purchasing. Each town, city, prefecture, and federal agency is now required to create and annually publicize its purchasing policy. In addition, it must report a summary of its purchasing records showing how it fulfilled the policy. Over 150 commodities are subject to the law. To evaluate product proposals, authorities use the GPN database, the Japanese national eco-labeling program (*Eco-mark*), and other third-party environmental labels.[40] The impact of the law has been substantial—a result one might expect given that governments in Japan purchase one-fifth of the nation's goods and services. A year after the law was enacted, one of every six green-product suppliers surveyed by the GPN reported a surge in sales of 50% or more. Over one-half of the electric appliance suppliers reported sales growth of 30 to 40%.[41]

Danish Programs[42]

Like Japan, Denmark has taken a multifaceted approach to green procurement. The foundation is the 1992 Danish Environmental Protection Act, which mandates that public authorities endeavor to promote the objectives of the law through procurement. An action plan for green public procurement was developed in 1994. The following year, a government circular was issued to all federal purchasing institutions reminding them to include environmental aspects on the same footing as price and quality when making procurement decisions. In 1998, the Minister for the Environment negotiated an agreement with county and municipal associations, committing local governments to adopt green procurement. By 2000, over two-thirds of the counties, one-half of the government purchasing institutions, and about one-third of municipalities had developed policies on it. To aid these authorities, the Danish Environmental Protection Agency (DEPA) has developed environmental purchasing guidelines covering about 50 different product groups. The agency also subsidizes the formation of green purchasing networks among smaller municipalities. It provides a handbook and seminars on green procurement for governmental purchasing professionals.

Besides DEPA, another important player in green procurement has been National Procurement Limited (NPL), a large group-buying organization for public entities with approximately 85 suppliers under contract. NPL collaborates with the DEPA, the Danish Labour Inspectorate, and the Danish Energy Agency to incorporate sustainability criteria into supplier agreements. NPL also maintains a website—Green Net—that provides guidance on green procurement and environmental information on products.

To spur market demand for green products, DEPA has organized several product-area panels. Panel members are drawn from across the supply chain, from raw material suppliers, product designers, manufacturers, and distributors, to retailers and consumers, and even waste processors and NGOs. The panel on textile products has been the most successful. Producers agreed to make textile products that conform to the green criteria of the European eco-label (the Flower); retailers agreed to buy and display them. The end result has been many more environmentally sensitive textile items on the market. Other panels have focused on electronics, transportation, and building and construction. Plans are to examine furniture, washing and cleaning agents, and cleaning and laundry services.

U.K. Programs[43]

In contrast with the national green procurement programs in Denmark and Japan, which are well underway, the programs in the United Kingdom are still generally at the planning and development stage. The British government is apparently serious about the effort, however—no doubt with encouragement from Prime Minister Blair. Each of the 19 central federal departments in Britain is required by government policy to develop and implement action plans and allocate resources for establishing sustainable procurement programs. Periodic progress reports are mandated. Departments are expected to use environmental criteria which have been issued for certain Quick Win product categories, while special product catalogues and Internet-based guidance are being prepared. Sustainable procurement information is being melded into a certification program for government purchasing agents. These efforts are being spearheaded by the DEFRA, along with the Office of Government Commerce (OGC), as part of a program called the *Framework for Sustainable Development on the Government Estate.*

What is noteworthy about the U.K. effort is the introduction of two elements that have received little attention in such programs elsewhere: (1) social criteria in purchasing decisions; and (2) risk assessments. OGC has been chartered to collaborate with other departments to develop recommendations on how social issues and risks should be considered in federal procurements. Environmental risk assessments are to be incorporated in each department's procurement process, with sign-off required by the department's green minister if risks exceed a certain threshold.

Some experimentation with risk assessments and social evaluations is being undertaken by the Environment Agency within DEFRA, which annually awards approximately 750 contracts worth $800 million.[44] To assess environmental risks, the agency identifies the life-cycle inputs and outputs. They do this by looking at the basic raw materials or components obtained during the premanufacture stage. They also examine the key environmental issues arising during the manufacture, use, and disposal stages. Significant environmental aspects or impacts are then identified for each of these four life-cycle stages and recorded in a matrix similar to that depicted in Figure 14.7. One social aspect is also evaluated: the likelihood that the stage of the life cycle would extend into the developing world. This social criterion is no doubt a flag for potential reputational and political risk. Who wants to become embroiled in an exposé involving the use of child labor and sweatshops by Third-World suppliers? To expedite the evaluation process, generic risk assessments based on this methodology have been prepared for about three dozen product classes.

Figure 14.6
Japan Green Purchasing Network's
Basic Principles for Green Purchasing[45]

1. Consider whether the product or service is really needed, and whether the quantity can be reduced.

2. Consider the various environmental impacts of the product over its life cycle—from raw-material extraction to disposal. Consider also the seriousness and geographical extent of the effects. Select products which:

    2.1 Use or emit fewer substances that have an adverse effect on the environment.

    2.2 Conserve resources and energy.

    2.3 Use renewable natural resources in a sustainable way.

    2.4 Provide long service life.

    2.5 Are reusable.

    2.6 Are recyclable.

    2.7 Contain recycled materials or reused parts.

    2.8 Ensure trouble-free treatment and disposal.

3. Select suppliers who have made a conscious effort to care for the environment, considering such factors as whether or not they:

    3.1 Have an EMS.

    3.2 Have proactive programs for resource savings, energy savings, waste reduction, management and reduction of chemical substances, green purchasing, green-product manufacture and distribution, and pollution and disaster prevention.

    3.3 Proactively disclose environmental information.

4. Collect environmental information on products and suppliers for evaluation. Product information may be available from various eco-label programs or third-party databases, or directly from the supplier.

	Figure 14.7 Matrix Used by U.K. Environment Agency to Identify Sustainability Impacts of Products[46]				
Aspect/ Impact	Life-Cycle Stage				Comments
	Raw Material/Pre-manufacture	Manufacture	Use	Disposal	
Resource Use					
Energy					
Water					
VOC					
Waste/End of Life Issues					
Hazardous Substances					
Packaging					
Noise					
Developing World Supply Chain					
Score for Stage (no. of significant impacts)					
Total Score for Product					

Once the sustainability risk is identified, it is married with the business risk of the transaction. If both risks are considered low, the Environment Agency simply adds provisions to the supplier's contract to address any significant issues. If either risk is high, the agency undertakes a more detailed risk assessment, ranking the issues and managing them. For example, high risks at the raw materials stage may be managed by requiring the supplier to adopt certain specifications, measures, management systems, or ethical supply chain management policies. High risks during manufacture may be addressed by a third-party site assessment. If high risks are identified under the use category, user specifications and education programs can be developed. High disposal risks may be mitigated by disposal specifications, supplier take-back programs, or end-user awareness.

As part of this assessment process, the Environment Agency also evaluates the strength of its bargaining position, or, in other words, how much influence it has within the market. If it has a strong position, the agency will demand sustainable performance of both the product and the supplier. If the influence is only moderate, the agency will focus on a few key areas and explore other opportunities for development. Where the influence is low, the agency will attempt to persuade the supplier to meet sustainability criteria as a way to differentiate itself and its products in the marketplace.

The agency's top-20 suppliers receive close evaluation, one-on-one discussions, and follow-up. The others within the top 500 are subject to a more systematic assessment of their sustainability standing. From a social perspective, this means looking at the working conditions, minimum age, pay, equal treatment, union membership, and diversity of a supplier's employees, as well as its management of overseas operations and subcontractors. At the conclusion of the evaluation, the top 500 are provided feedback and a CD training program covering corporate environmental and social responsibility.

The agency continues to experiment with its sustainable procurements program, doing its best to develop approaches that are innovative, fair, and reasonable. Still, questions remain. For example, will risk assessments and social criteria pass muster under the European Commission rules designed to assure free trade through fair, rational procurement criteria? Will selection processes become too bureaucratic? Whatever the outcome, the results will no doubt have an impact well beyond the United Kingdom.

Like the Environment Agency, a few other U.K. government agencies and institutions are also trying to adopt leading-edge practices involving green procurement. For instance, the Royal Mail conducts sustainable procurement workshops with its purchasing managers and their teams. It also incorporates environmental, social, and economic criteria into its supplier evaluations, and presents special awards to recognize superior supplier performance in these areas.[47]

Putting the Pieces Together

Of course, green procurement is just one aspect of turning government toward sustainability. To do so effectively, sustainability must be integrated into policy-setting, planning, and day-to-day decisionmaking at all levels. The challenge for those who want to see their governments pursue sustainability is first a challenge of education—showing government leaders what sustainability means and how it meshes with those leaders' own desires for their communities. With a vision in hand, then comes the planning, training, and tools to integrate the concept further into government's operations and services. While few governments have embraced sustainability fully, the pockets of activity that have emerged are encouraging. As more public officials become attracted to sustainability, they can use the best practices discussed above to help light the way forward.

Follow-up Checklist for Action:
Approach to Sustainability for Governmental Organizations

☐ Share with leaders of the government organization the potential benefits of pursuing sustainability through a simplified SOS. See Chapter 4 for ideas on how to do this communication. Also consider the value of sustainability for governmental entities as discussed in this chapter.

☐ After securing support from the leadership, form a sustainability team to coordinate sustainability planning, reporting, and other activities. Designate personnel from the planning and development department or some other function to lead the team. Also consider forming one or more multi-departmental sustainability working groups and a stakeholder advisory group.

☐ Identify the key sustainability aspects of the organization's operations and services, considering Figures 2.4, 2.5, and 13.1, other guidance from this chapter, and feedback from key stakeholders.

☐ Adopt a sustainability policy related to the key aspects of the organization's operations and services, drawing from the model policies in Figures 2.2 and 14.1-14.4, the Aalborg Charter, Global Compact, and other examples mentioned in this chapter. Include policy provisions on green buildings (including real estate development) and green procurement, as appropriate.

☐ Following the guidance of this chapter and Chapter 12, plan and implement an SOS appropriate for the organization's sustainability aspects, its size and risks. Consider the framework and tools of the LA 21 MCP and the ICLEI LA 21 Campaign. To be most effective, integrate sustainability planning into traditional community planning. Incorporate various goals and metrics in the plan, considering examples found in Appendix 7.2 and the guidance from Chapter 7.

☐ Consider establishing green building and green procurement initiatives, drawing from the examples discussed in this chapter.

☐ At least annually, measure performance against the organization's sustainability policy, plans, and goals. Prepare and communicate a sustainability report for the organization after considering this performance, the stakeholder feedback, the sustainability reports of other similar governmental bodies, and the guidance provided in Chapter 10 and this chapter.

☐ Periodically solicit input from various stakeholders on the organization's sustainability performance and communications, taking into account the guidance of Chapter 11 and this chapter. Focus particularly on employees, suppliers, and the public—especially those segments of the public the organization is obligated to serve. Determine what action should be taken on the feedback; at the very least, consider it during the next planning cycle.

Endnotes to Chapter 14

1. This quote is attributed to Abraham Lincoln, the 16th president of the United States, who lived from 1809 to 1865.

2. *See* GRI, PUBLIC AGENCY SUSTAINABILITY REPORTING: A GRI RE-SOURCE DOCUMENT IN SUPPORT OF THE PUBLIC AGENCY SECTOR SUP-PLEMENT PROJECT (2004), *available at* http://www.globalreporting.org/guidelines/resource/public.asp [hereinafter GRI PUBLIC AGENCY RE-SOURCE DOCUMENT].

3. ICLEI, *Local Agenda 21 Model Communities Program*, http://www.iclei.org/index.php?id=1202 (last visited Jan. 8, 2006) [hereinafter ICLEI, *Model Program*].

4. U.N. Conference on Environment and Development, Agenda 21, ch. 28, U.N. Doc. A/CONF.151.26 (1992), *available at* http://www.un.org/esa/sustdev/documents/agenda21/english/agenda21toc.htm. This chapter stipulates that "by 1996, most local authorities in each country should have undertaken a consultative process with their population and achieved a consensus on a [l]ocal Agenda 21 for the[ir] communities."

5. ICLEI, LOCAL AGENDA 21 PLANNING GUIDE (1996) and ICLEI, LO-CAL AGENDA 21 MODEL COMMUNITIES PROGRAM FINAL REPORT, VOLS. 1 and 2 (1998), *available at* http://www3.iclei.org/merchant/merchant2.cfm?id=6.

6. *See* ICLEI, *Model Program, supra* note 3.

7. ICLEI, *Local Agenda 21 Campaign*, http://www.iclei.org/index.php?id=798 (last visited Jan. 8, 2006).

8. CITY COUNCIL FOR HOBART, TASMANIA, AUSTRALIA, HOBART CITY COUNCIL MOVING FORWARD: ANNUAL REPORT 2003-2004 (2004), *available at* http://www.hobartcity.com.au/hccwr/lib86/2003-04%20annual%20report%20final.pdf [hereinafter HOBART REPORT 2003-2004].

9. DEFENCE ESTATES, MINISTRY OF DEFENCE, UNITED KINGDOM, MINIS-TRY OF DEFENCE SUSTAINABLE DEVELOPMENT REPORT: OCTOBER 2003-OCTOBER 2004 (2005), *available at* http://www.mod.uk/linked_files/dsc/env/mod_sd_report_03_04.pdf [hereinafter U.K. MINISTRY OF DEFENCE SD REPORT 2003-2004].

10. U.K. SECRETARY OF STATE FOR ENVIRONMENT, FOOD & RURAL AFFAIRS, SECURING THE FUTURE: DELIVERING U.K. SUSTAINABLE DEVELOPMENT STRATEGY: THE U.K. GOVERNMENT SUSTAINABLE DEVELOPMENT STRATEGY 184-86 (2005), *available at* http://www.sustainable-development.gov.uk/publications/uk-strategy/uk-strategy-2005.htm [hereinafter U.K. SUSTAINABLE DEVELOPMENT STRATEGY 2005].

11. ROYAL MAIL GROUP, CORPORATE SOCIAL RESPONSIBILITY REPORT 2004 (2004) and ROYAL MAIL GROUP, PLC, PASSION ABOUT PROGRESS—COR-

PORATE SOCIAL RESPONSIBILITY REPORT, APRIL 2004-MARCH 2005
(2005), *available at* http://www.royalmailgroup.com/aboutus/aboutus4.
asp [hereinafter ROYAL MAIL CSR REPORTS 2004, 2005].

12. Aalborgplus10.dk, *The Aalborg Charter*, http://www.aalborgplus10.dk/
    default.aspx?m=2&i=371 (last visited Feb. 14, 2006).

13. Leeds, U.K., City Council, *Sustainable Development Unit*, http://www.
    leeds.gov.uk/Sustainable%20Development%20Unit/page.aspx?style=
    (last visited Jan. 8, 2006).

14. City of Santa Monica, California, *Guiding Principles*, http://santa-
    monica.org/epd/scp/guiding.htm (last visited Jan. 8, 2006).

15. *See* ROYAL MAIL CSR REPORTS 2004, 2005, *supra* note 11.

16. *See* U.K. SUSTAINABLE DEVELOPMENT STRATEGY 2005, *supra* note 10.

17. *See* HOBART REPORT 2003-2004, *supra* note 8. *See* U.K. MINISTRY OF
    DEFENCE SD REPORT 2003-2004, *supra* note 8.

18. American Planning Association, *Policy Guide on Planning for Sustain-
    ability* (adopted by Chapter Delegate Assembly, Apr. 16, 2000, ratified
    by Board of Directors, Apr. 17, 2000, New York, N.Y.), *available at*
    http://www.planning.org/policyguides/sustainability.htm.

19. *See, e.g.,* AMBIENTE ITALIA RESEARCH INSTITUTE ET AL., EUROPEAN
    COMMON INDICATORS (European Commission, Eurocities, and Leg-
    ambiente (Italy), 2003), *available at* http://euronet.uwe.ac.uk/www.
    sustainable-cities.org/indicators/ECI%20Final%20Report.pdf, and
    World Bank Group, *Environmental Economics and Indicators: Publications*,
    http://lnweb18.worldbank.org/ESSD/envext.nsf/44ByDocName/
    Publications (last visited Jan. 8, 2006). *See* U.K. Sustainable Development
    Strategy 2005, *supra* note 10. See also the Millennium Development
    Goals discussed in Appendix 1.

20. GRI, PUBLIC AGENCY SUSTAINABILITY REPORTING: A GRI RESOURCE
    DOCUMENT IN SUPPORT OF THE PUBLIC AGENCY SECTOR SUPPLEMENT
    PROJECT (2004), *available at* http://www.globalreporting.org/guidelines/
    resource/public.asp.

21. GRI, *Sector Supplement for Public Agencies*, http://www.globalreporting.
    org/guidelines/sectors/public.asp (last visited Jan. 8, 2006).

22. WATERCARE SERVICES LTD., ANNUAL SUSTAINABILITY REPORT 2002:
    WATERCARE'S SCIENCE OF SAFETY (2003), *available at* http://www.
    Watercare.co.nz/default,publications.sm.

23. WATERCARE SERVICES LTD., ANNUAL REPORT 2004—CONSTANT
    PROGRESS, CONTINUOUS SUCCESS (2005) and WATERCARE SERVICES
    LTD., ANNUAL REPORT 2005—WATERSHED: AN INTEGRATED AP-
    PROACH (2006), *both available at* http://www.watercare.co.nz/default,
    publications.sm. See Chapter 7 for further discussion of Watercare's
    sustainability indexes.

24. WEC, 2004 PERFORMANCE REPORT: FOCUS ON CUSTOMER SATISFAC-
TION AND FINANCIAL DISCIPLINE, EXECUTION OF OUR BUSINESS PLAN,
AND INVESTMENT IN OUR FUTURE (2005), *available at* http://www.wec-
performancereport.com/.

25. WEC, BOARD OF DIRECTORS, CORPORATE GOVERNANCE GUIDELINES
(2005), *available at* http://www.wisconsinenergy.com/govern/governance.
htm.

26. WEC, CODE OF BUSINESS CONDUCT, EMPLOYEE COMPLIANCE, AND
CERTIFICATION (2005), *available at* http://www.wisconsinenergy.com/
govern/governance.htm.

27. *See* ROYAL MAIL CSR REPORTS 2004, 2005, *supra* note 11.

28. ADFCS, AUSTRALIAN GOVERNMENT, TRIPLE BOTTOM LINE REPORT
(2002-2003): OUR COMMITMENT TO SOCIAL, ENVIRONMENTAL, AND
ECONOMIC PERFORMANCE (2003), *available at* http://www.facs.gov.au/
internet/facsinternet.nsf/aboutfacs/triplebottomline.htm [hereinafter
Australian 2002-2003 Report]. ADFCS, AUSTRALIAN GOVERNMENT,
TRIPLE BOTTOM LINE REPORT 2003-2004: OUR COMMITMENT TO SO-
CIAL, ENVIRONMENTAL, AND ECONOMIC PERFORMANCE (2004), *available at* http://www.facs.gov.au/internet/facsinternet.nsf/aboutfacs/
triplebottomline.htm. It should be noted that this agency recently changed
its name to the Australian Department of Families, Community Services,
and Indigenous Affairs.

29. HKASD, ARCHSD SUSTAINABILITY REPORT 2004: FOUNDATIONS FOR
A SUSTAINABLE FUTURE (2004), *available at* http://www.archsd.gov.
hk/archsd_home01.asp?Path_Lev1=5.

30. *See* Australian 2002-2003 Report, *supra* note 28, at 9.

31. CITY OF PORTLAND, OREGON, GREEN BUILDING POLICY, BINDING CITY
POLICY BCP-ENB-9.01, Adopted by City Council, Resolution No. 35956
(2001), *available at* http://www.portlandonline.com/index.cfm?&a=
54355&c=34835&x=15&y=10.

32. *Id.*

33. U.S. Green Building Council, *Leadership in Energy and Environmental
Design*, http://www.usgbc.org/leed/leed_main.asp (last visited Jan. 8,
2006).

34. City of Chicago, Department of Environment, *Green Building*, http://
egov.cityofchicago.org/city/webportal/portalDeptCategoryAction.do?
BV_SessionID=@@@@1539750782.1100211410@@@@&BV_EngineID=
ccccadcmlmfkllhcefecelldffhdfgn.0&deptCategoryOID=-536887181&content
Type=COC_EDITORIAL&topChannelName=Dept&entityName=
Environment&deptMainCategoryOID=-536887205 (last visited Jan. 8,
2006).

35. ICLEI, PROCURA+ SUSTAINABLE PROCUREMENT CAMPAIGN (Freiburg, Germany, 2003), *available at* http://www.iclei-europe.org/index.php? id=519 [hereinafter ICLEI, PROCURA].

36. ATMOSPHERIC POLLUTION PREVENTION DIVISION, U.S. EPA, ENERGY STAR OFFICE PRODUCTS PROGRAM (1998).

37. OFFICE OF THE INSPECTOR GENERAL, U.S. EPA, RISK REDUCTION THROUGH VOLUNTARY PROGRAMS (1997).

38. *See* ICLEI, PROCURA, *supra* note 35.

39. GPN, *About GPN,* http://www.gpn.jp/English/aboutgpn.html (last visited Jan. 8, 2006).

40. For a good list of environmentally related labeling schemes, see European Commission, "Short Presentation of Existing Public and Private Eco-Label Schemes," *European Green Procurement Database,* http://europa. Eu.int/comm/environment/green_purchasing/html/general/ecoabel_en. cfm (last visited Jan. 8, 2006), and European Commission, "Short Presentation of Other Environmentally Related Labelling Schemes," *European Green Procurement Database,* at http://europa.eu.int/comm/environment/ green_purchasing/html/general/otherlabels_en.cfm (last visited Jan. 8, 2006).

41. Hiroyuki Sato, Secretary General, GPN, *Demand Side Approach and Green Purchasing Network in Japan,* 20 ECP NEWSL., JEMAI (2002), *available at* http://www.jemai.or.jp/english/dfe/pdf/20_1.pdf.

42. *See* RIKKE TRABERG, DEVELOPMENT DATA DIVISION, DANISH ENVIRONMENTAL PROTECTION AGENCY, DANISH MINISTRY OF THE ENVIRONMENT, GREENER PUBLIC PROCUREMENT IN DENMARK (2003), *available at* http://www.un.org/esa/sustdev/sdissues/consumption/denmark021127. pdf, and CHRISTOPH ERDMENGER ET AL., THE INTERNATIONAL COUNCIL FOR LOCAL ENVIRONMENTAL INITIATIVES, THE WORLD BUYS GREEN—INTERNATIONAL SURVEY ON NATIONAL GREEN PROCUREMENT PRACTICES (Freiburg, Germany, 2001), *available at* http://www.iclei-europe.org/index.php?id=1781.

43. Sustainable Development in Government Team, *Framework for Sustainable Development on the Government Estate,* http://www.sustainable-development.gov.uk/delivery/integrating/estate/estate.htm (last visited Jan. 8, 2006).

44. Christopher Browne, Procurement Strategy Manager, Environment Agency, U.K. DEFRA, presentation entitled, *U.N. Expert Meeting on Sustainable Public Procurement* (Copenhagen, Dec. 2, 2002), http://www. environment-agency.gov.uk/commondata/103603/un_presentation.ppt (last visited Jan. 8, 2006) [hereinafter Browne, U.K. Environment Agency Presentation].

45. GPN, GREEN PURCHASING BASIC PRINCIPLES (2001), *available at* http://www.gpn.jp/English/principle/index.html.

46. *See* Browne, U.K. Environment Agency Presentation, *supra* note 44.

47. *See* ROYAL MAIL CSR REPORT 2004, *supra* note 10.

Chapter 15

Approach to Sustainability for Colleges and Universities

"Human history becomes more and more a race between education and catastrophe."[1]
—H.G. Wells

Impact of Collegiate Institutions on Sustainability

To some people, colleges and universities may seem like distant, isolated ivory towers, offering little practical help in the fight for sustainability. Nothing could be further from the truth. Collegiate organizations, like their governmental, NGO, and business sisters, have both an operations and a services and products side to their activities that affect sustainability in a big way. The operations side for a college or university—the management of people, the running of buildings, the maintenance of grounds, streets, and utilities—is really not very different than that of a small city. Like municipal bodies, some universities have quite sizeable staffs, land holdings, and procurement and building programs. And like their municipal counterparts, they too can have a significant effect on the economic, social, and environmental aspects of their communities. In fact, a number of sustainability programs for governments are also quite suitable for academic institutions. For example, LA 21—a tool designed for governments—is being used by some European universities to guide their march toward sustainability.

The services and products side of the collegiate world—education and research—holds a special place in the quest for a sustainable society. As U.N. Secretary-General Annan noted on World Environment Day 2000:

> We need a major public education effort. Understanding of these challenges we face is alarmingly low. Corporations and consumers alike need to recognize that their choices can have significant consequences. Schools and civil society groups have a crucial role to play.[2]

Following up on the Secretary-General's remarks, the U.N. General Assembly declared 2005-2014 to be the *Decade of Education for Sustainable Development* to encourage national and international efforts on the matter (see Appendix 8.1.1).

To be sure, the world faces serious economic, social, and environmental problems that will require new solutions, new knowledge, and new, holistic ways of thinking—something collegiate institutions are best positioned to address. They have the focus, talent, and objectivity to evaluate sustainability issues of critical importance, and the credibility to help marshal public action on them. They are the ones who teach our decision-makers of tomorrow, the ones who must provide them with the information, tools, and skills essential in securing long-term well-being for all. That is the role of academic institutions—their moral imperative.

General Framework for Sustainability at Collegiate Institutions

Infusing sustainability into a college or university means infusing it into the institution's operations (buildings and grounds), products and services (research and education) as well as its student and community-outreach activities. This does not happen by simply wishing it so. Many obstacles must be overcome. As with companies, institutions of higher learning must find champions and leaders to move their organizations toward sustainability. In universities and colleges, champions are typically found among the faculty, although at few schools the president, chancellor, or other high-ranking administrator, a student activist, or a big financial donor has led the way. Regardless of where they come from, the champions and leaders must create a vision of what must be achieved and sell that vision to the movers and shakers of their organizations. But having a vision is meaningless without execution. That's where the real work begins. Schools must undertake the planning and build the operating, accountability, and reporting systems that will bring the vision to life. To perpetuate the initiative, the university must deploy, integrate, and align efforts across the organization, through its administration, faculty, staff, and student body. In that regard, the lessons of Chapter 8 are as germane to them as to a company that is trying to adopt a sustainability culture. The university, like a company, must incorporate sustainability considerations in its key decisionmaking, including purchasing and investment evaluations. Community outreach and other stakeholder engagement activities are important, too, since they generate the support of people who can make the institution successful. Such engagement also serves as a useful source of feedback on performance and priorities.

Fortunately, colleges and universities that seek sustainability have a wide range of support organizations to draw upon for advice and tools.

Such schools can also learn by studying the best SOS practices adopted by their fellow collegiate institutions. The encouraging news is that some of these institutions are well on the way to establishing comprehensive, well-integrated sustainability programs.

This chapter reviews the challenges and best SOS practices of collegiate sustainability initiatives and offers tips on how to sell the goal of sustainability to the school administration. Appendices 8.1, 8.2, and 8.3 present useful resources for those schools wanting to develop their own SOS programs. Appendix 8.1 identifies support organizations that can help. Appendix 8.2 lists sustainability-related codes that may be worth adopting. And Appendix 8.3 describes special assessment tools that have been used by universities to identify gaps in sustainability performance, to raise awareness about their sustainability-oriented risks and opportunities, and to pinpoint priorities for action. Readers should find that this chapter, when coupled with the lessons from other parts of this book, will provide a good review of the whys and hows of establishing a successful collegiate sustainability program.

The Challenges for Universities Seeking Sustainability

Visionaries who seek to align, deploy, and integrate sustainability across a collegiate setting will likely find the following institutional obstacles:

Creating a Multidisciplinary Approach

The first obstacle arises in attempting to build a strong multidisciplinary approach to teaching and research—something advocated in LA 21 under Chapter 36, *Education, Training, and Public Awareness*.[3] Such an approach is needed to overcome the complex, multidimensional problems standing in the way of sustainability. The trouble is, universities are organized by disciplines. Many of their grants and donations are earmarked for specific areas of study. Alumni are particularly interested in seeing their old departments highly rated since that enhances the status and value of their own education. School accrediting agencies reinforce traditional thinking, seeing no need to mandate cross-departmental courses on sustainability. Career advancement by faculty remains within disciplinary silos. The cultural bias reinforces these silos and discourages teamwork across them. Academics comfortable in their isolation may see little personal benefit to changing the status quo.

Because of the way universities work, a significant outside force may be required to prompt multidisciplinary action. An attractive research grant or alumni bequest demanding such collaboration can do the trick. Evidence that such cross-cutting programs are popular with students can also help. So can encouragement from governmental authorities and potential employers of graduates.

Granted, the move to integrated teaching must be done with balance. Specialization is required to reach the cutting edge of learning, and expertise by discipline must not be lost. But at the same time, disciplinary experts must become more team-oriented, and better grounded in how their specialty relates to others from the perspective of sustainability.

Creating a Multisector Approach

The second obstacle to instilling a sustainability mindset within academia comes in trying to implement sustainability programs across multiple sectors—operations, education, research, student activities, and community outreach. The idea is to identify initiatives that can serve more than one constituency for optimal benefit. If a program is to be created, why not make the most of it? Students can learn more about sustainable development if they are given hands-on experience in working with real-world issues. The university buildings and grounds department is one place to find such issues. What is more, operations staff, typically short on resources, can often use extra help. Both can join hands to address problems related to energy and water conservation, green buildings, biodiverse landscaping, on-campus violence, and binge drinking. Students can link with researchers on measures needed to bring about a sustainability culture within the institution. Community outreach efforts related to poor, elderly, or indigenous peoples can involve students and be incorporated into course work as well.

While much is to be gained from cross-sector initiatives, they require groups to adopt a new way of working. Administrative and operational staff may be reluctant to engage faculty and students in initiatives that the staff suspects will complicate decisionmaking, slow them down, impose extra costs or workloads, or otherwise be unreasonable. For this reason, faculty and students must be sensitive to the time, cost, and resource limitations of administrative and operations groups when designing a cross-sector program or crafting a sales approach for it. Advocates can lay a good foundation for these programs by finding a few enthusiastic, innovative, team-oriented participants from several sectors and bringing them together on a problem of great interest to all. Success there, followed by ample publicity and recognition from top management—subtly or overtly solicited if necessary—can encourage more cross-sector involvement later. For instance, students at the University of California at Berkeley started that school's comprehensive sustainability program by focusing on the campus recycling efforts. Operations personnel were keen to achieve the state-mandated recycling rate of 50% and pick up some recycling revenues in the process; students were anxious to promote recycling as part of their environmental ethic. By working together, the two groups forged relationships that made it easier to proceed to other sustainability programs. Their superb results also brought support from the school administration and faculty for further action on sustainability.[4]

Securing Funding

Money makes the world go round. As with the multidisciplinary approach, special funding pegged for multisector projects and programs can help. But funding is not always available. This is the third obstacle to pursuing sustainability at the collegiate level. In a 2001 survey commissioned by the National Wildlife Federation (NWF), over 1,100 presidents, provosts, and facilities chiefs at U.S. institutions of higher learning were asked to identify the key challenges to expanding their environmental programs. Nearly two-thirds of the respondents pointed to funding.[5]

Of course, finances are no problem if you can locate a generous, progressive benefactor interested in sustainability. The University of New Hampshire and University of British Columbia may have lessons to share in that regard: the former snared a $12 million endowment for its Sustainability Office; the latter arranged with its supplier, Fisher Scientific Canada, to annually fund committee-selected sustainability projects of up to $25,000, which benefit both sustainability and the university's scientific community—the main users of Fisher's products.[6] Unfortunately for most institutions, supporters like these are hard to find.

There are, of course, other funding alternatives. For example, at the suggestion of the vice president of Facilities at Harvard, the university established a $3 million interest-free revolving Green Campus Loan Fund for financing green projects. Under this program, projects with lower returns on investment can be funded if the total package of projects within a single submittal have a payback of five years or shorter. The program has exceeded expectations, producing an average annual return on investment of 40%, primarily through savings in costs for energy, water, waste management and disposal, and operation and maintenance.[7] At the Chapel Hill campus of the University of North Carolina, a student referendum was adopted accepting a $4 per semester increase in student fees, which raises approximately $200,000 annually to support the on-site installation of renewable energy technologies and the purchase of electricity from renewable resources. The school also used parking permit fees as a source of funding for fare-free mass transit on campus.[8]

Some national governments are stepping forward with modest financial support to help the cause. A few governments, such as those in Germany, the Netherlands, and the United Kingdom, have provided assistance to a wide range of organizations pushing sustainability in higher education.[9] In the United States, however, governmental support for such programs has been spotty at best. The states of Minnesota, New Jersey, Pennsylvania, and South Carolina each have provided small but significant funding for sustainability programs for higher education.[10] EPA issued a $250,000 grant to establish a sustainability program at Michigan State University, one of the largest university campuses in the country. The National Science Foundation funded a similar effort at Ithaca College in the state of New York. Four U.S. congressmen showed their support by introducing House Resolution 4664, the Higher Education Sustainability Act of 2004. If it had been enacted, this bill would have provided $50 million to create six demonstration centers of higher learning focusing on sustainability-oriented education, research, and outreach programs. Unfortunately, these examples are rare; the vast majority of national governments have taken little direct action to further the sustainability cause in universities and colleges.

Helpful Organizations

While most national governments haven't been particularly supportive, some other organizations have been. Many of them are listed in Figure 15.1 and profiled in Appendix 8.1. These networks can be useful sources for sustainability tools, benchmarking information, and advice for colleges and universities seeking their own sustainability programs.

Figure 15.1
Organizations That Can Help Universities Pursue Sustainability
(Appendix number for profile of each organization is noted below.)

8.1.1 Global Higher Education for Sustainability Partnership (UNESCO, ULSF, IAU, and COPERNICUS)	8.1.11 Technical University of Hamburg Consortium
	8.1.12 Alliance for Global Sustainability
8.1.2 U.S. Partnership for the Decade of Education for Sustainable Development (NCSE and ULSF)	8.1.13 U.K. Higher Education Partnership for Sustainability
	8.1.14 Philippines PATLEPAM
8.1.3 National Wildlife Federation's Campus Ecology® Group	8.1.15 Social Enterprise Knowledge Network
8.1.4 U.S. Environmental Protection Agency [or state counterpart]	8.1.16 New Jersey Higher Education Partnership for Sustainability
8.1.5 International Institute for Sustainable Development	8.1.17 Pennsylvania Consortium for Interdisciplinary Environmental Policy
8.1.6 Tertiary Education Facilities Management Association	
	8.1.18 Campus Consortium for Environmental Excellence
8.1.7 Oikos International	
8.1.8 Sierra Youth Coalition (SYC)	8.1.19 Associated Colleges of the South Environmental Initiative
8.1.9 Dutch CDHO	
8.1.10 Baltic University Program	8.1.20 South Carolina Sustainable Universities Initiative

Selling Sustainability to the Administration

To help ensure a collegiate sustainability program will be successful, advocates must convince school decisionmakers to support it. Such support is critical to securing the priority, funding, and personnel time needed to transform the institution in a permanent way. Indeed, prioritization, funding, and time were shown in two studies to be the biggest roadblocks to successful collegiate sustainability programs.[11] Given the importance of the discussions with upper management, some homework should be done. As with building a corporate program, the champion must begin by recruiting a core of solid supporters from diverse parts of the organization. One or more support organizations like those listed above may be able to provide helpful information and speakers. The presentation for management must then be carefully prepared, and presented by someone who is credible with the management team.

For starters, the presentation can explain sustainability and the SOS, and touch on many of the relevant sales points mentioned in Chapter 4. It can also speak to the special moral imperative of academic institutions to help others understand sustainability and the growing complexity of sustainability issues, such as those discussed in Appendix 1. LA 21, Chapter 36, and the U.N. Decade of Education for Sustainable Development can be cited to show that collegiate sustainability programs are being promoted at high levels. The presenter should explain how the drive for sustainability fits within the institution's own culture. The initiative should be couched not as a way to force new practices and thinking but rather as a new framework in which to empower and strengthen many existing programs. A point can be made about using an SOS to strategically position the school as an institution which both talks and walks along the ethical high ground—an argument that may have great appeal among school officials. These officials should also be sympathetic to points about regulatory compliance, and about cost savings through waste reduction, resource conservation, and accident prevention.[12] The benefit of strengthening community relations may resonate with management, too, especially if tensions have existed between the school and the surrounding community. The increasing interest of large corporate employers in sustainability can also be raised. In addition, advocates can relay any interest in sustainability topics that may have been expressed by students, government funders, and important private donors. Finally, the sales presentation can refer to the host of support organizations working on collegiate sustainability and cite some best sustainability practices at other schools to reinforce the academic and operational legitimacy of the initiative.

Best SOS Practices Among Collegiate Institutions

A wide range of best practices on various elements of an SOS can be found among colleges and universities.[13] Such practices exist in a number of elements, including: (1) structure and deployment; (2) personnel selection, development, and motivation; (3) policy and codes; (4) auditing; (5) planning; (6) sustainability programs within various sectors of university activity (campus operations, education, research, student activities, and community outreach); and (7) indicators and transparent reporting. These elements deserve a closer look.

Element 1: Structure and Deployment

Teams

To achieve sustainability objectives, a university must structure its organization to provide focus and accountability on these objectives and to facilitate their deployment down into the lower levels of the institution. But how can that be done so as to ingrain sustainability in the six key areas of concern: (1) curricula; (2) faculty development; (3) research; (4) operations; (5) student activities; and (6) community outreach? One way is to form six working teams—one around each area—with a small executive or steering committee providing oversight and coordination for all. The executive team can also help identify opportunities for inter-area collaboration, secure needed resources, and, if resources are short, decide priorities—or at least recommend them to management. It can also draft a master strategic plan on sustainability and monitor progress against it. For small schools, one or two working teams may handle it all. Regardless of school size, each working team should contain representatives from each relevant academic and administrative department and student group. Members of the various teams coming from the same department can also meet from time to time for further intradepartmental coordination across areas. External experts may be added to teams if desired. An executive director or other designated leader for sustainability can shepherd things along.

Other approaches can work, too. Ball State University of Muncie, Indiana, structured its sustainability planning around nine teams, each focusing on a provision of the Talloires Declaration (see Appendix 8.2.1). Each team was made up of faculty, students, operations personnel, and community representatives, as appropriate. A planning committee of two co-chairs and three support personnel oversaw and coordinated the work of the teams. A steering committee consisting of the planning committee and team chairs evaluated the team recommendations and selected 10 high-priority items for action. The Council on the Environment now oversees the implementation of the selected projects and serves as a clearinghouse for other sustainability initiatives. Council members, include people from each of the university's academic colleges and vice presidential areas, along with student and community representatives. The council meets once per month during the academic year.[14]

At the University of North Carolina at Chapel Hill, a cross-sector team, called the Sustainability Coalition, is organized into seven *task groups* focusing on: (1) academics; (2) business operations; (3) energy; (4) land and buildings; (5) transportation; (6) water; and (7) outreach, respectively. The coalition's job is to promote sustainability practices across the organization. The Sustainability Advisory Committee, which reports to the Vice Chancellor for Finance and Administration, guides the initiative from a strategic level. The committee is composed of high-level decisionmakers who broadly represent all constituencies in both the operations and academic sides of the institution. The purpose of this group is to recommend and provide management support for long-term sustainability goals and the strategies for implementing them.[15]

Unity College, a 600-student institution in Maine, formed a sustainability committee of faculty, staff, and students to prepare a sustainability plan for the school. The committee evaluated sustainability in its educational programs and named subcommittees to study four areas: (1) grounds; (2) food service; (3) energy and transportation; and (4) materials and purchasing.[16]

The University of Florida took a different approach, establishing a single multi-stakeholder task force for developing recommendations on how the university can become a recognized global leader on sustainability. The task force was staffed with faculty and student representatives; the vice presidents for public relations, finance, and administration; and the county director of community support services.[17] To guide its sustainability programs, Michigan State University created a University Committee for a Sustainable Campus with members drawn from operations, relevant student groups, and each of its colleges.[18] Similar teams also exist at Middlesex, Newcastle, and Queen's Universities in the United Kingdom; the University of British Columbia in Canada; and Harvard University and the University of California at Berkeley and Santa Barbara in the United States.[19]

Leaders, Staff, and Student Coordinators

A study of nine schools within the U.K. Higher Education Partnership for Sustainability (HEPS) program (see Appendix 8.1.13) identified several criteria for team success:

1. The team is actively chaired by a high-level administrator of the school, such as the vice chancellor or pro vice chancellor.
2. The team reports directly to the vice chancellor or senior management team.
3. The team is formally charged with planning and monitoring progress against a sustainability policy.
4. Progress is frequently and widely communicated.
5. Members of the team include senior representatives from the central planning office; grounds; and maintenance; purchasing and finance; human resources; marketing or press office; academic planning; and career services. Other members include the deans of key departments, student body leaders, and community representatives (governments, NGOs, and others).[20]

Top-level support of the type suggested by criteria 1 and 2 is a critical element identified in other studies, as well. According to an Australian survey of 52 universities from around the world, the lack of executive commitment was identified as one of the key obstacles to progress on sustainability. Others were the absence of a policy and, as previously noted, the shortage of funding.[21] Another study found that the universities most successful in implementing the Halifax Declaration (Appendix 8.2.2), a sustainability code for academic institutions, were those that enjoyed the full support of their president and had designated someone to oversee implementation.[22]

The importance of identifying someone to oversee implementation of collegiate sustainability programs should not be underestimated. Many programs jump off to a good start with the help of enthusiastic volunteers only to fail later because the volunteers leave the school or are diverted to other matters. By naming contacts with formal responsibility who are compensated by the school, the initiative can be institutionalized and momentum maintained. Sustainability coordinators have been named to manage programs at the University of Aberdeen, Liverpool John Moores University, and Sheffield Hallam University in the United Kingdom. They've also been established in the United States at Ball State, Brown, Carlton College, Emory, Portland State, Providence, Tulane, the University of Illinois at Champaign-Urbana, the University of Texas at Houston, Yale, and a few other schools. Michigan State has an Office of Campus Sustainability and the Universities of Florida, New Hampshire, and North Carolina at Chapel Hill have similar departments. Some collegiate sustainability departments consist only of one or two paid staff, but a few universities with strong, more sophisticated programs have more.

Harvard's Green Campus Initiative (HGCI), funded primarily through savings realized from eco-efficiency projects, includes a director and nine staff members drawn from various areas, such as building management, computer management, finance and administration, and communications. It is co-chaired by a faculty member from the School of Public Health, and by the associate vice president for Facilities and Environmental Services. The director of the HGCI also serves on the Sustainability Advisory Committee, a team of faculty, student, and administrative representatives that counsels on sustainability policy, planning, and progress measurement. A Green Campus Steering Group, consisting of the HGCI director and co-chairs as well as the director of EHS, meets frequently to help coordinate efforts and counsel HGCI staff.[23]

The Campus Sustainability Office at the University of British Columbia houses a director, energy manager, and communications manager, as well as a part-time strategy manager and support staff. The office is guided by a Sustainability Advisory Committee of faculty, student, and operations representatives. Approximately 130 "sustainability coordinators" each volunteer two to four hours per month to assist the Sustainability Office with communications, training, and other deployment of programs among the school's 300 departments. Student volunteers extend the program further, committing two to three hours a week to serve as "residence sustainability coordinators" at undergraduate student residence halls.[24]

The University of California at Berkeley has a similar network of students, called "residential recycling education coordinators." The university's operations group, student government, and housing departments jointly fund two students who identify, oversee, and train these coordinators.[25] The University of Melbourne and RMIT in Australia also provide part-time compensation for their student representatives.

While some higher education institutions have full-time sustainability directors or coordinators, many more have staff in other sustainability-related positions. A 2001 survey of 891 U.S. colleges and universities conducted for the NWF's Campus Ecology® Program found that 51% had recycling coordinators; 36%, energy conservation coordinators; 21%, environmental managers; and 7%, green purchasing coordinators.[26] The Australian survey cited earlier revealed that over one-half of the reporting institutions had a sustainability or environmental coordinator, the same amount that said they had an energy officer. Slightly less than half reported employing a director of sustainability or dean of environmental programs; however, no green purchasing coordinators were identified.[27] Some universities also have community relations officers, transportation coordinators, health and safety managers, sustainability research coordinators, and academic managers for sustainability curriculums. Those who are successful in these roles communicate plans and results clearly, involve others across the organization, and foster top-management support.

Element 2: Personnel Selection, Development, and Motivation

Academic organizations, like others, are only as good as the people in them. If an organization wants to enhance its chances of meeting some goal, it must coax the right people to join the effort, and ensure that they are properly trained and developed. But that is not all. It must motivate these people so they will do their best and stay involved. This is certainly true when the goal is infusing sustainability across an institution.

Selection Criteria

Selecting the right people at a university entails several objectives. It means hiring faculty and staff and accepting students who have the necessary education, skills, and experience required of the position. Granted, experience in a sustainability endeavor cannot compensate for a lack of required academic credentials; nevertheless, it should be an important selection factor. Such experience is often a sign of self-motivation, teamwork, and good citizenship—characteristics prized by any recruiter. Unfortunately, only one in five schools reporting in the Australian survey said they used a staff member's contribution to sustainability as a criterion in decisions involving hiring, tenure, and promotion.[28]

Selecting the right people also means picking those who possess values consistent with the culture the school wants to foster. These values would include, among others, accepting people of different backgrounds, embracing new ideas, and respecting the environment. Individuals with values and experiences that align with these and other sustainability-oriented attitudes can certainly make a difference for the school: approximately one-half of the U.S. schools in the NWF survey said that student, faculty, or staff interest had a role in encouraging the campus to implement environmental programs.[29]

Finally, selecting the right people means ensuring those who are chosen reflect a diverse mix of individuals across the organization. Campus diversity by gender, race, religion, ethnicity, age, sexual orientation, and physical ability is a positive force that encourages people to look at the world with new eyes. It enriches the non-classroom side of campus learning. Various studies reveal that students who interact with a diverse group of peers show greater growth in critical-thinking skills and greater satisfaction with their college experience. They are also more likely to stay enrolled in school and seek graduate or professional degrees.[30] Moreover, diversity is a catalyst for innovation and multifaceted thinking—the very things needed for sustainability solutions.

As mentioned in Chapter 2, diversity-oriented, nondiscriminatory hiring and promotion practices are essential for showing respect for others—practices at the core of sustainability. Yet few universities and colleges cover these topics on their sustainability website or in their sustainability reports. Most focus on environmental and community outreach activities, but not social issues like this. One institution that did openly discuss and address these topics is the University of Florida. In its 2002 *Sustainability Task Force Report*, it put forth the following goals and recommendations for implementing them:

Goals

> The University of Florida should set aggressive hiring and retention goals to ensure the University reflects society's racial, ethnic, and gender diversity. The University should also strive to ensure that all personnel are rewarded with at least a living wage with benefits appropriate to a world-class institution.

Recommendations

> 1. Require all academic and administrative units to develop student recruitment and faculty and staff hiring and retention policies that will bring the University of Florida to a position where its students, faculty, and staff reflect the State of Florida's racial, ethnic, and gender diversity.
> 2. Increase the levels of gender and equity training of all personnel working at or hired by the University of Florida.
> 3. Ensure that a minimum of a living wage with good benefits is paid to all University employees.
> 4. Engage University faculty and staff in decision-making and formalize this process.

5. Increase the level of investment in the training of University employees.
6. Take steps to improve campus climate by increasing the campus' exposure to diverse groups.[31]

Notwithstanding the U.S. debate about racial quotas on incoming students, institutions of higher learning that want to embrace the full spirit of sustainability cannot ignore this example. To do their part, the University of Miami created a Multicultural Student Affairs Office, and the University of Central Florida, an Office of Diversity Initiatives. The president of Emory University near Atlanta, Georgia, established a Commission on the Status of Minorities, a forum for recommending and supporting programs to improve the representation, development, and success of minority people at the school.[32] The University of Newcastle in Australia and the University of Victoria in Canada addressed diversity concerns directly in their institutionwide strategic plans.

Orientation; Introductory Workshops

Once people with the right skills, values, and diversity are on board, they must be developed so they can contribute to the sustainability effort. This is typically done by giving them appropriate training and learning experiences. Incorporating sustainability into orientation would seem an easy way to introduce students and new hires to the topic. However, only about one in eight U.S. schools indicated in the NWF study that they offered students, faculty, and staff orientation sessions related to their campus environmental programs. (As previously noted, the Australian survey showed somewhat better results, with slightly over one in four schools reporting sustainability orientation courses for students.)[33] More institutions had faculty development programs on environmental issues: half the schools questioned by the NWF and just under 40% of those covered in the Australian study said they provided them.[34] These programs may take the form of special workshops like those on environmental sustainability provided to instructors at Northern Arizona University. To help ensure good participation in an introductory workshop of this type, representatives of the group targeted for training should be engaged as much as possible in planning and presenting it. Without participant involvement and buy-in, turnout can be disappointing.

Research and Mentoring Programs

The development of faculty—as well as staff and students—may also be accomplished through participation in research teams on sustainability topics. Although more time-consuming than simple training, this hands-on learning can be highly effective. Students may benefit from mentoring programs, too. An innovative three-way mentoring arrangement is offered at the University of British Columbia. Its Sustainable Leaders Program matches any freshman interested in sustainability with a fourth-year student active in the field, and connects them with an outside professional practitioner.[35]

Motivational Techniques

Developmental learning for campus personnel is a never-ending process. So is motivating them to stay involved in sustainability initiatives. Without motivation, people lose interest, programs wither and die. Attention to sustainability must itself be sustainable. Motivating faculty and staff is in many respects similar to motivating company employees. As noted in Chapter 9, it turns on accountability, recognition, and caring. Of course, it's nice for faculty and staff to receive awards and write-ups for their contributions to sustainability, but if their activities are in addition to their current responsibilities and are not compensated, there may well be problems. One must not forget that these employees have bills to pay and families to support, and the pressures of money and time can be overwhelming. If the university is undergoing a budget cutback and employment is being trimmed, the intensity of these pressures can be compounded. Unfortunately, only one in six U.S. schools told the NWF that they held campus units accountable for environmental performance through incentives or penalties, or were planning to do so. One in eight said they did, or were intending to, formally evaluate or recognize how faculty have integrated environmental topics into their courses.[36]

Certainly more needs to be done to spur action toward sustainability on campus. Operations and academic managers can do much to create a climate for action by working with their subordinates to set clear expectations and performance goals and by regularly providing them fair and candid feedback. One expectation on campus should be that behavior aligns with the organization's sustainability policy. The City University in the United Kingdom does this by referring to its policy in the job description for each new position. Universities that really want to show sustainability is a priority will need to do what is done with any other highly valued area of study: reflect that priority in seeking grants and making budgetary decisions.

Motivating students can be more challenging since they are the "paying customers." Academic credits with good grades are the products they seek. Still, some will feel rewarded with internships, part-time jobs, or positions of leadership. And there are other less formal ways to stimulate a student's desire to excel, such as by openly recognizing their accomplishment, valuing their teamwork, or appreciating their altruism. Often it is enough that students see they can be a force for positive change. But when it comes to voluntary activities or service-learning opportunities for those who are less passionate, these people, too, may succumb to pressures of limited money and time. Those who design sustainability programs for students need to bear that in mind. Special funding for students can help. Modest student grants for environmental sustainability projects are available through the Campus Ecology Fellowship Program of the NWF. On-campus internships can sometimes be funded by corporations, as BC Hydro did at the University of British Columbia. The University of New Hampshire, Harvard, and others schools hire student interns for their own sustainability programs.

A number of rewards have been established to encourage excellence in sustainability performance in colleges and universities. The Australian National University created the Annual Environmental Achievement Award for the individual or group that has excelled in environmental management. Ball State University's Council on the Environment (COTE)—the benchmark institution regarding recognition—annually presents several types of sustainability awards. Their Green Initiative Awards are given to people who lead individual events or engage in other discrete everyday activities that move the university toward sustainability. Their Exemplar Awards recognize individuals or groups with significant accomplishments in promoting sustainability and environmental protection. The COTE Presidential Liaison's Award is presented for outstanding and continuing contribution in those areas.[37]

Awards from outside organizations can also be used to encourage university sustainability efforts. The Dutch Ministry of Education and the Ministry of Housing Spatial Planning and the Environment present a prize every two years to the institution of higher learning that has most successfully integrated sustainability into its activities. The NWF recognizes a number of campuses each year which have done exceptional work in demonstrating environmentally sustainable practices.

Element 3: Policy and Codes

Effective, efficient collegiate sustainability programs, like corporate ones, depend upon marshalling the right resources to address priorities planned around clear principles. Ideally, visionary principles would be identified first and endorsed by top management. Next would follow, in hierarchical order, strategic planning and then the tactical planning of projects and actions. In the real world, though, broad sustainability programs may evolve from the bottom up. They may start with a proclamation or noteworthy project pressed by some passionate faculty or student champion, which eventually catches the eye and imagination of management. At the University of Michigan a sustainability policy endorsed by student-body resolution played a prominent role in moving their programs forward.[38] At the University of North Carolina at Chapel Hill a similar resolution by the Faculty Council had the same effect.[39]

The Harvard program began not with a sustainability resolution or policy, but with a focus on waste reduction and resource conservation. These measures delivered attractive economic savings and built a foundation of broad-based support. Only later did the idea of developing a university-wide sustainability policy emerge, and that policy was clearly slanted toward the environment. Michigan is undertaking a similar strategy: it is focusing its management and reporting efforts on eight environmental indicators, with a plan to look at social indicators later.[40] Over time, as the concept of sustainability becomes better understood at Harvard and Michigan, their attention will likely shift to other aspects of sustainability—initiatives where the payback is more in risk-control, reputation, and ethics than in bottom-line savings. This step-by-step progression is not a bad thing. It's certainly better than adopting a broad sustainability policy only to find little institutional will or resources to implement it. Eventually, however, the target of all those efforts—the overall marching orders of the organization—must be defined in a policy, vision, or other statement. This is the document that will foster understanding and commitment from those who are helping make the university sustainable, the vision around which they will align their plans, goals, and tasks.

Institutions of higher learning that want to draft their own sustain-ability policy can obtain ideas from the Harvard policy, the North Carolina or Michigan resolutions, and the policies and resolutions of other universities.[41] The IISD maintains a website listing various colle-giate policies on sustainable development and the environment.[42] UNESCO, COPERNICUS, ULSF, IAU, and the collaborative regional groups profiled in Appendix 8.1 can also provide guidance and exam-ples. The model corporate sustainability policy presented in Figure 2.2 may help, too, if one considers the "products" of concern to be educa-tion and research, and the key stakeholders to include staff, faculty, stu-dents, funders, governments, and accreditation bodies. Ideally, the pol-icy should cover all dimensions of a collegiate program: curricula, fac-ulty development, research, operations, student activities, and commu-nity outreach.

Colleges and universities can also evaluate various external codes on sustainability, either as a source of ideas for their own policy or for con-sideration for endorsement. Over the years, several conferences of uni-versity representatives produced internationally recognized codes or, to be more accurate, "declarations" that defined the vision for sustainable development in higher education. Some of the more important docu-ments of this type are listed in Figure 15.2 and summarized in Appendix 8.2. The guidance presented in Chapter 4 for selecting codes applicable to business can also be used to evaluate these codes for possible endorse-ment. The advantages of endorsement in terms of reputation, peer sup-port, networking, and benchmarking may warrant a school to adopt one or more of these declarations even if they already have their own sustain-ability policy.

Figure 15.2 **Sustainability-Related Codes for Collegiate Institutions** (Appendix number for summary of each code is noted below.)	
8.2.1 Talloires Declaration (1990) 8.2.2 Halifax Declaration (1991) 8.2.3 Swansea Declaration (1993) 8.2.4 COPERNICUS Charter (1993) 8.2.5 Kyoto Declaration(1993) 8.2.6 Blueprint for a Green Campus (1994) 8.2.7 The Essex Report (1995)	8.2.8 Dutch Charter for Sustainable Development in Vocational Training (Higher Professional Education) (1999) 8.2.9 Lüneburg Declaration (2001) 8.2.10 Ubuntu Declaration (September 2002)

Element 4: Auditing

After the vision has been spelled out in an internal policy or external code endorsed by senior management, an assessment should be conducted to identify the gaps between that vision and the status quo. On the other hand, if it has been difficult convincing university authorities to adopt a vision, then an audit against best practices may be just the tool to persuade them that action is needed and that a vision should be articulated to guide the way. This is precisely what Penn State did. It jump-started its sustainability program with an extensive assessment led by a group of students, faculty, and staff which identified significant gaps in performance. With the audit report as a backdrop, the group drafted a sustainability policy or "ecological mission." The draft was circulated to 150 university leaders for input and finally shaped into a document that was unanimously adopted by the Faculty Council and signed by the university president. Next, a single, high-profile building on campus was selected for a detailed evaluation showing how its ecological footprint could be reduced while saving money. Finally, a series of short policy papers were drafted, routed for comment, and adopted, thus extending across the campus the lessons and practices derived from the building study. In this methodical way, the beginnings of an environmental sustainability culture were institutionalized at the school.[43]

Once a university decides to conduct an audit, it has a wide range of techniques to draw from. Formal internal or third-party audits of the type discussed in Chapter 9 may be conducted to evaluate operations with respect to compliance with legal and policy requirements, management system standards, and good risk management practices. If improvements in productivity are desired, waste, energy, and accident-reduction opportunities may be studied. Audit tools and processes used for business organizations can be readily adapted for this purpose with some adjustments for special issues such as campus transportation. Nearly half of the 63 international universities and colleges covered in the 2001 Australian survey reported that they conducted environmental audits. One in 10 was certified to the ISO 14001 EMS.[44]

But sustainability performance is not just about the environmental conditions of university operations. Fortunately, some assessment tools and processes can be used for evaluating collegiate institutions against a broader range of sustainability criteria, going beyond operations to consider education and research as well. Some of the more noteworthy tools for evaluating collegiate sustainability programs are listed in Figure 15.3 and summarized in Appendix 8.3.

Figure 15.3
Sustainability Assessment Tools for Collegiate Institutions
(Appendix number for overview of each tool is noted below.)

8.3.1 U.K.—EcoCampus	8.3.8 U.K. HEPS Reporting for Sustainability Guidance for Higher Education Institutions
8.3.2 ULSF's Sustainability Assessment Questionnaire	
8.3.3 Dutch Auditing Instrument for Sustainability in Higher Education	8.3.9 C2E2 Environmental Management System Self-Assessment Checklist
8.3.4 The Campus Sustainability Assessment Project	8.3.10 Campus Ecology Environmental Audit
8.3.5 NJHEPS Campus Sustainability: Selected Indicators Snapshot and Guide	8.3.11 The Ecological Footprint Analysis of Colorado College
8.3.6 Good Company's Sustainability Pathways Toolkit	8.3.12 EPA's 20 Questions for College and University Presidents
8.3.7 UCSB Campus Sustainability Assessment Protocol	

The selection of the audit tool to be used in a given situation will be based on a number of factors. The scope and objectives of the audit are two important considerations. A sophisticated audit of legal compliance and systems will demand a different tool than a review to provide a pre-liminary grasp of major issues. The time and money available for the re-view will dictate its detail and depth, which in turn should favor some types of tools over others. The qualifications of the auditor may make a difference, too, since some tools can only be effectively used by someone with considerable knowledge and experience. Finally, tool selection should be based in part on the degree of support and cooperation to be ex-pected from the audited entity. This is because some approaches require an extensive collection and explanation of data and therefore are only ap-propriate where this cooperation can be assured.

Element 5: Planning

After the current status is assessed against policy objectives, then strate-gic and tactical plans should be developed for closing the gaps. The plans can be organized in a variety of ways. The University of Florida's draft plan, consisting of broad strategic goals and detailed tactical recommen-dations to management, was framed around seven elements:

1. Campus operations (land management and biodiversity, buildings, energy and resource use, waste management, procurement, and investments)
2. Education
3. Research
4. Community outreach and integration
5. Campus community personnel (faculty, staff, and students)
6. Organizational policies and practices
7. Implementation[45]

The University of Michigan structured its plan around four elements: (1) guiding principles; (2) education and research; (3) administrative items; and (4) physical operations. Thirty recommended actions were presented, with eight identified as high priority. The plan was laid out in tabular form, showing the significance, benefits, implementing person-nel, and benchmark/reference institutions for each suggested action.[46] The sustainability plan for Unity College contained goals developed by each of its four planning subcommittees. Its plan also details specific ac-tions for implementing each goal, and names the people responsible for carrying them out. In addition, it includes a proposal for student-learning programs involving community service.[47]

Ball State University's Green Steering Committee used a modified *Delphi process* (see discussion of this process in Chapter 6) to identify 10 priority action items from the 186 items suggested by 9 working teams. Over the past few years, the university has been annually reporting on progress against the first 10 action items as well as a second tier of 10.[48] Ball State's sustainability initiatives were referenced generally in the universitywide strategic plan for 2001-2006, helping ensure the integration and alignment necessary for effective implementation. Eight of the U.K. HEPS universities and colleges have done the same.[49]

The schoolwide strategic plan for the University of Victoria in Canada specifically addresses sustainability issues. It contains text on assuring procedures are fair and equitable, promoting sustainability in planning and operations, and engaging the community through service programs. It also expressly supports equal opportunity and diversity among students and faculty, underscoring that commitment with a specific goal to increase the number of aboriginal graduates. The sustainability aspects of buildings, grounds, and transportation are addressed more specifically in the school's campus plan.[50]

The University of British Columbia's sustainable development strategy, called *Inspirations and Aspirations*, was drafted after stakeholder consultation with 20 departments, all of the faculties, and all major student organizations. The plan has nine key objectives organized around people, place, and process as follows:

Place
• Reduce pollution: air, water, and land
• Conserve resources: use energy, water, and materials wisely and efficiently
• Protect ecosystems: limit the impact on natural systems

People
• Improve health and safety: enhance quality of life
• Develop a vibrant community: enable everyone to achieve their highest potential
• Promote learning in the community: interact with Canada, Vancouver, and the world

Process
• Ensure economic viability: secure the financial resources to fund our vision
• Promote an open, inclusive model: keep stakeholders aware

of, and participating in, the university's sustainability plans
• Champion progress: develop an infrastructure that promotes
and embodies sustainability

The University of British Columbia's planning documents lists individual projects and other initiatives for each of the nine objectives.[51]

Regardless of how the sustainability plan is developed, its success will depend upon top management support and appropriate resources. Sound integration, alignment, and deployment of the type discussed in Chapter 8 will also be needed. But even with all of that, a collegiate sustainability program can still wither and die if the sustainability planning is viewed as a one-time exercise. Periodic reassessments and plan adjustments are essential to keep the program current, alive, and moving forward.

Element 6: Sustainability Programs Within Various Sectors of University Activity

Ultimately, a collegiate SOS and associated sustainability initiatives must be integrated into and implemented by various sectors of school activity. These activities can be categorized as campus operations, education, research, student activities, and community outreach activities. Below is a review of how a number of colleges and universities have addressed sustainability within these sectors of activity.

Campus Operations Sector

Operations—the support activities for the development and use of campus grounds and buildings—is typically the first focus of academic sustainability initiatives. Universities, like businesses, have seen the environmental aspects of their operations come under closer scrutiny by both regulators and the public. Many now realize that the reduction of energy use, resource consumption, and wastes in many cases translates into an attractive reduction in costs. The NWF survey of U.S. colleges and universities found the following percentages of respondents had at least some operational activities or goals concerning these environmental activities[52]:

Solid waste recycling	85%
Energy conservation	81
Water conservation	72
Environmental performance in building design	64
Environmental landscaping program	60
Goal on reducing solid waste disposal	56

Purchasing environmentally preferable goods	47
Reducing pollution	44
Making environmentally responsible investments	29
Managing transportation demand	24
Purchasing organic food	9

Recycling

Recycling remains the most popular campus environmental initiative—a finding by NWF that mirrors that from the Australian survey.[53] Roughly four out of five U.S. schools questioned by the NWF reported recycling aluminum containers and paper. Approximately half had recycling programs for glass, plastic, and construction materials. One-half also said they composted or mulched food scraps or landscape trimmings. Twenty-two U.S. colleges and universities reported they recycled 60% or more of their municipal waste.

Energy Conservation

As the NWF survey shows, energy conservation has been of significant and growing interest at universities and colleges. This has been due in part to the rising costs and usage of fossil fuels and electricity, and in part to the growing concern about the climate change effects of burning carbon-based fuels. (See Appendix 1.15 for a discussion on climate change.) These concerns—and tireless lobbying by student activists—led the Board of Regents and president of the University of California to adopt a policy and guidelines on clean energy and green buildings. These documents call for the university's 10 campuses to:

- surpass state-mandated energy-efficiency standards by 20% in all new construction;
- increase energy efficiency in existing buildings by 10% over the next decade:
- support use of on-site renewable energy to fulfill 10 megawatts of its energy demand;
- begin purchasing 10% of their energy from renewable resources, escalating to 20% by 2017; and
- erect buildings which are LEED-certified or equivalent.[54]

To encourage other higher learning institutions to take similar action, Greenpeace published *Greenpeace Clean Energy Now! Campus Guide: How to Stop Global Warming by Making Your Campus a Leader in Clean*

Energy. It's a toolkit of practical suggestions and useful references and forms for students who want to introduce energy/climate change programs at their schools.[55]

Several strategies have been used by universities to cut energy usage. According to the NWF study, upgrades in lighting and heating, ventilation, and air conditioning systems have been the most common actions. About half of the surveyed schools said they also developed energy-efficiency codes for new or existing buildings and used life-cycle analyses for evaluating energy projects.

Savings From Resource Conservation Projects

The NWF survey found that water conservation, like energy conservation, was accomplished primarily through system and equipment upgrades. The financial and environmental returns on both types of conservation projects can be quite attractive.[56] Portland State University in Oregon is expected to chop $275,000 a year from its water, energy, and green building projects.[57] By installing more efficient lighting systems, windows, fan and pump motors, and other equipment, the University of Vermont avoided 16 million kilowatt hours of electricity use in 2002. These measures saved $1.6 million and cut CO_2 emissions by 6,700 tons, the equivalent of taking 15,000 cars off the road.[58] The University of British Columbia's *EcoTrek* program, which involves the installation of water-conserving fixtures and the upgrade of lighting and heating systems, will save the university $2.5 million (Canadian) annually, cutting water use 30%, energy use 20%, and carbon emissions by 15,000 tons per year. This is in addition to the $5.4 million (Canadian) in energy costs it already recouped through energy conservation since 1998.[59] The University of Michigan cut its annual electricity usage by 25 million kilowatt hours—enough to power 1,600 average-size homes—and is saving nearly $10 million per year because of its energy conservation efforts.[60] Penn State found it could save 70 acres of trees, cut waste by 45 tons, and trim more than $120,000 per year from its paper costs by merely changing the default margin settings on university's word-processing software.[61]

Transportation Issues

Traffic congestion, space constraints on parking, and climate change and other air pollution have prompted a number of universities to reduce the environmental and social impacts of campus transportation. The University of Michigan has done this by acquiring a fleet of more than 500 vehicles operating on biodiesel fuel, ethanol, or electricity.[62] One in five schools surveyed by the NWF said they offered free or discounted bus passes to students, faculty, and staff. One in six had carpooling programs; one in eight offered incentives not to drive alone, and a like number provided bicycle paths. Sixty percent furnished bike racks.

Landscaping

Another aspect of university operations that affects sustainability is landscaping and other grounds work. The most popular environmental landscaping programs reported in the NWF study were integrated pest management and the use of native plants. About one-third of the survey respondents had programs to create food and shelter for wildlife, restore habitat, or remove invasive exotic species.

Green Purchasing

University programs on green purchasing and environmentally responsible investing are not nearly as common as other operational green programs, according to the NWF report. But U.S. universities are not the only academic institutions with large gaps in these areas. The Australian survey revealed the incidence of these programs to be even rarer among international schools. A notable exception was the purchase of organic foods, which was found to be four times more prevalent than reported for U.S. schools in the NWF study.[63]

Even so, a few universities have superb purchasing and investing initiatives. Leeds Metropolitan University in the United Kingdom is a long-time leader in environmentally preferable purchasing (EPP), having adopted a formal policy on it in 1993. The school published a *Green Purchasing Guide*, which contains background information, recommends certain products, and offers suggestions on how to select them. Leeds employs purchasing and environmental staff who incorporate environmental provisions into bid (tender) specifications and otherwise handle procurements.[64]

Rutgers University in New Jersey, like Leeds, uses EPP specifications and guidelines. It is well known for its EPP programs, and is frequently featured at conferences. The school has been assertive with its suppliers, pressing them to minimize and remove waste associated with their products, thus reducing the university's burden and costs. It mandated that waste contractors place educational advertisements in campus publications and routinely update the school on the latest industry trends, products, and recycling markets. Besides building an extensive EPP website, the university is also developing a green procurement training program for other schools, and a laboratory that can assess the environmental characteristics of products.[65]

Another type of contracting—the licensing of companies to produce items bearing school logos—also raises sustainability concerns. As noted in Appendices 2.3.8 and 2.3.9, over several hundred colleges and universities have committed to require their licensees to produce goods according to the workplace codes of conduct of the Fair Labor Association or Worker Rights Consortium. In contrast, most universities have not seemed too concerned about workplace codes or other social considerations when selecting vendors for their regular supplies and services. That situation is likely to change, however. The implications of university business on human rights is not an issue that will go unnoticed forever by NGOs and activist students.

Noteworthy programs also exist on the ethical investment of university endowments and pension funds. Columbia University in New York appointed an Advisory Committee on Socially Responsible Investing to advise the school trustees on this matter.[66] Duke University adopted SRI guidelines. Its students and those at Stanford, Yale, and other U.S. institutions of higher learning have lobbied their administrations, demanding disclosure of environmental and social impacts of university hedge fund investments—investments not subject to U.S. Securities and Exchange Commission rules on public disclosure.[67] FairPensions (formerly Ethics for USS), a university staff campaign with 4,000 supporters, promotes the ethical investment of the £19 billion ($36.8087 billion) (in pension funds in the U.K. Universities Superannuation Scheme (USS). As a result of FairPensions' efforts, USS adopted a "socially responsible and sustainable" investment policy, and hired a small staff to implement it and regularly report results. FairPensions has also taken shareholder action on issues such as climate change, pollution, large socially disruptive development projects, and access to vital medicines.[68]

Education Sector. Ideally, there are seven steps for incorporating sustainability into a university curriculum:

1. Identify and publicize the sustainability-related courses and degrees already in the curriculum.
2. Establish a network of academics who are interested in bringing sustainability to coursework in a more meaningful way, and work with them to achieve the following steps.
3. Integrate sustainability aspects into existing courses.
4. Work with communities, campus operations, businesses and others to establish "service-learning," internship, and other experiential courses.
5. Assess needs and create new academic degrees on sustainability.
6. Add sustainability to student orientation, and mandate certain sustainability coursework for all students.
7. Create opportunities for others outside the campus to learn about sustainability.

Let us examine each of these steps in more detail.

Step 1. Inventory and Publicize Courses. A first cut at identifying courses can be accomplished by doing an Internet search of university class listings for words such as "sustainability," "sustainable," "development," "globalization," "justice," "social," "community," "population," "peace," "women," "minority," "ecology," "biodiversity," "nature," "conservation," "environment," and "environmental." Courses on topics listed in Figures 2.4 and 2.5 are also worth considering. An exercise of this type by Michigan State University disclosed 287 classes related to sustainability.[69] According to the Australian survey, two-thirds of the responding schools had sustainability-related courses, a result that may have been higher if the survey had focused on more than just the environmental aspects.[70] Figure 15.4 shows the findings of the NWF study concerning the percentages of U.S. colleges and universities offering courses with environmental content in various departments.

Figure 15.4
Percentages of U.S. Colleges and Universities Offering Courses
With Environmental Content in Various Departments—2001[71]

Biology	68	Anthropology	15
Chemistry	47	History	14
Political science or sociology	33	Engineering (excluding	
Business or economics	25	environmental engineering)	
Philosophy or religion	22	or computer science	12
Literature	19	Education	11
		Communication or journalism	6

While the NWF study was undertaken in 2001, anecdotal evidence suggests that many of the issues it highlights still remain. A concern raised by the study was the lack of environmental content (let alone social content) in the coursework of future engineers and teachers—one group that is critical to designing sustainable solutions and the other, to bringing sustainable thinking to new generations. Clearly great change is needed here. Your own inventory may prove equally enlightening. Once it is prepared and edited, it can be posted under a sustainability umbrella and publicized among faculty, students, and management. But why do this? What does it change? Doesn't it just cast sustainability as all things to all people? While there may be some initial downsides to conducting this inventory, in the end it will help campus people understand the multifaceted aspects of sustainability and serve as a baseline for measuring progress to even more meaningful change.

Step 2. Establish Internal Network. The first place to recruit potential candidates for the network is among those who teach the courses on the sustainability list. Once formed, the network should open lines of communication with interested members of the school administration and student sustainability organizations. An early agenda item for the network is to inform members about the resources available from the Association of University Leaders for a Sustainable Future (ULSF) and other organizations listed in Appendix 8.1. If possible, a website with appropriate links to other useful sites should be established for reference. One with good links is that of the University of Technology, Sydney (UTS) in Australia.[72] To accelerate progress further, the school can follow the lead of UTS and Portland

State University by hiring an academic manager of sustainability teaching.[73] In any event, a network leader should be selected, and goals of the group clarified.

Step 3. Modify Course Content. After studying the issue, network members should meet with the university administration to discuss the meaning of sustainability and why it should be infused into the curriculum. Once any necessary management concurrence is obtained, network members can contact other faculty to orient them to the objective and consider how best to accomplish it. Funding can help move things along. At Ithaca College, $1,000 faculty grants were awarded to induce the integration of sustainability content into courses on history, philosophy, writing, recreation, management, biology, and physics.[74] Northern Arizona University established an interdisciplinary team, called the Ponderosa Group, to incorporate environmental sustainability into courses. Participants attend an intensive three-day training workshop to learn about the topic, and then put their knowledge to use in revising course content and syllabi. These efforts produced impressive results—as of 2006, the university had 31 departments that collectively offered 262 undergraduate courses, 116 liberal studies courses, and 97 graduate courses with an environmental orientation.[75] Examples like those developed by the Ponderosa Group can be persuasive, especially if the classes have proven highly successful. ULSF, the Baltic University Program, and other support organizations can provide information on how sustainability has been incorporated into other classes. Professional, trade, and regulatory groups may also assist with academic content. For instance, the Advertising Standards Authority in the United Kingdom has developed a training presentation on social responsibility for college marketing classes.[76]

The Sustainability Curriculum Framework prepared by the Boston-based NGO, Second Nature, presents a short, useful outline of the following seven critical sustainability themes to integrate into coursework:

1. *Scale of sustainability effects* (time and geography)
2. *Human connections to the physical and natural world* (relationship of population, consumption, technology, and carrying capacity to the biosphere, etc.)
3. *Ethics and values* (equity, justice, precautionary principle, development that is sustainable, measurement of societal well-being, etc.)

4. *How natural systems function* (natural laws, ecosystems, interdependence, holism, etc.)
5. *Technological and economic relationship to sustainability* (efficiency, pollution prevention, conservation, use of renewable resources, design for the environment, etc.)
6. *Motivating environmentally sustainable behavior* (legal, economic, spiritual, cultural, and other motivators)
7. *Pedagogical strategies for integrating sustainability* (research, experiential, interdisciplinary, real-world learning experiences)[77]

These themes should be incorporated in classes with several purposes in mind. First, the added content should help students understand the nature of sustainability. Second, the teaching materials should reveal what others have done around these themes, thus inspiring students to act. Finally, students should see what they themselves can do that will make a difference. Experience has shown that students are not receptive to classes that leave them with a feeling of helplessness in the face of bleak sustainability trends.

Step 4. Establish Service-Learning and Internship Courses. "Service-learning" is one pedagogical strategy for integrating sustainability into class work. It is a term first coined in the 1960s to describe a learning program in which students and faculty were linked with authorities in Tennessee to study development projects in a waterway area. It has come to mean teaching methods that engage students in structured community projects to help solve real-life problems. Besides practical learning, another objective of service-learning is to instill within students a sense of good citizenship and show them they can effect positive change in society. This teaching technique is particularly important in orienting future graduates to the grass-roots challenges posed by sustainability. The National Service-Learning Association offers a host of ideas on how the technique can be applied in various areas of study.[78] In one innovative service-learning program, Unity College of Maine aligned with local groups to create courses regarding water quality or other aspects of nearby Lake Winnewood. This theme was used in a wide range of classes, including drama, biology, environmental studies, ichthyology, chemistry, geology, composition, history, law, and statistics.[79]

With help from a National Science Foundation grant, Ithaca College in New York formed a three-way partnership with Tompkins County and Ecovillage at Ithaca (EVI)—a planned community dedicated to adopting sustainable practices—to develop service-learning opportunities. A number of courses were developed: (1) sustainable communities; (2) sustainable land use courses, which provide on-site learning at EVI; (3) an energy-efficiency and sustainable energy course taught by an EVI resident experienced in green building; and (4) an environmental futures course involving the calculation of *ecological footprints* for EVI and an inner-city neighborhood.[80]

The Center for Economic and Environmental Development (CEED) at Allegheny College in northwestern Pennsylvania created a broad array of service-learning programs around such topics as entrepreneurship for sustainability, watershed stewardship, educational outreach, energy, forestry, and environmental justice. In the *Read Between the Signs* project, art professors and student interns worked with the state department of transportation using discarded road signs to create an innovative sculptural mural along the fence around department property. Another project involved publishing an online journal of undergraduate environmental writing and art.[81]

Mini-grants from the South Carolina Sustainable Universities Initiative (SUI) helped launch two successful service-learning projects involving English classes. Clemson University's English Department developed a client-based service-learning program for its business and technical writing courses. Workshops were held with clients and teachers to provide guidance on the roles of each group in the program and to match the clients' sustainability-related writing projects to classes. The clients included a few corporations and a number of university groups, such as Student Housing, the Farmers Market, the Sustainable Agriculture Field Lab, the Environmental Committee, and a nearby elementary school. For client projects, students prepared manuals, announcements, brochures, advertisements, reports, presentations, and websites, among other things. After a surge in popularity, the program experienced some growing pains as it transitioned from grant funding to financial support from clients—a move designed to spread the economic burden and make the program sustainable.[82]

Encouraged by another SUI grant, the University of South Carolina created an optional course for the required freshman English 101 class.

Each class set reading and writing assignments and a 10-hour commu-
nity-service activity around a different topic related to environmental
sustainability. Between 2001 and 2004, over 1,000 students took the
course, contributing approximately 10,000 hours of community service.
The university also enriches the academic side of its sustainability program by using on-site buildings as green building "laboratories" for student master's theses, honors college theses, and other student projects.[83]

The University of British Columbia runs a successful service-learning
initiative that teams students with campus operations. Its Social, Ecological, Economic Development Studies (SEEDS) program has brought together over 1,000 students, instructors, and staff to work on projects such
as evaluating the feasibility of using biodiesel fuel in campus vehicles,
assessing strategies for non-chemical weed control, and mapping and analyzing vandalism.[84] Allegheny College appointed an Environmental
Science Internship Coordinator to arrange internship programs with
businesses, governments, and NGOs.

The NWF found from its survey that roughly one-half of the U.S. institutions offered undergraduate environmental courses involving service-
learning, and about the same number had classes around environmental
internships. Approximately two-thirds gave undergraduate students
credit for independent environmental research.[85] Over 95% of the colleges and universities surveyed in the Australian study said they permitted students to obtain academic credit for environmental research related
to the campus or local community.[86]

Step 5. Create New Courses and Degrees as Needed. The curriculum
should be reassessed periodically, taking into account the sustainability
challenges of society and its institutions. Input on academic needs
should be sought from students, alumni, and faculty peers as well as representatives of businesses, agencies, NGOs, and others likely to hire
graduates. The outcome of this review may single out courses that are an-
tiquated or of little value, which should be cut. Unfulfilled needs may
suggest new courses and degrees. Of course, new courses related to
sustainability need not have "sustainability" or other similar buzz words
in their name, although many do. Consider the courses listed in Figure
15.5, for example.

Figure 15.5
Examples of Collegiate Courses Related to Sustainability

1. Sustainability and the Law (University of Oregon Law School)
2. Sustainable Tourism, Sustainable Communities and Organizations, Sustainable Values and Strategies, Social and Environmental Entrepreneurship (George Washington University's School of Business and Public Management)
3. Sustainable Agriculture and Forestry (Oberlin College in Ohio)
4. Composition and Environmental Sustainability (University of South Carolina's English Department)
5. Corporate Strategies for Environmental and Social Responsibility (Vanderbilt University's Graduate School of Management)
6. Strategies for Sustainable Development; Systems Thinking for Sustainable Development; Badlands: Learning, Sustainability, and Systems; Sustainable Product Development (University of Michigan's School of Business)
7. Sustainable Enterprise; Financial Analysis: Integrating Sustainability; Business Strategy for a Sustainable World; Sustainable Operations; Global Context (University of North Carolina at Chapel Hill's School of Business)
8. Environmental Strategy and Sustainability; Ethics, Values, and Sustainability (University of Wisconsin's School of Business)
9. Sustainable Habits: Students and Systems at Stanford (Stanford University)
10. Social Entrepreneurship, Global Citizenship, Engineering for a Sustainable Society, Sociology of Sustainable Development, Building Sustainable Environments and Secure Food Systems, Sustainable Global Enterprise, Sustainable Development and the Global Hospitality Industry (Cornell University)
11. Contemporary Issues and Global Sustainability; Business Strategy: The Sustainable Enterprise (Illinois Institute of Technology's Graduate School of Business)
12. Citizenship and the Environment (University of Brighton in the U.K.)
13. Rural and Regional Sustainability (RMIT in Australia)
14. Principles and Practices of Sustainable Agriculture (Vassar College)
15. Corporate Social Responsibility (London Metropolitan University)
16. Sustainable Water Management, A Sustainable Baltic Region, Sustainable Community Development and Urban Planning (model courses developed by the Baltic University Programme)

Under its Business-Environment Learning and Leadership (BELL) program, the World Resources Institute convenes workshops and maintains a website for sharing the latest information on sustainability courses, issues, and teaching strategies at business graduate schools. The BELL website contains syllabi on a wide range of courses, including Business Strategies for Sustainability, Aboriginal Economic Develop-

ment Programs, Corporate Social Responsibility, Corporate Environmental Management, Environmentally Conscious Manufacturing and
Design, Business Ethics, and Accounting and the Environment. BELL's
highly regarded report series, *Beyond Grey Pinstripes*, benchmarks and
spotlights master's of business administration (MBA) schools and faculty who are at the forefront of incorporating social and environmental
stewardship into their programs.[87]

Some universities and colleges have gone beyond adding courses to
create entirely new academic certificates and degrees related to sustainability. Portland State University has a six-course certificate program,
entitled *Implementing Sustainability*, for post-graduate students interested in introducing a sustainability program at their own organizations.
The Stuart Graduate School of Business at the Illinois Institute of Technology has a four-course certificate program in Sustainable Enterprise.
Other schools are offering full degrees related to sustainability. Some examples are listed in Figure 15.6.

Figure 15.6
Examples of Collegiate Degrees Related to Sustainability

- Sustainable Futures (master's degree and Ph.D. from UTS in Australia)
- Sustainable Development (Ph.D. from Columbia University)
- International Management and Sustainability (master's degree from the University of Amsterdam)
- Corporate Governance and Company Social Responsibility (master's degree from the University of Verona in Italy)
- Sustainable Management (MBA from the School of Management, Presidio World College in California)
- Sustainable Business (MBA from the Bainbridge Graduate Institute in Washington)
- Sustainable Enterprise (MBA from New College in California)
- Corporate Social Responsibility (MBA and master's degrees from the Nottingham University's School of Business in the United Kingdom)
- Sustainable Systems (master's of science from Slippery Rock University of Pennsylvania)
- Globalization and Development (master's of science from the University of Manchester in the United Kingdom)
- Responsibility and Business Practice (master's degree from the University of Manchester's School of Management)
- Participation, Development, and Social Change (master's degree from the University of Sussex in the United Kingdom)
- Strategic Leadership Toward Sustainability (master's degree taught around the principles of The Natural Step, from the Blekinge Institute of Technology in Sweden)
- Implementation of Sustainable Technology (master's degree jointly developed by the University of Borås in Sweden, the University of Reading in the United Kingdom, and Gadjah Mada University in Indonesia)
- Social Responsibility (master's degree from St. Cloud College in Minnesota)
- Sustainable Development (bachelor's degree from the College of St. Mark and St. John in the United Kingdom)

Since sustainability issues cut across disciplinary lines, one avenue that should be explored in the curriculum review is whether the appropriate interdisciplinary approaches are being reflected in teaching. This is emphasized in LA 21, the Talloires Declaration, and other proclamations listed in Appendix 8.2. There are signs that this concern is beginning to be recognized. About half of the U.S. colleges and universities covered in the NWF survey said they allow undergraduates to design interdisciplinary degree programs incorporating the study of environmental issues.[88]

Two-thirds of the global institutions in the Australian survey reported they provided at least some interdisciplinary or multidisciplinary structures for research, education, and policy development on sustainability issues.[89] One of the leaders in multidisciplinary academics on sustainability is Ball State University. The school created a "clustered academic minor in Environmentally Sustainable Practices" under which students from different departments can obtain minor interdepartment degrees in such things as Environmental Policy, Sustainable Land Systems, Technology and the Environment, and the Environmental Context for Business.[90] The Vanderbilt Center for Environmental Management Studies was formed among students and faculty from Business, Engineering, Public Policy, and Law to create interdisciplinary degrees around environmental management.[91] Florida Gulf Coast University introduced team teaching between instructors from the English and Environmental Studies programs in a collaborative course on Environmental Literature.

Step 6. Mandate Training. A few universities with a serious commitment to sustainability have required students to take training on it. Over one-fourth of the institutions covered in the Australian survey reported having a student orientation session on the subject.[92] Eight percent of U.S. schools told the NWF they mandated that all students, regardless of major, complete at least one environmental course.[93] One school, Florida Gulf Coast University, requires that all students take *The University Colloquium: A Sustainable Future* as a condition for graduation. This interdisciplinary course reviews how the concept of sustainability applies to a variety of forces in southwestern Florida, including those that are environmental, social, ethical, historic, scientific, economic, and political.[94] A course on Leadership for Sustainable Development is mandated for all students by the Graduate School of Business Administration and Leadership at the Monterrey (Mexico) Institute of Technology.[95] By law, all students at state colleges and universities in Minnesota must take at least one course touching on a sustainability theme.[96]

Step 7. Provide Outreach Training. The final step to bringing sustainability to collegiate teaching is to share the school's sustainability learning and expertise with people outside the campus. This helps sharpen the skills of the instructors, exposes them to new ideas from the outside, and inspires them to improve their own programs. About half of the institutions covered in the Australian survey said they took an active role in disseminating information on sustainability to the wider community.[97]

Sharing may be done via regional partnerships with other schools, as discussed above. Or learning may be offered to people outside the regular student body through special extension courses. For instance, Harvard offers a course entitled, *Sustainability: The Challenge of Changing Our Institutions*, which is given to in-class and distance-learning Extension School students. Iowa State University provides an extension program on Sustainable Agriculture, which involves programs for farmers, agricultural professionals, and the public. A five-day summer course on *Sustainable Business* is available at the University of Vermont.

Sharing may also be achieved though hosting or delivering presentations at public conferences. For example, the University of Cambridge's Program for Industry has developed the *HRH The Prince of Wale's Business and the Environment Program*, which offers executive seminars to share ideas and best practices about sustainability within business.[98] Ithaca College in New York co-hosted a conference in which faculty, students, and staff joined with representatives of government, business, academia, and nonprofit and environmental groups to discuss the sustainability of local Tompkins County. Attendees heard reports on the outcomes of certain study-group and community discussions on sustainability topics that had been held earlier. At the end, attendees decided to form teams to undertake a number of regional projects. These projects included creating a sustainability information-resource hub and reviewing and reforming local resource and land use zoning regulations. Teams also agreed to develop regional sustainable transportation models and alternative fuel programs, and establish sustainability education and outreach programs with religious and arts groups.[99]

Other higher learning institutions provide training through conferences around the same sustainability theme over a period of years. Rutgers University co-sponsors and helps present an annual conference on green purchasing for governments, businesses, and academia. Ball State has been hosting a *Greening the Campus* conference for colleges and universities every year or two over the last decade.

Research Sector

Operational Concerns

Research has implications for sustainability in three ways. First, there are concerns related to research materials and operations. Materials used in research can be associated with a variety of environmental, safety, and ethical issues. Adverse effects should be considered and minimized to the extent practicable when the materials are being purchased. Testing and lab experiments may involve the use and disposal of dangerous substances that must be handled in a safe and environmentally responsible manner. Genetics studies and clinical evaluations with animals or human subjects are rife with ethical issues. An oversight group can be appointed to screen proposed research for these and other sustainability factors. Such a group exercising proper scrutiny can help the university avoid potential legal, ethical, and public relations nightmares.

Framework for Success

A second way research can affect sustainability is less obvious: the design of research teams can lay the groundwork for sustainable solutions. Sustainability projects that involve undergraduate students or individuals from campus operations, government, business, or NGO groups can bring useful insights to people inside and outside the school. Projects that employ a variety of disciplines can help researchers see problems in a more holistic way. In short, research, if properly structured, cannot only teach others, but encourage the type of multidisciplinary, cross-sector thinking that the complexity of sustainability demands.

A good example of collaborative research aimed at a sustainability issue is the Hydrogen Village being created at the University of British Columbia. This project, funded by a multimillion-dollar grant from Industry Canada, is a partnership among university, private-enterprise, and government to pilot operations using hydrogen-powered fuel cells. It includes testing various fuels in fuel cells, the creation of a hydrogen fueling station, and using hydrogen to power university trucks, campus-shuttle vehicles, and a campus building.[100]

Sustainability Solutions

Finally, research can do what research does best: find solutions to tough problems. And sustainability problems are some of the toughest. Solutions will require that we first improve our understanding of the issues, from a technological as well as sociological, economic, and political perspective. Then we need to understand what solutions—or, to be more precise, what *mix* of solutions—can solve our problems without causing even greater disruption. These problems are not just those associated with issues like climate change, resource depletion, population growth, world poverty, and AIDS. They also include the challenge of changing our institutions and culture. People and the organizations they run must appreciate the serious nature of sustainability issues and understand and accept the role they must play in solving them. But how can this be done? Research may be able to tell us. It is designed to sort fact from fiction and provide new insights to cause and effect. Hopefully it can deliver many of the answers we so desperately need.

Research Centers

Fortunately, some universities and colleges seem to be on the right track. Over 70% of the schools responding to the Australian survey said they had at least a moderate degree of research or scholarship activity across their institutions in various disciplines linked with the concepts of sustainability.[101] Often universities concentrate these efforts in a research center established to study sustainability or its environmental or social aspects. According to the NWF study, approximately one-quarter of U.S. universities and colleges house a research institute focusing on environmental issues.[102]

In fact, sustainability-related research centers exist all over the world, each with its own name and charter:

- The Global Sustainability Institute at RMIT (Australia) look for practical ways to implement the broad concepts of the TBL.
- The University of Michigan's Center for Sustainable Systems studies life cycle-based models and sustainability metrics, and generally promotes sustainable development through interdisciplinary research and education.
- The University of Queensland in Australia zeroes in on the application of sustainability to one industry with its Centre for Social Responsibility in Mining.
- The social aspects of sustainability are studied at the Institute for Social Responsibility, Ethics, and Education at San Jose State in California, as well as the Institute for Sustainable Fu-

tures at UTS.

• Business schools with sustainability centers can be found at the Illinois Institute of Technology, the University of North Carolina at Chapel Hill, the Monterrey Institute of Technology, Nottingham University (United Kingdom), and George Washington University. Many others have environmental centers.

• George Washington University also has an Institute for International Corporate Governance and Accountability at its law school.

• Georgia Tech's Institute for Sustainable Technology and Development, an independent group reporting directly to the vice provost of research, coordinates large technical projects on topics like environmentally conscious design and manufacture. It is also responsible for assuring that sustainability considerations are integrated in the research projects of other campus departments.

• The study of environmentally clean and sustainable production processes is the charge of special research centers at the Curtin University of Technology in Australia, Erasmus University in the Netherlands, and the University of Massachusetts at Lowell.

• In 2004, UNEP and Tongji University in Shanghai launched the UNEP-Tongji Institute for Environment and Sustainable Development. The institute was created to serve as a regional center for research and training on environmental sustainability. It provides a week-long leadership training course each year, which serves as the basis for new master's-level courses.[103]

• Costa Rica University conducts studies through its Institutional Program of Sustainability and Peace.

• The Office of Sustainability Programs at the University of New Hampshire has subgroups focusing on Climate Education, Biodiversity Education, Food and Society, and Culture and Sustainability.

• The Centre for Business Relationships, Accountability, Sustainability, and Society (BRASS), is a research center created through the Law and Business Schools at the University of Cardiff in the United Kingdom, and the Cardiff city and regional planning authorities.

• Sokoine University of Agriculture in Tanzania supports over 100 research projects on sustainable development issues. Its research motto is: "Management of natural resources for sustainable development and poverty alleviation."

Of course, without funding, research doesn't happen. A little seed money can go a long way, however. The University of South Carolina was able to use $215,000 in "mini-grants" to fund the preparation of proposals and other preliminary work needed for soliciting larger grants. While some sustainability projects didn't succeed, others did. By the end of 2003, the original mini-grant investment had spawned $2.27 million in additional external funding.[104] As with many things in life, if there's a will, there's usually a way.

Having a designated sustainability research center on campus can make it easier to find cash, however. The center can serve as a focal point for potential researchers and funders, alike—people who share a belief in the importance of the topic. With oversight from the center, good projects can be identified and properly managed. Center personnel can bring together various disciplines and sectors on individual projects to maximize benefits. They can widely publicize the results. Moreover, they can spend time with the administration to ensure that the sustainability agenda continues to receive top management support. If managed properly, sustainability research centers can become a source of great success, pride, and prestige for the school—a symbol of modern thinking.

Student Activities

The primary reason colleges and universities exist is to teach students. They affect learning in the classroom and through the experiences and environment they create for students outside it. These outside experiences are valuable because they provide other benefits as important as knowledge in solving our difficult sustainability problems—they provide students the confidence, passion, and tenacity to seek these solutions. Some schools of higher learning have done better than others as an incubator for this non-classroom learning, spawning student groups, campaigns, projects, and programs. Over 90% of the 52 domestic and foreign schools responding to the Australian survey said they had student groups involved in sustainability initiatives. Nearly three-fourths reported the presence of a student sustainability or environmental center on campus.[105]

Students for a Sustainable Stanford (SSS) is an example of what motivated students can do. The organization was formed by a small group of individuals who wanted to encourage green building and the reduction of greenhouse gas emissions on campus. They established a task force and mounted a large campaign to educate students, faculty, administrators, and the Board of Trustees. They published op-ed articles and lobbied graduate and undergraduate student organizations to adopt statements of support. Ultimately this led to the creation of the Environmental Stewardship Management Group, a committee of students, faculty, and operations and administrative staff that hammered out the *Stanford Guideline for Sustainable Buildings*. Later, SSS recruited student representatives to raise awareness in their residence halls about reducing waste and resource consumption. The organization is also working closely with the Dining Services Department to increase organic, local, and seasonal purchasing and to cut food and flatware waste. It is pressing the school administration to hire a full-time sustainability coordinator and to establish a Harvard-like revolving fund for financing eco-efficiency projects.[106]

Students at other universities and colleges have taken up activities like those of SSS. For example, the University of Victoria's Sustainability Project is a student-run organization that helps drive sustainability projects. Harvard established a Resource Efficiency Program, which hired student representatives to promote resource conservation in their dormitories. Their projects included improving energy efficiency, reusing discarded computers and furniture, and implementing green practices in laundry and dining rooms.[107]

The University of British Columbia has a similar student coordinator program staffed with volunteers, which helped save the school $225,000 in energy costs in 2002-2004.[108] Student Recycling Residential Coordinators at Berkeley joined with their counterparts from other University of California locations to successfully press the Board of Regents to adopt the clean energy and green building policy discussed earlier. Spurred by their great success, these students formed an intercampus organization, called the California Student Sustainability Coalition (CSSC), which created a student-run class with outside speakers. The course requires participants to complete a campus sustainability project. CSSC is also working on green transportation issues.

Student action was also behind the University of North Carolina initiative to assess students $4 per semester to pay for purchasing green energy and installing green power technology on campus.[109] The Student Environmental Action Coalition there campaigned for a student referendum which garnered support from 85% of the voters.[110] A student-led campaign at Michigan produced a Student Assembly resolution launching the school's sustainability program in 2001.

Student action on sustainability issues has also come in the form of protests. In the late 1990s, student sit-ins at Duke, Georgetown, Michigan, and Wisconsin persuaded school administrators to take more aggressive action on sweatshops that produced items bearing their school logo. Activists from these and other universities led the way in creating United Students Against Sweatshops and the Worker Rights Consortium (see Appendix 2.3.9). Student protests also helped convince Staples to begin selling forest-friendly paper and Dell to begin sponsoring local computer collection and recycling programs.

One student campaign has been more personal. The Graduation Pledge has been promoted and endorsed by students at more than 100 universities and colleges—everywhere from Ball State, Clemson, Columbia, Duke, Harvard, and Stanford in the United States, to Dalhousie and York in Canada, the Chinese Cultural University in Taiwan, and INSEAD in France and Singapore. The pledge reads: "I pledge to explore and take into account the social and environmental consequences of any job I consider and will try to improve these aspects of any organization for which I work." Thousands of students have signed this commitment over the years since it was created in 1987 at California's Humboldt State University. Manchester College in Indiana, now its chief advocate, is the center for the Graduation Pledge Alliance.[111] Besides tracking progress on the pledge, the alliance website helps students fulfill their pledge by providing an extensive list of links that can match students with socially responsible jobs, internships, and volunteer programs.

Community Outreach Activities

As we saw earlier, engaging with the outside community on sustainability initiatives can provide useful service-learning opportunities to augment classroom study. Community-based research can provide a rich learning experience, too. But what about traditional voluntary community service not linked to either classes or research? Can it be worthwhile? Yes. For one thing, it can strengthen problem solving, team building, leadership, and other skills for students, faculty, and staff alike. Moreover, most who are involved find such experiences popular and personally gratifying. When the University of Florida surveyed its students in 2001, it found over 80%—approximately 42,000 individuals—had participated in some community service activity. Many worked with Big Brothers/Big Sisters, Habitat for Humanity, or various clinics, crisis centers, and lower level schools. Student organizations there reported raising and donating nearly $1 million to local, state, and national charities.[112]

Universities can encourage voluntary community service in several ways. They can create websites that list community service opportunities, organizations, and contacts. They can also name coordinators to help identify community needs and match them with various campus organizations. And they can follow the University of Michigan in establishing an *Alternative Spring Break* program under which students take on community service projects during their time off instead of traveling to some popular watering hole.

Universities are increasingly extending their sustainability outreach activities beyond local borders. One of the most common ways they do that is through conferences and workshops open to outsiders. As noted in Figure 15.7, over the last few years, major conferences on sustainability have been hosted or sponsored by colleges and universities from all corners of the world.

Figure 15.7 Some Universities and Colleges Sponsoring or Hosting Sustainability Conferences Since 2003[113]	
Arab Academy for Science and Technology and Maritime Transport (Egypt) Auburn University Ball State University Chiang Mai University (Thailand) College of Menominee Nation (United States) Colorado State University Columbia University Dartmouth College Delft University of Technology (Netherlands) East China Normal University Freie Unversität Berlin Harvard University Illinois Institute of Technology Institut National Polytechnique de Grenoble (France) Instituto Superior Téchnico (Portugal) Islamic University of Gaza Jomo Kenyatta University of Agriculture and Technology (Kenya) Kuwait University McGill University Montclair State University (United States) National Technical University of Athens Oldenburg University (Germany)	RWTH Aachen University (Germany) San Francisco State University Stanford University Technical University of Crete University of Brunswick (Canada) University of California-Riverside University of Cambridge University of Cape Town University of Colorado University of East Anglia (United Kingdom) University of Geneva University of Heidelberg University of Malta University of Manchester (United Kingdom) University of Michigan University of Pennsylvania University of Pittsburgh University of Rome University of Sussex University of Tampere (Finland) University of Virginia Universidad Veracruzana (Mexico) University of Zagreb (Croatia) University of Zaragoza (Spain) Virginia Tech University

Where needs are great, the university has a strong interest, and the workload is too heavy for a volunteer, schools should consider paying their own participants for the extra time they devote to outreach activities. This might be appropriate if, for example, the local community needed one of the university's internal experts to provide extensive advice on community planning issues. Compensation would also be warranted for extra hours university staff members expend in communicating and promoting job openings and supplier and contractor opportunities to local citizens.

Element 7: Indicators and Transparent Reporting

Public, transparent sustainability reporting has not been a priority for academia. Most schools have seen little reason for it. Unlike corporations, universities are rarely the source of big national financial, social, or environmental scandals. NGOs don't write exposés about them. Legislators don't hold hearings on their potentially unethical practices. The Sarbanes-Oxley Act was not written with them in mind. Their most vocal critics have been their own students and faculty, and few of them have placed transparent reporting close to the top of their issues. What is more, those who have tried reporting don't receive much acclaim for it. With little hoopla over the matter, universities—unlike many corporations—usually feel no pressure to excel in publicizing their sustainability performance.

To compound the problem, the internal reasons for sustainability reporting have not been well appreciated in collegiate circles. Few university executives have seized sustainability as a tool for constructive change. Even fewer have taken the high moral ground, supporting transparent public reporting as a symbolic statement of the importance of open and honest communication by organizations. With internal and external spotlights off, progress on sustainability has been restrained at most schools. This is unfortunate because the lack of reporting has left institutions of higher learning without a focal point for stakeholder discussions, and without accountability for sustainability performance. Opportunities for improvement—and even leadership—in operations, education, and research have been lost.

Still, some enlightened colleges and universities are showing the way. As noted in Appendix 8.3, some have started by publicizing the results of their internal audits. A dozen or so have moved on to provide full reports on their sustainability or environmental programs and performance. The reports they have issued tend to fall in four categories: (1) infrequent sustainability reports with comprehensive metrics; (2) short anecdotal sustainability reports; (3) environmental reports; and (4) newsletter reports. Here are some examples of each:

Infrequent Sustainability Reports With Comprehensive Metrics

A few collegiate reports—some the result of student projects—have provided performance information on a broad array of sustainability metrics. However, because of the resources needed to produce these reports, they are typically not repeated on a regular basis. Some have simply served as one-time performance baselines for program planning. For example, Penn State's 100-page sustainability report for 2000 was prepared by 30 graduate and undergraduate students and several faculty members. It was a follow-up to the school's initial report two years earlier. The 2000 document shows the university's status under 33 indicators grouped in 10 areas: (1) energy; (2) water; (3) material resources and waste disposal; (4) food; (5) land; (6) transportation; (7) the built environment; (8) community; (9) research; and (10) decisionmaking. The results for each indicator are scored on a four-level scale. Of special note are the data on student diets and depression-related disorders, and the survey results on student ecological literacy. Besides the retrospective look at performance, the report offers recommendations for future program direction. These recommendations are in the form of a long-term goal and three short-term objectives for each of the 10 areas. They served as the basis for a "mission" or roadmap for a sustainable campus that was later endorsed by the student government, faculty senate, and university president.[114]

The University of Florida's 2001 report was the first of its kind to be prepared according to GRI reporting guidelines. This 50-page report was drafted by the director of the university's sustainability office and a doctoral candidate on the university's Greening UF Program—a grass-roots initiative of students, faculty, and staff. Data collection was aided by support from the assistant vice president of administrative affairs. Feedback on the draft was sought from 80 stakeholders on and off campus. Some noteworthy areas of the text cover diversity information, training budget, crime statistics, and sustainability-related research. In response to the report, the university president requested a follow-up publication with updated performance data, recommendations, and best practice information. That report was delivered the following year. This second report added data on community service, courses with sustainability content, and a few other topics.[115]

The GRI framework was also used by the University of Michigan in preparing its 2002 report—a mammoth at 200 pages with an equally long appendix. It was produced by four graduate students as a master's degree project, with the support of a steering committee of university, corporate, legislative, and NGO representatives. Data for the 50 reported indicators was collected from over 30 departments. Data of particular interest include that on employee grievances for harassment and discrimination, wage information relative to median household incomes for the community, and student enrollment in sustainability classes. In addition to communicating the status quo, the document provides extensive discussion on the rationale and methodology for each indicator and its context within the university. This was done with an eye to securing concurrence on these indicators for long-term use. In following up, the university's new president requested the school's Environmental Task Force to recommend a limited number of indicators to initially track and annually report. In response, eight environmental indicators were suggested in 2004. Over 30 supporting metrics linked to these indicators were identified for operational use. Reporting on social indicators was suggested for later consideration after the school gains experience with routine environmental reporting.[116]

Michigan State University's 75-page report for 2003 was prepared by the school's Office of Campus Sustainability with funding from the EPA. The report contains 67 graphs and 10 tables, providing detailed information on such wide-ranging subjects as types of food purchased and sources and types of livestock manure disposed. The information on campus crime, student drinking and its consequences, and staff and faculty employment deserve special attention. So does the candid discussion about the trade offs among sustainability issues, such as how much should be spent for cleaner fuels and how low thermostats should be set to save energy and costs.[117] A follow-up report is planned for late 2006.[118]

Short Anecdotal Sustainability Reports

In several reports, universities cover their sustainability programs with more story-line text and less graphs and charts than found among the large reports previously discussed. Two examples are the 23-page *Campus Sustainability Reports* published by the University of North Carolina at Chapel Hill for 2003 and 2005. These reports are framed around best practices in a variety of areas related to building and grounds, research, teaching, and public service. A section of one report discusses how sustainability concerns were incorporated into the school's master plan for development, prompting the school to hire new personnel to address architecture, historic preservation, water, and transportation issues. Another section talks about the university's research on regional smart-growth indicators and on community design, transportation, and architecture aimed at making it easy for people to be physically active.[119]

The 2005 report from the University of British Columbia—its third annual publication—runs 21 pages. The report contains program descriptions and data on a wide variety of initiatives, including operational efforts (air, water, climate change, energy, and green buildings), student program, research opportunities, and community outreach activities. The document generally describes the school's new sustainable development strategy and goals, discussed above. Presumably future reports will center on those new commitments.[120]

The University of Victoria's 14-page report for 2001, published by the student-led UVic Sustainability Project, is organized around individual projects, such as the social and green mapping used to help form a vision for a campus plan. It also reveals plans for addressing gaps discovered from a series of assessments that were conducted. A five-page progress report was issued in 2002.[121] The university institutionalized its reporting process for 2003-2004 by assigning it to the sustainability coordinator of its Facilities Management Department with oversight by the department executive director. The 13-page 2003-2004 report follows up on the sustainability aspects of the university's campus and strategic plans as it affects the campus grounds. It covers the management of energy, water, waste, transportation, green buildings, and natural areas.[122]

The four-page 2004 sustainability report by Sheffield Hallam University in the United Kingdom follows on to the seven-page document produced the previous year. These public reports, which were prepared for the university's Board of Governors, show how sustainability reporting can be done with a minimum of resources. This 2004 document communicates the school's performance data on waste generation and recycling, and water and energy consumption. It also describes the university's initiatives on community and social issues, as well as those aimed at encouraging transportation by something other than automobile. One particularly noteworthy project was the *Responsible Landlord Scheme* under which the school encouraged better standards for privately rented housing for students and other residents.[123]

Environmental Reports

A few schools keep their reports relatively brief and only focus on environmental issues. The 22-page environmental report for 2004 from

Royal Roads University in British Columbia is one example. It is unique for its coverage of biodiversity issues, including the preparation of an Invasive Species Management Plan. Academic institutions interested in establishing EMS may benefit from the text detailing the steps Royal Roads undertook to create theirs. The school's 16-page report for 2004-2005 provides additional information on the site's use of energy and natural resources, and its management of ecosystems and waste and transportation issues.[124]

As with the Royal Roads report, the 2004 report from Göteborg University in Sweden—its seventh annual edition—tells how it designed and implemented its EMS. In addition, the 49-page report lists its 12 environmental objectives for 2004-2006 along with the indicators used to track progress, the actions and tactics for implementation, and the results for 2004. It examines research and graduate programs, undergraduate programs, community interaction, and in-house operations, discussing the environmental aspects, objectives, indicators, and results for each of these areas of activity. The report also reviews the work of the university's Centre for Environment and Sustainability, and comments on the environmental and sustainable development content broadcast on university TV. The document provides an unusually candid report of its audit results and extensive detail on the environmental training provided.[125]

The University of Helsinki's 12-page environmental report for 2000 conveys the school's progress on various aspects of the environmental program. Like the Göteborg report, it too provides a table showing the specific objectives to be achieved (by 2005), the tactics to implement those objectives, and the indicators to be used to track progress.[126]

Tracking UVM, the University of Vermont's 25-page "report card," covers the school's environmental performance from 1990 to 2000, rating 12 measures for positive, negative, or little change. The text on best practices and on its extensive commuter-incentive program merit special attention. The UVM Environmental Council followed up to report progress in 2004 using a PowerPoint® presentation that included information on the school's ecological footprint. The presentation notes best practices from other schools and suggests future actions for the university itself.[127]

Newsletter Reports

Instead of doing periodic reports, some universities have elected to provide updates on programs and goals through sustainability newsletters. Michigan State University issues theirs monthly.[128] Harvard publishes one twice a year.[129]

As this review shows, sustainability reporting, even among some of the best collegiate performers, is erratic. Many of the schools that do publish a report often have the best of intentions but are unable to sustain the effort. Often the effort is ad hoc rather than institutionalized. When some passionate leader leaves the institution or internal or external funding is not renewed, reporting—and the accountability and focus it brings—disappears. Consequently, advocates must constantly keep their sustainability programs visible and foster support from a broad base of internal stakeholders, especially the upper level managers who decide budgets. Advocates also must keep in mind the lessons of Chapters 4 and 10 on how to marshal and maintain support for reporting and how to assure that the reporting effort is geared for continuation over the long term.

Looking at the few successful collegiate reporting programs suggests that a sustainability report for a college or university should be roughly between 20 and 35 pages and contain a good blend of metrics and program information. A longer comprehensive base-line report or audit may also be feasible for starters. But unlike some well-healed companies, institutions of higher learning cannot sustain a practice of regular lengthy reports. Tempering the report scope and production method can help, too, since this reduces the cost profile—and the attraction for budget cutters—as well as the likelihood of reporting fatigue. Better to have a short, low-tech report than none at all. If all else fails, newsletters and other school publications should be tapped for communicating plans, goals, and progress.

While some university reports have offered glimpses of program weaknesses, few could be characterized as models of transparency. In one sense, however, schools are well ahead of their business brethren on that score: many collegiate institutions have publicly posted their audit reports; one would be hard pressed to find many companies that do. Of course, transparency is not just about revealing problems, it is also about sharing an understanding of them so others may see the school's good intentions and learn from the difficulties they are facing. In that regard, the 2003 report on the South Carolina Sustainable Universities Initiative, with its discussion of lessons learned, presents an approach to be emulated.[130]

If universities are to report publicly, what parameters should they include? Appendices 7.3.1 through 7.3.4 show possible metrics. Many were drawn from the reports just discussed. Because university operations for buildings and grounds are comparable to office, research, or agricultural complexes in the private sector, the social and environmental indicators suggested for university operations are much the same as those recommended for companies in Appendix 7.1.

Appendices 7.3.1 through 7.3.4 provide more examples of indicators than any university could reasonably track. Like companies, schools must prioritize among their sustainability opportunities and risks to find those worthy of measurement and attention. Recall that this is what the University of Michigan did. The tools discussed in Chapter 6 and Appendix 4 can be used for this ranking exercise. When employing the tools provided in Appendix 4, "customers" can be considered students and potential funders; "sales" can be viewed as securing outside funding as well as attracting students and professors to the school's educational and research programs. Once the areas of focus are identified, performance indicators and goals can be selected using the lessons from Chapter 7. The best indicators are those that help the most in driving desired performance. For that reason, normalized metrics are worth considering, such as energy usage per square foot of building space, or grievance filings or water consumption based on the total campus population of students, faculty, and staff.

Integrated Programs

Creating the "sustainable university" is not just about infusing sustainable development into the curriculum, research, or operations. Nor is it only about auditing, planning, endorsing codes, or having a noteworthy program of community outreach. It is about doing all those things in an integrated way. It is about making sustainability part of the school culture—its lifeblood—rather than just stitching an extra appendage on the institution for appearance sake. Some schools—those mentioned most frequently in this chapter—are moving closer to that goal. However, the real test of a sustainable university is what the institution instills in the minds of its students, faculty, staff, and community members about sustainability—particularly how sustainability affects them and they affect it, and why these effects will likely become more pronounced in the future. It is about serving as an incubator for hatching new behaviors that will help us grasp and better address the big sustainability challenges we face today—and the even bigger ones of tomorrow. In this Decade of Education for Sustainable Development our collegiate institutions must step forward to do their part to help secure our well being and that of future generations. The road map is clear.

Follow-up Checklist for Action:
Approach to Sustainability for Colleges and Universities

☐ Identify those among the faculty, administration, operations, and student body who favor moving the school toward sustainability. Use this group to mobilize action on the steps below.

☐ Contact one or more of the support organizations mentioned in Appendix 8.1 and seek their guidance and tools for introducing, designing, and implementing a schoolwide sustainability program.

☐ Share with school administrative, faculty, and student leaders the potential benefits of pursuing sustainability through an SOS. See Chapter 4 for ideas on how to do this. Also consider the value of sustainability for collegiate institutions as discussed in this chapter.

☐ If appropriate, draft and seek approval of a student body resolution and/or one from the faculty council, calling for the school to establish an integrated sustainability program.

☐ After securing support from top management and others, identify a leader/coordinator for the sustainability program—preferably a full-time paid employee—as well as a sponsor from the top administrative ranks.

☐ Form a sustainability team to help coordinate sustainability planning, reporting, and other activities. Assure the team has appropriate support from management and that its representatives cover all the school's main activities, including operations (buildings and grounds), research, education, student programs, and community outreach. Also consider forming separate subteams for each of these areas of activity, or adopting one of the other structural examples described in this chapter.

☐ Identify the key sustainability aspects of the school's activities, considering Figures 2.4, 2.5, and other guidance from this chapter, and feedback from key stakeholders.

Follow-up Checklist for Action:
Approach to Sustainability for Colleges and Universities—Continued

☐ Adopt a sustainability policy related to the key aspects of the institution's operations, research, education, student programs, and community outreach,
drawing from the model policies in Figure 2.2, the codes of Appendix 8. 2, and
examples obtained from the IISD website, the support organizations, and
some of the schools mentioned in this chapter. For the reasons noted in this
chapter, consider endorsing one of the external codes of Appendix 8.2 in addition to having the school draft and adopt its own sustainability policy.

☐ Conduct a sustainability assessment of the school's operations, research, education, student programs, and community outreach activities. Use one or more
of the auditing tools mentioned in Appendix 8.3. Base the audit criteria on the
adopted sustainability policy, the best practices identified in this chapter, and
legal requirements, if possible.

☐ Following the guidance of Chapters 5, 6, and 12 and this chapter, plan and implement an SOS appropriate for the school's sustainability aspects, its size and
risks. Consider any audit results and stakeholder feedback that may have been
obtained. Emphasize multi-disciplinary and multisector initiatives. Incorporate various goals and metrics in the plan, considering examples found in Appendix 7.3 and the guidance from Chapter 7. Eventually, integrate
sustainability planning into the institution's regular planning process.

☐ Secure any needed funding to assure the continuation of the sustainability program. Consider the funding sources cited in this chapter and those mentioned
by the support organizations listed in Appendix 8.1.

☐ Assure that sustainability considerations are integrated in the selection, development, and incentive programs for teaching, research, and operations/ad-
ministrative personnel, and in student admissions policies.

☐ At least annually, measure performance against the school's sustainability
policy, plans, and goals. Prepare and communicate a sustainability report for
the school after considering this performance, the stakeholder feedback, the
sustainability reports of other universities and colleges, and the guidance provided in Chapter 10 and this chapter. Review the findings with upper management and the board and other groups as appropriate.

☐ Periodically solicit input from various stakeholders on the organization's
sustainability performance and communications, taking into account the
guidance of Chapter 11 and this chapter. Focus particularly on operations/ad-
ministrative, education, and research employees, students, and community
leaders. Determine what action should be taken on the feedback; at the very
least, consider it during the next planning cycle.

Endnotes to Chapter 15

1. This quote, attributed to H.G. Wells, was reportedly made during an interview by the *London Tribune*. Wells was an English novelist and historian who lived from 1866 to 1946.

2. Kofi Annan, *quoted in* SARAH BEKESSY ET AL., UNIVERSITIES AND SUSTAINABILITY, TELA ENVIRONMENT, ECONOMY, AND SOCIETY ISSUE II, at 1 (David Yencken ed., Australian Conservation Foundation, Inc., Carlton, Victoria, 2003), *available at* http://www.acfonline.org.au/uploads/res_ tp010.pdf [hereinafter AUSTRALIAN SUSTAINABLE UNIVERSITIES REPORT 2003].

3. U.N. Conference on Environment and Development, Agenda 21, U.N. Doc. A/CONF.151.26 (1992), §36.5, *available at* http://www.un.org/esa/ sustdev/documents/agenda21/english/agenda21toc.htm.

4. *See* Lisa Bauer, *Bridging the Great Divide at UC Berkeley*, presented at the Environmental Management for Sustainable Universities Conference, Monterrey, N.L., Mexico, June 9-11, 2004 [hereinafter Bauer Report on Berkeley Program].

5. Mary McIntosh et al., *State of the Campus Environment: A National Report Card on Environmental Performance and Sustainability in Higher Education* (survey for the National Wildlife Federation's Campus Ecology® program undertaken by Princeton Survey Research Associates, 2001), http://www.nwf.org/campusEcology/HTML/stateofthecampus report.cfm (last visited Jan. 11, 2006) [hereinafter NWF Campus Survey].

6. University of British Columbia, *Fisher Scientific Fund Calls for Proposals*, EOS NEWSL., Jan. 20, 2006, *available at* http://www.sustain.ubc. ca/home/aurora/V10/060120-18.html.

7. U.S. EPA, INSTITUTIONAL: FINANCIAL RESOURCES—DEDICATED REVOLVING LOAN FUND FOR ENVIRONMENTAL PROJECT (2003), *available at* http://www.epa.gov/NE/assistance/univ/pdfs/bmps/HarvardRevolving loanFund.pdf. Harvard University, *Harvard Green Campus Initiative*, HARV. GREEN NEWSL., Fall 2004, at 9, *available at* http://www.green campus.harvard.edu/newsletter/ [hereinafter Harvard Green Newsletter—Fall 2004].

8. SUSTAINABILITY OFFICE, UNIVERSITY OF NORTH CAROLINA AT CHAPEL HILL, UNC CHAPEL HILL CAMPUS SUSTAINABILITY REPORT (2003), *available at* http://sustainability.unc.edu/Index.asp?Type=C [hereinafter UNC-CH Sustainability Report 2003]. SUSTAINABILITY OFFICE, UNIVERSITY OF NORTH CAROLINA AT CHAPEL HILL, UNC CHAPEL HILL CAMPUS SUSTAINABILITY REPORT (2005), *available at* http://sustainability. unc.edu/Index.asp?Type=C [hereinafter UNC-CH SUSTAINABILITY REPORT 2005].

9. *See* Wynn Calder & Richard Clugston, *Education for a Sustainable and Secure Future*, PLANNING FOR A HIGHER EDUC., Mar./May 2003.

10. Wynn Calder & Richard M. Clugston, *Progress Toward Sustainability in Higher Education*, ELR NEWS & ANALYSIS, 33 ELR 10003, 10018 (Jan. 2003), *reprinted from a chapter in* JOHN C. DERNBACH, STUMBLING TOWARD SUSTAINABILITY (Envtl. L. Inst. 2002) [hereinafter Calder & Clugston 2003].

11. University Leaders for a Sustainable Future, *Research: Talloires in Action: Creating Leaders and Laggards in the U.S.*, PUBLICATIONS, Dec. 2002, *available at* http://www.ulsf.org/pub_declaration_resvol61.htm [hereinafter Talloires U.S. Survey]. *See* NWF Campus Survey, *supra* note 5, at 115.

12. *See* Talloires U.S. Survey, *supra* note 11.

13. For reports on best collegiate sustainability practices, see the following reports: University of Florida Sustainability Task Force, *Final Report* (approved Apr. 27, 2002), http://www.senate.ufl.edu/reports/sustainability/sustainability_task_force.html (last visited Jan. 8, 2006) [hereinafter University of Florida Sustainability Task Force Report 2002]. SARAH BEKESSY ET AL. ENVIRONMENTAL BEST PRACTICE IN AUSTRALIAN AND INTERNATIONAL UNIVERSITIES 18 (University of Melbourne 2001), *available at* http://www.unimelb.edu.au/staff/deansandheads/2002/Environmental BestPractise.pdf [hereinafter AUSTRALIAN BEST PRACTICES SURVEY]. *See* NWF Campus Survey, *supra* note 5. University of Michigan, *The Sustainable University of Michigan—A Student-Led Initiative: Sustainability at U of M and Other Institutions*, http://www.umich.edu/~usustain/sustain.html (last visited Jan. 8, 2006) [hereinafter Michigan Report on Collegiate Sustainability Practices].

14. GREEN COMMITTEE 2, BALL STATE UNIVERSITY, GREEN 2—FINAL REPORT: IMPLEMENTATION OF THE TALLOIRES DECLARATION (2001), *available at* http://www.bsu.edu/provost/ceres/g2/0main/finalrep.html [hereinafter BALL STATE TALLOIRES IMPLEMENTATION REPORT]. Ball State University, *Council on the Environment*, http://www.bsu.edu/provost/ceres/cote/ (last visited Jan. 8, 2006).

15. University of North Carolina and Chapel Hill, *UNC Sustainability Initiative*, http://sustainability.unc.edu/Index.asp?Type=C (last visited Jan. 8, 2006).

16. UNITY COLLEGE, THE 2001 SUSTAINABILITY REPORT (2001), *available at* http://www.unity.edu/sustainability/ [hereinafter UNITY COLLEGE SUSTAINABILITY PLAN].

17. University of Florida, *Office of Sustainability*, http://www.sustainable.ufl.edu/ (last visited Jan. 8, 2006). *See* University of Florida Sustainability Task Force Report 2002, *supra* note 13.

18. *See* OFFICE OF CAMPUS SUSTAINABILITY & UNIVERSITY COMMITTEE FOR A SUSTAINABLE CAMPUS, MICHIGAN STATE UNIVERSITY, CAMPUS SUSTAINABILITY REPORT (2003), *available at* http://www.ecofoot.msu.edu/files/pdfs/sustainability.pdf [hereinafter MICHIGAN STATE SUSTAINABILITY REPORT 2003].

19. SARA PARKIN ET AL., HIGHER EDUCATION PARTNERSHIP FOR SUSTAINABILITY, ON COURSE FOR SUSTAINABILITY: REPORT OF THE HIGHER EDUCATION PARTNERSHIP FOR SUSTAINABILITY 2000-2003 (Forum for the Future 2004), *available at* http://www.forumforthefuture.org.uk/publications/HEPSfinalreport_page1828.aspx (last visited Jan. 8, 2006) [hereinafter U.K. HEPS REPORT].

20. *Id.*

21. *See* AUSTRALIAN BEST PRACTICES SURVEY, *supra* note 13, at 18.

22. Tarah Wright, The Effect of the Halifax Declaration on Canadian Signatory Universities: A Tenth-Year Anniversary Retrospect, Policy, Change, and Environmental Sustainability in the University (2002) (unpublished Ph.D. dissertation, University of Alberta), *cited in* AUSTRALIAN SUSTAINABLE UNIVERSITIES REPORT 2003, *supra* note 2, at 25.

23. *See* Harvard Green Newsletter—Fall 2004, *supra* note 7. Harvard University, *Harvard University Green Campus Initiative*, http://www.greencampus.harvard.edu/index.php (last visited Jan. 8, 2006).

24. University of British Columbia, *The UBC Campus Sustainability Office*, http://www.sustain.ubc.ca/sc_prog.html (last visited Jan. 8, 2006). CAMPUS SUSTAINABILITY OFFICE, UNIVERSITY OF BRITISH COLUMBIA, ANNUAL REPORT: PROGRESS TOWARDS A SUSTAINABLE CAMPUS (2005), *available at* http://www.sustain.ubc.ca/ [hereinafter UNIVERSITY OF BC SUSTAINABILITY REPORT 2005]. CAMPUS SUSTAINABILITY OFFICE, UNIVERSITY OF BRITISH COLUMBIA, ANNUAL REPORT: PROGRESS TOWARDS A SUSTAINABLE CAMPUS (2004), *available at* http://www.sustain.ubc.ca/ [hereinafter UNIVERSITY OF BC SUSTAINABILITY REPORT 2004].

25. *See* Bauer Report on Berkeley Program, *supra* note 4.

26. *See* NWF Campus Survey, *supra* note 5.

27. *See* AUSTRALIAN BEST PRACTICES SURVEY, *supra* note 13, at 40.

28. *Id.* at 35, 39.

29. *See* NWF Campus Survey, *supra* note 5, at 115.

30. *See* University of Florida Sustainability Task Force Report 2002, *supra* note 13, app. xli-xlii and the various studies cited there.

31. *Id.* at 15.

32. *Id.*, app. xliv.

33. *See* AUSTRALIAN BEST PRACTICES SURVEY, *supra* note 13, at 35, 40.

34. *See* NWF Campus Survey, *supra* note 5, at 113, 120.

35. Campus Sustainability Office, University of British Columbia, *Sustainable Leaders Tri-Mentoring Program in Sustainability*, http://www.sustain. ubc.ca/leaders.htm (last visited Jan. 11, 2006).

36. *See* NWF Campus Survey, *supra* note 5, at 112, 120.

37. Council on the Environment, Ball State University, *Awards*, http://www. bsu.edu/cote/awards/ (last visited Jan. 8, 2006).

38. Student Assembly, University of Michigan, *Striving for Sustainable U of M* (resolution passed Dec. 11, 2001), http://www.umich.edu/~usustain/ msa_resolution.html (last visited Jan. 8, 2006).

39. University of North Carolina at Chapel Hill, *Faculty Council Resolution 2002-2006: A Resolution Urging the University to Commit Itself to Sustainability Measures in Its Institutional Policies and Practices*, http://www.unc.edu/faculty/faccoun/resolutions/Res2002-6.htm (last visited Jan. 8, 2006).

40. *See* ENVIRONMENTAL TASK FORCE, UNIVERSITY OF MICHIGAN, ENVIRONMENTAL TASK FORCE REPORT (2004), *available at* http://www.umich. edu/pres/committees/envrpt/ [hereinafter UNIVERSITY OF MICHIGAN ENVIRONMENTAL TASK FORCE REPORT 2004].

41. See, for example, the higher education institutions with sustainability mission statements listed in Michigan Report on Collegiate Sustainability Practices, *supra* note 13.

42. IISD, *Sustainability Campus Policy Bank*, http://www.iisd.org/educate/ policybank.asp (last visited Jan. 8, 2006).

43. *See* Joshua M. Pearce & Christopher Uhl, *Getting It Done: Effective Sustainable Policy Implementation at the University Level*, PLANNING FOR HIGHER EDUC., Mar./May 2003, *available at* http://www.bio.psu.edu/ greendestiny/publications/gdc-pfhe-31-3.pdf [hereinafter Pearce & Uhl on Penn State Program].

44. *See* AUSTRALIAN BEST PRACTICES SURVEY, *supra* note at 13.

45. *See* University of Florida Sustainability Task Force Report 2002, *supra* note 13.

46. UNIVERSITY OF MICHIGAN, THE "SUSTAINABLE UNIVERSITY OF MICHIGAN": SUGGESTED IMPLEMENTATION STRATEGIES (2000), *available at* http://www.umich.edu/~usustain/projects.html.

47. *See* UNITY COLLEGE SUSTAINABILITY PLAN, *supra* note 16,

48. *See* BALL STATE TALLOIRES IMPLEMENTATION REPORT, *supra* note 14. E-mail from Robert Koester, Chair, Ball State University Council on the Environment, to William R. Blackburn (Jan. 3, 2005).

49. *See* U.K. HEPS REPORT, *supra* note 19, at 25.

50. University of Victoria, Strategic Plan (2002), *available at* http://web.uvic.ca/strategicplan/introduction.html. University of Victoria, Campus Plan 2003 (2003), *available at* http://web.uvic.ca/fmgt/ sustain.html.

51. Campus Sustainability Office, University of British Columbia, Inspirations and Aspirations (2004), *available at* http://www.sustain. ubc.ca/framework.html.

52. *See* NWF Campus Survey, *supra* note 5.

53. *See* Australian Best Practices Survey, *supra* note 13, at 15, 39.

54. Office of Strategic Communications, University of California, Facts About the University of California: Green Building Policy and Clean Energy Standard (2003), *available at* http://www. ucop.edu/news/factsheets/greenbuildings.pdf. *See* Bauer Report on Berkeley Program, *supra* note 4, at 4-5.

55. Greenpeace, *Greenpeace Clean Energy Now! Campus Guide: How to Stop Global Warming by Making Your Campus a Leader in Clean Energy*, http://www.seac.org/energy/resources/cleanenergytoolkit.doc (last visited Jan. 8, 2006).

56. *See* D.J. Eagan & J. Keniry, National Wildlife Federation's Campus Ecology® Program, Green Investment, Green Return: How Practical Conservation Projects Save Millions on America's Campuses (1998).

57. David Santen, Portland State University, News: Portland State Recognized for Innovative Sustainability Practices (2004), *available at* http://www.pdx.edu/news/2845/.

58. Gloria Thompson et al., University of Vermont, *Tracking UVM: An Environmental Report Card for the University of Vermont for the Years 1990-2000*, at 14, http://www.uvm.edu/greening/trackinguvm.pdf (last visited Jan. 8, 2006) [hereinafter University of Vermont Environmental Report].

59. *See* University of BC Sustainability Report 2004, *supra* note 24, at 5-6. *See* University of BC Sustainability Report 2005, *supra* note 24, at 4-5. University of British Columbia, *APEGBC Award Nomination: University of British Columbia Campus Sustainability Office*, http://www. sustainability.ca/Docs/UBC%20Trek.pdf?CFID=10522550&CFTOKEN=49279066 (last visited Jan. 8, 2006).

60. *See* University of Michigan Environmental Task Force Report 2004, *supra* note 40.

61. *See* Pearce & Uhl on Penn State Program, *supra* note 43, at 53-61.

62. *See* University of Michigan Environmental Task Force Report 2004, *supra* note 40.

63. *See* Australian Best Practices Survey, *supra* note 13, at 16.

64. Leeds Metropolitan University, *Purchasing and Environment*, http://www.leedsmet.ac.uk/fin/pe/environmentpages/env_purchasing/env_purchasing.htm (last visited Jan. 8, 2006).

65. Rutgers University, *Environmentally Preferable Purchasing*, RUTGERS SUSTAINABLE, http://www.rusustainable.org/show_page.php?page=Purchasing (last visited Jan. 8, 2006). Rutgers University, *Green Purchasing*, http://procure.rutgers.edu/green.html (last visited Jan. 8, 2006). *See* Calder & Clugston 2003, *supra* note 10, at 10013-14.

66. *See* University of Florida Sustainability Task Force Report 2002, *supra* note 13, app. xxxii.

67. Corporate Social Responsibility Newswire Service, *Students Call for More Disclosure on University Hedge Fund Investments*, CSRWIRE, Jan. 8, 2006, *available at* http://www.csrwire.com/sfprint.cgi?sfArticleId=1357.

68. FairPensions, http://www.fairpensions.org.uk/index.htm (last visited Jan. 8, 2006).

69. *See* MICHIGAN STATE SUSTAINABILITY REPORT 2003, *supra* note 18, at 19.

70. *See* AUSTRALIAN BEST PRACTICES SURVEY, *supra* note 13, at 32, 38.

71. *See* NWF Campus Survey, *supra* note 5, at 116-17.

72. University of Technology, Sydney, *Conceptualizing Sustainability*, http://www.sustainability.uts.edu.au/resources/conceptualising_sustainability.html (last visited Jan. 8, 2006).

73. *See* AUSTRALIAN SUSTAINABLE UNIVERSITIES REPORT 2003, *supra* note 2, at 29.

74. *See* Peter Bardaglio & Edward Quevedo, *Building a Sustainable Future: The Positive Growth Initiative at Ithaca College*, SUSTAINABLE DEV., ECOSYSTEMS & CLIMATE CHANGE COMM. NEWSL., Oct. 2004, at 17-22 [hereinafter Bardaglio-Quevedo: Ithaca College].

75. Northern Arizona University, *The Ponderosa Project*, http://jan.ucc.nau.edu/ponderosa/ and Northern Arizona University, *Directory of NAU Environmental Programs and Courses*, http://www.mpcer.nau.edu/EnvironmentalCourses/ (both last visited Jan. 8, 2006). Center for Sustainable Environment, Northern Arizona University, *On-Campus Collaborators*, http://www.environment.nau.edu/collaborators/oncampus.htm (last visited Jan. 8, 2006).

76. U.K. Advertising Standards Authority, *ASA Schools and Colleges: Social Responsibility*, http://www.asa.org.uk/asa/about/Guided+Tours/Schools+and+Colleges/ (last visited Jan. 8, 2006).

77. Second Nature, *Sustainability Curriculum Framework*, http://www.secondnature.org/pdf/snwritings/factsheets/framework.pdf (last visited Jan. 8, 2006).

78. *See* National Service-Learning Ass'n, *National Service-Learning Clearinghouse: Higher Education*, http://www.servicelearning.org/hehome/index.php (last visited Jan. 8, 2006). At this website, you can do a search for *sustainable development*.

79. SECOND NATURE, EDUCATION FOR SUSTAINABILITY: CONTENT, CONTEXT, AND PROCESS OF LEARNING AND RESEARCH (2001), *available at* http://www.secondnature.org/pdf/snwritings/factsheets/EFSFactSheet.pdf.

80. Susan Allen-Gil et al., *Community Partnerships for Sustainable Education: The IC/EVI Model*, presented at the Conference on Environmental Management for Sustainable Universities (EMSU), Tecnológico de Monterrey, Campus Monterrey, Monterrey, Nuevo León, Mexico, June 9-11, 2004 [hereinafter Ithaca College-EVI 2004].

81. Allegheny College, *Opportunities*, ACAD.: ENVTL. SCI., http://www.allegheny.edu/academics/envsci/oppor.php (last visited Jan. 8, 2006).

82. CLEMSON UNIVERSITY, FINAL REPORT: INCORPORATING SUSTAINABILITY PROJECTS INTO BUSINESS AND TECHNICAL WRITING CLASSES: A WORKSHOP FOR FACULTY AND PROJECT CLIENTS (2003), *available at* http://www.sc.edu/sustainableu/2002HaqueSmithFinal.pdf. E-mail from Patricia Jerman, South Carolina Sustainable Universities Initiative, to William R. Blackburn (Jan. 10, 2005) [hereinafter Jerman E-mail].

83. *See* Jerman E-mail, *supra* note 82. E-mail from Patricia Jerman, South Carolina Sustainable Universities Initiative, to William R. Blackburn (Sept. 12, 2005).

84. *See* UNIVERSITY OF BC SUSTAINABILITY REPORT 2004, *supra* note 24, at 11, 12. *See* UNIVERSITY OF BC SUSTAINABILITY REPORT 2005, *supra* note 24, at 11, 12.

85. *See* NWF Campus Survey, *supra* note 5, at 118.

86. *See* AUSTRALIAN BEST PRACTICES SURVEY, *supra* note 13, at 32, 38

87. World Resources Institute, *WRI Project: BELL (Business-Environment Learning and Leadership) in North America, Latin America, and Asia*, RESEARCH TOPICS: BUS. AND ECON., http://bell.wri.org/ (last visited Jan. 8, 2006).

88. *See* NWF Campus Survey, *supra* note 5, at 118.

89. *See* AUSTRALIAN BEST PRACTICES SURVEY, *supra* note 13, at 32, 38.

90. Ball State University, *Interdepartmental Educational Program: Clustered Academic Minor in Environmentally Sustainable Practices*, http://www.bsu.edu/provost/ceres/Minors/ (last visited Jan. 8, 2006).

91. Vanderbilt Center for Environmental Management Studies, Vanderbilt University, *About VCEMS and Environmental Studies at Vanderbilt*, http://www.vanderbilt.edu/vcems/about.html (last visited Jan. 8, 2006).

92. *See* AUSTRALIAN BEST PRACTICES SURVEY, *supra* note 13, at 35, 40.

93. *See* NWF Campus Survey, *supra* note 5, at 118.

94. Joe Shepard et al., *The Challenges of Infusing Sustainability Across the Campus: The Curriculum and Campus Operations at Florida Gulf Coast University*, presented at the Environmental Management for Sustainable Universities Conference, Monterrey, N.L., Mexico, June 9-11, 2004.

95. Elisa Corbas-Flores & Karen Paul, *Teaching and Learning Sustainability in Business School*, presented at the Conference on Environmental Management for Sustainable Universities (EMSU), Tecnológico de Monterrey, Campus Monterrey, Monterrey, N.L., Mexico, June 9-11, 2004.

96. The course must touch on the "knowledge of the interaction and interdependence of the biophysical systems of the natural environment and human and social cultural systems." *See* University of Minnesota, *Research, Teaching and Outreach: Liberal Education Environmental Requirements*, SUSTAINABILITY AND U, http://www.uservices.umn.edu/sustainableU/liberaled.html (last visited Jan. 8, 2006).

97. *See* AUSTRALIAN BEST PRACTICES SURVEY, *supra* note 13, at 35, 40.

98. University of Cambridge Program for Industry, *HRH The Prince of Wales Business and the Environment Program*, http://www.cpi.cam.ac.uk/bep/ (last visited Jan. 11, 2006).

99. *See* Bardaglio-Quevedo: Ithaca College, *supra* note 74. *See* Ithaca College-EVI 2004, *supra* 80.

100. *See* UNIVERSITY OF BC SUSTAINABILITY REPORT 2005, *supra* note 24, at 7.

101. *See* AUSTRALIAN BEST PRACTICES SURVEY, *supra* note 13, at 32, 38.

102. *See* NWF Campus Survey, *supra* note 5, at 121.

103. Press Release, UNEP-Tongji University Offer New Approach to "Sustainability" (July 25, 2004), *available at* http://www.roap.unep.org/press/index.cfm.

104. SOUTH CAROLINA SUSTAINABLE UNIVERSITIES INITIATIVE, SOUTH CAROLINA SUSTAINABLE UNIVERSITIES INITIATIVE YEAR 4 ANNUAL REPORT 2, 9 (2002) [hereinafter SUI YEAR 4 REPORT].

105. *See* AUSTRALIAN BEST PRACTICES SURVEY, *supra* note 13, at 35, 40.

106. Students for a Sustainable Stanford, Stanford University, *Homepage*, http://sustainability.stanford.edu/ (last visited Jan. 8, 2006).

107. *See* Harvard Green Newsletter—Fall 2004, *supra* note 7, at 12.

108. University of British Columbia, *The UBC Campus Sustainability Office*, http://www.sustain.ubc.ca/sc_prog.html (last visited Jan. 8, 2006). *See* UNIVERSITY OF BC SUSTAINABILITY REPORT 2005, *supra* note 24. *See* UNIVERSITY OF BC SUSTAINABILITY REPORT 2004, *supra* note 24.

109. *See* Bauer Report on Berkeley Program, *supra* note 4.

110. *See* UNC-CH SUSTAINABILITY REPORT 2005, *supra* note 8, at 13.

111. Graduation Pledge Alliance, http://www.graduationpledge.org/index. html (last visited Jan. 8, 2006). *See also* Katharine Nicholson Ings, *Seniors Pledge Social Responsibility—At Large*, CHANGE, July/Aug. 2002, *available at* http://www.findarticles.com/p/articles/mi_m1254/is_4_34.

112. *See* University of Florida Sustainability Task Force Report 2002, *supra* note 13, app. xxxiii.

113. For a list of events see, Forum on Science and Technology for Sustainability, Harvard University, *Events*, http://sustsci.harvard.edu/events.htm (last visited Jan. 13, 2005). *See also* University Leaders for a Sustainable Future, *Events*, http://www.ulsf.org/resources_events.html (last visited Jan. 8, 2006).

114. PENN STATE GREEN DESTINY COUNCIL, PENN STATE INDICATORS REPORT—2000: STEPS TOWARD A SUSTAINABLE UNIVERSITY (2000), *available at* http://www.bio.psu.edu/greendestiny/publications/gdc-indicators_ 2000.pdf. *See also* Pearce & Uhl on Penn State Program, *supra* note 43, at 53-61.

115. David Newport & Thomas Chesnee, *University of Florida Sustainability Indicators August 2001* (The Greening UF Program, M.E. Rinker Sr. School of Building Construction and Planning, University of Florida), http://www.sustainable.ufl.edu/indicators.pdf (last visited Jan. 8, 2006). *See* University of Florida Sustainability Task Force Report 2002, *supra* note 13.

116. SANDRA RODRIGUEZ ET AL., UNIVERSITY OF MICHIGAN SCHOOL OF NATURAL RESOURCES & ENVIRONMENT, SUSTAINABILITY ASSESSMENT AND REPORTING FOR THE UNIVERSITY OF MICHIGAN'S ANN ARBOR CAMPUS (2002), *available at* http://css.snre.umich.edu/css_doc/CSS02-04.pdf. *See* UNIVERSITY OF MICHIGAN ENVIRONMENTAL TASK FORCE REPORT 2004, *supra* note 40.

117. *See* MICHIGAN STATE SUSTAINABILITY REPORT 2003, *supra* note 18.

118. Office of Campus Sustainability, Michigan State University, FOOTPRINTS, June 2005, at 6, *available at* http://www.ecofoot.msu.edu/.

119. *See* UNC-CH SUSTAINABILITY REPORT 2003, *supra* note 8. *See* UNC-CH SUSTAINABILITY REPORT 2005, *supra* note 8.

120. *See* UNIVERSITY OF BC SUSTAINABILITY REPORT 2005, *supra* note 24.

121. PENNY LLOYD, UNIVERSITY OF VICTORIA, THE UVIC SUSTAINABILITY PROJECT: ANNUAL REPORT 2001 (2001), *available at* http://uvsp.uvic. ca/about.php. ADAM MJOLSNESS, UNIVERSITY OF VICTORIA SUSTAINABILITY PROJECT, CAMPUS ECOLOGY COORDINATOR PROGRESS REPORT 2001/2002 (2002), *available at* http://uvsp.uvic.ca/about.php.

122. UNIVERSITY OF VICTORIA, FACILITIES MANAGEMENT, SUSTAINABILITY REPORT 2003-2004 (2004), *available at* http://web.uvic.ca/fmgt/sustain. html.

123. SHEFFIELD HALLAM UNIVERSITY, SUSTAINABILITY IN THE UNIVERSITY (2004), *available at* http://www.shu.ac.uk/services/facilities/ sustainability/linksdocs.html.

124. ROYAL ROADS UNIVERSITY, STATE OF THE ENVIRONMENT 2002-2004 ANNUAL REPORT (2004), *available at* http://www.royalroads.ca/about-rru/governance/sustainability/. ROYAL ROADS UNIVERSITY, PROGRESS TOWARDS SUSTAINABILITY: 2004-2005 FISCAL YEAR 3 (2005), *available at* http://www.royalroads.ca/about-rru/governance/sustainability/.

125. ENVIRONMENTAL UNIT, GÖTEBORG UNIVERSITY, GÖTEBORG UNIVERSITY: ENVIRONMENTAL REPORT 2004 (2005), *available at* http://www. mls.adm.gu.se/GU/handbok/4514rd1.htm.

126. University of Helsinki, *Environmental Report for 2000*, http://www.tekn. helsinki.fi/ymparisto/english.pdf (last visited Jan. 8, 2006).

127. GIOLA THOMPSON, UNIVERSITY OF VERMONT, TRACKING UVM: AN ENVIRONMENTAL REPORT CARD FOR THE UNIVERSITY OF VERMONT FOR THE YEARS 1990-2000 (2000), *available at* http://www.uvm.edu/greening/ trackinguvm.html. GIOLA THOMPSON, UVM ENVIRONMENTAL COUNCIL, DEVELOPING OUR ENVIRONMENTAL UNIVERSITY (2004), *available at* http://www.uvm.edu/greening/envcouncil/Develop_Env_Univ.pdf.

128. *See supra* note 118.

129. *See* Harvard Green Newsletter—Fall 2004, *supra* note 7.

130. *See* SUI YEAR 4 REPORT, *supra* note 104.

Chapter 16

Keeping the Initiative Alive: Making the SOS Sustainable

"The future is not some place we are going to, but one we are creating. The paths are not to be found, but made, and the activity of making them changes both the maker and the destination."[1]
—John Schaar

Sustaining the SOS

We have all seen inspired efforts go awry in all kinds of organizations. Plans are prepared but not executed. People promise to help, but later move or become sidetracked with other activities. Resources dry up. The excitement dims. Priorities shift. All these problems can plague an organization's commitment to sustainability, too. The chances of this happening are particularly great where there is no well-established process to assure ongoing follow-up.

An SOS is such a process. It provides a structure, a routine that people can follow to stay on track. But an SOS is not a perpetual motion machine. It is a dynamic system, a living machine that requires fuels—in this case, human involvement and resources. Follow-up is needed to ensure that these fuels are adequate and that the system is functioning properly to deliver the desired results. This follow-up, like the SOS itself, should be carefully planned. Here are some things that should be considered:

Anticipate the Future Internally and Externally

Sustainability leaders and advocates must keep an eye on the road ahead to anticipate and adjust for dips, turns, and other hazards. Are company sales and profits down? If so, the sustainability leader must anticipate working with fewer resources and find ways to emphasize sustainability projects which help the organization address its problems. Is a new CEO or board chairman coming on board? If that's the case, a sustainability initiative geared to her priorities should be brought forward. Executives who seem to have her ear should be assessed as potential allies for furthering the cause. Is the organization planning a big shift in strategy or structure? Then how can sustainability be framed to fit that new environment?

Anticipating the next moves of the organization is important, but so is anticipating changes outside the organization. What happens outside can affect what happens inside. A new, highly publicized corporate scandal or disaster is a sure sign that greater public and government scrutiny and expectations of business—including *your* business—will surely follow. In addition, studies continually emerge that offer new insights about sustainability trends. This is why a Big Picture Review was recommended in Chapter 6 as a part of strategic planning. But sustainability leaders and advocates should not wait until once a year to brush up on external affairs. This should be an ongoing task. General news publications like the *New York Times* and *Time Magazine* provide a good review of general current events. Those in business can follow publications like the *Wall Street Journal, Financial Times, Harvard Business Review*, the *Economist, Fortune*, and *Business Week*. The *ENDS Report* and *Ethical Corporation* from the United Kingdom and the *Environmental Forum* and *Crosslands Bulletin* from the United States are useful for staying up with issues on environmental sustainability. Free e-publication outlets like *EurActiv Update, Green.Biz.com, Planet Ark, Business and SD News* (WBCSD), and *Trendwatching.com*, provide a broader perspective on trends and developments that can affect your programs. The websites of business-related sustainability organizations such as the WBCSD, the BSR, CSR Europe, and Business in the Community, offer a wide range of news and tools for company sustainability practitioners. The latest presentations and articles on a variety of sustainability topics, including concepts drawn from this book, can be found on this author's website, at www.WBlackburnConsulting.com. Academic journals and conferences related to sustainability also abound. By tapping a few publications, websites, and conferences that are most germane to your organization, you can gain early warning about evolving issues and can factor that information into day-to-day decisionmaking and long-term planning.

Periodically Tune the System

People working within an organization over long periods tend to become myopic about the organization's weaknesses, and sometimes even its strengths. What is true about an organization is also true about an SOS. For this reason, an outsider should be brought in from time to time to review the SOS with fresh eyes. Such a review can prompt a shift of emphasis or resources that can improve performance or otherwise enhance the value delivered by the system.

Hone Skills and Knowledge

Periodically tuning the system won't do much good if the skills of the people who operate it have eroded. Organizations change, people leave, new people join, lessons fade. Strong training programs are needed to assure team members understand and can manage their assignments and, if talented, are ultimately developed for advanced responsibilities. Planning, team building, communications, and project management are just a few skills that can take on critical importance in the field of sustainability. Training must also be directed to keeping team members informed of changes in the SOS, the latest trends in sustainability, and the direction and challenges of their own organization.

Sustain Support and Resources

The job of selling the value of an SOS or other sustainability initiative never ends. Selling need not always be via a pre-rehearsed sales presentation, however. It's often more effective to "show and tell"—reveal successes to management as they occur, have outsiders comment on them, and use new problems as motivators for change. One of the most effective strategies, however, is to have a senior manager from a company facility or business unit personally share with her peers how the approach toward sustainability helped her own organization. Sustainability leaders and advocates must also collect little facts and figures about successes, problems, and opportunities, mastering sound bites than can come in handy during hallway conversations. Appropriate symbols, rituals, and routine events concerning sustainability can help, too, since these measures tend to drive the concept further into the culture of the organization.

When the organization faces difficult financial times, rallying support for the SOS can be particularly tough. As mentioned in Chapter 12, during such times, it is usually wise to make strategic adjustments, such as delaying lower priority projects in favor of those SOS-related initiatives that provide visible financial benefits, boost sales, or strengthen employee relations. Such adjustments can build credibility for the sustainability initiative over the long run.

Keep It Fresh and Inspiring

When programs become stale, participants can become apathetic. Sustainability leaders must find ways to keep the initiative fresh and inspirational. Individual and organizational recognition in the form of awards, certificates, commendation speeches by the CEO, newsletter articles, or other acknowledgment can go a long way. Participative strategic planning can also keep people involved and interested, while producing new projects or directions that can reinvigorate the troops. Changing the membership of the core team and other sustainability support groups can also inject new life into an organization's drive toward sustainability. Inspiring outside speakers can do that too, as can on-site fairs, conferences, and other special events.

Collaborate With Others

Sustainability leaders need to be on constant vigil for opportunities for win-win collaborations with other groups inside and outside the organization. Granted, good collaborations with external groups are not easy to find. But when properly selected and planned, drawing on the engagement tips from Chapter 11, they can achieve well beyond what either participant could accomplish alone. Collaborations can also bring new insights and skills to your own organization and thereby make your SOS more effective.

Continually Improve Performance

Sustainability leaders must continually monitor the output of their SOS, both formally through measurement and metrics, and informally through discussions with others. If results are lagging or some dysfunction is erupting in the organization that will eventually impede performance, the cause must be identified and addressed as soon as possible. If this is not done, the SOS and the organization's faith in it will be undermined. What is more, progress toward sustainability will be slowed, an effect that will compound each year the problem is allowed to linger. Given the importance of sustainability and what it can mean to the organization, this cannot be tolerated.

How Others Can Help

As this book has shown, companies can do much to move society toward sustainability while at the same time reaping benefits of their own. The

SOS is designed to help them do that. But the cause of sustainability will not be embraced across the business world merely by waiting for companies to stumble onto the wisdom of doing so. Some external encouragement is needed.

Organizations, like living organisms, evolve and grow in response to their environment. Just as a plant turns toward the light, businesses move in response to the stimuli around them. The environment in which organizations grow is, to a large extent, created by other organizations. Companies influence other companies as peers and customers. Governments shape the behavior of business through trade agreements, tax codes, and various human rights, environmental, and other laws. Companies can also be significantly affected by the expectations and preferences of investors. NGOs help define a firm's public image and influence the development of laws controlling corporate behavior, while academic institutions guide the thinking of future business leaders. Such institutions, along with various polling companies, continually provide new research on sustainability issues to business and other sectors. Academia also helps mold government policy and public opinion, which in turn can profoundly affect private enterprise. Indeed, entities of all kinds form an intricate web of relationships that can move business toward sustainability.

While many stakeholders are now pushing or pulling business in the right direction, others are not. Certainly much more can be done. For one thing, governments can more extensively use import duties, taxes, and other financial incentives to discourage unsustainable consumption, encourage sustainable practices, and stimulate innovative approaches toward sustainability. NGOs can publicly applaud those firms—especially the small ones—that adopt best sustainable practices. They can seek more opportunities for collaboration with business. And they can improve corporate transparency on, and accountability for, sustainability performance by focusing more attention on firms that don't candidly communicate this performance. Universities can strengthen their curriculums and research to better prepare their graduates for addressing the business challenges and opportunities related to sustainability. As shown in Chapters 13, 14, and 15, public bodies, NGOs, and academia can all demonstrate their commitment to sustainability—and encourage businesses to do the same—by developing an SOS and issuing sustainability performance reports of their own.

Investment groups and other financial institutions can aid the cause by understanding the business risks and opportunities posed by sustainability issues, and then use that knowledge to inject sustainability criteria into their loan and investment decisions. By basing such decisions on social and environmental factors as well as traditional economic considerations, these institutions can send a strong message of the practical importance of sustainability to business success.

Companies themselves can serve as role models among their peers by adopting an SOS and projecting a sustainability ethic. They can accelerate constructive change by sharing best practices through various business organizations and other forums. Through industrywide and business-sector collaborations, companies can involve other firms in addressing mutual sustainability problems that are too big for individual companies to resolve themselves.

But given the broad and complex nature of many sustainability matters, perhaps the most effective way to address them—and to bring business up to the learning curve on sustainability—is through joint efforts between business and other sectors of society. It is only by companies working together with governments, NGOs, academia, investors, and other stakeholders that we can turn the tide on some of the most serious issues of our day: poverty, climate change, resource depletion, discrimination, AIDS, and other enormous challenges to the sustainability of our society.

Of course, action by organizations depends on action by people. The purpose of this book has been to guide those people in shaping their organizations to meet the call of sustainability. As the great anthropologist Margaret Mead once said: "Never doubt that a small group of thoughtful committed people can change the world: indeed it's the only thing that ever has!"[2] You can be part of that change. This book has given you the tools. All you have to do is start—now!

Follow-up Checklist for Action: Keeping the Initiative Alive

☐ Drawing from the suggestions presented in this chapter, develop and implement steps for assuring the SOS continues to function effectively over the long term.

☐ Participate with others in encouraging more companies to take up the cause of sustainability.

☐ Take personal action as soon as possible to begin moving your own organization toward sustainability.

Endnotes to Chapter 16

1. This quote is attributed to John Schaar, an American writer and scholar, who is currently Professor Emeritus of Political Philosophy at the University of California at Santa Cruz.

2. Margaret Mead was an American anthropologist who lived from 1901 to 1978.

Appendix 1

Summary of Sustainability Trends

1.35.   Growing Power of NGOs/CSOs
1.36.   Increasing Global Terrorism

1.0 Introduction to Global Sustainability Trends; The Millennium Development Goals

"Don't it always seem to go, that you don't know what you've got till it's gone."[1]
                                    —Joni Mitchell

Seeing the Big Picture

Many of us rise each morning to sip our hot coffee and scan the headlines of the daily news. The articles may catch our attention but few alert us to the bigger picture being revealed. Like an observer in the Chicago Art Institute standing too close to Georges Seurat's stippled painting of *Sunday Afternoon on la Grande Jatte,* all we see is dots. To understand the full picture, we must stand back. As we do, soon a man, a tree, or an umbrella appear in the artwork. Only if we take a long view does the full masterpiece reveal itself. And so it is with the state of the world as it relates to sustainability. Events are the dots. Placed side by side, these dots paint a trend here, a trend there. When presented together, these trends give us the big picture in which business and society operate, a picture out of balance and in need of correction, a picture full of risks and opportunities.

The trends discussed in this appendix dictate much of the agenda for societal action in the drive for sustainability. People engaged in strategic and tactical planning must understand these trends and the specific risks and opportunities they hold for their organizations. Form C (Appendix 4) is designed to capture the planners' conclusions in that regard. The list below is not exhaustive, however. In assessing sustainability risks and opportunities during planning, companies are encouraged to add other sustainability issues and trends to Form C as relevant.

The Millennium Development Goals

The United Nations is keenly aware of the big picture of global sustainability trends. In 2002, the U.N. Member states unanimously adopted the Millennium Declaration acknowledging many of the serious problems concerning governance, poverty, disease, education, inequality, environmental degradation, and the lack of access to healthcare and technology in many corners of the globe.[2] The declarations reiterate a set of targets on these issues—the Millennium Development Goals (MDGs)—which were originally set out by international conferences and summits held in the 1990s and formerly referred to as the International Development Goals (see Figure A1.0.1). The U.N. Secretary-General issues a yearly report on progress toward implementation of the Millennium Declaration, including the goals, based on information drawn from across the U.N. organization. The first comprehensive review was produced in 2005.[3]

The Trends

This appendix summarizes a number of the important sustainability trends, including many associated with the MDGs. While some good progress is being made toward the goal on poverty reduction (Appendix 1.4), less than 20% of all countries are on track to meet the targets on child and maternal mortality (Appendix 1.5).[4] The Caribbean, East and Southeast Asia, and Latin America are positioned to meet their MDG on reducing hunger (Appendix 1.9), but progress has been slower in southern Asia and sub-Saharan Africa. Northern Africa has seen no improvement, and in western Asia conditions are worsening.[5] In five developing regions, 90% of children or more are enrolled in primary education (Appendix 1.11), and slight gains are being made in most other parts of the world. But nearly two out of five children in sub-Saharan Africa still get no schooling.[6] Good progress is being made in providing access to safe water, but the same cannot be said for improved sanitation—only East Asia and Latin America are likely to meet this goal, and nearly half of the people in developing nations still lack toilets (Appendix 1.18).[7] The picture is even less optimistic regarding the control of human immunodeficiency virus/acquired immune deficiency syndrome (HIV/AIDS), malaria, and other major diseases (Appendix 1.6).

In examining the state of our environment, many aspects of which are also summarized here, the U.N. 2005 Millennium Ecosystem Assessment concluded the following:

- The changes made to the ecosystems have contributed to substantial net gains in human well-being and economic development, to be sure, but these gains have been achieved at growing costs in the form of:

  1. The decline in many of the benefits provided by ecosystems, especially freshwater, fisheries, air and water purification, and the

control of regional and local climate, natural hazards, and pests;
2. Increased risk of accelerating abrupt and potentially irreversible
adverse changes in disease emergence, water quality, fishery
stocks, regional climate, and the creation of "dead zones" in
coastal waters; and
3. Greater poverty for some groups.

• These problems if unaddressed will substantially diminish the benefits that future generations obtain from ecosystems.

• The degradation of ecosystem benefits could grow significantly worse
during the first half of this century and is a barrier to achieving the MDGs.

• Reversing the degradation of ecosystems can be partially met, but
this would require significant changes in policies, institutions, and
practices that are not currently under way.[8]

Figure A1.0.1 United Nations Millennium Goals and Targets[9]

Goal 1. Eradicate extreme poverty and hunger

Target: Between 1990 and 2015, reduce by one-half the proportion of people living on less than $1 per day and the proportion who suffer from hunger.

Goal 2. Achieve universal primary education

Target: Ensure that by 2015 boys and girls everywhere will be able to complete primary education.

Goal 3. Promote gender equality and empower women

Target: Eliminate gender disparity in primary and secondary schools preferably by 2005 and at all levels of education by no later than 2015.

Goal 4. Reduce child mortality

Target: Between 1990 and 2015, reduce by two-thirds the mortality rate for children under five years old.

Goal 5. Improve maternal health

Target: Between 1990 and 2015, reduce by three-quarters the woman mortality rate in child birth.

Goal 6. Combat HIV/AIDS, malaria, and other diseases

Target: By 2015, halt and begin to reverse the spread of HIV/AIDS and the incidence of malaria and other major diseases.

Goal 7. Ensure environmental sustainability

Target: Integrate the principles of sustainable development into country policies and programs and reverse the loss of environmental resources.

Target: By 2015, halve the proportion of people without sustainable access to safe drinking water and basic sanitation.

Target: By 2020, achieve a significant improvement in the lives of at least 100 million slum dwellers.

Goal 8. Develop a global partnership for development

Target: Further develop open, rule-based, predictable, nondiscriminatory trading and financial systems, including improvements in good governance, development, and poverty reduction—both nationally and internationally.

Target: Address the special needs of the least developed countries, including tariff- and quota-free access for exports and enhanced financial assistance.

Target: Address the special sustainable development needs of landlocked countries and small island states.

Target: Deal comprehensively with the debt problems of developing countries to make debt sustainable in the long term.

Target: Work with developing countries to implement strategies for decent and productive work for youth.

Target: Work with pharmaceutical companies to provide access to affordable, essential drugs in developing countries.

Target: Work with the private sector to make available the benefits of new technologies, especially information and communications.

Indeed, current sustainability trends pose a great challenge to both society, its institutions and organizations—the challenge for prompt and effective action. Let us examine three dozen of these trends in more detail.

1.1. Growth in Global Business Competition

A drive through the parking lot of any U.S. supermarket tells the story. The automobile market is no longer simply the Chevy-Chrysler-Ford competition of 35 years ago. Notice the Audis, BMWs, Hondas, Mercedes, Mitsubishis, Nissans, and Toyotas. Global competition is clearly here to stay. The value of world exports of goods and services has grown tenfold since 1965.[10] Over the last three decades, the share of total world output by local factories of multinational or—to use the modern term—transnational corporations (TNCs) has doubled.[11] The number of TNCs jumped from roughly 7,000 to 65,000.[12] Their 850,000 affiliate operations and 54 million employees outside their home countries now compete everyday for the jackpot of world markets in everything from cars and cameras to costume jewelry and cantaloupes.[13] Even the National Basketball Association has gone global, selling over $500 million in merchandise outside the United States.[14]

These TNCs pack a wallop: of the 100 largest economies in the world, 51 are corporations.[15] Not only are they large, but they must continuously be fed. The success of their CEOs depends on them delivering an ever-increasing level of profits through global expansion, increased sales, cost competition, innovation, and brand strength. All the while competitors from every corner of the globe are hovering over them, waiting to steal their lunches. It's no simple job. In the end, local consumers benefit from the lower cost, superior quality products provided by the TNCs and try not to think much about the small local businesses they have let go hungry.

1.2. Opposition to Globalization

Globalization has come in many forms: the transnational reach of companies, unions, NGOs, governments, and other organizations; worldwide access to products, services, and people; international investment and other financial transactions; and the global exchange of technologies, information, and ideas—to name a few.[16] Nations like Ireland, Sweden, Switzerland, and many countries in Southeast Asia, have found a pot of gold at the end of their globalization rainbow. Others have not. Those that have successfully moved along the path to globalization have exhibited more stable governments, less corruption, and greater democratization and economic equality among their citizens than typically found in developing nations and other less globalized countries.[17] Proponents of globalization point to this as support for their cause.

Opponents say these positive characteristics of successful countries are not the results of globalizations but the contributing causes of both globalization and international economic achievement. Globalization flourishes where there is social stability, they say, and point to the fact that even socially disruptive events like 9/11 and the SARS outbreak can hurt both. More threatening is the backlash from those who feel they've been disenfranchised by globalization. These opponents cover a broad range: international terrorists at one end, arm-chair critics at the other, and protesters in Seattle somewhere in between. Their perception is that TNCs and the governments that support them are exercising excessive control over their lives by stealing their local culture, fouling their environment, pandering to consumerism, and taking away their jobs. According to Princeton historian Harold James, it is precisely this kind of backlash that helped derail globalization eras of the past.[18]

Regardless of where you stand on this chicken-or-egg argument, in the context of international business, the concepts of economic and social sustainability are mutually reinforcing. With the powerful force of business competition behind it and success stories all around, the globalization movement will be hard to stop. Says U.N. Secretary-General Kofi Annan: "[A]rguing against globalization is like arguing against the laws of gravity." The question here is not how to stop it, but how to make it work for everybody.

For business, the positive and negative implications of globalization are clear. From the positive side, companies may see globalization as the way to tap new markets, lower material and operational costs, recruit and develop new workers, and spread business risk. But business must also be prepared defensively—prepared to respond to the invasion of aggressive foreign competitors; prepared to deal with protests from employees, unions, and activist groups offended by the relocation of operations—and jobs—overseas. They must also be prepared to quickly handle public relations attacks from home and abroad over an environmental or ethical faux pas in some distant land. Fortunately, TNCs are armed with the modern tools of e-communication as they address these challenges. Unfortunately for them, so are their opponents.

1.3. Speed of Communications; The Digital Divide

The e-revolution has had a profound effect in shrinking the size of the globe. Masses of information now fly around the world at the speed of light, and more and more people are benefitting. From 1920 to 1990, the cost of a three-minute telephone call from New York to London plunged from $244.65 to $3.32.[19] As of 2002, over 600 million people were accessing the Internet through more than 170 million host computers, up over 100-fold from 10 years before.[20] One billion users were estimated for 2005. In 2000, there were 214 countries plugged into the internet, 17 times the number 12 years earlier.[21] This has led the high-income countries to a more knowledge-based economy with increased speed and efficiency for businesses of all kinds. It has also meant that TNCs have fewer places to hide when things go wrong. What happens at a company's Malaysia factory can be known within hours by the residents living near their Cincinnati headquarters and by their customers in Germany.

With Internet access, cell phones, faxes, personal digital assistants (PDAs), satellite imagery, and other new communications tools, the speed and breadth of communications will continue to increase—at least for some. The "digital divide" remains: only 10% of the world's citizens have access to the Internet; more than half have never used a phone.[22] This poses an opportunity for growth for computer and telecommunications businesses. But being successful in these markets is no easy task. Two billion people don't even have electricity.[23] And while it's noble to provide people with a new-found window-to-the-world, the first thing several billion of our destitute fellows want to know is where they can find their next meal. The problem is, the e-revolution may simply make the rich countries richer and do little for the poor. Finding the answer for these people will be the real business challenge. Companies like IBM, Hewlett Packard (HP), Microsoft, British Telecom (BT), Motorola, Intel, Ericsson, Cisco Systems, and Vodafone are making a valiant effort to do so.[24] Some creative initiatives have emerged—recall Grameen's telephone-ladies program discussed in Chapter 3, for example—but a viable long-term business strategy to address these potential customers is still elusive.

1.4. Widening Prosperity Gap

Without a doubt, the rich are getting richer, the poor, poorer. According to the World Bank, the wealthiest countries saw their economic output in gross domestic product per capita grow by two thirds—over $10,000—between 1975 and 1999 while the levels in low-income nations stayed relatively flat.[25] Sub-Saharan countries saw a 17% decline.

Approximately 1.1 billion people—one of every six in the world—live on less than $1 per day.[26] The good news is that this is 400 million fewer than the number of people at this poverty level in 1981—an improvement driven primarily by the economic boom in portions of East and South Asia.[27] Unfortunately the people of sub-Saharan Africa haven't seen a change for the better, and nearly half remain in severe poverty—almost double the number in 1981.[28] As of 2002, 45% of the world's population and 80% of those from India were earning less than $2 daily. This is 300 million more than in 1981.[29] While poverty levels should continue to improve worldwide, led primarily by gains in China, India, Indonesia, and Pakistan, they are projected to worsen in other parts of South Asia and in sub-Saharan Africa.[30]

If things weren't bad enough for the destitute, many of them are plagued with diseases and lack clean water, basic health care, stable governments, and other social services most of us take for granted. As renowned economist Jeffrey Sachs observed, 20,000 people die each day from extreme poverty.[31] The benefits of globalization have clearly passed them by. The rich-poor gap is also widening in population, with the number of people in low-income countries growing 50% since 1980, 3 ½ times the growth rate for those with high incomes.[32] That gap will stretch even further since almost all population growth over the next 10 years is expected to come from developing nations, raising the world's share of citizens there to 85%.[33]

So how do the struggling low-income countries dig themselves out of this hole? The problem is they are often burdened with crushing national debt and lack the resources to address the root causes of their plight: inadequate education; rapid population growth; destruction of natural resources; pervasive corruption; political instability; and the AIDS epidemic. Moreover, import duties and other trade restrictions imposed by industrialized nations have closed an important door to their economic improvement. And even if the income of these countries climbs, the effect on poverty will be limited because of the high levels of rich-poor inequality that exist.

The economies of countries with great economic disparity must grow twice as fast as countries with better equality if poverty is to be halved by 2015.[34]

The widening gap between rich and poor is not just a problem for the Third World, however; it's happening in the United States as well. Government data show that the richest 1% of U.S. citizens in 2000 had more money to spend after taxes than the poorest 40%, whereas in 1979 the wealthiest had just under half the after-tax money of the poorest 40%.[35] In fact, the income distribution in the United States is worse than that of India: In both countries, the richest 20% of the population have approximately 45% of the income. But in India, the poorest 20% have nearly 9% of the income, whereas in the United States they have only 5%.[36]

1.5. Population Growth; Mortality Rates

Looking at the developing and developed countries together, the U.N. populations division expects our current world's inhabitants to climb by half, from the current six million up to nine billion by mid-century.[37] That's another Beijing's worth of people every other month, another Australia every 4 months, another Mexico every 1 ½ years, another United States every 5 years.

Not only will we have more neighbors in the future, but older ones, too. Worldwide, the average life expectancy, which rose dramatically from 47 years in 1950 to 67 in 2003, should continue to climb, notwithstanding the dampening effect of the AIDS epidemic.[38] That trend should be fueled in part by ongoing improvements in child mortality in the Caribbean, Latin America, northern Africa, and southeastern Asia—the result of economic growth, better nutrition, and access to health care.

The increase in life expectancy should translate to business growth for companies associated with food, shelter, transportation, and other necessities. Given the graying of society, those businesses involving health care, retirement homes, and other services and products for the elderly should do particularly well. The marketing plans of many other industries will also need to give this segment of the population more attention.

The improvement in life expectancy is good news for most but not all regions. Unless conditions change significantly in the more impoverished regions of Africa, the average citizen there will continue to see death before age 40. There, tragedy is everywhere. In sub-Saharan Africa, one of every six children dies before the age of five from disease;

poor water, sanitation, or nutrition; or the lack of health care. In Niger and Sierra Leone the rate is one of every four.[39]

The death of women from pregnancy-related causes is quite high in Africa, too, reaching one in eight mothers in Angola, Niger, and Sierra Leone (as well as Afghanistan). This contrasts with a maternal death rate of less than 1 in 10,000 mothers in many parts of Europe. Overall, women in the least developed nations are over 130 times as likely to die from pregnancy or childbirth as those in industrialized countries. This higher risk is in large measure due to higher birth rates and the fact that only about half the women from least developed countries have skilled attendants present during childbirth.[40] But premature death is not just the result of poverty and disease. One in 10 deaths among adults is related to tobacco—a figure expected to rise to one in six by 2030.[41]

1.6. AIDS and Other Serious Diseases

Malaria, tuberculosis, and cholera and other water-borne diseases continue to take their deadly toll just as they have over the years. More than 9 million new cases of tuberculosis—some with new drug-resistant strains—caused an estimated 1.7 million deaths in 2003. Ninety-nine percent of those cases occurred in developing nations—three million in South and East Asia and two million in sub-Saharan Africa. The annual number of new tuberculosis cases is increasing about 1% per year due primarily to the emergence of drug-resistant strains, the spread of HIV/AIDS which reduces resistance to the disease, and the growing number of refuges and displaced people.[42]

Malaria claims 350 to 500 million victims each year, with over a million fatalities. In sub-Saharan Africa, where 90% of the malaria cases occur, the disease accounts for more than one-fourth of child mortality. With the introduction of insecticide-treated bed nets, the incidence of this mosquito-carried disease has decreased dramatically in places like Vietnam.[43]

The AIDS epidemic of the last few decades has brought even greater devastation. As of 2004, 39 million people worldwide were living with HIV—one-third of them ages 15 to 24. Globally, 4.9 million people were newly infected with the virus that year, and 3.1 million died from it.[44] Over half of the newly infected are under age 25. More than 95% of the HIV/AIDS cases were from developing nations, and 70% from sub-Saharan Africa. Between 35 and 40% of all adults in Botswana and Swaziland were carrying the disease in 2003 with little prospect for life-saving treatment.[45] Where it is spreading in sub-Saharan Africa, young women are three times as likely as young men to become infected.[46] AIDS is the world's number one killer for people ages 15 to 49. More than 15 million children have suffered the loss of one or both parents to the disease—a figure expected to climb to 25 million by 2010.[47] While Africa has been hardest hit, serious questions remain as to how the disease will play out in South and East Asia, home of seven million HIV/AIDS victims and a region where surveillance programs are weak.[48]

As more industrialized nations join the battle against AIDS and other deadly maladies—for moral reasons as well as for business growth—they will be increasingly looking to companies for solutions. Companies with the products, services, and experience to help should be in demand. Only 12% of AIDS/HIV victims in low- and middle-income countries are receiving the antiretroviral medicines they need.[49] But given the poverty of most victims and their countries, pricing will be a sticky issue that must be addressed to assure the solution is economically sustainable. Firms with operations in regions where AIDS is rampant must aggressively work to prevent and control the disease. Such actions are not only humanitarian but can help contain the business costs of AIDS—costs manifest in effects on absenteeism, recruitment, retraining, morale, and reputation. Firms seeking constructive strategies can look to the Global Business Coalition on HIV/AIDS for assistance. This organization is led by ex-U.S. Ambassador to the United Nations, Richard Holbrooke, and supported by 170 companies, the International Labour Organization, and World Economic Forum.

The devastation of AIDS, malaria, and tuberculosis could be dwarfed, however, by a flu pandemic of the type that killed 20 to 40 million people in 1918-1919. Although that Spanish Flu has not been a problem for more than 90 years, a virus of equal or greater virulence could emerge if the Avian Flu from Southeast Asia evolves to a more contagious type—something experts believe is quite possible. The mortality rate among the few who have contracted the Avian Flu has exceeded 50%. Companies should maintain contingency plans that lay out their response to such a disaster.

1.7. Mental Health Problems

According to the World Health Organization (WHO), over 400 million people had a mental or neurological disorder in 2001. This includes autism, Alzheimer's disease, schizophrenia, depression, sleep disorders, addiction, and substance abuse. It also encompasses bipolar affective disorder, panic and anxiety disorders, mental retardation, and epilepsy. Mental disorders account for approximately one-third of the time lost due to all disabilities. One of the most debilitating disorders is depression, which affects more than 120 million people worldwide. It is responsible for 12% of all disability time and likely to account for 15% by 2020. Severe depression or schizophrenia trigger many of the 1 million suicides and 10 to 20 million suicide attempts that occur annually.[50] Therapeutic drugs are available to control depression and other mental disorders—at least for those who have health care. Unfortunately, this rules out many of the poor around the world. And even if medications are available, a considerable number of the afflicted have trouble maintaining routine usage. This can be a serious problem. With the advent of therapeutic drugs, governments dramatically cut resources for mental health support forcing many previous institutional patients to fend for themselves.

1.8. Increased Immigration, Lower Fertility in Industrialized Nations

From 1990 to 1995, about 40% of the population growth in high-income countries was due to immigration.[51] That trend is expected to continue. Fertility rates are now below the replacement rate of 2.1 children per woman in Europe and in the United States. Rates are dropping in most other regions, too. Education and family planning have been big factors. Studies show that in Africa, Asia, and Latin America, women with seven or more years of schooling have two to three fewer children than those with three or less years.[52] By 2025, Africa is expected to be the only place where fertility has not dropped below the replacement level.[53]

If the trend toward declining fertility rates continues, this will help address concerns about the over consumption of the earth's resources. That's the good news. But there are challenges as well, especially for business. The number of working-age people in the developed countries is expected to shrink by 7% by 2025 while that in the low-income countries is expected to jump over 40%. This will mean the poor-country workers will outnumber their rich-country sisters five to one.[54] The United States and its industrialized partners will be looking to Africa, Central America, and other developing regions for new labor if they want to stay on the gravy train of business growth. They will also be seeking new consumers there. In the future, Third-World workers, armed with fresh wages, could well be the new markets for business. But to penetrate these markets, companies must have the right products for these new consumers—products suited to their needs and cultures.

Business leaders who want to position their companies to attract customers and potential employees from these growth regions would be advised to look to IBM, an organization that has effectively married its diversity programs and business strategy.[55] Other firms with superior diversity programs include Enterprise Rent-A-Car, Fifth Third Bancorp, Kraft Foods, PepsiCo, Pitney Bowes, Procter & Gamble (P&G), UPS, and Wells Fargo.

1.9. Hunger and Malnutrition

In 2000, 95% of the world's 840 million undernourished people—those consuming on average less than 1,900 calories per day—lived in the developing world. But the problem was not just confined to the poorest nations of Africa, Asia, and Latin America. Thirty million were from eastern Europe and the former Soviet Union, and 11 million from industrialized nations.[56] The WHO calls the lack of proper food "the silent emergency," and claims that some regions are running out of water necessary for adequate food production.[57]

Over the last decade, the number of undernourished people in industrialized countries fell by 20 million—worldwide by 3%. Good gains have been made in the Caribbean, eastern and southeastern Asia, and Latin America, but the problem remains severe in southern Asia. In sub-Saharan Africa, where hunger is worst, one-third of the population was found to be undernourished in 2002.[58]

Malnutrition, which is measured by comparing weight and height among populations of similar children, is improving slightly everywhere except South Asia. There, in 2000, nearly half of the children under age five were found to suffer from inadequate nutrition.[59] Worldwide, approximately five million children die of hunger each year—one every five seconds.[60]

1.10. Child and Forced Labor

Over 12 million people work as slaves or in other forms of forced labor. Such practices are present in all regions of the world—more than three-fourths of them in Asia Pacific, over 10% from Latin America, and even some (3%) in industrialized countries. Although most forms of forced labor are considered crimes in nearly all countries, often it is not well defined in the law. There are few prosecutions. Two-thirds of forced labor is for illegal economic gain by organized crime and other private parties. This includes traditional forms of the practice embedded in older beliefs and customs, such as slavery and slave raiding in parts of West Africa and the subjugation of tribal and caste minorities in Asia and indigenous peoples in Latin America. It also encompasses the more "modern" forms of debt bondage of workers, most prevalent in South Asia and commonly found among the labor-intensive businesses of agriculture, construction, garment-making, mining, packaging, and food processing. About 2.5 million people are forced to work by government or rebel military groups. Approximately the same number are the victims of cross-border trafficking. Most of the trafficking is for sexual reasons (43%) or economic exploitation (32%). Among the more egregious practices of this type is the smuggling of children by criminal networks for drug dealing, forced begging, or sexual purposes. Women and girls make up more than one-half of those subject to economic exploitation and 98% of those forced into the sex trade.[61]

The International Labour Organization (ILO) estimates that 250 million children ages 5 to 14 work in the developing world. Nearly half work full time. Three out of five child workers are from Asia; one-third are from Africa. In the United States, nearly 300,000 children worked illegally in 1997, 60,000 of them under age 14. Many of them were used in agricultural harvesting; more than 13,000 toiled in garment sweatshops. While the number of working children in the United States had declined dramatically from the two million of a century ago, the decline began to level off in 1995.[62]

For most TNCs, the issues of forced and child labor may not be visible in their own operations but hidden among the workforce of their suppliers and contractors. Given the high-publicity scandals that rocked the garment industry in the recent past, no company can afford to ignore this issue in its workplace or procurements.

1.11. Educational Needs for the Disenfranchised

As noted in Appendix 1.8, businesses will be increasingly relying on workers from developing countries to fill their labor needs. For many global companies, the question will be: Are the current general-education and skill-training programs adequate to produce the kind of workers required in our more knowledge-based and service-intensive economies? Currently, one of every five adults is illiterate—a dramatic improvement from 1970 when one of three could not read and write, but still a serious problem. In 2001, over 100 million children were not receiving primary schooling—96% of them from less-developed regions and 57% of them girls.[63] The good news is East Asia and the Pacific region, and Latin America and the Caribbean are close to universal primary education. But while conditions also improved in sub-Saharan Africa and South Asia, as of 2003, two in five children were still not achieving schooling in the former region, one in five in the latter.[64]

Domestic companies will need to be prepared to answer the education question, too. If business is to grow locally, more workers will be needed. This means more women, immigrants, and those from lower income communities will be pulled into the workforce to fill the shortage. It is in the self-interest of both domestic and international businesses to invest in schools and other institutions of learning that can help prepare the workers—and customers—of tomorrow.

1.12. Urbanization

For Third-World workers of tomorrow, staying at home won't be all sunshine and roses. Much of the population growth in low-income countries will be in urban areas. It's estimated that the proportion of urban dwellers will rise from the current level of almost 50% to 60% by 2030.[65] By then, the number of people living in slums—currently over 70% of the city populations in sub-Saharan Africa and around one billion people worldwide—could well double.[66] If the pollution and social ills of some cities are bad now, wait until you see them then.

Companies with operations in Third-World cities will need to be prepared for the problems that are sure to follow this population boom. Businesses with cost-effective solutions for transportation, water supply and treatment, housing, and other urban concerns may find opportunities there. The big issue is: who's going to pay for all this?

1.13. Overconsumption of Resources

Many in the industrialized decry the terrible state of our impoverished brethren in far-off lands. These poor souls need much but have little means to acquire it: low-income nations spent only 4% of the $19 trillion in total consumer spending in 1998.[67] Yet few of us from the industrialized world are willing to share our valuable resources with them in any meaningful way. We keep our compact discs (CDs), iPods, gasoline, and our flavored water because they are "basic necessities," and we clamor for more. Our consumer spending has been a feeding frenzy, soaring 68% between 1980 and 1998.[68] We think if the developing world was as smart and industrious as we and our ancestors have been, they could easily have these things too.

The fact is, though, we simply don't have enough goods and materials to sell these people even if they could afford them. How could we possibly provide even one-half of the world's population with a car, multiplying current global production fivefold? Consider what would happen if each of the one billion people of India were somehow able to consume at the same rate as the average American, who uses 15 times more energy, 25 times more meat, 40 times more coffee, 75 times more paper, and 180 times more motor fuel.[69] Each year, it takes between 45 and 85 tons of natural resources per person to support the economy of a typical industrialized country.[70] To provide that same level of consumption to the rest of the world would be a dream-come-true for TNC marketing people. One problem, though: it would take at least three earth's worth of resources. But the rate of consumption is not the only problem. Don't forget we will have another three billion mouths to feed worldwide in 50 years. In short, we'll have many more people consuming at ever-increasing rates.

To achieve sustainability of resources, the world must bring back into balance its consumption, technological development, resource reuse and recycling, and population growth. The relationships among the variables are as follows:

- *For nonrenewable resources*, such as fossil fuels and minerals, the critical requirement is that adequate supplies of substitutes be developed before the current resource is so depleted it causes economic or social disruption.[71] Depletion rates can be lengthened with greater recycling and reuse or through a lower rate of consumption. The consumption rate can be reduced by making the number of consumers or the usage rate per person smaller. Governments can do much to accelerate the introduction of substitutes and dampen consumption rates through wise tax policy and other financial incentives.
- *For renewable resources,* like wood, corn, and other biomass, the critical requirements are: (1) the harvest rate of the resource not exceed the rate of replanting or other replacement of the re-

source; and (2) the rate of consumption of the resource be no greater than the combined rates of harvest, reuse, and recycling of the resource. Here again, the rate of consumption can be reduced with a smaller usage rate per person or fewer consumers.

The point here is that the population (number of consumers) and the consumption rate per person (individual usage rate) are critical factors in achieving a sustainable balance for both types of resources. Another key factor for nonrenewables is the speed with which we develop and deploy new alternatives.

The good news is that we are beginning to address the population issue (except, perhaps, in sub-Saharan Africa), although, as discussed earlier, it will still take another half century or so to rein in that run-away horse. And technology is making great strides on many fronts to improve efficiency—which affects consumption rates—and introduce new alternative fuels and materials. Unfortunately, the low cost of materials and weak government policy—even creating disincentive subsidies in some cases—have removed the urgency for development in these areas.

Although many companies are working to increase the efficiency of their processes and products, the current intensity of that effort may not be enough. The Wuppertal Institute, a German think tank, claims that to achieve resource sustainability worldwide, industrialized nations must reduce their material and fuel consumption per unit of output value by 75 to 90%. In other words, they must improve their production efficiency by 4 to 10 times—termed, "Factor 4" and "Factor 10."[72] That sounds like a hopeless undertaking until you realize that by 1820, the Industrial Revolution had enabled one person to do what only 70 years earlier was the work of 200. In recent years, the "e-revolution" has also advanced productivity significantly, although our progress in many other areas hasn't been remarkable. If the folks from Wuppertal are right, we still have a long way to go. Opportunities in this area abound for corporations with technological innovation.

On the other hand, companies that try to ignore the problems of unsustainable consumption will likely regret it. As the competition for petroleum and other key materials grows, costs will rise and shortages of supply may adversely impact business growth. To be successful, companies must anticipate these trends, and respond proactively, substantially improving production efficiencies and planning a paced transition to alternative materials that are—or likely will be—readily available. Pollution must be aggressively attacked, not only to prevent the waste of materials, but also to minimize its effects in despoiling other unused resources. Because customers will also be facing the same challenges as their suppliers, companies must design new products which enable their users to accomplish the same ends with less material and energy. Producers may also need to recapture materials through the take-back of used products. These moves, where economically viable—remember, sustainability is about economics, too—will find support among consumers. They will be especially attractive to the small but growing number of followers of Voluntary Simplicity, a personalized sustainability philosophy aimed at, among other things, cutting consumption through educated buying.[73] Support for this philosophy is bound to grow considerably if society's rate of consumption overruns its supply and the shortage of resources becomes acute.

Addressing the overconsumption issue is not just a business imperative, but a serious threat to our society as a whole. Worldwide, critical resources are dwindling not just because of rising consumption rates and population growth, but also due to pollution, weak government policies, and poor development planning. The real question here is, at what point do we, the developed and the developing world alike, overrun the earth's carrying capacity for its inhabitants? Borrowing a page from finance, are we draining our bank account of resources faster than we can replenish it? Are we headed for a "cash flow" crisis where, even though we have the resources, they aren't available at the time and place needed? How well are we understanding and managing our "spending?" Is this the Kaibab Plateau all over again?

In a 1943 article, the great conservationist Aldo Leopold recounted the famous story of the mule deer of the Kaibab Plateau on the north rim of the Grand Canyon in northwestern Arizona. In the early 1900s, settlers brought cattle and sheep into the plateau to graze among the native mule deer. Mountain lions, wolves, and other predators were considered threats to the livestock and hunted aggressively. In 1906 the mule deer population in the area was roughly 4,000. Livestock grazing was reduced, although predator hunting wasn't, and soon the deer herds began to grow. By 1918, when the first signs of malnutrition and disease in the herds were being noticed, the deer population had already exploded to 50,000. It multiplied to 100,000 around 1924. Two years later it was decimated—cut back to 50,000. Then began a downward spiral until around

1940, when the deer population leveled off around 5,000. Leopold visited the area during the downfall and told what he saw:

> I have watched the face of many a newly wolfless mountain, and seen the south-facing slopes wrinkle with a maze of new deer trails. I have seen every available bush and seedling browsed, first to anaemic desuetude, then to death. I have seen every edible tree defoliated to the height of a saddlehorn. Such a mountain looks as if someone had given God new pruning shears, and forbidden him all other exercise. In the end the starved bones of the hoped-for deer herd, dead of its own too-much, bleach with the bones of the dead sage, or molder under the high-lined junipers.[74]

The mule deer overshot the self-restoring capability or "carrying capacity" of the range. They overconsumed and overreproduced to the point of throwing the plateau into ecological bankruptcy. Experts say that had action been taken when the herd was between 25,000 and 30,000, the carrying capacity and deer population may well have been maintained at that level. But action was not taken and the serious consequences which Leopold so vividly described were the result.

Over the years, Kaibab has had its human parallels. One of them was Easter Island—an example prominently featured in Jared Diamond's popular book, *Collapse*. This island in a remote part of the Pacific was settled by two or three dozen Polynesians sometime in the fifth century. The settlers found a lush, treed habitat that was ideal for raising sweet potatoes and chickens, their main staples. For a thousand years, the society grew and flourished. The islanders developed writing, sophisticated rituals, and knowledge of astronomy, and produced hundreds of huge stone statues for which they became famous. Archeologists estimate that by 1600, the island population had reached somewhere between 6,000 and 30,000—most likely around 15,000. By then, the stands of trees began to disappear, cut down to provide fuel for heating and cooking and for construction material for houses, canoes, and household goods. Large numbers of logs were also used to roll each massive stone statue across the island from quarry to erection site, an activity that intensified as clan rivalries grew.

By the time the first Europeans visited the island in 1722, the trees were gone. The inhabitants had retreated to flimsy reed huts or to stone shelters dug into hillsides. The wood for canoes was gone, and the reed boats being used were incapable of venturing out to dependable fishing waters. With the disappearance of the paper mulberry tree, good fishing nets could no longer be made. Denuded soils were eroded and depleted of nutrients, producing poor crops at best. The population had declined to a few thousand and was engaged in almost perpetual warfare over scarce resources. In the desperate search for food, cannibalism became common. Faced with an environmental disaster of their own doing, the island had regressed to ever more primitive conditions.[75]

Easter Island and the Kaibab Plateau hold many lessons for us on sustainability. For those spots in sub-Saharan Africa and a few other places on the globe, the carrying capacity may have already been exceeded or at least not wisely used. Like throwing bales of hay to starving deer, external aid to those regions is only a short-term solution—essential from a humanitarian perspective, but not really rebuilding or replenishing the capacity and balance needed for sustainability. Global economic institutions like the World Bank are currently wrestling with this short-term versus long-term dilemma.[76] Plans for debt relief and improved infrastructure and governance—key actions for rebuilding and preserving carrying capacity in impoverished regions—are receiving some attention, but not nearly enough for success.

And what about the smug industrialized countries? Does our current cornucopia suggest the Kaibab and Easter Island are of no relevance to us? Do we really know how far we are from the end of our carrying capacity, or are we simply consuming with no thought of the future.[77] Are we, as Leopold said, being destroyed by our "own too-much?" Will the demands of the masses drive us to "cut down our last tree?" Do we have the collective will to turn around our cultural norm for over-consumption?

Indeed, reversing cultural norms is a big and often overlooked part of the solution. Many of society's values about what is right, stylish, and desirable currently do not support sustainability. There aren't enough super stars like Bono bringing concern about the plight of Africa or other sustainability issues into the mainstream of popular culture. Efficiency rather than waste, modest consumption rather than over-consumption, need to come into vogue. University of Washington fish expert Dr. Ray Hilborn captured the point this way: "Most fishery problems are a result of not understanding how the fishermen behave rather than how the fish behave."[78] He was thinking of trawler operators who succumb to short-term economic pressures in adopting unsustainable fishing practices. But the lesson is a broader one.

If Dr. Hilborn is right, then how do we build into our resource management planning an adequate allowance for the human tendencies of ignoring long-term consequences and driving for ever greater wealth and consumption? What kind of incentives can we create to help re-set those norms. As Ford chairman Bill Ford said in 2003: "As long as gasoline is cheaper than bottled water in this country, people are saying: 'Give me the biggest engine you've got.' And we cannot fight that."[79] But governments can—starting with the elimination of subsidies that promote unsustainable consumption and technologies. Going a step further, they can realign tax policy to encourage the behavior and focus we need.

But there's a role for corporations, too. They must bring forth new technologies and demonstrate behaviors supporting sustainable consumption and the restoration of environmental carrying capacity. And while they do that, they must also find ways of achieving business growth—providing ever more value to their customers and society. Those that follow that formula will be the winners of tomorrow.

But will the needed changes in cultural norms, behaviors, and technologies come fast enough? If not, how will we be responding to the increasing competition for limited resources? In the end, can we avoid our own Easter Island?

1.14. Fossil Fuel Depletion

Balancing consumption rates with an eye to resource availability will be particularly important for some nonrenewable resources in high demand. Fossil fuels are good examples. Global energy demand climbed over fourfold since 1950 and is expected to increase by 60% between 2005 and 2030.[80] Fossil fuels now satisfy about 80% of the world's energy needs and are projected to cover approximately 90% of future demand.[81] According to BP, using known reserves at current consumption rates, we have about a 160-year supply of coal, maybe 70 years of natural gas, and only 40 years before oil becomes scarce.[82] Approximately 30% of the worldwide fossil fuel usage is met with coal, over 25% with natural gas, and nearly 45% with oil.[83]

Over the past 30 years, oil companies have been extracting significantly more oil than they have been finding. Experts predict world oil production to peak between 2015 and 2020, at which time we are likely to see a dramatic price surge.[84] Given that three-fourths of all oil reserves are in the Organization of Petroleum Exporting Countries (OPEC) nations, political conditions there also have the potential to cause big swings in oil supply and cost.[85] The United States is the largest consumer of oil, at over 20 million barrels per day—approximately one-fourth of the world's total. China is second at nearly seven million barrels but coming up fast as its economy expands. Their increasing use has helped push oil prices higher.

Growth in oil demand is attributed to automobiles, power plants, and industry.[86] Industry and power companies rely on oil when the use of gas or coal is not practicable. Over 500 million cars are on the road, with an additional 9 million being added annually. Changes in the driving habits of Americans haven't helped. The percentage of light-duty trucks on U.S. roads doubled between 1980 and 2001 as drivers switched from cars to less fuel-efficient sport utility vehicles, pickups, and mini vans. In that same period, the miles driven per capita went up by nearly one-half as did the number of people driving to work in private vehicles. People using car pools dropped over 25%.[87]

Both China and the United States are responsible for approximately one-fourth of the world's coal consumption.[88] Usage is growing rapidly in China. In the United States, coal remains the major source of power generation although growth in use has been restrained by environmental concerns. New pollution control technologies and the depletion in oil supplies should prompt greater reliance on coal in the future.

Natural gas has been increasingly used in commercial and industrial power plants because of its low pollutant properties. The U.S. consumes more than one-fourth of the world's production.[89] Over the last decade, new gas discoveries have generally kept pace with consumption levels. But with the growing attraction of this fuel, how long that can continue remains to be seen.[90]

Various companies will be expected to develop and deploy new energy technologies and renewable sources. This must come fast enough to provide a manageable economic transition as fossil fuel supplies dwindle and concerns about climate change grow (see Appendix 1.15). History provides some hope that this can be done. We've already survived the following technology waves for major power supplies over the last few centuries[91]:

Pre 1850s:	Direct energy—wood, wind, water, and animals
1830-1900:	Steam engine—coal
1900-1940:	Electric dynamo—coal

1910-1970:   Internal combustion engine—oil
1970-1990:   Nuclear
1990-to present: Gas turbine

The threats of climate change and future fuel shortages are bringing renewed attention to nuclear power, although challenges regarding cost and safety remain. These threats are also prompting some power companies to consider burning coal with sophisticated pollution controls, such as the integrated gasification combined-cycle technology, which bakes the coal, burns the emitted gasses, and captures most pollutants for later disposal.[92] Hydropower, which accounts for almost one-fifth of the world's electricity, is another possibility, especially in less developed regions. But like nuclear projects, they are costly and commonly face strong public opposition. Solar systems, wind turbines, and geothermal and other renewable energy sources are gaining in popularity. In fact, the solar market is projected to grow 35% annually until around 2010 or so, but the $20,000 to $25,000 price tag to convert a typical home to solar still is too rich for most people without a sizeable subsidy from the government or the utility company.[93] Denmark now relies on wind power for about 20% of its electrical needs.[94] An offshore wind farm with new high-efficiency windmills 35-stories high with rotor blades the length of a football field help meet Ireland's power needs. However, for cost and other reasons, all these alternatives together remain around 1% of total fuel use and are likely to address no more than 10% of global energy needs by 2025.[95]

Hydrogen fuel cells hold promise—they currently power public busses in nine European cities—but practical, widespread applications are still a long way off. We still need to determine how to store and transport hydrogen safely, conveniently, and economically on a large scale. According to the National Academy of Sciences, a complete transition from gasoline to hydrogen could take 50 years.[96]

Biomass energy, which includes ethanol, biogas, and biodiesel, is already being used to power vehicles in many locations. Ethanol from corn is currently blended with gasoline in the United States, and ethanol from sugar cane makes up one-half of Brazil's automobile fuels. Germany resorts to biodiesel to meet about 3% of its diesel needs. But to produce enough plant-based biofuels to power all vehicles around the globe would require a doubling of farm land.[97]

While there are many alternatives to petroleum, natural gas, and coal, none of them hold promise as the answer to our future fuel needs. Instead, each of these alternatives is likely to play a contributing role. Of course, if we are to find a sustainable balance between the supply and demand sides of the energy equation, we must do a better job of controlling fuel consumption, too. Fortunately, the focus on energy efficiency is growing, driven by increasing energy prices and environmental concerns—issues not likely to subside anytime soon. Much more attention to this will be needed, however. Tax policies and government funding on research and development, if properly focused, can do much to help.

New approaches for generating and using energy are needed to be sure. The pace of economic expansion, technological change, government policy, and social acceptance will determine whether the transition from the old to the new is a smooth one. Opportunistic companies will help move the transition along.

1.15. Climate Change

Scientists have confirmed that the burning of fossil fuels is the major reason greenhouse gases—carbon dioxide (CO_2) and other heat-trapping substances—have surged in the atmosphere with no end in sight.[98] Each year, humanity injects another 8 billion metric tons of carbon into the atmosphere. Roughly 80% of that is from the burning of fossil fuels; the remainder is associated with deforestation.[99] World carbon emissions from fossil fuels jumped 180% from 1960 to 2004—up fourfold since 1950—while the CO_2 concentration in the atmosphere increased 19%, putting it over 375 parts per million.[100] See Figure A1.15.1. This concentration is more than 30% greater than that of the mid-18th century and hasn't been exceeded in the last 420,000 years and probably in the last 20 million.[101]

What have been the consequences so far? That question and others related to climate change are periodically answered by the U.N.-sponsored Intergovernmental Panel on Climate Change (IPCC), the authoritative group of climate change experts from around the world who track and debate the peer-reviewed studies on the topic. The IPCC has reported that the global average surface temperature of the earth rose about 0.6 degrees Celsius (°C)—1 degree Fahrenheit (°F)—over the last century, more than any other century over the last 1,000 years.[102] The impact has been the greatest in the polar regions. A study commissioned by eight Arctic nations, including the United States, found that winter temperatures in

Alaska and western Canada increased 5 to 7°F over the past 50 years.[103] The northern tip of Antarctica, just south of Chile and Argentina, has risen nearly as much.[104] These temperature changes have caused a widespread retreat in mountain glaciers. Glacier National Park in the United States was a showcase of 150 glaciers in 1850. Only 37 remain, and they are likely to disappear within the next 30 to 50 years. The Portage Glacier 50 miles south of Anchorage is retreating at 165 feet per year and is now well out of site of the visitors viewing center.[105] The ice flows that George Washington dodged in his famous crossing of the Delaware River rarely occur today. During the last 30 years, the Arctic sea ice has retreated 8%—an area larger than Denmark, Norway, and Sweden combined.[106] The net effect of all this change has been a four- to eight-inch (0.1 to 0.2 meter) rise in sea levels over the last century.[107] This has alarmed many experts, including David Rind of the National Aeronautics and Space Administration's (NASA's) Goddard Institute for Space Studies. "Global warming is usually viewed as something that's 50 or 100 years in the future," he said. "But we have evidence that the climate of the Artic is changing right now, and changing rapidly. Whatever is causing it, we are going to have to start adapting to it."[108] Within the next half century, scientists say, the Arctic could be ice-free during the summer months.

Among respected scientists, there is no real disagreement that global warming is now underway and that human activity is in large part contributing to it, throwing off the natural balance of CO_2 generation and absorption. Even U.S. congressional experts and the leaders of the top-eight industrialized countries agree. The only serious debate is around the projected rate and extent of damage.[109] In 2001, the IPCC's experts evaluated numerous studies that used a variety of scientific models and scenarios to evaluate the effects of climate change. Based on that data, they estimated that by 2100, CO_2 concentrations in the atmosphere would likely increase 40 to 250% over 1990 levels, causing global average surface temperatures to become hotter by 2.5° to 10.4°F (1.4 to 5.8 °C)—quite shocking when you consider it took a shift of only 9°F to end the last ice age.[110] The European Union Environment Ministers, the European Commission, and British Prime Minister Tony Blair have all supported a goal to stabilize atmospheric CO_2 concentrations at the lower end of that range, that is, 1.4°C from 1990 levels, or 2°C from pre-industrial levels—a major undertaking by any view.[111]

Scientists have said that, notwithstanding some natural mitigating effects, it is probable the rate of CO_2 increase in the atmosphere will accelerate. Currently, one-half the CO_2 from the burning of fossil fuels is absorbed in "sinks" in the oceans, soil, and plants. The rise in carbon levels in the atmosphere has been mitigated by reforestation in the eastern U.S. and, ironically, by climate change itself, as the growing ranges for trees, shrubs, and other plants expand with warming. But the carbon uptake by that vegetation will stop once the new forests mature and reach a steady cycle of growth and decay. Even among existing forests, increased CO_2 levels will spur plants to become bigger and more lush, but as temperatures continue to climb and rainfall decreases in places, vegetation will die off—especially in the Amazon region—releasing more CO_2 into the atmosphere. Warmer climate will also increases microbial activity in the soil, which will give off more CO_2. As oceans soak up CO_2 and become warmer and more acidic, not only will this affect marine biodiversity, but it will considerably reduce the ability of the oceans to absorb more of the gas. Moreover, if the floor of deep cold oceans warms sufficiently, methane now trapped in the dense water there could be released. Since that methane has a potential greenhouse impact greater than all coal, oil, and natural gas reserves, release of a small fraction of it could rapidly accelerate climate change.[112]

The temperature change from higher atmospheric CO_2 levels is projected to cause a number of adverse effects. For one thing, it is expected to raise sea levels another 3.5 to 30 inches (0.09 to 0.88 meters) by 2100, largely as result of thermal expansion and melting glaciers.[113] Such a rise would not only worsen shoreline erosion, but if the higher end of this estimate is realized, densely populated areas in low-lying Florida, Louisiana, the Nile Delta, and Bangladesh would be flooded.[114] The effects could be particularly devastating for ocean islands like the Maldives, the Marshall Islands, and Tonga.[115] Risks to these areas have become more likely with the recent breakup of several huge ice shelves—one the size of Jamaica—floating off the Antarctic Peninsula. The loss of these shelves has not had a direct effect on the ocean level since they were already displacing sea water (like an ice cube in a glass of water); however, it will have an indirect effect because the shelves no longer block the flow of Antarctic glaciers from land to sea, thus accelerating their disintegration.[116]

In some regions, droughts may become more severe, while in others, the rate of evaporation and precipitation will likely increase, producing more floods.[117] Climate zones are already shifting away from the equator and toward the poles as average temperatures rise, causing displacement of certain plants, animals, and agricultural operations. With more warming, mosquitoes and other disease-carrying insects and rodents will broaden their range. Malaria, dengue fever, Lyme disease, and other maladies will find more victims.[118] These effects are not merely hypothetical: studies have shown that over the last few decades, climate change has helped spread tick-borne encephalitis northward into new regions of Europe.[119]

Another possible consequence, though more speculative, is that melting ice caps will alter the route of the ocean currents, especially the Gulf Stream which brings warm surface water and relatively mild temperatures to western Europe. Normally, the gulf currents lose water vapor as they move north and eventually sink in three different regions of the far North Atlantic as the water becomes cold, salty, and heavy. This cold water then moves south along the ocean floor, forming a type of continuous ocean conveyor system, called the North-Atlantic Thermohaline Circulation (THC) ("thermo" for heat; "haline" for salt). However, as the ice caps melt, freshwater pours into the North Atlantic, diluting the salt water. If diluted enough, the water can stop sinking, thereby halting the "pump" that drives this circulation, and altering the current flow. Thirteen thousand years ago, a gigantic lake formed of melted water from a glacier near Canada's Hudson Bay burst its banks, causing a huge flow of freshwater into the ocean. This in turn interrupted the THC, causing the Gulf Stream to flow east rather than north, plunging Europe into a colder period within a decade or so.[120] The bad news is that drops in salinity of certain North Atlantic currents—possible precursors to a THC collapse—have been occurring since the 1960s.[121] In 2005, a team of British researchers found from measurements on board a submarine that the downward currents in the Greenland Sea have been weakened to less than one-quarter of their former strength. (The other two THC pumps in the North Atlantic were not evaluated.)[122] Several studies have been undertaken of the relationship between the THC phenomenon and climate change—one suggesting that business as usual on greenhouse gas emissions would lead to a 2 in 3 chance of a THC collapse within 200 years. Another concluded that if the Gulf Stream was switched off, the U.K. annual temperature would cool as much as 5°C (9°F) within a decade or two; however, the author estimated the chance of that happening within the next 100 years as "low." Still, much uncertainty remains about where the tipping point is for such a collapse.[123] With the potentially huge adverse impacts on human habitation, health, and food sources, the stakes are high in this gamble.

The pressure on business to deal with climate change is emerging and will strengthen as the effects become more apparent. A number of initiatives are already urging action. The U.N. Framework Convention on Climate Change, which the United States and other countries signed at the 1992 Earth Summit in Rio, has as its objective the "stabilisation of greenhouse gas concentrations in the atmosphere at a level which would prevent dangerous anthropogenic interference with the climate system." The framework calls for industrialized nations to voluntarily control greenhouse gas emissions so as to cap them at 1990 levels by 2000. The 1997 Kyoto Protocol, which was adopted by over 150 countries but rejected by the United States, went further by establishing specific, legally binding greenhouse gas-reduction commitments for the parties designed to cut overall group emissions by at least 5% by 2012 relative to 1990 levels.[124] As part of its implementation plan, the European Union promptly adopted an emissions-trading system through which emitters can buy and sell the right to discharge certain capped levels of greenhouse gases (GHGs). The United States, which accounts for nearly one-quarter of all GHGs, announced its own voluntary program for reducing GHG intensity (GHG emissions per unit of gross domestic product) as well as another initiative for capturing methane emissions from landfills.

In an attempt to bring greater global attention and cooperation to the effort, Prime Minister Blair included climate change on the agenda of the meeting of the "Group of 8" countries—the United Kingdom, the United States, and six other major nations—held in Gleneagles, Scotland, in July 2005. That meeting resulted in a joint communiqué and action plan on climate change, clean energy, and sustainable development. While the Gleneagles plan set no specific targets or funding commitments, it did commit the signatories to explore a wide range of actions to see how they might be used to further the cause. These actions were related to renewable energy; new energy and pollution control technologies; building codes, appliance, and vehicle standards and labeling; emissions trading and other market mechanisms; and the practices of the World Bank and other development banks.[125] A joint declaration of support was also adopted by Brazil, China, India, Mexico, and South Africa—countries that also participated in the meeting.

Although U.S. federal efforts on climate change have not been as aggressive as those of Japan, the United Kingdom, and other modern nations, considerable action is being taken, especially by some states and cities. Over 28 states and Puerto Rico have issued or are developing strategies or action plans to cut greenhouse gas emissions. Forty states have either completed GHG emissions inventories or are doing so.[126] In July 2004, the Attorneys General from New York and seven other states sued the nation's largest utility companies, demanding that they cut their GHG emissions.

Although the case was dismissed by the lower court and the ultimate outcome is uncertain, it sent a clear political message that action must be taken.[127] In the aftermath of the dismissal, a memorandum of understanding was signed by seven Northeast states in 2005, indicating their intention to adopt a "cap-and-trade scheme for carbon dioxide emissions from large electric generators, leading to a 10% cut in GHGs by 2019."[128] In 2006, California enacted the Global Warming Solutions Act, requiring the reduction of statewide GHGs to 1990 levels by the year 2020 and imposing mandatory GHG emissions reporting by significant sources. Over half a dozen states have enacted California's GHG emissions standards for passenger vehicles, which will take effect with the 2009 model vehicles. The mayors of over 300 U.S. cities have endorsed the *U.S. Mayors Climate Change Agreement*, committing to meet or exceed the 7% emission reduction target under the Kyoto Protocol that the United States rejected, and calling for the federal government and state governments to do the same.[129] At the national level, since 2001, the Bush Administration has entered into over a dozen climate-related bilateral and regional partnership agreements with other nations. These agreements have been on issues ranging from climate change science to energy and sequestration technologies to policy approaches.[130] Over 200 companies and other organizations are annually reporting their greenhouse gas emissions reduction and sequestration projects under the U.S. Department of Energy's (DOE's) Voluntary Reporting of Greenhouse Gases Program.[131] A national GHG emissions trading program was launched on a pilot basis by the Chicago Climate Exchange and has been operating successfully since 2003.[132] More government programs, mandates, and incentives to act on climate change will surely follow over the years to come.

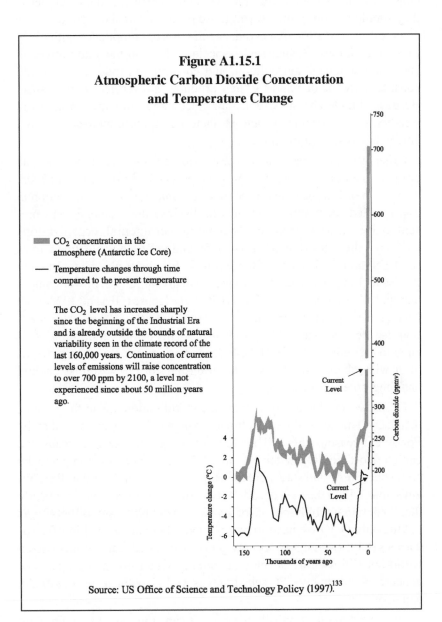

Figure A1.15.1
Atmospheric Carbon Dioxide Concentration
and Temperature Change

CO$_2$ concentration in the
atmosphere (Antarctic Ice Core)

Temperature changes through time
compared to the present temperature

The CO$_2$ level has increased sharply
since the beginning of the Industrial Era
and is already outside the bounds of natural
variability seen in the climate record of the
last 160,000 years. Continuation of current
levels of emissions will raise concentration
to over 700 ppm by 2100, a level not
experienced since about 50 million years
ago.

Source: US Office of Science and Technology Policy (1997).[133]

Companies would be wise to evaluate thoroughly their GHG emissions and explore actions that would reduce them. At the very least, they should promptly implement those projects that show good returns on investment or attractive avoidance of costs of compliance with likely future regulations. Businesses—especially those in the automotive, oil and gas, chemicals, agricultural, and construction industries—should consider how the demand for their products and services may change. Because climate change will also produce more dramatic variations in weather, those extremes should be factored into risk management and emergency response planning.

Other business impacts should be considered as well. For example, the pressure is mounting for companies to report GHG information. In 2005, a coalition of European and U.S. investors managing over $3 trillion in assets called for major companies to disclose the financial risks presented by climate change. Two nongovernmental organizations (NGOs)—the Coalition for Environmentally Responsible Economies (CERES) and the Friends of the Earth (FoE)—have also been pressing this issue. In response to these requests, many large U.S. power companies and other corporations such as General Electric (GE) and JP Morgan Chase have begun to report their climate change risks. The investor coalition also pledged to invest $1 billion in prudent business opportunities related to the reduction of GHGs. Indeed, markets are bound to grow for those with practical solutions to capturing and storing CO_2 emissions and handling other GHGs.

Even if we do find a way to break the world's addiction to fossil fuels, that doesn't mean the threat of climate change will go away immediately. For several reasons, this will be a long, ongoing battle. One is because we can't turn off the CO_2 switch over night. The emissions we pump into the atmosphere now will stay there for centuries. So even if we stabilize CO_2 emissions within the next decade or two, the high concentrations already there will remain for hundreds of years. [134] Another reason is that CO_2 is not the only GHG we have to worry about: there are also chlorofluorocarbons (CFCs)—substances now generally banned in the industrialized world but still used by developing nations. Other greenhouse gases of concern include many CFC substitutes as well as methane, nitrous oxide, and soot.

Still, the real question is how soon we can stop making the problem worse and begin to stabilize GHG concentrations in the atmosphere. Experts say that after stabilization occurs, global average surface temperatures would likely rise only a few tenths of a degree Celsius every 100 years rather than several degrees as projected for the 21st century.[135] Indeed, delay does not seem to be an option. The International Symposium on Stabilisation of Greenhouse Gas Concentrations, a world conference of climate change experts held in 2005 at the invitation of Prime Minister Blair, concluded:

> Different models suggest that delaying action would require greater action later for the same temperature target and that even a delay of 5 years could be significant. If action to reduce emissions is delayed by 20 years, rates of emission reduction may need to be 3 to 7 times greater to meet the same temperature target.[136]

Whether government acts or not, businesses will need to anticipate a growing public outcry to cut and control GHG emissions and begin to do its part to address these concerns now.

1.16. Deforestation

Forests cover only about half the areas of the globe that they did 8,000 years ago. The U.N. Food and Agriculture Organization estimates the world lost forest acreage roughly the size of Portugal each year of the 1990s. Losses would have been more than 50% greater, but were offset by plantation plantings and expansions in natural forests. Forty percent of Indonesia's tree cover was destroyed between 1950 and 2000, primarily from logging. Two-thirds of the lumber taken from that country's forests in 2000 was thought to have been illegally harvested. Between 2002 and 2003, the Amazon forests of Brazil were reduced more than 2.3 million hectares (5.6 million acres)—approximately half the size of Switzerland. Much of that loss was due to agricultural expansion. Nearly one-half of the world's forest depletion occurs in Brazil and Indonesia. The rate of deforestation is greatest in Africa and the Caribbean—roughly 0.8% per year.[137]

Agricultural development is by far the most common reason for forest loss, accounting for about 30% of the reduction.[138] Such development is often driven by population growth. Forests are also cleared for harvesting wood; building roads, railroads, and settlements; and constructing mines, oil wells, and dams. Poverty can play a role in prompting the harvest of wood and the development of settlements and agricultural

grounds. The growing demand for wood, paper, and other forestry products lies behind much of the logging.[139]

Deforestation has prevented the absorption of about a fifth of all annual carbon emissions, thereby exacerbating climate change. Moreover,
it has contributed to the loss of numerous plant and animal species. Without the trees to anchor the soil, erosion and flooding become a bigger risk
and surface waters are less likely to seep down to recharge aquifers.
Since trees give off moisture into the air which later falls as precipitation,
their removal can reduce rainfall. With less rain and more flooding, water
resources can become particularly tight. This is becoming an especially
acute problem in places like Colombia.[140]

With adoption of sustainable forestry practices, such as those promoted by the Forest Stewardship Council (FSC), much of this harm can
be avoided. But what about the poor people in developing nations? Won't
they just ravage the forests anyway? Nobel laureate Wangari Maathai has
shown that the answer need not be "yes." Recall from Chapter 2 how the
Kenyan activist mobilized women to plant 30 million trees across her
homeland while promoting human rights.

1.17. Threats to Biodiversity

Deforestation, along with population growth, pollution, and invasive
alien species, has accelerated the extinction of animal life. Over the
centuries, species with a limited range and no place to escape are primarily the ones that have suffered. A case in point is Hawaii, where at the
time of Captain Cook's visit in 1778, 93 species and subspecies of native
birds were breeding. Since then, 23 have gone extinct and another 13 are
imperiled.[141] Within the last two decades, however, continental extinctions have become as common as those on oceanic islands.[142]

Of course, some extinction is natural. Over the last 600 million years,
over 99% of species perished and were replaced by even larger numbers
that evolved from the survivors.[143] What is cause for concern, however, is
that we are losing species 50 to 500 times faster than in prehistoric
times.[144] Extinction expert Stuart Pimm of the University of Tennessee
tells us the world has seen five periods of mass extinction over the last
600 million years and, thanks to humankind, we are now working on
number six.[145] Unfortunately, it took from 20 to 100 million years for nature to restore the diversity of life after each collapse—a long time for the
fast-food generation to wait.[146]

According to the World Conservation Union (WCU)—a group of some 10,000 scientists and experts from 181 countries—more than 15,000 plants and animals are known to be threatened with extinction, including nearly one-third of all amphibians, one-fourth of all mammals, and one-eighth of all birds.[147] Our distant relative, the chimpanzee, may be extinct in the wild within the next 50 years.[148] Roughly 10% of all known plant species are under threat of permanent eradication.[149] For most plants and animals, habitat destruction is by far the most dominant threat. But the chief threat for about 30% of the amphibians is pollution, including climate change.[150] Here again we have valuable resources that are losing the battle with people.

Businesses could be adversely affected, too. Pharmaceutical companies dependent on diverse plants and animals as a source of new medicines may find the pickings much slimmer. Forest products companies are already being pressed to adopt more sustainable practices. Some have responded by seeking certification under the standards of the FSC. International Paper has taken a step further by signing a species conservation agreement with the U.S. Department of the Interior and the U.S. Fish and Wildlife Service. Under this 10-year pact, which covers 5.5 million acres of forestlands in nine U.S. states, the company agreed to work with the agency to protect water quality during forestry operations, help recover imperiled aquatic species, restore their habitat, and host workshops promoting awareness of the needs of these species.[151] Corporations like International Paper that step forward in a positive way to deal with biodiversity problems will receive public acclaim; those that worsen the situation won't be so popular.

1.18. Freshwater Depletion; Water Contamination

Only 2.5% of the earth's water is freshwater, the vast majority being ocean salt water. Seventy percent of the freshwater is trapped in glaciers and permanent snow cover (although, admittedly, climate change is doing its best to reduce that percentage). A little over 20% is used for irrigation, a use that is expected to increase by nearly 15% over the next 30 years. Unfortunately, one-half of the water withdrawn for irrigation never reaches the crops because of leakage or evaporation. Roughly 8% of freshwater is consumed for industrial and commercial uses, leaving less than 1% for human consumption.[152]

The late Sen. Paul Simon (D-Ill.) warned that the planet is facing a "catastrophic crisis" of water shortage and contamination.[153] Over the past century, the world has been withdrawing water nearly twice as fast as population growth. Global water demand tripled between 1950 and 1990 and is projected to double again by 2025. Six of every 10 European cities with populations over 100,000 are using groundwater faster than it can be replenished. Mexico City's use is causing its ground to sink 20 inches per year, and the city could go completely dry in the next decade.[154] In many other parts of Mexico, as well as parts of China, India and Yemen, watertables are falling as much as a meter per year.[155] Groundwater depletion is jeopardizing as much as a quarter of India's grain production.[156] The Arabian Peninsula, Cyprus, Jordan, Malta, and large parts of Israel use all their freshwater, leaving no room for growth. Algeria, Egypt, and Tunisia are expected to be in that same predicament within the next 10 years.[157] Over 40% of the world's people currently live in water-stressed areas. Within the next 20 years, the average supply of available freshwater per person is expected to drop by one-third.[158] Clearly the world is running headlong into a serious water crisis, a crisis that could severely limit business expansion in some regions, and cause significant population displacements and social unrest as well. Egypt has already announced it will go to war with any of the eight countries to the south that appropriate more than its share of the Nile. We may soon be reminded of the comment attributed to Mark Twain: "Whiskey is for drinking; water is for fighting."

More and more companies are beginning to see water supply and management as an area of important business risk and opportunity. This is certainly true for some large industrial users of water, such as those in beverages and bottling, textiles and apparel, biotechnology, electronics, and agricultural and food processing. Extractive businesses, like mining and forestry, and their down stream processors (refineries, paper mills, etc.) can also be particularly vulnerable. The Coca Cola Company—a business for which a plentiful water supply is critical—undertook a comprehensive inventory and risk assessment to determine whether enough water of the right quality and cost would be available to meet its future needs. The assessment included an evaluation of water sources and uses. It also examined the government restrictions on water use that will likely result as the struggle for supplies intensifies among the public, farmers, and industry. An action plan followed.[159] Indeed, facilities of all types often find it useful to conduct an accounting of water use and disposition through what is called a "water balance." This is sometime done with help from the local utility. A water balance involves identifying the source and quantity of water purchased or pumped into the site, determining where it is used, and ascertaining where and how much of that water is vaporized, discharged, and incorporated in outgoing products, respectively. Such an evaluation often uncovers piping or equipment leaks and wasteful practices that cause unnecessary losses of water and money. But correcting these problems is not the only way a company can improve its water-use efficiency. Because of current or impending water or wastewater restrictions, many firms are now reusing their own treated wastewaters for non-potable purposes, such as for irrigation or fire protection or in toilets or heating and air conditioning equipment. Companies are also finding good cost-saving opportunities can result by installing new water-saving equipment.

A business's water risks and opportunities may go beyond its own facility grounds, however, and extend up and down its supply chain, too. Anheuser-Busch found water shortages affecting its suppliers and hampering the company's brewery operations: A drought in Idaho limited irrigation for barley production. Low water levels at hydroelectric dams caused power shortages and soaring electricity prices, which in turn forced a drastic cut-back in aluminum production. A product assessment by P&G revealed that 85% of their sales were associated with consumer water use. Consequently, the company identified water as an area of company focus under its sustainability program. Among other water-related initiatives, the company developed the PUR water precipitant and filtering kits which offer a low-cost way for needy people in developing nations to kill viruses and bacteria and reduce parasites and other pollutants in drinking water.[160]

Businesses serious about reducing water are sometimes stymied by concerns that this may lower the amount of water they will have a right to use later. If a company fears this may happen, it should try to negotiate a satisfactory arrangement with the water supplier. Some creative solutions, such as leasing the saved water or banking water rights, may be available.[161]

Concern is not just for water withdrawals, though; it's also for the fouling of freshwater supplies through leaking underground tanks, the discharge of industrial pollution, the disposal of human wastes, and the runoff of contaminated storm water from streets, feedlots, and chemically doused agricultural lands. Among developing nations, the portion of the population using safe sources of water rose from 70% in 1990 to 79% in 2002. Unfortunately, more than one in six people worldwide still lack access to a safe water source. An estimated 2.6 billion people around the globe—nearly 70% of rural inhabitants in developing nations—lack toilets and other forms of improved sanitation. In 2000, diseases attributed to poor water sanitation killed 2.2 million—over twice the number of the World Trade Center fatalities each day. The majority of these victims were children under five.[162]

With freshwater moving ever closer to a crisis situation, something will have to give. Will the appropriate government policies, cultural change, and cost-effective technologies arrive in time? Let's hope so. In the meantime, corporations can help with their own solutions and philanthropy.

1.19. Wetlands Destruction

Wetlands—which include marshes, swamps, ponds, mudflats, mangrove forests, wet meadows, and bogs—cover up to 6% of the earth's surface. They are the most valuable of all ecosystems. They play important roles in recharging groundwaters; controlling floods; preventing sediment loss; and removing nitrates, salts, and other water pollutants. They also serve as home to a wide range of fish, birds, and other animals and plants. Many also serve as centers for recreation and tourism.

Unfortunately, many wetlands have been drained or filled to provide for housing, other construction, or agriculture. Others have been lost as a result of water diversion or man-made dams. Rising sea levels from climate change also threaten many of these ecosystems in coastal areas. In Europe, 60% of the wetlands have succumbed to agricultural use alone. Ninety percent of New Zealand's wetlands have disappeared. About 85% of the important wetlands in Asia are being jeopardized. India has lost 40 million hectares (100 million acres) of these lands to rice farming. Ninety percent of the Mesopotamian marshlands—the largest remaining wetland in the Middle East—have been intentionally drained or submerged by dams, increasing salinity in the soil and destroying nearby cropland. The United States loses approximately 24,000 hectares (60,000 acres) of these ecosystems each year. More than 50% of them in the lower 48 states have been destroyed over the last two centuries. It has been estimated that altogether, one-half of the world's wetlands have been lost since 1900.[163]

Since wetlands are not easily re-established, companies must be sensitive to how their activities—especially those related to agriculture and construction—can affect them. Firms must do their utmost to protect and preserve these sensitive but valuable ecosystems.

1.20. Fish Depletion

Nearly one billion people eat fish for their primary source of protein. The annual harvest, now over 130 million tons, surged nearly sevenfold from 1950 to 2002. The percentage from fish farming (aquaculture) climbed from 3% to 30%. Over that period, the annual fish consumption per person tripled to 21 kilograms (46 pounds). China provided the most fish in 2002—more than one-third of the total. Rounding out the top five were Peru, India, United States, and Indonesia. Developing nations catch three-fourths of wild fish but sell much of it to wealthier nations.[164]

Two-thirds of major fish stocks are being caught faster than they can reproduce. Ten percent have been so heavily fished they will take years to recover.[165] Eighty-two types of fish appear on the road to extinction, including halibut, sturgeon, grouper, skate, and several species of shark.[166] Marine experts estimate that these and other large ocean predators, such as tuna, marlin, swordfish, cod, and flounder have been fished down to only 10% of their levels of 50 years ago.[167]

One reason for the depletion of wild fish stocks has been the introduction of big factory trawlers, which track down fish using sophisticated electronics and scoop up 60 tons at a time. From 1850 to 1950, Atlantic cod was being netted by migratory seasonal fleets and local inshore small-scale fishers, routinely pulling in between 100,000 to 300,000 tons of fish per year. With the introduction of trawlers in the late 1950s, which could capture the deeper part of the stock, the annual take of cod soon soared, reaching a peak of 800,000 tons a decade later. But by 1992, stocks had virtually collapsed and a moratorium on commercial fishing was imposed. The Atlantic cod has yet to recover.[168]

Fishing operators each have a duty to follow responsible fishing practices and help prevent overharvesting. Unfortunately, only a few dozen fisheries have opted to be evaluated for certification under the Marine Stewardship Council's sustainable fishing standards.

But the burden is not just on operators. What's good for restaurants can spell disaster for fish stocks. New Orleans' chef Paul Prudhomme nearly wiped out the redfish species once his version, coated with Cajun spices and blackened with high heat, became the rage. Half of the Patagonian toothfish were depleted after they became a popular dish under the euphemistic label, Chilean sea bass.[169]

Freshwater fish have also taken the hit. About one-fifth of them—10,000 species—have become extinct, threatened, or endangered in recent decades. In many cases, species have come under pressure for one or more reasons, most commonly habitat alterations (71%), invasive non-native species (54%), overfishing (29%), and pollution (26%).[170] Dams and reservoirs have posed major problems for fish stocks in Canada, Europe, the former Soviet Union, and the United States. New dams planned for developing countries such as Brazil, Cambodia, China, Laos, and Thailand will worsen the situation there.[171]

Notwithstanding these growing threats, by 2010, the demand for fish is projected to climb an additional 40 to 60%, by 35 to 45 million metric tons.[172] However, even with careful management practices, experts say the catch of wild fish could only be increased by about 10 million tons.[173] Fish farms will be called on to make up the difference where they can, especially with shrimp, salmon, and catfish. By 2020, aquaculture could account for 3 of 10 fish put on the table.[174] Unfortunately, the large predator varieties simply can't be raised that way. Given the use of big trawlers, widespread deep-sea poaching, and the difficulties of enforcement, there seems little hope for some ocean fish species. Says Leon Panetta, head of the Pew Oceans Commission: "What's going on out there is the last buffalo hunt."[175]

1.21. Coral Reef Destruction

Coral reefs are formed by groups of tiny coral polyps encased in shells of calcium carbonate. They are the critical breeding and feeding grounds for 1,500 species of fish—10% of the global fish catch and a fourth of the catch for developing nations.[176] They also shelter coastal lands from storms, flooding, and erosion, and generate significant tourism revenues.

As of 2000, over one quarter of the world's coral reefs was severely damaged, up from 10% in 1992. The greatest destruction has been in the Indian Ocean, Arabian Sea, and Persian Gulf, as well as near Southeast Asia. Eleven percent of the reefs have been lost altogether. Six in ten remain threatened as direct result of human activities. Such activities include fishing, coastal development, coral mining, waste dumping, and vessel collisions. They also involve harmful runoff of sediments and nutrients from inland deforestation and farming. Three-fourths of Indonesia's reefs have been degraded by explosives used in "blast fishing."[177]

Climate change has an impact, too. As the oceans are warmed, the algae that support the coral polyps are expelled, causing the coral to bleach white and possibly die. Warming during the summers of 1998 and 2002 permanently damaged up to 5% of Australia's Great Barrier Reef.[178] Researchers believe that if ocean warming continues at its current pace, as many as 60% of coral reefs could be lost within the next three decades.[179]

Action to address climate change is critical to protecting reef ecosystems. Creating marine reserves where fishing and anchoring are banned can also help. Companies can contribute to the protection of reefs by taking responsible action on erosion control, coastal development, and waste discharges. Sound fishing and boating practices can prevent reef damage, too.

1.22. Spread of Hazardous Pollutants

Pollution not only limits fish stocks but affects their usefulness as human food. In an incident that shocked the world in the 1950s, fetal deformities were found to be common among pregnant women who consumed fish contaminated with methyl mercury from a metals plant near Minimata, Japan. Fetal brain growth was altered and nerve development damaged, causing the young victims to suffer uncontrollable shaking, muscle wasting, and other neurological damage. More recently, Minimata Disease was discovered in the villages around San Luis do Tapajos in the Brazilian rainforest. There, the cause was thought to be the consumption of fish contaminated with mercury discharged from gold processing operations or from the leaching of natural mercury from soils following slash-and-burn activities.[180]

Even though it's been five decades since Minimata, the issue still hasn't been mastered in the United States. The U.S. Environmental Protection Agency (EPA) reported that 630,000 of the 4 million babies born each year in the United States could have mercury levels in their blood above the agency's safety limit. The mercury comes primarily from fish eaten by the infants' mothers. For that reason, the U.S. Food and Drug Administration and EPA have urged women of childbearing years, and young children to limit their consumption of albacore or white tuna to six ounces (one can) a week and to restrict their consumption of swordfish, king mackerel, and tilefish. Some states urge similar caution about eating halibut, steak (yellowfin) tuna, and lobster as well as freshwater fish like flathead catfish, bass, sauger, saugeye, walleye, muskellunge, and northern pike.[181] Other fish that can also be risky include grouper, orange roughy, and marlin. EPA officials have said that between 60 and 70% of mercury in U.S. waters is from man-made pollution, and that emissions from coal-fired power plants contribute well over one-third of that.[182]

Mercury is not the only contaminant fouling our food chain, though. There is a whole class of toxic chemicals called persistent organic pollutants (POPs) that scientists link to birth defects, cancer, and other abnormalities. These substances include, for example, polychlorinated biphenyls (PCBs), at one time a popular coolant for electrical transformers; dioxin and furan, common pollutants from waste incinerators; and dichlorodiphenyltrichloroethane (DDT) and a whole range of other pesticides. Like mercury, POPs don't readily degrade in the environment but "persist." They contaminate water or vegetation and move up the food chain, building up or "bioaccumulating" along the way. Ultimately they concentrate in the fat and milk—or in the case of mercury, in the muscle—of various creatures, including humans. Studies of the breast milk of Inuit women, indigenous people of the Arctic region with diets rich in large fish and marine mammals, show unacceptably high levels of POPs. And these results occurred long after most industrialized countries banned the production and use of these substances.[183] That highlights another serious problem with these chemicals: they persist so well that within a relative short time, they can be transmitted through the air and water to all corners of the globe.

Most industrialized nations are well along the way toward controlling production, use, and emissions of POPS. In addition to national laws, added attention has been given to these chemicals under the Stockholm Convention on Persistent Organic Pollutants. This so-called POPs Treaty was signed by 150 countries and the European Union and took effect in 2004.[184] National and local governments in industrialized nations also typically regulate the disposal of these substances. They also control more than 80% of the 1 million tons of hazardous waste generated across the world each day.[185] Unfortunately government compliance programs aren't always adequate. Moreover, in parts of the world the illegal waste trade still flourishes. Over the years, spills and improper disposal have led to considerable contamination of soils and groundwater. Remediation costs in 13 Organization for Economic Cooperation and Development (OECD) countries have been estimated at $330 billion.[186]

Companies need to determine if they generate or emit hazardous chemicals from their operations, and if so, properly handle, control, and ultimately dispose of them in ways that won't harm people or the environment. When developing new chemicals, businesses not only need to assure their workers are properly protected, but that the risks have been properly assessed and communicated to customers and others who may be affected. For guidance, companies can look to programs like those outlined under the Toxic Substances Control Act or the European Union's law on the Registration, Evaluation, and Analysis of Chemicals (REACH). The challenge of controlling POPs and other hazardous substances is a difficult one, to be sure, but one that major businesses should be able to master. Companies in developed countries have already achieved great success in virtually eliminating the discharge of CFCs in the 10 years following 1986. There is no reason they can't be equally successful in attacking other hazardous substances as well.

1.23. Traditional Air Pollutants

According to the WHO, the six harmful air contaminants are sulfur dioxide (SO_2) (largely from power plants), nitrogen dioxide (NO_2) (associated with auto emissions), ground-level ozone (smog), carbon monoxide, lead, and suspended particulate matter or soot (usually as dust or smoke).[187] Over the last several decades, national regulations and international agreements have helped reduce and stabilize many of these pollutants in developed countries. A wide variety of strategies have been used to do this, including banning leaded gasoline and mandating pollution controls. Some results have been impressive. For example, sulfur oxide emissions have been cut dramatically since 1980—by 75% in many western European nations and by one-quarter in the United States.[188]

Still, air pollution remains a problem in certain regions, particularly in those developing countries like China that are experiencing rapid economic expansion. A World Bank survey of air quality in more than 100 cities in both wealthy and poor nations found that nearly 30% exceeded WHO's maximum allowable levels for SO_2 and over 70% exceeded those for nitrogen oxide (NO_x). The air quality in 22 of the 24 Chinese cities in the study showed levels beyond at least one of these limits.[189] An "Asian Brown Cloud" of soot, fly ash, and sulfuric acid has covered South Asia for more than a decade, fed by wood-burning stoves, forest fires, and, increasingly, the burning of fossil fuels.

Over the years, research has continually revealed ever greater threats posed by air pollution. Smog has been shown to significantly reduce crop yields, costing European farmers, for example, more than €6 billion annually.[190] Research on the impact of small dust and smoke particles on the respiratory system have led to new restrictions on smoking in public places. Lead exposures have been found to adversely affect cardio-vascular, reproductive, and nervous systems, as well as produce brain damage and behavioral problems in children. A study of over 1,700 school children in southern California from 1993 to 2001 found those who lived in cities with higher levels of NO_x, acid vapor, and soot suffered "clinically significant" damage to lung development that can lead to respiratory ailments and other health problems later in life.[191] Air pollution primarily from the use of fossil fuels is estimated to cause four to five million new cases of chronic bronchitis each year.[192] When transportation restrictions were imposed in Atlanta during the 1996 Olympics, cutting vehicle-related pollutant levels by almost one- third, the number of acute asthma attacks and health insurance claims tumbled by 40%.[193] World Bank researchers projected that air pollution will cause approximately 1.8 million premature deaths each year between 2001 and 2020—over half of them in China and India.[194]

Companies and governments alike must continue to refine their understanding of the dangers of air pollutants and craft creative, cost-effective strategies to prevent or control emissions causing harm.

1.24. Declining Soil Quality; Increasing Crop Yields

Overall, the earth could, in theory, provide enough food to support far more than its current population. The problem is, good soils and favorable growing conditions aren't always placed where they are needed, where the masses of people live. This is particularly true in many parts of Africa. There, soil quality has been degraded through wind and water erosion and overuse. A number of factors have contributed: poor management of croplands and watersheds, overgrazing of pastures; clearance of marginal lands for agricultural use; uncontrolled waste dumping and spills; and poor land use planning. Crop yields in the region could be cut in half within 40 years if these practices aren't corrected.[195]

Even though soil quality has declined worldwide, soil productivity has continued to rise, generally keeping pace with population growth. The yield per hectare climbed 90% in industrialized countries over the four decades following 1960. Although the yields remain about one-third less in undeveloped nations, they, too, saw an impressible improvement of 120% over that period. (One notable exception was sub-Saharan Africa, where yields remained relatively flat).[196] Worldwide grain production reached record levels in 2004, following a generally steady climb over previous decades.[197] This has been achieved through the conversion of more land to grains—much of it made possible by deforestation or irrigation. Improved crop hybrids and the liberal use of fertilizer, pesticides, and herbicides have also played important roles.

While soil quality and food shortage are serious problems in some regions, they are not yet worldwide crises. The price of meeting the food needs of a growing population has been a high one, though. Deforestation and the over use of water and chemicals are setting the stage for problems to come. In parts of Australia, India, Turkey, and the United States, irrigation, improper crop rotation, and other practices are leading to the increasing salinization of soils, which can eventually make the land unusable for agriculture.[198] Farmers, regardless of location, must aim for more sustainable practices. Industries that can help them along this path should enjoy increasing demand over the long term.

1.25. Ozone Depletion

Reduced crop yields, as well as more skin cancers, cataracts, and impaired immune systems, are all consequences of the thinning of the ozone layer—that protective layer of the atmosphere about 20 miles above the Earth's surface that filters out harmful ultraviolet radiation from the sun. Emissions of Freon®, halon, and other ozone-depleting substances destroyed much of the layer over the years, creating a hole over Antarctica the size of the United States. That destruction is continuing, albeit at a slower rate thanks to the Montreal Protocol, an international agreement banning the production and use of many ozone-depleting substances.[199]

Since 1986, worldwide use of CFCs has dropped dramatically. But considerable amounts of ozone-depleting substances are still leaking into the atmosphere from old refrigerators, fire extinguishers, air conditioners, and other ozone-depleting substances-containing equipment created before the ban became effective. Moreover, developing nations like China and India have seen a significant increase in usage, which in 2005 accounted for about half of total ozone-depleting substances emissions. Experts predict the ozone hole is not likely to recover until 2065.[200]

Companies using CFCs under treaty exemptions or in countries not bound by the treaty should diligently search for ways to phase out these substances as soon as possible.

1.26. Low Credibility of Corporations

Let's say there were four research scientists—one from the federal government, one from a corporation, one from an environmental organization, and one from a university—each expressing a different point of view about a major environmental issue. Which scientist would you believe? This was precisely the question asked in a U.S. survey conducted by *Business Week*/Harris poll in 2000. In response, 51% said they would believe the university scientist; 31%, the expert from an environmental group. Only 7% would believe the one from government. The corporate scientist fell to the bottom of the list at a lowly 5%—10 times less than the academic and 6 times less than the environmental activist.[201]

Other interesting results came from the survey as well. Less than one-third of the respondents said they would trust large corporations a moderate amount or more to protect the quality of the environment. Only about one-fourth said they thought large U.S. businesses did at least a pretty good job of being straightforward and honest in their dealings with consumers and employees.[202] Similarly dismal results came from a 2002 study of U.K. and U.S. workers: only about one-third of those surveyed said they would trust management to always communicate honestly.[203] A 2003 Gallup poll for *CNN/USA Today* found that a mere 18% of the respondents felt that the honesty and ethical standards of business executives were "high" or "very high."[204] That contrasted with an 82% rating given for nurses, the top-rated profession. In the game of "Who Do You Trust?" business is clearly losing.

A related worry voiced by the public concerns the responsible use of power by corporations as they drive for profits. Approximately three-fourths of those surveyed by *Business Week*/Harris poll indicated business had too much power over too many aspects of American life and too much political influence. Ninety-five percent agreed that corporations owe something to their workers and the communities in which they operate and should sometimes sacrifice some profit for the sake of making things better for these stakeholders.[205] This was consistent with a 2002 public opinion poll in 25 countries, where over four of five agreed to some extent that large companies should do more than give money to solve social problems.[206] Likewise, a 2003 survey by Market and Opinion Research International (MORI) in the United Kingdom found that four in five of those questioned believed that "large companies have a moral responsibility to society." The bad news was, over three in five felt "large companies don't really care."[207]

Unflattering public incidents concerning corporate behavior don't help; they merely reinforce the worst thoughts harbored by many about the irresponsibility of corporations on social and environmental issues. Consider the comment from the former general counsel of Monsanto, R. William Ide, who serves on the American Bar Association's Task Force on Corporate Responsibility. Here's what he said in the wake of the passage of the Sarbanes-Oxley law on corporate financial responsibility and after energy giant Enron was accused of concealing billions of dollars of debt in dubious partnerships:

> It is clear to me that ever since Enron and Sarbanes-Oxley, a revolution has been underway that has immensely increased the accountability of management.... Sarbanes-Oxley's requirement that the (chief executive officer) and the (chief financial officer) certify the quality of financial disclosures and internal controls is just the tip of the iceberg. It reflects the welling up of dissatisfaction by institutional shareholders and by stakeholders, including employees, creditors, regulators and consumers. ... All groups who feel they have a stake in our corporations are very upset about the behavior of boards and senior management . . . .[208]

Certainly incidents like the Enron scandal have left an impression on the public, causing them to question whether corporations can be trusted to do what's right. That view is reinforced when the bad publicity comes not just from one lone corporate maverick but in clusters: Arthur Andersen, Enron, ImClone, Tyco, and WorldCom all the subject of high-profile scandals within a period of a few years. While these bad actors may represent only a miniscule percentage of corporations, the impression looms large in the public eye. To the average citizen, improper corporate behavior seems rampant.

If it's not financial impropriety, it's something else in the news: genetically modified crops, Third-World labor practices, toxic air emissions, radiation releases, oil tanker spills, and unsustainable forestry practices. A wide range of product safety issues have also hit the papers, including those on tobacco, asbestos, sport utility vehicles, bottled water, soft drinks, and drugs. Several cases involving harm from the improper management of chemicals rose to become popular feature-length films. The list of incidents from the last few decades is extensive. Some involved actions taken in good faith by responsible companies but without full appreciation for how the public would respond. Others—particularly many of the financial scandals—involved the clear culpability of a few high-placed executives. For firms like Arthur Andersen, the blow has been fatal. However, regardless of the merits of each case, all contributed to public distrust. To quote the old saw, perception is reality.

The high-profile incidents of recent years certainly have poured gasoline on the fires of public distrust for corporations, but in a sense this is not a new development. U.S. antitrust laws were adopted several generations ago because of perceived abuses of economic power by Standard Oil and others. Even President Dwight D. Eisenhower complained of undue corporate influence by the so-called military-industrial complex. Since 1973, the Gallup Organization has never found more than one in three survey respondents who felt they had "a great deal" or "a lot" of confidence in big business. There was only one year in the last 20 when as many as a quarter of those polled in Gallup's national survey agreed that business leaders have high or very high ethical standards.[209] But what has changed in the modern era is the power of the transnational corporation as a shaper of global society and its values, the magnitude of the trouble corporations can cause, and the speed of worldwide communications. Those three factors have worked to magnify the warts of the corporation in the minds of citizens. Adding to this difficulty is the fact that the reputational risk of companies is not just single dimensioned but broad and complex. Each major stakeholder group—employees, customers, investors, communities, and the general public—has its own expectations about corporate responsibility. And a failing with regard to any one stakeholder group—say an employee strike over low wages—can have an impact on the views of others—investors and customers, for example.

For corporations, the message should be clear: the public really doesn't trust you to do the right thing. To overcome that bias, you must consistently demonstrate competent, trustworthy, caring behavior with a wide range of stakeholders. You must be open and honest in your communications. You must align yourself with academics, NGOs, and others who are trusted. And no matter how good you are in most of the things you do, you must never forget that a single corporate scandal can destroy the trust you have earned.

1.27. Extended Producer Responsibility

Public concern about the responsibility of corporations for their products has not gone unnoticed by government authorities, especially in Europe. There, regulators have embraced the concept of extended producer responsibility (EPR)—the idea that a manufacturer's responsibility for its products does not end upon delivery to the customer but extends from "cradle to grave," until the ultimate disposition of materials after use.[210] EPR encompasses several different producer obligations:

1. Minimizing adverse effects: Designing products to assure their safety and to minimize their adverse environmental and social effects all along their life cycle, from raw material extraction to disposal as shown in Figure 3.3.

2. Take-back responsibility: Assuming operational or financial responsibility for the take-back, disposal, recycling, or other disposition of the product and its packaging after use. Under this approach, if it costs $40 to dispose of an old computer, then that $40 should be added to its original price. That way a computer manufacturer will be motivated to find a more cost-effective way to recycle the computer—or develop a new one that is easier, less costly, more environmentally benign to dispose of—since by doing so, he can reduce his price and attract more buyers. This is a strong incentive to identify product and packaging designs and materials with lower volumes, weights, and hazards. Take-back programs may take various forms, including everything from company leasing programs to government-mandated take-back initiatives of the type discussed below.

3. Hazards information: Providing information to product handlers and customers so that the product can be used and handled safely and in an environmentally sound way. Pesticide containers often have this kind of information.

4. Assumption of liability: Assuming legal liability for any harm resulting from the proper use of the product, as well as from product defects. This also includes responsibility for mitigating the damage from those defects. For some products, meeting this obligation may be challenging. For example, hazardous materials may require molecular markers be added and registration systems and tests be established to track original ownership. This capability already exists to some extent with certain petroleum products and fertilizers (terrorist bomb material).

EPR is often called product stewardship. However, purists make a distinction between the terms, pointing out that under product stewardship, the responsibility for product disposition is not simply with the producer but is shared by all parties in the supply chain—from suppliers to producers, retailers, and consumers—as well as by governments.[211]

The Precautionary Principle

Some aspects of EPR touch on another concept: the precautionary principle.[212] This principle is captured prominently as Principle 15 of the Rio Declaration of the 1992 Earth Summit (U.N. Conference on Environment and Development). It was also mentioned in the European Community Treaty and the U.N. conventions on biodiversity, biosafety, climate change, and marine protection. It is described in concept in a number of U.S. environmental, safety, and medical product laws. While there is no broad consensus on its meaning, one frequently mentioned definition was offered at the 1998 Wingspread Conference of the Science and Environmental Health Network: "When an activity raises threats of harm to human health or the environment, precautionary measures should be taken even if some cause and effect relationships are not fully established scientifically." The principle acknowledges that society cannot be caught in "analysis paralysis" waiting for absolute scientific certainty before taking action on suspected threats that may pose serious harm. By the time scientific certainty arrives, the disastrous consequences may already be upon us.

EPR interpreted in the light of the precautionary principle suggests that the burden is on manufacturers to take appropriate precautions where there is reason to suspect their products cause harm. The emphasis is on prudent risk management rather than an absolute guarantee of safety. Ethical judgment must be called upon to fill the scientific void.

While the principle may help focus debate, it doesn't always end it. Disagreement commonly centers around the significance of the threat and potential consequence, and the appropriateness of the proposed precautionary measure. Think of the ongoing controversies over second-hand smoke, genetically modified crops, climate change, chemical safety, and polyvinyl chloride.

Various EPR programs have been around for a long time. Refillable glass bottles for beer and soft drinks were used by the U.S. beverage industry nearly a century ago. The concept of common-law liability for product defects began well before that. An aluminum can recycling program was imposed by Swedish law in 1979. Since then, 10 U.S. states, 1 U.S. city, most Canadian provinces and many European nations have adopted beverage container deposit-refund laws. Over the last quarter century, legislation has been enacted in European countries, the United States, and many other countries, requiring that "material safety data sheets" or "chemical information sheets" be sent to customers. These sheets provide information about the hazardous contents of products and how to handle and dispose of them. Over one-third of the U.S. states, the European Union, and several other countries have enacted laws on product packaging, limiting the concentration of heavy metals, such as lead, cadmium, mercury and hexavalent chromium. Product hazard warnings are now widespread. Labels providing detail on the contents of packaged foods and drugs are currently mandated by law. Environmental information labeling for such things as energy efficiency, recycled content, and CFC use is also common.

While EPR programs in some form have long been around, they've grown dramatically over the last few decades.[213] Their popularity was jump-started by Germany's Packaging Ordinance of 1991, stipulating certain packaging recycling targets and mandating that companies either take back their product packaging from their customers or pay for another nationwide service (a producer responsibility organization (PRO)) to do so. The effect of the law was to shift the cost of collecting, sorting, and recycling used packaging from the government to private industry, thus stimulating aggressive waste packaging reduction efforts and new waste sorting and recycling technologies. The ordinance was implemented through the "Green Dot" take-back system, so named for the logo placed on packaging of those producers who subscribed to the industry-designed waste recovery program. Despite claims of high costs and disruptions to markets for recycled materials, the German law proved popular and prompted the European Union to adopt its own similar packaging directive in 1994. Countries outside Europe, including Japan, Korea, and Taiwan, soon followed with their own versions. Twenty-eight countries now have packaging take-back laws.

The next major EPR initiative adopted by the European Union was the 2000 directive on end-of-life vehicles (ELVs). This law was built on the experience gained under ELV programs in Germany, France, Japan, and Sweden. Like the packaging directive, the European ELV law holds manufacturers responsible for take-back and sets target recycling rates.

But the European Union did not stop there. It continued its march toward EPR in 2003 with the adoption of the take-back directive on waste electrical and electronic equipment (WEEE) and a companion directive on the restriction of use of certain hazardous substances (RoHS) in such equipment. Lawmakers were encouraged by the government-mandated WEEE programs already in place in Italy, Japan, the Netherlands, Norway, Switzerland, and Taiwan. In 2003, California became the first U.S. state to adopt similar legislation, imposing a recycling fee on certain electronic goods and requiring manufacturers to report annually on their progress toward making their products more recyclable and with fewer hazardous materials. By 2005, several other states had adopted their own version of the law, and over half had proposed legislation of this type.

The legislative approach to EPR is spreading. Currently over two-thirds of the 29 industrialized nations in the OECD have either adopted such policies or are considering them. Around the globe, legally required EPR programs cover not only beverage containers, packaging, electronic equipment, and vehicles, but such things as nickel-cadmium batteries, tires, waste paper, and paint. The number and extent of the programs continues to grow.

Even where governments have not demanded EPR by law, they have often encouraged it. Germany's end-of-life vehicle ordinance proved unsuccessful and was replaced with an industrywide voluntary commitment supported by the government. Twenty-one states and 10 local agencies are members of the Product Stewardship Institute (PSI), a Massachusetts nonprofit organization that works with governments, industry, and others to promote EPR initiatives in the United States. PSI has developed proposals for pesticides, surplus paint, and small propane tanks. It is also exploring strategies for handling certain small devices containing radioisotopes, such as tritium exit signs and some manufacturing-process-control gauges.

Some industries have taken up the EPR torch on their own, either as an attempt to demonstrate good corporate citizenship, to respond to increasing public pressure, or to help shape programs they think may be mandated in the future. IBM, Dell, Epson, HP, Sony, and Xerox all have their own electronics take-back initiatives. DuPont, Interface, Honeywell, BASF, Shaw, and Collins & Aikman collect used carpeting for reprocessing. Toner and ink-jet cartridges from copiers are taken back for recycling by 16 different suppliers. The battery industry has a nationwide collection and recycling program in the United States for nickel-cadmium batteries, which it adopted after eight states and the Congress passed laws requiring such programs. Kodak successfully collects and recycles single-use cameras. The Vehicle Recycling Partnership, a collaboration among U.S. automobile makers, creates improved product designs, infrastructures, and technologies for the recycling and proper disposal of scrap vehicles. Benjamin Moore recovers surplus paint from its consumers. Armstrong World Industries reprocesses old ceiling tiles; Nike, old athletic shoes. Both accept brands other than their own. Tritium exit-sign manufacturers also have return programs. The list goes on.

Many companies understand the need to be on the EPR train. It is picking up speed as it rolls down the track. For those not on it, the risk is that their competitors or the government may impose a program that's not to their liking. It's simply an issue of whether a company wants a hand in shaping its own future. For industries untouched so far by this trend, it seems just a matter of time before success in a related field—or some special problem in their own—will focus the customer's or government's sights on them. Indeed, it has been the customer that has had to bear the waste problem. It's a burden they don't enjoy, and it's not getting lighter. They are seeing the merits of tossing this burden back in the laps of someone who can do something about it—business.

1.28. Green Products

Chapter 3 highlights the growing trend toward green products, those variations of regular products that better address environmental or social concerns. While organic foods, microcredit financial institutions, and certain energy-efficient equipment and recycled paper products have proven popular, some other green products have not. As noted in Figure

3.5, to be successful, a green product generally must be competitive on performance, convenience, and price, although some consumers are willing to pay a premium for products perceived as safer or healthier.

Let us explore in more depth how customers have responded to certain products that were subject to green claims (green energy and green buildings) and to green concerns (genetically modified crops and PVC medical products) to see what additional lessons can be learned.

Green Energy

Green-product strategies can be challenging, though. The marketing of green electrical power is a case in point. In the United States, a number of utilities have asked customers if they want to pay an incremental charge on their electricity bills for the purchase of energy from renewable sources—typically wind, solar, or hydro. Several states have allowed consumers to pick from several different suppliers, some of whom offered green power. A 1997 study by DOE and others examined nine of these utility green-pricing programs and found that in two-thirds of them, the customer participation was less than 1%. The best only had slightly more than 3% of its customers subscribed. While none of these programs was wildly successful, those with the greatest participation involved the local installation of wind turbines by nonprofit municipal utilities—something the customer could see and embrace as a community environmental initiative. For those with the least participation, the renewable energy source was provided by for-profit utilities and, in some cases, from facilities located outside the state. Local impact, clarity of message, and institutional credibility clearly made a difference. Overall, though, few consumers currently want to pay more for green energy from a power company.[214]

Contrast those local consumers with the Green Power Market Development Group, a group of a dozen companies brought together in 2001 by the World Resources Institute, a Washington-based sustainability think thank. These companies, which include General Motors, Dow Chemical, DuPont, Johnson & Johnson, IBM, Kinko's, and Staples, have committed to use renewable energy sources to supply over 100 megawatts of power for 250 facilities in 22 states. The program is a broad one, covering green power generated by the participants themselves from solar panels, landfill gas, and wind farms. Dow committed to use fuel cells to produce power from waste hydrogen generated as a process byproduct. The program also includes "energy credits" purchased by participants to support renewable energy projects by suppliers in other regions. A spokesperson for WRI explained that the companies were joining this initiative to help stimulate renewable energy development and as a hedge against volatile fossil fuel prices. These benefits, plus the positive public relations generated by the program, provided the value justifying the extra cost to these corporate customers. But the value apparently wasn't that compelling: like the individual consumers in the DOE study, these corporate customers also limited their green energy purchases to fill only a small part of their total energy needs.

Although the inflation-adjusted price of green energy has dropped significantly in recent years, without subsidies, it still cannot compete with coal and other traditional fuels in most locations. That's a major reason renewable energy sources other than hydro still account for less than 2% of U.S. total power production.[215] Certainly electrical utility companies should be pursuing green energy in preparation for tighter supplies of fossil fuels ahead—and tighter GHG restrictions. But no one should expect customers to be highly receptive to green power until its prices become competitive.

Green Buildings

The same is true about green building design. Surveys have repeatedly shown that buyers favor green building designs when all else is equal.[216] But the question is: Is all else—including price—equal? Homes and other buildings can be designed to be more energy and water efficient, with less indoor air contaminants and greater recycled materials and re-engineered lumber. When the savings more than offsets the added mortgage payment for the improvements, buyers will often snap up these green improvements.[217] If the net effect is a significant added cost, then the sale will be a tough one.[218]

Genetically Modified Crops

While price is important, the impact on personal health remains the trump card for green marketing, sometimes sinking products promoted as green based on other socially beneficial features. A case in point is Monsanto's difficulty in promoting genetically modified (GM) crops. These crops, with their improved yields, tolerance to herbicides and extreme weather, and natural resistance to diseases and pests, were touted by chief executive officer Robert Shapiro as a major breakthrough for sustainability—a solution to world hunger and the excessive use of pesticides and herbicides. Opponents countered that there were too many unknowns about the impact of these "Frankenfoods" on personal health from possible allergens and toxins and on surrounding fauna and flora, and consequently, their use should be banned. Instead of growing the seeds for the future, Monsanto sowed the seeds of doubt. An outcry from activists and a series of business setbacks led to Shapiro's resignation and the merger of Monsanto with Pharmacia in 1999. Since then, the business has reformed its agribusiness strategy under a new pledge focusing on dialogue, transparency, respect, sharing, and delivering benefits.[219] It has continued to successfully market genetically modified corn and soybeans which are used for animal feed or processed into sugars, oils, meal, or other substances used by manufacturers in food products. As of 2006, domestic sales were climbing nicely and demand in Brazil, Argentina, and India was picking up, too. However, the company shelved plans—at least for the near future—to introduce genetically modified herbicide-resistant spring wheat that would have been converted to flour for direct purchase by consumers.[220]

Despite Monsanto's problems and the strong opposition to genetically modified crops in Europe and Asia, where they are opposed by 70 to 80% of consumers, these crops remain popular with U.S. farmers. Over 85% of all soybeans, more than 70% of cotton, and over 45% of all corn planted in the states is of a genetically modified variety.[221] Some have speculated that this is because the U.S. public trusts agribusiness—or at least the farming industry—and its oversight agencies more than the Europeans trust theirs.[222] Perhaps European problems with Mad Cow Disease and other tragedies have undermined that trust. Whatever the cause, nothing has been very effective in addressing their concern—not even the Pope's endorsement of GM foods as the answer to world starvation and malnutrition.[223] In any event, it's clear that agribusiness, like the utility company peddling green power, depends upon the trust of the ultimate consumer as an essential ingredient for success.

Polyvinyl Chloride Products

Cross-Atlantic differences in public trust for industry and government may also help explain why medical products made with polyvinyl chloride (PVC) have become unpopular in many European countries while still enjoying good market support back in the United States. In the late

1990s, toys and medical products came under fierce attack from activists who claimed their use might be posing health risks for humans in light of studies showing certain plasticizers (ingredients in PVC) caused cancer and reproductive problems in rodents. These products were also criticized for contributing to the formation of toxic dioxin emissions from incinerators used to burn medical wastes. Many toy manufacturers, unencumbered by the rigorous and time-consuming process for changing medical products, quickly ditched PVC in baby teething rings and pacifiers in favor of other materials not in the spotlight. The European Union followed up somewhat anti-climactically by formally banning certain PVC plasticizers for use in such products and toys intended for children under age three. For all practical purposes, the adoption of tough pollution control standards for incinerators removed dioxin from the center of discussion. Later studies showed there were differences in the way humans and rodents metabolized PVC plasticizers, which explained why no cancers were found in primates or humans exposed to the material. That issue then slipped into the background, too. Since there was no convincing scientific or clinical proof that plasticizers could cause human reproductive problems, the U.S. Food and Drug Administration (FDA) and similar agencies in other countries did not ban use of PVC medical products. Instead, FDA asked for more studies on reproductive effects and recommended that non-PVC products be used for some high exposure procedures on infants until the final word was in.[224]

Notwithstanding all the public discussion of the issue, the vast majority of health-care customers still support PVC. This is so even though many non-PVC alternatives are readily available. Customers seem to have taken comfort from FDA and from the decades of use and familiarity with PVC products. What is more, many customers continue to prefer PVC products because they perceive these products offer superior performance and lower cost—two factors critical to a hospital's own sustainability these days. Producers of the non-PVC alternatives do not seem to have made much headway in the United States by marketing their products under the green banner.

Lessons for Business

The developments with PVC medical products and GM crops highlight the importance of earning and retaining customer and public trust to successfully execute both offensive and defensive marketing strategies associated with product sustainability claims. As these two examples show, where personal health is at stake, trust is of critical importance in overcoming the customer's hesitancy to change from what has worked in the past. GM organisms harnessed to make plastics—something currently being developed independently by DuPont, Dow-Cargill and little start-up Metabolix[225]—will not face the same scrutiny as GM foods unless the plastics are adopted for medical use. But even those companies would be wise to test early the waters of public opinion that Monsanto found so treacherous.

Soliciting and responding to public concerns about green products or other sustainability issues is best done on a proactive basis, before the issue becomes ripe. When the buying public feels a company has come up short on these issues, it won't hesitate to act. A 21-country survey in 2003 disclosed that approximately one-quarter of the respondents had punished companies they perceived as socially irresponsible, and a like amount considered doing so.[226] The total of these concerned consumers was up 9% from the results of a similar survey two years earlier.

So how can companies avoid the wrath of their customers on the "green-ness" of their products and services and on other sustainability issues? One way is to assure that market evaluations of new green products are realistic. Will a reasonable number of customers actually pay the proposed price for this new item? Another way is to use Form C (Appendix 4) to undertake a systematic assessment of companywide sustainability risks to identify vulnerabilities and then address the gaps. In making this assessment, it is important to consider not only scientifically determined risk, but also the public perception of it. As risk-communication expert, Peter Sandman points out:

> [T]he public defines "risk" more broadly than the risk assessment profession. It helps to stipulate new definitions. Call the death rate "hazard"; call everything else that the public considers part of risk, collectively, "outrage." Risk, properly conceived, includes both hazard and outrage.[227]

A third option is to give the customer control, that is, provide them a choice of alternative products and services as well as the information about each that they'll need to make an informed selection. In many cases, that's exactly what the customer wants. For example, a student survey taken in Japan, Norway, Taiwan, and the United States in 2001 revealed that many felt labeling GM food was "very important," with a high of 84% of the Norwegians saying so and a low of 49 percent of the Americans.[228] Making product information readily available can help the producer as well. Giving electrical service customers the choice of selecting green power or not, along with the information explaining the options, tends to switch the tables on them in the air pollution debate: No longer is it easy to make the utility the scapegoat for producing all that pollution.

1.29. Green Labeling/Marketing

Many producers began providing environmental information—or at least, claims—about their products in the early 1990s. By 1998, approximately 9% of all new products in the United States bore such claims.[229] But, because there were few regulations or guidance on these claims, many were confusing if not exaggerated, and consumer skepticism about them rose. How honest was it to say a product was "recyclable" when there was no local service to collect the used materials? What did "environmentally friendly" mean? The issuance of the *U.S. Federal Trade Commission Guides for the Use of Marketing Claims* in 1992, 1996, and 1998 helped somewhat.[230] So did the *Environmental Marketing Guidelines for Electricity* adopted in 2000 by the U.S. National Association of Attorneys General.[231] Other guidance has also been issued, but there is still a long way to go. Consumers, their activist groups, as well as producers themselves continue to press for more credible, effective environmental and other sustainability information about products and services. This objective has assumed more importance since the sale of green products began to gain traction in the late 1990s.[232]

Types of Environmental Labeling

Environmental labeling is of three types[233]:

> 1. Seal-of-approval labeling. Under this scheme, products are given seals of approval if their overall environmental performance meets certain standards or criteria of the approval authority. Standards exist for a broad range of products, including paints, adhesives, cleaners, paper products, computers, office furniture, and air conditioners. They even cover hotels and vehicle maintenance facilities. Germany started this effort when it issued its *Blue Angel* criteria in 1977. As of 2004, it had certified 3400 products under 90 categories of standards. The Japanese

Eco Mark has been granted to approximately 5,500 products in over 60 categories. Even the Czech Republic has 270 products certified under its 30 standards. The *Green Seal* is the U.S. label and the European Union has its program, *The Flower*. Twenty-three countries, the European Union, and several other multinational organizations with labeling programs now participate in the Global Ecolabelling Network (GEN), a nonprofit association designed to promote such labeling and elevate the quality and harmony among the various member programs. The European Union EcoLabeling Program has the same aims as GEN among the European Union countries. In 2001, the International Organization for Standardization (ISO) published ISO 14024, a standard covering this broad type of eco-labeling, which they call *Type 1*.[234]

One of the challenges with Type 1 labeling is determining when a product passes the certification test. Where do you draw the line if the product performs strongly against certain criteria but not so well against others? What happens if the product has superior environmental characteristics but the manufacturing process that produced it does not? To address the latter concern, some schemes involve some form of *life-cycle assessment* or LCA.[235] This involves a broad evaluation of the sum of environmental impacts starting at the initial stage of raw material and energy inputs and outputs and moving all along the production process to the disposition of the used product at the end. While this sounds quite scientific, it can actually be very subjective, especially in determining which environmental effects are more important than others, and in deciding where to set the boundaries in considering the life-cycle impacts of the supplies used in the production process.

2. Environmental-attributes labeling. These environmental claims are the kind regulated by the FTC's green marketing guidelines. This would include, for example, labeling about a product's recycled content and whether it is *biodegradable, compostable, recyclable,* or *CFC-free*. ISO designates this *Type 2* labeling.[236] It's covered under ISO 14021, which assumes the labeling claim will be self-declared by the producer rather than certified by an outside body. A number of countries have adopted this standard as their enforcement policy for fair environmental

labeling. Since this labeling is descriptive in nature, many consumers may still find it unclear. When it is self-declared, buyers may also question whether it's credible. This is why some producers retain independent organizations like Scientific Certification Systems (SCS) to certify their Type 2 claims.

3. Eco-profile labeling. This report-card-type labeling, sometimes called *product declarations, is* similar to the nutrition table found on food products. The idea is to provide a graph or table showing how the product stacks up against several different environmental-impact criteria. It is considered *Type 3* labeling under ISO 14025.[237] The concept is promising, but the difficulty is in developing measurable and meaningful environmental criteria that can be used by consumers to compare one product with the next. SCS, among others, is trying to develop such criteria.

Cause-Related Marketing

The rise of sustainability or "green" marketing has not just been limited to the direct promotion of products, however. Since the 1980s, it has been common to see companies try to strengthen their brands through association with some sustainability cause. A 2000 Cone/Roper executive survey of U.S. marketing, foundation, and corporate-giving directors showed that 91% believed cause-related marketing (CRM)—which associates a company or its products with some social, environmental, or other sustainability cause—can, in fact, enhance company or brand reputation.[238] The spending on CRM in 2004 was estimated at almost $1 billion—an increase of more than 50% from 1999.[239]

There are several types of CRM programs. Three of the more common types are as follows:

1. Sales-based donation programs. Under these programs, a company donates a percentage of its sales to a particular charity over a certain period. For example, in 2003, Target contributed $27 million to schools through a program, called *Take Charge of Education,* which donated a percentage of charges on the store credit card. The Co-operative Financial Services in the United Kingdom successfully uses CRM in its operations, drawing many high-income customers who are attracted to the wide variety of company programs that set aside a portion of the banking fees to fund various social and environmental causes. Carrying

CRM to an extreme is Newman's Own, the food products company established by American actor Paul Newman, which contributes *all* its after-tax profits—over $150 million since 1982—to various educational and charitable causes. The company's motto is to the point: "Shameless exploitation in pursuit of the common good."

2. Support for customer-aligned charities. Another approach to CRM is to target charities associated with customer segments the company wants to attract. Since 1995, Ford Motor has been a leading supporter of the annual Komen Breast Cancer Foundation's Race for the Cure, a sponsorship that helps a great cause while endearing the brand to a key customer segment—women. Nike, the athletic shoe and apparel company, gave $1 million to an initiative dear to the hearts of many of its customers—the cancer research foundation of biking champion Lance Armstrong. The company also helped add over $20 million more to the cause by producing $1 yellow *Live Strong* plastic bracelets that were offered for sale through the foundation's website. For more on customer-oriented philanthropy, see Chapter 3.

3. Support for causes aligned with business purpose. A third common CRM strategy is to endorse a cause that is a natural extension of the company's own business purpose. A good example is Feeding Children Better, an initiative aimed at ending childhood hunger. This program was a good fit for ConAgra, one of the nation's largest food companies, which established it through a joint effort with America's Second Harvest and other top anti-hunger organizations.

CRM programs are not without risk, however. In 1997, the American Medical Association (AMA) and Sunbeam were publicly criticized and eventually had to drop their proposed sales-based donation program. Under this program, the AMA would have endorsed nine Sunbeam health products, including blood-pressure monitors and thermometers, and Sunbeam would have paid a percentage of the sales to the AMA. Consumer groups and medical professionals saw this not as a way of supporting a good cause—the AMA—but as a conflict of interest by the AMA itself.[240] Because CRM programs can occasionally backfire, those planning to embark on them would be wise to first do some homework: Check the articles, case studies, and best practices provided on the Web sites for the Cause

Marketing Forum[241] and for the Cause Related Business Campaign of Business in the Community.[242] Still, as many companies will affirm, a properly designed CRM program can be well worth the investment.

1.30. Green Product Certification

Eco-labeling standards and certifying bodies geared to specific product areas have been increasingly popular. Chapter 3 examines some of the certification programs for forestry products, green buildings, chlorine-free products, and energy-efficient equipment, as well as for coffee and other produce.

1.31. Obesity; Food Nutrition

Ironically, while the number of malnourished people in the world exceeds 800 million, almost double that amount–one in four people worldwide—are overweight and contributing to the growing rates of diabetes, heart disease, and cancer.[243]

In the United States, obesity has reached epidemic proportions. A National Health and Nutrition Examination Survey conducted in 1999-2000 revealed that nearly two-thirds of American adults were either overweight or obese. A person is considered *overweight* if their body mass index (BMI)—the weight of a person in kilograms divided by the square of their height in meters—is 25 or greater but less than 30. A person is deemed *obese* if their BMI is 30 or more. People with a BMI of 40 or more are considered to suffer *extreme (morbid) obesity*. From 1960 to 2000 the prevalence of overweight people climbed slightly—from 31 to 34% of the U.S. population. However the incidence of obesity shot up nearly three-fold—from 13 to 31%. Extreme obesity almost doubled—rising from 2.9 to 4.7%. Approximately one in six U.S. youth ages 6 to 19 were found to be overweight—triple the 1970 level.[244] The percentage of children in the United Kingdom who are overweight is also surging.[245]

Health risks increase more steeply among people who have a BMI of 25 or greater and continue to escalate with increasing BMI. In the United States, excess weight is estimated to be responsible for 70% of the diabetes risk, as well as one in seven cancer deaths among men and one in five among women. The life expectancy of a moderately obese person could be two to five years less than for someone of normal weight. It could be up to 20 years less for the extreme obese. Most of the risk of premature death arises from the increased incidence of cardiovascular problems.[246]

The annual cost for treating medical problems associated with over-weight and obesity is over $90 billion—more than 9% of U.S. health expenditures. On average obese people incur medical expenses 36% higher than those incurred by people of normal weight.[247] This has led some employers to offer free or discounted weight-loss programs for employees, sometimes incorporated into the organization's overall employee wellness program.[248] For example, employees at Aetna can earn up to $345 a year in incentives for participating in the company's weight-management and fitness courses.

The large waistlines of Americans can be blamed on a number of causes, including but not limited to socioeconomic, sociocultural, behavioral, psychological, and genetic. Weight gain can be produced by certain medical conditions—hypothyroidism and depression, for instance—or result from the use of certain medications, such as steroids and antidepressants. The prevalence of overweight/obesity varies among races and genders. For example, the lowest incidence was found among Asian Americans; a 10% greater incidence was observed among white men than white women; and 17% more Afro-American women than Afro-American men were in these weight categories. However, the percentage increase in overweight/obesity has been steady over the decades among both genders, all racial and ethnic groups, all education levels, and all smoking levels.[249] This has led many to blame the increase on the sedentary lifestyle of the TV and video-game generation, and on the high fat and sugar content in fast foods and snacks.

McDonald's—the fast-food icon that sells over 1.5 billion double cheeseburgers a year—has felt the brunt of the criticism. It was featured in a controversial, unflattering documentary called "Super Size Me" showing the deterioration of the movie director's health after he spent 30 days eating nothing but McDonald's food. The company and some of its competitors, along with snack makers like Kraft Foods, have been named defendants in lawsuits alleging the unhealthy nature of some of their foods.

In 2005, McDonald's agreed to a $8.5 million settlement over its delayed efforts to remove trans fats (contained in partially hydrogenated oil) from its U.S. stores. Trans fats—called the worst heart-clogging fat in the American diet—are blamed for 30,000 to 100,000 cardiac deaths a year in the United States. They are commonly found in fast-food cooking oils, pot pies, donuts, granola bars, coffee creamers, cookies, crackers, frozen breakfast foods and dinners, and many other products.[250]

A number of actions are being taken in response to the growing concern about obesity, trans fats, and food nutrition in general. Some focus is being given to labeling and marketing. As of January 2006, US food companies must by law disclose trans-fat information on food labels. Snack-food makers Kraft and PepsiCo and U.K. supermarket giant Tesco have introduced new, expanded nutrition labels on their products. Kraft also agreed to phase out all its TV, radio, and print ads targeting 6- to 11-year-olds. Health-food grocery stores Wild Oats and Whole Foods have banned from their shelves any processed food that contains trans fat.[251] The U.K. Food and Drink Federation has adopted a manifesto committing its members to improve nutrition labeling, reduce portion sizes, and trim the level of sugar, fat, and salt in products.[252]

Another strategy by companies has been directed at the food itself. Many firms are introducing new or modified food products with improved nutritional content. Kraft is marketing reduced-sugar and reduced-fat versions of many of its products—including the popular Oreo cookie. The Pepperidge Farm division of Campbell Soup has replaced trans fat with sunflower oil in its Goldfish snack crackers. PepsiCo has eliminated the unhealthy oil from its Frito-Lay brand chips. General Mills is now using whole grains for all its breakfast cereals. McDonalds dropped its super-sized drinks and fries and added salads, fresh apples, and other healthier foods to its menu. It also negotiated with Newman to offer his Newman's Own brand of salad dressing, which contains all-natural ingredients and no preservatives. The company remains committed to cutting trans fats. Meanwhile, restaurant chains Ruby Tuesdays and Legal Seafoods have already begun using healthier substitutes in place of partially hydrogenated oils on griddles and in deep-fat fryers.[253]

Subway, the sub sandwich chain, took a comprehensive approach. It developed healthier menus, offered smaller portions, and posted its nutritional information prominently in its stores. It shifted its marketing strategy to position its sandwiches as the healthy fast food, using as its chief spokesperson a customer who achieved significant weight loss by dining on its sandwiches.

Some of these changes have been burdensome: trans fat substitutes often cost more; McDonald's salads and fruit can't be frozen for month-long storage. But other changes have brought business advantages. McDonald's salads earned the company $600 million a year in added sales in 2004, or 10% of its U.S. revenue. Cutting the super-sized portions was also a plus for the company since as it eliminated the cost and inconvenience of buying, storing, and handling the extra packaging for portion sizes only ordered by 5% of customers.[254]

The pressure will continue to grow on food suppliers to help reduce obesity and other health-care problems related to food nutrition. The key to long-term success for these suppliers will be to find food products that are healthier, appeal to consumer tastes, and, in the end, leave the company with a reasonable profit.

1.32. Rise in Socially Responsible Investing

From the birth of its popularity in the 1970s, socially responsible investing (SRI) has climbed to the point it now exceeds $2 trillion in the United States, comprising 1 of every 10 dollars of managed portfolio investments. This is up over 250% from 1995 levels. The practice is also taking hold in Australia, Brazil, Canada, Europe, Hong Kong, Japan, Malaysia, Singapore, South Africa, South Korea, and Taiwan.[255]

Types of SRI

There are three types of SRI:

1. Screened investments: Those publicly traded securities selected because of their financial performance as well as one or more ethical, social, or environmental factors.
2. Community investing and social venture capital: Investing in sustainability-oriented projects, especially those that provide resources or opportunities for economically underprivileged people who are underserved by traditional financial institutions.
3. Investor advocacy: A strategy of dialogue and the filing and voting of proxy resolutions with companies in order to bring some sustainability issue into the light for investors and the media.

Let us review each type in more detail.

Screened Investments

Approximately 70% of 2005 SRI moneys in the United States was devoted to socially screened investment portfolios, about one-fourth was for shareholder advocacy, another 5% involved both, and under one percent—$14 billion—went to community investing and social venture capital.[256] Screened investments are discussed further in Chapter 3. The other two strategies are reviewed below.

Community Investing

Community investing and social venture capital is the smallest but fastest growing segment of SRI, climbing over 150% between 2001 and 2005.[257] These funds go to provide resources and opportunities for economically underprivileged people who are not well served by traditional financial institutions. Investing of this type is through four channels: (1) community development banks; (2) loan funds; (3) credit unions; and (4) venture capital funds.

Community development banks may provide capital to rebuild lower-income communities. For instance, the Louisville, Kentucky Development Bank helped finance the new neighborhood of 450 owner-occupied homes, 600 rental units, schools, churches, and shops in place of a dirty, crime-ridden housing project.[258]

Community development loan funds, which jumped from $88 million in the United States in 1990 to over $3.2 billion 15 years later, may be extended at below-market rates to sustain very small (micro) enterprises and to otherwise promote local development. One such institution, the McAuley Institute Revolving Loan Fund, provided a $265,000 loan to a women's group in Pasadena, Texas, to build longer-term housings for battered, low-income women.[259] The International Fund Management group within Triodos Bank manages funds that provide debt (loans) and equity (stock) financial support to more than 50 microcredit institutions in approximately 25 countries in the developing world.[260]

Community development credit unions provide traditional banking services to the disadvantaged who otherwise may not have access to them. One good example, the Self-Help Credit Union in North Carolina, furnished the funds to repair an old Victorian house in Durham, North Carolina, so it could be used as a day-care center.[261] *Community development venture capital funds* offer equity funding to small businesses with the potential for rapid growth in order to create good jobs, entrepreneurial capacity, and wealth in distressed communities.

Investors may deposit capital money directly into these four types of organizations or provide it indirectly through specialized community investment portfolios, such as those available through the Calvert Foundation or Partners for the Common Good.

Investor Advocacy

A number of organizations carry SRI well beyond the screening of securities to advocate social and environmental change within companies. This advocacy may be achieved through a number of techniques. One approach is to engage in dialogue with companies. For example, through discussions, CalPERS helped persuade Glaxo to make their AIDS drug more affordable in impoverished areas.[262]

Advocacy may also be undertaken by filing and voting proposed corporate resolutions that bring issues of concern to light for other shareholders and the media. Activist shareholders find this approach attractive since it is so easy to do: in the United States, a shareholder need only hold $2,000 worth of stock for one year to be eligible to submit a resolution for consideration. Since management typically abhors public controversy, the mere suggestion that a resolution is being considered for submittal is often enough to prompt serious, constructive discussion between management and the concerned shareholder. Typically more than one-third of proposed resolutions are resolved this way before they ever come to a vote. In other cases, the confrontational nature of the resolution strategy drives the target company back into its defensive fortress, chilling the environment for constructive dialogue.

During 2004, shareholders filed nearly 1,200 proposed resolutions with U.S. companies on social and governance issues. Approximately 350 involved political contributions, sustainability reporting, climate change, equal employment opportunity, and other social issues. Nearly 850 covered governance issues related to executive compensation, board composition, anti-takeover provisions, and the like. See Figures A1.32.1 and A1.32.2. The total number of these resolutions for 2004 was up over 50% from three years earlier and over four-fold since 1999.[263]

Several factors are responsible for this growth. First, more activist groups are finding shareholder action an effective weapon in their arsenal for changing corporate behavior. Second, corporate scandals have angered many investors and prompted greater scrutiny of board policies and processes. Finally, regulatory changes and rulings by the U.S. Securities and Exchange Commission (SEC) have made it more difficult for corporations to reject proposed resolutions out of hand before a vote.[264] Interest in shareholder advocacy on sustainability issues has also been stimulated by the 2004 SEC regulations requiring mutual fund managers and investment advisers to disclose their voting record on all shareholder resolutions. A similar rule went into effect in Canada in 2006.[265]

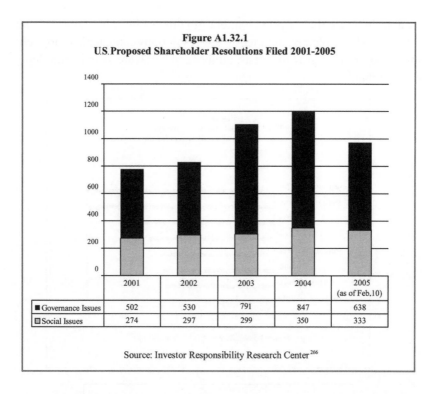

Figure A1.32.1
U.S. Proposed Shareholder Resolutions Filed 2001-2005

	2001	2002	2003	2004	2005 (as of Feb.10)
■ Governance Issues	502	530	791	847	638
▦ Social Issues	274	297	299	350	333

Source: Investor Responsibility Research Center[266]

Environmental resolutions of all types accounted for about 64 filing—about 30% of all social resolutions—in the United States during the
first two months of 2005. Climate change/energy efficiency was the subject of 32 of those proposals, an issue that pulled an average vote of
nearly 15% the year before. See Figures A1.32.2 and A1.32.3. Eleven filings covered genetic engineering. Global labor standards were the focus
of 23. Anti-bias policies concerning gays—bolstered by the 58% shareholder vote in 2002 in the long-fought battle at Cracker Barrel—were
covered in 22 of the 29 proposals on fair employment. Those anti-bias
petitions polled an average of almost 25% in 2004. Corporate reporting
on sustainability drew similar support in 2004 and was the subject of 20
proposals filed in early 2005.[267]

Even without a majority vote, shareholder advocacy can have an impact. In 2000 and 2001, proposed resolutions helped convince the lending industry to phase out mandatory credit insurance, GE to support
stronger energy efficiency standards for washing machines, and Coca-

Cola to increase the recycled content of some of its containers.[268] After 12% of its shareholders supported a 1999 resolution calling for it to stop selling wood from old growth forests, lumber and hardware giant Home Depot did just that.[269]

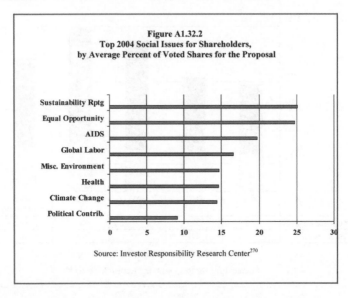

Figure A1.32.2
Top 2004 Social Issues for Shareholders,
by Average Percent of Voted Shares for the Proposal

Source: Investor Responsibility Research Center[270]

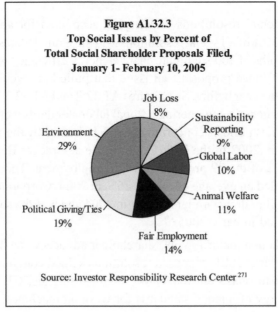

Figure A1.32.3
Top Social Issues by Percent of
Total Social Shareholder Proposals Filed,
January 1- February 10, 2005

Source: Investor Responsibility Research Center[271]

Other noteworthy advances on social and environmental issues have been made through stockholder advocacy as well, including the following:

- Forest preservation and paper recycling (Staples)
- Elimination of mercury thermometers (Cardinal Health, HCA, JC Penney)
- Nondiscrimination policies regarding sexual orientation (MBNA, Fifth-Third Bancorp, Wal-Mart)
- Climate change (American Electric Power, ChevronTexaco, GE, Cinergy)
- Help with HIV/AIDS pandemic (Coca Cola, ExxonMobil)
- Labor audits (Cintas, The Gap)
- Labor standards in developing nations (Unocal)[272]

Foreign activities of U.S. corporations have long been fair game in U.S.-based advocacy, going back to the apartheid issue in South Africa and the Bhopal disaster in India. Still, shareholder action on social issues has been largely a U.S. phenomenon, but that is beginning to change. The board of German-based Bayer came under fire from the Pesticide Action Network Peru for the 1999 deaths of 24 school children who accidentally drank the company's methyl parathion, mistaking the white powdered pesticide for powdered milk.[273]

Coalitions Among Ethical Investors

Another development in the SRI area has been the emergence of powerful coalitions among institutional investors. Labor union pension funds are supporting environmental resolutions, and environmental advocates are repaying the favor with votes on labor-related proposals. The American Federation of Labor-Congress of Industrial Organizations (AFL-CIO) has gone so far as to formalize its pro-environmental/pro-social voting policy into proxy voting guidelines for its pension funds.[274] Many coalitions represent broad range of investors and interests. Fifteen investor groups joined together to help convince Mitsubishi to abandon plans for a salt factory near a whale-calving site in Baja California. Over 140 investment organizations, representing $20 *trillion* in assets, backed the 2005 Carbon Disclosure Project, a survey of the world's 500 largest corporations on their practices and plans for dealing with climate change.[275] As these cases demonstrate, investor interest in corporate performance on sustainability issues is no longer restricted to a few fringe green funds of minor concern. Sustainability is not simply an issue of conscience; given the financial problems we have seen flow from the ethical missteps of companies, it's an issue of investment risk.

1.33. Investor Concerns About Corporate Governance

In 2004, U.S. investors filed nearly 850 shareholder resolutions on issues of corporate governance, the rules, policies and practices under which the company is managed through its board of directors. This was almost a 70% increase over the number filed only three years earlier.[276] (See Figure A1.32.1.)

Executive compensation was the popular governance topic for 2003-2005 resolutions (see Figure A1.33.1), supplanting proposals on anti-takeover measures and board composition which were in the spotlight in 2002. Labor funds were almost exclusively responsible for submitting more than 100 resolutions in 2003 on the expensing of stock options on the balance sheet. Unions also led the push for the separation of chairman and CEO positions at several dozen companies and in demanding that a few abandon their offshore tax havens and reincorporate back in the United States. Other governance issues commonly raised by stockholders involve the diversity, independence, and accountability of the board of directors.[277]

The attention to governance has led to the proliferation of laws, codes, and guidelines on the topic that provide corporations with a roadmap for developing their own internal programs.[278] A number of the governance codes are summarized in Appendix 2.6. The Cadbury Code, issued by a special commission in the United Kingdom in 1992, was among the earliest. It provides recommendations on board structure, financial reporting, and accountability.[279] (See Appendix 2.6.3 for more information on the United Kingdom governance codes.) In 1994, the Institute of Directors in South Africa produced the King Report, which included a code of corporate practice that covered a full range of financial, social, ethical, and environmental obligations (see Appendix 2.6.4). The code was updated in 2002. Also in 2002, Congress entered the arena in a big way with the adoption of the Sarbanes-Oxley Act, a law that imposes new responsibilities on board audit committees and expands the disclosure requirements of public companies. Now 50 countries—even places like Mauritius, Oman, the Philippines, Russia, and Turkey—have their own codes.[280] Pension funds CalPERS and TIAA-CREF each have issued standards on good governance. The National Association of Corporate Directors and the Council of Institutional Investors (see Appendix 2.6.2) have also produced international guidelines. Recommendations have come from the stock exchanges in Australia, London, New York, and Toronto. Business groups in Japan and France have published their guidance, too. The OECD has principles on the topic (see Appendix 2.6.1). Criteria have been produced for the good-governance award issued annually by *Business Week* and for the award granted jointly by the Wharton School of Business at the University of Pennsylvania and the international executive search firm, Spencer-Stuart. Companies like General Motors, Pfizer, GE, and Novo Nordisk, have developed model governance programs that have inspired their peers. A number of them have had their programs evaluated by one of the emerging governance-rating firms, such as GovernanceMetrics International and Institutional Shareholder Services.

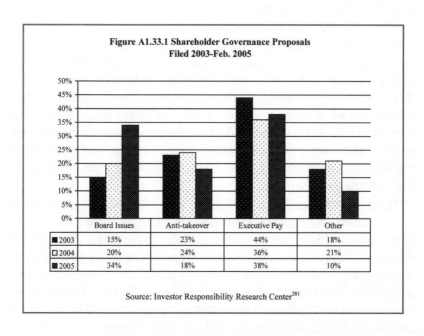

Figure A1.33.1 Shareholder Governance Proposals Filed 2003-Feb. 2005

	Board Issues	Anti-takeover	Executive Pay	Other
■ 2003	15%	23%	44%	18%
□ 2004	20%	24%	36%	21%
▨ 2005	34%	18%	38%	10%

Source: Investor Responsibility Research Center[281]

In the past, governance advocates were distinct from social-issue advocates, but that is changing. Social advocates, such as Domini Social Investments, Trillium Asset Management, Walden Asset Management, and various religious groups, are now wading in on governance resolutions as well.[282] The term "sustainable governance" is becoming more popular among all types of investors.

1.34. Increased Demands for Transparency, Public Reporting

A common theme underlying the governance codes, Carbon Disclosure Project, and a number of other SRI initiatives is the encouragement of proactive openness or "transparency" by companies about their financial, social, and environmental issues and performance. Stakeholders—investors, employees, consumers, activists and the general public—all want to know what they can expect from a company and its products. What are the issues and risks of concern? How is the company dealing with them? How might that affect me? The pleas for this information are growing louder.

One of the first big steps toward transparency outside the financial area occurred in the aftermath of two dramatic accidents: the release of methyl cyanide at the Union Carbide facility in Bhopal, India, in 1984 that killed over 3,000 people and injured 40,000,[283] and a similar incident a few months later at the company's facility in West Virginia that injured more than 100. In these cases, local residents were not aware that such deadly substances were being handled in their neighborhoods. These tragedies prompted a change in U.S. law establishing an annual toxic release inventory (TRI).[284]

Through TRI, companies provide the government information on the release and transfer of over 600 hazardous substances. In turn, the government makes this information readily available to the public in an Internet data base.[285] Local and nationwide activist groups often augment or reformat the data to make it more relevant to the public. The Scorecard website launched by Environment Defense in 1998, which links TRI data with information on health effects, census demographic data, and toxicological studies, has proven quite popular. TRI data taken directly from EPA or indirectly from the Scorecard or other sources is reported by the press. That publicity—or the threat of it—has provided a strong incentive for companies to reduce these harmful emissions.

After the first TRI data reached the papers, corporate executives across the country were shocked to read just how much toxic pollution their companies were emitting into neighboring communities. Most had taken comfort in their facilities' compliance with air permits and regulations. They soon learned, however, that the government's and public's expectations about safe levels of emissions were not the same. When EPA subsequently established its voluntary 33/50 Program, targeting a 33% and 50% reduction in 17 key TRI chemicals by 1992 and 1995, respectively, more than 1,200 companies quickly joined. They worked diligently to meet the goals, achieving the 50% reduction goal a year early. The clear lesson from TRI: light brings heat brings change. The success of TRI has given rise to similar programs in other countries, as discussed in Chapter 10.

The "light-brings-heat-brings-change" lesson about the effects of transparency also holds true with regard to green labeling, mentioned earlier. In that case, the "heat" comes from the consumer demand for products with the best combination of cost, performance, and environmental and social advantages. The lesson applies in the SRI area, too, with the heat coming from investors who are concerned about social and environmental issues that can pose ethical problems as well as real investment risk. As investors demand more information on the social and environmental performance of companies, some governments are responding by expanding corporate financial reporting laws to incorporate sustainability performance information. (See more on that in Chapter 10.)

Governments aren't the only ones advocating company transparency on sustainability issues. Many voluntary efforts are underway involving activists, investors, and companies, including the Global Reporting Initiative (GRI), a global coalition among these three groups and various professional associations. (See Chapter 10 for a discussion of GRI.) As of 2006, over 850 companies were using GRI Guidelines in some way to aid in reporting about their sustainability performance. Even more are expected to do so in the future.

1.35. Growing Power of NGOs/CSOs

As of 2000, there were approximately 25,000 active international non-governmental organizations (NGOs), a 150% increase from two decades earlier and a 60-fold growth from a century ago.[286] (See Figure 11.7.)

These groups, sometimes called civil society organizations (CSOs), display a wide variety of sizes, forms, and objectives. Millions of small local NGOs cover the globe. In many ways they help shape public policy and the direction of business. For a closer view of NGOs and their impact, see Chapter 11.

1.36. Increasing Global Terrorism

Terrorism is generally defined at "politically motivated violence perpetuated against noncombatant targets by sub-national groups of clandestine agents."[287] A study by San Jose State University showed that around the world there were only two terrorist attacks on buses, railroads, subways, and bridges that claimed 10 or more lives in the 1970s. That figure climbed to 8 the following decade and surged to 40 in the 1990s.[288] According to the U.S. government, significant incidents of terrorism were at a 20-year high in 2003.[289] Much of this violence seems to have arisen from resentment against a country or political order by groups that feel oppressed by them. Certainly, that has been the case for the al-Qaeda attacks against the United States, and for HAMAS and Hezbollah actions against Israel. Since the Iranian revolution of 1979 by Islamic Fundamentalists, more terrorists have also been motivated by religious extremism. This has led them to take more inspired, more dramatic acts of violence against their perceived oppressors, such as al-Qaeda's disastrous assault on the World Trade Center in New York.[290]

The typical terrorist organization is the evil twin of the NGO. Both groups see a need to right the wrongs they feel their governments cannot or will not address. Poverty and the lack of food, clean water, health care, and other essential services have exacerbated their discontent. For both, these wrongs have been primarily issues of sustainability—issues of resources and respect. While some terrorist groups rely on under-the-table state funding, an increasing number are—like their legitimate brethren—becoming more business like. In the case the terrorists, however, they have sought self sufficiency through criminal activities like drug dealing, smuggling, extortion, and kidnapping to supplement the contributions from various charities. Also, unlike NGOs, terrorist organizations seek their goals by inflicting severe pain and loss on others—most often innocent victims. So even though both groups may have visions of sustainability, the path chosen by the terrorist is the path to sustainability for only them and the path to destruction for others—certainly not the way to the sustainable world we need.

Endnotes to Appendix 1

1. JONI MITCHELL, *Big Yellow Taxi*, on BIG YELLOW TAXI (Reprise 1996).

2. United Nations Millennium Declaration, Resolution 55/2 adopted by the United Nations General Assembly, Sept. 18, 2000, http://www.un.org/ millennium/declaration/ares552e.pdf (last visited Jan. 7, 2006).

3. UNITED NATIONS, MILLENNIUM DEVELOPMENT GOALS REPORT 2005 (2005), *available at* http://unstats.un.org/unsd/mi/pdf/MDG%20Book.pdf [hereinafter MDG Report 2005].

4. *See, e.g.*, THE WORLDWATCH INSTITUTE, VITAL SIGNS 2005, at 108 (W.W. Norton & Co. 2005), *available at* http://www.worldwatch.org/pubs/vs/ [hereinafter Worldwatch Institute 2005].

5. *See* MDG Report 2005, *supra* note 3.

6. *Id.*

7. *See* MDG Report 2005, *supra* note 3. WORLD BANK GROUP, WORLD DEVELOPMENT INDICATORS 2005 (2005), *available at* http://devdata. worldbank.org/wdi2005/index2.htm [hereinafter World Bank 2005].

8. WALTER REID ET AL., *Ecosystems and Human Well-Being—Synthesis*, *in* MILLENNIUM ECOSYSTEM ASSESSMENT: 2005, at 1 (Island Press 2005), *available at* http://www.millenniumassessment.org/en/Products.Synthesis. aspx [hereinafter Millennium Ecosystem Assessment 2005].

9. *Millennium Project: About the Goals,* http://www.unmillenniumproject. org/goals/ (last visited Jan. 7, 2006).

10. *See* Worldwatch Institute 2005, *supra* note 4, at 49.

11. THOMAS L. FRIEDMAN, THE LEXUS AND THE OLIVE TREE 12 (Farrar, Straus & Giroux 1999) [hereinafter Friedman 1999].

12. UNITED NATIONS CONFERENCE ON TRADE AND DEVELOPMENT, WORLD INVESTMENT REPORT 2001: PROMOTING LINKAGES 108 (2001). UNITED NATIONS DEVELOPMENT PROGRAM (UNDP) ET AL., WORLD RESOURCES 2002-2004 (World Resources Institute 2003) [hereinafter World Resources Institute 2003]. UNITED NATIONS CONFERENCE ON TRADE AND DEVELOPMENT, WORLD INVESTMENT REPORT 1993: TRANSNATIONAL CORPORATIONS AND INTEGRATED INTERNATIONAL PRODUCTION (1993) (No. ST/CYC/159).

13. *See* World Resources Institute 2003, *supra* note 12, at 108.

14. *See* Friedman 1999, *supra* note 11, at 248.

15. SARAH ANDERSON & JOHN CAVANAGH, TOP 200—THE RISE OF CORPORATE GLOBAL POWER (Institute for Policy Studies 2000), *available at* http://www.ips-dc.org/downloads/Top_200.pdf.

16. For a good discussion on globalization, see THOMAS FRIEDMAN, THE WORLD IS FLAT: A BRIEF HISTORY OF THE TWENTY-FIRST CENTURY (Farrar, Straus & Giroux 2005).

17. A. T. Kearney, Inc., *Measuring Globalization: Who's Up, Who's Down*, FOR. POLICY, Jan./Feb. 2003, at 60-72. A. T. Kearney, Inc., *Globalization at Work: Measuring Globalization, Foreign Policy*, FOR. POLICY, Jan./Feb. 2001, http://www.foreignpolicy.com/users/login.php?story_id=1732&URL=http://www.foreignpolicy.com/story/cms.php?story_id=1732 (last visited Jan. 7, 2006).

18. *Id.* (both articles).

19. *See* World Resources Institute 2003, *supra* note 12, at 24.

20. *See* Worldwatch Institute 2005, *supra* note 4, at 60-61.

21. DON S. DOERING ET AL., TOMORROW'S MARKETS—GLOBAL TRENDS AND THEIR IMPLICATIONS FOR BUSINESS (World Resources Institute et al. 2002) [hereinafter Tomorrow's Markets 2002].

22. *Id.* at 45. *See* Worldwatch Institute 2005, *supra* note 4, at 60.

23. UNITED NATIONS EDUCATIONAL, SCIENTIFIC, AND CULTURAL ORGANIZATION (UNESCO) ET AL., WATER FOR PEOPLE, WATER FOR LIFE: EXECUTIVE SUMMARY OF THE WORLD WATER DEVELOPMENT REPORT (UNESCO Publishing & Berghahn Books 2003), *available at* www.unesco.org/water/wwap [hereinafter UNESCO 2003 Water Report]. *See also* UNESCO, *World Water Assessment Programme: Water and Energy*, http://www.unesco.org/water/wwap/facts_figures/water_energy.shtml (last visited Jan. 7, 2006)

24. *See, e.g., Is the Digital Divide a Problem or an Opportunity*, BUS. WK., Dec. 18, 2000 (special advertising section). *See also Digital Dividend*, http://www.digitaldividend.org/ (last visited Jan. 7, 2006) and the *Alliance for Digital Inclusion*, http://www.citizensonline.org.uk/adi (last visited Jan. 7, 2006).

25. *See* Tomorrow's Markets 2002, *supra* note 21, at 12. WORLD BANK, WORLD DEVELOPMENT INDICATORS 2001 (2001), *available at* http://web.Worldbank.org/WBSITE/EXTERNAL/DATASTATISTICS/0,,content MDK:20420198~menuPK:1170008~pagePK:64133150~piPK:64133175~theSitePK:239419,00.html [hereinafter World Bank 2001].

26. *See* World Bank 2001, *supra* note 25.

27. WORLD BANK GROUP, MILLENNIUM DEVELOPMENT GOALS (2004), *available at* http://ddp-ext.worldbank.org/ext/GMIS/home.do?siteId=2. *See* World Bank 2005, *supra* note 7. *See also* Jeffrey Sachs, *The End of Poverty*, TIME, Mar. 14, 2005, at 42-54 (adapted from JEFFREY SACHS, THE END OF POVERTY (Penguin 2005)) [hereinafter Sachs on Poverty].

28. UNITED NATIONS GENERAL ASSEMBLY, IMPLEMENTATION OF THE UNITED NATIONS MILLENNIUM DECLARATION: REPORT OF THE GEN-

ERAL ASSEMBLY 26 (2004), *available at* http://www.undp.org/mdg/
SGFirstProgressReportonMDGs.pdf [hereinafter Millennium Goals Report 2004]. *See* World Bank 2005, *supra* note 7.

29. *See* World Bank 2005, *supra* note 7.

30. *Id.*

31. *See* Sachs on Poverty, *supra* note 27, at 46.

32. *See* World Bank 2001, *supra* note 25, at 46.

33. *Id.*

34. L. Hanmer et al., *Will Growth Halve Global Poverty by 2015?*, Overseas Development Institute Poverty Briefing, 2000, *quoted in* Tomorrow's Markets 2002, *supra* note 21, at 12.

35. Lynnley Browning, *U.S. Income Gap Widening, Study Says*, N.Y. TIMES, Sept. 25, 2003, http://bernie.house.gov/documents/articles/20031001184819.asp (last visited Jan. 7, 2006).

36. *See* World Bank 2005, *supra* note 7. *See also* Worldwatch Institute 2005, *supra* note 4, at 89. The Gini Index for the United States is 40.8 compared to a 37.8 rating for India. The Gini Index measures the extent to which the distribution of income or consumption expenditures deviates from perfectly equal distribution, with a rating of 0 for perfect distribution and of 100 for perfect inequality.

37. UNITED NATIONS POPULATION DIVISION, WORLD POPULATION PROSPECTS: THE 2000 REVISION (2000) [hereinafter UNPD 2000].

38. *See* Tomorrow's Markets 2002, *supra* note 21, at 16. *See* World Bank 2005, *supra* note 7.

39. *See* Millennium Goals Report 2004, *supra* note 28, at 33. *See* World Bank 2005, *supra* note 7.

40. *See* World Bank 2005, *supra* note 7.

41. *See* Tomorrow's Markets 2002, *supra* note 21, at 16.

42. *See* MDG Report 2005, *supra* note 3. *See* World Bank 2005, *supra* note 7. *See* Tomorrow's Markets 2002, *supra* note 21, at 16.

43. *See* MDG Report 2005, *supra* note 3. *See* World Bank 2005, *supra* note 7. WORLD BANK, WORLD DEVELOPMENT INDICATORS 2003, at 11 (2003), *available at* http://web.worldbank.org/WBSITE/EXTERNAL/DATASTATISTICS/0,,contentMDK:20420198~menuPK:1170008~pagePK:64133150~piPK:64133175~theSitePK:239419,00.html [hereinafter World Bank 2003].

44. *See* MDG Report 2005, *supra* note 3. *See* World Bank 2005, *supra* note 7. *See* Tomorrow's Markets 2002, *supra* note 21, at 16.

45. *See* World Bank 2005, *supra* note 7.

46. *Id. See* MDG Report 2005, *supra* note 3.

47. *See* Worldwatch Institute 2005, *supra* note 4, at 68.

48. *See* World Bank 2005, *supra* note 7.

49. Associated Press, *The World Is Losing the Battle Against AIDS, U.N. Leader Says*, CHI. TRIB., June 3, 2005, at A4.

50. WORLDWATCH INSTITUTE, VITAL SIGNS 2002, at 144-45 (W.W. Norton & Co. 2002), *available at* http://www.worldwatch.org/pubs/vs/ [hereinafter Worldwatch Institute 2002].

51. *See* World Bank 2001, *supra* note 25.

52. *See* Tomorrow's Markets 2002, *supra* note 21 .

53. *See* UNDP 2000, *supra* note 37.

54. *Id.*

55. *See, e.g.,* David Thomas, Diversity as Strategy, HARV. BUS. REV., Sept. 2004, *Harvard Business Review OnPoint*, Reprint no. R0409G, *available at* http://www.hbr.org.

56. *See* World Bank 2003, *supra* note 43, at 6.

57. *See* Alex Kirby, *Hungry World "Must Eat Less Meat,"* BBC NEWS ON-LINE, Aug. 16, 2004, http://news.bbc.co.uk/1/hi/sci/tech/3559542.stm (last visited Jan. 11, 2006).

58. *See* World Bank 2003, *supra* note 43, at 6. *See* World Bank 2005, *supra* note 7. *See* MDG Report 2005, *supra* note 3.

59. *See* World Bank 2003, *supra* note 43, at 6.

60. UNITED NATIONS FOOD & AGRICULTURE ORGANIZATION (FAO), THE STATE OF FOOD INSECURITY IN THE WORLD 4 (2004), *available at* http://www.fao.org/documents/show_cdr.asp?url_file=/docrep/007/y5650e/y5650e00.htm.

61. ILO, A GLOBAL ALLIANCE AGAINST FORCED LABOR (2005), *available at* http://www.ilo.org/dyn/declaris/DECLARATIONWEB.DOWNLOAD_BLOB?Var_DocumentID=5059.

62. Elizabeth Larson & Bonnie Cox, *Social Accountability 8000: Measuring Workplace Conditions Worldwide*, QUALITY DIG., Feb. 1998, at 26-29.

63. *See* Tomorrow's Markets 2002, *supra* note 21, at 18. *See* World Bank 2003, *supra* note 43, at 7. WORLD BANK GROUP, MILLENNIUM DEVEL-OPMENT GOALS (2004), *available at* http://ddp-ext.worldbank.org/ext/GMIS/home.do?siteId=2.

64. *See* World Bank 2005, *supra* note 7.

65. *See* UNESCO 2003 Water Report, *supra* note 23.

66. *United Nations—Study: 1 in 6 Across Globe Live in Slums*, CHI. TRIB., Oct. 6, 2003, at A8.

67. *See* World Bank 2001, *supra* note 25.

68. *Id.*

69. WORLD RESOURCES INSTITUTE, EARTH TRENDS—RESOURCE CONSUMPTION 2005, at 1, *available at* http://earthtrends.wri.org/datatables/index.cfm?theme=6&CFID=377477&CFTOKEN=17083691.

70. UNEP, GEO-2000 GLOBAL ENVIRONMENTAL OUTLOOK (2000), *available at* http://www.unep.org/geo2000/english/index.htm [hereinafter Geo-2000].

71. We have had some success stories. For example, copper reserves were estimated at 280 million metric tons in 1970, but at 340 million metric tons in 2000 even though we consumed 270 million metric tons during the intervening 30 years. Several factors helped produce those results: the discovery of more copper and improved technologies to mine it, and the development of copper substitutes for some applications, such as fiber optic cable in lieu of copper wire. We are now unlikely to run out of the metal. *See* Clive Crook, *The Good Company*, ECONOMIST, Jan. 22, 2005, at 19.

72. Wuppertal Institute for Climate, Environment & Energy, http://www.wupperinst.org/Sites/home1.html (last visited Jan. 7, 2006). Michael Roberts & Peter Fairley, *Sustainable Development Is a New Global Agenda Attacking Overconsumption*, CHEM. WK., July 3, 1996, at 39. JEREMY GREENWOOD, THE THIRD INDUSTRIAL REVOLUTION: TECHNOLOGY, PRODUCTIVITY, AND INCOME INEQUALITY (1999), *available at* http://www.econ.rochester.edu/Faculty/GreenwoodPapers/third.pdf.

73. Christine Humphreys, *Escaping the Rat Race: More People Choosing Voluntary Simplicity*, ABCNEWS.COM—HEALTH AND LIVING, http://www.geocities.com/RainForest/6783/DalyNewsSimplicity980630 (last visited Jan. 7, 2006). Duane Elgin, *The Garden of Simplicity*, *in* THE SIMPLICITY LIVING NETWORK (2000), *available at* http://www.simpleliving.net/webofsimplicity/the_garden_of_simplicity.asp. *E.F. Schumacher Society: About the Society*, http://www.schumachersociety.org/about.html (last visited Jan. 7, 2006). Voluntary Simplicity (a list of publications), Mar. 19, 1998, http://members.aol.com/altsimliv/afslp027.html (last visited Jan. 7, 2006).

74. Aldo Leopold, *Deer Interruptions*, 321 WIS. CONSERV. DEP'T PUB. 3-11 (1943). ALDO LEOPOLD, A SAND COUNTY ALMANAC 139-40 (Ballantine Books 1970) (1949). *See also* JOHN LOGAN, PATCH DISTURBANCE AND THE HUMAN ANIMAL, Part 4 (1996).

75. *See* JARED DIAMOND, COLLAPSE: HOW SOCIETIES CHOOSE TO FAIL OR SUCCEED 79-119 (Viking Press 2005). Jared Diamond, *Easter Island Lessons*, AWAY.COM, http://away.com/features/easterisland.html (last visited Jan. 7, 2006). CLIVE PONTING, A GREEN HISTORY OF THE WORLD 168-70 (Penguin Books 1992), *excerpted at* http://www.eco-action.org/dt/eisland.html.

76. Facts on File News Service, *The Issue: What Role Does the World Bank Play in Eradicating Poverty in Developing Countries?*, Apr. 11, 2003, http://www.facts.com/facts-db-ref-modules.htm#issues (last visited Nov. 11, 2003).

77. Wackernagel and Rees of the University of British Colombia argue that the *ecological footprints* of most developed nations are currently unsustainable as they already exceed available biocapacity. The two popularized the concept of the ecological footprint, which they define as the "area of productive land and water ecosystems required to produce the resources that a population consumes and to assimilate the wastes that the population produces, whenever on earth that land and water may be located." MATHIS WACKERNAGEL & WILLIAM REES, OUR ECOLOGICAL FOOTPRINT: REDUCING HUMAN IMPACT ON THE EARTH (New Society Publishers 1996).

78. William K. Stevens, *Biologists Fear Sustainable Yield Is Unsustainable Idea*, N.Y. TIMES, Apr. 20, 1993, at C4.

79. Joan Muller, *Bill Ford's Next Act*, FORBES, June 23, 2003, at 74, 80.

80. G8 Countries, *Climate Change, Clean Energy, and Sustainable Development*, Communiqué From G8 Gleneagles Conference, Gleneagles, Scotland (July 6-8, 2005), http://www.fco.gov.uk/Files/kfile/PostG8_Gleneagles_CCChapeau.pdf (last visited Jan. 11, 2006) [hereinafter G8 Climate Change Communiqué 2005]. *See* Worldwatch Institute 2005, *supra* note 4, at 35.

81. *See* Worldwatch Institute 2005, *supra* note 4, at 34.

82. These reserve-to-production ratios are presented in BP, BP STATISTICAL REVIEW OF WORLD ENERGY (2005), *available at* http://www.bp.com/centres/energy/ [hereinafter BP Energy Report 2005].

83. *See* Worldwatch Institute 2005, *supra* note 4, at 31.

84. *Id.* at 30. From 1994 to 2004, the world consumed on average 70% more oil annually than it added as new-found reserves. *See* BP Energy Report 2005, *supra* note 82.

85. *See* BP Energy Report 2005, *supra* note 82.

86. *See* Worldwatch Institute 2005, *supra* note 4, at 30.

87. Timothy Egan, *Suddenly, It's Hip to Conserve Energy*, N.Y. TIMES, June 20, 2004, at D1, D13.

88. *See* Worldwatch Institute 2005, *supra* note 4, at 34.

89. *Id.*

90. *See* BP Energy Report 2005, *supra* note 82.

91. ROYAL DUTCH SHELL PETROLEUM CO., EXPLORING THE FUTURE: ENERGY NEEDS, CHOICES, AND POSSIBILITIES — SCENARIOS TO 2050 (2001).

92. For a discussion of the integrated gasification combined-cycle process, see Kenneth Stier, *Dirty Secret: Coal Plants Could Be Much Cleaner*, N.Y.

TIMES, May 22, 2005, at B3. *See also* Dave Orrick, *Clean Coal Conundrum*, DAILY HERALD (Arlington Heights, Illinois), June 11, 2005, at A1, A4.

93. Tim Gray, Suddenly, *Those Solar Panels Don't Look So 1970s*, N.Y. TIMES, Sept. 11, 2005, at B8.

94. Michael Parfit, *Future Power: Where Will the World Get its Next Energy Fix?* NAT'L GEOGRAPHIC, Aug. 2005, at 2-31 [hereinafter National Geographic—Future Power 2005].

95. *See also* SHELL, THE SHELL REPORT 2004: MEETING THE ENERGY CHALLENGE—OUR PROGRESS IN CONTRIBUTING TO SUSTAINABLE DEVELOPMENT 30 (2005), *available at* http://www.shell.com/static/investor-en/downloads/publications/2005/shellreport/shellreport_2005.pdf.

96. Ivan Lerner, *Fuel Cells: Long-Term Opportunity*, CHEM. MARKET REP., Mar. 22, 2004, at 14.

97. *See* National Geographic—Future Power 2005, *supra* note 94.

98. INTERGOVERNMENTAL PANEL ON CLIMATE CHANGE (IPCC), SUMMARY FOR POLICYMAKERS: A REPORT OF WORKING GROUP 1 OF THE INTERGOVERNMENTAL PANEL ON CLIMATE CHANGE (2001), *available at* http://www.ipcc.ch/pub/spm22-01.pdf [hereinafter IPCC 2001].

99. Tim Appenzeller, *The Case of the Missing Carbon*, NAT'L GEOGRAPHIC, Feb. 2004, at 94 [hereinafter Appenzeller, Missing Carbon].

100. *See* Worldwatch Institute 2005, *supra* note 4, at 41.

101. *See id.* at 40.

102. *See* IPCC 2001, *supra* note 98, at 2.

103. SUSAN JOY HASSOL, IMPACTS OF A WARMING ARCTIC: ARCTIC CLIMATE IMPACT ASSESSMENT 22 (2004) (Cambridge Univ. Press 2004), *available at* http://www.acia.uaf.edu/pages/overview.html [hereinafter Arctic Climate Assessment 2004].

104. NATIONAL AERONAUTICS & SPACE ADMINISTRATION (NASA), NASA EYES ICE CHANGES AROUND EARTH'S FROZEN CAPS (2004), *available at* http://www.nasa.gov/vision/earth/lookingatearth/icecover.html.

105. Timothy Egan, *The Race to Alaska Before It Melts*, N.Y. TIMES, June 26, 2005, at E1, E10, E11 [hereinafter NYT Alaska Melting 2005].

106. *See* Arctic Climate Assessment 2004, *supra* note 103, at 25.

107. *See* IPCC 2001, *supra* note 98, at 4.

108. Mike Toner, *Arctic Ice Thins Dramatically, NASA Satellite Images Show*, ATLANTA J.-CONST., Oct. 24, 2003, at A1.

109. *See* IPCC 2001, *supra* note 98. *See* John R. Justus & Susan R. Fletcher, *Global Climate Change*, CRS ISSUE BRIEF FOR CONGRESS, Order Code 1B89005 (updated June 10, 2005), http://ncseonline.org/NLE/CRSreports/

05jun/IB89005.pdf (last visited Jan. 11, 2006). *See also* G8 Climate Change Communiqué 2005, *supra* note 80. This document, which was agreed to by the leaders of the G8 countries (Canada, France, Germany, Italy, Japan, Russian, the United Kingdom, and the United States), stated as follows:

> Climate change is a serious and long-term challenge that has the potential to affect every part of the globe. We know that increased need and use of energy from fossil fuels, and other human activities, contribute in large part to increases in greenhouse gases associated with the warming of our earth's surface. While uncertainties remain in our understanding of climate science, we know enough to act now to put ourselves on a path to slow and, as the science justifies, stop and then reverse the growth of greenhouse gases.

110. *See* IPCC 2001, *supra* note 98, at 13.

111. *Dangerous Climate Change—Is the World on the Brink?*, THE ENDS REP., Feb. 2005, at 18.

112. DEFRA, STABILISING CLIMATE TO AVOID DANGEROUS CLIMATE CHANGE — A SUMMARY OF RELEVANT RESEARCH AT THE HADLEY CENTRE 6, 7 & 9 (2005), *available at* http://www.metoffice.com/research/ hadleycentre/pubs/brochures/ [hereinafter Hadley Research Summary 2005]. *See* Appenzeller, Missing Carbon, *supra* note 99, at 88-116.

113. *See* IPPC 2001, *supra* note 98, at 12, 13 & 16. The International Symposium on Stabilisation of Greenhouse Gas Concentrations, which was held in 2005 at the invitation of British Prime Minister Blair, reported that "in the absence of urgent and strenuous mitigation actions in the next 20 years (the world is) almost certainly committed to a temperature rise of between 0.5°C and 2°C (0.9° to 3.6°F) . . . by 2050." *Report of the International Scientific Steering Committee: Avoiding Dangerous Climate Change,* International Symposium on Stabilisation of Greenhouse Gas Concentrations, Hadley Centre, Exeter, U.K., Feb. 1-3, 2005, at 7, *available at* http://www.stabilisation2005.com/Steering_Commitee_Report.pdf (last visited Jan. 11, 2006) [hereinafter Hadley Centre Symposium 2005].

114. David Bjerklie et al. *Feeling the Heat: Special Report on Global Warming*, TIME, Apr. 9, 2001, at 24-29 [hereinafter Time Global Warming Report].

115. *See* Worldwatch Institute 2005, *supra* note 4, at 84.

116. *See* Hadley Centre Symposium 2005, *supra* note 113, at 10.

117. OFFICE OF AIR & RADIATION, U.S. EPA, GLOBAL WARMING AND OUR CHANGING CLIMATE: ANSWERS TO FREQUENTLY ASKED QUESTIONS (2000) (EPA 430-F-00-011) [hereinafter U.S. EPA Climate Change FAQs].

118. *See* Time Global Warming Report, *supra* note 114.

119. *See* Sarah Randolph, *Predicting the Risk of Tick-Borne Diseases*, 291 INT'L J. MED. MICROBIOLOGY 6-10 (2002) (Suppl. 33).

120. *See* Hadley Research Summary 2005, *supra* note 112, at 4, 5. *See* Hadley Centre Symposium 2005, *supra* note 113, at 10.

121. Robert B. Gagosian, *Abrupt Climate Change: Should We Be Worried?*, Paper Presented at the World Economic Forum, Davos Switz. (Jan. 27, 2003), *available at* http://www.whoi.edu/institutes/occi/images/ Abruptclimatechange.pdf.

122. Jonathan Leake, *Britain Faces Big Chill as Ocean Current Slows*, SUNDAY TIMES (Britain), May 8, 2005, http://www.timesonline.co.uk/ article/0,,2087-1602579,00.html (last visited Jan. 11, 2006).

123. *See* Hadley Centre Symposium 2005, *supra* note 113, at 10.

124. United Nations Framework Convention on Climate Change, Kyoto Protocol, http://unfccc.int/essential_background/kyoto_protocol/items/2830. php (last visited Jan. 11, 2006). The framework entered into effect March 21, 1994. The Kyoto Protocol became legally binding February 16, 2005.

125. *See* G8 Climate Change Communiqué 2005, *supra* note 80.

126. *See* PEW CENTER ON GLOBAL CLIMATE CHANGE, CLIMATE CHANGE AC-TIVITIES IN THE UNITED STATES: 2004 UPDATE (2004), *available at* http:// www.pewclimate.org/what_s_being_done/us_activities_2004.cfm.

127. *See* Connecticut v. American Elec. Power Co., No. 04-5669, 2005 U.S. Dist. LEXIS 19964 (S.D.N.Y. Sept. 19, 2005), *consolidated with* Open Spaces Inst. v. American Elec. Power Co. (No. 04-5670).

128. *See Regional Greenhouse Gas Initiative*, http://www.rggi.org/ (last visited Jan. 11, 2006).

129. *U.S. Mayors Climate Protection Agreement*, http://www.ci.seattle.wa. us/mayor/climate/ (last visited Oct. 12, 2006).

130. U.S. DEPARTMENT OF STATE, SUSTAINABLE DEVELOPMENT PARTNERS, USA ENERGY NEEDS, CLEAN DEVELOPMENT AND CLIMATE CHANGE—PARTNERSHIPS IN ACTION (2005), *available at* http://www. state.gov/documents/organization/57489.pdf.

131. Energy Information Administration, U.S. DOE, *Voluntary Reporting of Greenhouse Gases Program*, http://www.eia.doe.gov/oiaf/1605/frntvrgg. html (last visited Feb. 9, 2006).

132. *Chicago Climate Exchange*, http://www.chicagoclimatex.com/ (last visited Jan. 9, 2006).

133. *See* U.S. EPA Climate Change FAQs, *supra* note 117.

134. *See* Time Global Warming Report, *supra* note 114. DANIEL L. ALBRITTON ET AL., CLIMATE CHANGE 2001: SYNTHESIS REPORT (Cambridge Univ. Press 2001).

135. *See* IPPC 2001, *supra* note 98, at 17.

136. *See* Hadley Centre Symposium 2005, *supra* note 113, at 7.

137. *See* Worldwatch Institute 2005, *supra* note 4, at 92-93.

138. *See* Tomorrow's Markets 2002, *supra* note 21, at 34.

139. *See* Worldwatch Institute 2005, *supra* note 4, at 92-93.

140. *See id.*

141. Robert Pyle, Bishop Museum, Hawaii, *Birds of Hawaii*, http://biology. usgs.gov/s+t/noframe/t017.htm (last visited Jan. 11, 2006).

142. WORLD CONSERVATION UNION (WCU), SPECIES SURVIVAL COMMISSION, THE 2004 IUCN RED LIST OF THREATENED SPECIES: EXECUTIVE SUMMARY (2004), *available at* http://www.iucn.org/themes/ssc/red_list_ 2004/GSA_book/Red_List_2004_exec_summary.pdf [hereinafter 2004 IUCN Red List Summary].

143. EDWARD WILSON, THE DIVERSITY OF LIFE 187-94 (W.W. Norton & Co. 1992, 1999 ed.) [hereinafter Wilson on Biodiversity 1992].

144. *See* 2004 IUCN Red List Summary, *supra* note 142.

145. John Fleischman, *Mass Extinctions Come to Ohio*, DISCOVER, June 1997, at 82-90.

146. *See* Wilson on Biodiversity 1992, *supra* note 143, at 31.

147. *See* 2004 IUCN Red List Summary, *supra* note 142.

148. *See* Worldwatch Institute 2005, *supra* note 4, at 86.

149. *See* Tomorrow's Markets 2002, *supra* note 21, at 32.

150. *See* 2004 IUCN Red List Summary, *supra* note 142.

151. Aspen Publishers, *International Paper Protects and Manages Aquatic Resources*, BUS. & ENV'T, July 2004, at 8.

152. *See* UNESCO 2003 Water Report, *supra* note 23. UNEP, THE COMPREHENSIVE ASSESSMENT OF THE FRESHWATER RESOURCES OF THE WORLD (1999) [hereinafter UNEP Water Report 1999]. UNEP, *Freshwater Resources,* http://www.unep.org/vitalwater/freshwater.htm (last visited Jan. 11, 2006). *See* Tomorrow's Markets 2002, *supra* note 21, at 36.

153. Michael Kilian, *A Crusader's Last Appeal*, CHI. TRIB., Mar. 1, 2005, at A6.

154. Melissa Master, *Just Another Commodity?*, ACROSS THE BOARD, Aug. 18, 2002, at 18-24 [hereinafter Master 2002].

155. WORLDWATCH INSTITUTE, VITAL SIGNS 2001, at 110 (W.W. Norton & Co. 2001), *available at* http://www.worldwatch.org/pubs/vs/ [hereinafter Worldwatch Institute 2001].

156. *See id.* at 134.

157. *See* Master 2002, *supra* note 154, at 18-24.

158. *See* UNEP Water Report 1999, *supra* note 152.

159. Personal Communication with Vail T. Thorne (Dec. 9, 2003). *See also* Vail T. Thorne, *Water Scarcity and Its Impact on Water Rights: A Real Concern for Multinational Companies?*, 33 ELR 10617-25 (Aug. 2003).

160. GLOBAL ENVIRONMENTAL MANAGEMENT INITIATIVE (GEMI), CONNECTING THE DROPS TOWARD CREATIVE WATER STRATEGIES 24 (2002), *available at* http://www.gemi.org/ConnectingTheDrops.pdf [hereinafter GEMI Water Report 2002]. P&G, SUSTAINABILITY REPORT 2005—LINKING OPPORTUNITY WITH RESPONSIBILITY 4-8 (2005), *available at* http://www.pg.com/company/our_commitment/sustainability. jhtml.

161. See GEMI Water Report 2002, *supra* note 160, at 38-39, for other suggested approaches.

162. *See* MDG Report 2005, *supra* note 3. *See* UNESCO 2003 Water Report, *supra* note 23. C. REVENGA ET AL., 2000, PILOT ANALYSIS OF GLOBAL ECOSYSTEMS: FRESHWATER SYSTEMS (World Resources Institute 2000).

163. *See* Worldwatch Institute 2005, *supra* note 4, at 90-91. *See* Worldwatch Institute 2001, *supra* note 155, at 96-97.

164. *See* Worldwatch Institute 2005, *supra* note 4, at 26-27.

165. *Id.* at 26-27.

166. *Emptying the Oceans*, WEEK, June 20, 2003, at 13 [hereinafter Emptying the Oceans].

167. *See* Worldwatch Institute 2005, *supra* note 4, at 26-27.

168. *See* Millennium Ecosystem Assessment 2005, *supra* note 8, at 12.

169. *See* Emptying the Oceans, *supra* note 166.

170. *See* Tomorrow's Markets 2002, *supra* note 21.

171. *See* Worldwatch Institute 2001, *supra* note 155, at 96-97.

172. *See* Geo-2000, *supra* note 70.

173. *Id.*

174. *See* Worldwatch Institute 2005, *supra* note 4, at 26-27.

175. *See* Emptying the Oceans, *supra* note 166.

176. *See* NYT Alaska Melting 2005, *supra* note 105, at 10.

177. *See* Worldwatch Institute 2001, *supra* note 155, at 92.

178. *See* NYT Alaska Melting 2005, *supra* note 105, at 10.

179. *See* Worldwatch Institute 2001, *supra* note 155, at 92.

180. Reuters, *Mercury Poisoning Disease Hits Amazon Villages* (Feb. 4, 1999).

181. Michael Hawthorne, *Pregnant Women Get New Mercury Warning*, CHI. TRIB., Feb. 7, 2004, at A1, A15. Michael Hawthorne & Sam Roe, *U.S. Safety Net in Tatters*, CHI. TRIB., Dec. 12, 2006, at A1, A18.

182. Environmental Media Services, *Mercury Is a Major Public Health Problem*, May 8, 2001. Jeffery R. Holmstead, *Multi-Pollutant Legislation and the Clear Skies Act*, TRENDS, May/June 2003.

183. Environmental Media Services, *Experts Urge Ban on Production, Use of World's Most Toxic Chemicals*, June 29, 1998.

184. Stockholm Convention on Persistent Organic Pollutants, May 22, 2001 (entered into force May 17, 2004), http://www.pops.int/ (last visited July 26, 2005).

185. *See* Worldwatch Institute 2002, *supra* note 50, at 112-13.

186. *See* Tomorrow's Markets 2002, *supra* note 21, at 27.

187. WHO & EUROPEAN ENVIRONMENTAL AGENCY, AIR AND HEALTH—LOCAL AUTHORITIES, HEALTH, AND ENVIRONMENT 3 (1997), *available at* http://reports.eea.eu.int/2599XXX/en/page019.html.

188. *See* Tomorrow's Markets 2002, *supra* note 21, at 27.

189. *See* World Bank 2003, *supra* note 43, at 168-69. *See* World Bank 2005, *supra* note 7. *See* Worldwatch Institute 2005, *supra* note 4, at 94.

190. Fred Peace, *Smog Crop Damage Costs Billions*, NEW SCIENTIST, June 11, 2002.

191. *See* Michael Hawthorne, *Dirty Air Fouling Up Kids' Lungs, Study Finds*, CHI. TRIB., Sept. 9, 2004, at A15.

192. *See* Tomorrow's Markets 2002, *supra* note 21, at 26.

193. *See* Worldwatch Institute 2005, *supra* note 4, at 94-95.

194. WORLD BANK, FUEL FOR THOUGHT: AN ENVIRONMENTAL STRATEGY FOR THE ENERGY SECTOR 98 (2002).

195. *See* Geo-2000, *supra* note 70.

196. *See* Tomorrow's Markets 2002, *supra* note 21, at 15.

197. *See* Worldwatch Institute 2005, *supra* note 4, at 22-23.

198. *See* DIAMOND, *supra* note 75, at 47-49.

199. U.S. EPA, ENVIRONMENTAL INDICATORS: OZONE DEPLETION (2006), *available at* http://www.epa.gov/ozone/science/indicat/index.html. Andrew Revkin, *Ozone Layer Is Improving, According to Monitors*, N.Y. TIMES, July 30, 2003, at A11.

200. *See* Tomorrow's Markets 2002, *supra* note 21, at 27. Usha Lee McFarling, *Ozone Layer Unlikely to Recover Until 2065*, CHI. TRIB., Dec. 7, 2005, at 17.

201. Business Week/Harris Poll, *How Business Rates: By the Numbers*, Sept. 11, 2000, *available at* BUS. WK. ONLINE, http://www.businessweek.com/ (last visited Jan. 7, 2006) [hereinafter Business Week/Harris Poll 2000].

202. *Id.*

203. Mercer Human Resource Consulting, *Britain at Work Survey* (London, Oct. 21, 2002), http://www.mercerhr.com/pressrelease/details.jhtml/dynamic/idContent/1072265 (last visited Jan. 7, 2006).

204. Joseph Carroll, *Poll Analyses: Public Rates Nursing as Most Honest and Ethical Profession*, (Gallup News Service, Dec. 1, 2003), http://www.massnurses.org/News/2003/12/gallup_poll.htm (last visited Jan. 7, 2006).

205. *See* Business Week/Harris Poll 2000, *supra* note 201.

206. GLOBESCAN INC. (TORONTO), CORPORATE SOCIAL RESPONSIBILITY MONITOR 2002 (2002), *available at* http://www.globescan.com/ and e-mail: research@globescan.com.

207. *Research Unveils Deep Mistrust of Business*, PR WK. (United Kingdom), Oct. 10, 2003, at 4.

208. Interview with R. William Ide, *Sarbanes-Oxley: Does Your Law Department Have the Resources to Meet The New Challenges?*, METRO. CORP. COUNSEL, Sept. 2003, at 1.

209. JAROL B. MANHEIM, BIZ-WAR: ORIGINS, STRUCTURE AND STRATEGY OF FOUNDATION-NGO NETWORK WARFARE ON CORPORATIONS IN THE UNITED STATES (American Enterprise Institute for Public Policy Research 2003).

210. PAT FRANKLIN, EXTENDED PRODUCER RESPONSIBILITY: A PRIMER (Container Recycling Inst. 1997). U.S. EPA, PRODUCT STEWARDSHIP (2003), *available at* http://www.epa.gov/epaoswer/non-hw/reduce/epr/. BETTE K. FISHBEIN, EPR: WHAT DOES IT MEAN? WHERE IS IT HEADED? (INFORM, Inc. 2003), *available at* http://www.informinc.org/eprppr.php, *also published in Issue Brief: Green Product Design*, 8 P2: POLLUTION PREVENTION REV. 43-55 (1998), *available at* http://www.bsr.org/CSRResources/IssueBriefDetail.cfm?DocumentID=50105. (The four citations of this footnote are hereinafter EPR Sources.)

211. JAMIE MAXNER ET AL., PRODUCT STEWARDSHIP: SHARED ENVIRONMENTAL CONCERN (2003), *available at* http://www.writers.net/writers/26294.

212. Commission of the European Communities, *Communication From the Commission on the Precautionary Principle*, COM (2000)1, Feb. 2, 2000, http://europa.eu.int/eur-lex/en/com/cnc/2000/com2000_0001en01.pdf (last visited Jan. 7, 2006). Joel Tinkner et al., *The Precautionary Principle in Action—A Handbook*, http://www.biotech-info.net/handbook.pdf (last visited Jan. 7, 2006). David Appell, *Precautionary Principle: The New Uncertainty Principle*, SCI. AM., Jan. 2001, *available at* http://www.biotech-info.net/uncertainty.html. NOVARTIS CORP., NOVARTIS POSITION PAPER: THE PRECAUTIONARY APPROACH—HOW TO APPLY THE PRECAUTIONARY PRINCIPLE (2000). OECD, *Uncertainty and Precaution: Implications for Trade and Environment*, no. COM/ENV/TD(2000)114/FINAL (Paris Cedex, France, Sept. 5, 2002), http://www.olis.oecd.org/olis/

2000doc.nsf/LinkTo/com-env-td(2000)114-final (last visited Jan. 7, 2006).

213. *See* EPR Sources, *supra* note 210.

214. RUDD MAYER ET AL., PROMOTING RENEWABLE ENERGY IN A MARKET ENVIRONMENT: A COMMUNITY-BASED APPROACH FOR AGGREGATING GREEN DEMAND (Land & Water Fund of the Rockies/U.S. DOE 1997).

215. H. Josef Hebert, *Some Companies Attracted to "Green" Energy*, ASSOCIATED PRESS, Sept. 17, 2003.

216. David Ritchey Johnston, *Building Green in a Black and White World—Chapter 1*, *excerpted in* NATIONAL ASS'N OF HOME BUILDERS, TRENDS RELATED TO GREEN BUILDING (2003), *available at* http://www. housingzone.com/topics/nahb/green/nhb00ca004.asp.

217. David Ritchey Johnston, *Building Green in a Black and White World—Chapter 3*, *excerpted in* NATIONAL ASS'N OF HOME BUILDERS, ACTUAL COSTS—IS BUILDING GREEN TOO EXPENSIVE? (2003), *available at* http://www.housingzone.com/topics/nahb/green/nhb00ca029.asp.

218. Hugo H. Ottolenghi, *Not Easy Building Green: Construction That Makes Minimal Demands on the Environment Is Barely Visible in Florida*, DAILY BUS. REV. (Miami), Oct. 10, 2002.

219. Allesandra Pome & Elizabeth Ayres, *The Rise and Fall of Monsanto*, ESM 210, May 24, 2002, http://www.esm.ucsb.edu/academics/courses/210/Final%20Projects/Monsanto.doc (last visited Jan. 7, 2006).

220. Elizabeth Weise, *Monsanto Drops Biotech Wheat*, USA TODAY, May 11, 2004, at 7D [hereinafter Wiese 2004].

221. *Id.* Reuters Environmental News Service, *Factbox: What are Genetically Modified Crops?*, PLANET ARK, Mar. 11, 2004, http://www.planetark. com/dailynewsstory.cfm/newsid/24227/story.htm (last visited Jan. 11, 2006). *See also* Wen S. Chern et al., *Consumer Acceptance and Willingness-to-Pay for Genetically Modified Vegetable Oil and Salmon: A Multiple-Country Assessment*, AGBIOFORUM, 2003, art. 5, http://www. agbioforum.org/v5n3/v5n3a05-chern.htm (last visited Jan. 7, 2006) [hereinafter GM Food Survey].

222. Richard Edelman, *NGOs and Corporate Citizenship, in* EXECUTIVE PANEL DISCUSSION ON NGOs AND GLOBAL CORPORATE CITIZENSHIP (2001).

223. Organic Consumers Ass'n, *The Pope Comes Out in Favor of Frankenfoods*, Aug. 4, 2003, http://www.organicconsumers.org/ge/pope.cfm (last visited Jan. 7, 2006).

224. Baxter Healthcare Corp., *PVC in Medical Products*, http://www.baxter. Com/about_baxter/news_room/positions_policies/sub/pvc_position_ statement.html (last visited Jan. 7, 2006).

225. Stuart F. Brown, *Bioplastic Fantastic*, FORTUNE, July 21, 2003, at 92-94.

226. GLOBESCAN INC. (TORONTO), CORPORATE SOCIAL RESPONSIBILITY MONITOR 2003 (2002), *available at* http://www.globescan.com/ and e-mail: research@globescan.com.

227. PETER SANDMAN, RISK = Hazard + Outrage; Summary (1998), *available at* http://www.psandman.com/handouts/sand47.pdf.

228. *See* GM Food Survey, *supra* note 221.

229. Jennifer Janke, *Increasing Benefit of Voluntary Eco-Labeling Schemes*, Mar. 16, 2000, http://www.commercialdiplomacy.org/pdf/ma_projects/jahnke.pdf (last visited Jan. 11, 2006) [hereinafter Janke, Benefit of Eco-Labels 2000].

230. 16 C.F.R. 260, http://www.ftc.gov/bcp/grnrule/guides980427.htm (last visited Jan. 7, 2006).

231. *See, e.g.*, STATE OF OREGON, DEPARTMENT OF JUSTICE, MEDIA RELEASES: ENVIRONMENTAL MARKETING GUIDELINES FOR ELECTRICITY (2000), *available at* http://www.doj.state.or.us/releases/rel010500.htm.

232. Over one-half of Americans bought at least one green product in 1999, up from 35% only six years earlier. *See* Janke, Benefit of Eco-Labels 2000, *supra* note 229.

233. DK-Teknik Energy and Environment, Applications of LCA Methodological Framework: Marketing (1998). ISO, *ISO 14000 Information Zone*, http://www.iso-14001.org.uk/iso-14021.htm and NSF Bookstore, http://www.techstreet.com/cgi-bin/browsePublisher?publisher_id=133&subgroup_id=216 (last visited Jan. 7, 2006). James L. Connaughton, *Memorandum to Members of U.S. SubTAG3 to ISO TC 207 SC3: Status Report and Upcoming Meetings in Stockholm*, May 23, 2000, http://www.nsf.org/business/standards_and_publications/pdf/report6-2-01.pdf (last visited Jan. 7, 2006). GREEN SEAL, PRODUCT STANDARDS AND CERTIFICATION (2003), *available at* http://www.greenseal.org/standards.htm. Global Eco-Labelling Network, *Homepage*, http://www.gen.gr.jp/ (last visited Jan. 7, 2006) [hereinafter Global Eco-Labelling Network]. National Environmental Education & Training Foundation, *GreenBiz.com: Verifying Environmental Product Claims*, http://www.greenbiz.com/toolbox/howto_third.cfm?LinkAdvID=4197 (last visited Jan. 7, 2006).

234. ISO, ISO 14024: 1999: ENVIRONMENTAL LABELS AND DECLARATIONS — TYPE I ENVIRONMENTAL LABELLING — PRINCIPLES AND PROCEDURES (1999), *available at* http://www.iso.org/iso/en/CatalogueDetailPage.CatalogueDetail?CSNUMBER=23145&ICS1=13&ICS2=20&ICS3=50.

235. For standards, examples, and other guidance on life-cycle assessment, see ISO, *ISO 14040-14049 Series*, http://www.iso.org/iso/en/CatalogueListPage.CatalogueList?ICS1=13&ICS2=20&ICS3=10&scopelist= (last vis-

ited Jan. 7, 2006). See also the LCA publications of the Society of Environmental Toxicology and Chemistry (SETAC), http://www.setac.org/htdocs/who_intgrp_lca.html (last visited Feb. 10, 2006). A number of different terms have been used to describe the life-cycle assessment process. One of the first was life-cycle analysis. More recently though, two terms that have generally replaced it are: life-cycle inventory and the previously mentioned, life-cycle assessment, which better reflect the different stages of the process. Other terms such as eco-balancing and material flow analysis are also used.

236. ISO, ISO 14021: 1999: ENVIRONMENTAL LABELS AND DECLARATIONS—SELF-DECLARED ENVIRONMENTAL CLAIMS—TYPE II ENVIRONMENTAL LABELLING (1999), *available at* http://www.iso.org/iso/en/CatalogueDetailPage.CatalogueDetail?CSNUMBER=23146&ICS1=13&ICS2=20&ICS3=50.

237. ISO, ISO14025: 2000: TECHNICAL REPORT: ENVIRONMENTAL LABELS AND DECLARATIONS—TYPE III ENVIRONMENTAL DECLARATIONS (2000), *available at* http://www.iso.org/iso/en/CatalogueDetailPage.CatalogueDetail?CSNUMBER=26956&ICS1=13&ICS2=20&ICS3=50. *See also* ISO, DRAFT ISO 14025: 2005: STANDARD: ENVIRONMENTAL LABELS AND DECLARATIONS—TYPE III ENVIRONMENTAL DECLARATION—PRINCIPLES AND PROCEDURES (2005), *available at* http://www.Iso.org/iso/en/CatalogueDetailPage.CatalogueDetail?CSNUMBER=38131&scopelist=PROGRAMME.

238. Business for Social Responsibility (BSR), White Papers: Cause-Related Marketing (2001/2003). For many companies, the question no longer is whether they will engage in cause-related marketing, but which cause to embrace. BSR, ISSUE BRIEF: OVERVIEW OF BUSINESS AND MARKET PLACE (2003), *available at* http://www.bsr.org/CSRResources/IssueBrief Detail.cfm?DocumentID=49040.

239. Laren Gard, *We're Good Guys, Buy From Us: Companies Are Trying Out Innovative Charity Drives to Burnish Their Brands*, BUS. WK., Nov. 22, 2004, http://www.businessweek.com/magazine/content/04_47/b3909095.htm (last visited Jan. 7, 2006).

240. Philip Holmes, *Cause-Related Marketing Makes You the Customer's Choice*, IMPRINT, Summer 2002, http://www.logomall.com/imprintPM/issues/Summer-2002/SM.htm (last visited Jan. 7, 2006).

241. Cause-Marketing Forum, *Cause Marketing Resource Center*, http://www.causemarketingforum.com/page.asp?ID=73 (last visited Jan. 7, 2006).

242. Business in the Community, *Cause-Related Business Campaign*, http://www.bitc.org.uk/programmes/programme_directory/cause_related_business/index.html (last visited Jan. 7, 2006).

243. *United Nations: Obesity Strategy Contested*, CHI. TRIB., May 19, 2004, at A6.

244. Ioana Carabin & George Burdock, *Obesity in the United States: An Overview*, UPDATE: FOOD & DRUG L., REGULATION & EDUC., Jan./Feb. 2005, at 9-14 [hereinafter Obesity in the U.S. 2005].

245. *U.K. Food and Drinks Industry Issues Own "Manifesto,"* BUS. & ENV'T, Nov. 2004, at 9 [hereinafter U.K. Food Manifesto].

246. *See* Obesity in the U.S. 2005, *supra* note 244.

247. *Id.*

248. *See* Amy Joyce, *Bosses Working Harder to Cut Fat, Build Health of Employees*, CHI. TRIB., Mar. 30, 2004, at C4.

249. *See* Obesity in the U.S. 2005, *supra* note 244.

250. Kim Severson & Melanie Warner, *Fat Substitute, Once Praised, Is Pushed Out of the Kitchen*, N.Y. TIMES, Feb. 13, 2005, at A1, A23 [hereinafter Fat Substitute].

251. Delroy Alexander, *Kraft to Stop Advertising Its Sugary Snacks to Kids*, CHI. TRI., Jan. 13, 2005, at A1, A26 [hereinafter Kraft Sugary Snacks]. Aspen Publishers, *Tesco Acts as Food Industry Battles Against Junk Food Pressure*, BUS. & ENV'T, July 2004, at 8. *See* Fat Substitute, *supra* note 250. *See also* Kraft Sugary Snacks, *id.*

252. *See* U.K. Food Manifesto, *supra* note 245.

253. *See* Fat Substitute 2005, *supra* note 250. Melanie Warner, *You Want Any Fruit With That Big Mac?*, N.Y. TIMES, Feb. 20, 2005, at C1, C8 [hereinafter McDonald's Fruit].

254. *See* McDonald's Fruit, *supra* note 253.

255. SOCIAL INVESTMENT FORUM, 2005 REPORT ON SOCIALLY RESPONSIBLE INVESTING TRENDS IN THE UNITED STATES (2006), *available at* http://www.socialinvest.org/areas/research/trends/sri_trends_report_2005.pdf [hereinafter 2005 U.S. SRI Study].

256. *Id.*

257. *Id.* For more information on community investing, see the website of the Community Investing Center, a project of Co-op America and the Social Investment Forum Foundation, http://www.communityinvest.org/index.cfm (last visited Jan. 11, 2006).

258. Co-op America and the Social Investment Forum Foundation, *Community Investment Success Stories: Building Healthy Communities*, BUILDING COMMUNITIES (2003) [hereinafter Community Investment Success Stories].

259. *Id.*

260. Triodos Bank, Triodos Bank Actively Involved in UN Year of Microcredit, Triodos Press Release (November 18, 2004), *at* http://www.triodos.com/com/whats_new/latest_news/press_releases/119721?lang= (last visited Jan. 11, 2006). See more in Chapter 3 on microcredit banks.

261. *See* Community Investment Success Stories, *supra* note 258.

262. Peggy Anne Salz, *Redefining Corporate Value*, FORTUNE, July 21, 2003, at S2-3.

263. MEG VOORHES, KEY SOCIAL ISSUES: 2005 PROXY SEASON (2005) [hereinafter Voorhes IRRC 2005]. *See* 2005 U.S. SRI Study, *supra* note 255. *See* Worldwatch Institute 2001, *supra* note 155, at 115.

264. Philip R. Stanton, *SEC Reverses Cracker Barrel No-Action Letter*, 77 WASH. U. L.Q. 979-92 (1999).

265. *See* 2005 U.S. SRI Study, *supra* note 255.

266. *See* Voorhes IRRC 2005, *supra* note 263. E-mail from Michele Soule, IRRC, to William Blackburn (Mar. 18, 2005) [hereinafter Soule IRRC E-mail 2005]. Investor Responsibility Research Center, *Homepage*, http://www.irrc.org/ (last visited Jan. 11, 2006). *See* 2005 U.S. SRI Study, *supra* note 255.

267. *See* Voorhes IRRC 2005, *supra* note 263.

268. *See* 2005 U.S. SRI Study, *supra* note 255.

269. *See* Worldwatch Institute 2001, *supra* note 155, at 115.

270. *See* Voorhes IRRC 2005, *supra* note 263.

271. *Id.*

272. SOCIAL INVESTMENT FORUM, HAWKEN CRITIQUE OF SOCIALLY RESPONSIBLE INVESTING MISSES KEY TRENDS AND IMPACTS (2004), *available at* http://www.socialinvest.org/areas/news/041005.html.

273. *Shareholders Challenge Pesticide Companies*, NATURAL LIFE, Oct. 2003, at 24, 25.

274. JOHN ENTINE, CAPITALISM'S TROJAN HORSE: HOW THE "SOCIAL INVESTMENT" MOVEMENT UNDERMINES STAKEHOLDER RELATIONS AND EMBOLDENS THE ANTI-FREE MARKET ACTIVITIES OF NGOS (American Enterprise Institute for Public Policy 2003) [hereinafter Entine NGO Critique].

275. Letter from Paul Dickinson, Project Coordinator, Carbon Disclosure Project, to CEOs of the world's 500 largest corporations, re: *Greenhouse Gas Emissions* (Feb. 1, 2005), *available at* info@cdproject.net.

276. *See* Voorhes IRRC 2005, *supra* note 263. *See* Soule IRRC E-mail 2005, *supra* note 266.

277. *See* Voorhes IRRC 2005, *supra* note 263. *See* 2005 U.S. SRI Study, *supra* note 255. SOCIAL INVESTMENT FORUM, REPORT: 2003 PROXY SEASON EXPECTED TO SET RECORDS, WITH CEO PAY AND GLOBAL WARMING AMONG TOP ISSUES (2003), *available at* http://www.socialinvest.org/Areas/News/030212_san_proxy.htm [hereinafter 2003 Proxy Report].

278. *Id.*

279. Elisabeth Ribbans, *The Director Will See You Now*, TOMORROW, July 2002, at 42-46.

280. McKinsey & Co., *Evaluating Governance Codes*, CNET NEWS.COM, Apr. 18, 2004), http://news.com.com/2030-1014-5191872.html?tag=cd. top (last visited Jan. 8, 2006).

281. *See* Voorhes IRRC 2005, *supra* note 263.

282. *See* 2003 Proxy Report, *supra* note 277.

283. *See* World Resources Institute 2003, *supra* note 12.

284. 42 U.S.C. §§11001-11050, ELR STAT. EPCRA §§301-330.

285. *See* www.epa.gov/enviro and www.epa.gov/triexplorer.

286. Helmut Anheier & Nuno Themudo, *Chapter 8: Organizational Forms of Global Civil Society: Implications of Going Global, in* GLOBAL CIVIL SOCIETY 2002 (Centre for the Study of Global Governance 2002), *available at* http://www.lse.ac.uk/Depts/global/yearbook02chapters.htm#part4 [hereinafter Organizational Forms of CSOs]. James A. Paul, *NGOs and Global Policymaking*, GLOBAL POL'Y F., June 2000, http://www.global policy.org/ngos/analysis/anal00.htm (last visited Jan. 8, 2006) [hereinafter NGOs and Global Policy].

287. *See* Raphael Perl, *Terrorism and National Security: Issues and Trends*, CRS ISSUE BRIEF FOR CONGRESS, Order Code IB10119 (updated Dec. 21, 2004), http://www.fas.org/irp/crs/IB10119.pdf (last visited Feb. 13, 2006).

288. *Target: Ground Transportation*, N.Y. TIMES, July 10, 2005, at D4.

289. U.S. DEPARTMENT OF STATE, REVISED TERROR REPORT SHOWS CONTINUED VALIDITY OF SALIENT POINTS (2004), *available at* http://usinfo. State.gov/xarchives/display.html?p=washfile-english&y=2004&m= June&x=20040623182536adynned0.7506678&t=xarchives/xarchitem. html.

290. *See* Perl, *supra* note 287 and Bruce Hoffman, *Terrorism Trends and Prospects*, *in* COUNTERING THE NEW TERRORISM (Rand Publications 1999), *available at* http://www.rand.org/publications/MR/MR989/.

Appendix 2

Sustainability-Related Codes of Organizational Behavior

List of Codes Summarized in this Appendix 2	
2.1 General Sustainability Codes 2.1.1 U.N. Global Compact 2.1.2 The Earth Charter 2.1.3 Global Sullivan Principles of Corporate Social Responsibility 2.1.4 OECD Guidelines for Multinational Enterprises 2.1.5 Social Venture Network's Standards for Corporate Responsibility 2.1.6 Caux Round Table's Principles for Business 2.1.7 Principles for Global Corporate Responsibility: Benchmarks for Measuring Business Performance 2.1.8 U.S. Department of Commerce Manual of Business Ethics for Emerging Markets 2.1.9 Nippon Keidanren's Charter of Corporate Behavior **2.2 Environmental Codes** 2.2.1 The CERES Principles 2.2.2 ICC Charter for Sustainable Development 2.2.3 Position Statement of Pew Center's Business Environmental Leadership Council 2.2.4 Responsible Care® Global Charter **2.3 Human Rights, Labor, and Other Social Codes** 2.3.1 U.N. Universal Declaration of Human Rights 2.3.2 Amnesty International's Human Rights Principles for Companies	**2.3 Human Rights, Labor, and Other Social Codes—continued** 2.3.3 U.N. Norms on the Responsibilities of Transnational Corporations and Other Business Enterprises With Regard to Human Rights (draft) 2.3.4 U.S.-U.K. Voluntary Principles on Security and Human Rights 2.3.5 ILO Tripartite Declaration of Principles Concerning Multinational Enterprises and Social Policy 2.3.6 European Union Charter of Fundamental Rights 2.3.7 Social Accountability 8000 2.3.8 Fair Labor Association's Workplace Code of Conduct 2.3.9 Worker Rights Consortium's Model Code of Conduct 2.3.10 WRAP Apparel Certification Principles 2.3.11 Ethical Trading Initiative's Base Code **2.4 Marketing and Advertising Codes** 2.4.1 ICC International Codes of Marketing and Advertising Practice 2.4.2 Better Business Bureau and Other U.S. Marketing and Advertising Codes 2.4.3 British Code of Advertising, Sales Promotion, and Direct Marketing 2.4.4 Canadian Direct Marketing Association Code of Ethics and Standards of Practice

List of Codes Summarized in this Appendix 2—Continued	
2.5 Anti-Corruption Codes	**2.6 Governance Codes**
2.5.1 OECD Convention for Combating Bribery of Foreign Officials in International Business Transactions	2.6.1 OECD Principles of Corporate Governance
2.5.2 U.N. Convention Against Corruption	2.6.2 Council of Institutional Investors' Corporate Governance Policies
2.5.3 ICC Rules of Conduct to Combat Extortion and Bribery	2.6.3 The U.K. Combined Code
2.5.4 Transparency International's Business Principles for Countering Bribery	2.6.4 King II Code of Corporate Practices and Conduct
2.5.5 AS 8001-2003 Fraud and Corruption Control Standard	2.6.5 AS 8000-2003 Australian Good Governance Principles
	2.6.6 Sarbanes-Oxley Act
	2.6.7 Other Governance Codes
	2.7 Industry-Specific Codes

2.1 General Sustainability Codes

2.1.1 <u>U.N. Global Compact</u> (www.unglobalcompact.org)
The *Global Compact* was announced in 1999 by U.N. Secretary General Annan and formally launched the following year. It is administered by the U.N.'s Global Compact Office with the support of six U.N. agencies. The compact's 10 principles for business encompass support for human rights, labor rights, environmental responsibility, and anti-corruption measures. More specifically, they call for companies to uphold freedom of association and collective bargaining; to eliminate child labor, forced labor, and employment discrimination; and to embrace the precautionary approach and the development and sharing of environmentally friendly technologies. The principles also ask that companies work against bribery, extortion, and other forms of corruption. The principles were derived from three important documents: (1) the *Universal Declaration of Human Rights*; (2) the International Labour Organization's *Declaration on Fundamental Principles and Rights to Work*; and (3) the *Rio Declaration on Environment and Development*. Given their source and underpinnings, the compact is the most prestigious of all global sustainability codes. It has been adopted by over 2,500 companies and several dozen international NGOs and labor federations. Endorsing companies are encouraged to participate in U.N. partnerships, projects, and dialogues related to the principles. Some companies see this access to a broad global stakeholder network as one of the advantages to participation. But not ev-

erybody has unreserved praise for the compact: groups like Amnesty International, Oxfam, Friends of the Earth, and Human Rights Watch have criticized it for not having a system to transparently assess and report what the endorsing companies have done to implement the principles. In response, the organization adopted a policy and practical guide calling for endorsers to issue annual progress reports. The effectiveness of this approach is being assessed. Some companies have opposed the code because of sensitivity about the precautionary principle and labor union activities.

2.1.2 The Earth Charter (http://www.earthcharter.org/)

In 1987, the U.N. World Commission on Environment and Development called for the creation of a charter setting forth the principles of sustainable development, an objective reaffirmed at the Rio Earth Summit five years later. With the help of the Dutch government, the initiative to draft the Earth Charter was finally launched in 1994 by Maurice Strong (the secretary general of the Earth Summit and chairman of the Earth Council) and Mikhail Gorbachev (president of Green Cross International and former president of the Soviet Union). The international Earth Charter Commission approved the document in 2000. The charter is arranged in 16 principles under the following 4 themes:

> 1. *Respect and Care for the Community of Life:* This includes not only respecting the dignity of all human beings, but building democratic societies and assuring that the needs of future generations are addressed.
> 2. *Ecological Integrity:* Among other things, this covers adopting sustainable development plans and regulations. It also entails preventing the release of harmful genetically modified organisms. It requires that renewable resources be consumed no faster than they can be regenerated, and that the use of non-renewables be minimized. The precautionary approach must be followed, which requires, among other things, avoiding military activities that could damage the environment. In addition, ecological integrity means ensuring universal access to health care services that foster reproductive health and responsible reproduction.
> 3. *Social and Economic Justice:* The principles encompassed

within this theme touch on a number of objectives. Poverty must be eradicated and wealth equitably distributed. People should be guaranteed the right to potable water, clean air, food security, uncontaminated soil, and safe sanitation. Universal access to education, health care, and economic opportunity are to be provided. Multinational corporations must act transparently. Discrimination should be eliminated and the rights of indigenous peoples affirmed.

4. *Democracy, Nonviolence, and Peace:* This set of principles requires transparency and accountability in governance. It calls for other things, too. Everyone should have the right to receive timely information about environmental matters and help development plans that may affect them. All people should receive education on the knowledge, values, and skills for a sustainable way of life. Corruption should be avoided. Animals must not be treated cruelly. Weapons of mass destruction should be eliminated, and military resources converted to peaceful purposes. Cultural tolerance must be promoted.

The secretariat that supports the charter and facilitates its adoption is located at the University of Peace in Costa Rica. Guidelines entitled, *What Can I Do With the Earth Charter in Business*, are available on the organization's website. The charter has been endorsed by over 2,300 organizations—primarily cities, schools, other governmental bodies, and NGOs from around the world.

2.1.3 Global Sullivan Principles of Corporate Social Responsibility (http://www.globalsullivanprinciples.org/principles.htm)

The late Rev. Leon Sullivan, a Philadelphia clergyman and civil rights leader, was a pioneer in corporate social responsibility, having developed his famous *Sullivan Principles* in 1977. Those principles—a code of conduct for human rights and equal opportunity for companies operating in South Africa—were credited with helping dismantle apartheid in that country. Building on that work 20 years later, Rev. Sullivan joined with world and industry leaders to create the *Global Sullivan Principles of Social Responsibility*. The new principles were "globalized" under the United Nations in 1999. Organizations adopting the principles commit to support human rights, especially with respect to employees, customers, suppliers, and communities. More specifically, such organizations promise to eliminate the exploitation and discrimination of workers, and to respect freedom of association. They agree to provide workers a safe and healthy workplace and an opportunity to improve their skills. Moreover, they promise to pay wages that enable employees to meet their basic needs. Although the principles are framed around "social responsibility," they reflect a broad view of that term by including provisions on protecting the environment and promoting sustainable development.

Collaboration with governments and communities is stressed with the aim of improving the quality of life. Implementation is to be specifically addressed through policies, procedures, training, and reporting. For accountability, endorsing parties must annually submit a simple progress update for posting on the Sullivan website. Approximately 300 organizations have signed on to this global code—roughly two-thirds of them companies and the remainder a mix of big-city governments and other civic and educational institutions.

2.1.4 OECD Guidelines for Multinational Enterprises
(http://www.oecd.org/document/28/0,2340,en_2649_34889_2397532_1_1_1_1,00.html)

The Organization for Economic Co-operation and Development (OECD) was formed by international agreement in 1961 to promote economic growth, employment, financial stability, and the expansion of trade among its Member countries. Currently it has 30 Members, including Australia, Japan, Mexico, New Zealand, South Korea, the United States, and many European countries—all developed democratic nations that favor free markets. OECD's main function is to spot emerging issues and use dialogue, peer review, and consensus to identify effective strategies and policies for its Member countries. In 1976, the organization adopted its *Guidelines for Multinational Enterprises*—voluntary standards of behavior recommended by the OECD governments for international businesses and other entities. The standards were significantly amended in 2000 by a committee of government delegates working with business and trade-union advisory groups and various NGOs. The guidelines are comprehensive, containing detailed provisions on labor practices and human rights; environmental management and responsibility; bribery; consumer information and protection; technology transfer; fair competition; and the disclosure of economic, social, and environmental information. Some of the more interesting—and controversial—provisions urge endorsing enterprises to promptly pay their taxes and to refrain from seeking or accepting special exemptions not contemplated in the law, including exemptions related to environment, health, and safety (EHS), labor, and tax requirements. The guidelines also ask that organizations provide information and facilities for employee union representatives, adhere to the precautionary principle, and adopt management systems to prevent bribery. The promotion of the standard is left to designated national contacts (National Contact Points) and to the committee and advisory groups responsible for its development.

Companies may declare adherence to the guidelines but there is no formal listing of those that do. However, if someone thinks a company in an OECD country is violating a guideline provision, she may notify the National Contact Point. If the contact believes the issue has merit, she will attempt to mediate a resolution among the parties or, if no resolution can be reached, she will issue a statement or recommendation. Her decision carries no legal weight but may have political and public-relations value. Since the guidelines were first issued three decades ago, only one case has ever been accepted by the U.S. Department of State, which serves as the U.S. contact. The Netherlands and Sweden have used the process more frequently. The Dutch government requires that companies comply with the OECD guidelines as a condition to obtaining export credits.

2.1.5 Social Venture Network's Standards for Corporate Responsibility (http://www.svn.org/initiatives/standards.html)

The Social Venture Network (SVN), formed in 1987, is a San Francisco-based nonprofit network that promotes new models and leadership for socially and environmentally sustainable business. Its 400 members are primarily socially responsible entrepreneurs and investors. It helped found Business for Social Responsibility, and in 1999, worked with more than 200 individual contributors to produce its *Standards of Corporate Responsibility*. The standards are organized around nine major principles: three on general topics (ethics, accountability, and governance) and six on topics related to the interests of various stakeholder groups (investors, employees, business partners, customers, communities, and the environment). They indicate that companies should, among other things—

> 1. Compensate their providers of capital with an attractive and competitive rate of return while protecting company assets and the sustainability of these returns.

2. Respect their employees' right to fair labor practices and competitive wages and benefits.
3. Promote and monitor the corporate social responsibility of their business partners.
4. Integrate environmental considerations into day-to-day management decisions.

In addition, the standards say that stakeholder need-to-know must take precedence over inconvenience and cost to the corporation. SVN also provides recommended practices, measures, and a list of resources to supplement each principle.

2.1.6 Caux Round Table's Principles for Business
(http://www.cauxroundtable.org/principles.html)

The Caux Round Table, named for its meeting place in Caux-sur-Montreux, Switzerland, is a group of 25-50 principled business leaders from around the world—primarily, Europe, Japan, and North America—who promote moral capitalism. The organization was founded in 1986 to reduce escalating trade tensions. It later took up global corporate responsibility. In 1994, it launched its *Principles for Business* to spur dialogue and action by business leaders and others on the issue of responsible corporate behavior. The principles call for businesses to contribute to human rights, education, welfare, and the vitalization of countries in which they operate. Charitable donations and participation in civic affairs is encouraged. Other provisions commit companies to use resources prudently, improve the environment and promote sustainable development. Still others advocate free and fair competition. More specifically, businesses are to support the WTO and efforts to relax domestic measures that hinder global commerce—obligations that no doubt rankle some NGOs. Under the principles, companies are to fulfill their promises and be truthful, sincere, and transparent. They are to shun bribery, other corrupt practices, and industrial espionage. They are to treat customers with dignity, upholding the integrity of their cultures and showing respect for human dignity in marketing and advertising. Products are to sustain or enhance the environment and the customer's health and safety. Businesses must listen to and honestly communicate with employees, treat them in a nondiscriminatory manner, and provide them the compensation necessary to improve their living conditions. The employment of "differently abled people" is to be promoted. Businesses must also provide shareholders the information they need, and respect their formal resolutions. Suppliers must be paid on time. A preference must be given to suppliers with employment practices that respect human dignity.

The Caux Round Table has developed a model Self-Assessment and Improvement Process to help companies adopt the principles. However, the organization doesn't track endorsers or require progress reports.

2.1.7 Principles for Global Corporate Responsibility: Benchmarks for Measuring Business Performance
(http://www.bench-marks.org/index.shtml and
http://www.iccr.org/publications/)

The *Principles for Global Responsibility*, first issued in 1995, was developed by three coalitions of faith-based organizations: (1) the Interfaith Center on Corporate Responsibility of the USA (ICCR); (2) the Ecumenical Council for Corporate Responsibility of the United Kingdom (ECCR); and (3) the Taskforce on the Churches and Corporate Responsibility of Canada (TCCR, now KAIROS-Canada). These northern NGOs were joined by several from the South in producing the updated version of the principles in 2003. Most members of the coalitions are also large investors in company stocks.

This code is one of the most exhaustive, aggressive, and controversial. It covers 38 pages of principles of business philosophy (principles), company policies and practice (criteria), and reference points for measuring company performance (benchmarks). The principles examine company obligations from an external perspective—termed "The Wider Community," and an internal one—"The Corporate Business Community." The Wider Community is further divided into four subparts—the ecosystem and national, local, and indigenous communities. The Corporate Business Community addresses obligations with respect to employees, such as those concerning working conditions, health and safety, women, minorities, the disabled, child labor, and forced labor. A number of other stakeholders are addressed, too, including suppliers, contractors, shareholders, joint ventures/partnerships/subsidiaries, and customers. The internal perspective also covers financial integrity, ethics, and governance.

Some of the more noteworthy obligations under the principles are the following:

1. *Human Rights:* If there is a movement within a country calling for a company to withdraw because of gross and system-

atic violations of human rights, the company will do so. The board of directors will annually review operations in countries that consistently violate the Universal Declaration on Human Rights. A wide range of international human rights codes must be followed.

2. *Labor Practices:* Employees must be paid a sustainable living wage to meet basic needs, plus some discretionary income to invest in the "ongoing sustainability of local communities." The company will provide employees with child- and elder-care services or otherwise support these services. It should have a clear policy on employee stress. Paid maternity, paternity, family, and compassionate leave must be provided. Employees should not be required to work overtime on a regular basis. Workers will have the right of access to health care, including accessible and affordable therapies and medicines. The company will provide HIV/AIDS drugs if the government doesn't. The company must practice nondiscrimination, including fair treatment for the disabled and those with different sexual orientations or political opinions. The diversity of the labor force and managerial employees must be proportionally representative of the local community.

3. *Supplier Relations:* The company must have a strong code of conduct on labor practices for its suppliers. It must accept independent monitoring of its practices, as well as those of its suppliers, by NGOs and local community organizations.

4. *Products and Services:* The company may not market harmful products or products which denigrate or supplant sustainable natural products. The precautionary principle must be invoked prior to developing a genetically modified organism. Patent rights must not supersede the rights of farmers to pursue traditional sustainable agriculture or forestry. Tobacco companies must support smoke-free enclosed spaces. If the company produces arms, it should allow independent monitoring of its operations by NGOs and eventually convert to some other socially useful product. It may not engage in military or war activities. Returned, second-hand, and reject goods and outlet samples must be made available through local independent distributors.

5. *Environmental Responsibility:* The board of directors must establish an environmental committee, and World Health Organization (WHO) codes should be followed. Environmental per-

formance must be independently audited, and the results reported to stakeholders.

6. *Stakeholder Relations:* The company must have a process for
inclusive and thorough consultation with stakeholder groups,
and integrate their interests into business plans. Indigenous peoples should be allowed full participation in business decisions
concerning their ancestral lands and way of life.

7. *Accountability, Reporting:* Employee compensation—especially that of senior management—must be linked to sustainability performance. The company's financial auditors must
publicly report the consultancy fees and commissions they received from the company. An oral and written report must be
provided to communities on the company's impact on them. The
company should provide independently verified, transparent
public reports on its sustainability performance. A report on the
company's performance under the principles should be made
available to all shareholders.

8. *Other:* The company's legislative lobbying efforts must support responsible environmental protection and social, labor, and
human rights. The organization must regularly report its lobbying activities to its stakeholders. A mechanism must be available
for the company to address unethical conduct by its joint ventures. In addition, the company must offer stock options to a
broad cross-section of employees, and account for these options
as an expense.

As this list shows, the principles are rigorous. Because they are so
tough, companies haven't adopted them. Nevertheless, they remain a
good source for companies wanting to conduct a self-assessment against
leading-edge—or beyond leading-edge—practices. Members of the
sponsoring investor coalitions have assessed companies against the principles using research, surveys, and dialogue.

2.1.8 U.S. Department of Commerce Manual of Business Ethics for
Emerging Markets
(http://ita.doc.gov/goodgovernance/business_ethics/manual.asp)

The International Trade Administration of the U.S. Department of Commerce worked with Transparency International, the Ethics Officer Association, American and Russian business groups, and various experts
from eastern Europe to develop its 2004 *Manual for Managing a Respon-*

sible Business Enterprise in Emerging Market Economies. This 245-page document contains guidance, checklists, and worksheets to be used by business in designing and implementing ethical practices for its operations, particularly in developing nations. The manual offers suggestions on organizational structure, management standards, procedures, and accountability mechanisms related to responsible governance. It presents ideas on how to integrate ethical considerations into business planning and strategies. A sample outline and provisions for a business code of conduct are also presented.

2.1.9 Nippon Keidanren's Charter of Corporate Behavior
(http://www.keidanren.or.jp/english/policy/pol052.html)

Nippon Keidanren (The Japan Business Federation) was created in 2002 by the merger of Keidanren (Japan Federation of Economic Organizations) and Nikkeiren (Japan Federation of Employers' Associations)—two organizations born in the late 1940s. Originally formed to help war-devastated Japan rebuild its economy, Keidanren eventually began addressing corporate environmental and social responsibility. This direction fit well with that of Nikkeiren, an organization championing sound labor-management relationships. Their revised *Charter of Corporate Behavior*, issued by the combined organization in 2004, commits their 1,300 corporate members to meet 10 basic environmental and social obligations. These obligations include producing safe, socially beneficial goods and services; promoting fair trade and competition; and respecting human rights and cultural differences. Other obligations cover employee safety and diversity and the support for community development and philanthropic causes. The charter also calls for members to address environmental issues in a positive way. It encourages the active and fair disclosure of "corporate information" to shareholders and the public, although no guidance is provided on what type of information that entails. The unique aspect of this code is its attention to those things that can bring about real change within a company. The charter asks companies to establish systems to achieve the desired corporate behavior, and for the highest levels of their management to assume responsibility for implementing its provisions. If a member company violates one of the charter obligations, it must investigate the cause, develop preventive actions, and promptly report these actions to the public. Responsibility for the violation is to be assessed and disciplinary action taken, "which includes the highest level of management where necessary." Nippon Keidanren does not collect these nonconformance reports or track the progress of members in fulfilling the charter. That is left to the members themselves.

2.2 Environmental Codes

2.2.1 The CERES Principles (http://www.ceres.org/)

The Coalition for Environmentally Responsible Economies (CERES) was formed in Boston in 1988 as a coalition of environmental advocacy groups, socially responsible investment firms, and public pension funds. Its purpose was to find ways to use investment dollars to promote a healthy environment. A year after its founding, in the wake of the *Exxon Valdez* oil spill, CERES published its Valdez Principles, later renamed the CERES Principles. The principles cover a full range of company environmental responsibilities, addressing biodiversity protection, sustainable use of natural resources, energy conservation, and risk reduction. They also call for the development of safe products and services and the restoration of the environment where damaged by the company. The most notable parts concern public disclosure and dialogue. Each endorsing company is required to engage in regular dialogue with its neighbors and to notify them promptly if they may be endangered by conditions caused by the company. Companies also must annually assess their progress in implementing the principles, and produce a public performance report meeting CERES' criteria. This reporting requirement has been a sticking point with many companies. After the development of the GRI reporting guidelines, which CERES spearheaded, the organization dropped its own environmental reporting criteria, substituting the broader GRI sustainability criteria instead. Each year CERES reviews and critiques the sustainability reports issued by its 70-plus endorsers.

2.2.2 ICC Charter for Sustainable Development
(http://www.iccwbo.org/home/environment_and_energy/sdcharter/
charter/principles/principles.asp)

The International Chamber of Commerce (ICC) is a global business organization headquartered in Paris with thousands of member companies in 130 nations. Since its founding in 1919, its aim has been to serve world business by promoting trade and investment, open markets, and the free flow of capital. In keeping with its policy favoring self-regulation, in 1991 the organization developed its *Charter for Sustainable Development*. The charter has proved quite popular, having been adopted by more than 2,300 companies and business associations. The 16 principles of the charter address a wide range of business obligations concerning the EHS aspects of products, services, and operations. The principles call for employee awareness and the involvement of customers, suppliers, and contractors. Businesses are to take a proactive approach in researching ways to reduce environmental effects and in assessing the impacts of activities prior to undertaking them. They are asked to have open discussions with employees and the public about potential environmental hazards their organizations may cause. Emergency preparedness plans are required to deal with hazards that may arise outside normal operations. Endorsing companies are expected to go beyond their own operations to contribute to the development of public environmental policy and the spread of environmentally sound technology. A number of the principles focus on implementation, calling for endorsers to recognize environmental management as among their highest corporate priorities, and to integrate the charter obligations into each business function. The principles promote continual improvement through audits and the reporting of performance to the board, employees, governmental authorities, and the public.

2.2.3 Position Statement of Pew Center's Business Environmental Leadership Council (http://www.pewclimate.org/companies_leading_ the_way_belc/)

The Pew Center for Global Climate Change is an independent, nonpartisan, nonprofit organization established by the Pew Charitable Trust in 1998. The center's mission is to provide credible information, answers, and innovative solutions in addressing global climate change. Forty-two major corporations have joined its Business Environmental Leadership Council. Council members endorse four "beliefs" concerning the threat of climate change and what should be done about it. Among these beliefs is a commitment that businesses "take concrete steps now to assess opportunities for emission reduction; establish and meet emission-reduction objectives; and invest in new, more efficient products, practices, and technologies."

2.2.4 Responsible Care® Global Charter
(http://www.responsiblecare.org/)
(http://www.rctoolkit.com/globalcare.asp)
(http://www.rctoolkit.com/pdfs/RCMSTech_012504.pdf)
(http://www.americanchemistry.com/s_acc/sec_statistics.asp?CID=
176&DID=304)

The Responsible Care® program originally started in Canada in 1985
and spread to 52 countries representing over 85% of the world's chemical
production. The program is coordinated by the International Council of
Chemical Associations (ICCA) but implemented through individual
country organizations like the American Chemistry Council (ACC).
ICCA's *Responsible Care Global Charter* details the minimum requirements for country-level chapters of the organization as well as for member companies. Among other things, the charter calls for companies to
implement initiatives in support of sustainable development. More specifically, members are expected to continuously improve their EHS performance; engage and address the concerns of their stakeholders; coop-
erate with governments in developing effective rules; and foster responsible management of chemicals along the supply chain. In addition, companies must improve product stewardship, which includes among other
things, supporting education, research, and testing on chemical risks and
benefits. Members are also asked to development externally verified
management systems covering the charter obligations. At least every two
years, they must report to their national chapters on performance under a
designated set of measures. In turn, the chapters must compile this data
and report it to the public. A number of national programs have established additional requirements for their members as well. For example,
ACC's Responsible Care® program requires its members to establish a
third-party-certified EHS and security management system conforming
to the ACC's ISO-like management standards. These standards are further discussed in Appendix 3.8. The Responsible Care® program has
done much to raise the visibility of key sustainability issues among those
in the chemical industry and has no doubt stimulated improved performance among many. Still, success has not been universal, as evidenced
by a 2004 report by the NGO Environmental Defence that was critical of
the Canadian chapter, and by ICCA's own status report on Responsible
Care® implementation and progress issued in 2005.[1]

2.3 Human Rights, Labor, and Other Social Codes

2.3.1 U.N. Universal Declaration of Human Rights
(http://www.unhchr.ch/udhr/)

This declaration was adopted by the United Nations in 1948, when the horrors of the Holocaust and other human rights indignities of World War II were still fresh in the public's mind. It recites a long string of rights that every person should enjoy. Most rights are of the type that must be acknowledged and protected by the state, but some have implications for companies. Those implications are spelled out in the proposed U.N. *Norms on the Responsibilities of Transnational Corporations and Other Business Enterprises With Regard to Human Rights* and in Amnesty International's *Human Rights Principles for Companies*, both of which are discussed below. Among the rights spelled out in the declaration are freedom from discrimination based on race, color, sex, language, or other status, as well as freedom from slavery and other inhumane treatment. Many provisions of the U.S. Bill of Rights are included, such as the freedoms of religion, speech, and to peacefully assemble and associate. Freedom from arbitrary arrest and the right to a fair public trial are provided. The declaration also recognizes a personal right of privacy. Among the document's more challenging provisions is one declaring the right to a standard of living that provides adequate food, clothing, housing, medical care, and social services. Another recognizes the individual's right to security in the event of unemployment, sickness, disability, widowhood, and old age. Under the document, workers are entitled to join trade unions and earn equal pay for equal work. They must be provided just and favorable working conditions, periodic holidays with pay, and reasonable limitations in working hours. The "moral and material interests" of those who produce scientific, literary, or artistic works is to be protected. The Universal Declaration of Human Rights served as one of the foundations for the U.N. Global Compact.

2.3.2 Amnesty International's Human Rights Principles for Companies
(http://web.amnesty.org/library/index/ENGACT700011998)

Amnesty International's Principles, adopted in 1998, provide practical guidance on the implications of certain human rights standards, including the OECD guidelines, the *Universal Declaration of Human Rights*, and various International Labor Organization conventions and declarations. Here are highlights from Amnesty's nine Principles:

1. *Company Policy:* Companies should have an explicit policy on human rights which includes support for the *Universal Declaration of Human Rights.*

2. *Security:* Security arrangements made by companies should assure human rights are protected, and that certain U.N. codes on the use of force and firearms are met. Security personnel with serious human rights violations in the past should not be hired. Clear rules should be established for calling in state security forces. Torture and inhuman treatment is banned.

3. *Engagement With Communities:* Companies should make sure their activities don't adversely affect human rights within their communities. They must also promote human rights locally, such as through education, training, and citizenship programs.

4. *Discrimination:* Company policies and practices should prevent discrimination based on sex, color, ethnic origin, language, or beliefs.

5. *Forced Labor:* Businesses, their suppliers, and partners should not use forced labor.

6. *Health and Safety:* Companies should assure safe and healthy working conditions and products.

7. *Labor Rights:* Companies should respect the rights of employees to speak, peacefully assemble, associate and unionize, bargain collectively, and, if necessary, strike.

8. *Job Security and Pay:* Employees should have reasonable job security and fair pay that provides an adequate standard of living for workers and their families.

9. *Monitoring:* Companies should monitor their compliance with human rights standards with appropriate participation by employees, communities, and NGOs. Independently verifiable performance reports should be prepared.

In addition to the principles, Amnesty International joined with leading academic institutions to form the Business and Human Rights Resource Centre, which maintains an extensive website of business-related human rights information.[2]

2.3.3 U.N. Norms on the Responsibilities of Transnational Corporations and Other Business Enterprises With Regard to Human Rights (draft) (http://www1.umn.edu/humanrts/links/norms-Aug2003.html)

The U.N. norms interpret how the *Universal Declaration of Human Rights* should be applied to transnational corporations. In August 2003, the U.N. Sub-Commission on Promotion and Protection of Human Rights approved the norms, passing them to the U.N. Commission on Human Rights with certain recommendations. One recommendation was that comments on the norms be solicited from various U.N. agencies, businesses, and other external parties, and that after the comments are received, a working group be established to explore how the norms should be implemented. The comment period closed at the end of 2006.

In many ways, the norms are like Amnesty International's *Human Rights Principles for Companies*. In some respects, they go beyond that document. For example, the norms address discrimination based on disability and age. They would allow discrimination, however, if it favored children, related to inherent requirements to perform the job, or was used under an affirmative action program to overcome past discrimination against certain groups. Employee pay should not only provide an adequate standard of living, but also enable workers to make progressive improvement. Bribery is banned. Companies are to refrain from encouraging governments to abuse the human rights of others, and must ensure that the products and goods they provide are not used for that purpose. The norms also expand on the implementation provisions of Amnesty International's principles, calling for businesses to adopt internal rules of operation on human rights, to incorporate the norms into procurement contracts, and to open themselves to periodic monitoring by the United Nationas itself. Companies are also to provide adequate reparations to parties that are harmed by the organization's breach of the norms.

2.3.4 U.S.-U.K. Voluntary Principles on Security and Human Rights (http://www.state.gov/g/drl/rls/2931.htm)

The U.S. Department of State and U.K. Foreign and Commonwealth Office convened a dialogue with a number of oil and mining companies, several unions that serve those companies, and eight NGOs to explore how companies might maintain safety and security of their operations while also respecting human rights. This dialogue gave birth to the *Voluntary Principles* in 2000. The principles are presented in three parts:

1. *Risk Assessment:* This part presents factors to be used in evaluating situations for security risks. It lists considerations for assessing the potential for violence and other adverse consequences that may arise from a particular situation and the response to it.

2. *Interactions Between Companies and Public Security:* This text spells out the type of communication, oversight, and involvement companies should have when asking governments to provide security services. This includes, among other things, supporting human rights training for the security forces and requesting that no security force members implicated in human rights abuses provide services for the company. Businesses are also expected to report to the host government any claims of human rights abuses by the assigned security forces, and to monitor the investigations that follow.

3 *Interactions Between Companies and Private Security:* This section on private security forces contains provisions similar to those on public forces. Some additional requirements are included as well. Security firms should be selected which have a well-trained staff that is representative of the local population. Such firms should also have firm polices and a good track record of respecting human rights and refraining from the excessive use of force. The voluntary principles should be incorporated into the service agreement. Contracted private security forces are to be used only for preventive and defensive purposes.

2.3.5 ILO Tripartite Declaration of Principles Concerning Multinational Enterprises and Social Policy
(http://www.ilo.org/public/english/standards/norm/sources/mne.htm)

The International Labour Organization (ILO), headquartered in Geneva, Switzerland, is the only surviving major creation from the 1919 Treaty of Versailles which established the League of Nations. ILO's original purpose was to deal with the labor conditions involving "injustice, hardship and privation" that existed in the wake of World War I. This was not just an altruistic measure; addressing these issues was thought to be critical to avoiding civil unrest of the type that had led to the Russian Revolution. By the time it became the first specialized agency of the United Nations in 1946, the ILO had broadened its scope to also encompass social policy and human and civil rights.

ILO develops consensus documents, typically in the form of treaties or "Conventions," which must be ratified by Member states; nonbinding "Recommendations"; and less formal codes of conduct, resolutions, and declarations. Conventions and Recommendations are proposed by various committees and voted on by Members at an annual ILO conference. Conference Members comprise 4 representatives from each of 272 countries. These four include two representatives from government and one each from business and labor. This government-business-labor "tripartite" structure is unique among U.N. agencies.

The *Tripartite Declaration of Principles Concerning Multinational Enterprises and Social Policy* was adopted by the ILO in 1977. It provides principles concerning employment, training, conditions of work, and industrial relations within multinational companies. Under these principles, companies are to provide equal opportunities in employment, except for preferences which may be given for correcting historical patterns of discrimination and for hiring national workers and suppliers from the host country. Companies are urged to promote employment, especially in developing nations, using technologies likely to lead to job growth. They must try to provide stable employment and avoid arbitrary dismissals. If jobs must be eliminated because of production transfers or plant closings, workers are to be given due notice and their incomes protected by companies and governments. Training is to be provided for all levels of employees to improve skills and enhance career opportunities. Companies are encouraged to offer their own skilled people to train others outside their organizations through government-sponsored training programs. The declaration says that wages and benefits should be competitive, at a minimum providing for the basic needs of workers and their families. It calls for businesses to maintain the highest global standards of health and safety for their employees, and to provide them with benchmark information on foreign standards that may be helpful. Companies must recognize the freedom of association of workers and their rights to organize trade unions and bargain collectively without the threat of closing operations. Companies are urged to arrange with worker groups to establish an employee-management consultation process, fair grievance procedures, and arbitration or other dispute-resolution mechanisms. The declaration also incorporates the principles of the *Universal Declaration of Human Rights* and a number of ILO Conventions and Recommendations. It urges governments to enact laws and collaborate with companies and employer and worker organizations using the declaration as a guide to further social progress.

2.3.6 European Union Charter of Fundamental Rights
(http://www.europarl.europa.eu/charter/default_en.htm)

The European Union's *Charter of Fundamental Rights*, adopted in 2000, incorporates all the human rights found in the international conventions of the Council of Europe, ILO, and the United Nations, as well as those found in European national laws. Besides the more common rights discussed above in this Appendix 2.3, the document also captures some that are less frequently expressed, such as the freedom of the arts and sciences, the freedom to choose an occupation, the right to marry and found a family, and the promotion of linguistic diversity. Others include the right to vote and stand as a candidate for election to the European Parliament, the right of a fair trial with defense and the presumption of innocence, and the freedom of movement and residence. The provisions of the charter were incorporated in full in the draft Constitution of Europe, which was rejected when the French and Dutch failed to ratify it in 2005. The Constitution is now being reconsidered. Even without formal legal status, the charter has on several occasions influenced decisions of the Court of Justice of the European Communities.

2.3.7 Social Accountability 8000
(http://www.sa-intl.org/index.cfm?fuseaction=Page.viewPage&pageId=710&parentID=540&grandparentID=473&nodeID=1)

As mentioned in Appendix 3.22, Social Accountability (SA) 8000 is a management system standard for addressing workplace conditions and independently verifying factory compliance. But it is a code of conduct as well. The standard was written in 1997 by a board of 25 people from NGOs, industry, and consulting firms under the charge of New York-based nonprofit, Social Accountability International (SAI). SAI—formerly the Council on Economic Priorities Accreditation System—was created at the request of the ILO. While the management standards within SA 8000 are based on the ISO standards, the portions related to workplace conditions and labor rights spring from various ILO and U.N. documents.

The SA 8000 standard bans the employment of forced labor and children. It demands that an endorsing company remedy situations where children are employed and assure they are provided proper schooling. The standard also provides detailed requirements on factory safety and health programs. It prohibits discrimination and demands that companies respect the freedom of association and right to collective bargaining by workers. It insists that physical and verbal abuses not be tolerated. Regular work is capped at 48 hours per week, with a 12-hour limit on overtime. Employees are to be paid enough to meet their basic needs and provide some discretionary income. An endorsing company must select suppliers and contractors based on their ability to meet the SA 8000 standards, and require by contract that they conform to the standards. Frequent announced and unannounced inspections must be conducted to assure contracted home-workers are complying.

Over 400 sites have been certified under SA 8000, primarily from the apparel, textile, and chemical industries in Brazil, China, India, Italy, and Vietnam. These certifications are provided by independent auditors accredited by SAI. Local NGOs, unions, and individuals are encouraged to report any observed nonconformances to the standard by certified facilities.

2.3.8 Fair Labor Association's Workplace Code of Conduct
(http://www.fairlabor.org/all/code/)

The Fair Labor Association (FLA) was formed in 1997 by the Apparel Industry Partnership, a coalition of labor and human rights NGOs, and various industries and "university licensees" associated with the clothing business. The FLA created a *Charter Document* containing the one-page *Workplace Code* and a companion document, *Principles of Monitoring*, which together cover much of the same scope as SA 8000. Like SA 8000, the FLA Code and Principles serve as the basis for a facility assessment and certification program. Audited production sites are drawn from the lists used by FLA participant organizations. These participants include 12 leading brand-name apparel corporations and over 175 colleges and universities that license production of goods bearing their logos. Audits are undertaken by pre-qualified company representatives according to a monitoring plan, with a certain percentage of sites assessed by independent external auditors accredited by the association. FLA audit reports, which identify the company but not the site, consist of completed

THE SUSTAINABILITY HANDBOOK

checklists with brief commentary. The FLA refers any third-party complaints back to the company for 45 days. If the matter has not been satisfactorily resolved after that time, the FLA executive director may request an investigation by an independent monitor acceptable to both it and the company.

2.3.9 Worker Rights Consortium's Model Code of Conduct
(http://www.workersrights.org/coc.asp)

The Worker Rights Consortium (WRC) was formed in 2000 by United Students Against Sweatshops (USAS) and other international student and labor activists advocating improved working conditions in garment and other factories. Over 150 colleges and universities are affiliated members. The WRC and its model code of conduct were created in reaction to what these activists perceived were weaknesses in the FLA. The WRC board, unlike that of the FLA, contains no industry representatives but only representatives from USAS, member universities, and labor-allied NGOs. The WRC does not issue company certifications of compliance but simply evaluates a site against the provisions of its model code, and publishes detailed reports of the findings. It also issues updates on progress. The WRC may audit any site of the target company, with some interviews held outside the factory. Its investigation teams include a WRC delegate and local workers or community members. The WRC establishes and trains workers on local complaint mechanisms, and often bases its audits on issues raised though those channels. Although some rivalry exists between the WRC and the FLA, the two groups occasionally work together on projects, with the WRC undertaking a comprehensive audit and the FLA working with the company on corrective and preventive action.[3]

2.3.10 WRAP Apparel Certification Principles
(http://www.wrapapparel.org/modules.php?name=Content&pa=
showpage&pid=3)

Worldwide Responsible Apparel Production (WRAP) is an independent body formed by the American Apparel and Footware Association (AAFA) in 2000. The AAFA is the largest U.S. trade association of the sewn products industry, with over 700 member companies representing more than 85% of such products sold at wholesale in the country. The process of certifying an apparel production facility under WRAP begins with the company submitting an application and paying a registration fee. The applicant then adopts the WRAP principles, conducts a self-assessment against WRAP's requirements, and documents it has implemented certain procedures. The required principles and procedures cover compliance with work-hours and minimum-wage laws, customs rules, and other legal requirements; safe and healthy working conditions; freedom of association and collective bargaining; security of shipments; environmental practices; and prohibition of forced and child labor, harassment, abuse, and discrimination. After the company notifies WRAP its site has remained in compliance with the requirements for at least 45 days, WRAP authorizes the company to hire one of the WRAP-accredited consultants to conduct an on-site verification audit. Once the consultant's favorable recommendation is received and reviewed by WRAP, it is passed to the WRAP certification board for final approval. Board certifications are good for one year, during which the facility may be subject to unannounced inspections.

2.3.11 Ethical Trading Initiative's Base Code
(http://www.ethicaltrade.org/Z/lib/base/index.shtml)

The aim of the Ethical Trading Initiative (ETI) is to improve workplace conditions among retailers and suppliers that buy or sell food, clothing, and other products in the United Kingdom. The organization was formed in 1998 as an alliance among these companies, trade unions, and NGOs. Approximately 35 companies participate. Forty percent of the funding is provided by the U.K. government, with the rest coming from membership fees. The ETI Base Code is similar to SA 8000 and the FLA's Workplace Code, which should not be surprising since all are based on most of the same ILO and U.N. documents. ETI is similar to FLA in other respects, too. Member companies must develop and implement work plans. These plans must set forth how they will monitor and independently verify site performance and report progress to ETI annually. In addition, each company member must collaborate with other members and the ETI Secretariat in designing and implementing a pilot scheme to identify good practices in code implementation, monitoring, or independent verification.

2.4 Marketing and Advertising Codes

2.4.1 ICC International Codes of Marketing and Advertising Practice
(http://www.iccwbo.org/home/menu_advert_marketing.asp)

The ICC has issued a wide range of international codes of practice on marketing and advertising. Its code on advertising practice was first issued in 1937. It also has standards on sales promotion, direct marketing, direct selling, and environmental advertising. Other ICC standards include those on advertising and marketing on the Internet, advertising to children, sponsorship, and responsible food and beverage communications.

2.4.2 Better Business Bureau and Other U.S. Marketing and Advertising Codes
(http://www.bbb.org/BizEthics/)

The Better Business Bureau is a nonprofit organization founded in 1912 to foster honest relationships between business and consumers, instilling consumer confidence, and contributing to an ethical business environment. It has over 150 branches and 300,000 local business members throughout Puerto Rico and the United States. One of its missions is to evaluate businesses and issue reliability reports on them to consumers. It assists in resolving business-customer disputes, too. The bureau has developed several standards of practice including a *Code of Advertising, Code of Online Business Practices, Charitable Solicitation Standards, Guidelines for Children's Advertising*, and other related documents. Its *Code of Advertising* provides guidance on the proper use of various enticing phrases in promoting products and services, such as "sale," "free," "list price," "rebate" and "easy credit." The code spells out conditions for fair advertising layouts and illustrations as well as for advertised warranties, contests, and games. It also addresses "bait and switch" practices—ads making an alluring offer to sell one product when the advertiser really intends to switch the customer to another.

The Council of American Survey Research Organizations, a national trade association of commercial survey research companies, has a *Code of Standards and Ethics for Survey Research* (http://www.casro. org/codeofstandards.cfm). Another U.S.-based trade association, the Direct Marketing Association has *Guidelines for Ethical Business Practice* as well as a privacy code that allows potential customers to opt out of future solicitations (http://www.the-dma.org/guidelines/). The American Marketing Association, an organization of 38,000 marketing professionals primarily from Canada and the United States, maintains a general set of ethical norms and values for all kinds of marketers (http://www.marketingpower.com/content435.php). While their code applies to individual professionals, many provisions are also appropriate for organizations.

2.4.3 British Code of Advertising, Sales Promotion, and Direct Marketing (CAP Code)
(http://www.cap.org.uk/)

The British Code was adopted by the Committee of Advertising Practice (CAP), a self-regulating body formed in 1961 by organizations from the advertising, sales promotion, direct marketing, and media businesses. The code includes specific provisions on advertising related to alcoholic drinks, children, motoring, environmental claims, health and beauty products, weight control, financial products, gambling, and tobacco. It supplements the law, providing a more complete and easier way to resolve advertising and marketing disputes. Complaints under the code are investigated and adjudicated by an independent group, the Advertising Standards Association (ASA).

Violators of the code may be penalized in several ways. They may suffer adverse publicity from rulings published by the ASA on their website. In addition, CAP may issue alerts to its members, advising them to withhold services to noncompliant parties and to deny them advertising space. CAP trade associations and professional bodies may withhold their recognition and membership privileges, too. CAP and ASA may also require persistent offenders to have their marketing communications pre-screened by the CAP Copy Advice Team. In severe cases, the matter may be referred to the government's Office of Fair Trade for legal enforcement under British consumer and advertising laws.

Complaints from European locations outside the country are coordinated through the European Advertising Standards Alliance (EASA), a group that includes ASA and it counterparts from other countries throughout Europe. EASA's statement of common principles serves as the core values of its members, helping create a generally consistent approach to self regulation of sales and marketing across the European Union.

2.4.4 Canadian Direct Marketing Association Code of Ethics and Standards of Practice
(http://www.the-cma.org/regulatory/codeofethics.cfm)

The members of the Canadian Marketing Association include Canada's major financial institutions, insurance companies, publishers, marketers, and charitable organizations. Its code and standards (Code) address a wide range of marketing media, including broadcast, print, telephone, and the Internet. The Code contains provisions on marketing content and accuracy, and product guarantees and shipment. It also covers product safety, marketing to children, and personal privacy. The Code mandates that marketers respect the environment by minimizing unwanted mailings and other waste. The association relies on mediation as the primary tool for resolving complaints. However, if a member does not implement specific recommendations issued by the association's president and board, the member may be subject to a publicly announce expulsion.

2.5 Anti-Corruption Codes

2.5.1 OECD Convention for Combating Bribery of Foreign Officials in International Business Transactions
(http://www.oecd.org/document/21/0,2340,en_2649_34859_2017813_
1_1_1_1,00.html)

OECD adopted its Convention on Combating Bribery in 1997, ratifying and bringing it into force two year later. The convention requires each Member country to adopt laws making it a crime to offer, promise, or give a bribe to a foreign public official, either directly or indirectly, or to conspire or attempt to do so. Money laundering in connection with bribing a foreign official is also to be made a criminal offense. These laws are to impose tight financial recordkeeping requirements on companies. Those breaching these laws are to be subject to extradition and to seizure of their property. The convention provides for mutual legal assistance among signatory countries in investigating and enforcing violations. The OECD Working Group on Bribery, the organization responsible for implementing the convention, conducts follow-up monitoring on the adequacy of country legislation and the effectiveness with which it is being enforced. One consequence of this monitoring has been to eliminate the tax deductibility of bribes previously allowed in certain signatory countries.

2.5.2 U.N. Convention Against Corruption
(http://www.unodc.org/unodc/en/crime_convention_corruption.html?
print=yes)

In 2003, the U.N. General Assembly adopted the *Convention Against Corruption*, laying out a comprehensive framework for dealing with international corruption. Like the OECD Convention, the U.N. version requires its Member countries to establish criminal offenses for directly or indirectly offering or giving bribes, as well as for conspiring or attempting to do so. But the U.N. convention goes beyond that of OECD by extending this prohibition to soliciting and accepting bribes as well, and making it applicable to both public officials and business employees. Furthermore, crimes under the U.N. provisions encompass the bribing of both foreign and domestic public authorities, and officials of public international organizations. Like its OECD counterpart, the U.N. document provides for international mutual legal assistance and asset recovery—two key tools for combating corruption across the world. However, the U.N. convention also promotes preventive measures, such as educational programs, the adoption of codes of conduct for public officials, and the strengthening of public recruitment, procurement, and reporting procedures. Member countries are urged to promote similar codes for businesses, and to ensure they have sufficient internal auditing controls. Like the OECD convention, the U.N. document prohibits off-the-book accounts and other shady accounting practices. The tax deductibility of bribes is specifically proscribed, too. While some criticize the U.N. convention for being loosely worded in places, most agree it has been a big step forward in dealing with international corruption in government and business. It should prove particularly important among those countries not covered by the OECD or other regional conventions on bribery and extortion.

2.5.3 ICC Rules of Conduct to Combat Extortion and Bribery
(http://www.iccwbo.org/policy/anticorruption/)

The ICC published its *Rules of Conduct to Combat Extortion and Bribery* in 1977 and expanded them in 1996. Three years later the rules were reissued with *Recommendations to Governments and International Organizations* and supplemented with a manual of best corporate practices, entitled *Fighting Corruption—A Corporate Practices Guide.*[4] The rules were again amended in 2005. The rules are a set of good commercial practices intended to be used as a method of self-regulation by international businesses, both profit and nonprofit, and including state-run companies. These organizations are urged to adopt their own codes consistent with the rules, which should apply to all parts of the organization, including its domestic and foreign subsidiaries. The rules focus on the behavior of company employees, agents, and other intermediaries, covering many of the same prohibitions and practices addressed in the U.N. Convention on Bribery. Specific prohibitions include extorting bribes from others, kicking back a portion of a contract payment to someone from the other contracting party, and paying bribes disguised as consulting, agency, or subcontracting fees or charitable or political contributions. Payments through sales representatives, customs agents, lawyers, joint venture partners, and outsourcing firms are singled out for special scrutiny. Contracts with agents are to include a provision making bribery grounds for termination. The board of directors is charged with maintaining proper systems of control to prevent bribes and extortion. Such systems should include confidential channels through which employees and other parties may raise concerns, seek advice, and report violations. The board is to take action against any director or employee who violates the rules and make appropriate public disclosure of the enforcement of its anti-corruption policies or codes. The board's audit committee or other similar body is to conduct independent reviews of compliance with the rules. The highest priority for action is to be eliminating large-scale extortion and bribery involving politicians and senior officials. Also to be prohibited but of secondary concern are small "facilitation payments" made to low-level officials to secure or expedite approvals or other routine or necessary actions which the payer is already entitled to receive. The ICC has established a standing Commission on Anti-Corruption to promote and guide the adoption and implementation of the rules.

2.5.4 Transparency International's Business Principles for Countering Bribery
(http://www.transparency.org/tools/business_principles/about)

Transparency International (TI) is a global NGO founded in 1993 for the purpose of combating corruption in a proactive way. It is headquartered in Berlin, but it also has 85 independent national chapters around the world. The organization works through a coalition of other activist groups, businesses, and governments to further its cause. TI does not expose individual cases of corruption, but rather monitors their aftermath, and studies and proposes reforms that that can prevent recurrences. The organization has developed several tools to help raise awareness of corruption hot spots. These tools include the *Corruption Perceptions Index*, which captures the degree of corruption perceived by international and domestic businesses, and the *Bribe Payers Index*, which measures the propensity of leading exporting companies to bribe abroad. Its *Integrity Pact* is a model agreement between governments and bidders aimed at preventing corruption in public procurement. TI also organizes conferences and publishes an annual *Global Corruption Report* to bring focus to the issue. In 2000, it joined with 11 of the world's leading banks, convincing them to adopt the *Global Anti-Money Laundering Guidelines for Private Banking*, also called the *Wolfsberg AML Principles*. One of TI's most important achievements was the development of the 2002 *Business Principles for Countering Bribery*, a task undertaken with Social Accountability International and a steering committee of other NGOs, companies, academia, and trade unions. The principles were designed to complement and give practical effect to the OECD Convention and ICC Rules on Bribery.

Like the ICC Rules, the TI principles provide a comprehensive list of good practices for businesses in countering bribery of public officials and in private business transactions. The document prohibits paying, arranging, and receiving bribes of any type, either directly or through other parties. Parties specifically mentioned are government officials, customers, agents, contractors, suppliers, the employees of these organizations, as well as the employees' families, friends, associates, and acquaintances. The principles are to apply to all of a company's operations, including its subsidiaries and joint ventures. Companies are expected to publicly disclose their charitable and political contributions and assure these payments are not a subterfuge for bribery. They are to ban the offer or receipt of gifts, hospitality, or expenses that could affect the outcome of business transactions. Companies must work to identify and eliminate small "facilitation payments." (In contrast, the ICC says these payments are a concern but admittedly may take time to address.) Due diligence reviews concerning the potential for bribery should be undertaken before the company enters a joint venture or agreement with an agent, contractor or supplier. Those known to pay bribes are not to be hired. Those who are hired should receive training on the company's anti-bribery program. To facilitate compliance, the company should provide a hotline or other confidential channel for reporting violations and seeking advice. It should assure employees they won't be penalized for refusing to pay bribes, even if this results in loss of business.

No formal mechanism exists for a company to "adopt" the principles as is. However, businesses are asked to commit to "apply" them to the extent relevant, borrowing from them as needed in establishing their own specific policy and program that addresses the company's greatest bribery risks. The policy should be issued by the board of directors or equivalent body. The board, along with the CEO, is expected to demonstrate a visible and active commitment to implement it. Businesses should monitor performance against their anti-bribery policies, something that can be done either internally or through certification of compliance by an external body. The anti-bribery program—including audits, management systems, and other measures geared to continuous improvement—should be periodically reviewed by senior management. Reports on these reviews should be presented to the board of directors or its audit committee. The board, in turn, should disclose its own findings in the annual report to shareholders.

2.5.5 AS 8001-2003 Fraud and Corruption Control Standard
(http://www.standards.com.au/catalogue/script/Result.asp?PSearch=
false&SearchType=simple&Status=all&DegnKeyword=8000&Db=
AS&Max=15)

AS 8001 is one of five standards issued by Standards Australia as part of its Governance Standards series. The series, which includes both behavioral codes and management system standards, are further described in Appendices 2.6.5 and 3.12. Like the other AS standards, those on fraud and corruption control are framed around structural, operational, and maintenance elements. Among other things, they cover processes for detecting, reporting, and addressing fraud and corruption; the development of a control plan; and the assessment of program effectiveness.

2.6 Governance Codes

2.6.1 OECD Principles of Corporate Governance
(http://www.oecd.org/dataoecd/32/18/31557724.pdf)

The non-binding *OECD Principles of Corporate Governance*, first issued in 1999 and updated in 2004, provide guidance to governments for allocating rights and responsibilities among a company's management, its board, shareholders, and other stakeholders. The principles also present a structure for corporations in setting and pursuing objectives and monitoring performance. The principles have been widely adopted as a benchmark by regulators, stock exchanges, investors, corporations, and others around the world. They are used by the World Bank to help improve corporate governance in emerging markets, and are one of the 12 key standards used by the Financial Stability Forum for ensuring international financial stability. The OECD document is organized around six principles, with sub-principles and commentary provided for each:

1. *Foundation for Governance Framework:* The framework for corporate governance is to be based on transparent and efficient markets, the law, and the clear allocation of responsibilities.
2. *Shareholder Rights:* Shareholders have the right to own and transfer stock, share in company profits, vote at general shareholder meetings, and elect and remove board members. They also have the right to be sufficiently informed about decisions concerning fundamental corporate changes and to participate in those decisions. They should be allowed to consult with each other concerning their rights.
3. *Equitable Treatment of Shareholders:* Minority and foreign shareholders must be treated the same as other shareholders. Insider trading and conflicts of interest by board members and executives harm shareholders and therefore should be prohibited.
4. *Stakeholder Rights:* The governance framework must recognize the rights of stakeholders, including the right to timely access to relevant information and the right to communicate with the board about illegal and unethical practices without suffering adverse consequences. Employee participation in governance should be encouraged, such as through works councils, employee stock ownership plans, and the solicitation of employee feedback. Creditor rights are to be effectively enforced.
5. *Disclosure and Transparency:* A company must make timely, accurate, and complete disclosure concerning its financial situation, performance, ownership, and governance. It should communicate its commercial objectives as well as its positions on ethics, the environment, and other public issues. It should reveal foreseeable risk factors that may affect the business as well as material issues regarding employees and other stakeholders.

The compensation paid board members and key executives must be disclosed. An independent auditor accountable to the shareholders should conduct an annual audit of the company's financial statements. The company should make available the views of unbiased analysts, brokers, rating agencies, and others if relevant to investor decisions.

6. *Board Responsibilities:* The board must use its independent judgment to guide the company strategically, to effectively monitor the company's management, and to ensure its own accountability to shareholders. Among other duties, the board is expected to review and guide the company's risk policy and oversee the effectiveness of the company's governance practices. In exercising its duties, the board must apply high ethical standards and take into account the interests of stakeholders.

The OECD, in cooperation with the World Bank and other international partners, organized regional roundtables in Asia, Latin America, and Russia to facilitate the implementation of the principles. It has an ongoing commitment to capture and share best practices.

2.6.2 Council of Institutional Investors' Corporate Governance Policies (http://www.cii.org/dcwascii/web.nsf/doc/policies_index.cm)

The Council of Institutional Investors is a U.S.-based association of more than 130 corporate, public, and union pension funds collectively holding in excess of $3 trillion in pension assets. In 2003, the council updated its model governance policies. These policies serve as a suggested benchmark by which its members can judge the governance programs of companies targeted as potential investments. The council sees the promotion of good corporate governance as consistent with the fiduciary duty of its members in protecting their long-term investments. It has found these guidelines to be appropriate in most situations.

The council's *Corporate Governance Policies* include general provisions as well as specific ones on board responsibilities, shareholder voting rights, shareholder meetings, and director and management compensation. Some of the policies warrant special note: companies are to practice good corporate citizenship. They are expected to establish and disclose their governance policies and procedures as well as their ethics codes. A mechanism is to be created under which shareholders can communicate directly with all directors on non-trivial matters. Incentive stock options should be expensed in accounting records. Boards must assess themselves on a regular basis to determine whether they possess the diversity of skills, backgrounds, experiences, ages, races, and genders appropriate to their company's ongoing needs. Limits are set on the number of other boards that the CEO and board members may join. Two-thirds of the board directors should be "independent," according to criteria set forth in the policies. Board auditing, nominating, and compensations committees should have all independent members. The audit committee is to select the company's financial auditor. Shareholder expense and convenience are to be the primary concerns in choosing the time and place of shareholder meetings.

2.6.3 The U.K. Combined Code
(http://www.fsa.gov.uk/pubs/ukla/lr_comcode2003.pdf)

The Financial Reporting Council (FRC), the body that regulates financial reporting and accountancy in the United Kingdom, published *The Combined Code: Principles of Good Governance and Code of Best Practice* in 1998 and updated it in 2003. The code was based on several earlier codes and guidance developed by the FRC, the London Stock Exchange (LSE), and the accounting profession. The LSE adopted Listing Rules requiring all companies on the LSE to explain in their annual financial reports how they applied the Combined Code and to detail any noncompliance. The code contains a set of principles on director responsibilities and compensation, shareholder relations, and accountability and audit. The code also includes principles on the role of institutional investors that are not tied to the Listing Rules. Each principle is explained in more detail in a supplemental collection of guidance documents and good practices suggestions.

The Combined Code emphasizes the need for a balance of power within the board. No individual or small group is to dominate decision-making. According to the code, the same person should not serve as both board chairman and chief executive officer. Nor should the CEO later become chairman. A senior independent director is to be named for the purpose of receiving complaints that cannot be resolved through regular channels.

Special guidance is provided on internal control systems, which the code mandates in order to safeguard shareholders' investment and company assets. Such systems must ensure legal compliance and the quality of internal and external reporting. They must enable the company to respond appropriately to significant business, operational, financial, compliance, and other risks. The systems must include control activities and processes for gathering and communicating information. A monitoring process is needed to determine whether the control measures are effective. The Institute of Chartered Accountants in England and Wales has issued additional guidance on an enterprise risk management (ERM) process that can be used to help satisfy this code requirement.[5]

Supplemental guidelines have also been developed on another important provision of the code: the board's rigorous annual assessment of its own performance. Checklists are available on the evaluation and induction of board members. Additional guidelines are provided on the roles of the board chairman and non-executive directors, and the audit, remuneration, and nomination committees. The FRC has established a Committee on Corporate Governance to monitor and report on code implementation and emerging best practices in corporate governance.

2.6.4 King II Code of Corporate Practices and Conduct
(http://www.ecseonline.com/PDF/King%20Committee%20on%20
Corporate%20Governance%20-%20Executive%20Summary%20
of%20the%20King%20Report%202002.pdf)

In 1992, former South African Supreme Court judge Mervyn E. King was asked by the Institute of Directors in South Africa to chair the Committee on Corporate Governance. The committee produced the 1994 King Report, which included a code of corporate practice that went beyond traditional financial and regulatory concerns to embrace a full range of financial, social, ethical, and environmental obligations. The code was subsequently reassessed and revised by a second King Committee in 2002. The *Code of Corporate Practices and Conduct* published with the King II Report is intended for large companies listed on the Johannesburg Stock Exchange and certain other organizations. Besides the usual governance provisions, the code also has sections on risk management and integrated sustainability reporting. Under the code, the board of directors is responsible for ensuring "that the company has implemented an effective ongoing process to identify risk, to measure its potential impact against a broad set of assumptions, and then to activate what is necessary to proactively manage these risks." Every company is expected to report annually on "the nature and extent of its social, transformation, ethical, safety, health, and environmental management policies and prac-tices," with the board making the final determination on report content. In addition, companies are urged to engage their stakeholders in deter-mining the organization's standards of ethical behavior.

2.6.5 AS 8000-2003 Australian Good Governance Principles (http://www.saiglobal.com/shop/script/Details.asp?DocN= AS964071607297)

The Good Governance Principles issued by Standards Australia include both management system standards (which are discussed in Appendix 3.13) and a code of behavior for establishing and maintaining a robust governance program within a company or other organization. The code includes broad governance principles for incorporation in an organiza-tion's own governance policy, practices, and procedures. It addresses the role, powers, and responsibilities of the board; disclosure and transpar-ency obligations; the rights and equitable treatment of shareholders: and the role of stakeholders in corporate governance. Special guidance for nonprofits and a model set of ethical principles—termed "Underlying Values"—are also provided. Australian Standard (AS) 8000 was pre-pared through a multistakeholder process involving industry, govern-ments, consumers, and others. It is the lead standard for a set of other re-lated AS management and behavioral standards. These other standards include those on fraud and corruption control (AS 8001), which are de-scribed in Appendix 2.5.5. They also include standards on organizational codes of conduct (AS 8002), corporate social responsibility (AS 8003), and whistleblower protection programs for entities (AS 8004), all of which are discussed in Appendix 3.13.

2.6.6 Sarbanes-Oxley Act

Although this Appendix 2.6 is devoted to governance codes developed outside formal legislative bodies, the Sarbanes-Oxley Act adopted by Congress in 2002 in many respects carries the same if not more weight outside the United States as a model code.[6] Sarbanes-Oxley Act contains extensive requirements aimed at preventing conflicts of interest and en-hancing disclosure concerning corporate financial matters. It places great emphasis on the integrity of a corporation's internal controls of its finances and related disclosures. These controls must assure that infor-mation material to financial performance is made known to the CEO and

chief financial officer (CFO). These corporate officers must certify to investors that the controls meet the statutory criteria and that the financial
reports fairly present the company's financial picture. An independent
auditor approved by an audit committee of independent directors must
attest to these representations. The audit committee is also required to
oversee the controls, and establish financial risk management and assessment policies. It must identify and review risks relevant to the business,
including those related to sustainability, to determine which ones may
materially affect the company's financial performance. A process for assessing these risks is detailed in *Enterprise Risk Management—Integrated Framework*, published by the Committee of Sponsoring Organizations, a group of five major U.S. financial professional associations.[7]

2.6.7 Other Governance Codes

The following organizations also have issued noteworthy governance
codes or guidance:

- New York Stock Exchange and National Association of Securities Dealers (http://www.sec.gov/rules/sro/34-48745.htm)
- S&P
  (http://www2.standardandpoors.com/NASApp/cs/Content
  Server?pagename=sp/Page/SiteSearchResultsPg&search=
  2&b=10&r=1&l=EN&vqt=Corporate+Governance+Scores%
  2DCriteria%2C+Methodology+and+Definitions&vns=1)
- California Public Employees Retirement System (CalPERS)
  (http://www.calpers-governance.org/principles/default.asp)
- National Association of Corporate Directors
  (http://www.nacdonline.org/publications/default.asp?user=
  7CDECBDFFEB14291BE86CD1756A08968)
- F&C Asset Management
  (http://www.isisam.com/aboutus.asp?pageID=1.1.3.1.1)
- Pension Investment Association of Canada
  (http://www.piacweb.org/assets/piac_gov_standards.pdf)

2.7 Industry-Specific Codes

A host of codes have been published that apply to specific industries.
Some have been developed by the Forest Stewardship Council, the Marine Stewardship Council, and other similar organizations that certify the
sustainability practices of particular industries.[8] Others have been issued

as guidance documents by the industries themselves or in collaboration with others. The timber industry in Alberta has the *Forestcare Guiding Principles*.[9] The American Petroleum Institute has its own *Environmental, Health, and Safety Mission and Guiding Principles*.[10] The *London Principles* were developed for the U.K. banking industry.[11] Another set of principles for financial institutions, the *Wolfsberg Standards* (see Appendix 2.5.4), was prepared by the Wolfsberg Group, an association of large international banks.[12] Special environmental and sustainability statements prepared under the UNEP Financial Initiative are available for endorsement by companies in the finance and insurance sectors.[13] The BSR lead a group of major electronics companies in developing an *Electronic Industry Code of Conduct*.[14] Companies involved in sustainable agriculture can subscribe to the *Asilomar Declaration for Sustainable Agriculture*.[15] Those in the fishing industry have the U.N.'s *Code of Conduct for Responsible Fisheries*.[16] The International Council on Mining and Metals has a Sustainable Development Framework with principles for its industry members.[17] Sustainability guidelines have been developed for members of the International Hydropower Association.[18] "Diversity in the Workplace: A Statement of Principle" was drafted to promote diversity at law firms.[19] A number of sustainability codes for those in education are discussed in Appendix 8.2. A quick Internet search may reveal specialty codes for your type of organization.

Endnotes to Appendix 2

1. ICCA, RESPONSIBLE CARE 1985-2005 (2005), *available at* http://www. icca-chem.org/section04.html. ENVIRONMENTAL DEFENCE, SURVEY SAYS . . . AN EVALUATION OF THE EFFECTIVENESS OF RESPONSIBLE CARE (2004), *available at* http://www.environmentaldefence.ca/reports/survey-report-reponsible-care.htm.

2. Business & Human Rights Resource Centre, *Homepage*, http://www. business-humanrights.org/Home (last visited Jan. 11, 2006).

3. *See also* USAS, COMPARISON OF THE WORKER RIGHTS CONSORTIUM (WRC) AND THE FAIR LABOR ASSOCIATION (FLA) (2004), *available at* http://www.studentsagainstsweatshops.org/docs/wrc_fla_04.doc.

4. RIGHTING CORRUPTION — A CORPORATE PRACTICES MANUAL (Francois Vincke & Fritz Heimann eds., 2003), *available at* http://www.iccbook susa.com/index.cfm?fid=55&bookid=100.

5. MARTYN E. JONES & GILLIAN SUTHERLAND (DELOITTE & TOUCHE), IMPLEMENTING TURNBULL: A BOARDROOM BRIEFING (1999), *available at* http://www.aeat.com/consulting/flyers/index.pdf.

6. Sarbanes-Oxley Act of 2002, Pub. L. No. 107-204, 116 Stat. 745 (2002) (codified as amended at scattered locations of 15 U.S.C.).

7. COMMITTEE OF SPONSORING ORGANIZATIONS OF THE TREADWAY COMMISSION, ENTERPRISE RISK MANAGEMENT — INTEGRATED FRAMEWORK, EXECUTIVE SUMMARY (2004), *available at* http://www.coso.org/publications. htm.

8. See Chapter 3 for more on the Forest Stewardship Council, the Marine Stewardship Council, and other organizations that certify green products.

9. Alberta Forest Products Ass'n, *Stewardship/ForestCare*, http://www. albertaforestproducts.ca/industry/forestcare.aspx (last visited Jan. 11, 2006).

10. American Petroleum Institute, *API Environmental Health and Safety Mission and Guiding Principles*, http://api-ep.api.org/environment/index.cfm? Objectid=AFE6B092-90E1-11D5-BC6B00B0D0E15BFC&method= display_body&er=1&bitmask=002008000000000000 (last visited Jan. 11, 2006).

11. FORUM FOR THE FUTURE, CENTRE FOR SUSTAINABLE INVESTMENT, FINANCING THE FUTURE: THE LONDON PRINCIPLES — THE ROLE OF U.K. FINANCIAL SERVICES IN SUSTAINABLE DEVELOPMENT (DEFRA 2002), *available at* http://www.forumforthefuture.org.uk/uploadstore/London%20_ principles_full_report.pdf.

12. The Wolfsberg Group, *Wolfsberg Standards*, http://www.wolfsberg-principles. com/standards.html (last visited Jan. 11, 2006).

13. UNEP Finance Initiative, *UNEP FI Statements*, http://www.unepfi.org/signatories/statements/index.html (last visited Jan. 11, 2006).

14. ELECTRONIC INDUSTRY CODE OF CONDUCT, VERSION 2.0 (2005), *available at* http://www.eicc.info/docs/EICC_code.pdf.

15. ECOLOGICAL FARMING ASS'N, THE ASILOMAR DECLARATION FOR SUSTAINABLE AGRICULTURE (1990), *available at* http://www.eco-farm.org/efa/declaration/declaration.html.

16. FISHERIES DEPARTMENT, U.N. FOOD & AGRICULTURE ORGANIZATION, CODE OF CONDUCT FOR RESPONSIBLE FISHERIES (2000), *available at* http://www.fao.org/documents/show_cdr.asp?url_file=/DOCREP/005/v9878e/v9878e00.htm.

17. International Council on Mining & Metals, *Sustainable Development Framework*, http://www.icmm.com/sd_framework.php (last visited Jan. 11, 2006).

18. INTERNATIONAL HYDROPOWER ASS'N, SUSTAINABILITY GUIDELINES (2004), *available at* http://www.hydropower.org/sustainable_hydropower/sustainability_guidelines.html.

19. CHARLES R. MORGAN, DIVERSITY IN THE WORKPLACE: A STATEMENT OF PRINCIPLE (American Corporate Counsel Ass'n 1999), *available at* http://www.acca.com/gcadvocate/diversitystmt.html.

Appendix 3

Sustainability-Related Management System Standards

List of Codes Summarized in this Appendix 3	
3.1 ISO 9001 Quality Management System Standard	3.15 IFC Social and Environmental Management System
3.2 ISO 14001 Environmental Management System Standard	3.16 Austrian Model CSR Management System Guide ON-V 23
3.3 ISO 26000 Social Responsibility Guidance Standard (proposed)	3.17 Mexican Standard IMNC SAST 004 Social Responsibility System Guideline (draft)
3.4 OHSAS 18001	
3.5 ILO Guidelines on OSH Management Systems	3.18 AFNOR Guide SD 21000
3.6 ANSI Z10 OHS Management System	3.19 Q-RES Management Model
3.7 EMAS	3.20 German Values Management System Standard
3.8 Responsible Care® Management Standards	3.21 U.K. Investors in People Standard
3.9 SIGMA Management Framework	3.22 SA 8000
3.10 BS 8900 Sustainability Management Guidelines (proposed)	3.23 The Natural Step Framework
	3.24 Reitaku Ethics Compliance Standard 2000
3.11 Baldridge Award Criteria	3.25 ISO 27001 and 28000 Security Management System Standards
3.12 Australian Business Excellence Framework	3.26 Compliance Program Elements of the U.S. *Sentencing Guidelines*
3.13 AS 8000-8004 Australian Governance Series Standards (including CSR Standard)	3.27 U.S. EPA Compliance-Focused Environmental Management System
3.14 U.S. DOE Performance-Based Management Handbook	

3.1 ISO 9001 Quality Management System Standard
(http://www.iso.ch/iso/en/iso9000-14000/index.html)

This quality management system standard, the most famous of all management system standards, was developed by a technical committee of the International Organization of Standardization (ISO). It defines a process for continual improvement in operational performance aimed at meeting product requirements. The standard is organized around the following elements: (1) management responsibility; (2) resource management; (3) product realization, including the establishment of product-related objectives, processes, communications, monitoring, validation, and recordkeeping; and (4) measurement, analysis, and improvement. Registration bodies around the world are empowered to authorize certain auditing firms to evaluate facilities and issue formal certifications of conformance to the standard. Certification of production facilities is now a common requirement imposed on suppliers by their large customers. Unfortunately, ISO 9001 does not say how much improvement must be made or require any mechanism for holding employees accountable for results. Also, because ISO 9001 applies only to facilities, it doesn't address the role of division and corporate staff or of the use of teams of people from the facility and other business units. These omissions can sometimes hamper the ability of the standard to drive results. More than 500,000 facilities around the world hold ISO 9001 certification. China, the country with the most certifications, has over 7%.

As of 2006, ISO was in the preparatory stages of developing an updated version of its 9004 standard, a 9001-related document entitled *Quality Management Systems—Guidelines for Performance Improvement*. The new version, labeled *Managing for Sustainability—A Quality Management System Approach*, would adapt the 9001 approach to address sustainability.

3.2 ISO 14001 Environmental Management System Standard
(http://www.iso.ch/iso/en/CatalogueDetailPage.CatalogueDetail?
CSNUMBER=31807&ICS1=13&ICS2=20&ICS3=10)

This is ISO's environmental management system (EMS) standard for continually improving performance. The standard is organized around (1) the environmental policy, (2) planning, (3) implementation and operation, (4) checking and corrective action, and (5) management review. It is similar to ISO 9001 in many ways. However, it introduces the planning concept of an "environmental aspects analysis" under which a determination is made about the relative importance of various *aspects*—things like air pollution equipment and waste generation that can have either a positive or negative effect on the environment. Some customers, including many automobile makers, require ISO 14001 certification of their suppliers. ISO 14001 has many of the same weaknesses of ISO 9001. Another shortcoming is that certification to the standard can be achieved even though there are existing unresolved violations of environmental law so long as there is a clear "commitment to comply." There are over 100,000 sites certified to ISO 14001, with approximately 20% of them from Japan.

3.3 ISO 26000 Social Responsibility Guidance Standard (proposed)
(http://isotc.iso.org/livelink/livelink/fetch/2000/2122/830949/3934883/3935096/home.html?nodeid=4451259&vernum=0)

In October 2004, the ISO Technical Management Board adopted a New Work Item Proposal calling for the development of an international standard that provides guidance to organizations of all types on how "to formulate social responsibility systems taking into account communication of stakeholders." More specifically, the guidelines will address methods and options for "operationalizing social responsibility, identifying and engaging with stakeholders, and enhancing credibility in claims made about social responsibility." Technically, however, the standard is not intended to be a formal management system standard or a standard for third-party certification. The guidance standard will cover the social responsibility (SR) context in which organizations operate, common SR issues, SR principles drawn from a variety of sources, and practical guidance on how to implement and integrate SR within an organization. The standard is targeted for completion in 2008.

3.4 OHSAS 18001
(http://www.ohsas-18001-occupational-health-and-safety.com/)

The Occupational Health and Safety Assessment Series (OHSAS) 18001 standard is often mistaken for an official ISO standard although it is not. However, it was developed by a consortium of accredited third-party ISO certification organizations, consulting firms, and the ISO-designated national standards bodies from Australia, Ireland, South Africa, Spain, and the United Kingdom. OHSAS resembles ISO 14001, but instead of requiring an aspects analysis, OHSAS calls for the identification of hazards and the assessment of risks. (In this respect, OHSAS is like the BS 8800, the occupational health and safety management system standard of the BSI.) A "risk" is a potentially negative impact caused by an aspect, such as the risk of fatality caused by a leaking cylinder of chlorine gas or the risk of amputation from an assembly machine without safety guards. Also, OHSAS, unlike ISO, requires the involvement of employee representatives (via a safety committee or otherwise) in deciding policies, procedures, and operational changes that may affect the health and safety of employees.

3.5 ILO Guidelines on OSH Management Systems
(http://www.ilo.org/public/english/protection/safework/ managmnt/guide.htm)

The International Labour Organization (ILO), the specialized U.N. agency that promotes human and labor rights, developed its *Guidelines on Occupational Safety and Health Management Systems* drawing on input from government, business, and labor. The ILO guidelines are similar to OHSAS 18001 but have some noted differences. The ILO requires companies to evaluate employee comprehension and retention of training lessons and to assure risk assessments are undertaken before any modification is made to work methods, materials, processes, or machinery. Safety issues must be addressed in procurements and leases. Extensive provisions are provided on contractor safety and auditing. The guideline also says that workers should be allowed to participate in all stages of the OSH audit, including, "as appropriate," the selection of the auditor and analysis of results.

3.6 ANSI Z10 OHS Management System
(http://www.aiha.org/Content/InsideAIHA/ANSI/z10.htm)

In 1999, the American National Standards Institute (ANSI) authorized its Accredited Standard Committee Z10 to commence work on an Occupational Health and Safety (OHS) Management System standard. The American Industrial Hygiene Association was designated as secretariat. The resulting standard Z10 issued in 2005 is similar to OHSAS 18001 but has some unique provisions as well. Organizations adopting the standard commit to provide employees and employee representatives with the time and resources necessary to participate in OHS programs, including planning, implementation, evaluation, and corrective and preventive action. Processes must be established to identify, evaluate, and control health and safety risks related to contractor activities and procurements.

3.7   EMAS
(http://www.europa.eu.int./comm/environment/emas/tools/
sitemap_en.htm) (http://www.emas.org.uk/)

The European Eco-Management and Audit Scheme (EMAS) is a voluntary EMS certification process created under a regulation of the European Community. Certification under EMAS can be obtained if a site has an ISO 14001 certification and, in addition, issues a public, externally verified report on its environmental performance. It must also have a verified audit program and no apparent regulatory noncompliances. There are over 4,100 sites certified to EMAS, nearly one-half of which are in Germany.

3.8   Responsible Care® Management Standards
(http://www.responsiblecare- us.com/about.asp)
(http://www.rctoolkit.com/pdfs/RCMSTech_012504.pdf)
(http://www.americanchemistry.com/s_acc/sec_employment.asp?
CID=374&DID=1256)

The international and U.S. Responsible Care® programs are described in Appendix 2.2.4. Company membership in the U.S. Responsible Care® program of the American Chemistry Council (ACC) is granted to those ACC companies that establish an EHS and security management system conforming to the ACC's ISO-like management standards. Third-party certification of the system is required and must be undertaken by auditors meeting ACC's qualifications. Unlike an ISO audit which focuses on facilities, a Responsible Care® certification review also must evaluate the corporate oversight function. ACC members that desire certification under both Responsible Care® and ISO 14001 may obtain a combined 14001 certification that covers both in a single process. To gain certification under Responsible Care®, companies must, among other things, involve employees in the development of the management system, and undertake dialogue with them and external stakeholders about operational and product risks. In addition, such companies must conduct risk-appropriate reviews of the Responsible Care® performance of transporters, suppliers, contractors, distributors, and customers as part of any evaluation of qualifications. Members must also adhere to a special security code. In addition, they must publicly report performance using certain economic, environmental, health and safety, societal, and product-related metrics. Through its Partnership Program, ACC also offers Responsible Care® status to those outside the organization that are involved in the chemical business.

3.9   SIGMA Management Framework
(http://www.projectsigma.com/Guidelines/Framework/Default.asp)

The British Sustainability-Integrated Guidelines for Management (SIGMA) is the government-sponsored project of the BSI, the Institute for Social and Ethical Accountability (AccountAbility), and the Forum for the Future. SIGMA includes a four-phase management framework for furthering sustainability within a company with regard to five "capitals": (1) natural; (2) social; (3) human; (4) manufactured; and (5) financial. (See further discussion on those capitals in Chapter 2 and Appendix 8.3.8.) The management framework follows the traditional plan-do-check-act approach but is expressed as phases involving: (1) leadership and vision; (2) planning; (3) delivery; and (4) monitoring, reviewing, and reporting. The first phase includes, among other things, making the business case to secure top management support. As part of the last phase, the company must assure that publicly reported information is relevant, material, complete, and reliable, and that it responds to stakeholders concerns in a timely and transparent way.

3.10   BS 8900 Sustainability Management Guidelines (proposed)
(http://www.bsi-global.com/British_Standards/sustainability/index.xalter)

The British Standards Institution (BSI) is planning to develop a series of standards and publications providing practical advice to organizations developing sustainability strategies and programs. The first of these documents, the *Guidance for Managing Sustainable Development* (BS 8900), was issued in draft in September 2005. The draft recommends that organizations interested in pursuing sustainability first issue a set of sustainability principles consistent with its values, decisionmaking, and behavior. These principles may include such things as inclusivity, integrity, stewardship, and transparency. A model *maturity matrix* is presented which shows how these principles may be translated to general practices, which in turn may be tracked along four stages of program maturity from minimum involvement to full engagement. A statement of the organization's purpose, vision, and values is suggested, too, to provide a framework for operations at all levels on the various aspects of sustainability. BS 8900 also offers guidance on identifying and engaging stakeholders, and on improving the organization's ability to put sustainability into practice. The document discusses existing management systems that may be used, and urges that organizations assess their sustainability risks and opportunities and establish performance indicators and targets for measuring progress. Guidance is provided on integrating sustainability into performance review and reporting processes, including a recommendation that the sustainability strategy be updated every three to five years.

3.11   Baldridge Award Criteria
(http://www.quality.nist.gov/Business_Criteria.htm)

The Baldridge Criteria were designed to define operational excellence in business. They serve as the standard for determining which businesses receive the prestigious Malcolm Baldridge National Quality Award. The criteria are grouped in seven categories that make up a Performance Excellence Framework: (1) leadership (including social responsibility); (2) strategic planning; (3) customer and market focus (customer knowledge, relationships, and satisfaction); (4) measurement, analysis, and knowledge management; (5) human resource focus (work systems and employee learning, motivation, well-being, and satisfaction); (6) process management; and (7) business results (traditional customer, product, financial, and human-resource results as well as those concerning organizational effectiveness, governance, and social responsibility).

3.12   Australian Business Excellence Framework
(http://www.businessexcellenceaustralia.com.au/GROUPS/ABEF/)

The framework is the Australian counterpart to the U.S. Baldridge Criteria. It focuses on seven performance categories similar to those contained in the U.S. standard. Performance against each category is evaluated by examining it from four "assessment dimensions": (1) approach (how the organization puts plans and structures into place); (2) deployment (how it deploys those plans and structures); (3) results (how it measures and analyzes the outcomes); and (4) improvement (how it learns from the experience). To complement the categories and assessment dimensions, the organization has a set of 12 principles of business excellence, which address such things as providing clear direction, fostering continual learning, using data effectively, and delivering value to stakeholders. Like Baldridge, the Australian Business Excellence Framework serves as the basis for a national business excellence award.

3.13   AS 8000-8004 Australian Governance Series Standards
(including CSR Standard) (http://www.standards.com.au/catalogue/
script/Result.asp?PSearch=false&SearchType=simple&Status=all
&DegnKeyword=8000&Db=AS&Max=15)

The Australian *Good Governance Principles* include both codes of behavior (see Appendix 2.6.5) and management system standards for establishing and maintaining a robust governance program within a company or other organization.   The AS 8000 management systems are
framed in terms of *structural elements* (commitment, policy, responsibility, and continuous improvement); *operational elements* (issues identification, procedures, systems for addressing breaches and complaints,
recordkeeping, and reporting); and *maintenance elements* (education
and training, visibility and communication, monitoring and assessment,
review, and liaisons with stakeholders). The AS 8000 Governance Standard is the lead standard for a set of other related AS standards on fraud
and corruption control (AS 8001), organizational codes of conduct (AS
8002), corporate social responsibility (AS 8003),   and whistleblower
protection programs for entities (AS 8004). Each of these other standards
is also framed around structural, operational, and maintenance elements.
The CSR Standard (AS 8003) also contains unique provisions on transparency, stakeholder engagement, and third-party verification of compliance with the standard.

3.14   U.S. DOE Performance-Based Management Handbook
(http://www.orau.gov/pbm/pbmhandbook/pbmhandbook.html)

The *Performance-Based Management Handbook* is a hefty six-volume
compilation of techniques and tools for implementing the *Government
Performance and Results Act of 1993*, a law calling for federal agencies
to establish effective performance measurement and management systems. The handbook was prepared in 2001 for the U.S. Department of
Energy (DOE) by the Oak Ridge Associated Universities, a multi-uni-
versity consortium. It is one of a long series of guidance documents issued by DOE on the topic. *Performance-based management*, as defined
in the handbook, is "a systematic approach to performance improvement
through an ongoing process of establishing strategic performance objectives; measuring performance; collecting, analyzing, reviewing and reporting performance data; and using that data to drive performance improvement." The handbook addresses how to do this. It also highlights 11

areas that must be maintained if the management system is to be successful. These areas include, among other things, leadership, a sense of purpose, commitment, involvement, communication, and resources.

3.15 IFC Social and Environmental Management System
(http://www.ifc.org/ifcext/policyreview.nsf/content/home)

The International Finance Corporation (IFC) is the investment arm of the World Bank that funds private sector projects in developing countries. The IFC imposes certain environmental and social responsibilities on those who borrow its funds. In 1998 it adopted "Safeguard Policies" setting forth its standard loan conditions concerning social and environmental matters. In 2006, it updated and recast these conditions in a *Policy on Social and Environmental Sustainability*, which includes new "Performance Standards." The new Performance Standards require IFC loan projects to undergo an assessment of environmental and social risks and opportunities. Projects with significant environmental or social impacts require a social and environmental management system. The system must include an action plan based on the assessment, organizational capacity (resources, management support, structure, roles and responsibilities, etc.), training, community engagement, monitoring, and reporting.

3.16 Austrian Model CSR Management System Guide ON-V 23
(http://www.on-norm.at/publish/221.html)

In May 2004, the Austrian Standards Institute issued its *Guidance for the Implementation of Corporate Social Responsibility* (CSR Guidelines). The CSR Guidelines contain a model CSR management system based on the plan-do-check-act process. The system covers top management commitment and leadership, the initial review and periodic management reviews, communications, and planning. It also covers implementation, monitoring, measuring, and corrective and preventive actions. A chapter is devoted to the process of preparing and issuing a sustainability report. The guidance also provides recommendations on the type of economic, social, and environmental obligations companies may be expected to assume under corporate social responsibility. These recommendations are framed in terms of (1) common *requirements,* which are often reflected in law or international agreements, and (2) *recommendations for the company's voluntary commitment,* which suggest commitments beyond the requirements that a company may want to voluntarily assume.

3.17 Mexican Standard IMNC SAST 004 Social Responsibility System Guideline (draft)
(http://www.imnc.org.mx/#;Email:normalizacion@imnc.org.mx)

The Mexican Institute of Standardization and Certification (Instituto Mexicano de Normalización y Certificación or IMNC) has drafted *Guidelines for the Implementation of a Social Responsibility Management System* (NMX-SAST-004-IMNC-2004). The document approaches the management of social responsibility much as ISO approaches the management of the environment under ISO 14001. The IMNC standard calls for companies to adopt a process of continual improvement to manage their social responsibilities. The process is to be framed around a social responsibility policy, planning, implementation and operation, verification and corrective action, and periodic management review. Companies are to identify and prioritize their social responsibility aspects and impacts, and assure that those aspects with significant impacts are considered when the organization establishes its objectives. The annex to the standards contains a model set of social responsibility obligations relative to human rights, the environment, and various stakeholders.

3.18 AFNOR Guide SD 21000
(http://www.afnor.fr *and* http://www.qres.it/documenti/backoffice/scroll/EU%20final%20report%202004%20_intro.doc)

The French Industrial Standards Authority (AFNOR) convened teams from governments, companies, consultants, unions, and NGOs to develop Guide SD 21000 (FD X 30-021). The guide, issued in May 2003, aims at helping various enterprises incorporate sustainability concerns into their strategies and management. The SD 21000 management process commences with the organization defining its vision, values, ethical rules, and management principles in a way that reflects the sustainability concept. The enterprise then identifies the expectations, interests, and issues (stakes) of its key stakeholders, and prioritizes each stake taking into account the risks and opportunities flowing from it, the strengths and weaknesses of the organization, requirements of law and international conventions, and best sustainability practices. At the conclusion of this evaluation, top management issues a policy communicating its strategic vision and commitment to continually improve sustainability performance. The organization's values, vision, and strategy are adjusted as appropriate and new objectives and indicators are developed. The organization also reviews its approaches for managing various support activities to assure they consider sustainability concerns. These activities include the design, construction, and operation of buildings and other structures; the design of products and services; internal and external communications; and purchasing. Short-term and multiyear plans are prepared for achieving the objectives. Progress is periodically monitored, measured, and recorded. Results are then reviewed by management and reported internally and externally. Additional stakeholder feedback is sought, and the plan-do-check-act process of continual improvement repeats.

3.19   Q-RES Management Model
(http://www.qres.it/Q-RES%20Guidelines%20January%202002.pdf)

In 1999, the Centre for Ethics, Law, and Economics (CELE) at the University of Castellanza in Varese, Italy, initiated a project to develop quality standards for social and ethical responsibility (RES). Joining them in the effort were a number of companies, professional associations, consulting companies, and nonprofit organizations. Three years later, the initiative produced a document entitled, *The Q-RES Project: The Quality of the Social and Ethical Responsibility of Corporations—Guidelines for Management*. These guidelines present a model system designed around six tools for managing social and ethical matters: (1) corporate ethical vision; (2) code of ethics; (3) ethical training; (4) organizational systems of implementation and control; (5) social and ethical accountability; and (6) external verification. For each of these tools, the guidelines offer a definition and an explanation of the tool's function, content, development methodology, auditing evidence, and excellence criteria.

3.20   German Values Management System Standard
(http://www.dnwe.de/dnwe/redax/files/1006502972557-1/Final%20 Version%20WMS%20English%20.pdf)

The Values Management System (VMS) standard was the product of a cooperative effort by the Center for Business Ethics (Zentrum für Wirtschaftsethik—ZfW), the research institute of the German Network for Business Ethics (Deutsches Netzwerk Wirtschaftsethik—DNWE), and a number of companies and economic associations. The aim of the standard is to help produce sustainability of business success through a self-imposed values-driven governance of organizational behavior. The focus is on four different values: (1) moral values (e.g., integrity, fairness, sincerity, responsibility); (2) cooperation values (e.g., loyalty, team spirit, openness); (3) performance values (e.g., benefit, competence, flexibility, creativity, innovation, quality); and (4) communication values (e.g., respect, affiliation, transparency, communication). The standard is organized in two parts. *Part I: Principles* describes the aim of the VMS process and how it is to be applied. This part covers values and compliance orientation; the application of VMS to, and integration in, all areas of management; continual improvement; building internal competence; management responsibility; and self-assessment. *Part II: Constituents* lays out the process elements. This part addresses the company vision, mission, values, and strategy, as well as implementation tools, and individual commitment and incentives. It also covers resources, communications, documentation, and management review.

3.21   U.K. Investors in People Standard
(http://www.investorsinpeople.co.uk/IIP/Web/Homepage1.htm)

The Investor in People program was formerly operated by the U.K. Department of Education and Employment but is now administered by an independent entity, Investors in People (IIP) U.K. IIP maintains a 10-step management system standard aimed at continuously improving organizational performance though a focus on employee learning, development, and involvement. Organizations apply to IIP for certification, which is granted after a successful assessment by a third-party auditor. Over 35,000 IIP certifications have been granted, primarily to U.K. organizations.

3.22   SA 8000
(http://www.sa-intl.org/index.cfm?fuseaction=Page.viewPage&
pageId=473)

Social Accountability (SA) 8000 was written by the Council on Economic Priorities Accreditation Agency—now Social Accountability International—with the help of two dozen other activist groups, consultants, and companies. The standard, which is based on a number of ILO and U.N. conventions, focuses on a wide range of workplace conditions. It calls for the establishment of a basic management system with external reporting. It goes beyond ISO and OHSAS to mandate compliance with law and conformance with certain performance requirements concerning child labor, forced labor, health and safety, and freedom of association. Other requirements cover collective bargaining rights, discrimination, discipline, working hours, and compensation. Approximately 600 facilities have been certified under this standard by auditors accredited by Social Accountability International.

3.23   The Natural Step Framework
(http://www.naturalstep.org) (http://www.naturalstep.ca/framework.html)

The Natural Step is a global organization founded by Dr. Karl-Henrik Robert of Sweden based on his first-hand observations about the links between human illness and toxins. The Natural Step Framework refers to a set of principles and a strategy for acting on them. The four principles or conditions of sustainability are: (1) substances from the earth's crust must not systematically increase in nature (such as by contaminating waters with toxic heavy metals); (2) substances produced by society must not systematically increase in nature (as do persistent, bioaccumulative toxic chemicals); (3) the physical basis for the productivity and diversity of nature must not be systematically destroyed (such as through the destruction of rain forests); and (4) resources must be used fairly and efficiently in order to meet basic human needs globally. The implementation strategy for continual improvement starts with understanding current sustainability trends. Once that is accomplished, the organization must "back cast," that is, assess where it stands relative to achieving the four principles, visualize what it would look like if it met these principles, and identify steps needed to achieve that vision. Thereafter, the organization prioritizes opportunities for action, sets goals to achieve those priorities, and manages and assesses progress.

3.24   Reitaku Ethics Compliance Standard 2000
(http://www.ie.reitaku-u.ac.jp/~davis/assets/applets/ecs2k-e.pdf)

The Reitaku Centre for Economic Studies at Reitaku University in Japan produced ECS 2000 as a business ethics research project in 1999. The standard is based on an ISO-type plan-do-check-act process geared to assuring compliance with ethics-related laws and company standards. A comprehensive internal audit is the cornerstone of the process. ECS 2000 contains an unusual provision for addressing "emergency situations"

where executive officers are involved in unethical behavior or the organization violates the law. The standard requires that in such circumstances, the organization "submit to consultation by an external body and
initiate a (thorough) reform of the organization."

3.25   ISO 27001 and 28000 Security Management System Standards
(http://www.iso.org/iso/en/CatalogueDetailPage.CatalogueDetail?
CSNUMBER=42103&ICS1=35&ICS2=40&ICS3=)
(http://www.iso.org/iso/en/CatalogueDetailPage.CatalogueDetail?
CSNUMBER=44641&scopelist=PROGRAMME)

ISO has developed several management systems standards related to security, including the 27001 standard on information security management systems (ISMS) adopted in 2005 and the 28000 security management systems standard for the supply chain issued in draft in 2006. Both
standards require an assessment of security risks and the adoption of objectives and measures to control them as needed. In other respects these
standards display a basic framework similar to that of ISO 9001 and
14001. ISO 27001 and 28000 are supported by companion standards providing best practice approaches for their implementation—ISO 17799
(being redesignated 27002) for the former and ISO 28001 for the latter.

3.26   Compliance Program Elements of the U.S. *Sentencing
Guidelines*[1]

The U.S. Sentencing Commission, a separate agency within the U.S.
government's judicial branch, develops sentencing guidelines and policies to be used by U.S. federal courts in sentencing offenders of federal
crimes. The 2004 guidelines indicate that the severity of penalties for
federal crimes can be reduced where companies show they have an "effective compliance and ethics program." The commission defines that
phrase to include many elements of a management system, namely: responsible high-level leader; adequate resources; standards and procedures; effective training; incentives and discipline; compliance risk assessment; monitoring and auditing; and corrective and preventive action.

3.27   EPA Compliance-Focused Environmental Management
System[2]

The Compliance-Focused Environmental Management System
(CFEMS) was originally developed by the EPA's National Enforcement
Investigations Center in 1997, prompted by its finding that many viola-

tions of U.S. environmental laws were due to inadequate management systems. It was last revised in 2001. The guidance document which describes the system requirements also contains model language for a consent decree through which implementation of the system would be mandated in a negotiated settlement of a violation of federal environmental law. A CFEMS is also geared to fulfilling the management systems requirements of the U.S. *Sentencing Guidelines* (see Appendix 3.6) as it applies to environmental law. The 12 prescribed elements of the CFEMS are: (1) policy; (2) organization, personnel, and oversight of an environmental management system; (3) accountability and responsibility; (4) requirements; (5) assessment, prevention, and control; (6) incident and noncompliance investigations; (7) training, awareness, and competence; (8) planning and organizational decisionmaking; (9) maintenance of records and documents; (10) pollution prevention program; (11) continuing program evaluation and improvement; and (12) public involvement/community outreach.

Endnotes to Appendix 3

1. U.S. SENTENCING GUIDELINES. U.S. DEPARTMENT OF JUSTICE, U.S. AT-
   TORNEYS MANUAL tit. 9 (Criminal Resource Manual), §163, http://www.
   usdoj.gov/usao/eousa/foia_reading_room/usam/title9/crm00162.htm (last
   visited Jan. 8, 2006).

2. OFFICE OF CRIMINAL ENFORCEMENT, U.S. EPA, COMPLIANCE-FO-
   CUSED ENVIRONMENTAL MANAGEMENT SYSTEM—ENFORCEMENT
   AGREEMENT GUIDANCE (2001) (330/9-97-002R), *available at*
   http://www.epa.gov/Compliance/resources/policies/criminal/cfems_01.
   pdf.

Appendix 4

Planning Forms for Assessing and Prioritizing Sustainability Risks and Opportunities

Comments on Forms A, B, and C

When completing the forms, a rating system of 1 to 5 is suggested but other rating scales can also be used. Ratings of overall importance or priority for a line item entered in column i of Forms A or B may be calculated as a sum or multiple of the other scores entered on the line, or alternatively, may be merely a reflection of the general feeling about the importance of the item obtained after glancing at those other scores. While scores from Form C (impact assessment of sustainability trends) should be reviewed in completing column f on Form A, this will not usually warrant a straight transfer of scores. That's because there may be several trends from C—or none at all—that are linked with a given sustainability topic listed in A. For example, the trend involving "Fresh Water Depletion; Water Contamination" (see Appendix 1.18); and the one on the "Spread of Hazardous Pollutants" (see Appendix 1.22) may both be relevant to the topic of addressing soil contamination. Formal mathematical rigor is not required, and scoring can be based on individual judgment after scanning any relevant information from Form C. In the end, though, trends with high ratings for business risk or business opportunity should merit action.

Appendix 4

Form A
Business Prioritization of Sustainability Topics

Rating Scale
1=Top Priority, Very Important, To Greatest Extent
5=Lowest Priority, Not Important, To Least Extent

Priority Ratings

a. Sustain-ability Topic (From Figures 2.3-2.5)	b. Importance to Business Success (From Form B)	c. Importance to Management	d. Consistent With Company Culture	e. Public Visibility of Topic/ External Pressure to Act	f. Responsive to Sustainability Trend (Consider Form C as Relevant)	g. Extent of Potential Impact	h. Ease of Implemen-tation ($, Time)	i. Overall Priority

Appendix 4

Form B
Importance Rating of Sustainability Topics
to Business Success

Rating Scale
1=Top Rating, Very Important
5=Lowest Rating, Not Important

Importance To Business Success

a. Sustainability Topic (From Figures 2.3-2.5)	b. Improves Productivity, Lowers Costs	c. Strengthens Employee Relations	d. Enhances Reputation	e. Reduces Risk	f. Improves Sales, Customer Appeal	g. Heightens Innovation	h. Extends or Preserves License to Operate, Community Appeal	i. Overall Importance Rating

Appendix 4

Form C

Business Impact Assessment of Sustainability Trends

Rating Scale
1=Top Rating, Very Important
5=Lowest Rating, Not Important

a. Trend	b. Business Risk (Legal, Financial, Reputational, Competitive, Operational)		c. Business Opportunity (Innovation, Sales, Productivity, Reputation, Employee Relations, Risk Reduction, License to Operate,)	
	Rating	Description / Comments	Rating	Description / Comments
1. Growth in Global Bus. Competition				
2. Opposition to Globalization				
3. Speed of Communications; the Digital Divide				
4. Widening Prosperity Gap				
5. Population Growth; Mortality Rates				
6. AIDS and Other Serious Diseases				
7 Mental Health Problems				
8. Increased Immigration; Lower Fert. in Ind. Nations				
9. Hunger and Malnutrition				
10. Child and Forced Labor				
11. Education Needs for the Disenfranchised				
12. Urbanization				
13. Over-consumption of Resources				
14. Fossil Fuel Depletion				
15. Climate Change				
16. Deforestation				
17. Threats to Biodiversity				
18. Fresh Water Depletion; Water Contamination				

Appendix 4

Form C --continued

Business Impact Assessment of Sustainability Trends

Rating Scale
1=Top Rating, Very Important
5=Lowest Rating, Not Important

a. Trend	b. Business Risk (Legal, Financial, Reputational, Competitive, Operational)		c. Business Opportunity (Innovation, Sales, Productivity, Reputation, Employee Relations, Risk Reduction, License to Operate,)	
	Rating	Description / Comments	Rating	Description / Comments
19. Wetlands Destruction				
20. Fish Depletion				
21. Coral Reef Destruction				
22. Spread of Hazardous Pollutants				
23. Traditional Air Pollutants				
24. Declining Soil Quality				
25. Ozone Depletion				
26. Low Credibility of Corporations				
27. Extended Producer Responsibility				
28. Green Products				
29. Green Marketing/ Labeling				
30. Green Product Certification				
31. Obesity; Food Nutrition				
32. Rise in Socially Responsible Investing				
33. Investor Concerns about Corporate Governance				
34. Increased Demands for Transparency, Pub Rpting				
35. Growing Power of NGOs/CSOs				
36. Increasing Global Terrorism				

Method for Calculating Savings and Cost Avoidance for Baxter's Environmental Financial Statement

The Baxter Environmental Financial Statement is show in Figure 3.7. This Appendix 5 demonstrates how savings and cost avoidance are usually calculated for that statement. As used in the statement, *savings* has its ordinary meaning: the reduction in actual cost between the report year and the prior year. When costs go up, savings is negative. *Cost avoidance,* on the other hand, is the additional cost, other than the report year's savings, which was not incurred but would have been if the waste reduction in material/energy usage or waste had not taken place. Figure A5.1 below presents a scenario demonstrating how savings and cost avoidance are computed.

Figure A5.1. Example of Waste Savings and Cost Avoidance Calculations

Scenario assumptions:
- **Base Year:**
    - Waste disposal cost = $1,000
    - Waste material cost = $9,000
- **Annual Changes in Years 1 & 2:**
    - Production increase = 10%/yr.
    - Waste reduction = 15%/yr.
    - Per-unit disposal cost increase = 5%/yr.
    - Per-unit material cost increase = 7%/yr.

Financial Measure	Report Year		
	Base Year	**1**	**2**
a. Waste cost (material + disposal)	$10,000	$9,079	$8,242
b. Savings	---	921	837
c. Cost avoidance due to waste-reduction project initiated in report year	---	1,748 (From Project 1)	1,587 (From Project 2)
d. Cost avoidance due to waste-reduction project in prior year	---	---	3.136 (From Project 1)
e. Total savings and cost avoidance (b + c + d)	---	$2,669	$5,560

The scenario assumes that in our base year, the waste disposal cost was $1,000 and the cost of the material in the waste was $9,000, making the total cost of waste $10,000. If production increases 10% in year 1, waste volumes would normally go up the same percentage. If, in addition, waste disposal costs per ton increase 5%, the cost of waste disposal in the first year would be: $1,000 × (1 + 0.10) × (1 + 0.05) = $1,155. With a 10% production increase and a 7% increase in the price of the material, the value of material wasted in the first year is $9,000 × (1 + 0.10) × (1 + 0.07) = $10,593. Adding the two amounts gives the total cost of waste in year 1, which is $1,155 + $10,593 = $11,748. So if no waste reduction projects are initiated, we will see a $1,748 increase in the cost of waste.

In our scenario, however, we improve our production process so that even with the production increase, our waste quantities in year 1 are 15% lower than in the base year. This means our disposal cost in year 1 would be $1,000 × (1 - 0.15) × (1 + 0.05) = $893. Our waste material cost would equal $9,000 × (1 - 0.15) × (1 + 0.07) = $8,186, resulting in a total waste cost in year 1 of $893 + $8,186 = $9,079. The savings would be the base year cost of $10,000 minus the year 1 cost of $9,079, which equals $921. This savings is represented by the light gray triangle on the left in Figure A5.2. But that is not the only financial benefit we see from our project. We have also avoided paying the cost increase—$1,748—which we would have incurred if no waste reduction project had been undertaken. This cost avoidance is shown in the diagram as the black triangle on the left. Thus our total financial benefit of the project in year 1 is the savings ($921) plus the cost avoidance ($1,748), or $2,669.

To complicate the problem a little more, we have the same changes in year 2 that we experienced the previous year, namely, another 10% increase in production, 5% increase in per-unit disposal cost, and a 7% increase in per-unit material cost. If we take no action to further cut our waste, our disposal cost would drift up to $893 × (1 + 0.10) × (1 + 0.05) = $1,031 and our waste material loss would rise to $8,186 × (1 + 0.10) × (1 + 0.07) = $9,635, producing a total waste cost of $1,031 + $9,635 = $10,666. In other words, our total waste costs would have risen in year 2 by $10,666 - $9,079 = $1,587.

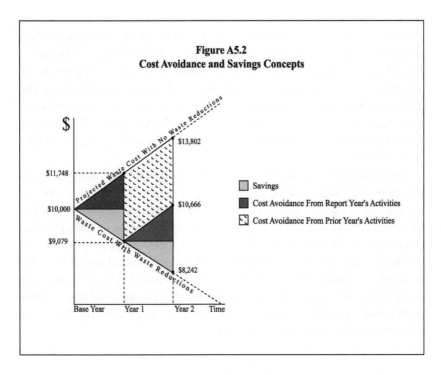

Figure A5.2
Cost Avoidance and Savings Concepts

Once again, however, in year 2 we implement a second project that cuts our waste another 15%. This means our disposal cost in year 2 would be $893 × (1 - 0.15) × (1 + 0.05) = $797. Our waste material loss would be $8,186 × (1 - 0.15) × (1 + 0.07) = $7,445. This leaves us with a total waste cost in year 2 of $797 + $7,445 = $8,242. Our savings for year 2 would be $9,079 - $8,242 = $837, represented by the light gray triangle in the lower right of Figure A5.2. We also have cost avoidance in that year because we didn't have to pay the $1,587 increase that would have been incurred had we not pursued our second project. This is depicted as the black triangle in the lower right of our diagram. Our total financial benefit in year 2 due to our second project would be the savings ($837) plus cost avoidance ($1,587), or $2,424. But in that year we are still reaping the benefit of the first waste-reduction project. If we hadn't undertaken either project 1 or 2, our year 3 waste disposal cost would have climbed to $1,155 × (1 + 0.10) × (1 + 0.05) = $1,334, and our waste material loss would have reached $10,593 × (1 + 0.10) × (1 + 0.07) = $12,468 for a total waste cost of $13,802, as shown on the top line in Figure A5.2. Remember that if we hadn't completed the second waste project in year 2, our total waste cost would have been $10,666. So the continuing effect (cost avoidance) of the first project in year 2 is $13,802 - $10,666 = $3,136. This is represented in the pattern area of the graph in Figure A5.2. Therefore, the total financial benefit in year 2 from both projects can be calculated by adding savings ($837), plus cost avoidance from project 2 undertaken in year 2 ($1,587), plus cost avoidance in year 2 from project 1 initiated the previous year ($3,136). This gives us a total benefit in year 3 of $5,560.

For a company like Baxter where each factory makes many different products, the companywide production growth rate is determined by using the rate of growth in cost of goods sold (COGS) as adjusted for inflation and inventory changes. Inflation adjustments are based on a blend of three relevant U.S. Producer Price Indexes. Once the growth rate is calculated for the year, it is averaged with those determined for the two previous years. This rolling three-year average is used in the calculations to avoid distortions due to startups and delayed environmental effects from production changes. The three-year rolling average used for 2004 was 8%; the one for 2003, 9%; and 2002, 7%.

Appendix 6

Examples of Sustainability Issues for Various Functional Groups

List of Functional Groups Covered in this Appendix 6	
6.1 Business Development (Mergers and Acquisitions)	6.11 Human Resources/Employee Relations
6.2 Business Planning	6.12 Information Technology (IT)
6.3 Charitable Giving; Foundation	6.13 Internal Audit
6.4 Communications; Public Relations; Community Relations	6.14 Investor Relations
6.5 Corporate Governance; Corporate Secretary	6.15 Law; Corporate Compliance
	6.16 Manufacturing
6.6 Environment, Health, and Safety (EHS)	6.17 Quality
	6.18 Research and Development; Product Design
6.7 Ethics/Business Practices	6.19 Risk Management
6.8 Facilities Engineering; Energy Management	6.20 Sales and Marketing; Distribution
6.9 Finance	6.21 Security
6.10 Government Affairs/Public Policy	6.22 Supply Chain (Supplier Management; Purchasing)

Listed below are examples of sustainability-related issues that may be faced by various functional groups within an organization:

6.1 Business Development (Mergers and Acquisitions)

The following issues are with regard to business operations to be acquired or sold:

• Conducting financial due diligence assessments; evaluating financial strengths and risks and compliance with securities regulations

• Conducting social due diligence assessments, including evaluating claims and risks concerning ethical improprieties; product problems; child and forced labor; union issues; antitrust compliance; serious safety and health problems; governance issues; diversity, harassment, and discrimination; community relations and public credibility; securities law compliance; employee morale; political contributions; and supplier-related sustainability risks

• Conducting environmental due diligence assessments to evaluate traditional environmental compliance, liabilities, and risks; emerging issues arising from operations; product-related issues; and long-term natural resource availability
• Integrating sustainability policies and programs into new acquisitions

6.2   Business Planning

• Assuring that sustainability considerations are incorporated into the organization's strategic planning process and final plan

6.3   Charitable Giving; Foundation

• Aligning policies for charitable giving with sustainability objectives
• Providing financial support to encourage employee participation in community activities
• Providing funds to match employee donations to organizations that support sustainability causes
• Properly balancing contributions across all geographic regions of business
• Contributing products, materials, and equipment to charitable and other nonprofit organizations
• Partnering with NGOs to further sustainability initiatives
• Assuring the size of charitable giving is appropriate in light of profits generated
• Emphasizing giving that helps create long-term solutions

6.4   Communications; Public Relations; Community Relations

• Transparently reporting to the public the company's sustainability performance
• Participating in GRI; using the GRI reporting guidelines
• Developing communication strategies to improve the credibility of the company on sustainability issues
• Conducting media-relations and stakeholder-engagement training that emphasizes open and honest communication
• Developing community-outreach programs on sustainability issues (education, health, environmental issues, etc.)
• Participating in organizations that focus on business sustainability programs

• Partnering with NGOs to further sustainability causes
• Identifying and managing significant public issues with potentially serious ramifications for the business
• Creating, or encouraging the formation of, public advisory councils or other forums through which community members can provide feedback on company operations or help the company address sustainability issues of mutual concern

6.5   Corporate Governance; Corporate Secretary

• Proactively identifying and disclosing to the board potentially serious business risks (including those arising from sustainability issues) as part of an enterprise risk management (ERM) program (see Appendices 2.6.3 and 2.6.6 for further discussion on ERMs)
• Complying with financial disclosure laws
• Assuring the board has an effective check and balance on management and that it thoroughly reviews the company's strategic and tactical/operating plans (including plans to address sustainability issues), resources, and structure
• Adopting and enforcing conflict of interest, ethics, and governance standards that apply to the board
• Adopting a board membership and structure that assures good coordination with management while preserving independence from them
• Assisting with recruitment of independent directors
• Aligning management incentives with the long-term interests of the company; adopting processes that ensure that executive compensation is in line with peer groups and performance
• Adopting procurement practices that ensure independence of outside financial auditing firms
• Conducting board member training and oversight on governance and sustainability issues
• Adopting effective mechanisms for managing crises
• Periodically assessing performance versus recognized standards of good governance (see, for example, the governance codes mentioned in Appendices 1.33 and 2.6)
• Responding to governance investigations and queries
• Apprising the board and management on the latest governance trends

6.6   Environment, Health, and Safety (EHS)

• Properly controlling and reducing waste generation and disposal and natural resource use in products, services, processes and operations; incorporating environmental concerns into design decisions
• Protecting wetlands, coral reefs, water resources, and soils
• Reducing the degree of hazard of materials used; eliminating ozone-depleting substances and persistent organic pollutants; minimizing and offsetting greenhouse gases (GHGs)
• Participating in GHG trading programs
• Protecting biodiversity, especially in agricultural activities and property development
• Addressing the environmental concerns of customers (see Appendix 1.27 on Extended Producer Responsibility); assisting with environmental labeling for products
• Preventing unauthorized release of pollutants
• Complying with environmental and occupational health and safety laws and permits
• Independent auditing of compliance with EHS laws and standards
• Adopting an ISO 14001 EMS and an OHSAS 18001 health and safety management system
• Engaging in employee awareness and community outreach programs on environmental matters and wellness
• Restoring contaminated sites
• Preventing occupational injuries and illnesses, reducing their incidence and severity, and generally assuring the health and safety of employees, contractors, and visitors
• Using Six Sigma, Lean Manufacturing, and other programs to improve EHS performance
• Preventing, detecting, and controlling indoor air pollution
• Working with supply chain personnel to develop EHS criteria for supplier evaluation and to help suppliers reduce their EHS risks and impacts

6.7   Ethics/Business Practices

• Enacting ethics policies for employees, suppliers, distributors, and the board of directors
• Establishing confidential hotlines for filing ethics complaints; independent oversight of complaint resolution

• Adopting policies on the protection of "whistleblowers" (those who file ethics complaints)
• Adopting bioethics policies if applicable to the business
• Using annual management letters of assurance or other mechanisms to help assure ethics policies are being communicated, understood, and followed

6.8   Facilities Engineering; Energy Management

• Adopting procurement standards to ensure new equipment is energy efficient and meets environmental, health, safety, and other sustainability requirements
• Incorporating energy efficiency, environmental, health, safety, and other social concerns into the design of new facilities and processes; adopting standards for this purpose
• Adopting a combined energy conservation-climate change policy
• Conducting pollution-prevention and energy-conservation audits
• Undertaking internal and external benchmarking of best energy and environmental management practices for utilities operations at facilities, and communicating those practices among the organization's facilities
• Installing and procuring renewable sources of energy
• Promoting the use of public transportation and ride sharing by commuting employees

6.9   Finance

• Considering sustainability issues in the review and approval of major capital expenditures
• Promoting financially attractive sustainability initiatives
• Fulfilling the CFO's obligations under applicable governance standards
• Assuring the financial sustainability of the company

6.10   Government Affairs/Public Policy

• Communicating the company's performance, activities, and policies on sustainability to lobbyists and appropriate governmental officials and legislators
• Pursuing lobbying efforts in support of government policies that further sustainability
• Developing position papers on sustainability topics of public

and company concern
• Assuring political contributions are legal and ethical

6.11   Human Resources/Employee Relations

• Incorporating sustainability information and materials into new employee recruitment and orientation
• Identifying and addressing employee development needs
• Adopting special recruitment and equal opportunity programs for minorities, women, older workers, and the handicapped
• Enacting nondiscrimination programs
• Addressing and preventing sexual harassment and other employee intimidation
• Protecting the privacy of employees
• Incorporating sustainability objectives into employee roles and responsibilities and annual performance objectives
• Prohibiting forced labor and child labor and other similar employee exploitation
• Promoting the use of public transportation and ride sharing by commuting employees
• Paying fair wages and benefits, including adequate, nondiscriminatory dependent-care benefits
• Encouraging employee work-life balance
• Adopting sensitive layoff policies that show respect for impacted employees
• Respecting employee rights of association and collective bargaining
• Fostering open, honest dialogue between employees and management
• Conducting employee surveys and dialogue, openly communicating the issues and responses, and helping assure action plans are developed and implemented to address concerns
• Preventing worker violence and establishing emergency procedures to address it
• Assuring that proper policies, procedures, and arrangements are in place to protect the health records and other private information of employees and other workers

6.12 Information Technology (IT)

• Assuring that the company's information systems are properly secure and respect the privacy of individuals

• Assisting others in developing and maintaining IT systems used for sustainability monitoring and reporting (see Chapter 9 for a discussion of these systems)

6.13 Internal Audit

• Strengthening compliance with legal, ethical, governance, and accounting requirements; assuring the integrity of compliance systems
• Working with external auditors or others to assess and verify certain sustainability performance data
• Helping develop compliance self-assessment tools for use by company business units, functions, departments, and other groups

6.14 Investor Relations

• Engaging in dialogue with investor groups and investor-rating organizations, including socially responsible investors; establishing methods for openly responding to investor concerns and for properly respecting shareholder rights
• Communicating the company's performance, activities, and policies on sustainability to shareholders
• Disclosing to investors in a timely and transparent way the serious business risks—including those related to sustainability issues—that may have a material impact on the company's short- or long-term financial performance
• Assuring financial information is disclosed in accordance with financial reporting laws, relevant codes of ethics, and principles of transparency

6.15 Law; Corporate Compliance

• Overseeing companywide legal compliance programs to assure they include tracking legal developments, communicating relevant developments to those who may be affected, and creating and implementing programs for compliance (see, for example the compliance program elements required under the U.S. *Sentencing Guidelines* discussed in Appendix 3.26)

• Developing compliance policies for the company's adoption
• Undertaking independent audits, self-inspections, and other measures to assess legal compliance
• Establishing non-compliance logs or other mechanisms to track noncompliance until resolution
• Adopting disciplinary and reward policies and practices demonstrating that the company considers legal compliance a serious matter
• Developing and implementing programs for complying with securities and antitrust rules and other areas of legal compliance not handled by other functions
• Assuring appropriate training is provided on compliance
• Providing a hotline for anonymously reporting illegal activities within the organization
• Instituting corrective and preventive actions to address compliance problems

6.16   Manufacturing

• Assuring that the issues identified for the relevant functions at manufacturing sites are addressed. See, for example, the issues related to Communications, EHS, Facilities Engineering, Finance, Human Resources, Research and Development, Supply Chain, Quality, and Security

6.17   Quality

• Assuring products and services (including those donated to charitable causes) are safe, effective, and meet labeling and advertising representations
• Preventing product defects and waste
• Taking responsibility for any unexpected harm caused by the company's products or services
• Adopting ISO 9001 or some other quality management standard
• Respecting animal rights; minimizing the use of animals in product testing

6.18   Research and Development; Product Design

• Incorporating sustainability concerns into the selection of materials and designs, looking at economic, social, and environmental impacts along the full life cycle of the product from raw

material extraction to ultimate disposal
• Reducing the degree of hazard and quantity of materials needed for products and packaging
• Improving the ergonomics and energy efficiency of products
• Designing products for disassembly and reuse
• Identifying new products to address sustainability issues
• Adopting the precautionary principle in design (see Appendix 1.27 for further discussion on this)
• Respecting animal rights; minimizing the use of animals in product testing
• Adopting responsible practices for the use of humans in product testing

6.19   Risk Management

• Identifying potential liabilities and losses (including those arising from sustainability issues) that could significantly affect the company
• Raising awareness and otherwise promoting programs to reduce and control those risks
• Securing insurance or other financial protection to cover significant risks that can't otherwise be addressed
• Working with corporate governance personnel and others to establish an effective enterprise risk management program that considers sustainability risks

6.20   Sales and Marketing; Distribution

• Using sustainability performance to help build brand strength
• Communicating the company's performance, activities, and policies on sustainability to customers and distributors
• Periodically soliciting feedback from customers on their sustainability concerns related to the company's products, services, and operations, and forwarding those concerns to those within the company who can respond
• Identifying new products and markets—especially those for low-income regions—that can improve sales and help the cause of sustainability
• Aligning with sustainability causes in caused-related marketing (CRM)
• Providing information to product handlers and customers so

that the company's products can be used and handled in a safe and environmentally sound way
• Providing complete and fair product labeling and advertising that identifies product attributes as well as any significant risks to health, safety, and the environment
• Obtaining product certifications related to sustainability

6.21   Security

• Assuring that security staff respects the human rights of employees, protesters, local citizens, and others they may confront
• Protecting employees from workplace violence
• Addressing bioterrorism risks
• Adopting security management standards, such as the Security Code of Management Practices under the Responsible Care® program of the American Chemistry Council[1] or the standards discussed in Appendix 3.25.

6.22   Supply Chain (Supplier Management; Purchasing)

• Communicating the company's performance, activities, and policies on sustainability to suppliers and contractors
• Allocating more procurements to minority- and women-owned businesses and small businesses
• Incorporating sustainability concerns into procurement decisions
• Collaborating with suppliers, distributors, and internal groups to address customers' concerns about sustainability issues related to products and services, and to generally improve the economic, social, and environmental characteristics of products, services, and operations
• Considering fuel economy and alternative fuels in fleet procurements
• Assuring distributors, suppliers, and contractors adhere to company supply-chain standards concerning ethics, environment, health and safety, human rights, child and forced labor, security, antitrust compliance, emergency response, and other sustainability matters.

Endnote to Appendix 6

1. AMERICAN CHEMISTRY COUNCIL, RESPONSIBLE CARE SECURITY CODE OF MANAGEMENT PRACTICES (2002), *available at* http://www.american chemistry.com/s_acc/sec_employment.asp?CID=373&DID=1254.

Examples of Sustainability Metrics

Appendix 7.1 Examples of Sustainability Metrics for Companies

Appendix 7.1.1
Company Sustainability Metrics:
Standard Units of Production Activity and Service Value (SUOPs)

- Sales revenue
- Cost of goods sold
- Adjusted cost of goods sold (adjusted for inventory changes and inflation as determined by the change in the applicable U.S. Producer Price Index(es))
- Value of production (cost of materials and subassemblies processed plus estimated value added by process)
- Number of product units produced or sold
- Number of indexed statistical product units produced or sold by multi-product companies (such as widget equivalents (WE) where for example, Product A = 1 WE; larger Product B = 1.6 WE; and even larger Product C = 3.4 WE, etc.)
- Number of major product units produced or sold (ignores minor products)
- Liter equivalents of liquid products produced or sold
- Cubic meters of natural gas sold
- Metric tons of product produced or sold
- Pallets of product shipped
- Truck loads of product shipped
- Kilometers of shipments made
- Number of transactions processed
- Number of customers served
- Number of employees
- Labor hours
- Number of 100 full-time equivalent employees (FTEs) (100 FTE = 200,000 work hours)
- Giga (billion) watt hours or mega (million) watt hours of electricity generated, transmitted, or distributed
- Miles of wire
- Loads of laundry washed
- Acres planted or treated
- Units cleaned or processed
- Square feet or square meters of building space
- Bushels or tons harvested
- Board feet of lumber
- Metric tons of ore processed
- Carats mined

	Appendix 7.1.2 Company Sustainability Metrics: General Performance	
Sustainability Topic	**Unit of Sustainability Performance**	**Ratio Metric** **(Average, Per-unit, Normalized, etc.)** **(SUOP= selected total standard units of production for the company. See Appendix 7.1.1 for examples.)**
Regulatory compliance	-Number and amount of fines paid, by type -Number of agency inspections -Number of agency inspections due to employee and community complaints -Number of government notices alleging violation (NOV) -Number of regulatory items in audits -Number of regulatory items open more than 90 days	-Amount of fines paid per billion dollars revenue -Amount of fines paid per SUOP -Percent of agency inspections resulting in NOVs -Percent of agency inspections due to employee or community complaint that resulted in NOVs/
Liability	-Number of unresolved lawsuits filed against company -Amount of reserves set aside for litigation	
Operating/management systems standards	-Number of sites and business units committed to implementing sustainability operating system standards (SOS, ISO, OHSAS, etc.) -Number of sites and business units achieving sustainability operating system standards	-Average percent of operating system standards implemented, overall and by system element -Percent of sites and business units achieving sustainability operating system standards -Percent of audited sites receiving various audit scores -Average percent of sites adopting identified best practices
Audits	-Number of site and business unit audits by subject matter -Number of open audit items; number of major items open	-Percent of sites audited, by size or risk category -Average number of audit items per site by category -Percent of facilities conducting self audits -Average time for completing corrective and preventive actions
Costs	-Capital costs for sustainability programs, by program subject -Operating costs for sustainability programs, by program subject	-Sustainability expense, including amortization, (or a certain component of that expense) per SUOP
Planning		-Percent of sustainability objectives met, by program subject -Percent of managers with personal performance objectives or bonuses tied to sustainability objectives

Appendix 7.1.2—Continued Company Sustainability Metrics: General Performance		
Sustainability Topic	**Unit of Sustainability Performance**	**Ratio Metric** **(Average, Per-unit, Normalized, etc.)** **(SUOP= selected total standard units of production for the company. See Appendix 7.1.1 for examples.)**
Supplier issues	- Money spent on local suppliers (including service providers and contractors) - Number of local suppliers - Number of suppliers used who are owned by minorities or women, who are small businesses or who employ a high percentage of women, minority, older and disabled workers - Money paid for purchases from these suppliers - Number of suppliers included in sustainability training - Number of suppliers rejected by the company as a result of sustainability screening - Money spent on purchase of goods from sustainability-certified or sustainability-screened sources	-Percent of purchasing moneys spent with small, minority and women-owned suppliers or those with a high percentage of disabled workers -Percent of suppliers who are local -Percent of purchasing spend on local suppliers -Percent of suppliers who have undergone sustainability (environmental, ethics, human rights, etc.) screening or training, and percent of purchasing cost these suppliers represent -Percent of supplies sourced from ISO 14001- and 9001-certified sites -Percent of purchased wood and agricultural products from sustainability-certified sources
Stakeholder relations	- Ratings from surveys of stakeholder groups (government, investors, communities, NGOs, etc.) - Number of community complaints received by type	-Per ent of community complaints that received responses and percent that were adequately resolved.
Training		-Percent of employees trained on the SOS and sustainability in general and on specific sustainability topics
Investment/transactions	- Number of investments/transactions rejected because of ethical or other sustainability issues	
External recognition	- Number of external awards received by subject	

	Appendix 7.1.3 Company Sustainability Metrics: Economic Performance	
Sustainability Topic	**Unit of Sustainability Performance**	**Ratio Metric** (Average, Per-unit, Normalized, etc.) (SUOP= selected total standard units of production for the company. See Appendix 7.1.1 for examples.)
Company performance	*All of the following should be expressed in appropriate monetary units:* -Sales (turnover) - Size of average sale - Earnings before interest and tax - Net profit/earnings/income - Value added (net sales- cost of goods purchased) -Economic Value-Added (EVA) (profit less taxes and cost of capital) - Gross margin (net sales-cost of goods sold) - Dividends paid - Stock price - Cash flow generated - Liabilities - Debt and lease obligations - Depreciation and amortization - General and administrative overhead expenses - Total payroll and benefits - R&D costs - Employee training costs - Capital expenditures - Cost of goods sold - Interest paid - Reserves - Total assets - Retained earning *Other non-financial metrics include the following:* - Number of shares - Credit ratings - Ratings by socially responsible investment groups	-Percent of worldwide and regional market share for major products -Percent of total sales revenue from domestic sales, percent from each global region - Percent return on invested capital -Total shareholder return benchmarked to appropriate industry index -Earnings per share -Net debt-to-capital ratio -Cash to earnings ratio Market Value-Added (MVA) (ratio of capital invested to market value of equity and debt) -Percent growth in sales -Percent growth in earnings per share -Percent return on capital employed -Percent return on equity after tax -Ratio of cost to income -Sales per square foot -Sales per employee -Average training cost per employee -Ratio of sales revenue to general and administrative cost -Percent profit margin -Debt to equity ratio -R&D expense as a percentage of sales revenue -Total company tax as a percentage of sales revenue -Average days payment for sales are outstanding (DSO) -Average days payment of accounts payable (invoices) are outstanding (DPO) -Ratio of average days for collection of payments for sales to average days for payment of invoices (DPO/DSO or "accounts payable to sales") -Inventory turns (average period for selling and replacing inventory)
Community support	- Taxes paid - Number of local suppliers - Moneys paid to local suppliers	-Percent of suppliers that are local -Percent of supply costs paid to local suppliers

Appendix 7.1.4 **Company Sustainability Metrics:** **Social Performance**		
Sustainability Topic	**Unit of Sustainability Performance**	**Ratio Metric** **(Average, Per-unit, Normalized, etc.)** **(SUOP= selected total standard units of production for the company. See Appendix 7.1.1 for examples.)**
Workplace safety and health	- Number of lost-time occupational injuries and illnesses - Number of days lost due to occupational injuries and illnesses - Number of days workers could not do originally assigned job because of injuries and illnesses (restricted days) - Number of recordable injuries and illnesses under US OSHA - Number of injuries requiring more than simple first aid - Number of serious injuries (fatalities, amputations, hospitalizations) - Number and cost of vehicle accidents - Number of agency inspections - Number of workers' compensation claims for occupational injuries and illnesses, total WC payment made, and actual and projected cost for injuries occurring in report year - Number of accidental fires and explosions and cost of damage from them - Number of employee wellness events - Number of safety training sessions - Number of safety suggestions received from employees	-Employee and contractor injuries and illnesses per 100 FTE (200,000 work hours) compared with benchmarks -Percent of total days lost due to occupational injuries and illnesses -Average lost days per occupational injury and illness case - Average no. of sick days claimed per employee -Vehicle accidents per 100,000 km driven -Vehicle accidents per 100 fleet vehicles -Percent of employees completing special driver safety training -Percent of agency inspections resulting in notice of violation -Average cost per claim of workers' compensation cases -Percent of employees trained on safety -Percent of sites/departments completing a health and safety audit/assessment -Percent of job hazard analyses completed -Percent of sites with trained health and safety leaders -Percent of sites with behavior-based safety programs -Percent of sites with OSHA VPP certification -Percent of sites completing health and safety risk assessments
Product/customer issues, producer responsibility	- Customer satisfaction rating from surveys - Number of complaints and lawsuits concerning function or quality of company's products and services or the labeling or promotion of them - Number of product recalls and special warnings issued - Length of increase in average product life -Cost of major product recalls -Sales volume lost through recalls	-Percent of customer complaints resolved within a set time -Product defects per million products -Percent of products recalled - Percent of purchases by repeat buyers -Percent of production facilities with ISO 9001 certification -Percent of production facilities with Six Sigma Black Belt professionals

Appendix 7.1.4--Continued Company Sustainability Metrics: Social Performance		
Sustainability Topic	**Unit of Sustainability Performance**	**Ratio Metric** (Average, Per-unit, Normalized, etc.) (SUOP= selected total standard units of production for the company. See Appendix 7.1.1 for examples.)
Charitable donations	- Money donated to charitable/public causes (companywide and regional) - Money value or quantity of in-kind donations (products or services) - Number of grant recipients by type	-Percent of pre-tax profits donated
Community outreach	- Total employee volunteer hours - Number of outreach programs by type	-Percent of employees participating in community volunteer programs
Corporate governance	- Number of board members completing training on company and regulatory governance rules - Number of independent board members - Number of resolutions filed on environmental, social and governance issues	-Percent of board members completing training on company and regulatory governance rules -Percent of board directors who are independent non-executive directors -Percent of shareholder votes received on environmental, social and governance resolutions
Employee compensation	- Total salaries and benefits paid -Number of workers paid less than the statutory minimum wage	-Average salary paid by employee category -Ratio of average salary to per capita gross national income or to industry average -Ratio of lowest wage and benefits paid to statutory minimum -Ratio of CEO pay to average worker pay -Percent of workers who are supervised temporary/contacted workers - Average salary paid for temporary workers -Percent of all workers (regular, supervised temporary and supervised contracted) without benefits granted to regular workers
Employee development and well-being	- Number of employees and supervised contracted workers - Number of days or hours of training provided - Cost of training - Number of employees receiving training - Employee satisfaction rating from surveys - Number of job applicants	-Average training days, hours, or cost per employee or per FTE -Percent of employees trained -Percent of employees leaving company (turnover) -Training cost as a percentage of sales revenues
Union rights	- Number of facilities that have unions - Number of union workers	-Percentage of employees who are in union -Percentage of sites that are unionized

Appendix 7.1.4--Continued Company Sustainability Metrics: Social Performance		
Sustainability Topic	**Unit of Sustainability Performance**	**Ratio Metric** (Average, Per-unit, Normalized, etc.) (SUOP= selected total standard units of production for the company. See Appendix 7.1.1 for examples.)
Human rights	-Number and value of investments rejected by company because of human rights issues -Number of suppliers rejected by company at least in part because of human rights reasons -Number of training sessions on human rights issues -Number of workers under 18 engaged in hazardous jobs (for company and suppliers) -Number of workers under 16 who are not receiving regular schooling (for company and suppliers) -Number of workers under 14 (for company and suppliers) -Number of workers engaged in forced labor (for company and suppliers)	-Percent of suppliers evaluated for human rights performance - Percent of suppliers rejected by company at least in part because of human rights concerns -Percent of purchasing, human resources and security employees trained on relevant human rights issues
Diversity/non-discrimination	-Number of employees -Number of women, aboriginal workers, other visible minorities, disabled workers and those over-55 in board, management, general employee and intern positions - Number of discrimination charges that were filed against the company, and number upheld	- Percent of total employees, board members, management, general employees and intern positions held by women, aboriginal workers, other visible minorities, disabled workers and those over-55 compared to industry benchmarks and general local population - Percent of workers who were laid off who were in these categories -Percent of new hires who are in these categories -Percent of franchises owned by people of these categories -Percent of non-domestic management who are expatriates
Business practices/ethics	-Number and value of reported bribes -Number of employees who signed certificate of conformance with ethics code -Number of anti-competition cases filed against company and number of unfavorable rulings in such cases -Number of ethics complaints by type, reported to ethics office or company hotline -Employee survey results on ethics questions	-Percent of employees who signed certificate of conformance with ethics code

Appendix 7.1.5 Company Sustainability Metrics: Environmental Performance		
Sustainability Topic	**Unit of Sustainability Performance**	**Ratio Metric** **(Average, Per-unit, Normalized, etc.)** **(SUOP= selected total standard units of production for the company. See Appendix 7.1.1 for examples.)**
Energy usage	- Giga(billions)joules or trillions of joules of energy used, by type - Millions of liters of gasoline or fuel oil burned - Millions of cubic meters of natural gas burned - Millions of kilograms of propane or wood burned - Millions of metric tons of coal burned - Millions of joules of electricity or steam generated on site for use by company and for use by other consumers - Cost of energy - Number of facilities with incentives for commuting by other than single-occupancy auto - Number of employees participating in ride-share programs or commuting in other than single-occupancy vehicle, and amount of subsidy company paid for this - Number of alternate-fuel vehicles in fleet - Cost saved and avoided because of energy conservation measures	-Energy used per SUOP -Energy use per square meter or foot of building space -Percent of electricity from green/renewable sources -Percent of energy obtained from various categories of sources -Percent of energy used for various purposes -Average fuel economy of company fleet -Percent of fleet vehicles that exceed certain fuel economy levels -Percent of fleet fueled with other than gasoline or regular diesel fuel -Percent of employees participating in ride share programs or commuting via public transportation -Average commuting distance per employee
Solid and hazardous waste; hazardous substances	- Metric tons of regulated/hazardous and non-regulated/non-hazardous waste generated, by type - Metric tons of materials recycled, reused or recovered, by type - Metric tons of wastes disposed, by type of disposal (incineration, land-based, deep well, etc.) - Value of material generated as waste - Disposal cost - Recycling revenue - Revenue from sale of surplus equipment - Disposal, material and other cost saved or avoided because of waste reduction efforts - Maximum amount of hazardous waste and other hazardous substances on site at any one time, by hazard category - Volume of waste generated from product recalls and other off-spec product	-Percent of generated waste that is recycled or reused -Percent of waste incinerated -Percent of waste landfilled, land-applied or injected to deep well -Waste generated per SUOP -Percent of waste generated from product recalls and other off-spec product

Appendix 7.1.5--Continued
Company Sustainability Metrics:
Environmental Performance

Sustainability Topic	Unit of Sustainability Performance	Ratio Metric (Average, Per-unit, Normalized, etc.) (SUOP= selected total standard units of production for the company. See Appendix 7.1.1 for examples.)
Solid and hazardous waste; hazardous substances--continued	- Number of pollution prevention suggestions received from employees - Number of pollution prevention projects completed	
Greenhouse gas emissions	- Millions or thousands of metric tons of greenhouse gases (in CO_2 equivalents) emitted by the company from vehicles and operations, by source category - Quantity of greenhouse gas emissions from energy suppliers that was associated with production of electricity or steam purchased by the company - Cost saved and avoided because of emission-reduction efforts	-Emissions per SUOP -Percent of greenhouse gas emissions by source category
Other air emissions	- Metric tons or kilograms of specific pollutants emitted (e.g., NOx, SO2, particulates, volatile organic compounds, dioxin, US Toxic Release Inventory substances, persistent organic pollutants) - Metric tons or kilograms of environmental impact potentials for ozone-depleting substances (in CFC equivalents), for acidic gases (in SO2 or proton equivalents) and nutrient pollution (in NO3 equivalents) - Metric tons or kilograms of ozone depleting substances used - Number of days of exceedances of regulatory or permit limits - Metric tons of hazardous air emissions from significant incidents - Cost saved and avoided because of emission reduction efforts	-Emissions per SUOP
Soil contamination, waste-site clean-ups	- Number and total volume of significant oil, fuel and chemical spills reportable under law Number of such spills over a certain volume - Estimated liability/cost to clean up contaminated sites - Number of waste disposal and recycling sites evaluated	-Percent of waste disposal and recycling sites evaluated and approved by company -Concentration of key pollutants in soil and groundwater

Appendix 7.1.5--Continued Company Sustainability Metrics: Environmental Performance		
Sustainability Topic	**Unit of Sustainability Performance**	**Ratio Metric** (Average, Per-unit, Normalized, etc.) (SUOP= selected total standard units of production for the company. See Appendix 7.1.1 for examples.)
Biodiversity, land use, wetlands/natural habitat protection	- Amount of owned, leased or managed land impacted by operations - Acres or hectares of biodiversity-rich habitats owned, leased or managed by company - Number of sites with significant biodiversity issues -Number of sites with significant cultural heritage issues - Number of UICN Red List species with habitats in areas affected by operations - Area of land rehabilitated/improved - Number of sustainability-certified acres/hectares under cultivation -Area of land used for various purposes -Number of protected areas, as defined by the World Conservation Union, that have been environmentally affected in an adverse way by the company's operations	-Percent of sites completing biodiversity surveys -Percent of land impacted by operations -Percent of land rehabilitated -Percent of land that is permeable -Percent of land that is open -Percent of land used to grow crops -Percent of acres/hectares under cultivation that are sustainability-certified -Percent of land used for various purposes -Volume or weight per acre/hectare of various hazard classes of chemicals applied to land (e.g., pesticides, herbicides, fertilizers) -Weight per kilometer of salts and other chemicals applied to roads
Wastewater	- Millions of gallons or liters or thousands of cubic meters of wastewater discharged, by type of disposition - Millions of gallons or liters of wastewater reused or reclaimed - Number of exceedances of regulatory or permit limits - Metric tons of key pollutants in wastewater (e.g., BOD5, COD, suspended solids, phosphorus and nitrogen compounds, heavy metals, other toxic substances) - Cost saved and avoided because of the reduction of wastewater pollutants	-Amount discharged per SUOP -Amount discharged per employee -Percent of wastewater reused or recycled -Percent of tested samples exceeding wastewater limits
Water	- Cubic meters or millions of liters of water used, by type of source of supply - Cubic meters or millions of liters of water used for various purposes - Number and total volume of significant oil, fuel and chemical spills to surface waters - Cost saved and avoided because of water conservation efforts	-Water use per SUOP -Percent of water obtained from various sources -Average annual absolute and percentage change, in volume, flow or level of any groundwater sources used -Percent of total water used that is in product -Maximum concentration of various pollutants in well water, waterway, drinking water relative to established standards -Percent of tested samples exceeding limits

Appendix 7.1.5--Continued Company Sustainability Metrics: Environmental Performance		
Sustainability Topic	**Unit of Sustainability Performance**	**Ratio Metric** **(Average, Per-unit, Normalized, etc.)** **(SUOP= selected total standard units of production for the company. See Appendix 7.1.1 for examples.)**
Natural resource use	- Metric tons of each major type of materials used - Tree equivalents of paper used - Metric tons of purchased materials with recycled content - Metric tons or cubic meters of waste substances from off-site sources used in process - Cost saved and avoided because of the reduced use of natural resources	-Average percent recycled content in various products (or product families) purchased or sold -Volume or weight of major materials used per SUOP -Total hectares or acres, and hectares or acres per SUOP, needed to supply company with necessary energy and materials (ecological footprint)
Product/customer issues	- Number of products requiring animal testing -Number of animals purchased for testing purposes -Number of products converted from animal testing to another evaluation method - Number of products undergoing sustainability/environmental evaluation - Number of product and packaging take-back programs - Number or total weight of products and materials returned for reclaiming or reprocessing - Total take-back fees paid to authorities - Energy consumed by product in joules - Product emissions in kilograms of CO_2 equivalents -Total weight of packaging and of amount reduced	-Percent of products requiring animal testing -Percent of products formerly requiring animal testing that have been converted to other evaluation methods -Percent of products for which sustainability/environmental life-cycle impact and risk evaluations have been completed -Percent reduction of product and packaging material -Average percent reduction of product and packaging material per unit of product -Percent of product or packaging material recovered in take-back programs -Percent of products that can be recycled, reused or reclaimed -Energy consumed and waste and emissions produced by each major energy-consuming product sold (e.g., vehicles, production equipment) -Percent of procurement expense devoted to goods screened against sustainability criteria -Percent of procurement transactions screened against sustainability criteria
Green design	- Number and type of awards won for design - Number of buildings meeting green design criteria (e.g., LEED certification)	-Percent of building space designed to meet green criteria -Percent of new buildings meeting green design criteria

Appendix 7.2. Examples of Sustainability Metrics for General Governments

In addition to the tables below, other useful sources of information on sustainability indicators for communities are the following websites:

- Sustainable Measures database of indicators, at http://www. sustainablemeasures.com/
- Sustainable Communities Network, *Inventories & Indicators*, at http://www.sustainable.org/creating/indicators.html

Appendix 7.2.1 Sustainability Metrics for General Governments: Economic Performance[1]				
Governmental Entity	**Metrics**			
Hamilton, Ontario	-Percent population in labor force -Unemployment rate -Percent permanent, temporary, and self-employed workers	-Percent families with low income -Personal bankruptcies per 100,000 population	-Business bankruptcies per 100,000 establishments -Average donation amount per tax filer	-Average rent of a two-bedroom apartment as a percent of median family income -Percent families spending more than 50% of income on housing
Seattle, Washington	-Number and percent of employees at top 10 companies -Unemployment rate -Percent share of total community income by personal income quintile	-Health care expenditure per capita -Average monthly hours worked to meet basic needs	-Percent market price for housing is above affordable cost for median, low-income, and first-time buyers -Percent children in poverty	-Percent Emergency Room visits not admitted to hospital -Percent banks meeting various Community Reinvestment Act lender ratings
Santa Monica, California	-Percent total wages by business sector -$ Reinvestment by business -Ratio of jobs to housing -Percent residents employed in city	-Average household income relative to city cost of living -Percent new jobs paying more than the local cost of living -Percent households earning more than $100,000 and less than $25,000	-Percent city employees living in city -Average distance city employees travel to work -Percent new and existing housing available to families within various income categories	-Low-income housing units by neighborhood -Number of homeless and percent served by city shelter -Percent residents working more than 40 hours per week to meet basic needs

Appendix 7.2.1--Continued Sustainability Metrics for General Governments: Economic Performance[665]				
Governmental Entity	**Metrics**			
Southern California Council on Env. & Development	-No. of employed -Unemployment rate	-Average annual personal income -Number and percent households with income below poverty level	-Number and percent households paying more than 30 percent of income for shelter -Estimated $ health care savings if particulate levels in air are reduced	-Percent and $ per person of benefits from transportation plan allocated to various categories of household income
Pittsburgh, PA	-Average prices per square foot for commercial property on main street	-Average length of time for-sale property on market	-Number of vacant properties	-Percent of business buildings in good or better condition
Southeast Louisiana	-Tons of cargo and thousands of visitors passing through -Patents issued -Average entry-level wage rate	-Gross domestic regional product -FDIC bank deposits per capita -Percent difference between median house price and affordable house price -Percent difference between fair market rent and affordable rent	-Ratio of degrees awarded to new jobs requiring degrees -Percent growth in jobs -Regional business climate ranking (per survey) vs. national ranking	-Median household income -Venture capital invested in region

Appendix 7.2.2 Sustainability Metrics for General Governments: Social Performance[666]				
Governmental Entity	**Metrics**			
Hamilton, ON	-Population -Population density -Housing starts -Percent housing units that are substandard -Cars per capita -Housing permits issued -Visits to cultural centers	-Infant mortality rate -Deaths of people under 75 -Percent births that are low weight -Percent work hours lost due to illness or disability -Hospitalizations for falls by people over 65 -Rate of mortality due to heart disease	-Number of robberies -Property, violent and youth crimes per 100,000 population -Pedestrians and cyclists injured -Percent people achieving various levels of schooling -Percent 18 year-olds receiving high school diplomas	-No. high school equivalency diplomas granted -Percent Grade 3 students performing at levels 3 and 4 -Voter turnout for municipal elections -Shelter occupancy rate -Contacts (hits) on the city's Web site for volunteer programs
Seattle, WA	-Population -Percent population with weak, limited and strong literacy -Percent people completing high school by ethnicity -Ratio of staff representation to student representation by ethnicity	-Volunteer hours per student -Students doing volunteer work -Juvenile crime cases -Ratio of ethnic groups' representation in juvenile system to representation in population -Percent births with low weights by ethnicity	-Child asthma hospitalizations per 100,000 residents -Library books checked out per capita -Community center visits per capita -Attendance at art institutions/events -Students per art teacher -Number of arts organizations	-Community garden plots -Percent population engaging in various neighborly activities/behaviors -Percent survey responses in each rating category on community as place to live and quality of life -Percent population living within 3 blocks of open space
Santa Monica, CA	-Percent residents volunteering at city events and total volunteer hours -Percent residents in neighborhood organizations by neighborhood	-Percent households within ¼ and ½ mile of park -Percent new housing within ¼ mile of transit stop, open space and grocery store	-Percent residential mixed-use projects within ¼ mile of transit stop -Percent streets and intersections with unacceptable congestion	-Capacity of local health care service providers to meet the basic needs of residents -Average response times for fire and police

Appendix 7.2.2--Continued Sustainability Metrics for General Governments: Social Performance				
Governmental Entity	**Metrics**			
Santa Monica, California-- continued	-Number of women, minorities, and disabled in leadership positions in city, business, and nonprofit orgs. -Percent registered voters who voted -Percent residents who attended city meetings and events -Percent residents who feel they have the opportunity to voice concerns (per survey) --Vehicle collisions with bikes and pedestrians	-Crime rate per capita by type and neighborhood -Percent residents who think the city is safe (per survey) -Incidents of domestic, child, and elder abuse and percent prosecuted -Incidents of employment and housing discrimination and number prosecuted -Percent rehabbed affordable housing designed for people with special needs	-Percent students who are suspended from, and drop out of, school -Percent students with substance abuse -Percent students who feel safe at school (per survey) -Percent students in advanced placement courses who received passing grades -Percent new housing in non-residential zones	-Percent students enrolling in college -Percent residents who believe (per survey) that needs are not being met for counseling; emergency food, shelter, and clothing; employment and job training services; recreation and youth programs; health care; substance abuse services; affordable housing; seniors and the disabled; transportation -Percent residents with health insurance
Southern California Council on Environment & Development	-Population -Number and percent households in defective or overcrowded housing	-Current baseline level, and projected level after transportation plan is implemented, of: total vehicle miles per day, average vehicle speed, millions of hours per day of delay from traffic congestion, and average time for a 20-mile trip and 12-mile commuter trip		

Appendix 7.2.2--Continued **Sustainability Metrics for General Governments:** **Social Performance**			
Governmental Entity	**Metrics**		
Pittsburgh, Pennsylvania	-Participation of children in organized activities -Number of residents who know four or more neighbors by name	-Satisfaction of residents with day care and after-school options (per survey) -Number of auto mobile break-ins and thefts	-Resident satisfaction with city cleanliness, on-street parking and public transportation (per survey) -Percent of owner-occupied houses	-Number of positive versus negative new stories about city -Average length of residency at same address
Southeast Louisiana	-Percent of residents who could name 3 things they expect to appreciate about the community in 10 years -Uninsured Emergency Room visits -Heart disease death rate, by race -Percent adults reading at level 1	-Percent of 2nd and 3rd graders reading at or above their grade level - Ranking of community versus an "equity index" on treatment of minorities -Percent kindergartners and first graders held back	-Percent of college freshmen taking remedial classes -Percent of children living in poverty -Percent of high school students held back -Total combined incidence of drug episodes in Emergency Rooms, suicides, and child abuse	-Births per 1,000 teenage girls -Percent infant mortality by race - Percent of total births under 2,500 grams -Crimes per 100,000 people committed by adults and juveniles -Percent residents satisfied with quality of life (per survey)

Appendix 7.2.3 **Sustainability Metrics for General Governments:** **Environmental Performance**[3]				
Governmental Entity	**Metrics**			
Hamilton, Ontario	-Hectares of agricultural land lost -Cumulative area of significant natural protected areas -Total loading of nitrogen and phosphorus in the waterway	-Number of days all beaches open for swimming -Total water consumption -Total solid waste generated -Residential recycling rate	-Average residential electricity consumption -Number of ground-level ozone exceedances -Average concentrations of SO_2, NO_2, and inhalable particulate matter	-Hospitalization rate for respiratory illness per 100,00 people -Greenhouse gas emissions from municipal operations (CO_2 equivalents) -Transit ridership per capita
Seattle, Washington	-Wild salmon returns -Rating of biological health of local streams -Average turbidity levels at five sites on waterways (measures erosion) -Percent watershed area that is urban, rural, agricultural, and park/forest	-Days of various air quality index ratings -Total water consumption -Pounds of solid waste generated, disposed, and recycled per capita per day	-Pounds of heavy metals in sewage, and toxic materials released per day -Acres zoned for agriculture -Certified organic farms -Miles of bicycle lanes	-Miles driven and gallons of gas consumed per capita -Trillions of BTUs of gasoline, natural gas, and renewable-sourced and nonrenewable-sourced electricity used -BTUs of energy used per \$ of personal income
Santa Monica, California	-Percent residents who know of city's ecological footprint and sustainable development plan and how they affect it (per survey)	-Percent new and rehabbed housing that meets city green building code	-Number and percent of residents using city household hazardous waste collection center -Amount of household hazardous waste collected	-Number of facilities permitted to release toxic air contaminants (TACs) -Total volume TACs emitted

Appendix 7.2.3--Continued Sustainability Metrics for General Governments: Environmental Performance				
Governmental Entity	**Metrics**			
Santa Monica, California— cont.	-Ratio water use to total economic activity by business sector -Total solid waste generated, land-filled, and diverted from landfill -Total water use and per capita use by sector -Percent water from local and imported sources -Percent water potable and non-potable -Acres of open space and percent permeable -Percent tree canopy by neighborhood -Percent new trees meeting sustainability criteria -Percent new landscaped city grounds planted with regionally appropriate plants	-Total and per capita greenhouse gas emissions, by source and sector -Ratio energy use to total economic activity by business sector -Total energy (electricity) use and per capita by sector -Total renewable energy (electricity) use and by sector -Energy (electricity) use from clean distributed generation sources -Percent new construction with LEED green building certification -Days beach health warnings posted in dry and wet weather months -Total and per capita wastewater generation, and by sector -Demographic profile and percent of residents living within one-half mile of significant emissions source	-Volume and toxicity of hazardous materials purchased by city -Percent produce served at city-operated facilities that is locally grown organic produce -Total produce sold at farmers' markets and percent organically grown, grown with low chemicals, and conventionally grown -Percent restaurants purchasing produce from local farmers' markets -Percent residents who report that vegetable-based protein is primary protein for at least half of their meals (per survey) -Percent city non-emergency fleet using alternative fuels	-Total vehicle miles, and local-resident versus drive-through miles -Number of trips by bike, bus, walking, rail, and car -Average ridership per vehicle for companies of 50+ employees -Percent residents using other than car for transportation in last month (per survey) -Percent residents satisfied with available sustainable modes of transportation (per survey) -Total and percent street miles with bike lanes -Vehicles per person and per driver -Percent vehicles with low emissions or alternate fuels -Total and percent ridership of city buses

Appendix 7.2.3—Continued Sustainability Metrics for General Governments: Environmental Performance[671]				
Governmental Entity	**Metrics**			
Southern California Council on Env. & Development	-Actual and projected days exceeding federal and state clean air stds. - Actual and projected percent inhalable particulates are above state stds. - Actual and projected percent peak ozone concentrations are above federal stds. - Actual and projected total tons per day of VOC, nitrogen oxides, and inhalable particulate emissions, and by stationary sources and on-road and off-road vehicles	- Actual and projected percent VOC, nitrogen oxides and particulate emissions attributed to autos/motorcycles, light trucks and heavy trucks -Total children and asthma-afflicted children exposed to dangerous air pollutants -Est. deaths from air particulates -Actual and projected gallons per day of fuel consumption by light and medium duty vehicles	- Actual and projected percent vehicles using various types of fuel - Actual and projected percent of various types of energy used -Actual and projected amount water used and amounts imported from various sources - Actual and projected percent water recycled -Percent total days beach water met various quality levels -Percent urban and rural lands used for various purposes	- Actual and projected total pounds solid waste produced per capita per day and sent to landfill and recycled - Actual and projected percent solid waste recycled - Actual and projected percent families recycling and participating in green waste diversion -Current baseline level, and projected level after transportation plan is implemented, of percent workers driving alone, using car pool and public transportation, walking or biking, and working at home
Pittsburgh, PA	-Percent of zoning and code enforcement cases won	-Energy use in buildings	-Domestic water use	
Southeast Louisiana	-Total financial loss from flood damage -Percentages of the poor and minorities who live within 3 miles of a pollutant emitter versus percentages of these people in the local population	-Percent of area covered by urban development, water and vegetation -Percent of days air quality was rated good, and percent rated moderate	-Regional waste generation and recycling rates, vs. national averages	-Millions of pounds of toxic air releases -Millions of pounds of soil and water pollutants

Appendix 7.3. Examples of Sustainability Metrics for Universities

Appendix 7.3.1 Sustainability Metrics for Universities: General Performance				
Function	**Metrics**			
Education	-Number and percent of courses with sustainability content by department -Percent courses assessed for sustainability content	-Number and percent of students enrolled in courses with sustainability content -Number students enrolled in service-learning courses	-Total hours of service-learning -Percent students receiving orientation or other training on sustainability	-Percent students who correctly answered basic questions about sustainability (per survey) -Percent students who know of school's sustainable development plan and how they affect it (per survey)
Research	-Number and percent of research projects related to sustainability	-Percent research projects that are interdisciplinary		
Operations	-See Appendix 7.1 for standard operational metrics	-Number of sustainability training courses by subject, given to staff		
Student Activities/ Issues	-Number of student organizations and number of students participating in them	-Percent students volunteering for charities, and total volunteer hours		
Community Outreach	-Number of the school's community outreach projects involving students, faculty or staff -Number and type of charities aided by students, faculty and staff, and hours contributed	-Number of students, faculty and staff participating in community outreach/charitable initiatives	-Number and percent of suppliers that are local	-Percent favorable rating for university on community survey

**Appendix 7.3.2
Sustainability Metrics for Universities:
Economic Performance**

Function	Metrics			
General	-Total accrued payroll and benefits -Average wage/salary of university employees, by type, vs. university minimum wage	-University revenues by type of source -Amount of private financial support by type of source -Royalty and licensing income	-University expenditures by major type/activity -Scoring on economic items on sustainability audit	-Amount and percent of investments screened for sustainability factors -Investment income -Allocation of investment assets by type
Education	-Number and percent of courses with economic sustainability content by department	-Average student tuition and instruction costs -Amount of student financial aid by source	-Estimated average total costs per year of attendance for undergraduate resident and non-resident students	- Average hours of work at the school's minimum wage needed for undergraduate student to pay for studies
Research	-Total amount of research funding raised and expenditures made	-Amount and percent of research funding for projects related to sustainability	-Amount and percent of research funding for projects that are interdisciplinary	
Operations	-Median income for various levels of faculty and staff vs. median household income for community	-Percent employees who are local residents -Budget for employee training	-Budget for university hospital indigent care -Total annual health-care cost paid by the university	-Employee contributions to university capital campaigns
Student Activities/ Issues	-Total sum of charitable donations collected by student groups			
Community Outreach	-Total funds contributed by students, faculty and staff to charitable causes	-Total and percent of supplier money paid suppliers that are local		

Appendix 7.3.3
Sustainability Metrics for Universities:
Social Performance

Function	Metrics			
General	- Number and percent of tenured, tenure-track and temporary faculty who are women and minorities - Percent undergraduate and graduate students by ethnicity/race and gender	-Student population by class year - Total school population by type (students, faculty, administrative and clerical staff)	- Number and percent of undergraduate and graduate students who are residents, non-residents and foreign -Scoring on social items on sustainability audit	- Percent graduates at each level by gender who obtain jobs within one year of obtaining degree - Percent graduates at each level by gender who seek additional education within one year of obtaining degree
Education	- Number and percent of courses with social sustainability content by department - Total student credit hours from study abroad	-Average GPA and SAT/ACT scores for incoming freshmen - Number of undergraduate and graduate program applicants vs. enrollment	- Percent retention of all enrolled students and minority students after one year	-Percent enrolled students graduating from undergrad and grad school -Percent enrolled minorities, women and male non-minorities graduating from undergrad and grad school
Operations	-See Appendix 7.1 for standard operational metrics -Total school employment by type of job -Percent employees retained -Average response times for campus fire and police	- Number of servings per day of various food groups consumed by students vs. US Dept of Agriculture recommendation -Quantity of food purchased for dining halls by category -Quantity and percent of food purchased for dining halls that is organic	-Crime rate per capita by type -Percent students, faculty and staff who think the campus is safe (per survey) - Number of traffic accidents -Percent staff by ethnicity/race and gender - Average age and seniority of staff	-Number and percent of senior executive, senior and middle management positions filled by women, minorities and the disabled - Percent of staff and faculty who are disabled -Percent minorities and women at various levels of faculty -Number of labor, harassment and discrimination grievances filed on campus, and their disposition

Appendix 7.3.3--Continued Sustainability Metrics Used by Universities: Social Performance				
Function	**Metrics**			
Student Activities/ Issues	-Percent students with substance abuse problems -Percent students reporting various ranges of days of alcohol, cigarette, and marijuana use over the last 30 days (survey)	-Average number of alcoholic drinks consumed per month per student by gender and year (per survey) -Percent students by gender and year who consumed more than five drinks at an outing at least three times in the last two weeks (per survey)	-Percent students by gender, race, and location who engaged in specified adverse behaviors as a result of drinking (per survey)	-Percent students diagnosed with depression-related disorders

Appendix 7.3.4
Sustainability Metrics for Universities:
Environmental Performance

Function	Metrics			
General	- Scoring on environmental items on sustainability audit			
Education	-Number and percent of courses with environmental sustainability content by department	-Percent students who know of school's ecological footprint and how they affect it (per survey)		
Research	-Amount of hazardous and infectious wastes produced from research			
Operations	-See Appendix 7.1 for standard operational metrics - Number of environmental training courses, by subject, given to staff -Number and percent non-emergency vehicles using alternative fuels - Number of trips and average trip distance by motor pool vehicles	-Average commuting distance by students, faculty and staff -Passenger trips using campus public transportation - Number of parking stalls - Number of parking decals sold - Number of vehicles registered by students, employees and commercial groups	- Percent students driving alone, using car pool and public transportation, and walking or biking to school (per survey) -Percent campus population regularly traveling to campus by means other than single occupant auto (per survey) -Miles of bicycle lanes -Number of bicycle permits issued	-Percent student housing that meets green building criteria -Percent new trees meeting sustainability criteria -Percent new landscaped grounds planted with regionally appropriate plants -Percent exotic and percent native woody vegetation on campus

Endnotes to Appendix 7

1. HAMILTON, ONTARIO, VISION 2020: HAMILTON'S COMMITMENT TO SUS-
TAINABILITY COMMUNITY—ANNUAL SUSTAINABILITY INDICATORS RE-
PORT (2003), *available at* http://www.vision2020.hamilton.ca/indicators/
2003report.asp. SEATTLE, WASHINGTON, SUSTAINABLE SEATTLE: INDI-
CATORS OF SUSTAINABLE COMMUNITY: 1998 (1999). *See also* Sustainable
Seattle, *Toward a Sustainable Future: The King County/Seattle Indica-
tor and Strategies for Action Project*, http://www.sustainableseattle.org/
Programs/RegionalIndicators/IndUpdate (last visited Jan. 8, 2006). Santa
Monica, California, *Sustainable City Plan*, http://santa-monica.org/epd/
scp/index.htm (last visited Jan. 8, 2006). SOUTHERN CALIFORNIA COUN-
CIL ON ENVIRONMENT & DEVELOPMENT (SCCED), ANNUAL INDICATOR
REPORT: THE STATE OF THE LOCAL ENVIRONMENT AND ECONOMY: 1997
(1998), *available at* http://www.scced.org/scced/sccedinfo/indic97.html.
SUSTAINABLE PITTSBURGH, SWPA COMMUNITY INDICATORS HAND-
BOOK (2002), *available at* http://203.147.150.6/pdf.cfm. ALAN ATKISSON
ET AL., TOP 10 BY 2010, REGIONAL INDICATORS OF SUSTAINABLE DEVEL-
OPMENT FOR SOUTHEAST LOUISIANA: EXECUTIVE SUMMARY (2002),
available at http://indicators.top10by2010.org/pdf/T10ExecSum.pdf.
(These reports are hereinafter collectively referred to as Six Government
Indicator Reports.)

2. *Id.*

Appendix 8

Sustainability Resources for Universities

Appendix 8.1. Organizations That Can Help Universities Pursue Sustainability

List of Organizations Described in this Appendix 8.1	
8.1.1 Global Higher Education for Sustainability Partnership (UNESCO, ULSF, IAU, and COPERNICUS)	8.1.11 Technical University of Hamburg Consortium
	8.1.12 Alliance for Global Sustainability
8.1.2 U.S. Partnership for the Decade of Education for Sustainable Development (NCSE and ULSF)	8.1.13 U.K. Higher Education Partnership for Sustainability
	8.1.14 Philippines PATLEPAM
8.1.3 National Wildlife Federation's Campus Ecology® Group	8.1.15 Social Enterprise Knowledge Network
8.1.4 U.S. Environmental Protection Agency	8.1.16 New Jersey Higher Education Partnership for Sustainability
8.1.5 International Institute for Sustainable Development	8.1.17 Pennsylvania Consortium for Interdisciplinary Environmental Policy
8.1.6 Tertiary Education Facilities Management Association	
	8.1.18 Campus Consortium for Environmental Excellence
8.1.7 oikos International	
8.1.8 Sierra Youth Coalition	8.1.19 Associated Colleges of the South Environmental Initiative
8.1.9 Dutch CDHO	
8.1.10 Baltic University Programme	8.1.20 South Carolina Sustainable Universities Initiative
	8.1.21 Net Impact

8.1.1 Global Higher Education for Sustainability Partnership (UNESCO, ULSF, IAU, and COPERNICUS)

The United Nations Educational, Scientific, and Cultural Organization (UNESCO)[1] is the task manager for implementing Chapter 36 of Agenda 21[2]—the chapter on education found in this action plan emerging from the 1992 Earth Summit in Rio. The organization launched *Educating for a Sustainable Future* in 1994 to follow up on the recommendations concerning education that came from major U.N. conferences and conventions on various sustainability topics in the 1990s. In 2002, UNESCO was designated as the lead agency for the promotion of the *Decade of Education for Sustainable Development (2005-2014),* a program adopted by the U.N. General Assembly to encourage national and international efforts on this matter.[3] One part of UNESCO's strategy for the program has been to join forces with three university coalitions to form the Global Higher Education for Sustainability Partnership (GHESP). The member coalitions include the U.S.-based Association of University Leaders for a Sustainable Future (ULSF) (see Appendix 8.1.2), the UNESCO-based International Association of Universities (IAU), and COPERNICUS Campus (the Cooperation Program in Europe for Research on Nature and Industry through Coordinated University Studies—see Appendix 8.2.4). All have been quite visible in furthering the sustainability agenda among their 1000-plus university members. Together the GHESP partners are developing strategies, tools, and resources, including an online resource center, to aid in building collegiate sustainability programs.[4]

8.1.2 U.S. Partnership for the Decade of Education for Sustainable Development (NCSE and ULSF)

ULSF has also joined with the National Council for Science and Environment (NCSE) and others to form the U.S. Partnership for the Decade of Education for Sustainable Development (USPDESD), which will develop a multi-stakeholder action plan for implementing the program in the United States.[5] ULSF, with a membership of over 70 universities and colleges, has been a leader in its own right. In addition to offering sustainability workshops, case studies, and self-assessment tools, it consults directly with academic institutions on a variety of sustainability issues related to operations, curricula, faculty development, and research. Its website provides links to information on over 115 campus programs.

8.1.3 National Wildlife Federation's Campus Ecology® Group

The National Wildlife Federation's (NWF's) Campus Ecology® group maintains best practices and other useful information about collegiate environmental sustainability programs on its website. The group also publishes a newsletter, provides speakers, and presents annual awards.[6]

8.1.4 U.S. Environmental Protection Agency

A National Colleges and Universities Sector within the U.S. Environmental Protection Agency (EPA) works with six college and university national organizations to develop tools and approaches for advancing the use of environmental management systems (EMS), reducing regulatory performance barriers, and measuring environmental progress.[7]

8.1.5 International Institute for Sustainable Development

The International Institute for Sustainable Development (IISD) maintains an online interactive tool kit for greening the campus.[8]

8.1.6 Tertiary Education Facilities Management Association

An Australian organization, Tertiary Education Facilities Management Association (TEFMA), has prepared a useful guide for incorporating sustainability into university operations.[9]

8.1.7 oikos International

A few student-led organizations have helped promote university sustainability programs. Among the more prominent groups is the International Student Organization for Sustainable Economics and Management (oikos International), founded as a local student group at the University of St. Gallen, Switzerland. It is supported by corporations like ABB, Deutsche Telekom, Dow, SAM, and Shell. The main objective of oikos is to increase university student awareness about sustainable development and to integrate it into teaching and research worldwide. Particular emphasis is placed on schools of economics and management. The organization hosts conferences, operates an "international winter school" for high potential students, assesses curriculum, and provides other resources to help its members with their sustainability initiatives. Over 50,000 economics and management students from universities in Europe, India, and the United States participate in local oikos chapters.[10]

8.1.8 Sierra Youth Coalition

In Canada, an active student organization, the Sierra Youth Coalition (SYC), has helped infuse sustainability practices into higher education through its Sustainable Campuses Project. SYC has provided support to over 40 campuses in the form of conferences, workshops, student-led audits, and other assistance.

8.1.9 Dutch CDHO

The Dutch National Environmental Student Platform was formed by students at several Dutch universities to promote sustainable campus operations and curriculum reform. In 1998, it was melded into the Commissie Duurzaam Hoger Onderwizs (CDHO), commonly translated into English under various names, including the Dutch Committee on Sustainability in Higher Education, the Committee on Sustainable Higher Education, and the Network for Higher Education and Sustainable Development. The new organization added members from university faculty, staff, and boards, as well as representatives from various government ministries.[11]

8.1.10 Baltic University Programme

The Baltic University Programme (BUP) is a network of 180 institutions of higher learning in 14 countries in the Baltic Sea region of eastern Europe. Uppsala University in Sweden serves as BUP's secretariat. Thirteen other institutions serve as contacts in the other countries in the region. The organization is primarily funded by the Swedish Development Agency and the Swedish Institute. BUP is helping implement Agenda 21 in the academic sector in the Baltic region, offering educational materials, interdisciplinary courses, and teacher and mentor training. It also provides workshops, seminars, summer camps, and other aid. BUP promotes similar activities in Africa and Latin America, too.[12]

8.1.11 Technical University of Hamburg Consortium

The Technical University of Hamburg (TUH) Consortium in Germany leads a consortium of universities in a European Union-funded program aimed at integrating sustainability into curricula and research at European collegiate institutions. Universities in Latin America are also involved with their European counterparts in information sharing, faculty exchanges, and other activities.[13]

8.1.12 Alliance for Global Sustainability

Alliance for Global Sustainability (AGS) is a coalition among four leading science and technology universities: Swiss Federal Institute of Technology, Zurich; Massachusetts Institute of Technology; University of Tokyo; and Chalmers University of Technology in Sweden. The organization also partners on an ad hoc basis with universities and governments in China, Mexico, and other countries. Its purpose is to collaborate through multi-disciplinary research teams to develop leading-edge research and education on sustainability issues in science, technology and the social sciences. AGS's research has covered topics involving energy and climate, transportation/mobility, urban systems, water and agriculture, and cleaner technologies. Other projects have addressed policy and communications. The organization hosts annual and special technical meetings where the latest ideas are shared and discussed. One of its more popular programs, Youth Encounter on Sustainability (YES), brings together a diverse group of graduate and senior undergraduate students from around the world. At these forums, attendees learn from each other and form multi-disciplinary working groups to address various sustainability problems.[14]

8.1.13 U.K. Higher Education Partnership for Sustainability

The U.K. Higher Education Partnership for Sustainability (HEPS) is a collaboration of 18 U.K. universities led by the NGO Forum for the Future. Funded by member institutions and U.K. regional governments, this initiative is designed to help bring a lasting sustainability culture to member schools. It uses a flexible process to bring about change, starting with a one-day Opening Sustainability Review with students, faculty, and operations and management personnel. During the review, participants gain an understanding of sustainability, assess expectations, and develop a sustainability work plan for their institution. HEPS representatives serve as facilitators, promote partnership projects, and provide a framework for sustainability reporting. The organization has developed guidelines for establishing specific sustainability programs, including those related to green purchasing, commuter transportation, sustainability reporting, other program communications, and sustainable resource and asset management. It has published tools for incorporating sustainability into course work and for integrating environmental and social considerations into traditional financial accounts.[15]

8.1.14 Philippines PATLEPAM

The Philippine Association of Tertiary Level Educational Institutions in Environmental Protection and Management (PATLEPAM) is a government-sponsored network of 380 universities and colleges that works to further education, training, and research on environmental and sustainability issues. It chairs the Subcommittee on Information and Education for the Philippine Council for Sustainable Development in its implementation of Agenda 21. It also networks with NGOs and youth groups to help deliver environmental education to local communities.[16]

8.1.15 Social Enterprise Knowledge Network

The Social Enterprise Knowledge Network (SEKN) is a collaboration of nine Latin American business schools, ESADE Business School of Spain, Harvard Business School, and the AVINA Foundation. Its aim is to strengthen research, teaching, and management practice in "social enterprise" in Latin America. A "social enterprise" is any kind of organization or undertaking engaged in activities of significant social value or in the production of items with an embedded social purpose. SEKN emphasizes the use of case studies in teaching and as the basis for research.[17]

8.1.16 New Jersey Higher Education Partnership for Sustainability

The New Jersey Higher Education Partnership for Sustainability (HEPS) is a consortium of 37 New Jersey colleges and universities hosted by a foundation within the New Jersey Institute of Technology. The partnership is supported by foundation, corporate, and state funding and by membership fees. It holds seminars, develops toolkits, publishes a newsletter, and otherwise facilitates the exchange of information among its members about sustainable practices at the collegiate level. It has established cross-institutional teams focusing on energy use, green design, sustainability education and awareness, and environmentally preferable purchasing. Faculty liaison and sustainability coordinators have been designated at each member institution. Among its accomplishments, the organization convinced all 56 collegiate presidents within New Jersey to sign a "Sustainability Covenant" committing to a GHG reduction goal. It also assisted in the development and support of the New Jersey Sustainable State Institute, which provides information, analysis, and practical strategies to help the state develop along a sustainable path. The partnership has programs on outreach and publicity and student involvement. To maintain support, the group has an effective working relationship with the New Jersey President's Council, which includes the leaders of its member institutions. In addition, New Jersey's HEPS is developing an advisory committee of outside experts who can provide advice on projects and funding.[18]

8.1.17 Pennsylvania Consortium for Interdisciplinary Environmental Policy

The Pennsylvania Consortium for Interdisciplinary Environmental Policy collaborates on research, academic courses, and policy development concerning the environment and sustainable development. Members include 52 Pennsylvania colleges and universities as well as the state department of environment and the department of conservation and natural resources.[19]

8.1.18 Campus Consortium for Environmental Excellence

Thirty colleges and universities from the northeastern U.S. and Alaska joined together with Pfizer to form the Campus Consortium for Environmental Excellence (C2E2). Its main purpose is to improve environmental performance in higher education through professional networking, information exchange, and the development of resources and tools. Among its work products are audit tools for evaluating university laboratory practices and EMS. It has also produced a white paper on using hand-held electronic devices for gathering and managing EHS data on campus.[20]

8.1.19 Associated Colleges of the South Environmental Initiative

The Associated Colleges of the South (ACS) comprises 16 private liberal arts colleges and universities scattered among 12 states in the southern U.S. Under its Environmental Initiative, ACS serves as a forum for collaborative action. Like the New Jersey HEPS, ACS has established interinstitutional teams. Three teams, called "Alliances," have been formed: one on curriculum and faculty development; another on student development and engagement; and the third on operations, entitled "Campus as Lab for Sustainability." ACS has recruited liaisons from all member institutions and has helped them establish on-campus teams. To encourage progress, the organization issues grant funding to its members for the development of environmental and sustainability programs concerning curriculum, operations, student activities, and campus-community partnerships.[21]

8.1.20 South Carolina Sustainable Universities Initiative

The South Carolina Sustainable Universities Initiative (SUI) is led by three major research institutions: the Medical University of South

Carolina, the University of South Carolina, and Clemson University. The statewide network includes a total of 16 colleges and universities. The organization's primary function is to help its members lead the way to a more sustainable future through teaching, research, community service, and facilities management. It has worked toward this goal by preparing an introductory video, hosting conferences, and sharing information about member programs. Additionally, SUI has offered sustainability mini-grants for new courses, faculty training, student projects, and conferences. SUI grants have also been awarded to jump-start campus resource-conservation and pollution-reduction programs.[22]

8.1.21 Net Impact

Net Impact, formerly Students for Responsible Business, is a network of more than 10,000 master's of business administration (MBA) students, graduate students, and professionals dedicated to using the power of business to further sustainability. Founded in 1993 by MBA students, the organization operates through a central office in San Francisco and more than 125 chapters in cities and graduate schools around the globe. It provides members with various resources, including publications, conferences, teleconferences, and other networking opportunities.[23]

Appendix 8.2. Sustainability-Related Codes for Collegiate Institutions

List of Codes Summarized in this Appendix 8.2	
8.2.1 Talloires Declaration (1990) 8.2.2 Halifax Declaration (1991) 8.2.3 Swansea Declaration (1993) 8.2.4 COPERNICUS Charter (1993) 8.2.5 Kyoto Declaration(1993) 8.2.6 Blueprint for a Green Campus (1994) 8.2.7 The Essex Report (1995)	8.2.8 Dutch Charter for Sustainable Development in Vocational Training (Higher Professional Education) (1999) 8.2.9 Lüneburg Declaration (2001) 8.2.10 Ubuntu Declaration (September 2002)

8.2.1 Talloires Declaration (1990)[24]

In 1990, Tufts University President Jean Mayer asked presidents, rectors, and vice chancellors from 22 universities around the world to meet at the Tufts European Center in Talloires (pronounced Tal-Whar), France, to discuss the role of higher education institutions in environmental management and sustainable development. With the help of some internationally respected environmental experts, they produced the *Talloires Declaration*, an action plan committing their institutions to the following actions:

1. Raise awareness with industry, the public, government, and foundations about the urgent need to move toward a sustainable future; involve these groups as well as NGOs and communities in helping find sustainable solutions.
2. Develop interdisciplinary approaches toward sustainability in university curricula, research, operations, outreach programs, and policy formation.
3. Develop faculty expertise and programs that help assure that all students at all levels have the awareness and understanding to become ecologically responsible citizens.
4. Establish good ecological practices and policies in university operations.
5. Partner with primary and secondary schools to bring interdisciplinary teaching about sustainability to those institutions.
6. Collaborate with national and international organizations to promote a worldwide university effort toward a sustainable future.

A secretariat was established to assure follow-up on these commitments. That responsibility now resides with the ULSF. Over 300 colleges and universities have signed the declaration—approximately one-third of them from Canada and the United States, one-third from Latin America and the Caribbean, and one-third from other regions.

8.2.2 Halifax Declaration (1991)[25]

A year after the Talloires conference, a similar meeting was convened at Dalhousie University in Halifax, Nova Scotia, Canada, among the presidents and senior representatives from 33 universities in 10 countries. Representatives of several university associations also participated. The resulting *Halifax Declaration* expresses many of the same themes identified at Talloires, but injects new points as well. Those points concern the need to address sustainability issues in education as an ethical obligation, focusing not just on environmental degradation but on inter-generational inequity and the disparities between peoples of the North and those of the

South. The document asserts that "intolerable human disparity . . . lie(s) at the root of environmental *unsustainability*."

8.2.3 Swansea Declaration (1993)[26]

Agenda 21 was the action plan on sustainability that was adopted at the Earth Summit (U.N. Conference on Environment and Development) in Rio de Janeiro in 1992. Disappointed by the poor showing of universities at Rio and inspired by the examples of Talloires and Halifax, the Association of Commonwealth Universities (ACU) used its meeting in Swansea, Wales a year later to add its voice to the cry for sustainable universities. The ACU, which draws its membership from 400 universities in 47 countries, emerged from the meeting with the *Swansea Declaration*. This declaration was substantively the same as its two predecessors, but added a provision asking ACU member institutions to establish and disseminate a clearer understanding of sustainable development.

8.2.4 COPERNICUS Charter (1993)[27]

This Germany-based organization was founded in 1988 by CRE, a group that would later become the European Universities Association. The mission of the Cooperation Program in Europe for Research on Nature and Industry Through Coordinated University Studies (COPERNICUS) is to share knowledge and expertise on sustainability among member institutions. It also encourages university-industry partnerships. The *COPERNICUS University Charter for Sustainable Development* was drafted in 1993 as a follow-up to CRE's "Urgent Appeal" presented at the Earth Summit in Rio. The charter has been signed by well over 300 universities in 37 European countries. It includes many of the same commitments as the earlier declarations, but has some that are unique. Special provisions cover educating university staff employees; fostering collaborations among teachers, researchers and students; and promoting technology transfer. There are also commitments on participating in audits and providing continuing education to business, governments, NGOs and the media. One part of the charter candidly speaks of the need to overcome competitive instincts between disciplines and departments in order to successfully introduce interdisciplinary programs.

8.2.5 Kyoto Declaration (1993)[28]

The Kyoto Declaration—not to be confused with the Kyoto Protocol on Climate Change—was adopted by some 90 international universities at the Ninth Round Table meeting of the IAU held at Kyoto, Japan. This declaration embodies the substance of both the Halifax and the Swansea documents. It adds a cautionary note that "sustainable development . . . not be interpreted in a manner that would lead to 'sustained *undevelopment*' for certain systems, thus blocking their legitimate aspiration to raise their standard of living." The Kyoto Declaration has been endorsed by over 650 IAU member institutions.

8.2.6 Blueprint for a Green Campus (1994)[29]

In 1994, a student-inspired conference, termed the Campus Earth Summit, was hosted by Yale University. It attracted Teresa Heinz (wife of 2004 U.S. presidential candidate John Kerry), a host of big-name environmental leaders, and over 400 faculty, staff, and students from 22 countries and all U.S. states. The resulting report, *Blueprint for a Green Campus*, offers 10 recommendations for greening college campuses. Suggestions on curricula include improving the quality of environmental courses, integrating environmental considerations into all disciplines, and using campus and local environmental issues as teaching opportunities. From an operations perspective, the report recommends campus environmental audits, environmentally responsible purchasing policies, and energy and waste-reduction programs. It also urges universities to incorporate environmental considerations into planning on land-use, transportation, and buildings. In addition, the report advocates student environmental centers and greater support for students seeking environmental careers. It provides useful best-practice cases supporting each recommendation.

8.2.7 The Essex Report (1995)[30]

A year after the Yale summit, 32 educators and other professionals with environmental expertise gathered at a workshop in Essex, Massachusetts to discuss sustainability and how best to incorporate it into higher education. The meeting was sponsored by the NGO Second Nature and Tufts University, and held under the auspices of the President's Council on Sustainable Development. The report which emerged identifies some serious ecological and social trends and the role that universities should play in helping address them. It cites difficult problems with the current approach to education that must be overcome, and paints a detailed vision of the content and strategies for education that should be adopted. For example, the report calls for changes in requirements for faculty tenure and promotion aimed at encouraging interdisciplinary work on sustainability. While the *Blueprint for a Green Campus* focuses on the environment, the *Essex Report* goes well beyond that to outline the interrelated nature of environmental, social, and economic issues and how society and educational institutions must address them holistically through systems thinking. The report concludes with specific recommendations for institutions of higher learning, mirroring many of those recited in the documents previously mentioned. In addition, it calls for each institution to develop a 10- to 20-year plan to make environmentally just and sustainable action a goal and central thrust of its education, research, operations, investment, recruiting, and community outreach activities. It also lists the actions that various stakeholders can take to help.

8.2.8 Dutch Charter for Sustainable Development in Vocational Training (Higher Professional Education) (1999)[31]

The Dutch CDHO (see Appendix 8.1.9) includes over 1,000 representatives from university faculty, research, and management, as well as NGOs, governments, and business. It is funded by the Dutch Ministry of Environment and coordinated by the Expertise Centre for Sustainable Development at the University of Amsterdam. In 1999, CDHO drafted a national "charter" among Dutch institutions of higher learning under which they agreed to integrate sustainable development into their classrooms, policies, and operations. The charter has been signed by 170 departments from 31 colleges. The charter arose out of dissatisfaction with the lack of an accountability mechanism in the COPERNICUS Charter. Consequently, the Dutch document includes a protocol containing specific obligations regarding sustainability. Each institution's compliance with the protocol is to be assessed every two years. Star ratings are issued, with four stars being the highest "Quality Mark" granted for sustainable development in higher education. The five private bodies which accredit Dutch universities every six years are also authorized to issue formal sustainable development accreditation to schools that achieve at least a two-star performance.

8.2.9 Lüneburg Declaration (2001)[32]

A meeting was held at the University of Lüneburg, Germany in October 2001 in anticipation of the World Summit on Sustainable Development held in Johannesburg the following year. In attendance were representatives of the four GHESP partners—UNESCO, COPERNICUS, ULSF, and IAU—as well as the European University Association. The outcome of this meeting was a joint position statement signed by the GHESP partners, re-affirming their commitment to Agenda 21, Chapter 36 and the Talloires, Kyoto, and COPERNICUS declarations. The Lüneburg Declaration calls for higher education institutions, NGOs, and other stakeholders to focus particularly on nine obligations from those documents. The Lüneburg group urged the United Nations to use Johannesburg as an opportunity to give greater attention to the "indispensable role of education in general, and higher education in particular, in achieving sustainable development."

8.2.10 Ubuntu Declaration (September 2002)[33]

At the Johannesburg World Summit in Johannesburg, the GHESP parties joined with other academic and scientific associations in endorsing the *Ubuntu Declaration on Education and Science and Technology for Sustainable Development.* The declaration follows up on the Lüneburg proclamation, urging governments of the world to integrate a sustainable development focus into the curriculum at every level of education. Besides curriculum development, Ubuntu emphasizes other measures, including North-South networking, strategic educational planning and policy-making, and capacity building in scientific research and learning.

Appendix 8.3. Sustainability Assessment Tools for Collegiate Institutions

List of Assessment Tools Summarized in this Appendix 8.3	
8.3.1 U.K.- EcoCampus 8.3.2 ULSF's Sustainability Assessment Questionnaire 8.3.3 Dutch Auditing Instrument for Sustainability in Higher Education 8.3.4 The Campus Sustainability Assessment Project 8.3.5 NJHEPS Campus Sustainability: Selected Indicators Snapshot and Guide 8.3.6 Good Company's Sustainability Pathways Toolkit 8.3.7 UCSB Campus Sustainability Assessment Protocol	8.3.8 U.K. HEPS Reporting for Sustainability Guidance for Higher Education Institutions 8.3.9 C2E2 Environmental Management System Self-Assessment Checklist 8.3.10 Campus Ecology Environmental Audit 8.3.11 The Ecological Footprint Analysis of Colorado College 8.3.12 EPA's 20 Questions for College and University Presidents

8.3.1 U.K.- EcoCampus[34]

The U.K. EcoCampus is a modular, phased approach with software for assessing and building an ISO-like management system around eight themes: (1) resource use (including energy and water); (2) local environmental quality/built environment; (3) waste; (4) community involvement; (5) transport; (6) curriculum greening; (7) ethical and sustainable procurement; and (8) health, welfare, and safety. It's being developed by the U.K.-based Environmental Association for Universities and Colleges (EAUC) in partnership with Nottingham Trent University. Fourteen institutions of higher learning, the British Standards Institution, and others have helped shape the tool. Universities that use EcoCampus may be eligible for any of five different levels of award, depending on the stage of development of their program. They achieve the highest award when they earn ISO 14001 certification.

8.3.2 ULSF's Sustainability Assessment Questionnaire[35]

The Sustainability Assessment Questionnaire (SAQ) is a 12-page qualitative questionnaire by the University Leaders for a Sustainable Future (ULSF). The tool helps institutions of higher learning assess the extent to which they are sustainable. It focuses on the following dimensions of higher education: (1) curriculum; (2) research and scholarship; (3) operations; (4) faculty and staff development and rewards; (5) community outreach and service; (6) student opportunities; and (7) institutional mission, structure, and planning. It is designed to be used by a group of 10 to 15 representatives drawn from faculty, staff, administration, and students. The questionnaire is filled out either individually or by small teams working on particular sections. The entire group then has a facilitated discussion on each section of the questionnaire to formulate impressions. Finally, the group brainstorms possible next steps for strengthening sustainability on campus. The whole process takes a few hours.

8.3.3 Dutch Auditing Instrument for Sustainability in Higher Education[36]

The Dutch CDHO developed the Auditing Instrument for Sustainability in Higher Education (AISHE), an assessment tool to measure the progress toward sustainability in education at colleges and universities. The tool was created to assist academic institutions in meeting their obligations under the Dutch Charter discussed in Appendix 8.2.8, but can be used by schools not affiliated with that proclamation. The AISHE process is similar to that used for SAQ. However the AISHE tool—a 119-page book of evaluation forms, scoring diagrams, and guidance—is much more elaborate than SAQ. AISHE is organized according to a model developed by the European Foundation of Quality Management, which uses the plan-do-check aspects of the Deming Quality Circle.[37] The tool provides textual descriptions of 20 criteria arranged in 5 levels of progress, as shown in Figure A8.3.3.1.

Figure A8.3.3.1		
AISHE Criteria for Five Levels of Progress for Sustainability Programs[38]		
PLAN	**DO**	**CHECK**
1. *Vision and policy* Vision Policy Communication Internal environmental management 2. *Expertise* Network Expert group Staff development plan Research and external services	3. *Educational goals and methodology* Profile of the graduate Educational methodology Role of the teacher Student examination 4. *Education contents* Curriculum Integrated problem handling Traineeship graduation Specialty	5. *Result assessment* Staff Students Professional field Society

After individual scoring of the criteria, a group discussion is held to develop two consensus scores for each item: one reflecting the current situation and the other the desired state. Three to five priorities are then selected and recommended to management for immediate action. The process takes two half-day meetings. It is to be repeated every year or two to track progress.

8.3.4 The Campus Sustainability Assessment Project[39]

The Campus Sustainability Assessment Project (CSAP) is an extensive, easily sortable database of sustainability and environmental audit reports on colleges and universities. It also contains useful lists of other resources related to collegiate sustainability auditing. The site was initiated by Andrew Nixon and Harold Glasser of Western Michigan University in 1999. Nixon's undergraduate honors thesis, *Improving the Campus Sustainability Assessment Process*, provides background information on CSAP as well as a review of best practices and a model assessment questionnaire and process.[40]

8.3.5 NJHEPS Campus Sustainability: Selected Indicators Snapshot and Guide[41]

The guide consists of a list of audit questions arranged under 10 categories: (1) solid waste; (2) energy; (3) water/sewage; (4) transportation; (5) indoor air quality; (6) landscape; (7) food service; (8) new structures/renovations; (9) procurement; and (10) curriculum. After the questions are answered, a summary sheet (snapshot) is completed, giving each of the 10 general categories an overall rating of 1 to 7, depending upon the auditor's estimate of the level of sustainability attained. Three sub-elements under each category are also rated. Once the ratings are completed, each general category is prioritized on a 1-to-10 basis, according to the current likelihood of the school successfully addressing the sustainability issues involved. An audit of Princeton University using the NJHEPS tool was conducted in 2000 by two graduate students, and is available on the Internet.[42]

8.3.6 Good Company's Sustainability Pathways Toolkit[43]

The Pathways Toolkit is an audit framework developed by the Good Company consulting firm. It focuses on the core and supplementary indicators shown in Figure A8.3.6.1. Reports on audits using the Toolkit show the intent for each indicator, note the audited institution's performance, and compare it with benchmark performance. The report completed by Good Company in 2002 for the University of Oregon can be viewed on the Internet.[44] The company's own website provides additional information.[45]

8.3.7 UCSB Campus Sustainability Assessment Protocol[46]

This assessment protocol was prepared by four graduate students to evaluate the environmental sustainability of the University of California at Santa Barbara (UCSB). It covers building design, energy, waste management, transportation, air quality, water management, and landscape management. The Protocol report, which runs over 170 pages, provides an introduction and background information as well as assessment results, analysis of results, and recommendations for each topic. Letter ratings of performance are provided in a "report card."

8.3.8 U.K. HEPS Reporting for Sustainability Guidance for Higher Education Institutions[47]

This Guidance, which was developed by the Forum for the Future and the U.K. HEPS, provides higher learning institutions with a framework for identifying sustainability targets and reporting progress against them online. It incorporates elements found in another Forum product: the SIGMA Project. (See Chapter 2 and Appendix 3.9 for a discussion of

SIGMA.) The tool presents a 3 x 5 appraisal grid by which the university considers its roles in (1) campus operations, (2) teaching and research, and (3) community outreach. The tool also identifies ways to enhance its "stock" in five resources or "capitals" for each role. These capitals are *natural capital* (the environment), *human capital* (people), *social capital* (social relationships and structures), *manufactured capital* (fixed assets), and *financial capital* (money). The grid is used to identify sustainability targets or objectives against which progress can be measured. To aid in the completion of this grid, the tool presents 12 questions tied to "features" that define a sustainable world. Those questions and the features are shown in Figure A8.3.8.1. The guide also contains a list of 24 possible sustainability performance indicators—8 for data likely to be available, 8 that should be reported as a matter of best practice, and 8 more that could be used if desired. An online tool enables a university to insert its targets, objectives, and performance data, and immediately compare its results with those of other universities and colleges.

Figure A8.3.6.1
Good Company Sustainability Assessment Indicators
Core Indicators

Environment	*Health and Safety*
1. Campus energy intensity	13. Ergonomic safety
2. Campus water intensity	14. Indoor air quality (IAQ)
3. Energy- and water-use monitoring and feedback	15. Core benefits for employees
4. Recycling infrastructure	16. Pro-rated benefits for part-time employees
5. Recycling rate (share of total waste stream)	
6. Hazardous materials	*Campus community and beyond*
7. Computer hardware purchasing and disposal	17. Curriculum for environmental and sustainability studies
8. True-cost print charging	18. Governance and leadership for sustainability and environmental performance
9. Paper use and purchasing	
10. Custodial chemical use	19. Purchasing tools and strategies
11. Low-impact grounds maintenance (chemical and water use)	20. Planning and policy for campus construction and development
12. Transportation infrastructure	

Supplementary Indicators	
S-1. Purchasing policy for wood products	S-6. "Green chemistry" curriculum
S-2. Renewable energy purchasing	S-7. Stakeholder involvement in new construction
S-3. Greenhouse gas (GHG) inventory	S-8. Labor policy for campus licensing
S-4. Low VOC paints and finishes	S-9. Investment policy for endowment funds
S-5. Extended benefits and employee assistance programs (EAPs)	S-10. Food procurement and disposal by campus units

Source: The Good Company.[48]

8.3.9 C2E2 Environmental Management System Self-Assessment Checklist[49]

This tool by the Campus Consortium for Environmental Excellence (C2E2) poses 33 questions designed to help a university assess its EMS. The questions are arranged under four topics according to an ISO 14001 framework: (1) policy; (2) planning; (3) implementation and operations; and (4) checking and corrective action. Descriptions of four levels of development are provided for each question so evaluators can rate performance on a scale of 0 to 3. Universities can tally all their ratings and compare the total with the maximum potential score of 99 to obtain a rough idea of the overall condition of its EMS.

Figure A8.3.8.1 **Forum for the Future/U.K. HEPS Sustainability Features and** **Assessment Questions**[50]			
TBL Aspect	**Captl.**	**Sustainability Feature** (Defines what a sustainable world would look like.)	**Question to Be Answered About the Strat Plan or Other Sustainability Initiative** (How does your plan/initiative contribute to . . . .)
Economic	Financial	Financial capital accurately represents the value of natural, human, social, and manufactured capital.	. . . the valuation of all forms of capital?
	Manufactured	All infrastructure, technologies, and processes make a minimum use of natural resources and maximum use of human innovation and skills.	. . . the maximization of resource use-efficiency through human innovation?
Social	Human	At all ages, individuals enjoy a high standard of health.	. . . ensuring human health?
		Individuals are adept at relationships and social participation, and throughout life set and achieve high personal standards of their development and learning.	. . . the empowerment of individuals and promotion of life-long learning?
		There is access to varied and satisfying opportunities for work, personal creativity, and recreation.	. . . the encouragement of employability, creativity and recreation?
	Social	There are trusted and accessible systems of governance and justice.	. . . ensuring trusted governance and justice systems?
		Communities and society at large share key positive values and a sense of purpose.	. . . the increase of mutual respect and positive values?
		The structures and institutions of society promote stewardship of natural resources and development of people.	. . . the promotion of positive institutional change?
		Homes, communities, and society at large provide safe, supportive living and working environments.	. . . creating a safe and supportive living and working environment?

TBL Aspect	Captl.	Sustainability Feature (Defines what a sustainable world would look like.)	Question to Be Answered About the Strat Plan or Other Sustainability Initiative (How does your plan/initiative contribute to . . . .)
Environmental	Natural	In their extraction and use, substances taken from the earth do not exceed the environment's capacity to disperse, absorb, recycle, or otherwise neutralize their harmful effects (to humans and/or the environment).	. . . the reduction of the use of non-renewables?
		In their manufacture and use, artificial substances do not exceed the environment's capacity to disperse, absorb, recycle, or otherwise neutralize their harmful effects (to humans and/or the environment).	. . . the reduction of waste, emissions and persistent chemicals?
		The capacity of the environment to provide ecological-system integrity, biological diversity, and productivity is protected or enhanced.	. . . the maintenance and enhancement of biodiversity?

Figure A8.3.8.1—continued
Forum for the Future/U.K. HEPS Sustainability Features and Assessment Questions

8.3.10 Campus Ecology Environmental Audit[51]

This auditing tool sprang from a 1989 thesis project by Amy Smith and a group of graduate students in Urban Planning at the University of California, Los Angeles (UCLA). Building on that work product, in the early 1990s Amy and the Student Environmental Action Committee formally developed this audit guide framed around 200 assessment questions. The questions involve general campus information as well as common environmental issues, such as solid waste, hazardous substances, radioactive and medical waste, wastewater and stormwater runoff, pest control, air quality, water, and energy. They also cover less obvious issues like workplace environment, food, procurement policies, transportation, campus growth and design, research, investment polices, business ties, environmental education and literacy, and job placement and environmental ca-reers. Reports on the audits conducted using this tool at the University of Pennsylvania (1996)[52] and University of California, Chico (2000)[53] are available on the Internet. The report on the University of Pennsylvania, though somewhat dated, is still worth noting. Besides listing the audit questions and findings, each topic section has an introduction, an over-view of the situation at the university, and a discussion of how various as-pects of the topic impact the environment. Each section also contains best practices at other universities, recommendations, and conclusions. Links to helpful websites are listed as well.

8.3.11 The Ecological Footprint Analysis of Colorado College[54]

Ecological Footprint Analysis (EFA), was developed in the mid-1990s by Mathis Wackernagel and William Rees. It is macro measurement of relative environmental efficiency and sustainability. The analysis in-volves assessing energy and material consumption on campus, and using various conversion factors to determine the minimum land necessary to provide these resource flows. The resulting footprint is typically ex-pressed as hectares or acres per capita. Although it isn't as useful as some other tools in pinpointing needed improvements, it can be beneficial in raising awareness about the meaning of environmental sustainability and the need to address it. A copy of the 2002 EFA of Colorado College is available on-line.

8.3.12 EPA's 20 Questions for College and University Presidents[55]

This list was developed by the U.S. Environmental Protection Agency's Mid-Atlantic Region at the request of university leaders. The document lists high-level questions related to environmental systems for managing compliance and improving programs, touching on such things as poli-cies, procedures, tracking, and auditing.

Endnotes to Appendix 8

1. UNESCO, *Homepage*, http://portal.unesco.org/en/ev.php-URL_ID= 15006&URL_DO=DO_TOPIC&URL_SECTION=201.html (last visited Jan. 8, 2006).

2. *See* DIVISION FOR SUSTAINABLE DEVELOPMENT, U.N. DEPARTMENT OF ECONOMIC & SOCIAL AFFAIRS, AGENDA 21, CHAPTER 36, PROMOTING EDUCATION, PUBLIC AWARENESS, AND TRAINING (1992), *available at* http://www.un.org/esa/sustdev/documents/agenda21/english/agenda21 chapter36.htm.

3. ULSF, *Resource Partners and Events: United Nations Decade of Education for Sustainable Development (2005-2014)*, http://www.ulsf.org/ resources_decade_usa.htm (last visited Jan. 8, 2006) [hereinafter Education for a Sustainable Future].

4. GLOBAL HIGHER EDUCATION FOR SUSTAINABILITY PARTNERSHIP, MEMORANDUM OF UNDERSTANDING (2002), *available at* http://www.unesco. org/iau/sd/pdf/mou.pdf.

5. *U.S. Partnership for the Decade of Education for Sustainable Development*, http://uspdesd.sinapseconsulting.com/index.php?USPDESD=18d 72ea945b41856bc6184d114cb895b (last visited Jan. 8, 2006).

6. NWF, *National Wildlife Federation Campus Ecology®*, http://www.nwf. org/campusEcology/index.cfm (last visited Jan. 8, 2006).

7. U.S. EPA, *Sectors: Colleges and Universities*, http://www.epa.gov/sectors/ colleges/index.html (last visited Jan. 8, 2006).

8. IISD, *Sustainable Development on Campus: Tools for Campus Decision Makers*, http://www.iisd.org/educate/ (last visited Jan. 8, 2006).

9. TEFMA, A GUIDE TO INCORPORATING SUSTAINABILITY INTO FACILITIES MANAGEMENT (2004), *available at* http://www.tefma.com/PDFs/ SustGuideFinalWeb.pdf.

10. oikos: International Student Organization for Sustainable Economics and Management, *oikos International-Welcome*, http://oikosinternational.org/ pages/index.html (last visited Jan. 8, 2006).

11. Niko Roorda, *Research: Assessment and Policy Development in Sustainability in Higher Education With AISHE*, PUBLICATIONS, May 2002 (excerpt from an expanded article from the International Journal of Sustainability in Higher Education), *available at* http://www.ulsf.org/pub_ declaration_resvol52.htm [hereinafter Roorda Overview of AISHE].

12. *The Baltic University Program*, at http://www.balticuniv.uu.se/index.htm (last visited Jan. 8, 2006). *See also* Ea Maria Blomqvist et al., *The Baltic University Programme (BUP)—A Network of 180 Universities in 14 Countries Supporting Education for Sustainable Development in the Baltic Sea Region*, presented at the Conference on Environmental Manage-

ment for Sustainable Universities (EMSU), Tecnológico de Monterrey, Campus Monterrey, Monterrey, N.L., Mexico, June 9-11, 2004.

13. *See* Education for a Sustainable Future, *supra* note 3. Sarah Bekessy et al., *Universities and Sustainability*, 2 TELA: ENV'T, ECONOMY & SOC'Y 22 (2003), *available at* http://www.acfonline.org.au/uploads/res_tp010.pdf.

14. Alliance for Global Sustainability, *Homepage*, http://globalsustainability. org/content.cfm?uNav=27&uLang=1 (last visited Jan. 8, 2006).

15. *Higher Education Partnership for Sustainability*, http://www.forumforthe future.org.uk/aboutus/HEPS_page1509.aspx (last visited Jan. 8, 2006).

16. Philippine Environmental Management Bureau, *Philippine Association of Tertiary Level Educational Institutions in Environmental Protection and Management (PATLEPAM)*, http://www.emb.gov.ph/eeid/PATLEPAM. htm (last visited Jan. 8, 2006). *See also* Education for a Sustainable Future, *supra* note 3.

17. SEKN, *Homepage*, http://www.sekn.org/ (last visited Jan. 8, 2006).

18. New Jersey HEPS, *Homepage*, http://www.njheps.org/ (last visited Jan. 8, 2006). *See also* Wynn Calder & Richard M. Clugston, *Progress Toward Sustainability in Higher Education*, ELR NEWS & ANALYSIS, 33 ELR 10003, 10015 (Jan. 2003), reprinted from a chapter in JOHN C. DERNBACH, STUMBLING TOWARD SUSTAINABILITY (Envtl. L. Inst. 2002) [hereinafter Calder & Clugston 2003].

19. Pennsylvania Consortium for Interdisciplinary Environmental Policy, *Homepage*, http://www.paconsortium.state.pa.us/ (last visited Jan. 8, 2006). *See also* Calder & Clugston 2003, *supra* note 18, at 10015.

20. C2E2, *Homepage*, http://www.c2e2.org/ (last visited Jan. 8, 2006).

21. Associated Colleges of the South, *Homepage*, http://www.colleges.org/ (last visited Jan. 8, 2006). *See also* Calder & Clugston 2003, *supra* note 18, at 10014.

22. South Carolina SUI, *Homepage*, http://www.sc.edu/sustainableu/ (last visited Jan. 8, 2006).

23. Net Impact, *Homepage*, http://www.netimpact.org/ (last visited Oct. 4, 2006).

24. ULSF, PROGRAMS (TALLOIRES DECLARATION) (1990), *available at* http://www.ulsf.org/programs_talloires.html.

25. IISD, THE HALIFAX DECLARATION (1991), *available at* http://www.iisd. org/educate/declarat/halifax.htm.

26. IISD, THE SWANSEA DECLARATION (1993), *available at* http://www.iisd. org/educate/declarat/swansea.htm.

27. COPERNICUS CAMPUS, UNIVERSITY CHARTER (1993), *available at* http://www.copernicus-campus.org/sites/mission_index.html.

28. IAU, KYOTO DECLARATION ON SUSTAINABLE DEVELOPMENT (1993), *available at* http://www.unesco.org/iau/sd/sd_dkyoto.html. *See also* IAU, IAU KYOTO DECLARATION—ACTION PLAN: DRAFT ACTION PLAN FOR INDIVIDUAL UNIVERSITIES (1993), *available at* http://www.unesco.org/iau/sd/rtf/sd_akyoto.rtf.

29. HEINZ FAMILY FOUNDATION, BLUEPRINT FOR A GREEN CAMPUS: THE CAMPUS EARTH SUMMIT INITIATIVES FOR HIGHER EDUCATION (1995).

30. SECOND NATURE, THE ESSEX REPORT: WORKSHOP ON THE PRINCIPLES OF SUSTAINABILITY IN HIGHER EDUCATION (1995), *available at* http://www.secondnature.org/aboutsn/aboutsn_writings.htm.

31. DUURZAAM HOGER ONDERWEIJS, CHARTER FOR SUSTAINABLE DEVELOPMENT IN VOCATIONAL TRAINING (1999), *available at* http://dho21.nl/index.php?mid=2. *See also* Education for a Sustainable Future, *supra* note 3 and Roorda Overview of AISHE, *supra* note 11.

32. COPERNICUS CAMPUS, THE LÜNEBURG DECLARATION ON HIGHER EDUCATION FOR SUSTAINABLE DEVELOPMENT (2001), *available at* http://www.lueneburg-declaration.de/.

33. IAU, Ubuntu Declaration: Seeks Global Educational Alliance for Sustainable Development (2002), *available at* http://www.icsu.org/Gestion/img/ICSU_DOC_DOWNLOAD/194_DD_FILE_10.3.1_Ubuntu_Declaration.pdf.

34. Environmental Ass'n for Universities & Colleges, *EMS Projects*, http://www.eauc.org.uk/index.cfm?zID=23 (last visited Jan. 8, 2006). ANN GALBRAITH, UNIVERSITY OF GLASGOW, SUSTAINABLE DEVELOPMENT AND ENVIRONMENTAL MANAGEMENT SYSTEMS: REPORT FOR SUNS PROJECT 2004, at 4-5 (Scottish Universities Network for Sustainability 2004), *available at* http://www.suns.org.uk/Documents/report%20environmental%20management%20systems%200304.pdf.

35. ULSF, *Programs (SAQ)*, http://www.ulsf.org/programs_saq.html (last visited Jan. 8, 2006).

36. NIKO ROORDA, DUTCH COMMITTEE ON SUSTAINABLE HIGHER EDUCATION, AISHE: AUDITING INSTRUMENT FOR SUSTAINABILITY IN HIGHER EDUCATION (2001), *available at* AISHE@dho.nl [hereinafter AISHE Auditing Tool]. *See* Roorda Overview of AISHE, *supra* note 11.

37. *See* European Foundation for Quality Management, http://www.efqm.org (last visited Jan. 8, 2006).

38. *See* AISHE Auditing Tool, *supra* note 36, at 8.

39. Campus Sustainability Assessment Project, *Homepage*, http://csap.envs.wmich.edu/index.html (last visited Jan. 8, 2006).

40. Andrew Nixon, Improving the Campus Sustainability Assessment Process, (undergraduate honors thesis, Environmental Institute, Western

Michigan University, May 2002), http://www.ulsf.org/nixon/contents. htm (last visited Jan. 8, 2006).

41. New Jersey HEPS, Campus *Sustainability Selected Indicators Snapshot and Guide*, http://www.njheps.org/assessment/instructions.htm (last visited Jan. 8, 2006).

42. ELIZABETH BERNIER & BROOKE JACK, PRINCETON UNIVERSITY, 2000 ENVIRONMENTAL AUDIT OF PRINCETON UNIVERSITY (Environmental Institute 2001), *available at* http://web.princeton.edu/sites/pei/PDF/EAD. pdf.

43. Good Company, *Campus Sustainability Assessments*, http://www.good company.com/campus/assessmentinfo.htm (last visited Jan. 8, 2006) [hereinafter Good Company Website].

44. GOOD COMPANY, SUSTAINABILITY ASSESSMENT OF THE UNIVERSITY OF OREGON BASED ON GOOD COMPANY'S SUSTAINABLE PATHWAYS TOOLKIT: FINAL REPORT (2002), *available at* http://darkwing.uoregon. edu/~eic/UO-finalreport-051502.pdf.

45. *See* Good Company Website, *supra* note 43.

46. TARLIE HARRIS ET AL., UNIVERSITY OF CALIFORNIA, SANTA BARBARA, GREENING UCSB: DEVELOPMENT OF AN ASSESSMENT PROTOCOL AND POLICY STATEMENT TO IMPROVE CAMPUS SUSTAINABILITY (Donald Bren School of Environmental Management 2001), *available at* http://www. Bren.ucsb.edu/research/2001Group_Projects/Final_Docs/greening_ final.pdf.

47. ANDY JOHNSTON ET AL., U.K. HIGHER EDUCATION PARTNERSHIP FOR SUSTAINABILITY AND FORUM FOR THE FUTURE, REPORTING ON SUSTAINABILITY: GUIDANCE FOR HIGHER EDUCATION INSTITUTIONS (2003), *available at* http://www.forumforthefuture.org.uk/uploadstore/reporting. pdf [hereinafter U.K. HEPS Sustainability Performance Guide].

48. *See* Good Company Website, *supra* note 43.

49. TOM BALF ET AL., CAMPUS CONSORTIUM FOR ENVIRONMENTAL EXCELLENCE, ENVIRONMENTAL MANAGEMENT SYSTEM SELF-ASSESSMENT CHECKLIST, VERSION 1.0 (2000), *available at* http://www.c2e2.org/ems_ assessment/emsassess.htm.

50. *See* U.K. HEPS Sustainability Performance Guide, *supra* note 47.

51. APRIL SMITH & STUDENT ENVIRONMENTAL ACTION COALITION, CAMPUS ECOLOGY: A GUIDE TO ASSESSING ENVIRONMENTAL QUALITY & CREATING STRATEGIES FOR CHANGE (Living Planet Press 1993).

52. MICHAEL ISENBERG, SCHOOL OF ENGINEERING AND APPLIED SCIENCE, UNIVERSITY OF PENNSYLVANIA, CAMPUS ENVIRONMENTAL AUDIT (1996), *available at* http://dolphin.upenn.edu/~pennenv/audit/.

53. Shelley Orteneau, California State University, Chico, *Environmental Audit 1999-2000: California State University, Chico*, http://www.csuchico.edu/eac/enviroaudit/exec_sum.html (last visited Jan. 8, 2006).

54. EMILY WRIGHT, ENVIRONMENTAL SCIENCE, COLORADO COLLEGE, THE ECOLOGICAL FOOTPRINT OF THE COLORADO COLLEGE: AN EXAMINATION OF SUSTAINABILITY (2002), *available at* http://www.coloradocollege.edu/Sustainability/EcoFootprint.pdf. The Colorado College assessment was based on MATHIS WACKERNAGEL & WILLIAM REES, OUR ECOLOGICAL FOOTPRINT: REDUCING HUMAN IMPACT ON THE EARTH (New Society Publishers 1996).

55. U.S. EPA, *20 Questions for College and University Presidents*, MID-ATLANTIC COMPLIANCE ASSISTANCE, *available at* http://www.epa.gov/region03/compliance_assistance/questpres.htm.

Acronyms

Index